TEXAS
POLITICS
TODAY

2011–2012
EDITION

TEXAS POLITICS TODAY

2011–2012 EDITION

William Earl Maxwell   **San Antonio College**
Ernest Crain   **San Antonio College**
Adolfo Santos   **University of Houston–Downtown**

with

Elizabeth N. Flores   Del Mar College
Joseph Ignagni   The University of Texas at Arlington
Cynthia Opheim   Texas State University–San Marcos
Christopher Wlezien   Temple University

WADSWORTH
CENGAGE Learning™

Australia • Brazil • Japan • Korea • Mexico • Singapore • Spain • United Kingdom • United States

WADSWORTH
CENGAGE Learning™

Texas Politics Today, 2011–2012

William Earl Maxwell, Ernest Crain, Adolfo Santos

Executive Editor: Carolyn Merrill

Development Editor: Rebecca Green

Associate Development Editor: Katherine Hayes

Assistant Editor: Laura Ross

Editorial Assistant: Angela Hodge

Media Editor: Laura Hildebrand

Marketing Manager: Lydia LeStar

Marketing Coordinator: Josh Hendrick

Marketing Communications Manager: Heather Baxley

Art Director: Linda Helcher

Print Buyer: Fola Orekoya

Rights Acquisition Specialist, Image: Amanda Groszko

Rights Acquisition Specialist, Text: Katie Huha

Production Service: Cadmus

Cover designer: Pier Design Co.

Cover Image credits: Troyek/©istockphoto; BrandonJ74/©istockphoto

Compositor: Cadmus Communications

For product information and technology assistance, contact us at
Cengage Learning Customer & Sales Support, 1-800-354-9706

For permission to use material from this text or product,
submit all requests online at **www.cengage.com/permissions**.

Further permissions questions can be e-mailed to
permissionrequest@cengage.com

Library of Congress Control Number: 2010941826

Student Edition:
ISBN-13: 978-0-495-90948-4
ISBN-10: 0-495-90948-3

Wadsworth
20 Channel Center Street
Boston, MA 02210
USA

Cengage Learning is a leading provider of customized learning solutions with office locations around the globe, including Singapore, the United Kingdom, Australia, Mexico, Brazil and Japan. Locate your local office at **international.cengage.com/region**

Cengage Learning products are represented in Canada by Nelson Education, Ltd.

For your course and learning solutions, visit **www.cengage.com.**

Purchase any of our products at your local college store or at our preferred online store **www.cengagebrain.com.**

Instructors: Please visit **login.cengage.com** and log in to access instructor-specific resources.

Printed in Canada
2 3 4 5 14 13 12 11

CONTENTS

CHAPTER 1

TEXAS HISTORY AND CULTURE 1

PREFACE

Although you and other intelligent, well-meaning Texans may strongly disagree about public policies, the policies of Texas state and local governments dramatically affect each of our lives—every day. If you refuse to participate, you relinquish your role in our democracy and your natural right to control your own future. The real losers in the political game are those who do not play.

Human beings are political by their very nature. Understanding government is necessary for intelligent development of a political ideology and for acceptance of conflicting ideologies as legitimate. We hope that this book's fact-based discussion of recent controversial issues will engage your interest and that its explanation of ongoing principles of Texas politics will help you understand opposing views in context. *Texas Politics Today* is your invitation to join the dynamic conversation about politics in the Lone Star State. You should be impressed neither by what the authors know nor by what your professors know, but by your own opportunities to become part of civil discourse and by what you can do for yourself and for others as you become a part of this political world of ours.

We designed the 2011–2012 edition of *Texas Politics Today* to meet your needs as students in introductory college and university-level courses. We wrote this reader-friendly text for you to use in courses specializing in Texas government as well as those that integrate state and national politics.

We explain the background, rules of the game, political players, and framework of political institutions that give birth to the public policies that most affect you, and you can explore major historical, demographic, political, and cultural trends and the role of political interest groups throughout the text. You can use vignettes, figures, tables, diagrams, and photos as active visual learning tools, and enjoy the humor of Ben Sargent's Pulitzer Prize-winning **cartoons**, which illustrate important issues that you will recognize in Texas politics.

You can exploit student-centered learning aids: Each chapter opens with an **outline** and **learning objectives** that preview the chapter's themes and content. You should focus on **key terms and concepts** set in boldfaced print, listed at the end of each chapter, and defined in the Glossary. **Marginal definitions** conveniently guide you through the text.

Expanded **chapter summaries** bullet important points that you should understand and remember. **How Texas Compares** sections help you put some of the main chapter themes into perspective by summarizing how other states compare with Texas. **Review questions** focus on main themes that you should think about. Provocative **Join the Debate** features at the end of each essay raise broad questions that you should raise in class discussions and consider for debate and research on contemporary political issues.

NEW TO THIS EDITION

Instructors will recognize the most effective elements of previous editions, but this edition also analyzes the latest available data and discusses current issues, recent legal and structural changes, as well as contemporary demographic and political developments. In addition, nearly all essays in the book have been revised or replaced. Here is some of the enticing new material in the 2011–2012 edition:

* **Enhanced visuals** make every photo, chart, and cartoon a teaching tool and a learning opportunity. Captions explain how students should read and use the graphics, what they should take away from the images, and which general conclusions they should draw or which analytical questions they should think about.

* **Using the new media** to participate in politics is a special focus of our "Join the Conversation" feature inside the front cover and of the new article following Chapter 3. "Tips on Becoming a Smart Consumer of State Services" inside the back cover has new ideas about how students can make state government work for them, and the e-government article after Chapter 9 puts Internet access to state agencies in perspective.

* New topics in "**How Does Texas Compare**?" put Texas political institutions into context and direct students to debate the merits of alternative institutions and policies.

* **Get Active!** sections are rich in fresh online resources that put tools into students' hands to link up with activist groups in Texas politics; to sample liberal, conservative, and libertarian opinion; and to decide where they stand on the ideological spectrum.

* The impacts of the "stimulus bill," health care reform, "tea party" movement, secessionism, states' rights, and immigration issues are covered throughout the chapters.

* Results of the 2010 elections are incorporated into the political chapters, especially Chapters 3, 4, and 6.

* The influence of recent U.S. Supreme Court rulings about the *Miranda* decision, corporate contributions, and conflicts of interest generated by campaign contributions are discussed in Chapters 3, 4, 5, and 11.

* The companion website accessible through **cengagebrain.com/shop/ISBN/0495909483** offers a full array of online study tools, including learning objectives, glossary flashcards, practice quizzes, and web links. It also houses an evolving online library of news articles and additional resources so students can apply the concepts they learn in the book to the current events around them.

Each chapter contains important new contents:

Chapter 1 A provocative description of women's social position in Texas since the time of the Republic of Texas. The political struggles of women since Minnie Fisher Cunningham took a leading role in the battle for suffrage rights and the impeachment of Governor Jim Ferguson. The treatment of Latinos as "a class apart" before *Hernandez* v. *Texas* (1954) and a new essay about the Mexican-American civil rights movement in Texas. Efforts to suppress African Americans during the historic *Mansfield* school desegregation case and a new essay about the incredible resurgence of the Texas KKK during the 1920s. Secession politics before the Civil War and current political conflicts between Texas and the national government. *Roe* v.

Wade (1973) and the right to privacy, results of the 2009 legislative session, and current conflicts between Texas's political leaders and the national government. New discussion of the Texas–Mexico border as a special region that is impacted by internationalism in security, economic, and cultural matters.

Chapter 2 Clear discussion of contemporary views of national powers, the Tenth Amendment, states' rights, and secessionism. The health care reform controversy as a case study in conflicting views of federalism. New essay showing the impact of E. J. Davis on Texans' attitudes about government and how it influenced the shape of the Texas Constitution.

Chapter 3 The latest on elections, campaign spending, and changes in election law, including the impact of *Citizens United* v. *FEC* (2010) legalizing corporate contributions in Texas election campaigns. An essay about how media are changing Texas politics and campaigns. Get Active! and Logging On sections featuring websites that offer new opportunities for student participation.

Chapter 4 Latest changes in major party platforms, the 2010 Texas election results, and new data about party identification in Texas. A new map of the presidential election of 2008 showing which counties voted for Obama and McCain. Discussion of the concept of "tipping" in the description of Texas party realignment process.

Chapter 5 Discussion of Texas's biggest-spending interest groups and their lobbying contracts; special focus on energy industry lobbying and the development of "Astroturf" lobbying. Expanded coverage of noneconomic interest groups, including a new essay that shows the political importance of social interest groups and their positions on God, gays, guns, and immigration.

Chapter 6 Joe Straus's unprecedented rise to the House speakership and conservative Republican resistance to his bipartisan leadership style. The increasing role of women in legislative politics, including a new essay about how Judith Zaffirini has become a role model for powerful state legislators.

Chapter 7 Selection of committee chairs. Comparative features about the results of recent legislation likely to be revisited in future legislative sessions such as statutes dealing with property taxes and with texting while driving. Special discussion of maneuvers such as "chubbing" in determining the fate of the recent Voter ID bill. New essay about the importance of legislative procedure and the partisan rancor and antics surrounding the "blocking bill."

Chapter 8 Updated ranking of the Texas governor's power compared to governors in the 49 other states. New essay about how the governor's strategic use of the appointive power as a formidable political tool amidst such controversies as the Forensic Science Commission dispute.

Chapter 9 Discussion of the impact of state agencies on individuals' lives such as the State Board of Education as it adopted the new social science curriculum for public school students. New article to engage students with some of the state's main websites and to put the state's Internet access efforts into perspective.

Chapter 10 Possible impacts of U. S. Supreme Court rulings on conflicts of interest (*A. T. Massey* v. *Caperton*) in judicial campaigns and corporate contributions (*Citizens United* v. *FEC*) on Texas courts. Essay about the role of campaign contributions in judicial decisions and how the partisan divide on tort reform affects judicial outcomes.

Chapter 11 Texas lawsuit climate, new U.S. Supreme Court decisions diluting *Miranda* requirements, and new feature about how Texas compares to other states on the death penalty.

Chapter 12 Reorganization of topics to simplify a difficult subject and enhanced visuals to explain how to use the tables and figures. Fresh coverage of the stimulus bill and its impact on the Texas budget.

Chapter 13 The social science curriculum and the culture wars. Expanded discussion of tuition deregulation. The future of health insurance in Texas. New essay about teaching evolution and religious influences in the public school curriculum.

Chapter 14 Enhanced focus on issues of national importance facing Texas's local governments. Expanded coverage of immigration and Texas cities. New coverage of other issues of national consequence facing local governments such as environmental quality and homelessness. A new article providing an insider's view of the mayor's office and how cities compete to attract businesses such as sports franchises.

STUDENT AND INSTRUCTOR SUPPLEMENTS

* A variety of student and instructional aids are available separately. Contact your Cengage sales representative for details about the following products and more print and online resources.

* On **CengageBrain.com** students can save up to 60 percent on their course materials through our full spectrum of options. Students have the option to rent their textbooks or purchase print textbooks, e-textbooks, or individual e-chapters, and audio books, all at substantial savings over average retail prices. CengageBrain.com also includes access to Cengage Learning's broad range of homework and study tools, including the student resources discussed here. Go to **cengagebrain.com/shop/ISBN/0495909483** to access your *Texas Politics Today* resources.

* The **Companion website** for *Texas Politics Today* accessible through **cengagebrain.com/shop/ISBN/0495909483** offers a full array of online study tools, including learning objectives, glossary flashcards, practice quizzes, and web links, and houses an evolving online library of news articles and additional resources so students can apply the concepts they learn in the book to the current events around them.

* **PowerLecture (ISBN-10: 0840035195 | ISBN-13: 9780840035196)** is a one-stop lecture, class preparation, and exam tool that makes it easy for you to assemble, edit, publish, and present custom lectures for your course and prepare your examinations. The PowerPoint® lectures bring together text-specific outlines; tables, statistical charts, graphs; and photos from the book. In addition, you can add your own materials to create a powerful, personalized presentation. A Microsoft® Word test bank and ExamView® computerized testing offer a large array of well-crafted multiple-choice and essay questions, along with the answers and page references. An Instructor's Manual includes a chapter summary, learning objectives, chapter outlines, discussion questions, and suggestions for stimulating class activities and projects. The test bank, instructor manual, and PowerPoints have all been updated with new content. New photos, figures, graphs, and charts are found on PowerLecture as well.

* **WebTutor™ ToolBox for Printed Access Card**
  Blackboard® (ISBN-10: 0534274897 | ISBN-13: 9780534274894)
  WebCT™ (ISBN-10: 0534274889 | ISBN-13: 9780534274887)
  WebTutor™ ToolBox offers a full array of online study tools, including learning objectives, glossary flashcards, practice quizzes, web links, and a daily news feed from NewsEdge, an authoritative source for late-breaking news.

* **Mexican American Politics Supplement (ISBN-10: 0495793159 | ISBN-13:**

9780495793151) by Fernando Pinon of San Antonio College is a 32-page booklet that can either be bound in or bundled with the purchase of a new text.

★ **Texas Political Theater DVD (ISBN-10: 0495573108 | ISBN-13: 9780495573104)** enables instructors to integrate current and historically poignant *ABC News* footage into classroom presentations, offering real-world application to the concepts studied in *Texas Politics Today* and serving to spark class discussion.

ACKNOWLEDGMENTS FOR THE 2011–2012 EDITION

The authors thank the following reviewers for their useful suggestions toward this revision:

Sarah Binion, Austin Community College
Malcolm L. Cross, Tarleton State University
Kevin T. Davis, North Central Texas College
Brian R. Farmer, Amarillo College
Robert Paul Holder, McLennan Community College
Mel Laracey, The University of Texas–San Antonio
John David Rausch, Jr., West Texas A&M University

ACKNOWLEDGMENTS FOR EARLIER EDITIONS

The following reviewers also contributed greatly through feedback on recent prior editions of *Texas Politics Today*:

Larry E. Carter, The University of Texas–Tyler
Neil Coates, Abilene Christian College
Laura De La Cruz, El Paso Community College
Frank J. Garrahan, Austin Community College
Glen David Garrison, Collin County Community College–Spring Creek
Timothy Hoye, Texas Woman's University
Casey Hubble, McLennan Community College
Charles R. Knerr, The University of Texas–Arlington
Dennis B. Martinez, The University of Texas–San Antonio
Jalal K. Nejad, Northwest Vista College
J. D. Phaup, Texas A&M University–Kingsville
Jo Marie Rios, Texas A&M University–Corpus Christi
Allan Saxe, The University of Texas–Arlington
Charles Vernon Wilder, Texarkana College

Chapter 1

Texas History and Culture

CONTENTS

LEARNING OBJECTIVES

* Describe the social and cultural groups that migrated to Texas from early European settlement to modern-day migration from other states and other countries.
* Trace the relations between Texas's ethnic and gender groups and the struggle for equality among Latinos, African Americans, and women.
* Explain the important political conflicts during Texas's major political epochs, including the days of the Republic, early statehood, the Civil War and its aftermath, the era of Democratic Party dominance, and the emergence of Republican control.
* Describe the distinctive social, economic, and political characteristics of major Texas regions.
* Distinguish between moralistic, traditionalistic, and individualistic cultures.
* Describe the social changes that are likely to define Texas's political future.

★ GET ★ ACTIVE ★

Learn more about your own culture. Talk to grandparents, parents, uncles, and aunts to learn what they know about your culture and family history. Record as much oral history as you can about their personal lives, experiences, and political recollections, as well as family myths and traditions. You may find this information priceless as you talk to your own children and grandchildren about their culture.

Broaden your cultural and political experiences. Participate in activities and organizations of ethnic, religious, and ideological groups that are different from your own. This will help you better understand and appreciate the rich diversity of modern American life.

Go to the library and log onto the Internet to research the background and richness of your family culture. Pick a hero who shares your culture. Here are a few reliable sources:

★ Institute of Texan Cultures: **http://www.texancultures.utsa.edu/public/**

★ Texas State Library and Archives Commission: **http://www.tsl.state.tx.us** (click on "Online Exhibits")

★ Houston Institute for Culture: **http://www.houstonculture.org**

★ Texas State Historical Association and Center for Studies in Texas History: **http://www.tsha.utexas.edu**

★ Texas Beyond History: **http://www.texasbeyondhistory.net**

Almost 500 years ago Spanish explorer Alonzo Alvarez de Pineda first set foot on what was to become Texas. During the next three centuries, land-hungry settlers pushed the Cherokees and the Caddos from the eastern pine forests; the Karankawas from the sands of the coast; and the Comanches, Apaches, and Kiowas from the western plains. Texas culture and history have been made under 37 Spanish governors, 15 Mexican governors, five presidents of the Republic of Texas, and 48 state governors.

The successful end of the Texas Revolution in 1836 saw the English/Scotch–Irish culture, as it had evolved in its migration through the southern United States, become the dominant culture of the state. Anglo Americans were the most numerous population group and controlled most of the political and economic systems in Texas.

Sam Houston About 1850 ☞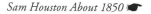

Why is Sam Houston still revered as a Texas politician?

Library of Congress Prints and Photographs Division Washington, D.C./LC-USZ62-110029

Latinos and Native Americans stood in the way of the Anglo-Saxon concept of "Manifest Destiny" and, by various methods, hundreds of old Latino families throughout Texas were driven from their property as waves of Anglo settlers poured into the new republic. Even Latino heroes of the Texas Revolution, with names like Navarro, Seguin, de Zavala, and de Leon, lost much of their property.

San Antonio Latinos were spared the worst of this onslaught because of the opposition by the city's strong German community, which considered such actions to be contrary to republican values. Still, by 1856 half the city's Latino population was gone.[1]

---

[1]See David Montejano, *Anglos and Mexicans in the making of Texas, 1836–1986* (Austin: University of Texas Press, 1987), pp. 26–29.

Anglo-American Protestant sects also became the dominant religious groups in Texas. As evidence of the dominance of this Anglo-Scotch culture, all the presidents of the Republic and the governors of the state have been Protestant and had surnames linked to the British Isles.

Politics and Government: The Early Years

Politics in the Republic of Texas were simpler than politics in Texas today. There were no political parties, and conflict revolved around pro-Houston and anti-Houston policies. Sam Houston, the hero of the battle of San Jacinto (1836), advocated peaceful relations with the eastern Native Americans and U.S. statehood for Texas. The anti-Houston forces were led by Mirabeau B. Lamar, who believed that Native American and Anglo-American cultures could not coexist. He also envisioned Texas as a great nation extending from the Sabine River to the Pacific.[2]

> Sam Houston, Davy Crockett, Jim Bowie, and others were of Scotch–Irish descent and culture. Scotch–Irish immigrants from the Scots–English border, by way of Northern Ireland, led the Anglo-American movement west and had a major impact on the development of modern mid-American culture.

WOMEN IN THE REPUBLIC

Although women could neither serve on juries nor vote, unmarried women retained many of the rights that they had enjoyed under Spanish law, which included control over their property. Married women also retained some Spanish law benefits because, unlike Anglo-Saxon law, Texas marriage did not create one legal person with the husband as the head. Married women could own inherited property, share ownership in community property, and legally make a will. However, the husband legally had control of all the property, both separate and community (including earned income), and an employer could not hire a wife without her husband's consent.[3]

Divorce laws were restrictive on both parties, but a husband could win a divorce if for the wife's "amorous or lascivious conduct with other men, even short of adultery," or if she had committed adultery only once, although he could not gain a divorce for concealed premarital fornication. On the other hand, a wife could only gain a divorce if "the husband had lived in adultery with another woman." Physical violence was not grounds for divorce unless the wife could prove a "serious danger" that might happen again. In practice, physical abuse was tolerated if the wife behaved "indiscreetly" or had "provoked" her husband. Minority and poor wives had little legal protection from beatings because the woman's "station in life" and "standing in society" were also legal considerations.[4]

JOINING THE UNION

Texas voters approved **annexation** to the United States in 1836, almost immediately after Texas achieved independence from Mexico. However, because owning human property was legal in the Republic and would also be legal once it became a state, the annexation of Texas

Annexation

The incorporation of a territory into a larger political unit, such as a country, state, county, or city.

---

[2]The information in this and subsequent sections depends heavily on Seymour *v.* Connor, Texas: *A History* (New York: Thomas Y. Crowell, 1971); Rupert N. Richardson, *Texas: The Lone Star State,* 3rd ed. (Englewood Cliffs, NJ: Prentice Hall, 1970); T. R. Fehrenbach, *Lone Star: A History of Texas and the Texans* (New York: Collier Books, 1980).
[3]Elizabeth York Enstam, "Women and the Law," *Handbook of Texas Online,* http://www.tshaonline.org/handbook/online/articles/jsw02
[4]Ibid.

would upset the tenuous balance in the U.S. Senate between pro- and anti-slavery senators. This and several other political issues, primarily relating to slavery, postponed Texas's annexation until December 29, 1845, when it officially became the 28th state.

Several articles of annexation were more or less peculiar to Texas. Most important was that Texas retained ownership of its public lands because the U.S. Congress refused to accept them in exchange for payment of the republic's $10 million public debt. Although many millions of acres were eventually given away or sold, the remaining public lands continue to produce hundreds of millions of dollars in state revenue, mostly in royalties from the production of oil and natural gas. Today, this revenue primarily benefits the Permanent University Fund and the Permanent School Fund. The annexation articles also granted Texas the privilege of "creating . . . new states, of convenient size, not exceeding four in number, in addition to said State of Texas."[5]

EARLY STATEHOOD AND SECESSION: 1846–1864

Secession

The separation of a territory from a larger political unit. Specifically, the secession of southern states from the Union in 1860 and 1861.

The politics of early statehood immediately began to revolve around pro-Union and secessionist forces. Sam Houston, a strong Unionist, was alarmed at the support for **secession** in Texas, resigned his seat in the U.S. Senate and in 1857 ran for the office of governor of Texas. He was defeated primarily because secessionist forces controlled the dominant Democratic Party. However, he was elected governor two years later.

After Abraham Lincoln was elected president of the United States in 1860, a Texas secessionist convention voted to secede from the Union. Governor Sam Houston used his considerable political skills in the vain attempt to keep Texas in the Union. He declared the convention illegal, but it was upheld as legitimate by the Texas legislature. Although only approximately five percent of white Texans owned slaves, the electorate ratified the actions of the convention by an overwhelming 76 percent majority.[6] Although defeated by the secessionists, Houston adamantly continued to fight what he considered Texans' determination to self-destruct. Although he reluctantly accepted the vote to secede, Houston tried to convince secessionist leaders to return to republic status rather than joining the newly formed Confederate States of America—a plan that might have saved Texas from the tragedy of the U.S. Civil War. Texas's convention repulsed this political maneuver and petitioned for membership in the new Confederacy. Houston refused to accept the actions of the convention, which summarily declared the office of governor vacant and ordered the lieutenant governor into the position. Texas was then admitted to the Confederacy.

The politics during the Civil War primarily concerned the military. Besides supplying large numbers of troops to the conflict (primarily Confederate, but also Union), Texas was responsible for the defense of the frontier and the Mexican border. Thus, the state—not the central Confederate government—filled the military vacuum created by the withdrawal of federal troops.

Juneteenth, or Emancipation Day, long celebrated by Texas African Americans, became an official state holiday in 1979.

POST–CIVIL WAR TEXAS: 1865–1885

After the collapse of the Confederacy, relative anarchy existed in Texas until it was occupied by federal troops on June 19, 1865. Only then were government functions and stability

---

[5]The Annexation of Texas, Joint Resolution of Congress, March 1, 1845, *U.S. Statutes at Large, Vol. 5,* pp. 797–798. This document can be found online at http://www.pbs.org/weta/thewest/resources/archives/two/texannex.htm

[6]See *A Declaration of the Causes Which Impel the State of Texas to Secede from the Federal Union,* http://avalon.law.yale.edu/19th_century/csa_texsec.asp

restored to the state. Radical Republicans gained control of the U.S. Congress and enacted punitive legislation that strictly limited both voter registration and eligibility to hold public office for former Confederate soldiers and officials. This restriction even included former mayors and school board members.

The Reconstruction of Texas Under E. J. Davis From 1865 through 1869, Texas government was under the military rule of the U.S. Army. After the adoption of the constitution of 1869, E. J. Davis, a Texan and radical Republican who had fought for the Union in the Civil War, was elected governor of Texas in an election in which the former slaves could vote—but the former leaders of the state could not. Texas was then readmitted to the Union and governed by civilian authority under Davis, who served for a single four-year term, from 1870 through 1873. Under the 1869 Texas Constitution, political power was centralized in the office of the governor, and the state police and the militia were placed under his direct control.

Charges of corruption were common during the Davis administration, and state indebtedness drastically increased. Regardless of the accuracy of these allegations, Republican domination of Texas politics was "a world turned upside down" for most white Texas citizens.

The Fall of Governor Davis The perception of the Davis administration as a government imposed on a defeated people in itself made it unpopular and prompted a strong anti-Republican reaction. In 1873, former Confederates were allowed to vote, and in 1874, Democrat Richard Coke was overwhelmingly elected governor in a hotly contested campaign. The Texas Supreme Court, handpicked by Davis, invalidated the election on the basis of a technicality.

Davis locked himself in the capitol, surrounded it with the state police, requested the support of federal troops from President Ulysses S. Grant, and refused to leave office. In the predawn hours of January 13, 1874, however, Democratic legislators managed to gain access to the unoccupied legislative chambers, declared a quorum present, and officially validated the election of Coke as governor of Texas. Despite Grant's refusal to send in troops and with tension mounting, Davis still refused to leave the capitol. Only when serious violence seemed imminent between the state police and the numerically superior Coke forces did Davis withdraw.

The End of Republicanism The new Texas officials immediately began to remove the last vestiges of radical Republicanism. One of the first steps was to rewrite the state constitution. A constitutional convention of 90 members was elected (75 Democrats and 15 Republicans) that included many former officials of both the Union and Confederate governments. Forty members of the 1875 convention also belonged to the Grange, a nonpartisan organization of farmers. Ratified in 1876, the new constitution cut expenditures, decentralized state government, and strictly limited the flexibility of elected officials. Although often amended, it is still in use. Davis established a law practice in Austin and continued to head the Republican Party and control patronage from Washington until his death in 1883. He remained unpopular with most Texans, and his death created a racial division between African-American and white Republicans. The African-American forces,

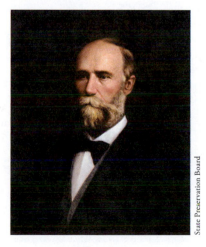

State Preservation Board

Reconstruction Governor E. J. Davis

What were some of the political forces working against Governor E.J. Davis?

under Norris Wright Cuney of Galveston, gained control of both the state party machinery and party patronage from Washington. The political consequence of Reconstruction and the policies of E. J. Davis was one-party dominance by an all-white Democratic Party with the numerically smaller, predominantly black Republican Party in opposition.

Politics and Government: 1886–1945

After 1886, increasing demands for change forced the Democratic Party to make political adjustments. Many reform measures were enacted and enforced in Texas in the 1880s, especially **antitrust legislation**. The election of James Stephen Hogg as attorney general in 1886 ensured the vigorous enforcement of the new laws against abuses by insurance companies, railroads, and other corporate interests.

Antitrust legislation

Legislation directed against economic monopolies.

GOVERNOR HOGG

Hogg, who had strong support among small East Texas farmers, played an important reformist role in Texas politics and rapidly developed a reputation as a champion of the common people. Feeling that he needed more power to regulate the railroad interests that dominated many state governments, Hogg ran for governor. The 1890 Democratic State Convention nominated him as its candidate for governor in spite of opposition from powerful political and corporate business interests. A major issue in the campaign that followed was a proposed amendment giving the Texas legislature the power to establish a commission to regulate railroads. The voters gave both Hogg and the amendment a clear victory.

Governor Hogg's daughter, Ima Hogg (Miss Ima), was a major benefactor and philanthropist to Texas institutions and charities. Contrary to popular belief, Governor Hogg did not have another daughter named Ura.

The Railroad Commission As governor, Hogg was able to persuade the legislature to establish a three-member Railroad Commission, despite intense opposition from special interest legislators. His appointment of respected political figures to the commission, notably John H. Reagan as chairman, enabled it to become one of the most important railroad regulatory bodies in the United States.

The constitutionality of a railroad commission still had to be tested in the federal courts, but it was upheld after two years of litigation. The commission was later given the power to regulate the production and transportation of oil and natural gas and to regulate rubber-tired vehicles used in intrastate commerce. In 1994, however, the U.S. Congress determined that the commission's *intrastate* trucking regulations were an obstacle to *interstate* commerce and mandated gradual deregulation of the trucking industry in Texas.

Edward M. House In 1894, an early Hogg supporter, Edward M. House, was able to take control of the Democratic Party from Hogg on a "promote unity" platform. House established himself as a behind-the-scenes

James Stephen Hogg was a progressive newspaperman, a politician, and the first Texas-born governor of Texas.

What were some of Jim Hogg's programs that labeled him a "progressive"?

The State Publishing Company, Austin, Texas, 1905/ The University of Texas at Austin, Center for American History

political power in Texas for the next 40 years. House also wielded significant influence in national politics, first as a supporter and later as chief confidant of President Woodrow Wilson (1913–1921). Although he never sought elective office, he was one of the most astute politicians ever to operate in Texas.

Throughout the early 1900s, programs enacted by the legislature continued to identify Texas as one of the most progressive states in the nation. Texas pioneered the regulation of monopolies, railroads, child labor, and other employer abuses, as well as reform of prisons, taxes, and insurance companies. In 1905, state conventions were replaced with direct primaries to nominate major party candidates.

FARMER JIM: 1914–1918

James E. Ferguson entered the Texas political scene in 1914, and was a controversial and powerful force in Texas politics for the next 20 years. He had worked as a migrant laborer in California, Nevada, Colorado, and Texas. Although Ferguson had little formal education and only a few months of studying law, he was admitted to the Texas bar in 1897.

By 1914, when he announced his candidacy for governor, Ferguson owned varied business interests and was the president of the Temple State Bank. Ferguson was an anti-prohibitionist ("wet") at a time when **Prohibition** was a major political issue, and although his strongest opponent in the Democratic primary was a prohibitionist ("dry"), Ferguson tried to ignore the liquor issue. Although sensitive to the problems and interests of the business community, Ferguson called himself "Farmer Jim" to emphasize his rural background and focused his campaign on the difficulties of the numerous **tenant farmers** in Texas.

Farmer Jim as Governor The legislature was unusually receptive to Ferguson's programs, which were in the best tradition of the **progressive movement**, and enacted legislation designed to help alleviate problems of tenant farmers, rural schools, and state courts. Governor Ferguson was reelected in 1916, and although rumors of financial irregularities in the office had begun to gain credibility, his progressive legislative programs were again successful. This was especially true in the areas of public school and college education and the proposal to create a state highway commission. The latter agency was formed to take the construction and maintenance of state roads away from the counties, where there was great variation in quality and consistency.

The Fall of Farmer Jim Rumors of financial irregularities such as bribery and embezzlement continued during Ferguson's second term. His fatal step, however, may have been "declaring war" on The University of Texas. After the legislature had adjourned, Ferguson issued an **item veto** of the entire appropriation for the university, apparently because the board of regents had refused to remove certain faculty members whom the governor found objectionable. This step alienated many politically powerful graduates. They immediately demanded action, and Ferguson was indicted by the Travis County grand jury for illegal use of public funds.

Women also joined in the groundswell of opposition to Ferguson. Led by Minnie Fisher Cunningham, Texas suffragists had organized, spoke out, marched, and

Prohibition
Outlawing of the production, sale, and consumption of alcoholic beverages.

Tenant farmer
A farmer who does not own the land that he or she farms but rents it from a landowner.

Progressive movement
A political movement within both major parties in the early 20th century. Progressives believed that the power of the government should be used to restrain the growing power of large corporations, as well as to provide services for its citizens.

Item veto
The power to veto particular sections or items of an appropriations bill while signing the remainder of the bill into law. The governors of most states have this power.

Texan Minnie Fisher Cunningham was a champion for women's suffrage in the state.

Why were people opposed to women having the right to vote?

Library of Congress

lobbied for the right to vote during the Ferguson years but gained no real political traction as Farmer Jim strongly opposed their cause. Suffragists effectively lobbied state legislators "through the back door," and organized rallies advocating his impeachment.[7]

Ultimately, Farmer Jim was impeached on 21 charges. In August 1917, after three weeks of hearings by the state senate, Ferguson was convicted on 10 of the charges, removed from office, and barred from holding public office in Texas.

Ferguson was found guilty of accepting funds from secret sources, tampering with state officials, depositing state funds in the Temple State Bank (which he partly owned), and using public funds for personal gain. His successor was Lieutenant Governor W. P. Hobby, Sr.

Again, women actively participated in the political arena although they lacked the right to vote. William P. Hobby, considered receptive to women's suffrage, was touted as "The Man Whom Good Women Want." This tactic ultimately proved successful and women, with some delays won the legislative battle and gained the right to vote in the 1918 Texas primaries.[8]

National suffrage momentum precipitated a proposed constitutional amendment establishing the right of women to vote throughout the United States. Having endured more than five years of "heavy artillery" by Cunningham and the Texas Equal Suffrage Association, legislative opposition crumbled and Texas became one of the first southern states to ratify the Nineteenth Amendment. Texas women received full voting rights in 1920.[9] The same legislature, in another called session, ratified the Eighteenth Amendment to the U.S. Constitution, establishing national Prohibition. The prohibitionists had won.

WORLD WAR I, THE TWENTIES, AND THE RETURN OF FARMER JIM: 1919–1928

As did the rest of the nation, Texas saw boom years during World War I. Its favorable climate and the Zimmerman Note (in which Germany allegedly urged Mexico to invade Texas) prompted the national government to station additional troops in the state. Texas became an important training area for the military, and many of the training camps later became permanent bases.

Progressive political programs, however, suffered during the war. Several of Governor Hobby's proposals to use the state's credit to help citizens purchase homes and to write a new constitution were defeated either by the legislature or by the voters.

In 1921, Pat M. Neff became governor of Texas. His proposals to reorganize the executive branch to eliminate duplication and waste, and to rewrite the Texas Constitution both failed. Meanwhile, bootleggers—traffickers in illegal alcohol—often circumvented Prohibition. Governor Neff, an avid prohibitionist, used the Texas Rangers to find and destroy private stills used to produce illegal spirits. The Rangers were too few in number to be effective and the legislature refused to give Neff the police powers necessary to enforce Prohibition effectively. Crime, education, and the **Ku Klux Klan (KKK)** emerged as issues that demanded attention from the politicians and voters. Progressive measures enacted during this period included free textbooks for public schools, the establishment of several colleges, and the beginning of the state park system.

CIVIL RIGHTS

Civil rights remained an elusive concept during this period for racial minorities. African Texans were legally denied the right to vote in the Democratic **white primary** and public

Ku Klux Klan (KKK)
A white supremacist organization. The first Klan was founded during the Reconstruction era following the Civil War.

White primary
The practice of excluding African Americans from Democratic Party primary elections in Texas. First enforced by law and later by party rules, this practice was found unconstitutional in *Smith* v. *Allwright*, 321 U.S. 649 (1944).

---

[7]Women of the West Museum, "Western Women's Suffrage—Texas," www.http://theautry.org/research/women-of-the-west
[8]Ibid.
[9]Ibid.

facilities, such as theaters, restaurants, beaches, and so forth, were segregated by race. Segregation laws were enforced both by official law enforcement agents and by unofficial organizations using terror tactics. Although these laws were not specifically directed at Latinos, who were legally white, they were effectively enforced against them through social custom and coercion. The Ku Klux Klan, local law officers, and the Texas Rangers actively participated in violence and intimidation of both Latinos and African Texans to keep them "in their segregated place." Lynching was also used against both groups, often after torture.[10]

The KKK (first organized in the late 1860s to intimidate freed African slaves) was reborn in the 1920s with a somewhat modified mission. The new Klan saw itself as a patriotic, Christian, fraternal organization for native-born white Protestants. Its members perceived both a general moral decline in society, precipitated by "modern" young people, and a basic threat to the Protestant white Christian "race" and its values by African Americans, Jews, Catholics, Latinos, German Americans, and other "foreigners." Acting on its paranoia, the 1920s Klan set out to force society to comply with its version of fundamentalist Christian morality. It used intimidation, violence, and torture—tarring and feathering, branding, beating, threats of castration—as means of coercion. As many as 80,000 Texans may have joined the "invisible empire" in an effort to make the world more to their liking. Many elected officials—U.S. and state legislators as well as county and city officials—were either avowed Klansmen or friendly neutrals. In fact, the Klan influenced Texas society to such an extent that its power was a major political issue from 1921 through 1925.

> The University of Texas (UT) changed the names of Simkins Hall and Simkins Park on July 15, 2010 to Creekside Hall and Park. The dorm and park were named after former UT law professor William S. Simkins and former UT System Regent Eldred J. Simkins. The brothers were active organizers and members of the Ku Klux Klan. The dorm was originally built and named in the 1950s.

In response to this racially charged atmosphere, a number of organizations committed to equality were founded or grew larger during the 1920s. Among these were the National Association for the Advancement of Colored People (NAACP), established in 1909, and the League of United Latin American Citizens (LULAC), which was formed in Corpus Christi in 1929.

When Dr. L. H. Nixon, an African-American citizen of El Paso, was denied the right to vote in the Democratic primary, the NAACP instituted legal action and the U.S. Supreme Court found in *Nixon* v. *Herndon* (1927) that the Texas White Primary law was unconstitutional. However, the Texas legislature transferred control of the primary from the state to the Democratic State Executive Committee and the discrimination continued. Dr. Nixon again sought justice in the courts, and the U.S. Supreme Court in 1931 also ruled the new scheme unconstitutional. Texas Democrats then completely excluded African Texans from party membership. In *Grovey* v. *Townsend* (1935), the U.S. Supreme Court upheld this ploy, and the Texas Democratic primary remained all white. Although it had suffered a temporary setback in the episode, the NAACP had proven its potential as a viable instrument for African Americans to achieve justice.[11]

The Return of the Fergusons The strongest anti-Klan candidate in the gubernatorial election of 1924 was Miriam A. "Ma" Ferguson, wife of the impeached (and convicted)

> "Ma" Ferguson was governor in name only and Farmer Jim exercised the real power of the office.

---

[10]Texas State Historical Association, *Handbook of Texas Online*, http://tshaonline.org/handbook/online/
[11]Connor, pp. 378–379.

Farmer Jim. Running successfully on a platform of "Two Governors for the Price of One," she became the first female governor of Texas. Ma's election indicated that Texas voters had forgiven Farmer Jim. Her success in getting legislation passed that prohibited wearing a mask in public led to the end of the Klan as an effective political force in Texas. Ma was criticized, however, for her lenient pardoning policy (occasionally a convicted felon was pardoned before reaching prison) and a highway scandal. In the 1926 election, she was defeated by Attorney General Dan Moody, also a reformer and an anti-Klan candidate.

In 1928, national politics exerted more influence than usual on Texas politics when Al Smith became the Democratic nominee for president. Smith was a Roman Catholic, a "wet," and a big-city politician; Herbert Hoover, the Republican nominee, was a Protestant, a "dry," and an international humanitarian. Hoover won the electoral votes from Texas—the first Republican ever to do so.

THE GREAT DEPRESSION: 1929–1939

When the stock market crashed in 1929, Texas, along with the entire nation, was crushed under the blow. Almost overnight, prices dropped, farm products could not be sold, mortgages and taxes could not be paid, and many jobs ceased to exist. Numerous businesses and bank accounts were wiped out.

The Independent Oil Crisis The discovery of the East Texas oil field near Kilgore in 1930 helped to alleviate the situation until overproduction of oil forced the price to drop to as low as 10 cents a barrel (about $1.60 in today's currency). Unlike earlier discoveries, the East Texas field was developed and controlled largely by "independents"—oil producers not associated with the major oil companies. The "majors" owned the oil refineries, however, and because of the oil surplus, they often refused to purchase oil from independents for refining. Independents requested assistance from Governor Ross Sterling, but instead he ordered the East Texas field closed because of its threat to the entire oil industry. Outraged independents claimed that he had overreacted and refused to stop production.

Sterling declared martial law and sent in the National Guard. Eventually, the Railroad Commission (RRC) was given the power to control production of oil in Texas (first by executive order, later by law). To give the RRC some authority, the Texas Rangers were pressed into service in 1933 in an attempt to enforce the RRC guidelines. Despite the work of the Rangers, some East Texas independents still circumvented RRC orders by building their own refineries for processing illegal ("hot") oil and selling gasoline through independent retail outlets. A legislative act in 1934 that required refineries to divulge their sources of crude oil eventually ended the expansion of independent operators and refiners. The whole enforcement question soon became unimportant, however, because by 1938 the major oil companies had gained control of 80 percent of the production in the East Texas fields.

> Governor Sterling was one of the founders of Humble Oil Company (later Exxon), and the commander of the Texas National Guard was employed by Texaco Oil Company as an attorney.

"Ma" Ferguson Again In 1932, Ma Ferguson, using economy in government as her campaign issue, was reelected governor. In 1933, the ratification of the Twenty-first Amendment to the U.S. Constitution brought an end to nationwide Prohibition. Prohibition ended in Texas two years later with the adoption of local option elections, although selling liquor by the drink was still forbidden statewide. A board was established to administer taxing and licensing of liquor dealers.

"PASS THE BISCUITS, PAPPY": 1938–1945

W. Lee O'Daniel, certainly one of the most colorful and unusual characters in Texas politics, entered the Democratic gubernatorial primary in 1938. "Pappy" O'Daniel was a highly successful flour salesman and the host of a radio hillbilly music show that was liberally sprinkled with homespun poetry and moral advice. O'Daniel's show had more daily listeners than any show in the history of Texas radio. The leader of O'Daniel's band, the Light Crust Doughboys, was Bob Wills.

In his gubernatorial campaign, O'Daniel used the slogan, "Pass the biscuits, Pappy!" Touring Texas in a bus with the Light Crust Doughboys, O'Daniel ran on a platform of the Ten Commandments, the Golden Rule, and increased old-age pensions.

He had never run for public office, had never voted in Texas, had never paid a poll tax (saying that no politician was worth $1.75), and admitted that he knew nothing about politics. With no campaign manager and no campaign headquarters, and without a runoff, he defeated 13 candidates in the Democratic primary—some of whom were well-known, prominent political figures.

"Pappy" as Governor Governor O'Daniel was not successful as a legislative leader, but he was reelected easily in 1940 against strong opposition in the Democratic primary. Again, he was notably unsuccessful in getting his proposals passed by the legislature. When a U.S. senator from Texas died, O'Daniel appointed Andrew Jackson Houston, the last surviving son of Sam Houston. Andrew Jackson Houston, at age 87, became the oldest man ever to enter the U.S. Senate.

> Pappy O'Daniel was resurrected, buffoonized, and reincarnated as a Mississippi governor in the hit 2000 movie *O Brother, Where Art Thou?* by Joel and Ethan Coen. The character was played by Charles Durning, who also played Texas Governor Dolph Briscoe in the movie version of *The Best Little Whorehouse in Texas*.

Indeed, there was some question as to whether he could survive the trip to Washington! He did, but he died 18 days later.

"Pappy" as Senator Pappy then entered the special election for the Senate seat and won, defeating 29 other candidates. (His closest competitor was a young congressman from Central Texas, Lyndon B. Johnson.) Lieutenant Governor Coke R. Stevenson succeeded Pappy as governor. O'Daniel served with a notable lack of distinction in the Senate but was reelected to a full six-year term in 1942. His ineffectiveness in Washington was possibly related to his habit of making derogatory remarks about other politicians, such as "Washington is the only lunatic asylum in the world run by its own inmates."

Texas State Library and Archives Commission

"Pappy" O'Daniel and the Hillbilly Boys. For all his failings politically and personally, "Pappy" O'Daniel was an important figure in the development of western swing music. Because of his talent for publicity and his business acumen, his bands, the Light Crust Doughboys and the Hillbilly Boys, became nationally recognized performers.

Why was Pappy O'Daniel so successful at winning elections?

Politics and Government Since World War II

LYNDON B. JOHNSON ENTERS CENTER STAGE

Beauford Jester easily won the gubernatorial election of 1946 after an especially bitter primary victory over Homer P. Rainey, the former president of The University of Texas. A major campaign issue was university autonomy and academic freedom.

The 1948 senatorial campaign for the seat of the retiring Pappy O'Daniel is worth special note. Several qualified people announced their candidacies for the position. The runoff in the Democratic primary pitted former governor Coke R. Stevenson against U.S. Congressman Lyndon B. Johnson.

The campaign was especially controversial, and the election was the closest in the state's history, with both candidates charging election fraud. At first, the election bureau gave the unofficial count as 494,330 votes for Stevenson and 493,968 for Johnson; then the revised returns for counties began to be reported, most of which favored Johnson. The final official election results were 494,191 for Johnson and 494,104 for Stevenson—a difference of 87 votes.

Historian T. R. Fehrenbach, writing about Lyndon Johnson's 87-vote victory over Coke Stevenson for the U.S. Senate in 1948, said, "There was probably no injustice involved. Johnson men had not 'defrauded' Stevenson, but successfully "out-frauded' him."[12]

"Box 13" in Jim Wells County, one of several "machine" counties dominated by political boss George Parr (the "Duke of Duval"), was particularly important in these new figures. This box revised Johnson's vote upward by 202 votes and Stevenson's upward by only one. Box 13 was also late in reporting. In the end, after various bitter political and judicial battles, Johnson was certified the victor.

CIVIL RIGHTS REVISITED

Latino Texans Returning World War II veterans, fresh from fighting to make the world safe for democracy, found discrimination still existed in the homeland. A decorated veteran, Major Hector Garcia settled in Corpus Christi and became convinced by conditions in the Latino-American community in South Texas that still another battle was yet to be fought—and in his own backyard. Garcia, a medical doctor, found farm laborers enduring inhuman living conditions; deplorable medical conditions in slums; disabled veterans starving, sick, and ignored by the Veterans Administration; and an entrenched unapologetic Anglo-Texan elite maintaining public school segregation.

To begin his war, Dr. Garcia needed recruits for his "army." With other World War II veterans, Dr. Garcia organized the American GI Forum in a Corpus Christi elementary school classroom in March 1948. This organization spread throughout the United States and played a major role in giving Latino Americans full citizenship and civil respect.[13]

One of the most incendiary sparks to ignite Latino Texans to fight for civil rights was Felix Longoria's funeral. Private Longoria was a decorated casualty of World War II whose body was returned to Three Rivers for burial in the "Mexican section" of the cemetery, which was separated from the white section by barbed wire. But an obstacle developed—the funeral home's director refused the Longorias' request to use the chapel because "whites would not like it." Longoria's widow asked Dr. Hector Garcia for support, but the director also refused his request. Dr. Garcia then sent a flurry of telegrams and

---

[12]Fehrenbach, *Lone Star*, p. 659.
[13]http://www.justiceformypeople.com/drhector2.html

letters to Texas congressmen protesting the actions of the funeral director. Senator Lyndon B. Johnson immediately responded and arranged for Private Longoria to be buried at Arlington National Cemetery.[14]

African Texans The Texas branch of the NAACP remained active during this period and served as a useful vehicle for numerous legal actions to protect African-American civil rights. African Texans at last won the right to participate in the Texas Democratic primary when the U.S. Supreme Court ruled in *Smith* v. *Albright* (1944) that primaries were a part of the election process and that racial discrimination in the electoral process is unconstitutional. Twenty years later, the first African Texans since Reconstruction were elected to the Texas legislature.

World War II veteran Heman Sweatt applied for admission to The University of Texas Law School, which by Texas law was segregated. State laws requiring segregation were constitutional so long as facilities serving blacks and whites were equal. Because Texas had no African-American law school, the Texas legislature hurriedly sought to establish a law school for Sweatt—conveniently located in his hometown of Houston. Although established, but lacking faculty and a library for the new law school, the NAACP sued Texas. Ruling that the new law school was indeed not equal, the U.S. Supreme Court ordered Sweatt admitted to The University of Texas. It is worth noting that "separate-but-equal" facilities remained legal because the court did not overturn *Plessy* v. *Ferguson*, which granted the constitutional sanction for legal segregation. Instead the court simply ruled that the new law school was not equal to The University of Texas.[15]

THE 1950s: SHIVERCRATS AND THE SEEDS FOR A REPUBLICAN TEXAS

Lieutenant Governor Allan Shivers became governor in 1949 after the death of Governor Jester. He was easily elected as governor in 1950, setting the stage for the 1952 Texas political extravaganza in which a president, the governor, and a U.S. senator would be elected.

Both state and national political issues captured the interest of the 1952 Texas voters. Harry Truman, a Democrat, had succeeded to the presidency in 1945 after the death of Franklin Roosevelt. Several scandals marred the Truman administration, and many conservative Texas Democrats were disillusioned with the New Deal and Fair Deal policies of the Roosevelt–Truman era.

The Tidelands Controversy Another major issue was the **tidelands** question. After the discovery of oil in the Gulf of Mexico, a jurisdictional conflict arose between the government of the United States and the governments of the coastal states. Texas claimed 3 leagues (a Spanish unit of measure equal to about 10 miles) as its jurisdictional boundary; the U.S. government said that Texas had rights to only three miles. At stake were hundreds of millions of dollars in royalty revenue.

Joseph Scherschel/Time Life Pictures/Getty Images

Tidelands

A submerged area that extends 3 leagues (about 10 miles) off the Texas coast. The tidelands controversy developed when offshore oil was discovered and the federal government contended that Texas's jurisdiction extended only three miles into the Gulf of Mexico.

Heman Sweatt successfully integrated Texas public law schools after the U.S. Supreme Court began to chip away at the "separate-but-equal" doctrine in the landmark case Sweatt *v.* Painter, *339 U.S. 629 (1950).*

Why was there so much opposition to integrated education?

---

[14]V. Carl Allsup, "Felix Longoria Affair," *Handbook of Texas Online,* http://www.tshaonline.org/handbook/online/articles/vef01

[15]*Sweatt* v. *Painter,* 339 U.S. 629 (1950); *Plessy* v. *Ferguson,* 163 U.S. 537 (1892).

Governor Shivers and Attorney General Price Daniel, who were campaigning for the U.S. Senate, both attacked the national Democratic administration as being corrupt and soft on communism, eroding the rights of states, and being outright thieves in attempting to steal the tidelands oil from the schoolchildren of Texas. State control would direct much of the oil income to the Permanent School Fund used for public education and would mean a lower school tax burden for Texans. The Democratic presidential nomination of Adlai Stevenson of Illinois, who disagreed with the Texas position on the tidelands, only intensified this opposition.

Loyalists and Shivercrats The Republicans nominated Dwight Eisenhower, a World War II hero who was sympathetic to the Texas position on the tidelands issue. Eisenhower was born in Texas (but reared in Kansas), and his supporters used the campaign slogan "Texans for a Texan." The presidential campaign crystallized a split in the Texas Democratic Party that lasted for the next 40 years. The conservative "Texas Democrats" faction of the party, led by Shivers and Daniel, advocated "splitting the ticket"—voting for Eisenhower for president and for Texas Democrats for state offices (for some time afterward adherents of this sort of split voting came to be known as **"Shivercrats"**). The liberal faction, or "Loyalist Democrats of Texas," led by Judge Ralph "Raff" Yarborough, campaigned for a straight Democratic ticket.

Texas voted for Eisenhower, and the tidelands dispute was eventually settled in favor of Texas. Shivers was reelected governor, and Daniel succeeded in entering the U.S. Senate. Shivers, Daniel, and the Democratic candidates for several other statewide offices (including those of lieutenant governor and attorney general) were also nominated by the Republican Party. Running as Democrats, these candidates defeated themselves as Republicans in the general election.

Governor Shivers also sought and won an unprecedented third term in 1954, but the fallout from the U.S. Supreme Court's *Brown* v. *Board of Education* (1954) public school desegregation decision would loom large during the Shivers term.[16] In 1956, when Mansfield school district, just southeast of Fort Worth, was ordered to integrate, angry whites surrounded the school and prevented the enrollment of three African-American children. Governor Shivers declared the demonstration an "orderly protest" and sent the Texas Rangers to support the protestors. Because the Eisenhower administration took no action, the school remained segregated. The Mansfield school desegregation incident "was the first example of failure to enforce a federal court order for the desegregation of a public school." Only in 1965, when facing a loss of federal funding, did Mansfield desegregate.[17]

Important to Latino Americans and ultimately other whites facing discrimination, was *Hernandez* v. *State of Texas* (1954). Pete Hernandez was convicted of murder in Edna, Jackson County, Texas, by an all-Anglo jury. Latino attorneys Gustavo (Gus) Garcia, Carlos Cadena, John Herrera, and James DeAnda challenged the conviction, arguing that the systematic exclusion of Latinos from jury duty in Texas violated their rights to equal protection of the law guaranteed by the Fourteenth Amendment of the U.S. Constitution. Texas courts ruled that Latinos

Shivercrat

A follower of Governor Allan Shivers of Texas (1949–1957). Shivercrats split their votes between conservative Democrats for state office and Republicans for the U.S. presidency.

Governor Allan Shivers delivering his speech to the convention floor. ☛

What were the events and political currents that enabled Allan Shivers to become such a successful politician?

John Dominis/Time Life Pictures/Getty Images

---

[16] *Brown* v. *Board of Education of Topeka,* 347 U.S. 483 (1954).

[17] George N. Green, "Mansfield School Desegregation Incident," *Handbook of Texas Online,* http://www.tshaonline.org/handbook/online/articles/jcm02

were white, so all Anglo (white) juries could not be discriminatory. To change the system, the Latino team of lawyers would have to change the interpretation of the U.S. Constitution. The stakes were high, for if they failed, Latino discrimination throughout the southwestern United States could legally continue for decades. Garcia argued that Latinos, although white, were "a class apart" and suffered discrimination on the basis of their "class." The U.S. Supreme Court agreed, overturned the Texas courts, and ruled that Latinos were protected by the Constitution from discrimination by other whites. The Hernandez decision established the precedent of Constitutional protection by class throughout the United States and was a forerunner for future decisions prohibiting gender, disability, or sexual preference discrimination.[18]

The veterans' land and insurance scandals also surfaced to mar the Shivers administration and scandals continued well into the administration of his successor, Price Daniel, Sr. Lobbyists' use of the "three Bs" of lobbying ("booze, beefsteak, and babes"), campaign contributions, and all-expense paid vacations for influential administrators and legislators continued to buy weak laws and lax regulation. In 1959, public outrage forced the legislature to adopt (minimal) controls on lobbyists. During the Daniel administration, Texas's first broadly based tax, the general sales tax, was enacted.

Gus Garcia, legal advisor for the American G.I. Forum, is shown during a visit to the White House. Garcia was also the lead attorney in the U.S. Supreme Court case that established Latinos as a "class apart."

Why is the "class apart" designation important to people other than Latinos?

Library of Congress

THE 1960s: TEXAS HAS A PRESIDENT AND DISCOVERS THE EQUAL PROTECTION CLAUSE

When Lyndon B. Johnson, majority leader of the U.S. Senate and one of the most powerful men in Washington, lost his bid for the Democratic presidential nomination to John F. Kennedy in 1960, he accepted the nomination for vice president. By the grace of the Texas legislature, Johnson was on the ballot of the general election as both vice-presidential and senatorial nominee. When the Democratic ticket was successful, he was elected to both positions, and a special election was necessary to fill the Senate seat he chose to vacate. In the special election, Republican John Tower was elected to fill Johnson's vacated seat in the Senate—the first Republican since Reconstruction to serve as a U.S. senator from Texas.

After the assassination of President Kennedy in 1963, Lyndon B. Johnson became president and was then easily elected for a full term in 1964. He chose not to run again in 1968, however, largely because of urban race riots, anti-Vietnam War sentiment, and poor health.

In 1962, John B. Connally, the Secretary of the Navy in the John F. Kennedy administration, returned to Texas and was elected governor. Connally became a dominant force in Texas politics and was easily reelected to second and third terms. He did not seek reelection for a fourth term and, in 1969, was succeeded by Lieutenant Governor Preston Smith.

The 1960s is known for the victories of the national civil rights movement. Texan James Farmer was cofounder of the Congress of Racial Equality (CORE), and along with Dr. Martin Luther King, Jr., Whitney Young, and Roy Wilkins, was one of the "Big Four" African Americans who shaped the civil rights struggle in the 1950s and 1960s. Farmer, who followed the nonviolent principles of Mahatma Gandhi, initiated both sit-ins as a means of integrating public facilities and freedom rides as a means of registering African Americans to vote.

---

[18] 347 U.S. 475 (1954); V. Carl Allsup, "Hernandez v. State of Texas," *Handbook of Texas Online*, http://www.tshaonline.org/handbook/online/articles/jrh01. Also see *A Class Apart;* the excellent documentary on Hernandez by PBS American Experience, produced and directed by Carlos Sandoval and Peter Miller.

Members of the Congress of Racial Equality (CORE) plan their journey to protest segregated restaurants and restrooms in bus terminals in the South. Texas civil rights activist James Farmer (second from the left) was one of the founders of CORE. ☞

Why were restrooms and restaurants segregated?

AP Photo/Byron Rollins

The first sit-in to protest segregation in Texas was organized with CORE support by students from Wiley and Bishop Colleges in the rotunda of the Harrison County courthouse in Marshall, Texas. The founder of CORE, James Farmer was himself a graduate of Wiley College and was a member of its 1935 national champion debate team, which served as the inspiration for the popular movie *The Great Debaters* starring Denzel Washington.[19]

Most African Americans and Latinos were relegated to the lowest-paid jobs as either service workers or farm workers. The fight to organize into labor unions was the primary focus for much of the Latino civil activism in the 1960s. In rural areas, large landowners controlled the political as well as the economic system and were largely united in opposition of labor unions. The United Farm Workers (UFW) led a strike against melon growers and packers in Starr County in the 1960s, demanding a minimum wage and other grievances. Starr County police officers, the local judiciary, and the Texas Rangers were accused of brutality as they arrested and prosecuted strikers for minor offenses.

On February 26, 1977, members of the Texas Farm Workers Union (TFWU), strikers, and other supporters began a march to Austin to demand the $1.25 minimum wage and other improvements for farm workers. Press coverage intensified as the marchers made their way north in the summer heat. Politicians, members of the American Federation of Labor–Congress of Industrial Organizations (AFL-CIO), and the Texas Council of Churches accompanied the protestors. Governor John Connally, who had refused to meet them in Austin, traveled to New Braunfels with then House Speaker Ben Barnes and Attorney General Waggoner Carr to intercept the march and inform strikers that their efforts would have no effect. Ignoring the governor, the marchers continued to Austin and held a 6,500-person protest rally at the state capitol. The rally was broken up by Texas Rangers and law enforcement officers.

Texas Southern University students stage a sit-in at a Houston supermarket lunch counter, 1960. ☞

What did sit-ins accomplish?

AP Photo

Legal action was taken against the Rangers for their part in the strike and the protest. The eventual ruling of the U.S. Supreme Court held that the laws the Rangers had been enforcing were in violation of the U.S. Constitution.[20] The Rangers were reorganized as a part of the Texas Department of Public Safety.

Women were given the right to serve on juries in 1954. The 1972 ratification of Texas's Equal Rights Amendment together with the passage of a series of laws titled the Marital Property Act amounted to be a revolution for women. The act granted married women equal

---

[19]For more information, see http://CORE-online.org
[20]See Robert E. Hall, "Pickets, Politics and Power: The Farm Worker Strike in Starr County," *Texas Bar Journal* 70(5); *Allee* v. *Medrano*, 416 U.S. 802 (1974); Texas Farm Workers Union, *Handbook of Texas Online*.

rights in insurance, banking, real estate, contracts, divorce, child custody, and property rights. This was the first such comprehensive family law in the United States.[21]

In 1972, Texas's Equal Rights Amendment was ratified by the voters. Also, *Roe* v. *Wade*, a Texas case tried by Texas lawyer Sarah Weddington before the U.S. Supreme Court, still stands in the center of national debate. The *Roe* decision overturned Texas statutes that criminalized abortions and in doing so established a limited, national right of privacy for women to terminate a pregnancy. *Roe* followed a 1965 Connecticut privacy case, *Griswold v. Connecticut,* that overturned a state law that criminalized the use of birth control.[22]

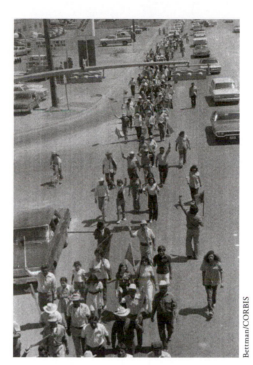

Bettman/CORBIS

About 300 United Farm Workers march to McAllen as a prelude to their attorneys answering charges against the organization made by La Casita Farms in Star County.

How did marches like this and the United Farm Workers' march to Austin attract attention to the grievances of farm workers?

THE 1970s: SCANDAL AND REFORM

The Sharpstown scandal erupted in 1971. It began when attorneys for the U.S. Securities and Exchange Commission (SEC) filed a suit alleging stock fraud against a series of elected Texas officials. The SEC also filed suit against Frank Sharp, owner of the Sharpstown State Bank. Buried in the SEC's supporting material was the allegation that several prominent politicians, including Governor Smith and House Speaker Gus Mutscher, had accepted bribes to support legislation favorable to Sharp. Although Governor Smith was not found guilty of any wrongdoing, Mutscher, along with others, was convicted of conspiracy to accept a bribe.[23]

In the wake of the scandal, a large number of "reform" advocates were elected in 1972. Dolph Briscoe, a wealthy Uvalde rancher and banker, won the governorship by a plurality of less than 100,000 votes over his Republican and Raza Unida opponents—the first general election since the institution of the party primary in 1906 in which the Democratic gubernatorial candidate did not receive a majority of the votes. Briscoe was easily reelected in 1974.

In 1974, state legislators served as delegates to a constitutional convention but failed to propose a new constitution to the voters, primarily because of conflict over a proposed *right-to-work* provision. (Under right-to-work laws passed in many states, union membership cannot be a requirement for employment.) The legislature in the next regular session proposed an extensive revision of the Texas Constitution in the form of amendments, but voters rejected them by a margin of almost three to one.

In 1979, William P. Clements became the first Republican governor of Texas since E. J. Davis had vacated the office in 1874. The election of a Republican governor did not affect legislative–executive relations, however, since Clements received strong political support from conservative Democrats.

---

[21]Enstam, "Women and the Law."

[22]*Roe* v. *Wade*, 410 U.S. 558 (1973); *Griswold* v. *Connecticut,* 381 U.S. 479 (1965); Sarah Weddington, "Roe v. Wade," *Handbook of Texas Online,* http://www.tshaonline.org/handbook/online/articles/jrr02

[23]For further discussion of the Sharpstown scandal, see Charles Deaton, *The Year They Threw the Rascals Out* (Austin, TX: Shoal Creek Publishers, 1973); Sam Kinch, Jr. and Ben Procter, *Texas under a Cloud: Story of the Texas Stock Fraud Scandal* (Austin, TX and New York: Jenkins, 1972).

THE 1980s: EDUCATION REFORM

In 1982, Democratic Attorney General Mark White displaced incumbent governor Bill Clements despite Clements' unprecedented campaign spending. Teachers overwhelmingly supported White, who promised them salary increases and expressed support for education. Clements opposed the salary increases and was perceived as unsympathetic to education.

In 1984, House Bill 72, the first comprehensive educational reform since 1949, became law. The reform increased teacher salaries, made school district revenue somewhat more equitable, and—controversially—raised standards for students and teachers. Public school teachers were required to pass a competency test to continue to teach ("no pass, no teach"), and students who failed a course were barred from extracurricular activities for six weeks ("no pass, no play").

In 1986, voter unhappiness with education reform, a sour economy, and decreased state revenue was enough to return Republican Bill Clements to the governor's office in a sweeping victory over Democrat Mark White. In 1988, three Republicans were elected to the Texas Supreme Court and one to the Railroad Commission—the first Republicans elected to state-wide office (other than governor or U.S. senator) since Reconstruction.

In 1989, the Texas Supreme Court unanimously upheld an Austin district court's ruling in *Edgewood* v. *Kirby*[24] that the state's educational funding system violated the Texas constitutional requirement of "an efficient system" for the "general diffusion of knowledge." After several reform laws were also declared unconstitutional, the legislature in 1993 enacted a complex law that left the property tax as the basic vehicle for school funding but required wealthier school districts to share their wealth with poorer districts. Critics called the school finance formula a "Robin Hood" plan.

THE 1990s: TEXAS ELECTS A WOMAN GOVERNOR AND BECOMES A TWO-PARTY STATE

In 1990, the state board of education adopted the first elementary and high school biology texts since the 1960s that contained a thorough explanation of Darwin's theory of evolution. In 1994, however, the board removed pictures of male and female reproductive systems and discussions of changes that occur at puberty from high school health books.

Down-ticket

Describes a candidate for political office relative to others located higher on the ballot.

With the 1990 election of Dan Morales (attorney general), Kay Bailey Hutchison (treasurer), and Rick Perry (agriculture commissioner), Texas elected the first Latino ever, and the first Republicans since Reconstruction, to **down-ticket** executive offices. (You will learn more about such offices in Chapter 9.) Austin voters elected the first openly gay legislator in 1991.

Texans also elected Ann Richards as their first female governor since Miriam "Ma" Ferguson. Through her appointive powers, she opened the doors of state government to unprecedented numbers of women, Latinos, and African Americans. In 1992, Texas elected Kay Bailey Hutchison as its first female U.S. senator. She joined fellow Republican Phil Gramm, and they became the first two Republicans to hold U.S. Senate seats concurrently since 1874.

Two-Party Politics When the smoke, mud, and sound bites of the 1994 general election settled, a new political age had dawned—Texas had truly become a two-party state. Republican candidates won victories from the top to the bottom of the ballot. For the first time since Reconstruction, with the election of George W. Bush, Republicans held the governor's office and both U.S. Senate seats.

Although both Democratic and Republican incumbents were reelected to down-ticket administrative positions, Republicans held all the Railroad Commission seats and a majority on the state board of education and the Texas Supreme Court.

In 1996, Republicans won a majority in the Texas Senate for the first time since Reconstruction. The 1997 legislature failed to enact campaign finance reform, nonpartisan

---

[24]777 S.W.2d 391 (Tex. 1989).

election of judges, and Governor Bush's tax initiative to reduce public schools' reliance on local property taxes. The state's first comprehensive water management plan was enacted, however, along with voluntary surgical castration for child molesters, prohibition of tobacco possession by minors, and authorization for patients to sue health maintenance organizations (HMOs) for malpractice. Voters also ratified an amendment to the Texas Constitution that allows them to use their *home equity* (the current market value of a home minus the outstanding mortgage debt) as collateral for a loan.

Republican Dominance The 1998 general election was a sweep year for Republicans, who won every statewide elective office. This overwhelming achievement also positioned Governor George W. Bush as the front-runner for the Republican nomination for president in 2000. In the 76th Texas legislature (1999), however, Democrats narrowly retained control of the state house of representatives, and Republican control of the state senate was diminished to a one-vote margin.

Legislators deregulated electric companies in Texas and required parents' permission for underage girls to obtain an abortion or have their bodies pierced (except for ears). Physicians were also given the right to collectively bargain with HMOs. The legal blood-alcohol level for driving drunk was reduced to 0.08 percent; cities and counties were prohibited from suing gun manufacturers; and the state's city annexation law was made more restrictive.

Public school teachers received a pay raise, but not enough to bring them up to the national average. A plan for taxpayer-funded vouchers to be used by families to pay for their children's private school education failed. To take advantage of federal grants that had been made available, Texas adopted a program to provide basic health insurance to some of the state's children who lacked health insurance coverage. Despite passage of this Children's Health Insurance Program (CHIP), more than 20 percent of Texas's children remained uninsured.

THE 2000s: TEXAS BECOMES A REPUBLICAN STATE

The 2001 legislature enacted a "hate crimes" law that strengthened penalties for crimes motivated by a victim's race, religion, color, gender, disability, sexual preference, age, or national origin. The legislature also criminalized open alcohol containers in most motor vehicles, established partial funding for health insurance for public school employees, and made it easier for poor children to apply for health-care coverage under Medicaid. With little conflict, the legislature increased subsidies to corporations by agreeing to reimburse school districts that grant **tax abatements** to corporations. A Republican proposal to redraw U.S. congressional districts preoccupied the 2001 legislature as major state issues were left unresolved.

The Republicans Consolidate Their Power The Republicans swept Texas statewide offices and both chambers of the legislature in the 2002 elections. A Republican governor, lieutenant governor, and speaker of the house ensured Republican proposals a sympathetic hearing in the 2003 legislative session. A nonpartisan policy, however, remained in effect in the legislature, as the lieutenant governor and speaker appointed some Democrats to committee chair and vice-chair positions.

A projected $10 billion budget deficit created an uncomfortable environment for the Republicans. Politically and ideologically opposed to both new taxes and state-provided social services, the legislature and the governor chose to reduce funding for most state programs but especially education, health care, children's health insurance, and social services for the needy.

Attempts to close some tax loopholes failed. For example, businesses and professions of all sizes continued to organize as "partnerships" to avoid the state corporate franchise tax. The legislature did place limits on pain-and-suffering jury awards for injuries caused by physician

Tax abatement

A reduction of or exemption from taxes (usually real estate taxes); typically granted by a local government to businesses in exchange for bringing jobs and investments to a community.

malpractice and hospital incompetence and made it more difficult to sue the makers of unsafe, defective products.

The legislature's social agenda was ambitious. It outlawed civil unions for same-sex couples and barred recognition of such unions even when they are registered by other states. In addition, a 24-hour wait to be "educated" about the fetus is now required before a woman can have an abortion.

The Redistricting Controversy Although the districts for electing U.S. representatives in Texas had been redrawn by a panel of one Democratic and two Republican federal judges following the 2000 census, Texas Congressman and U.S. House Majority Leader Tom DeLay was unhappy that more Texas Republicans were not elected to Congress. Governor Rick Perry agreed to call a special session to further redraw the new court-approved districts to increase Republican representation. Minority party Democrats argued that the districts had already been drawn to accommodate the decade's population shifts and that the Republicans were only trying to gerrymander Texas voters. (See Chapter 6 for a further discussion of the gerrymander.)

During Special Session One (June 30, 2003), most house Democrats (dubbed the "Killer Ds") left the state for Oklahoma to deny the state house of representatives the required two-thirds quorum necessary to conduct its business.

Special Session Two (July 28, 2003), saw Republican Lieutenant Governor David Dewhurst change the senate rule that had required a two-thirds majority vote for bills to be heard on the senate floor. This denied the minority senate Democrats a procedural tool to block congressional redistricting. In response, most senate Democrats left the state for New Mexico so that the Texas Senate would not have the required quorum. For Special Session Three (September 15, 2003), senate Democrats were unable to muster enough members to block the quorum, and the new district lines were drawn. The redistricting generated numerous lawsuits challenging its legality, but the U.S. Supreme Court refused to overturn most of the actions of the Texas legislature; affirming that states could redistrict more than once each decade and rejected the argument that the redistricting was an illegal partisan gerrymander.

Congressman Tom DeLay was indicted for money laundering and forced to resign his seat in Congress. The voters elected former Democratic Congressmen Nick Lampson to DeLay's old seat. The 2007 legislature saw almost continuous battle between the house and the speaker, the senate and the lieutenant governor, the senate and the house, and the legislature and the governor. Legislators did find time to restore some needy children to the Children's Health Insurance Program.

The 2009 legislature seemed almost placid after the unprecedented house revolt against Speaker Tom Craddick and election of Joe Straus as new speaker. However, consideration of the contentious voter identification bill caused conflict in the senate and a parliamentary shutdown of the house of representatives in the last days of the legislative session. The house adjourned without a voter identification bill resolution, leaving several important matters to be resolved by special session. Other bills that failed included proposals to legalize casino gambling, increase the legal age to purchase tobacco products, needle exchange programs, guns on campus, medical marijuana, and increased strip club fees. The legislature passed new laws, including limited restrictions on using a cell phone when driving through a school zone and a tax increase on smokeless tobacco.

In 2010, much of the state's political attention was focused on disputes about Texas's acceptance of federal funds. Texas accepted federal stimulus money to help balance the state's budget but turned down more than $500 million in federal stimulus money for unemployed Texans. The state declined to apply for up to $700 million federal grant money linked to Race to the Top, a program to improve education quality and results. Governor Perry believed that the money would result in a federal takeover of Texas's education. Texas also joined Alaska as the only two states refusing to participate in a National Governors Association effort to rewrite national curriculum standards.

Texas Culture and Regions

POLITICAL CULTURE

A political culture reflects the political values and beliefs of a people. It explains how people feel about their government—their expectations of what powers it should have over their lives and what services it should provide. A political culture is largely developed through agents of socialization such as family, religion, peer group, and education and is characterized by its levels of ethnic and religious diversity and political tolerance. Shaped by culture, individual participation in the political system depends on people's view of their place within it.

MORAL, TRADITIONAL, AND INDIVIDUALISTIC CULTURES

A number of different approaches have been used to study diversity in nations, regions, states, and communities. One popular approach is that of Daniel J. Elazar, who depicted American political culture as a mix of three distinct subcultures, each prevalent in at least one area of the United States.

Elazar used the term *moralistic* to describe a culture whose adherents are concerned with "right and wrong" in politics. *Moralistic culture* views government as a positive force, one that values the individual but functions to the benefit of the general public. Discussion of public issues and voting are not only rights but also opportunities to better the individual and society alike. Furthermore, politicians should not profit from their public service. Moralistic culture is strongest in New England, and although a product of the Puritan religious values, it is associated with more secular (nonreligious) attitudes.

Individual culture embodies the view that government is practical, its prime objective being to further private enterprise, but whose intervention into people's lives should be strictly limited. Blurring the distinction between economic and political life, individualistic culture sees business and politics as appropriate avenues by which an individual can advance her or his interests. Accordingly, business interests play a very strong role and running for office is difficult without their support. Conflicts of interest are fairly commonplace, and political corruption may be expected as a natural political activity. The individualistic culture predominates in the commercial centers of the Middle Atlantic States, moving west and south along the Ohio River and its tributaries.

Widespread throughout America, in Texas *traditional culture* derives primarily from the plantation society of the Old South and the patron system of northern Mexico and South Texas. Government is seen to have an active role but primarily to maintain the dominant social and religious values. Government should also help maintain accepted class distinctions and encourage the beliefs of the dominant religion. Traditionalistic culture views politics as the special preserve of the social and economic elite—as a process of maintaining the existing order. Believing in personal rather than public solutions to problems, it views political participation as a privilege and accepts social pressure and restrictive election laws that limit participation.[25]

Moralistic culture

A political subculture that views government as a positive force, one that values the individual but functions to benefit the general public.

Individual culture

A political subculture that views government as a practical institution that should further private enterprise but intervene minimally in people's lives.

Traditional culture

A political subculture that views government as an institution to maintain the dominant social and religious values.

---

[25]Daniel J. Elazar, *American Federalism: A View from the States*, 3rd ed. (New York: Harper & Row, 1984).

POLITICAL CULTURE AND POLITICAL PARTICIPATION

Elazar considered Texas a mix of traditional and individualistic cultures. The traditional overrides the individualistic in East Texas, which was initially settled by immigrants from the Upper Old South and Mexican border areas, where the patron system dominated early Texas. The individualistic supersedes the traditional throughout the rest of the state. As a result, in Texas, participation in politics is not as highly regarded as in those states with a moralistic culture. Voter turnout in Texas is in fact well below the national average. Texans see politics largely as the domain of economic interests, and most tend to ignore the significance of their role in the political process and how it might benefit them.[26]

TEXAS CULTURAL REGIONS

D. W. Meinig found that the cultural diversity of Texas was more apparent than its homogeneity and that no unified culture has emerged from the various ethnic and cultural groups that settled Texas. He believed that the "typical Texan," like the "average American," does not exist but is an oversimplification of the more distinctive social, economic, and political characteristics of the state's inhabitants.[27]

Both Meinig and Elazar see modern regional political culture as largely determined by migration patterns, for people take their culture with them as they move geographically. Meinig believed that Texas had evolved into nine fairly distinct cultural regions. However, whereas political boundaries are distinct, cultural divisions are often blurred and transitional. For example, the East Texas region shares political culture with much of the Upper South, whereas West Texas shares a similar culture with eastern New Mexico, and so forth (Figure 1.1.)

The effects of mass media, the mobility of modern Texans statewide and beyond, and immigration from Mexico also blur the cultural boundaries within Texas, between its bordering states, and with Mexico. Although limited because they do not take into account these modern-day realities, both Meinig and Elazar's explanations are useful guides to a general understanding of contemporary Texas culture, attitudes, and beliefs.

East Texas East Texas is a social and cultural extension of the Old South. It is basically rural and biracial. Despite the changes brought about by civil rights legislation, black "towns" still exist alongside white "towns," as do many segregated social and economic institutions, such as churches, fraternal lodges, and chambers of commerce.

East Texas counties and towns are often dominated by old families, whose wealth is usually based on real estate, banking, construction, and retail merchandising. Cotton—once "king" of agriculture in the region—has been replaced by beef cattle, poultry, and timber. As the result of a general lack of economic opportunity, young East Texans migrate to metropolitan areas, primarily Dallas–Fort Worth and Houston. Seeking more tranquility and solitude, retiring urbanites have begun to revitalize some small town and rural communities that lost population to the metropolitan areas. The region is dominated spiritually by fundamentalist Protestantism, which permeates its political, social, and cultural activities.

Spindletop

Spindletop was a major oil discovery in 1901 near Beaumont that began the industrialization of Texas.

The Gulf Coast Before 1900, Texas was an economic colony; it sold raw materials to the industrialized North and bought northern manufactured products. In 1901, however, an oil well named Spindletop was drilled near Beaumont, and the Texas economy began to change. Since **Spindletop**, the Gulf Coast has experienced almost continuous growth, especially

---

[26]Ibid.

[27]Information for this section is adapted from D. W. Meinig, *Imperial Texas: An Interpretive Essay in Cultural Geography* (Austin, TX and London: University of Texas Press, 1969).

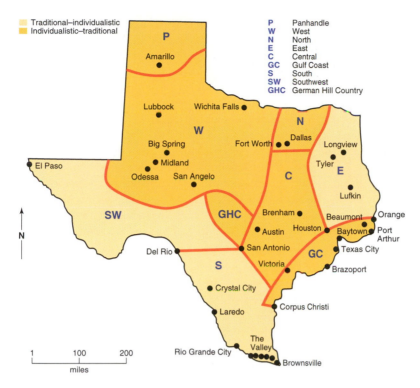

Figure 1.1

Texas Political Culture.
Maxwell's original figure
is based on Elazar and
Meinig concepts.

In which political cultural area
do you reside? Do you agree
with the assumptions of the
author about your area?

during World War II, the Cold War defense buildup, and the various energy booms of the late 20th and early 21st centuries.

In addition to being an industrial and petrochemical center, the Gulf Coast is one of the most important shipping centers in the nation. Spindletop was backed by out-of-state investors, largely from the northeastern states, and its success stimulated increased out-of-state investment. Local wealth was also generated and largely reinvested in Texas to promote long-range development. Nevertheless, much of the economy is still supported by the sale of raw materials.

A Boom Based in Houston Through boom and bust, the petrochemical industry, which is concentrated on the Gulf Coast, has experienced unprecedented growth, producing a boom-town psychology. Rapid growth has fed real estate development and speculation throughout the region. The Houston area especially has flourished, and Harris County (Houston) has grown to become the third most populous county in the United States.

The initial growth of Houston was fueled by the influx of job seekers from East Texas and other rural areas of the state after World War II. This growth tended to give the Gulf Coast the flavor of rural Texas in an urban setting. Houston's social and economic elite were generally composed of second- and third-generation rich whose wealth came from oil, insurance, construction, land development, or banking. This rural flavor diminished, however, as migration to Texas from the Frost Belt (Great Lake and Mid-Atlantic states). Frost Belt migration was to a large extent a result of the economic difficulty resulting in the metamorphosis of the U.S. economy from an industrial to a service base. This migration included both unskilled and unskilled workers and added large numbers of well-educated young executives and professionals to the Houston elite pool. The Gulf Coast economy also attracts heavy immigration from the Americas, Africa, Europe, and Asia, giving modern Houston a culture as international as that of Los Angeles or New York. In fact, modern Houston has street signs in

Vietnamese, Chinese, and English in areas with large Vietnamese and Chinese populations. There are still many large ranches and plantations in the Gulf Coast region. They are owned either by wealthy business executives who live in the large cities or by "old families."

The collapse of the oil boom and drastic declines in the price of oil and other petroleum products in the 1980s and 1990s struck especially hard at the Gulf Coast economy, which relies heavily on the petrochemical industry. Conversely, rising prices in the 2000s have resulted in another oil-based boom for the region.

The implosion of Houston-based Enron Corporation in the early 2000s affected financial markets and political attitudes nationwide, but it was especially damaging to Houston's economy, labor force, and national image. Enron was intertwined into the fabric of Houston's political, social, cultural, and financial existence to an extent rarely seen in corporate America. A dynamic corporate citizen, Enron made significant contributions to almost every aspect of Houston life. Its collapse left many Houstonians with dramatically decreased retirement incomes and investments. Despite the Enron collapse, the Gulf Coast continues to be a remarkably vibrant and energetic region. Houston, the worldwide oil and gas capital, boasts many corporate headquarters.

Although negatively affected, Texas's economy weathered the 2008 economic and financial meltdown much better than other urban states. Texas real estate also suffered fewer home foreclosures, primarily because the state did not experience a housing boom comparable to the West Coast, East Coast, or Nevada and Arizona.

South Texas The earliest area settled by Europeans, South Texas developed a **ranchero culture** on the basis of livestock production that was similar to the feudal institutions in faraway Spain. **Creoles**, who descended from Spanish immigrants, were the economic, social, and political elite, whereas the first Texas cowboys, the **Mestizos** and the Native Americans, did the ranch work. Anglo Americans first became culturally important in South Texas when they gained title to much of the real estate in the region following the Texas Revolution of 1836. However, modern South Texas still retains elements of the ranchero culture, including some of its feudal aspects. Large ranches, often owned by one family for several generations, are prevalent; however, wealthy and corporate ranchers and farmers from outside the area are becoming common.

South Texas Agriculture Today Because of the semitropical South Texas climate, **The Valley (of the Rio Grande)** and the **Winter Garden** around Crystal City became major producers of vegetable and citrus products. These areas were developed by migrants from the northern United States in the 1920s and continue to be important multi-use agricultural assets. The development of citrus and vegetable enterprises required intensive manual labor, which brought about increased immigration from Mexico. Modern South Texas Latinos can usually trace their U.S. roots to the 1920s or later because much of the Latino population was driven south of the Rio Grande after the Texas Revolution.

Southwest Texas Southwest Texas exhibits many of the same **bicultural** characteristics as South Texas. Its large Mexican-American population often maintains strong ties with relatives and friends in Mexico. The Roman Catholic Church strongly influences social and cultural attitudes on both sides of the border.

Southwest Texas is a major commercial and social passageway between Mexico and the United States. El Paso, the "capital city" of Southwest Texas and the fifth largest city in

---

Ranchero culture

A quasi-feudal system whereby a property's owner, or patron, gives workers protection and employment in return for their loyalty and service. The rancher and workers all live on the *ranchero*, or ranch.

Creole

A descendant of European Spanish (or in some regions, French) immigrants to the Americas.

Mestizo

A person of both Spanish and Native American lineage.

The Valley (of the Rio Grande)

An area along the Texas side of the Rio Grande River known for its production of citrus fruits.

Winter Garden

The Winter Garden is an area of South Texas known for its vegetable production.

Bicultural

Encompassing two cultures.

The *La Raza Unida* political movement of the 1960s began in Crystal City. *La Raza Unida* literally means "A United People." This party was organized in the late 1960s as a means of getting Mexican Americans to unite politically and to identify ethnically as one people. Its name is derived from *La Raza Cosmica* ("The Cosmic Race"), written by Mexican intellectual Jose Vasconcelos. For more information, see http://larazaunida.tripod.com

Texas, is a military, manufacturing, and commercial center. El Paso's primary commercial partners are Mexico and New Mexico. The economy of the border cities of Southwest Texas, like that of South Texas, is closely linked to Mexico and has also benefited from the economic opportunities brought about by NAFTA. The agricultural economy of much of the region depends on sheep, goat, and cattle production, although there is some irrigated row-crop agriculture. Most of the labor on ranches, as well as in manufacturing and commerce, is Latino.

Latino pioneers are depicted in a model by Laredo sculptor Armando Hinojosa that is to be placed atop a memorial commemorating early Texas Latinos.

Why are monuments important to people?

AP Photo/Harry Cabluck

The Texas Border South and Southwest Texas together comprise the area known as the "Texas Border." A corresponding "Mexico Border" includes parts of the Mexican states of Chihuahua, Coahuila, Nuevo León, and Tamaulipas. It can be argued that the Texas Border and the Mexico Border are two parts of an economic, social, and cultural region with a substantial degree of similarity that sets it off from the rest of the United States and Mexico. The Border region, which is expanding in size both to the north and to the south, has a **binational**, bicultural, and bilingual subculture in which **internationality** is commonplace and the people, economies, and societies on both sides constantly interact.[28]

South and Southwest Texas are "mingling pots" for the Latino and Anglo American cultures. Roman Catholic Latinos often retain strong links with Mexico through extended family and friends in Mexico and through Spanish-language newspapers. Many Latinos continue to speak Spanish; in fact, Spanish is also the commercial and social language of choice for many of the region's Anglo Americans.

The Texas Border cities are closely tied to the Mexican economy, on which their prosperity depends. Although improving economically, these regions remain among the poorest in the United States.

The economy of the Texas Border benefits economically from *maquiladoras*, which are Mexican factories through which U.S. corporations employ inexpensive Mexican labor for assembly and piecework. Unfortunately, lax environmental and safety standards result in high levels of air, ground, and water pollution in the general area. In fact, the Rio Grande is now one of America's most ecologically endangered rivers.

The ongoing **North American Free Trade Agreement (NAFTA)**, which has helped remove trade barriers between Canada, Mexico, and the United States, is an economic stimulus for the Texas Border because it is a conduit for much of the commerce with Mexico.

Immigration and National Security Poverty, military conflicts, crime, political disorder, and suppression of civil liberties in Central America and Mexico have driven hundreds of thousands of immigrants into the border regions of the United States. This flow of immigrants continues despite the tightened security measures and fence construction after the September 11, 2001, terror attack on New York City and Washington, D.C. The Texas Border is a major staging ground for the migration of both legal and illegal immigrants into the interior of Texas and the rest of the United States. The government's immigration control expenditures economically benefit the regions.

Binational
Belonging to two nations.

Internationality
Having family and/or business interests in two or more nations.

Maquiladora
A factory in the Mexican border region that assembles goods imported duty-free into Mexico for export. In Spanish, it literally means "twin plant."

North American Free Trade Agreement (NAFTA)
A treaty between Canada, Mexico, and the United States, that calls for the gradual removal of tariffs and other trade restrictions. NAFTA came into effect in 1994.

---

[28]John Sharp, Texas Comptroller of Public Accounts, "Bordering the Future: Challenge and Opportunity in the Texas Border Region," July 1998, p. 3; Jorge Bustamante, "A Conceptual and Operative Vision of the Population Problems on the Border," in *Demographic Dynamics on the U.S.-Mexico Border*, ed. John R. Weeks and Roberto Ham Chande (El Paso, TX: Texas Western Press, 1992), cited in Sharp, "Bordering the Future."

The U.S.-Mexico Border Fence Near Hidalgo, Texas ☛

What is the purpose of the border fence? Do you think that it will be successful?

Scott Olson/Getty Images

Military expenditures by the U.S. government are also important to the economy of the region. A decision by the U.S. Navy to station a contingent of naval vessels in Ingleside has been an economic boost to the upper South Texas coast, and Fort Bliss continues to economically benefit the El Paso area.

The American craving for illegal, mind-altering, addictive chemicals provides a steady flow of American capital through the Texas Border into Mexico and South America. Basically, the drug traffic is uncontainable as long as its U.S. market exists, but newspapers and other media virtuously trumpet feel-good headlines about "record drug busts" and arrests while the drug trade continues unabated.

This "invisible trade," because of its illegal status, inevitably results in violence as surely as did the American experiment prohibiting the sale and consumption of alcoholic beverages from 1919 to 1933. The collateral damage of the drug trade is readily visible and all too common as stories of death and destruction are lead stories for evening news and provide villains and endless plots for movies and television detective programs. Although the worst of the violence is confined to the border areas of Mexico and the United States, its political, economic, lawless, and violent extension is increasingly evident throughout both countries.

Collateral to the drug traffic and its companion violence is a reverse cash flow from Mexico to the United States for weapons purchases. This illegal traffic moves easily obtained weapons, ammunition, and explosives from Texas and other states into Mexico and South America minimally balancing the outflow of capital from the United States to Mexico and South America for drugs.

When the expenditures by the Mexican, Texas, and U.S. governments for narcotics and immigration agents, prison construction and operation, related military operations, and increased police employment are combined with the expenses, wages, and bribe money spent by drug, weapons, and immigrant traffickers, the result is increased employment and a significant but unwholesome economic infusion to both sides of the border. Immigration, illegal traffic, and border security will be major political issues for both Democrats and Republicans in the foreseeable future.

German Hill Country The Hill Country was settled primarily by immigrants from Germany but also by immigrants who were Czech, Polish, and Norwegian. Although they mixed with Anglo Americans, Central European culture and architecture was dominant well into the 20th century. Skilled artisans were common in the towns; farms were usually moderate in size, self-sufficient, and family owned and operated. Most settlers were Lutheran or Roman Catholic, and these remain the most common religious affiliations for modern residents.

The German Hill Country is still a distinct cultural region. Although its inhabitants have become "Americanized," they still cling to many of their Central European cultural traditions. Primarily a farming and ranching area, the Hill Country is socially and politically conservative and has long been a stronghold of the Texas Republican Party.

Migration into the region, primarily by Anglo Americans and Latinos, is increasing. The most significant encroachment into the Hill Country is residential growth from rapidly expanding urban areas, especially San Antonio and Austin. Resorts, country homes, and retirement villages for well-to-do urbanites from the Gulf Coast and Dallas–Fort Worth area are also contributing to the cultural transformation of the German Hill Country.

> Comfort, Texas, was settled by German "Freethinkers" seeking freedom *from* religion. They were both abolitionists and opponents of secession, and many were massacred by pro-Confederate raiders during the U.S. Civil War. A monument to these pioneers was erected in Comfort.

West Texas The defeat of the Comanches in the 1870s opened West Texas to Anglo-American settlement. Migrating primarily from the southern United States, these settlers passed their social and political attitudes and southern Protestant fundamentalism on to their descendants.

There are relatively few African Americans in modern West Texas, but Latinos migrated into the region in significant numbers, primarily to the cities and the intensively farmed areas. West Texas is socially and politically conservative, and its religion is Bible Belt fundamentalism. West Texas voters traditionally supported conservative Democrats but today favor the Republican Party. Indeed, this is true of most conservative Texans throughout the state.

The southern portion of the area emphasizes sheep, goat, and cattle production. In fact, San Angelo advertises itself as the "Sheep and Wool Capital of the World." Southern West Texas, which is below the Cap Rock Escarpment, is the major oil-producing area of Texas. The cities of Snyder, Midland, and Odessa owe their existence almost entirely to oil and related industries.

Northern West Texas is part of the Great Plains and High Plains and is primarily agricultural, with cotton, grain, and feedlot cattle production predominating. In this part of semiarid West Texas, the outstanding agricultural production is due to extensive irrigation from the **Ogallala Aquifer**. The large amount of water used for irrigation is gradually depleting the Ogallala. This not only affects the present economy of the region through higher costs to farmers but also serves as a warning signal for its economic future.

The Panhandle Railroads advancing from Kansas City through the Panhandle brought Midwestern farmers into this region, and wheat production was developed largely by migrants from Kansas. Because the commercial and cultural focus of the region was Kansas City, the early Panhandle was basically Midwestern in both character and institutions.

The modern Texas Panhandle shares few cultural attributes with the American Midwest. Its religious, cultural, and social institutions function with little discernible difference to those of northern West Texas. The Panhandle economy is fed through extensive irrigation of cotton and grains from the Ogallala Aquifer. Feedlots for livestock and livestock production were established because of their proximity to the region's grain production but are major economic enterprises in their own right. Effective conservation of the Ogallala Aquifer is critical to the economic future of both northern West Texas and the Panhandle.

Ogallala Aquifer

A major underground reservoir and a source of water for irrigation and human consumption in northern West Texas and the Texas Panhandle, as well as other states.

North Texas Located between East and West Texas, North Texas exhibits many characteristics of both regions. Early North Texas benefited from the failure of the French socialist colony of **La Réunion**, which included many highly trained professionals in medicine, education, music, and science. (La Réunion was located on the south bank of the Trinity River, across from modern downtown Dallas.) The colonists and their descendants helped give North Texas a cultural and commercial distinctiveness. North Texas today is dominated by the Dallas–Fort Worth **Metroplex**. Dallas is a banking and commercial center of national importance, and Fort Worth is the financial and commercial center of West Texas.

When railroads came into Texas from the North in the 1880s, Dallas became a rail center, and people and capital from the North stimulated its growth. Fort Worth became a regional capital that looked primarily to West Texas. The Swift and Armour meatpacking companies, which moved plants to Fort Worth in 1901, became the first national firms to establish facilities close to Texas's natural resources. More businesses followed, and North Texas began its evolution from an economic colony to an industrially developed area.

North Texas experienced extraordinary population growth after World War II, with extensive migration from the rural areas of East, West, and Central Texas. The descendants of these migrants are now third- and fourth-generation urbanites and now tend to have urban attitudes and behavior. Recently, migration from other states, especially from the North, has been significant. Many international corporations have established headquarters in North Texas. Their executive and support staffs contribute to the region's diversity and cosmopolitan environment.

Although North Texas is more economically diverse than most other Texas regions, it relies heavily on the defense and aerospace industries. It also produces electronic equipment, computer products, plastics, and food products.

Central Texas Central Texas is often called the "core area" of Texas. It is roughly triangular in shape, with its three corners being Houston, Dallas–Fort Worth, and San Antonio. The centerpiece of the region is Austin, one of the fastest-growing metropolitan areas in the nation. Already a center of government and education, the Austin metropolitan area has become the "Silicon Valley" of high-tech industries in Texas. Although the worldwide downturn in the high-tech sector after 2000 dealt a serious blow to the area's economy, high-tech industries still make a major economic contribution.

Austin's rapid growth is a result of significant migration from the northeastern United States and the West Coast, as well as from other regions in Texas. The influx of well-educated persons from outside Texas has added to the already substantial pool of accomplished Austinites, making it the intellectual and political capital of the state, as well as economic center of Central Texas. The cultural and economic traits of all the other Texas regions mingle here, with no single trait being dominant. Central Texas is a microcosm of Texas culture.

Politics and Diversity

Voter participation in Texas is historically low, even by United States standards. Social scientists argue that this is attributable to political conditioning as well as social and economic reality. And Latino participation is low even by Texas standards. However, Latino voter turnout surged during the 2008 primary and election. Is this sleeping political giant really awake or was this level of political participation simply an anomaly. What would be the impact of substantial Latino political participation on the Texas political system? We look at differing attitudes among Latinos in this chapter's *Politics and Diversity* feature.

La Réunion

A failed French socialist colony of the 1800s located within the city limits of modern Dallas. Its skilled and educated inhabitants benefited early Dallas.

Metroplex

The greater Dallas–Fort Worth metropolitan area.

POLITICS AND DIVERSITY IN TEXAS

HISPANICS VERSUS MEXICAN AMERICANS

In 2002, Democrat Tony Sanchez unsuccessfully challenged Republican Rick Perry for the Texas governor's seat. Sanchez sought to "make history" by becoming the first Hispanic governor of Texas. To that end, Sanchez, a wealthy businessman, put up almost $60 million of his own money.

Nevertheless, Sanchez received only 39 percent of the votes. This was lower than the 44 percent received in 1996 by Victor Morales, a Mexican-American schoolteacher who ran for the U.S. Senate against incumbent Republican Phil Gramm. Unlike Sanchez, Morales campaigned on a shoestring budget. Why then, did Morales turn in a noticeably better performance than Sanchez?

THE PROBLEM WITH THE "HISPANIC" LABEL

One possible answer is that Rick Perry may have been a more popular, less polarizing figure than Phil Gramm. Another answer, however, is that Morales was more effective than Sanchez in mobilizing Mexican-American voters. One problem with Sanchez's approach was the very fact that he billed himself as the "Hispanic" candidate and as a direct descendant of the original Spanish settlers of Laredo, Texas. A majority of Latinos are not particularly fond of the Hispanic label and prefer to identify with their actual country of origin. Cuban Americans, for example, usually prefer to be called exactly that.

THE MEANINGS BEHIND THE LABELS

Fernando Pinon, a professor at San Antonio College, argues that the two appellations—Hispanic and Mexican American—represent alternative frameworks by which Latinos in Texas view themselves in relation to the dominant Anglo population. The term *Mexican American* brings to mind resistance to the majority that "stole their land and ha[s] since then denied them their culture, suppressed their rights, and turned them into second-class citizens." The word *Hispanic,* in contrast, brings to mind accommodation rather than confrontation. Hispanics have "made it" within the system. "Hispanic Texans represent a Latinized version of Anglo Texan suburbanites," writes Pinon, "and, as such, do not connect with the mostly blue-collar Mestizo Mexican American of the barrio."

Given these considerations, it is easy to understand the greater success that Morales enjoyed in mobilizing the Latino vote. Morales presented himself as a cultural maverick fighting the establishment. He was able to tap into the historical grievances of the Mexican–American population. Tony Sanchez, wealthy and successful, was unable to do the same.

LATINOS, HISPANICS, TEJANOS, AND MEXICAN AMERICANS

People with Spanish surnames and descendants of people from Spain, Mexico, Central America, parts of the Caribbean and South America are popularly referred to as *Latinos* or the feminine *Latinas*. The U.S. Census Bureau uses *Hispanics*, and both terms include the substantial numbers of Cuban Americans and Central Americans that have recently immigrated to Texas. On the other hand, the use of *Hispanics* sometimes overgeneralizes and ignores the specific contribution Americans of Mexican descent have made to the state's history and culture. The term *Tejano* (or *Tejana*) is sometimes used to refer specifically to a Texan of Mexican descent. The term *Chicano* (or *Chicana*) was popular with Mexican–American civil rights activists in the 1960s and 1970s but is less commonly used today.

FOR DEBATE

In the years to come, we can expect that the existing Mexican-American population of Texas will become better educated, earn more, and be more completely integrated into the majority culture. What effect will these developments have on Latino political attitudes? Could continued high rates of immigration from Mexico have an effect on the political attitudes of Mexican Americans who are already here? If so, how?

*Fernando Pinon, "The Political Culture of Hispanics and Mexican Americans in Texas," *Texas Politics Today*, 11th ed. (Belmont, CA: Thomson Wadsworth, 2004), p. 27.

Cultural Diversity

Texas is one of the fastest-growing states in the nation. No longer predominantly rural and agrarian, Texas is becoming more culturally diverse than ever as immigrants continue to find it a desirable place to call home. The 2000 Census showed a significant trend toward greater ethnic diversity (Table 1.1). During the 10-year period, the Anglo majority declined from 60.7 to 53.1 percent, whereas Latinos increased from 25.5 to 32.0 percent, and the rapidly growing "Other" classification (primarily Asians, Pacific Islanders, Middle Easterners, and Native Americans) grew from 2.1 to 3.3 percent. The African-American percentage of the total population also decreased marginally, from 11.7 to 11.6 percent.

TABLE 1.1 SCENARIO 0.5 POPULATION* 1990 AND 2000, AND PROJECTED POPULATION 2005–2040 (IN THOUSANDS AND PERCENTS** BY RACE/ETHNICITY FOR STATE OF TEXAS, 2004)

Year	Total	Anglo American	%	African American	%	Latino	%	Other	%
1990*	16,987	10,308	60.7	1,981	11.7	4,340	25.5	357	2.1
2000*	20,852	11,075	53.1	2,422	11.6	6,670	32.0	686 (231)***	3.3
2005	22,556	11,328	50.2	2,589	11.5	7,820	34.7	819	3.6
2010	24,331	11,534	47.4	2,755	11.3	9,080	37.3	961	4.0
2015	26,157	11,695	44.7	2,913	11.1	10,437	39.9	1,113	4.3
2020	28,006	11,796	42.1	3,052	10.9	11,883	42.4	1,274	4.5
2025	29,897	11,831	39.6	3,171	10.6	13,448	45.0	1,447	4.8
2030	31,831	11,789	37.0	3,269	10.3	15,140	47.6	1,633	5.1
2035	33,790	11,682	34.6	3,345	9.9	16,934	50.1	1,828	5.4
2040	35,761	11,525	32.2	3,403	9.5	18,804	52.6	2,029	5.7

* Census population.
** Percent and population have been rounded.
***The 2000 Census was the first with a "two or more races" category. This table includes these approximately 231,000 respondents in the "Other" classification with Asians, Native Americans, Pacific Islanders, and Middle Easterners.

Sources: Adapted from "Projections of Texas and Counties in Texas by Age, Sex, and Race/Ethnicity for 1990–2040" and U.S. Census Bureau, Census 2000 Redistricting Data Summary File. Texas State Data Center and Office of the State Demographer; Institute for Demographic and Socioeconomic Research, College of Business, The University of Texas at San Antonio, 6900 North Loop 1604 West, San Antonio, Texas 78249-0704, http://txsdc.utsa.edu/tpepp/. Copyright © 1998–2004. For more information contact txsdc@utsa.edu, phone (979) 845-5115, or fax (979) 862-3061.

What does Table 1.1 tell us about Texas's changing cultural makeup?

The Texas State Population Estimates and Projections Program aids government and corporate planners by developing estimates of Texas's future population growth. This group of researchers has proposed a number of possible population scenarios. One scenario assumes that net migration into Texas will be zero. We find this assumption to be unrealistic and therefore do not include that scenario here. Another scenario assumes that the relatively high immigration levels of the 1980s will continue. Although possible, this table is also not included in this text. The middle-of-the-road scenario is printed in Table 1.1, and is the one Texas statisticians recommend for long-range business and governmental planning. This mid-range scenario, which assumes a moderate degree of immigration, predicts a Texas population of slightly more than 35 million by 2040, with a Latino plurality by 2025 and a Latino majority by 2035. In contrast, the high-immigration scenario projects a Texas population of more than 51 million by 2040. Latinos achieve plurality status by 2015 and majority status by 2030. Furthermore, the "Other" classification surpasses African Americans and collectively becomes the third largest group by 2040. All scenarios show Anglo Texans losing their numerical majority by 2010.

Clearly, Texans are becoming more diverse and now have the opportunity to continue to build on their already rich cultural pluralism. Increasing diversity could also have a significant impact on the political culture of Texas because the interests of more groups would have to be seriously considered as public policy is formulated and implemented.

A downside of Texas diversity is an unequal distribution of wealth and access to medical care. As shown in Figures 1.2, 1.3, and 1.4, Latino/Hispanic Americans, African Americans, and "Others" are more likely to live in poverty, have significantly lower family income, and have lower levels of health insurance than Anglo Americans.

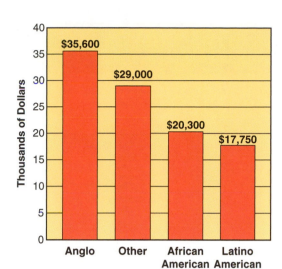

Figure 1.2

Net Family Income in Texas

Source: The Henry J. Kaiser Family Foundation, "State Health Facts Online," www.statehealthfacts.kk.org

Which of these groups will benefit the most from income tax reduction?

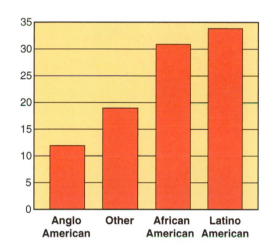

Figure 1.3

Percentage of Persons in Poverty in Texas

Source: The Henry J. Kaiser Family Foundation, "State Health Facts Online," www.statehealthfacts.kk.org

Why do you think that each group falls along these economic lines?

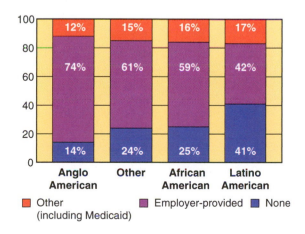

Figure 1.4

Health Insurance Status of Persons Under the Age of 65 in Texas

Source: The Henry J. Kaiser Family Foundation, "State Health Facts Online," www.statehealthfacts.kk.org

Which of these groups do you think will benefit the most from healthcare reform?

HOW DOES TEXAS COMPARE?
HOW TEXAS RANKS AMONG THE 50 STATES

Texas is often ranked among the 50 states to make a political point or further a political agenda. However, these rankings can also be used to illustrate Texas's distinctive political culture, to offer insights into the state's policy priorities and to offer perspective on the state's population and its quality of life.

50th = Lowest, 1st = Highest	Texas's Rank	Did You Know . . .
Tax Revenue		
Tax revenue raised per capita	49th	*That Texas requires low-income families (the bottom 20%) to pay three times the share of their incomes in taxes as the wealthy?
Tax expenditures per capita	50th	
Progressiveness of tax revenues	44th	
Per Capita Spending on		
Mental health	48th	
Medicaid	37th	
Percent public schools funding from state	47th	
Education		
Public school enrollment	2nd	*That Texas does not require sex education programs to teach students about preventing pregnancy or sexually transmitted diseases by any means other than abstinence?
Average teacher salary	49th	
Scholastic Assessment Test (SAT) scores	46th	
Percentage of population over age 25 with high school diplomas	50th	*That 143 of 1,000 Texas high school graduates scored in the top 20 percent nationally on the SAT and ACT tests, as compared to 265 students in top-performing states?
High school graduation rates	41st	
Percentage of adults with bachelor's degree	30th	
Current expenditures per student	44th	
Teenage birth rate	1st	
Health Care		
Percentage with health insurance	50th	*That one in four Texans has no health insurance?
Percentage of population with employer-based health insurance	46th	*That 33 percent of poor children in Texas are uninsured compared with 20 percent nationwide?
Percentage of uninsured poor covered by Medicaid	47th	
Percent of population who visit the dentist	43rd	*That in Texas, 65 percent of Latino children and 57 percent of African-American children live in low-income families compared with 24 percent of Anglo-American children?
Percent of women receiving prenatal care in first trimester	29th	
Financial Security		
Percentage living below poverty level	3rd	*That 49 percent of Texas children live in low-income families?
Percentage malnourished	3rd	
Amount of welfare and food stamp benefits paid	47th	
Home mortgage delinquency rate	4th	
Average net worth of household	48th	

HOW DOES TEXAS COMPARE?
HOW TEXAS RANKS AMONG THE 50 STATES

50th = Lowest, 1st = Highest	Texas's Rank	Did You Know ...
Children		
Birth rate	2nd	*That 46 percent of Texas children in low-income families live with a single adult?
Percentage of children living in poverty	7th	
Percentage of uninsured children	1st	
Environment		
Air pollution emissions	1st	*That Texas has the tenth-largest economy in the world?
Pollution released by manufacturing plants	1st	
Greenhouse gases released	1st	*That one in seven of Texas infants is born prematurely?
Toxic chemicals released into water	1st	
Toxic chemicals released into air	5th	
Known carcinogens released into air	1st	
Known carcinogens released into water	7th	
Amount of hazardous waste generated	2nd	
Energy consumption per capita	5th	
Quality of Life		
Income inequality between rich and poor	9th	
Income inequality between rich and middle class	5th	
Homeowners insurance affordability	50th	
Percent of households with Internet access	36th	
Public Safety		
Number of executions	1st	*That Texas spends $7,142 per public school student and $20,232 per prison inmate?
Rate of incarceration	2nd	
Total crime rate	8th	
Violent crime rate	15th	
Rape rate	18th	
Percent of murders involving firearms	14th	
Workers		
Average hourly earnings	42nd	*That 17.6 percent of Texans live in poverty?
Percentage of workforce represented by a union	47th	*That only 5.7 percent of Texas workers are covered by a union?
State minimum wage rates	33rd	
Workers' compensation benefit payment per covered worker	48th	

(continued)

HOW DOES TEXAS COMPARE?
HOW TEXAS RANKS AMONG THE 50 STATES (CONTINUED)

FOR DEBATE

Discuss each category and recommend what Texas needs to do to improve its rankings. How likely are Texans to support these changes? Which of these rankings reflect Texas's conservative, low-tax, low-spending, tough-on-crime political culture? Give examples of conservative social views in Texas public policy. Which of these rankings best reflect Texans' pro-business approach to public *policy? What is the proper role of government in solving social and economic problems? Should Texas strive to develop policies more like those in other states, or should Texas continue to implement policies based on self-reliance and limited government?*

Source: *Texas on the Brink, 2009: How Texas Ranks among the 50 States.* This publication can be accessed at the website of Senator Eliott Shapleigh (from El Paso), http://www.shapleigh.org/reporting_to_you

CHAPTER SUMMARY

★ Originally part of Mexico, Texas was largely settled by migrants from the American South. Texas declared its independence from Mexico in 1836 and joined the United States in 1845. Early politics revolved around the slavery issue and the possibility of secession from the Union, which was strongly opposed by Sam Houston, one of the founders of the Texas Republic and the hero of the battle of San Jacinto (1836). After the election of Abraham Lincoln as U.S. president, Texas left the Union and joined the Confederacy. The collapse of the Confederacy meant anarchy until Union troops occupied Texas in June 1865.

★ After a period of military occupation, radical Republican E. J. Davis (1870–1873) became governor in an election in which African Americans could vote but many former Confederates could not. The Davis administration was enormously unpopular with the white majority in Texas, and after the former Confederates regained the franchise, Davis was swept from office. The Democratic Party was to control Texas politics for more than 100 years.

★ While conservatives normally dominated the Democratic Party, Texas experienced a degree of progressive reform with the election of several progressive governors between 1890 and 1939, including James Hogg (1891–1895) and both "Farmer Jim" and "Ma" Ferguson (1915–1917, 1925–1927, and 1933–1935). Another colorful governor was radio announcer W. "Pappy" Lee O'Daniel, a popular figure who nonetheless had little legislative success.

★ A key figure in the era following World War II (1939–1945) was governor Allan Shivers (1949–1957). A conservative Democrat, Shivers advocated voting for Republican presidents and conservative Democrats for all other offices. In 1960, Lyndon B. Johnson, U.S. senator from Texas and the Senate majority leader, became vice president under John F. Kennedy. In a special election in 1961, Republican John Tower filled Johnson's seat. Tower was the first Republican since Reconstruction to be elected to an important position in Texas, but he would not be the last. In 1963, after Kennedy's assassination, Johnson became president of the United States.

★ Civil rights have always been an issue, and the primary purpose for both African Americans and Mexican Americans being in Texas was seen by the dominant Anglo Americans as sources of cheap labor. Modern Texans can take no pride in the historical treatment of both these groups, who were undereducated and exploited for their labor and lived under a state-enforced caste system. The enduring consequences of discrimination are still with us, as illustrated by lower levels of health care, education, and income.

★ The election of Republican William Clements as governor in 1979 was a sign of the growing importance of the Republican Party. By 1994, Texas was clearly a two-party state. By 2002, the Republicans were in complete control of all levels of state government, including both chambers of the legislature. Texas seemed headed toward a one-party system again, but under a different party. In 2003, the Republicans consolidated their power by redistricting the U.S. House seats. As a result, in 2004, they gained control of the Texas delegation to the U.S. House.

★ Texas can be divided into a series of cultural regions with differing characteristics and traditions: (1) East Texas, (2) the Gulf Coast, (3) South Texas, (4) Southwest Texas, (5) the German Hill Country, (6) West Texas, (7) the Panhandle, (8) North Texas, and (9) Central Texas. These regions display varying combinations of moral, traditionalistic, and individualistic cultures.

★ Projections of population growth and immigration predict a gradual shift in Texas's population away from an Anglo American majority toward a Latino-American majority. Increased political clout can come with increased population, and Latino-Americans could begin to challenge the political and economic dominance of Anglo Americans. Regardless of the political outcome of population shifts, Texas is becoming more culturally diverse and now has an opportunity to build on its already rich cultural pluralism.

HOW TEXAS COMPARES

★ Beginning in the 1820s Texas's settlers came from the "Anglo" political culture of the Old South, and Texas political history can best be compared to that of other former Confederate states. Like other southern states, the Texas political culture has been traditionalistic and individualistic.

★ Like other southern states, Texas politics was dominated by mostly conservative Democrats between Reconstruction and the 1960s. As with other one-party states in the South during this period, politics revolved around personality as much as issues, and racial politics was a major undercurrent in campaigns and public policy.

★ With the other southern states, Texas politics became more competitive in the later part of the 20th century, and these states have now come to be Republican party strongholds in the 21st century.

★ Meanwhile, Texas public policies have remained conservative. Per capita, only one state has lower taxes, and no state spends less on public services than Texas. The state has more business-friendly economic policies and culturally traditional social policies than most states.

★ Texas economy has become more industrialized than most states, and with less vigorous environmental limits than states like California, Texas ranks first among the states in emission of greenhouse gases released into the air and toxins released into the water.

★ With three of America's ten largest cities, Texas has become the second most populous state, and one of the most metropolitan. Texas ranks among the top ten states in population growth and today it has twice the percentage of Latinos in its population as the nation as a whole.

KEY TERMS

annexation
antitrust legislation
bicultural
binational
Creole
down-ticket
individual culture
internationality
item veto

Ku Klux Klan (KKK)
La Réunion
maquiladora
Mestizo
Metroplex
moralistic culture
North American Free Trade
    Agreement (NAFTA)
Ogallala Aquifer

progressive movement
Prohibition
ranchero culture
secession
Shivercrat
Spindletop
tax abatement
tenant farmer
tidelands

traditional culture
The Valley (of the Rio Grande)
White primary
Winter Garden

REVIEW QUESTIONS

1. Describe the general cultural characteristics of Texas's regions. Does the description fit your home area?

2. Describe the Texas political system before the Civil War.

3. Describe the Progressive period in Texas politics. What roles did James Stephen Hogg and James E. and Miriam A. Ferguson play?

4. What role did the Ku Klux Klan play in Texas politics in the 1920s?

5. Describe the politics of W. Lee O'Daniel.

6. What was Texas politics like in the 1950s, and how did the Shivercrats lay the groundwork for the current success of Republican candidates?

7. What are the predictions concerning Texas's population growth and its future ethnic makeup?

LOGGING ON

Welcome to cyberpolitics in Texas. The Internet creates unprecedented opportunities for research, communication, and participation in Texas politics. Today, students can easily communicate with the authors of their textbooks, government leaders, and fellow students all across Texas. To facilitate this, Wadsworth, Cengage Learning has developed a companion website available at www.cengage.com/politicalscience/maxwell/texaspoliticstoday15e

Recent study of French explorer Robert La Salle's ship La Belle, sunk in 1686, has revealed new insights into the early European exploration of Texas. The Texas Historical Commission has information about this state project at **http://www.thc.state.tx.us/belle/**

Look at the state of Texas home page for information on Texas history, early native populations, historical events and dates, historic sites, and population information, projections, and demographics: **http://www.state.tx.us**. A useful site for all purposes is the Texas State Library and Archives Commission (TSLAC) at **http://www.tsl.state.tx.us**

The *Handbook of Texas Online* is a great source for information on Texas history, culture, and geography. A joint project of the Texas State Historical Association and The University of Texas at Austin, it is an encyclopedia of all things Texan. It can be found online at **http://www.tsha.utexas.edu/handbook/online**

Factual information and statistics can be found in the *Texas Fact Book 2006,* written by the Bob Bullock Texas State History Museum for the Legislative Budget Board, at **http://www.lbb.state .tx.us/Fact_Book/Texas_Fact_Book_2006_0106.pdf**

The Ku Klux Klan in Texas

Brian R. Farmer
Amarillo College

INTRODUCTION

After two decades of progressivism and political reforms that began the 20th century in Texas politics, it was perhaps to be expected that a reactionary movement would arise to counter what many Texans viewed as too much reform, too fast. When the moral crusade that accompanied the calamity that was World War I was added to the mix, seemingly out of nowhere, the Ku Klux Klan (KKK) experienced a resurgence in Texas during the 1920s. It was able to extend its reach far beyond anything the Klan had achieved in the 19th century.

Under William J. Simmons, a Methodist minister from Georgia, the KKK combined multilevel marketing, patriotism, nativism, and fundamentalist Protestantism into a potent form of organized hate that attracted more than 150,000 members in Texas and millions of sympathizers. The KKK built its organization in each community from the top down by targeting leading members of Texas communities for Klan leadership and then recruiting downward. The Klan courted the leading Protestant ministers, the Chiefs of Police, and the leading businesspeople in each community as well as elected city officials, giving the Klan political power on the local levels. The Texas KKK was not an entirely local phenomenon but part of a nationwide movement that had 700,000 members across the country. The KKK became so widespread across the southern United States that it even included a strong presence in the northern states of Ohio and Indiana by 1922.

The Klan in Texas was led by Grand Dragon A. D. Ellis, an Episcopal priest from Beaumont. Under Ellis, the KKK recruited members mainly from the Protestant, white middle class, and membership was limited to white, native-born, Protestants. The KKK built its membership by paying field organizers (Kleagles) $4.00 of each $10.00 initiation fee paid (Klecktoken) by inductees. Of this, $1.00 went to the "King Kleagle." Another $0.50 went to the local Cyclops of the local Klavern that the new member joined. The Imperial Kleagle, Edward Clarke, received $3.00 and the remaining $1.50 went to the Imperial Wizard, William J. Simmons. Members had to purchase official robes from the Klan for $6.50, and inductees were anointed with KKK Holy Water that was purchased for $6.00 a quart (water that Simmons later admitted was sold in jars simply dipped in the Chattahoochee River in Georgia).

Klan members were told to practice "Vocational Klanishness," meaning that they were to patronize each other's businesses in preference to nonmembers. Businesses of nonmembers were often vandalized as an incentive for all businessmen to join the Klan. Klan-friendly businesses placed "AKAI" (A Klansman Am I) signs in their windows both to invite business from Klansmen and to ward off Klan vandalism.

Stated KKK goals included the preservation of patriotism, the preservation of the purity of women, white supremacy, and "enforcing law at a time of lawlessness." The Klan was pledged to "return America to its Godly heritage and purge America of un-American and un-Godly influences." The political platform of the KKK included the Protestant fundamentalist-friendly planks of the Golden Rule, the teaching of the Ten Commandments in schools, prayer in public schools, and opposition to the teaching of Darwin's evolution. Additionally, the Klan advocated that textbooks in schools should explain the evils of liquor.

KKK targets were not limited to blacks, and included almost everyone and everything other than white, fundamentalist Protestants. The Klan officially opposed Catholics, Jews, blacks, Mexicans, short skirts, abortions, immorality, adultery, divorce, "demon rum," dance halls, movie theaters, and immigration. The KKK identified paintings and books that it viewed as immoral, and opposed beauty contests, carnivals, and jazz clubs.

Victims of KKK violence included blacks, but also Catholics and other minorities, doctors who performed abortions, businessmen charged with corrupting young women, husbands who abandoned their wives, divorcees who set immoral examples, pimps, prostitutes, gamblers, thieves, and bootleggers.

The political power of the KKK and Protestant fundamentalism led to the passage of the Blue Laws that closed businesses on Sundays in an effort to allow everyone the opportunity to attend Church. Municipal laws in Texas were passed prohibiting public flirting, women smoking in public, and the playing of jazz after midnight. Restrictions were also passed on the brevity of bathing suits, and a bill was introduced in the Texas legislature banning women's heels to no more than one inch. In 1923, a bill was introduced to ban evolution in education, but the bill died in the senate.

The Klan, however, did not limit its efforts to influencing public policy. Newspapers reported 80 floggings in Texas in 1921 alone. In Houston, a white merchant was whipped for "bothering" high school girls. In Beaumont, a doctor was whipped for performing abortions. In Bay City, a banker was whipped for adultery. In Goose Creek, two oil field workers were whipped for being "undesirable citizens." In Houston, a black dentist was castrated for "associating with a white woman." In the bloody month of May 1922, nine black citizens were killed across Texas by KKK mobs. The KKK denied involvement, and these incidents were ignored by KKK-dominated law enforcement officers in many areas. Klan penetration was so great that grand juries generally refused to indict Klansmen.

The KKK may have reached its peak in Texas in 1922, when Dallas dentist Hiram Wesley Evans became Imperial Wizard (national leader) of the entire KKK. Texas even had its own women's chapter, and in June 1923, 1,500 female Klanswomen held a Klan parade in Fort Worth. Governor Pat Neff was accused of KKK membership by his political opponents in 1922, a charge that Neff would neither confirm nor deny, but he was reelected that same year regardless. Also in 1922, KKK member Earle B. Mayfield, a Texas railroad commissioner, won the election to the U.S. Senate against former Texas governor James Ferguson. Ferguson made the KKK the central issue of his campaign, but most Texans refused to vote for Ferguson, who had been impeached and removed from the Texas Governor's Office in 1918. In 1923, whites-only primaries, supported by the Klan, began in Texas under Governor Pat Neff. Academics across Texas condemned the practice of white-only primaries and Neff and the legislature retaliated by cutting faculty salaries at state colleges and universities 20 percent. Neff retired in 1924 after two terms as governor to become the president of Baylor University.

In 1924, Ferguson attempted to get back into the governor's mansion by backing his wife, Miriam Amanda (M. A. "Ma") Ferguson in a campaign for governor with opposition to the Klan as part of their platform. Ma's opponent in the Democratic primaries was Judge Felix Robertson of Dallas, a candidate of the KKK. According to Robertson, he stood for the "God-given right and supremacy of white Christian men." Robertson also stated that "America and Texas have forgotten God, and can stop their drift into ruin only by returning to the rugged cross of Christianity."

Robertson garnered more votes than Ma Ferguson in the Democratic primary, but on the day of the primary election, a rock-throwing, white-sheeted crowd attacked the Fergusons' home in Temple. The Klan's attack backfired, since conservatives in Texas generally viewed a white man's property as sacrosanct and the attack was also viewed by many as an unmanly attack on a woman. Robertson had to face Ma the next month in a runoff, when Ferguson defeated the Klan candidate by 98,000 votes. Ma then defeated Republican George Butte in the general election and became the first female governor of Texas.

After 1924, the KKK began to decline, partially as a result of overreach, since the KKK targets had been expanded to approximately one-half of the population, and partially because of public revulsion at KKK violence. In the most celebrated case, the Klan's Grand Dragon of Indiana, David Stephenson, born in Texas in 1891, was accused of brutally kidnapping and raping a woman on a Chicago-bound train from Indiana. The woman, Madge Oberholzer, was terribly mutilated, and toxicologists testified that the lacerations made on her body by human teeth were sufficient to cause her death. But she died after ingesting a lethal dose of bichloride of mercury tablets after Stephenson took her back to his mansion and tried to hide her in a loft above his garage. Stephenson was convicted of second-degree murder and a tidal wave against the Klan swept the nation until the KKK, so powerful in 1922, became almost nonexistent by 1930.

In Texas, Ma Ferguson contributed to the Klan's demise in 1925 by ushering through the legislature an "Anti-Mask" law that prevented Klansmen from wearing their hoods in public. Texas Attorney General Dan Moody gained a reputation for vigilance in his enforcement of the Act, and subsequently defeated Ferguson for governor in 1926 on an anti-Klan platform.

Given that a good percentage of people will do sordid things in secret that they will not do when their identities are known, the "undedicated" members of the KKK quickly abandoned the organization in an overt sense after the Stephenson scandal and the enforcement of the Anti-Mask bill. It is much easier to destroy an organization, however, than an ideology, and while the Klan as an organization was essentially discredited and defeated in the late 1920s, the ideas that spawned the Klan survived the organization's demise and would weave their way in and out of Texas politics in different forms for decades to come.

BIBLIOGRAPHY

Anderson, Ken. *You Can't Do That Dan Moody: The Klan-Fighting Governor of Texas* (Austin, TX: Eakin Press, 1999).

Alexander, Charles C. *The Ku Klux Klan in the Southwest* (Norman, OK: University of Oklahoma Press, 1995).

Campbell, Randolph B. *Gone to Texas* (New York: Oxford University Press, 2003).

Calvert, Robert A., Arnoldo De Leon, and Gregg Cantrell. *The History of Texas*, 3rd ed. (Wheeling, IL: Harlan Davidson, 2002).

Chalmers, David M. *Hooded Americanism: The History of the Ku Klux Klan* (New York: Doubleday, 1965).

Fehrenbach, T. R. *Lone Star: A History of Texas and the Texans* (Cambridge, MA: Da Capo Press, 2000).

Lay, Shawn. *The Invisible Empire in the West: Toward a New Historical Appraisal of the Ku Klux Klan in the 1920s* (Champaign, IL: University of Illinois Press, 1992).

Pearson-Haas, Ben. *KKK: The Hooded Face of Vengeance* (Evanston, IL: Regency, 1963).

Richardson, Rupert, Adrian Anderson, Gary D. Wintz, and Ernest Wallace. *Texas: The Lone Star State*, 9th ed. (Upper Saddle River, NJ: Prentice-Hall, 2004).

JOIN THE DEBATE

1. Have any KKK ideas survived into modern day Texas politics? How do they manifest themselves today?

2. What ideas did the Klan use to present itself as a wholesome organization that people would want to be a part of? In what ways was the KKK a successful business enterprise in its day?

3. What factors led to the demise of the KKK as an organization? Was the Klan discredited more because of its ideas or because of its tactics?

The Mexican–American Civil Rights Movement in Texas

Robert Ballinger
South Texas College

INTRODUCTION

This chapter mentions the formation of the American G.I. Forum and how the incident regarding the funeral of Private Felix Longoria helped to spark the Mexican-American civil rights movement. Although most people are familiar with the struggle for equality for Mexican Americans led by Cesar Chavez in California, few people realize that several events tied to the Mexican-American struggle for equal rights took place in Texas, mainly in the Rio Grande Valley. These events were often inspired by, and modeled on, the larger national movement.

FARM WORKERS' STRIKE

In June of 1966, while Cesar Chavez was leading his strike against grape growers in California, labor organizers led a strike of farm workers against farms located in Starr County, Texas. The workers demands included a raise to $1.25 per hour and an end to the use of day laborers from Mexico. In response to the strike, county officials asked the state to send in the Texas Rangers. The Rangers arrested many of the strikers, and allegations of police brutality were widespread. On July 4, the striking workers began a march to the Basilica in San Juan and from there on to Austin. Strike leaders had said that they wanted to meet with Governor John Connally, but the governor refused to meet with them officially. He did visit with the strikers informally before they reached Austin, telling them that their strike was not going to change anything. While the strike was underway, members of the U.S. Senate Subcommittee on Migratory Labor, including Senator Edward Kennedy, held hearings in Rio Grande City and Edinburg. Picketing ended shortly after these hearings. Although the strike did not result in specific improvements for farm workers in Texas, it did result in a ruling by the United States Supreme Court in 1974 (*Medrano* v. *Allee*)[1] that placed

restrictions on how the state could use the Texas Rangers during labor disputes.

EL PARTIDO DE LA RAZA UNIDA

Attempts to increase voter turnout and to challenge Anglo dominance of the political system in Crystal City in the late 1960s led to the formation of a political party to represent the interests of Mexican Americans: *El Partido de La Raza Unida*. Chapters of *La Raza Unida* formed throughout south Texas and other southwestern states. The party was successful in winning many local elections, especially in south Texas. In 1972, the party nominated Ramsey Muñiz to run for governor of Texas. Muñiz received approximately six percent of the vote. In the latter part of the 1970s, *La Raza Unida*'s success declined and it turned its attention more toward voter turnout efforts.

EDCOUCH-ELSA HIGH SCHOOL WALKOUT

Inspired by school walkouts in East Los Angeles protesting inferior education, seniors at Edcouch-Elsa High School staged a walkout of their own. In retaliation, the school said that it would not allow these students to graduate. Only one other school in the region would allow some of the students to transfer so that they could graduate.

THE PHARR RIOT

In February 1971, a demonstration was organized to protest police brutality in Pharr. Like other cities in deep South Texas, Pharr was divided geographically, economically, and socially along ethnic lines, and there were no Mexican Americans represented in government office. During the demonstration, both sides accused the other of aggressive behavior. The police grabbed one protestor and pulled him into the police station. They also used high-pressure water hoses on the protestors. However, the police said that the protestors began throwing rocks at the police and at bystanders. The demonstration quickly degenerated into a riot, which lasted four hours. By the time it ended, 40 people had been arrested, and a bystander was killed when a deputy sheriff fired into the crowd.

A previously planned visit to the Rio Grande Valley by Cesar Chavez three days later turned into a memorial for the victim of the riot. Chavez used the opportunity to call for a boycott of Pharr businesses. A month later, 1,000 people marched from the San Juan Basilica to the cemetery where the victim was buried. The march was called to again protest police brutality and as a memorial for the victim. The next couple of months saw picketing of the Pharr police station and a boycott of prominent businesses in Pharr. It was hoped that business owners would pressure the city to address the complaints of the Mexican-American community.

---

[1] *Allee v. Medrano*, 416 U.S. 802 (1974).

The consequences of the Pharr riot were widespread and long-lasting. The riot ushered in a period of increased political awareness and political activity by Mexican-American residents of the Rio Grande Valley. Increased voter turnout among Mexican Americans led to the first election of Mexican-American government officials in Pharr and other Valley cities.

JOIN THE DEBATE

1. How did these early South Texas civil rights movements set the stage for Latino participation in modern Texas politics? How has the Latino struggle for equality reflected in Texas politics today?

2. How do Anglo reactions to these Latino protests reflect the state's political culture?

RESOURCES

The farm workers' strike in Starr County is discussed on the Wikipedia page for the United Farm Workers (http://en.wikipedia.org/wiki/United_Farm_Workers).

Three short videos about the Pharr riot are available on YouTube. Unfortunately, the fourth video of the set has not been posted at the time of this writing (http://www.youtube.com/view_play_list?p=E5C5873D29FC25D9&search_query=pharr+riot).

An excellent resource for those wanting to know more about the Mexican-American struggle for equal rights, including the school walkouts, and *El Partido de La Raza Unida* is the four-part *Chicano!* video series that originally aired on PBS.

Chapter 2

The Texas Constitution in Perspective

CONTENTS

LEARNING OBJECTIVES

* Explain the functions of constitutions.
* Identify which powers are assigned to the national government and which are assigned to the states.
* Identify Texas's historic constitutions and the cultural and political forces that shaped each of their distinctive features.
* Identify the rights protected by the Texas Bill of Rights and distinguish those that are also protected by the U.S. Constitution.
* Describe the major constitutional structures, functions, and limits of Texas's legislative, executive, and judicial branches.
* Describe the constitutional functions and limits of the three major types of local government.
* Identify Texas voter qualifications and restrictions on the right to vote.
* Explain the process of amending and revising the Texas constitution and the reasons that amendments are frequently necessary.

★ GET ACTIVE ★

Link up with groups active in supporting your view of constitutional rights.

Conservative Groups

★ The National Rifle Association (**http://www.nra.org/**) supports a broader right to keep and bear arms.

★ Students for Concealed Carry on Campus (**http://concealedcampus.org/**) fights to repeal restrictions on campus firearms.

★ Texas Alliance for Life (**http://www.texasallianceforlife.org/**) is a pro-life group.

★ Texas Eagle Forum (**http://texaseagle.org/**) and the Federalist Society (**http://www.fed-soc.org/**) broadly advocate conservative views of personal liberties.

Liberal Groups

★ Texas Freedom Network (**http://www.tfn.org/**) and the Anti-Defamation League (**http://www.adl.org/**) focus on religious liberty.

★ NARAL Pro-Choice America (**http://www.naral.org/**) supports abortion rights.

★ The Brady Campaign (**http://www.bradycampaign.org/**) advocates gun control.

★ Texas Coalition to Abolish the Death Penalty (**http://www.tcadp.org/**) fights capital punishment.

★ Texas Civil Liberties Union (**http://www.aclutx.org/**) supports liberal positions on civil liberties.

Tune into the continual rewriting of the state's fundamental law by voting in Texas elections to ratify state constitutional amendments. Note that proposals are sometimes detailed and confusing, and beware of biased special-interest group television and newspaper ads describing them. Good amendment summaries and analyses are available in news sections of local papers, and the websites of

★ The League of Women Voters at **http://www.lwvtexas.org** and

★ The Legislative Council at **http://www.tlc.state.tx.us**

The real character of a government is determined less by the provisions of its constitution than by the minds and hearts of its citizens. Government is a process of decision making conditioned by its history, its people, and pressures exerted by citizens, interest groups, and political parties.

Still, our national, state, and local governments would be vastly different were it not for their constitutions. Although the exact meaning of constitutional provisions may be

The Archives Division/Texas State Library

🖐 *Austin around the time that Texas's state constitution was written. The Texas Constitution was the product of a very different era, and numerous amendments have been necessary to accommodate dramatic changes in the state since it was first written.*

Since 1875, what social changes have affected the way the state is governed?

disputed, there is general agreement that constitutions should be respected as the legal basis controlling the fundamentals of government decision making. Constitutions serve as a rationalization for the actions of courts, legislatures, executives, and the people themselves. Indeed, the very idea of having a written constitution has become part of the political culture—the basic system of political beliefs in the United States.

Constitutions establish major governing institutions, assign them power, and place both implicit and explicit limits on the power they have assigned. Moreover, because Americans respect constitutions, they promote **legitimacy**, *the general public acceptance of government's "right to govern."*

Legitimacy

General public acceptance of government's right to govern; also, the legality of a government's existence conferred by a constitution.

The National Constitution and the States: Federalism

State government is limited by the larger system in which it operates. The U.S. Constitution allocates power between the two levels of government, state and national, and limits the power of both. Such a constitutional **division of powers** is the essential characteristic of a federal system.

Division of powers

In a federal system, the granting of certain powers to the national government and others to the regional or state governments.

DIVISION OF POWERS

Because the U.S. Constitution does not draw a bright line between the power of the national government and the states, there has been enormous conflict as the political and legal environments sometimes support growth in national power and, at other times, tilt toward the states. In this epic struggle for power, the national courts have acted as an umpire between the two levels of government.

Delegated powers

Powers granted to the national government by the U.S. Constitution.

Expressed powers

Powers explicitly granted by the U.S. Constitution to the national government; also known as *enumerated powers.*

Implied powers

Powers delegated to the national government as a result of interpretation of the "necessary and proper" clause in the U.S. Constitution.

National Powers The powers granted to the national government are **delegated powers**; some are explicit, and others are implied. The U.S. Constitution (mostly in Article I) gives Congress an explicit list of **expressed** or **enumerated powers**. The national government has powers to regulate interstate and foreign commerce, establish uniform rules for naturalization and bankruptcies, raise and support armies and navies, wage war, conduct international relations, tax and borrow money, and do many other things, all of which are specifically stated in the U.S. Constitution.

The national government also has **implied powers** associated with its authority to do whatever is "necessary and proper" to carry out its expressed powers. Thus the government's *delegated powers* consist of its *expressed powers* plus its *implied powers*. The question of how much power is granted to the national government depends largely on interpretation of the implied-powers clause of the Constitution. Except in a few recent cases, the U.S. Supreme Court has generally interpreted the "necessary and proper" clause broadly, allowing the national government to act far beyond the literal language of the Constitution.

Congress has exercised its implied powers in broad and sweeping ways, occasionally using even war powers and national defense to justify domestic programs. Among the most important of the policy areas where the national government has grown are interstate commerce, taxation, social services, health care, civil rights, and the war on terror. By establishing conditions for receiving federal grants, Congress has also exerted considerable influence on state and local policies.

HEALTH-CARE REFORM: A QUESTION OF FEDERALISM

In March 2010, Congress passed the Patient Protection and Affordable Care Act of 2010, also known as health-care reform. Among its numerous provisions is an individual mandate that requires uninsured citizens to buy health insurance or pay a fine to the federal Internal Revenue Service. The act also provides for state exchanges through which citizens and small businesses may purchase health insurance. Those without employer-based insurance may be eligible for federal subsidies on a sliding scale depending on their income. The Medicaid program will be expanded to cover individuals and families with incomes up to 133 percent of the federal poverty level.

THE CASE THAT HEALTH-CARE REFORM IS UNCONSTITUTIONAL

Several provisions in health-care reform legislation have raised issues about the scope and power of the federal government. Critics of the controversial legislation have derided it as "Obamacare" and have argued that it is a federal "takeover" of medical care and a violation of state and individual rights. Texas Attorney General Gregg Abbott and a dozen other Republican state attorneys general have challenged the constitutionality of the law.*

Their central argument is that the federal government does not have the constitutional power to mandate citizens to buy qualifying health insurance. Congress passed the individual mandate under its authority to regulate interstate commerce, but Gregg Abbott argues that the federal government cannot twist "commerce" to include "every possible activity under the sun," including failing to buy health insurance—the "act of doing absolutely nothing" does not constitute an act of commerce.

The U.S. Supreme Court has found that, indeed, there are limits to what constitutes interstate commerce. When the federal government tried to create gun-free zones around public schools, the court ruled that it was too much of a stretch of the national government's power to regulate interstate commerce to say that it could control the threat of gun violence around schools as a threat to economic activity. The Court ruled that gun possession is essentially a noneconomic activity, and therefore, not subject to regulation as interstate commerce.** The more conservative tilt of the current Supreme Court suggests that it might hold that failure to buy health insurance is not an act of interstate commerce, and therefore, cannot be punished by the national government.

THE CASE THAT HEALTH-CARE REFORM IS CONSTITUTIONAL

In contrast, many constitutional lawyers argue that the national government has the broad power to regulate the health insurance market because it is part of interstate commerce. Advocates argue that failure to buy health insurance is a decision that is clearly commercial in nature and that widespread lack of insurance has a direct and sweeping impact on interstate commerce.

Historically, the U.S. Supreme Court has allowed the national government considerable latitude to regulate individual economic decisions when they have an impact on interstate commerce. When a farmer raised wheat for his own personal use in excess of the quota assigned to him by the national government, the U.S. Supreme Court ruled that his actions were interstate commerce because by growing his own wheat he affected the interstate market by denying it his purchases. Therefore, the national government has the power to compel him to comply with its policies to limit wheat production.*** Similarly, the Supreme Court ruled that cultivation of marijuana for personal use can be regulated by the national government because it affects the national market for this product.**** In both cases, the national government was allowed to regulate individual choices because their personal decisions affect interstate commerce. The court could rule that individuals' decision not to buy health insurance has a similar effect on the interstate market.

FOR DEBATE

Should the national government have the power to regulate citizens' choices that affect interstate commerce? Which national government policies would change if it had no such power?

---

*Attorney General Abbott Challenges the Constitutionality of Federal Health Care Takeover, Office of Attorney General of Texas, News Release, March 23, 2010, http://www.oag.state.tx.us/oagNews/release.php?id=3273

**United States v. Lopez, 514 U.S. 549 (1995).

***Wickard v. Filburn, 317 U.S. 111 (1942).

****Gonzales v. Raich, 545 U.S. 1 (2005)

State Powers Despite this growth of the national government, states remain a vital and vibrant part of the federal system. Although federal budgets have grown during the last half-century, state budgets have grown even more rapidly. The 50 states today have more civilian employees than the federal government, and local governments employ almost four times as many people as the national government. State governments are primarily responsible for defining and punishing crime; planning and building highways; and administering welfare, Medicaid, higher education, and unemployment compensation. Local governments are primarily responsible for law enforcement, public schools, flood control, public utilities, sewage treatment, and mass transportation. The federal government has grown considerably in the last century, but state and local governments are engaged in programs, such as building sports

Figure 2.1

Division of State and National Power. This figure illustrates that there is some sharing of powers between the states and national government in a federal system.

Give specific examples of these concurrent powers as well as those that are exclusive to the national government and those that are reserved to the states. Why do some political groups support greater power for the national government while others favor more power for the states?

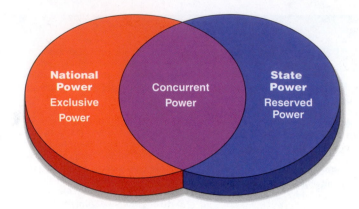

Exclusive powers

Powers delegated to the national government but not to the states.

Concurrent powers

Powers shared by the national government and the states.

Supremacy clause

Article VI of the U.S. Constitution, which makes the national constitution and laws supreme when they conflict with state rules and actions.

Tenth Amendment

U.S. Constitution provision that all powers not delegated to the national government are reserved for the states and the people—the basis for states' rights arguments.

Reserved powers

Powers belonging only to the states and not shared with the federal government.

arenas and enforcing seat-belt laws, that were inconceivable in 1900. Americans are definitely governed more at all levels—federal, state, and local.

Much state power overlaps with the national government. Although the national government has some **exclusive powers** that are powers not permitted to the states (to make treaties, establish a currency system, or conduct war), there is a broad range of **concurrent powers** (see Figure 2.1) shared between the national government and the states. Concurrent powers include the powers to tax, borrow, and regulate commerce. If a conflict develops within the scope of these shared powers, the courts will use the **supremacy clause** (Article VI of the U.S. Constitution) to invalidate state policies in favor of those adopted by the national government.

In addition to these concurrent powers, the states also have reserved powers. According to the **Tenth Amendment** in the U.S. Constitution "the powers not delegated" to the national government are **reserved** for the states and the people. The Tenth Amendment is not specific about which powers are reserved only to the states and not shared with the federal government.

As they interpret the general language in the U.S. Constitution, the federal courts have rarely used the Tenth Amendment to invalidate federal actions, but the courts have struck down the federal attempts to compel states to enforce federal laws. For example, the U.S. Supreme Court ruled that it is unconstitutional for the federal government to force states to clean up nuclear waste or to do background checks on gun buyers—these are attempts to "commandeer" state agencies in the service of the federal government.[1]

Instead of protecting a specific list of reserved powers, the Tenth Amendment simply reaffirms that the national government only has those powers that are delegated by the Constitution, but it does not mean that the national government has no implied powers. For political reasons, pundits frequently misquote the Tenth Amendment as saying "all powers not *explicitly* delegated to the national government" are reserved to the states. If this had been the actual language of the Constitution, the national government would not be able to provide such popular national programs as Social Security, Medicare, and environmental protection because they are not explicitly mentioned in the U.S. Constitution and would have been reserved to the states.

However, early in the nation's history, the U.S. Supreme Court in the case of *McCulloch* v. *Maryland* (17 U.S. 316, 1819) set the precedent that the national government could act beyond its expressed powers. Chief Justice John Marshall pointed out that unlike the Articles of Confederation, which provided that all powers not explicitly delegated to the national government were reserved to the states, the Tenth Amendment deliberately excludes the word "explicitly," leaving implied powers intact.

---

[1]*New York* v. *United States*, 505 U.S. 144 (1992); *Printz* v. *United States*, 521 U.S. 898 (1997).

LIMITS ON STATES

Texas must not only contend with the growth of the national government but must also deal with significant U.S. constitutional limits on state action. Neither the states nor the national government may enact bills of attainder (legislative punishment without court trial) or ex post facto laws (retroactive criminal laws) or grant titles of nobility. State governments (but not the national government) are forbidden to impair the obligations of contract. State governments are required to grant full faith and credit to the public acts, records, and judicial proceedings of every other state; for example, state courts in one state must recognize deeds, wills, and contracts from another. However, one state is not required to punish violators of another state's criminal laws; instead, it should provide for the rendition (often less properly called "extradition") of criminal fugitives to the states having jurisdiction.

Even more important guarantees are contained in the **Fourteenth Amendment**, which provides that no state shall "deprive any person of life, liberty, or property without due process of law" or deny any person the "equal protection of the laws." The federal courts interpreted the "due process" clause to extend most of the provisions of the U.S. Bill of Rights to state governments, and the "equal protection" clause served as the legal basis for desegregation and for outlawing other discriminatory state policies. The Fourteenth Amendment fundamentally altered the character of the federal union by setting up certain national standards for state governments.

The following are subsequent amendments that protect various political rights and limit the powers of state governments:

★ The Fifteenth Amendment prohibits states from denying the right to vote to anyone because of race, color, or previous condition of servitude.
★ The Seventeenth Amendment provides for the election of U.S. senators by the voters rather than by state legislatures.
★ The Nineteenth Amendment forbids the states from prohibiting persons from voting on the basis of sex.
★ The Twenty-fourth Amendment limits the powers of the states by forbidding state poll taxes as a condition for voting in *national* elections.
★ The Twenty-sixth Amendment forbids states from using age in setting suffrage requirements, as long as the voter is at least 18 years old.

U.S. constitutional standards for state action are interpreted by the courts. Although it is not specifically provided for in the U.S. Constitution, federal courts have assumed the power of **judicial review** to declare state action unconstitutional (in *Fletcher* v. *Peck*, 10 U.S. 87, 1810).[2] Although the U.S. Constitution restrains state action, perhaps the greatest limitation on the growth of state power in Texas may be the state's conservative political culture and its constitution.

Fourteenth Amendment

The amendment to the U.S. Constitution that places restrictions on the states and set certain national standards for state action. Its "due process" clause and "equal protection" have been used to void many state actions.

Judicial review

The power of the courts to rule on the constitutionality of government actions.

The Texas Constitution

Texas's constitution is one of the most restrictive in the nation—it limits the powers of every major state institution. Why has Texas developed such a constitution?

Because its writers were skeptical of government power, the constitution sets meager legislative salaries, establishes short and infrequent sessions, and contains many statute-like details that circumscribe the legislature's ability to make policy. Because Texans had bitter memories of Governor E. J. Davis's abuse of executive authority, they wrote constitutional provisions

---

[2]The U.S. Supreme Court had earlier assumed the power to declare national government action unconstitutional in *Marbury* v. *Madison*, 5 U.S. 137 (1803).

ONE NATION INDIVISIBLE: DOES TEXAS HAVE THE RIGHT TO SECEDE FROM THE UNION?

Texas Governor Rick Perry stunned the national news media by reviving secessionism after a 2009 "Tea Party" rally when he said, "Texas is a unique place. When we came into the Union in 1845, one of the issues was that we would be able to leave if we decided to do that." It is clear that the governor's statement was an emotional rhetorical flourish after an intense rally of antitax, antifederal government protesters, but his words may have been surprising given the state's history.

Unlike other states such as Alaska and Vermont, which have modern secessionist movements, Texas's secessionist sentiment once led to war with the United States in 1861. As recently as 1997, Texas Rangers confronted the "Republic of Texas" group in their armed mountain fortress in West

Texas—members believed that Texas remained an independent nation because it was not legally annexed by the United States Today, almost every Texan has seen a "Texas Secede" bumper sticker, and a major polling organization found that 31 percent of Texas voters say that the state has the right to secede from the United States—in fact, almost one in five of them would actually vote to leave the Union.* And a separate poll showed more than one-third believe that Texas would be better off as an independent nation.**

In fact, Texas has no legal right to secede. The governor was wrong that secession was an issue settled at the time Texas joined the United States in 1845. The United States did grant Texas the power to divide itself into five states by spinning off four new ones within its territory; there was never any agreement that Texas could withdraw from the Union once it had joined.***

The historical event more relevant to the question of secession was the U.S. Civil War in which 600,000 died to settle the issue. During its aftermath in 1869, the U.S. Supreme Court invalidated the state's ordinances of secession and clearly ruled that the U.S. Constitution does not allow Texas to leave the United States. The court ruled that the union between Texas and the other states was complete, perpetual, and indissoluble.****

FOR DEBATE

★ Today's secessionism is motivated by the by the view that the national government has become too powerful relative to the states? Is it true that the power of the national government has grown faster than state governments?

★ Research what Texas would look like as an independent nation. How would its population and economy compare with other nations? How would the nation of Texas conduct international relations with the United States, Mexico, and international terrorists?

*Rasmussen Reports, April 17, 2009, http://www.rasmussenreports .com/public_content/politics/general_state_surveys/texas/

**Daily Kos/Research 2000 Poll, April 20–22, 2009, http://www .dailykos.com/statepoll/2009/4/22/TX/288

***Joint Resolution for Annexing Texas to the United States, Approved March 1, 1845, Texas State Library and Archives Commission.

****Texas v. White, 74 U.S. 700 (1869).

☛ *Anxious about the growth of national government power, some Texas Tea Party protestors have been sympathetic to secessionist rhetoric.*

What drives such antifederalist sentiments?

---

for a weak governor who shares power with several other elected and appointed administrators. Fearful of government authority, Texans wrote a constitution that divides judicial power and restrains local governments, especially counties. Conservative in financial matters, the constitution's framers constrained state spending with rather strict balanced budget requirements, outlawed income taxes except for very limited purposes, and elevated property rights.

The Texas constitution is one of the longest, most detailed, and most frequently amended state constitutions in the nation. It is the second longest, and with 467 amendments, it is the fourth most amended state constitution as Texans have often responded to emerging challenges by further amending their constitution. About 90,000 words in length, the Texas constitution is longer than that of any state except Alabama. The constitution, critics charge, is poorly organized and confusing to most of the state's citizens.

THE TEXAS CONSTITUTION IN HISTORY

Like all state constitutions, the Texas Constitution reflects the interests and concerns of the people who have written and amended it. Many of its changes parallel those of other state constitutions; others are unique to Texas.

Republic of Texas Constitution The first Texas Constitution after independence from Mexico was written in 1836 for the Republic of Texas. The constitutional convention, in reaction to policies experienced under the government of Mexico, provided a constitution with careful separation of church and state, forbidding clergymen of any faith from holding office. It changed the antislavery policies of the old Mexican government by forbidding masters to free their own slaves without consent of the Republic's congress. Remembering the abuses of Mexican President Santa Anna, Texans limited the terms of their presidents to three years and prohibited them from being elected to consecutive terms. Aside from the reactions to Mexican rule, it established a **unitary government** (a central government with no provisions for states).

Otherwise, the constitution was an almost word-for-word copy of the U.S. Constitution and those of several southern states. It was clearly the product of the political culture from which the early Texans came—the Anglo-American culture of southern planters.

Constitution of 1845 A new constitution was written in 1845 in preparation for Texas's admission to the United States. Although much like other southern state constitutions, it also incorporated elements of the Spanish political culture (which would later be adopted by other states): exempting homesteads from foreclosure, protecting a wife's property rights, and providing for community property, meaning that property acquired during marriage would be owned equally by husband and wife. It also required a two-thirds vote in the Texas House to establish any corporation and made bank corporations illegal altogether. The governor served a two-year term, and the legislature was allowed to meet once every two years.

Constitution of 1861 The constitution of 1861 was basically the same as that of 1845 except that it reflected that Texas had become one of the Confederate states at war with the Union: it increased the debt ceiling and prohibited the emancipation of slaves.

Constitution of 1866 After the Civil War, Texans wrote the constitution of 1866, which they thought would satisfy the Unionists and permit the readmission of Texas under President Andrew Johnson's mild Reconstruction program. This document nullified secession, abolished slavery, and renounced Confederate war debts. Under its terms, a civilian government was elected and operated for several months despite some interference from the Freedmen's Bureau. Under the authority of the Reconstruction Act passed by the Radical Republicans in Congress, the military purged civilian-elected authorities and effectively restored military rule.

Constitution of 1869 With most whites either barred from the election or boycotting it, voters elected members of a constitutional convention in 1868. It produced a document that centralized state power in the hands of the governor, lengthened the chief executive's term to four years, and allowed the governor to appoint all major state officers, including judges. It provided annual legislative sessions, weakened planter-controlled local government, and centralized the public school system. The convention in 1868 reflected little of the fear of centralized government power that was later to become the hallmark of the Texas government. The constitution it proposed was ratified in 1869.

Unitary government

A system of government that places primary authority in a central government. Subordinate governments have only as much authority as is permitted by the central government.

The constitution of 1869 was to serve as the instrument of government for an era that most Texans and traditional historians would regard as the most corrupt and abusive in the state's history. Under Republican Governor E. J. Davis, large gifts of public funds were made to interests such as railroads, tax rates skyrocketed to pay for ambitious and wasteful public programs, landowners refused to pay high property taxes (amounting to as much as one-fifth of personal income), many Texans refused to pay exorbitant taxes, and government accumulated what was for that time an incredible public debt. Law and order collapsed, and much of the state fell prey to desperados and Native American attacks on white settlers. Instead of using the state police and militia to maintain the peace, Governor Davis made them a part of his powerful political machine and a symbol of tyranny. He took control of voter registration, intimidated unsupportive newspapers, and arrested several political opponents. In 1874, his handpicked supreme court used the location of a semicolon in the state constitution as a pretext for invalidating the election of Democrat Richard Coke, and wired President Grant to send federal troops to thwart the overwhelming Democratic victory. Grant refused, and Democrats slipped past guards at the capitol and gathered in the legislative chambers to form the new government.

According to legend, Davis, determined not to give up his office, surrounded himself with armed state police in the capitol. Only when a well-armed group of Coke supporters marched toward the capitol singing "The Yellow Rose of Texas" did Davis finally vacate his office. For most Texans, Reconstruction left a bitter memory of a humiliating, corrupt, extravagant, and even tyrannical government.

Revisionist historians argue that Governor Davis was not personally corrupt and that Reconstruction brought progressive policies and built roads, railroads, and schools while protecting the civil and political rights of former slaves. Some see it as a period in which an activist government attempted to play a positive role in people's lives. The period that followed was characterized by a conservative white reaction to these policies.

The Constitutional Convention of 1875 Whichever historical view is more accurate, it is clear that most Texans of the day were determined to strip power away from state government by writing a new constitution. The Texas Grange, whose members were called Grangers, organized in 1873. Campaigning on a platform of "retrenchment and reform," it managed to elect at least 40 of its members to the constitutional convention of 1875. Like most of the 90 delegates, they were Democrats who were determined to strike at the heart of big government, which had served Reconstruction minority rule.

> Only 15 of the 90 elected delegates were Republicans; however, during the course of the convention, one of the Republican delegates was declared insane and replaced by a Democrat.

To save money, the convention did not publish a journal—reflecting the frugal tone of the final constitution. The convention cut salaries for governing officials, placed strict limits on property taxes, and restricted state borrowing; it was also miserly with the power it granted government officials. Most of the governor's powers were stripped, the term was reduced from four to two years, and the salary cut. In addition, the new constitution required that the attorney general and state judges be elected rather than appointed by the governor.

Nor did the legislature escape the pruning of the convention. Regular legislative sessions were to be held only once every two years, and legislators were encouraged to limit the length of the sessions. Legislative procedure was detailed in the constitution, with severe restrictions placed on the kinds of policies the legislature might enact. In fact, a number of public policies were written into the constitution itself. Local government was strengthened, and counties were given many of the administrative and judicial functions of the state. Although the Grangers had opposed the idea of public education, they were persuaded to allow it if segregated schools were established by local governments.

The Center for American History/The University of Texas at Austin

🖐 *Delegates to the constitutional convention of 1875 substantially limited the power of state government.*

What would delegates have considered to be abuses of state power that needed to be prevented in the future?

The convention had largely reacted to the abuse of state power by denying it. When the convention ended, some of the money appropriated for its expenses remained unspent. Despite opposition from blacks, Republicans, most cities, and railroad interests, voters ratified the current state constitution of 1876.

THE TEXAS CONSTITUTION TODAY

Many students begin their examination of state constitutions with some kind of ideal or model constitution in mind. Comparisons with this ideal then leave them with the feeling

The Texas Constitution was adopted in 1876 by a rural society reacting to Reconstruction. ☞

What historical factors led to the writing of the Texas Constitution? What should Texans do to modernize and streamline it?

Courtesy Texas State Library and Archives Commission

that if only this or that provision were changed, state government would somehow find its way to honesty, efficiency, and effectiveness. In truth, there is no ideal constitution that would serve well in each of the uniquely diverse 50 states, nor is it possible to write a state constitution that could permanently meet the dynamically changing needs and concerns of its citizens. Further, because government is much more than its constitution, honest and effective government must be commanded by the political environment— leaders, citizens, parties, interest groups, and so forth—constitutions cannot guarantee it. Scoundrels will be corrupt and unconcerned citizens apathetic under even the best constitution.

However, this pragmatic view of the role of state Constitutions should not lead to the conclusion that they are only incidental to good government. A workable constitution is necessary for effective government even if it is not sufficient to guarantee it. Low salaries may discourage independent, high-caliber leaders from seeking office, constitutional restrictions may make it virtually impossible for government to meet the changing needs of its citizens, and institutions may be set up in such a way that they will operate inefficiently and irresponsibly.

The events preceding the adoption of the 1876 Texas Constitution did not provide the background for developing a constitution capable of serving well under the pressures and changes that would take place in the century to follow. The decade of the 1870s was an era of paranoia and reaction, and the constitution it produced was directed more toward solving the problems arising from Reconstruction than toward meeting the challenges of generations to follow. It was literally a reactionary document.

BILL OF RIGHTS AND FUNDAMENTAL LIBERTY

In many ways, the Texas Constitution reflects basic American political culture. For example, its bill of rights contains provisions that are similar to those found in other state charters and the U.S. Constitution. In fact, the U.S. Supreme Court has interpreted the Fourteenth Amendment to extend many national constitutional guarantees to the states. State constitutional guarantees are not redundant, however, because the U.S. Constitution establishes only *minimum* standards for the states. The Texas Bill of Rights (Article 1) guarantees additional rights not specifically mentioned by the U.S. Constitution.

Notably, Texas has adopted an amendment to prohibit discrimination based on sex. A similar guarantee was proposed as the Equal Rights Amendment to the U.S. Constitution, but it was not ratified by the states. The Texas Constitution also guarantees victims' rights and forbids imprisonment for debt or committing the mentally ill for an extended period without a jury trial. It also prohibits monopolies and the suspension of the writ of habeas corpus under any circumstances. Article 16 protects homesteads and prohibits garnishment of wages except for court-ordered child support.

Texas's courts have interpreted some state constitutional provisions to broaden basic rights beyond the minimum standards set by the U.S. Constitution. Although the U.S. Supreme

Court refused to interpret the Fourteenth Amendment as guaranteeing equal public school funding,[3] Texas's supreme court interpreted the efficiency clause of Texas's constitution (Article 7, Section 1) as requiring greater equity in public schools.[4] By using Texas constitutional and **statutory law** (passed by the legislature), Texas courts have struck down polygraph tests for public employees, required workers' compensation for farm workers, expanded free-speech rights of private employees, and affirmed free-speech rights at privately owned shopping malls. Although the state constitution has been the target of considerable criticism, there is general agreement that the Texas Bill of Rights and other provisions guarantee the average citizen a greater variety of protections than most other state constitutions.

SEPARATION OF POWERS

Like the state bill of rights, Article 2 of the Texas Constitution limits government. To prevent the concentration of power in the hands of any single institution, the national government and all states have provided for a **separation of powers** among three branches: legislative, executive, and judicial.

Because there is still the potential for any of these three branches to abuse whatever powers they have been given, the Texas Constitution also follows American tradition in subsequent constitutional articles: it sets up a system of **checks and balances**. Under certain circumstances, a function normally assigned to one branch of government is given to another. For example, the veto power that deals with lawmaking (a legislative function) is given to the governor (an executive). Impeachment and conviction, which deal with determining guilt (a judicial function), are given to the legislature. The state senate (a house of the legislature) confirms appointments the governor makes in the executive branch. Although there is a separation of powers, the checks-and-balances system requires that each branch have the opportunity to influence the others. The three branches specialize in separate functions, but there is some sharing of powers as well.

LEGISLATIVE BRANCH

The legislative article (Article 3) is by far the longest in the Texas Constitution. It assigns legislative power to a **bicameral** (two-house) legislative body consisting of the 31-member senate and the 150-member house of representatives. Elected for a four-year term from single-member districts, each senator must be at least 26 years old, a citizen, and must have resided in the state for five years and in the district for one year. A representative serves only two years and must be at least 21 years old, a citizen, and a resident of the state for two years and of the district for one year.

Although populous industrialized states are usually much more generous, the Texas Constitution sets annual salaries at $7,200 unless the Texas Ethics Commission recommends an increase and voters approve it. The Ethics Commission has made no such recommendation but has exercised its power to increase the per diem allowance (for daily expenses) to $150 while the legislature is in session. No other large state sets legislative salaries so low (Figure 2.2 illustrates legislative salaries and sessions in the 50 states).

Texas restricts the legislature to **biennial regular sessions** (convened once every two years). Because sessions are also limited to 140 days, important legislation may receive inadequate consideration, and many bills are ignored altogether. The 2009 legislature introduced an incredible 12,238 bills, concurrent resolutions, and joint resolutions (87 per day). It passed 5,910 (49%) of these legislative proposals, and it spent $1.3 billion for every day in session—more than any in modern history.

Except to deal with rare matters of impeachment, Texas's legislature may not call itself into **special sessions** or determine the issues to be decided. Lasting no more than 30 days,

---

[3] *San Antonio Independent School District* v. *Rodriguez*, 411 U.S. 1 (1973).
[4] *Edgewood* v. *Kirby*, 777 S.W. 2d 391 (Tex. 1989).

Statutory law

Law passed by legislatures and written into code books.

Separation of powers

The principle behind the concept of a government with three branches—the legislative, executive, and judicial.

Checks and balances

The concept that each branch of government is assigned power to limit abuses in the others, for example, the executive veto could be used to prevent legislative excesses.

Bicameral

Consisting of two houses or chambers; applied to a legislative body with two parts, such as a senate and a house of representatives (or state assembly). Congress and 49 state legislatures are bicameral. Only Nebraska has a one-house (unicameral) legislature.

Biennial regular session

Regular legislative sessions are scheduled by the constitution. In Texas, they are held once every two years, hence they are biennial.

Special session

A legislative session called by the Texas governor, who also sets its agenda.

LEGISLATIVE HONORS FOR THE BOSTON STRANGLER

Many of the thousands of bills and resolutions passed by Texas legislative bodies are local, honorary, or otherwise have little impact on the state and are passed with little or no debate. The Texas House of Representatives, in the rush of its 1971 regular session, passed one such resolution to honor Albert De Salvo, otherwise known as the "Boston Strangler," for "pioneering efforts in population control techniques." Such an embarrassing vote raises serious questions about how much attentive deliberation is given to more serious matters during the short legislative sessions. For example, do legislators have enough time and expertise to evaluate state spending?

HOW DOES TEXAS COMPARE?
LEGISLATIVE TERMS, SALARIES, AND SESSIONS

Terms Like 34 other states, Texas does not limit the number of terms legislators may serve. Voters are left to decide whether to retain experienced incumbents or replace them with fresh legislators.

Salaries Figure 2.2 shows that the Texas Constitution is much more restrictive than most states with respect to legislative salaries and sessions. Although New Hampshire pays its legislators only $200, no other populous state sets legislative pay as low as Texas. Most larger states pay their legislators more like ordinary middle-class employees, and many allow legislators to set their own salary by statute.

Sessions Most states provide annual regular legislative sessions and 15 states place no limit on their length. Texas is among only five states with biennial legislative sessions. Unlike most legislatures, the Texas legislature may not call itself into a special session or determine its own agenda. Low salaries and limited sessions make it difficult for the Texas legislature to function as a professional institution and may make members more dependent on interest groups for income and research on public policy.

FOR DEBATE

★ *Should Texas limit the number of terms legislators serve? Or, would term limits also restrict legislators' experience and, therefore, make them more vulnerable to the influence of lobbyists?*

★ *Should Texas consider increasing legislative salaries and the length of their sessions? Or, would doing this give legislators too much power?*

Figure 2.2

State Legislative Sessions and Annual Salaries. Compare Texas's legislative salaries with those in other states. Note that, unlike in most large states, Texas legislative sessions are limited in length, and they are held only once every two years—only five states have biennial (B) regular sessions.

Source: Based on data from *The Book of the States, 2009* (Lexington, KY: Council of State Governments, 2009), pp. 83–86, 99–101.

What are the consequences of low salaries and short and infrequent sessions?

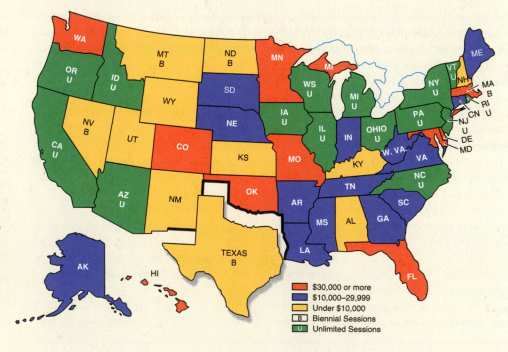

special sessions are convened by the governor to consider only the legislative matters he or she presents. Special sessions are more restricted in Texas than in any other state.

The Texas Constitution establishes more specific procedural requirements than most other state constitutions. Although the provision is often suspended, the constitution requires that a bill must be read on three separate days unless four-fifths of the legislature sets aside the requirement. It stipulates when bills may be introduced and how they will be reported out of committee, signed, and entered in the journal once enacted. It even specifies how the enacting clause will read.

Although most states legally require a balanced budget, Texas's constitutional restriction seems more effective than most. Article 3, Section 49, strictly limits the legislature in authorizing state debt except under rare conditions. The comptroller of public accounts is required to certify that funds are available for each appropriations measure adopted. Although specific constitutional amendments have authorized the sale of bonds for veterans' real estate programs, student loans, parks and water development, and prison construction, Texas's per capita state debt remains among the lowest in the nation.

Constitutional detail further confines the legislature by making policies on subjects that normally would be handled by legislative statute. Much of the length of Article 3 results from its in-depth description of the Veterans' Land Program, Texas park and water development funds, student loans, welfare programs, a grain warehouse self-insurance fund, and the municipal donation of outdated firefighting equipment. The constitution establishes the design of the great seal of Texas, authorizes the legislature to pass fence laws, and even explains how the state must purchase stationery! Article 16 authorizes the legislature to regulate cattle brands; Article 11 permits the building of seawalls. By including such **statute-like details** in the Texas Constitution, its framers guaranteed that even relatively unimportant decisions that could easily be handled by the legislature must be changed only by constitutional amendment.

Events may outstrip detailed constitutional provisions, leaving **deadwood** (inoperable provisions) that voters must constantly approve amendments to remove. For example, Article 9, Section 14, provides for the establishment of county poorhouses. Although no county elected an inspector of hides and animals in modern times, the position remained a constitutional office until 2007. The basic distrust of the legislature, however much it may have been deserved in 1876, put a straitjacket on the state's ability to cope with the challenges of the 21st century.

EXECUTIVE BRANCH

Article 4 establishes the executive branch, with the governor as its head. The governor must be a citizen, at least thirty years of age, and a resident of the state for five years immediately preceding his or her election to a four-year term. The constitution no longer limits the governor's salary, and according to statute, it is $150,000.

Provisions for terms, qualifications, and salary may be somewhat less restrictive than in most states, but there are much more severe constitutional restrictions on the power of the office. Although the constitution provides that the governor shall be the chief executive, it actually establishes a **plural executive** by dividing executive powers among a number of independently elected officers—the governor, lieutenant governor, attorney general, comptroller of public accounts, commissioner of the general land office, and three railroad commissioners. There are also provisions for a state board of education to be either elected or appointed. The constitution stipulates that the governor appoint the secretary of state.

In the tradition of the constitutional plural executive, the legislature by statute has also established an elected commissioner of agriculture and has exercised its option to make the

Statute-like detail
Detailed state constitutional policies of narrow scope, usually handled by statutes passed by legislative bodies.

Deadwood
State constitutional provisions voided by a conflicting U.S. constitutional or statutory law; also provisions made irrelevant by changing circumstances.

Plural executive
An executive branch with power divided among several independent officers and a weak chief executive.

HOW DOES TEXAS COMPARE?
CHIEF EXECUTIVES' QUALIFICATIONS, TERMS, TERM LIMITS, AND SALARIES

The Texas governor's salary is typical among the states. Although qualifications to be governor are similar to most states, Texas does not impose term limits on its chief executive. Many states limit the governor to a maximum of two consecutive terms. In most states, Governor Rick Perry would not have been allowed to run for reelection in 2010.

CONSTITUTIONAL PROVISIONS FOR CHIEF EXECUTIVES' QUALIFICATIONS

Provisions	Texas Governor	U.S. President	The 50 States' Governors
Age	30 years	35 years	34 states set the minimum age at 30
Residence	5 years	14 years	5 years or less in 37 states
Terms	4 years	4 years (limited to 2 terms or 10 years)	48 states allow a 4-year term, but unlike Texas, 36 states also impose term limits

FOR DEBATE

Should Texas follow the lead of the national government and most states imposing constitutional term limits on its chief executive? Or, should voters be left the right to decide how many terms their governor may serve when they decide to reelect or defeat the incumbent?

Source: Data from *The Book of the States, 2009* (Lexington, KY: Council of State Governments, 2009), pp. 187, 200–201.

HOW DOES TEXAS COMPARE?
PLURAL EXECUTIVES

Like the national government, Alaska, Hawaii, and Maine have hierarchical executive systems in which the chief executives appoint important executive officers as subordinates. Most other states have a plural executive system in which several major executives are independently elected and are not answerable to the governor. However, few states elect as many executive officers as Texas. Seven states have abolished the office of lieutenant governor as an executive elected statewide, and some have made offices as important as the attorney general appointed rather than elected. Rarely are comptrollers or land, educational, or agricultural officers elected as they are in Texas. Critics charge that electing so many executives creates a *long ballot* that confuses voters about lines of administrative responsibility and about whom they should hold accountable for problems in state government.

The Texas Constitution mentions even public notaries, thereby making them constitutional officers even though they are not elected.

FOR DEBATE

Does a hierarchical executive system allow for streamlining, coordination, and efficiency in a highly visible chief executive's office that the public can easily hold accountable? Or, does a centralized executive system concentrate too much power in the hands of the governor and allow the chief executive to appoint officers that the public should be allowed to elect?

Removal powers

The authority to fire appointed officials. The Texas governor has limited removal powers; they extend only to officials he or she has appointed and are subject to the consent of two-thirds of the state senators.

Indirect appointive powers

Texas governor's authority to appoint supervisory boards but not operational directors for most state agencies.

state board of education elected independent of the governor. Most of the remaining agencies that the legislature establishes to administer state programs are headed by appointed multimember boards with substantial independence from the governor. Generally, the governor appoints only supervisory boards with the approval of two-thirds of the state senate. The board in turn appoints its agency's director. The governor does not appoint the agency administrator directly. Furthermore, Texas is one of seven states that lacks a formal cabinet.

The governor has limited **removal powers** to supplement these **indirect appointive powers**. The governor may fire his own staff and advisors at will, but removal of state officers is more difficult. The governor may fire appointed officers only if two-thirds of the senators agree that there is just cause for removal, making firing almost as difficult as impeachment and conviction. Furthermore, the governor may not remove anyone appointed by a preceding governor. **Directive authority** (to issue binding orders) is still quite restricted, and **budgetary power** (to recommend to the legislature how much it should appropriate for various executive agencies) is limited by the competing influences of the Legislative Budget Board.

The statutes and the constitution combine to make the governor a relatively weak executive, but the veto gives the governor effective influence over legislation. Texas's legislature has not mustered the necessary two-thirds vote to override a governor's veto in more than 40 years. The Texas legislature often lacks the opportunity to override a veto because major legislation may be adopted during the last days of the session. The Texas Constitution allows the governor 10 days to act during the session and 20 days after it adjourns. During the last 10 days, the governor may avoid the threat of an override by simply waiting until the legislature adjourns before vetoing the bill.

Texas is among 43 states that give the governor the **item veto** power to strike out particular sections of an appropriations bill without vetoing the entire legislation; several states also allow its application to matters other than appropriations. The governor of Texas lacks both the **reduction veto** (to reduce appropriations without striking them out altogether) and the **pocket veto** (to kill bills simply by ignoring them after the end of the session). Despite the access to publicity and broad appointive and legislative powers of the Texas governor, the office remains among the weakest in the nation.

COURTS

Just as the constitution limits the power of the chief executive, Article 5 also fragments the court system. Texas is the only state other than Oklahoma that has two courts of final appeal—the highest court for civil matters is the nine-member Texas Supreme Court; the other, for criminal matters, is the nine-member court of criminal appeals. Leaving some flexibility as to number and jurisdiction, the constitution also creates courts of appeals, as well as district, county, and justice of the peace courts. The same article describes the selection of grand and trial juries and such administrative officers as sheriff, county clerk, and county and district attorneys.

The number and variety of courts is confusing to the average citizen, and coordination and supervision are minimal. State courts have also come under attack due to the lack of qualified judges. The constitution specifies only general qualifications for county judges and justices of the peace, who need not be lawyers. There may have been good reasons for laypeople to serve as judges in a simple, rural setting, but today many Texans regard them as an anachronism.

The manner of selecting judges is another factor that affects their qualifications, in that Texas judges are chosen in **partisan elections**, in which they run as Democrats or Republicans. Trial judges are elected to serve for four years and appeals court judges for six, but judges traditionally leave office before the end of their last term. The governor has the power to fill most vacancies until the next election—a power that gives the governor enormous influence over the makeup of the courts because, once in office, judges are usually returned to office without serious challengers in the next election.

LOCAL GOVERNMENT

The state constitution decentralizes governmental power by assigning many functions to units of local government, especially counties. Much of the counties' rigid organizational structure is described in Articles 9 and 16. As a result, voters of the entire state were once required to approve amendments so individual counties could abolish unneeded offices like treasurer, weigher, or surveyor. The constitution now authorizes county voters to abolish a few

Directive authority
The power to issue binding orders to state agencies; the directive authority of Texas's governor is severely limited.

Budgetary power
The power to propose a spending plan to the legislative body; a power limited for Texas's governor because of the competing influences of the Legislative Budget Board.

Item veto
Executive authority to veto sections of a bill and allow the remainder to become law.

Reduction veto
The power of some governors to reduce amounts in an appropriations bill without striking them out. Texas's governor does not have this power.

Pocket veto
Chief executive's power to kill legislation by simply ignoring it at the end of the legislative session; this power is not available to Texas's governor.

Partisan elections
General elections in which candidates are nominated by political parties and their party labels appear on the ballot.

HOW DOES TEXAS COMPARE?
SELECTING JUDGES

Methods of Selection Although citizens of most states elect their judges, some critics regard this effort at popular control as undesirable. A judge may become too much the politician and too little the independent magistrate to apply the law uniformly. Several states have attempted to solve these problems by providing for nonpartisan election of judges. Other states make their judges independent of electoral politics altogether by giving their governors or legislators the power to appoint and reappoint high court judges without direct voter input.

The Merit Plan Others have attempted to combine the advantages of appointment with the benefits of election by allowing the governor to make an appointment for an initial term after which voters decide whether to retain the appointed judge based on his or her record. Many of those using an appointive-elective system require the governor to make an initial appointment from a list nominated by a judicial qualifying commission—a **merit system** also commonly known as the Missouri Plan. Figure 2.3 shows the methods used to select supreme court judges in various states.

Life Terms Like the founders of the U.S. Constitution, 2 of the original 13 states continue to strive for complete judicial independence by setting no term length at all for their supreme court judges. Rhode Island allows its supreme court judges to serve for life while Massachusetts high court judges serve for terms of good behavior until age 70 with no need to be reappointed or reelected.

FOR DEBATE

★ *Should Texas consider adopting a merit plan in an effort to focus the judicial selection process on qualifications and reduce the effects of special interest campaign contributions? Or, should voters be allowed to select judges as they select other elected officials?*

★ *How would Texans react to lifetime terms for its highest court judges? Why?*

Merit Plan

A method of selecting judges based on the candidate's qualifications rather than politics. Under this system, the governor fills court vacancies from a list of nominees submitted by a judicial commission, and these appointees later face retention elections. Also known as the *Missouri Plan*.

Figure 2.3
State-by-State Selection of Supreme Court Judges

Sources: Based on data from Bureau of Justice Statistics, *State Court Organization, 2004* NCJ 212351, National Center for State Courts, February 2009; *The Book of the States, 2009* (Lexington, KY: Council of State Governments, 2009), pp. 303–305.

What are the advantages of the partisan election of judges? Why would some reformists support a merit plan for their selection?

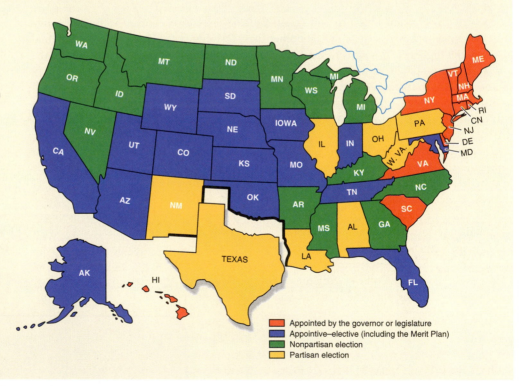

Appointed by the governor or legislature
Appointive–elective (including the Merit Plan)
Nonpartisan election
Partisan election

General-law charter

A document authorizing the establishment of a city with a population of 5,000 or less whose structure and organization are prescribed and limited by state law.

offices, but there is no provision for county home rule. As in state government, the constitution divides and diffuses county powers through a plural executive system.

The legislature, which has the power to set up structures for city governments, has offered municipalities several standard alternative **general-law charters**. Cities with populations of more than 5,000 may adopt **home-rule charters** and establish any organizational structure or program that does not conflict with state law or the constitution.

Generally, the legislature has the power to provide for the establishment of limited-purpose local governments known as special districts. Numerous special districts are also established by the constitution itself, and to eliminate one of these requires an amendment. Many of them have been created to perform functions that general-purpose local governments, such as counties and cities, cannot afford because of constitutional tax and debt limits. Arising out of constitutional restrictions, **special districts** have multiplied taxing and spending authorities and, except for school districts, operate largely outside the public's view.

SUFFRAGE

A major function of the state and local governments is to determine the character of democracy in America as they set requirements for **suffrage** (the legal right to vote) and administer elections. Article 6 of the Texas Constitution deals with suffrage requirements. It denies the right to vote to persons under age 18, certain convicted felons, and individuals found mentally incompetent by a court of law.

Although constitutional restrictions on their qualifications are now as minimal as any in the nation, Texas voters still lack certain opportunities to participate in state government. **Initiative** (registered voters proposing statutory or constitutional changes by petition), **referendum** (voters approving changes in law by election), and **popular recall** (citizens petitioning for a special election to remove an official before his or her term expires) are available in most other states and even in some Texas cities, but not for statewide issues in Texas.

Texas permits voters to decide directly on only three matters: constitutional amendments, the state income tax, and legislative salaries. Texas's political parties sometimes place referenda on their primary ballots, but the results are not legally binding.

AMENDING THE TEXAS CONSTITUTION

Article 17 of the Texas Constitution provides that the **proposal of constitutional amendments** must be by two-thirds of the total membership of each house of the legislature (at least 21 senators and 100 representatives). **Ratification** of constitutional amendments requires approval by a majority of those persons voting on the amendment in either a general or a special election. Because such an extraordinary majority of legislators must agree merely to propose constitutional amendments, a number of them are relatively uncontroversial. Historically, voters have approved more than 70 percent of proposed constitutional amendments.

Critics argue that the state must resort to the amendment process often because the Texas Constitution is badly written. About 90,000 words long, it is one of the least concise state constitutions in the nation. One sentence rambles on for 765 words, and several approach 300 words in length. The content is ambiguous, overlapping, and poorly organized. For example, provisions dealing with local government are scattered throughout Articles 3, 5, 8, 9, 11, and 16. This poor draftsmanship has led to a restrictive interpretation of its provisions, public ignorance of its contents, and confusion as to its intentions.

Although only two state constitutions (along with the U.S. Constitution) contain fewer than 10,000 words, few are as restrictive as the Texas Constitution. The continuing need to amend detailed and restrictive state constitutions means that citizens are frequently called on to pass judgment on proposed amendments. Although some of the constitution's defenders maintain that giving Texas voters the opportunity to express themselves on constitutional amendments reaffirms popular control of government, voters display little interest in amendment elections. Faced with trivial, confusing, or technical amendments, often only 10 to 15 percent of the voting-age population votes on constitutional amendments, and turnout has occasionally dropped into the single digits.

Home-rule charter

A document organizing a municipality with a population greater than 5,000 and allowing it to use any organizational structure or institute any program that complies with state law.

Special district

A limited-purpose local government that provides a narrow range of services not provided by general-purpose local governments such as cities or counties. Examples of special districts include municipal utility districts, hospital authorities, and transit authorities.

Suffrage

The legal right to vote.

Initiative

An election method that allows citizens to place a proposal on the ballot for voter approval. If the measure passes, it becomes law (permitted in some Texas cities but not in state government).

Referendum

An election that permits voters to determine if an ordinance or statute will go into effect.

Popular recall

A special election to remove an official before the end of his or her term, initiated by citizen petition (permitted in some Texas cities but not in state government).

Proposal of constitutional amendments

In Texas, the proposal of a constitutional amendment must be approved by two-thirds of the total membership of each house of the Texas legislature.

Ratification

Approval of a constitutional amendment by a majority of voters.

HOW DOES TEXAS COMPARE?
AMENDING STATE CONSTITUTIONS

Although the process of amending the Texas Constitution is about as difficult as in other states, Texans have amended their constitution 467 times since 1876, more than twice the average for all 50 states. Only three state constitutions— those of South Carolina (493), California (518), and Alabama (807)—have more amendments than Texas.

COMPARING CONSTITUTIONAL AMENDMENT PROCEDURES

Amending Procedure	Texas Constitution	U.S. Constitution	The 50 States' Constitutions
Proposal	Two-thirds of the entire membership of both houses of the legislature is required.	Two-thirds of the vote in both houses of Congress may propose an amendment, or two-thirds of the states may petition Congress to call a national constitutional convention to propose amendments.	Twenty-one states require a two-thirds vote, but 9 set the level at three-fifths, and 20 require a simple majority; 18 permit proposal by initiative.
Ratification	A simple majority of the votes cast on the amendment is required.	Three-fourths of state legislatures or three-fourths of state ratifying conventions (currently, 38 states) is required.	Forty-three states are like Texas; four require a majority of the total number of all voters; New Hampshire and Florida require more than a simple majority; Delaware requires no ratification by voters; some states allow alternative methods.

Source: *The Book of the States, 2009* (Lexington, KY: Council of State Governments, 2009), pp. 14–16.

ATTEMPTS TO REVISE THE TEXAS CONSTITUTION

Attempts to revise the constitution have met with successive failures. Ironically, in 1972, Texas voters had to amend the constitution to provide for its revision. Under the provisions of that amendment, the legislature established a constitutional revision commission of 37 members appointed by the governor, lieutenant governor, speaker of the house, attorney general, chief justice of the supreme court, and presiding judge of the court of criminal appeals. The commission made several proposals. Meeting in 1974, the legislature acted as a constitutional convention and agreed to many of these recommendations. However, the convention divided over the issue of a right-to-work provision to restrict organized labor, and the final document could not muster the two-thirds vote needed to submit the proposal to the electorate.

In the 1975 regular session, the legislature proposed eight constitutional amendments to the voters. Together, the proposed amendments were substantially the same as the proposal it had previously defeated. If they had been adopted, the amendments would have shortened the constitution by 75 percent through reorganization and by eliminating statute-like detail and deadwood. The legislature would have been strengthened by annual sessions, and a salary commission would have set the legislators' salary. Although limited to two terms, the governor would have been designated as the chief planning officer and given removal powers and certain powers of fiscal control. The court system would have been unified and its administrative procedure simplified. Local governments would have operated under broader home-rule provisions, and counties would have been authorized to pass general ordinances and to abolish unneeded offices.

Opponents' chief arguments were against more power for the legislature, greater government costs, and the possibility of an income tax—all of which are serious issues for many

Texans. Since the legislature had written the proposals, it was easy for the Texas voter to see such things as annual sessions and flexibility concerning their salaries as a "grab for power" that would substantially increase government expenditures. Despite an emotional campaign, only 23 percent of registered voters cast ballots in the election, and they overwhelmingly rejected the proposed amendments.

HOW DOES TEXAS COMPARE?
CONSTITUTIONS' LENGTH, DETAIL, AND THEIR NEED FOR AMENDMENTS

As of 2011, the U.S. Constitution had been in effect for 222 years but had been formally amended only 27 times. It has endured mammoth and fundamental changes in government and society largely because it does not lock government into a rigid framework. Because the U.S. Constitution addresses only with the most basic elements of government and leaves much to Congress, the president, and the courts, few formal amendments have been necessary.

Although the U.S. Constitution provides for a basically representative government, it was hardly democratic in the early years. During the Jeffersonian and Jacksonian eras, however, government became more democratic as political parties developed, states lowered suffrage requirements, and voters were allowed to choose electors in the electoral college.

The 19th century saw the growth of the new nation from 13 fledgling agricultural states on the Atlantic coast to a vast industrial and commercial nation stretching across a continent. In the 20th century, America moved from the position of a third-rate international power to a dominant role in the world. Since the New Deal of the 1930s, government has been further transformed into a highly developed welfare state. Much of the nature of the national government is determined by statute, executive order, and court interpretation, so these changes did not require changing the language of the U.S. Constitution.

Although there is considerable variation among state constitutions (see Figure 2.4), most are much longer than the national constitution, and they frequently deal with details of both structure and policy. Consequently, as changing political and social conditions require changes in government structure and policy, formal constitutional amendments are necessary. There are several reasons for both the details and the frequent amendments to state constitutions:

1. Public officials, interest groups, and voters seem to view their state constitutions as more than the basic law of the state. They fail to make a clear distinction between *what ought to be* and *what ought to be in the constitution*. Thus all sorts of inappropriate details are included in the documents. A constitution is fundamental law; it deals with the basic principles of government. It is organic law—the superior law that establishes governing institutions and organizes their formal power relationship. Accordingly, constitutions ideally should describe how decisions will be made but not actually establish policies, which must change with political and social conditions.

2. States have added detailed amendments to overturn the effects of controversial court interpretations of general constitutional provisions. For example, supreme courts in Hawaii, Massachusetts, Iowa, New Jersey, and Vermont found that denying the benefits of marriage to same-sex couples was a violation of their state constitutions. As a result, Hawaii and a majority of other states (including Texas) added amendments to define marriage as an exclusively heterosexual right.

3. Institutions and interest groups frequently feel safer when their interests are protected in a constitution (which is more difficult to change than ordinary law). This has caused many state constitutions to become long lists of protections for vested interests.

4. State governments have a peculiar position in the federal system. They are presumed to have all the powers that have not been explicitly prohibited them. Thus citizens who are wary of strong governments have felt the need to impose detailed constitutional restrictions.

5. When state governments misuse their powers, the response is usually to place constitutional limitations and restriction on those powers. The result is a longer constitution but probably not a more responsible government. A government bound by a rigid constitution cannot respond effectively to changing needs. Excessive restrictions may actually guarantee unresponsive and hence irresponsible government.

State constitutions are poorly written and arranged. Some provisions are so poorly drafted that they are interpreted to be even more restrictive than the constitution's framers intended and as a result, new amendments must be added to authorize states to perform vital functions in a modern society.

(continued)

HOW DOES TEXAS COMPARE?
CONSTITUTIONS' LENGTH, DETAIL, AND THEIR NEED FOR AMENDMENTS (CONTINUED)

THE 50 STATES' CONSTITUTIONS COMPARED

Characteristic	Texas Constitution	U.S. Constitution	50-State Average*
Length (words)	90,000	7,575	38,288
Amendments	467	27	144
Age (years)	135	222	109
Frequency of amendment	3.5 per year	Once every 8 years	1.3 per year

FOR DEBATE

★ Critics argue that Texas's constitution should be written in general language, details should be omitted, and day-to-day decisions should be left to the legislature, the governor, and the courts. Would shortening the constitution give too much power to state government?

★ Does the frequent need to amend the state's constitution empower the people?

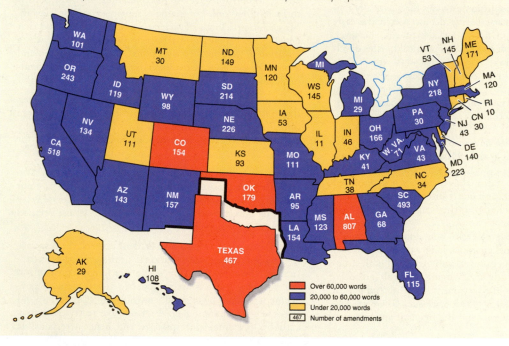

Figure 2.4

State Constitutions: Length and Number of Amendments, 2009

Source: Based on data from *The Book of the States, 2009* (Lexington, KY: Council of State Governments, 2009), pp. 12–13.

What are the advantages and dangers of a short constitution, written in general language?

CHAPTER SUMMARY

★ State government operates within a federal system whereby a constitutional division of powers delegates some power to the national government and reserves some to the states. National and state governments share such concurrent powers as taxing, spending, and regulating commerce. States are bound by certain constitutional restrictions, but modern government powers and programs have grown at all levels—federal, state, and local.

★ Constitutions are always the result of a political process in which framers reflect their values, hopes, and fears. The current Texas Constitution was written in the period following Reconstruction after the U.S. Civil War. Most white Texans viewed the Reconstruction state government as extravagant, tyrannical, and abusive. In 1875, an elected state constitutional convention reacted to the Reconstruction regime by limiting state government in almost every imaginable way. Voters overwhelmingly approved the convention's work in 1876.

★ The Texas Constitution includes a bill of rights that is more expansive than those in most state constitutions, including protections for homesteads, debtors, and the mentally ill. The Texas Constitution includes an Equal Rights Amendment to forbid discrimination by sex.

★ The Texas Constitution follows the national pattern by establishing a separation of powers between legislative, executive, and judicial branches.

★ The Texas Constitution strictly limits the sessions and salaries of state legislators and includes many statute-like details that the legislature cannot change without a constitutional amendment. Special sessions are especially restricted, and procedures in both regular and special sessions are circumscribed.

★ The governor of Texas is limited in his or her role as chief executive because Texas has a plural executive system that includes many independently elected executives over which the governor has no control. The governor lacks most of the powers of typical executives to hire, fire, direct, and budget. Although Texas has had some powerful governors, such as Allan Shivers and John Connally, they became effective despite the constitution—not because of it.

★ The power of the courts to interpret the Texas Constitution is limited by its detail. Texas divides its final court of appeal into two bodies—the court of criminal appeals and the Texas Supreme Court—and also establishes intermediate courts of appeals and district, county, and justice of the peace courts. Judges are chosen in partisan elections. Critics say that judges elected in this way may become too concerned with political matters.

★ County and special district governments are particularly limited by constitutional and statutory requirements. Only larger cities have the considerable flexibility of home rule and some allow citizen participation by initiative, referendum, or recall. All local governments face debt and tax restrictions.

★ A constitution sets forth fundamental law that establishes essential governing principles and structures. Some state constitutions, like that of Texas, also go beyond to establish many details of routine government and require frequent amendment to reflect new realities. It is difficult for the state government to develop effective programs without first amending the constitution. Numerous amendments dealing with minor issues are added, like patches, to the constitution.

★ Critics find the Texas Constitution confusing. It contains not only the fundamentals of government but also detailed provisions concerning matters that might better be left to the ongoing institutions of government. It is long, it contains much deadwood, and many say that it is poorly drafted and disorganized. Reformers argue that a constitution should include only organic law; that is, it should organize responsible institutions of government. If it goes beyond fundamentals, it becomes a rigid legislative code, difficult to change and can be baffling to voters.

HOW TEXAS COMPARES

Texas has one of the longest, most detailed, and most frequently amended state constitutions in the United States. More than most state constitutions, the Texas Constitution reflects a political culture that is skeptical of government.

★ Most large state legislatures meet annually for longer sessions, have more flexibility in passing statutes and budgets, and receive higher salaries than in Texas.

★ Most states have a stronger chief executive who can appoint, remove, direct, and budget more effectively than can the Texas governor.

★ Most top state judges are selected using either nonpartisan elections or some type of merit plan rather than the Texas system of partisan election.

★ Many states allow initiative, referendum, and popular recall; these are unavailable to Texas voters at the state level.

KEY TERMS

bicameral	expressed powers	Merit Plan	reserved powers
biennial regular session	Fourteenth Amendment	partisan elections	separation of powers
budgetary power	general-law charter	plural executive	special district
checks and balances	home-rule charter	pocket veto	special session
concurrent powers	implied powers	popular recall	statute-like details
deadwood	indirect appointive	proposal of constitutional	statutory law
delegated powers	powers	amendments	suffrage
directive authority	initiative	ratification	supremacy clause
division of powers	item veto	reduction veto	Tenth Amendment
enumerated powers	judicial review	referendum	unitary government
exclusive powers	legitimacy	removal powers	

REVIEW QUESTIONS

1. Define *federalism*. Specifically define division of powers by showing which powers are given to the national government and which to the states.

2. How does the Texas Constitution differ from the constitutions of other states and the U.S. Constitution?

3. What are the historical reasons for restrictions in Texas's constitution? What benefits did the state constitution's writers hope to achieve by limiting state government?

4. Discuss the major constitutional provisions that restrain state government. What are the consequences of such restrictions?

5. What are the strengths and weaknesses of the Texas Constitution? Should it be revised? Why or why not?

LOGGING ON

The U.S. Constitution sets the context for the powers of the state of Texas in relationship to the national government and the other 49 state governments. Search the Supreme Court landmark case pages of **http://www.findlaw.com** for *Marbury* v. *Madison* (1803) to read about the rationale for judicial review of national action; search for *Fletcher* v. *Peck* (1810) to find the justifications for judicial review of state actions. At the same site, find articles about *McCulloch* v. *Maryland* (1819) and how it interpreted the implied powers clause and the Tenth Amendment. Search the U.S. Constitution for Articles IV and VI and the Tenth and Eleventh Amendments. Click on annotations to read U.S. Supreme Court interpretations of these important constitutional provisions. Describe the states' relations with each other and the national government.

The complete text of the Texas Constitution, all 17 articles, is at **http://www.constitution.legis.state.tx.us/**. In the index, click on Article 3, "Legislative Department." Click on Section 29 and notice that even the enacting clause for legislation is included in the constitution. Click on Article 16, Section 6, and notice the level of detail. Read the deadwood provision in Article 9, Section 14. Contrast the legislative and executive articles (3 and 4) of Texas's constitution with those of Illinois (Articles 4 and 5) at **http://www.ilga.gov./**. Read constitutional amendments that have been recently proposed by the Texas legislature and a history of state constitutional amendments published at **http://www.tlc.state.tx.us/**

Reconstituting Texas: E. J. Davis and His Legacies

Timothy Hoye
Texas Woman's University

INTRODUCTION

During the decade that followed the Civil War, Texas went from a period of Reconstruction to one of reconstitution. In the aftermath of the war, the drive to guarantee former slaves their political and civil rights created racial resentment among many white Texans, and the centralization of state power at the same time created an antigovernment political environment that resulted in the writing of Texas's current constitution. The restrictiveness in the state constitution is a direct result of the attitudes of those who wrote and ratified it.

Louis Menand begins his Pulitzer Prize–winning study of post–Civil War America by observing the "remarkable fact" that the United States fought a civil war "without undergoing a change in its form of government" (Menand, ix). The same cannot be said of Texas.

After the war, Texans faced the daunting task of reconstituting themselves in the shadow of defeat and occupation by Union forces. When Union troops began to occupy Texas, in May and June of 1865, a four-year period began of military rule punctuated by clashes between former secessionists and Unionists. Early postwar attempts to reestablish order were frustrated by conflicting agendas between and among the Union army, the newly established Freedmen's Bureau, President Andrew Johnson, a resurgent Democratic Party in Texas, and Radical Republicans in both the United States Congress and in Texas.

Clear Reconstruction policies would be established when, on March 2, 1867, the Radical Republicans in Washington prevailed among the contending postwar factions. With passage of the First Reconstruction Act, military rule was strengthened, many local officials were removed from office by order of the military, and their replacements were required to take a Test Oath that they had never borne arms against the United States. Radical Reconstruction would also require former Confederate states to ratify of the Thirteenth, Fourteenth, and Fifteenth Amendments

👆 *E. J. Davis remained loyal to the United States, and his service in the Union army was a bitter reminder of Texas's defeat in the Civil War.*

How did resentments against Governor Davis lead to the writing of the current Texas Constitution?

Texas State Library and Archives Commission

to the U.S. Constitution, and Texas would be required to write a constitution to replace the one it had ratified in 1866.

In 1867, Texas held its election to select delegates for a state constitutional convention—the first statewide election in which African Americans could vote in Texas (Baggett, 450). From June 1868 to February 1869, delegates met in convention at Austin. Eventually, in July 1869, a new constitution was ratified by Texas voters. With support from President Ulysses S. Grant, Edmund J. Davis was elected governor in December 1869, and assumed office the following January. The 12th Texas Legislature was also elected and in February 1870, the new legislature voted to adopt the Fourteenth and Fifteenth Amendments to the U.S. Constitution, chose two United States senators, and completed requirements for readmission to the Union. On March 30, 1870, President Ulysses S. Grant signed an act restoring Texas to the Union.

E. J. DAVIS, THE 1869 CONSTITUTION, AND *EX PARTE RODRIGUEZ*

The implementation of the new constitution and Governor Davis's actions under it would create much resentment within more traditional circles in Texas and in time lead to considerable reaction and, by most readings, a considerable reactionary reconstituting of Texas in the mid-1870s. Much of the resentment was race based and "violence against blacks was both widespread and brutal" (Cantrell, 335).

The previous 1866 constitution had denied African Americans the right to vote, to hold office, to serve on juries, and provided for segregated schools. The 11th Texas legislature, meeting in the fall of 1866, had passed laws denying African Americans the right to testify in court cases involving whites, denied them service in the state militia, created a separate insane asylum for freedmen, and established segregation on the railroads (Pitre, 341).

The constitution of 1869, by comparison, provided that "all freemen" have "equal rights" (Article 1, Section 2), and that no citizen will "ever be deprived of any right, privilege, or immunity, nor be exempted from any burdens, or duty, on account of race, color, or previous condition" (Article 1, Section 21). In fact, although African-American Republicans outnumbered white Republicans after 1867, they "did not dominate the party" in

leadership positions. No African Americans received a cabinet post in the Davis administration (Pitre, 341). Of the 90 delegates at the constitutional convention of 1868/1869, only nine were African American. In addition, the highest government position achieved by African-American Republicans during this time was to the office of state senator, and only three were elected (Baggett, 442).

Other resentments derived from the Davis administration's response to the problem of increased violence and lawlessness in Texas. The legislature created both a state militia and a state police force, with the former often assisting the latter. Complaints of inappropriate police behavior were numerous, such as using police to protect and promote Republican candidates and voters while neglecting the opposition. Governor Davis, similarly, used martial law to enforce order in Madison, Hill, Walker, Limestone, and Freestone counties.

The creation of a "highly centralized" system of public schools was also heavily criticized. The state selected teachers, shaped the curriculum, made attendance compulsory, and included the education of African Americans. Other actions of the Republican-dominated legislature delayed the first election to be held after the readmission of Texas to statehood, gave the governor numerous additional appointive powers at the local level, provided considerable subsidies to railroad interests, raised taxes, encouraged immigration, made homesteads easier to obtain, and tended to be soft regarding Indian policies (Moneyhon, s.v. "Reconstruction").

Opponents regarded these policies as excessive, and they saw the root problem as a constitution that granted too much power to the legislature, the executive branch, the judiciary, and to government in general. The constitution of 1869 provided for annual sessions of the legislature, and gubernatorial appointment of the attorney general, the secretary of state, and all judicial positions, including appointments to the supreme court, a detail that would become especially important in the *Ex Parte Rodriguez* case that will be discussed later. Most importantly, for critics, the constitution of 1869 was the product of pressure from Washington and what were perceived by many to be "radical" Republicans more concerned with punishing than reconstructing the southern states.

Growing opposition to the centralization of power established by a constitution of questionable legitimacy and to actions of a legislature counter to antebellum sentiments in Texas led to a coalition of moderate Republicans and Democrats who managed to gain control of the Texas House after the 1872 elections. The following year, on December 2, Texas voters elected Democrat Richard Coke governor by a two-to-one margin. Governor Davis, however, refused to step down, claiming that the election had been ruled unconstitutional by the Texas Supreme Court and that he was duty bound to enforce the court's decision.

The case in question was *Ex Parte Rodriguez*, better known to history as the semicolon case. The constitution of 1869, in Article 3, Section 6, provided that elections "shall be held at the county seats of the several counties, until otherwise provided by law; and the polls shall be opened for four days. . . . ." The state's position, supported by the newly elected Democrats, was that the legislature had "provided by law" new places and new times, both within the legislature's power under the constitution's language. Lawyers for Rodriguez, who was accused of voting twice in Harris County, argued that their client was not guilty because the election was illegal. The semicolon in the constitutional language, they argued, set the requirement for "four days" apart from the previous section and thereby beyond the legislature's power to change. The court sided with the Rodriguez claim and voided the election.

All of this became a moot point, however, when newly elected Democrats, in defiance of the court, took control of the legislative chambers under the protection of guards sent by Governor Davis to arrest them and declared the election valid. Governor Coke was sworn in on January 15, 1874, and Governor Davis resigned four days later. Democrats would control state government for the next hundred years.

THE 1876 RECONSTITUTION OF TEXAS

For the better part of the last 147 years, it has been commonplace to see the present Texas Constitution as a reaction to the failings and outright corruption of Governor E. J. Davis and his radical Republican friends. Among the first tasks of the new Democrat-controlled legislature was to begin preparations for the rewriting of what nearly all in Austin thought a disastrous constitution of 1869. In the summer of 1875, Texas voters approved a constitutional convention, which began deliberations on September 6. Ninety delegates, three from each of the then 30 senatorial districts, gathered in Austin. Seventy-five of the delegates were Democrats, and 15 were Republicans, including six African Americans.

What resulted from the convention was the constitution of 1876, a constitution routinely criticized as being too long, poorly organized, badly written, and containing too much statutory material. It has been amended more than 450 times, most recently with the addition of 11 amendments in November 2009. The biggest criticism, however, is that it is the product of reaction rather than proaction, of avoiding past errors rather than planning for the challenges of a modern Texas.

The Texas Constitution provides for a biennial legislature (Article 3), a weak chief executive (Article 4), an elected plural executive (Article 4), and elected judges (Article 5), none of which contributing to efficiency of government for a diverse, complex, and dynamic environment such as one finds in 21st century Texas. All of this suggests that the challenge of reconstituting Texas continues to the present day and that a closer look at the constitutional legacy of E. J. Davis might be in order.

Numerous revisionist and post-revisionist scholars have "demonstrated nuances that need to be considered" (Crouch, 282) in evaluating Governor E. J. Davis and his legacy. A more complex

picture has emerged of Davis's impact on the Texas political landscape during the Reconstruction period. Traditionally, his legacy is one of tyranny and corruption, the legacy of an ambitious, overreaching governor. Increasingly, he is less the vilified governor and more a leader in the attempt to reconstitute Texas with a modern constitution providing strong institutions of government.

BIBLIOGRAPHY

Baggett, James Alex. "Origins of Early Texas Republican Party Leadership," *The Journal of Southern History* 40 (August 1974), 441–454.

Cantrell, Gregg. "Racial Violence and Reconstruction in Texas, 1867–1868," *Southwestern Historical Quarterly* 93 (July 1989–April 1990), 333–355.

Constitution of the State of Texas, 1876.

Constitution of the State of Texas, 1869.

Crouch, Barry A. "'Unmanacling' Texas Reconstruction: A Twenty-Year Perspective," *Southwestern Historical Quarterly* 93 (July 1989–April 1990), 275–302.

Menand, Louis. *The Metaphysical Club: A Story of Ideas in America* (New York: Farrar, Straus, and Giroux, 2001).

Moneyhon, Carl H. "Reconstruction," *Handbook of Texas Online*, http://www.tshaonline.org/handbook/online/articles/mzr01

Pitre, Merline. "A Note on the Historiography of Blacks in the Reconstruction of Texas," *Journal of Negro History* 66 (Winter 1981–1982), 340–348.

JOIN THE DEBATE

1. Which state government policies led to the antigovernment sentiment that dominated the political environment during the writing of Texas's constitution of 1876? Which constitutional provisions reflect these antigovernment sentiments today?

2. How can a constitution balance fear of excessive government power with the need for responsible government action?

3. If Texans were to reconstitute its state political system today, how would it differ from the one established in 1876? Would Texans agree with Governor E. J. Davis's vision of a modern state?

Chapter 3

Voting and Elections

CONTENTS

LEARNING OBJECTIVES

* Describe different forms of political participation.
* Identify the leading predictors of whether or not a person votes.
* Describe some of the ways that politicians have restricted the right to vote in Texas over the years.
* Why is voter turnout so low in Texas?
* Describe the historical importance of the primary in Texas politics.
* Describe how open and closed primaries differ.
* Describe how candidates get on the ballot.
* Identify the factors that most advantage candidates in Texas state elections.
* Discuss why it is so difficult to control spending in Texas election campaigns.

★ GET ACTIVE ★

- Act out, join the movement, start a street team, register to vote at Rock the Vote website: **http://www.rockthevote.com/home.html**

- Register to vote at the Texas Secretary of State's website: **http://www.sos.state.tx.us/elections/voter/reqvr.shtml**

- Check out election results at **http://www.sos.state.tx.us/elections/historical/index.shtml**

- Keep up with public opinion in Texas at **http://www.pollingreport.com/** and **http://www.rasmussenreports.com/public_content/politics/general_state_surveys/texas/**

- Follow Professor Rick Hasen's popular and well-respected election law blog at **http://electionlawblog.org/**

One of the distinguishing features of Texas politics is the number and variety of elections held in the state. Texas elects a very large number of officials to do different things at different levels of government. See for yourself: go to your county website and locate a sample ballot. To find your county's URL, go to: **http://www.state.tx.us**. On this home page, under "Living," click on "Texas Cities and Counties" and then open the "County Directory."

Once you have located your county website, find a sample ballot. Ballots are usually stored on the county clerk's section of the site. You may be able to click on a link marked "Elections" or "County Clerk," although a site's structure is sometimes not so straightforward. In some instances, you may find that your county simply does not post a sample ballot. You might mention this in an email to the county clerk. Perhaps the clerk's office will send you one.

If your county website does not have a sample ballot, try another county's, such as Bexar, Dallas, Denton, El Paso, Harris, Jefferson, or Travis, all of which include a full sample ballot before primary and general elections. Examine the ballot from top to bottom, keeping in mind that it may take some time. Indeed, in some areas, people may be asked to vote for more than 100 different offices, from governor to railroad commissioner, from state representative to city council members, from state judges to county judges, justices of the peace, and constables. There are other offices as well, and often a constitutional amendment or two is included.

Learn about current elections at **http://www.localvoter.com**. Here you will find information about candidates and issues in your community, learn how to get involved, and get links to other resources.

Fact check Texas politicians' claims at **http://www.politifact.com/texas**

---

*D*emocracy makes demands on its citizens, in terms of both time and money. A sacrifice of time is required if voters are to inform themselves of the qualifications of the large number of candidates who compete in the spring for nomination in the party primaries. Then, in November, roughly 4,200 of these party nominees ask the voters to elect them in the general election to numerous local, state, and national offices.

Political Participation

Voting in elections is the most basic and common form of political participation. Many people take part in other ways, by discussing political issues with friends and coworkers, writing letters to local representatives or to newspaper editors, distributing campaign literature or contributing money to a campaign, and placing bumper stickers on cars. Some people are members of interest groups, whether neighborhood or trade associations, serve on political party committees, or act as delegates to conventions. Yet others participate in demonstrations or sit-ins, such as the flurry of Tea Party protests.

THE PARTICIPATION PARADOX

Elections, of course, are the defining characteristic of representative democracies. It is through our votes that we hold elected officials accountable. After all, votes are what matter to politicians, at least those interested in winning and holding office. If we vote—and reward and punish elected officials for what they do while in office—politicians have an incentive to do what we want. If we do not vote, elected officials are largely free to do what they want. Clearly, voting is important in a representative democracy.

The problem is that individuals' votes typically do not make a difference in elections. Imagine that you voted in the 2008 presidential election. Did your vote matter? That is, did your vote swing the election, ensuring Barack Obama's victory or dooming him to defeat? No, it didn't. President Obama won the election despite your vote. The point is that our individual votes rarely have any effect on the outcome. This fact begs the question: Why do people vote? Among political scientists, this is known as the **participation paradox**. The point of this paradox is not that you or other people should not vote but rather that people vote for other reasons (and therefore chiding people to vote because their votes "make a difference" is probably not very effective).

Participation paradox

The fact that citizens vote even though their votes rarely influence the result of an election.

Who Votes?

Over the years, political scientists have learned quite a lot about why people go to the polls. It is now clear that a relatively small number of demographic and political variables are especially important.[1] The most important demographic variables are education, income, and age. The more education a person has, the more likely the person is to vote. The same is true for income, even controlling for education. Age also matters. As people grow older, they are more likely to vote, at least until they become very old. Why do these factors matter? The answer is straightforward: people who are educated, have high incomes, and are older are more likely to care about and pay attention to politics. Thus, they are more likely to vote.

In addition to demographic factors, certain political factors influence the likelihood of voting, especially one's expressed interest in politics and intensity of identification with political parties. The more a person is interested in politics, the more likely the person is to vote. The effect is fairly obvious but nevertheless quite important. A person who does not have a lot of education or income is still very likely to vote if the person has a strong interest in politics.

Identification with either of the major political parties also makes a person more likely to vote. This pattern reflects the fact that strong partisan identifiers, on average, care a lot more about who wins than people who do not identify with the parties. It also reflects the mobilization of identifiers by the political parties. That is, the more one identifies with a party, the more likely it is that the person will be contacted by the party and its candidates during election campaigns.

[1] Raymond E. Wolfinger and Steven Rosenstone, *Who Votes?* (New Haven, CT: Yale University Press, 1980). Also see Sydney Verba and Norman H. Nie, *Participation in America* (New York: Harper & Row, 1972).

MORE THAN VOTING

Although voting is the most common form of political participation, a much smaller number of Americans participate in other ways. In 2008, surveys indicate that 20 percent wore a button or displayed a bumper sticker, 13 percent donated money to a political party or campaign, 9 percent attended a political meeting or rally, and 5 percent worked for a political party or candidate.[2]

A Voter and Future Voter Exercising Their Right. Parental socialization is how most people learn to become active in politics. ☞

Why do voters case their ballots when a single vote is very unlikely to determine the winner of an election?

Tom Carter/PhotoEdit

In one sense, deciding to vote is much like deciding to attend a sporting event, for example, a professional baseball game. We do not go to a game to affect the outcome. We go for other reasons, because we like baseball and care about it. The same is true for voting; education, income, age, interest, and party identification are important indicators of our desire to participate.

Of course, other factors are also important for explaining electoral participation, but the small set of demographic and political variables tells us quite a lot. With this information, we can pretty much determine whether a person will or will not vote in a particular election. We also can account for most of the differences in turnout among different groups, such as African Americans, Asian Americans, Latinos, and whites.

THE PRACTICE OF VOTING

The legal qualifications for voting in Texas are surprisingly few and simple. Anyone who is (1) a citizen of the United States, (2) at least 18 years of age, and (3) a resident of the state is eligible to register and vote in Texas. The only citizens prohibited from voting are those who have been declared "mentally incompetent" in formal court proceedings and those convicted of a felony whose civil rights have not been restored by a pardon or by the passage of two calendar years from the completion of the sentence.

Meeting these qualifications does not mean that a person can simply walk into the voting booth on election day. In order to vote, a person must be registered. As a result of the Voting Rights Acts of 1965 and 1970, a number of U.S. Supreme Court rulings, and recent congressional action, the registration procedure is almost as simple as voting itself. (This was not always true—see the list of "Legal Constraints" below.) A person may register in person or by mail at any time of the year up to 30 days before the election. Since the passage of federal "motor voter" legislation, a person can also register when renewing a driver's license; indeed, every person renewing a driver's license is asked whether he or she wants to register to vote. Spouses, parents, or offspring also can register the applicant, provided that they are qualified voters.

---

[2]American National Election Studies, University of Michigan, http://www.electionstudies.org. Note that these numbers may overstate the actual levels of participation, as they are difficult to verify, and we know that survey respondents tend to exaggerate turnout.

The present Texas registration system is as open and modern as that of any other state that requires advanced registration. (Note that a number of states, including Maine, Minnesota, and Wisconsin, permit election-day registration, and North Dakota has no registration at all. There, one just walks in, shows identification, and votes.) The Texas system, established by law in 1975, provides for the mailing of a new two-year voter registration certificate to every voter by January 1 in even-numbered years. The system is permanent in that once a voter is on the rolls, he or she will not be removed unless the nonforwardable certificate is returned. Since 1977, Texas law requires that the secretary of state make postage-free registration applications available at any county clerk's office. They are also available at various other public offices.

Names on returned certificates are stricken from the eligible voters list and placed on a strike list. The strike list is attached to the list of voters for each precinct; for three months the previously registered voters whose names are on the strike list can vote in their old precincts if they have filled out a new voter registration card for the new residence. They can vote, however, only for those offices that both residences have in common. Thus, the person who has moved can vote on at least a portion of both the first and runoff primary ballots. The coroner's reports, lists of felony convictions, and adjudications of mental incompetence are also used to purge the list of eligible voters. Anyone can purchase the computer-generated voter list for each county in the state. Political parties and candidates make extensive use of voter lists when trying to identify likely voters during election campaigns.

Establishing residence for voting is no longer a matter of living at a place for a specified time. Residence is defined primarily in terms of intent (that is, people's homes are where they intend them to be). No delay in qualifying to vote is permitted under U.S. Supreme Court rulings except for a short period of time in which the application is processed and the registrant's name is entered on the rolls. In accordance with the Court's ruling, that delay in Texas is fixed at 30 days.[3]

Once registered, voting is easy. This is especially true in Texas, which has passed a number of laws facilitating the act of voting. In 1975, for example, the legislature required that all ballots and election materials be printed in Spanish as well as English in counties with a five percent or more Latino population. In 1991, the legislature authorized early voting, which allows people to vote at a number of different sites before election day.[4] Thus it is now very easy to register and vote in Texas.

VOTER TURNOUT IN THE UNITED STATES AND IN TEXAS

Making registration and voting easier was expected to result in increased **voter turnout**—the proportion of eligible Americans who vote. Such has not been the case; indeed, the reverse has been true. Since 1960, turnout has actually declined. This is not to suggest that the actual number of voters has diminished. In fact, the number has steadily increased, from 70.6 million votes for president in 1964 to an estimated 131 million votes in 2008—an increase of 86 percent. However, the number of voting-age Americans increased from 114.1 million to 231 million during the same period—an increase of more than 100 percent. Thus the **voting-age population** (VAP) has grown at a much faster rate than the actual voting population.[5]

Voter turnout

The percentage of people who are eligible to vote that actually vote.

Voting-age population

The total number of persons in the United States who are 18 years of age or older regardless of citizenship, military status, felony conviction, or mental state.

---

[3]In two 1973 cases (*Burns* v. *Fortson*, 410 U.S. 686, and *Martson* v. *Lewis*, 410 U.S. 679), the U.S. Supreme Court upheld delays of up to 50 days in Georgia and Arizona, respectively.
[4]Texas was one of the first states to institute early voting for all voters.
[5]The VAP is an imperfect measure of the voting-eligible population (VEP) because it includes people who cannot vote (noncitizens and felons) and excludes people who can (eligible citizens living overseas). Because the number of noncitizens and felons are large and the sum of these far exceeds the number of overseas eligibles, the VAP tends to exaggerate the actual VEP. In 2008, for example, the difference was substantial (approximately 18 million people). The VAP measure will therefore understate rates of participation. Unfortunately, reliable measures of VEP over long stretches of time are not readily available, particularly at the state level, which is why VAP is used here. For more information on measuring turnout, see the United States Elections Project at http://elections.gmu.edu

Figure 3.1

How Many People Vote in the United States? Presidential Election Turnout, 1932–2008. Here we see that turnout declined in the early 1970s but has not changed much during the last 30 years. Only a little more than 50 percent of the voting-age population now votes in presidential elections.

Sources: *Congressional Quarterly Report*, October 1, 1988, 2002; Federal Election Commission, "National Voter Turnout in Federal Elections: 1960–2000," http://www.fec.gov. Data for 2004 and 2008 are from the United States Elections Project, http://elections.gmu.edu/Voter_Turnout_2004.htm; [http://elections.gmu.edu/Turnout_2008G.html]

Describe the groups that are most likely to vote. Does one party or the other benefit more when there is a high turnout of voters?

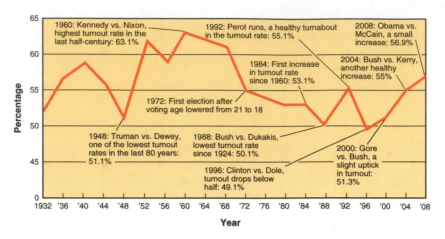

Figure 3.1 shows voter turnout in presidential elections from 1932 to 2008. Apart from a decrease in turnout in 1944 and then again in 1948, turnout increased from 1932 through 1960. After hitting an all time high of 63.1 percent in 1960, the presidential vote declined steadily until the late 1970s. After that time, turnout among the VAP hovered above 50 percent, with the exception of 1992, when it jumped to 55.1 percent.[6] Turnout actually fell below 50 percent in 1996, meaning that fewer than half of the voting-age population went to the polls, and rose slightly to just above 51 percent in 2000. In 2004, turnout surged to 55.4 percent. In 2008, it went up further still, to 56.9 percent.[7] A similar overall pattern is evident in nonpresidential, or "midterm" elections, although voting rates are always 15 to 20 percent lower in those years. Turnout decreased from 45.4 percent in 1962 to 35.3 percent in 1978. Since that time, turnout in midterms has averaged just over 35 percent, though it has fluctuated from election to election. In 2006, just above 36 percent of the voting-age population voted.

Among persons between the ages of 18 and 24, the turnout rate has remained fairly steady. These young people are still much less likely to vote than the average American. About 37 percent voted in the 2000 presidential election, and less than 20 percent voted in the 2002 midterm election. In 2004, there was a sizable increase of nearly six percentage points, although this jump was only slightly greater than the increase in other age groups.[8] In 2008, turnout jumped another two points, again only slightly greater than for the rest of the population.

There are two main reasons for the decrease in voter turnout in the United States after the 1960s. The first reason can be traced to the Twenty-sixth Amendment, which lowered the voting age from 21 to 18 in 1972. The amendment was passed at the height of the Vietnam War, with proponents arguing that a person who could be drafted and sent off to war should be able to vote. By extending the vote to 18- to 20-year-old citizens, the amendment expanded the eligible voting population. As we have already seen, however, these young people are less likely to vote than are older persons. Thus, adding the age group to the lists of eligible voters in 1972 slightly reduced the overall turnout rate. Second, identification with the two major political parties dropped substantially after the 1960s, and

---

[6]Survey data suggest that the temporary increase in turnout in 1992 was due to the candidacy of Ross Perot, which drew people (approximately 5% of the population) to the polls who otherwise would not have voted.

[7]When the VEP is used (see footnote 5), estimated turnout in 2008 was 61.7 percent, almost 5 points greater than estimated with the VAP.

[8]For more information on voting among young people, see the Center for Information and Research on Civic Learning and Engagement (CIRCLE) report at http://www.civicyouth.org/PopUps/FactSheets/FS-PresElection04.pdf

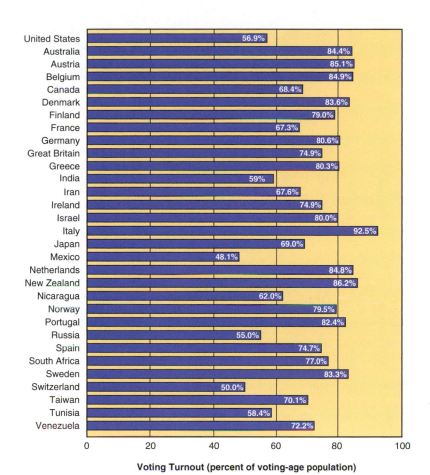

Figure 3.2

Voter Turnout from Around the World. The United States is most similar to India, Russia, and Tunisia.

Source: International Institute for Democracy and Electoral Assistance, http://www.idea.int/

Why is turnout so far below what we observe in other established, industrialized democracies?

Voting Turnout (percent of voting-age population)

approximately one-third of all Americans now consider themselves "independents."[9] (The proportion is even greater for younger voters.) As noted earlier, these voters are less likely to vote than are partisans.[10]

Turnout in American general elections is significantly lower than that in other industrialized democracies of the world. A study found that in the 13 most comparable nations—those without compulsory voting—the turnout between 1972 and 1980 averaged 80 percent, fully 25 to 30 percent above the rate in the United States.[11] The more recent numbers in Figure 3.2 show much the same pattern. Interestingly, American political attitudes seem more conducive to voting than those in countries with far higher turnouts. Low voter turnout in the United States is caused by other factors, including institutional structures (primarily the strength of political parties) and the fact that we require voters to register.

---

[9]See Paul R. Abramson and John H. Aldrich, "The Decline of Electoral Participation in American," *American Political Science Review* 76 (June 1982), pp. 502–521.

[10]Some scholars attribute part of the decline in turnout to the increasing tendency toward divided government at the national level, where the president is from one political party and the majority in Congress is from the other. The argument is that divided government makes it more difficult for voters to assign responsibility for policy decisions and that, as a result, voters cannot easily reward or punish specific elected officials at the polls. See Mark N. Franklin and Wolfgang P. Hirczy de Mino, "Separated Powers, Divided Government, and Turnout in U.S. Presidential Elections," *American Journal of Political Science Review* 42 (January 1998), pp. 316–326.

[11]G. Bingham Powell, Jr., "American Voter Turnout in Comparative Perspective," *American Political Science Review* 80 (March 1986), pp. 17, 23. Switzerland, the only country studied where turnout is lower than in the United States, was not included in this computation.

HOW DOES TEXAS COMPARE?
VOTER TURNOUT

In partial contrast to the national trend, voter turnout in Texas (and in most of the South) has not declined since 1960. Instead, it has remained fairly stable at levels below the national average. In presidential elections, turnout actually increased somewhat through the 1960s and leveled off thereafter until 1996, falling to 41.3 percent (see Table 3.1). In 2000, it jumped up slightly to 43.1 percent and then again in 2004 to 45.6 percent, about 10 percent less than the national rate. In that year, only one state posted a lower turnout rate than Texas, and the same was true in 2008.

In midterm elections, turnout has bounced around a lot from election to election and exhibits little pattern (see Table 3.2). The turnout rate typically has been between 20 and 30 percent, and only Louisiana has consistently vied with Texas for the dubious honor of the lowest turnout in the nation.[12] Turnout in Texas did exceed 30 percent in 1994, when Governor Ann Richards lost to George Bush. In 2006, turnout actually dipped to 26 percent despite an open field of four gubernatorial candidates, including Republican Governor Perry and Democrat challenger Chris Bell and two independent candidates as well—Republican State Comptroller Carole Keeton Strayhorn (who ran as an Independent) and singer-writer Richard "Kinky" Friedman. In 2010, voter participation was 27.3 percent, lower than any other state.

TABLE 3.1 PERCENTAGE OF THE VOTING-AGE POPULATION CASTING BALLOTS IN PRESIDENTIAL GENERAL ELECTIONS, 1960–2008

	1960	1964	1968	1972	1976	1980	1984	1988	1992	1996	2000	2004	2008
United States	62.8	61.9	60.6	55.5	53.3	52.6	53.1	50.1	55.2	49.1	51.3	55.4	56.9
Texas	41.8	44.4	48.7	45.3	46.2	44.9	47.2	45.5	49.1	41.3	43.1	45.5	45.6
Difference (Texas vs. United States)	21.0	17.5	11.9	10.2	7.1	7.7	5.9	4.7	6.1	7.8	8.2	10.0	10.3
Rank of Texas among the 50 states	44th	48th	43rd	43rd	44th	44th	45th	46th	46th	48th	48th	49th	49th

Sources: Lester Milbrath, "Participation in the American States," in Herbert Jacob and Kenneth N. Vines (eds.), *Politics in the American States*, 2nd ed. (Boston: Little, Brown, 1971), pp. 38–39; *Statistical Abstract of the United States, 1976, 1979, 1983, 1986, 1989, and 1993* (Washington, DC: U.S. Government Printing Office); Federal Election Commission, "Voter Registration and Turnout," http://www.fec.gov; United States Elections Project, http://elections.gmu.edu/Turnout_2004G.html, http://elections.gmu.edu/Turnout_2008G.html

---

TABLE 3.2 PERCENTAGE OF THE VOTING-AGE POPULATION CASTING BALLOTS IN NONPRESIDENTIAL GENERAL ELECTIONS, 1962–2006

	1962	1966	1970	1974	1978	1982	1986	1990	1994	1998	2002	2006
United States	45.4	45.4	43.5	36.1	35.3	38.0	33.4	33.1	36.0	36.4	36.2	37.1
Texas	25.8	20.9	27.5	18.4	24.1	26.2	25.5	26.8	31.3	6.1	28.8	25.8
Difference (Texas vs. United States)	19.6	24.5	16.0	17.7	11.2	11.8	7.9	6.3	4.7	10.3	7.4	11.3
Rank of Texas among the 50 states	43rd	50th	47th	49th	46th	48th	45th	42nd	45th	47th	49th	50th

Sources: *Statistical Abstract of the United States, 1976, 1979, 1983, 1989,* and *1996* (Washington, DC: U.S. Government Printing Office); Federal Election Commission, "Voter Registration and Turnout," http://www.fec.gov; United States Elections Project, http://elections.gmu.edu/Turnout_2002G.html; http://elections.gmu.edu/Turnout_2006G.html

Why does Texas have among the lowest voter turnout statistics in the nation? Should Texas adopt policies that encourage voters to participate? Suggest changes that would make it easier for citizens to participate in state elections.

REASONS FOR LOW VOTER TURNOUT IN TEXAS

Most Texans probably think that Texas is in the mainstream of American society. Why, then, is there such a difference between Texas and other urbanized and industrialized states in its political behavior? Why does Texas compare more closely with states of the Deep South in voter turnout? The answer may lie in its laws, socioeconomic characteristics, political structure, and political culture.

---

[12]In Louisiana, the state and local contests are decided before the general election, so the motivation for voting is low. Louisiana's "blanket primary" ballot lists all candidates from all parties. If no one receives a majority of the votes in a given race, the top two vote recipients compete in a September runoff primary, irrespective of political party affiliation, and the winner of the primary is elected. No other state uses this system.

AP Photos/Smiley N. Pool, Pool

Peter Silva/Reuters/Landov

Republican State Comptroller Carole Keeton Strayhorn (left) and singer-writer Richard "Kinky" Friedman (right) ran for governor in 2006 as independent candidates and received 18 percent and 13 percent of the vote, respectively. Despite an open field of four candidates, including Republican Governor Rick Perry (middle) and Democrat challenger Chris Bell, voter turnout was only 26 percent.

Why do so few voters turn out in nonpresidential elections in Texas? Would a larger number of Texans cast their ballots for governor if the election were held at the same time as presidential elections?

Legal Constraints Traditionally, scholars interested in the variation in turnout across the American states have focused on laws regulating registration and voting. Clearly, the most important of these laws were the restrictions on who may vote, such as the poll tax, property ownership requirements, or the outright exclusion of African Americans and women.

Although these restrictions disappeared some time ago, other barriers to registration and voting persisted, and some remain in effect today.[13] One can ask: Does a state promote political participation by setting the minimum necessary limitations and making it as convenient as possible for the citizen to vote? Or, does a state repeatedly place barriers on the way to the polls, making the act of voting physically, financially, and psychologically as difficult as the local sense of propriety will allow? There is no doubt into which category Texas once fell—the application has been uneven, but historically Texas was among the most restrictive states in its voting laws.

However, nearly all of these restrictions have been changed by amendments to the U.S. Constitution, state and national laws, rulings by the U.S. Department of Justice, and judicial decisions. Even a cursory examination of these restrictions and the conditions under which they were removed makes one appreciate the extent to which Texas's elections were at one time closed. Consider these changes in Texas voting policies:

1. *Poll tax.* The payment of a poll tax as a prerequisite for voting was adopted in 1902. The cost was $1.75 ($1.50 plus $0.25 optional for the county) and represented more than a typical day's wages for some time. Many poor Texans were kept from voting. When the Twenty-fourth Amendment was ratified in 1964, it voided the poll tax in national elections. Texas and only one other state kept it for state elections until it was held unconstitutional in 1966 (*United States* v. *Texas,* 384 U.S. 155).
2. *Women's suffrage.* An attempt was made to end the denial of the ballot to women in 1917, but the effort failed by four votes in the Texas legislature. Women were allowed to vote in the primaries of 1918, but not until ratification of the Nineteenth Amendment in 1920 did full suffrage come to women in Texas.

---

[13]See Glenn Mitchell, II and Christopher Wlezien, "The Impact of Legal Constraints on Voter Registration, Turnout, and the Composition of the American Electorate," *Political Behavior* 17 (June 1995), pp. 179–202.

3. *White primary.* African Americans were barred from participating when the first party primary was held in 1906. When movement toward increased participation seemed likely, Texas made several moves to avoid U.S. Supreme Court rulings allowing African Americans to vote. Not until 1944 were the legislature's efforts to deny African Americans access to the primaries finally overturned (*Smith* v. *Allwright,* 321 U.S. 649).

4. *Military vote.* Until 1931, members of the National Guard were not permitted to vote. Members of the military began to enjoy the full rights of suffrage in Texas in 1965, when the U.S. Supreme Court voided the Texas constitutional exclusion (*Carrington* v. *Rash,* 380 U.S. 89).

5. *Long residence requirement.* The Texas residence requirement of one year in the state and six months in the county was modified slightly by the legislature to allow new residents to vote in the presidential part of the ballot, but not until a 1972 ruling of the U.S. Supreme Court were such requirements abolished (*Dunn* v. *Blumstein,* 405 U.S. 330).

6. *Property ownership as a requirement for voting in bond elections.* Texas held to this requirement until the U.S. Supreme Court made property ownership unnecessary for revenue bond elections in 1969 (*Kramer* v. *Union Free District No. 15,* 395 U.S. 621), and for tax elections in 1969 (*Cipriano* v. *City of Houma,* 395 U.S. 701), and in 1975 (*Hill* v. *Stone,* 421 U.S. 289).

7. *Annual registration.* Even after the poll tax was voided, Texas continued to require voters to register every year until annual registration was prohibited by the federal courts in 1971 (*Beare* v. *Smith,* 321 F. Supp. 1100).

8. *Early registration.* Texas voters were required to meet registration requirements by January 31, earlier than the cutoff date for candidates' filings and more than nine months before the general election. This restriction was voided in 1971 (*Beare* v. *Smith,* 321 F. Supp.1100).

9. *Jury duty.* Texas law provided that the names of prospective jurors must be drawn from the voting rolls. Some Texans did not like to serve on juries, and not registering to vote ensured against a jury summons. (Counties now use driver's licenses for jury lists.)

Texas used almost every technique available except the literacy test and the grandfather clause[14] to deny the vote or to make it expensive in terms of time, money, and aggravation. This is not the case today. Most barriers to voting in Texas have been removed, and as was mentioned previously, the legislature has instituted a number of provisions that make voting easier than in most states. Thus, the laws in Texas may help us understand why turnout was low in the past and, with the relaxing of restrictions, why turnout has increased somewhat since 1960. The current laws do not help us understand why turnout in Texas remains low today. For this, we need to look elsewhere.

Socioeconomic Factors   Texas is known as the land of the "big rich" cattle barons and oil tycoons. What is not so well known is that Texas is also the land of the "big poor" and that more than 4 million persons—more than in any other state—live in poverty here. Although nationally the proportion of people living below the poverty level in 2008 was 13.2 percent, in Texas the proportion was 15.8 percent. For African-American and Latino Texans, almost 25 percent have incomes below this level. Of the more than 3 million individuals in Texas living in poverty, more than one-third are children. Understandably, formal educational achievement is also low. Of Texans older than 25 years of age, one in four has not graduated

[14]The grandfather clause gave white citizens who were disenfranchised by poll tax or literacy requirements the right to vote if they had been eligible to vote before the passage of the restricting legislation. These laws were found unconstitutional by the U.S. Supreme Court in *Guinn* v. *United States,* 238 U.S. 347 (1915).

👆 *Signing petitions and attending rallies are important forms of political participation. Although people are less likely to vote in the United States and especially Texas by comparison with people in other countries, they are more likely to take part in other ways.*

Identify forms of participation other than voting. Which forms of participation have the greatest impact on Texas's political system?

from high school. Among African Americans, the ratio is just less than one of three, and among Latinos, it is almost one of two.[15]

Given that income and education are such important determinants of electoral participation, low voter turnout is exactly what we should expect in Texas. Because income and education levels are particularly low among African Americans and, especially, Latinos, turnout is particularly low for these groups. Voting by Texas minorities is on the rise, however, and this has led to much greater representation of both groups in elected offices, as we will see. These trends should continue as income and education levels among minorities increase.

Political Structure Another deterrent to voting in Texas is the length of the ballot and the number of elections. Texas uses a long ballot that provides for the popular election of numerous public officers (whom some people believe should be appointed). In an urban county, the ballot may call for the voter to choose between 150 and 200 candidates vying for 50 or more offices. The frequency of referendums on constitutional amendments contributes to the length of the ballot in Texas. Voters are also asked to go to the polls for various municipal, school board, bond, and special-district elections. Government is far more fragmented in Texas than in other states, and this makes particular elections a lot less meaningful and perhaps a lot more frustrating for voters.

Political Culture Insights into voter participation levels have been derived from the concept of **political culture**, which describes the set of political values and beliefs that are dominant in a society. Borrowed from social anthropologists, this concept has been found to be applicable to all political systems, from those of developing countries to modern industrial democracies. It has been especially useful in the study of American politics, where federalism

Political culture

The political values and beliefs that are dominant in a nation or state.

[15]U.S. Census Bureau, http://www.census.gov/cgi-bin/saipe/saipe.cgi; U.S. Census Bureau, http://www.census.gov/hhes/www/poverty/data/threshld/thresh08.html. The definition of *poverty* depends on the size and composition of the family. For a family of four (two adults and two children), the threshold in 2008 was an annual income of $22,570 or less.

has emphasized the diversity among regions, states, and communities—a diversity that cries out for some approach that can effectively explain it.

As we saw in Chapter 1, the American political culture is actually a mix of three sub-cultures, each prevalent in at least one area of the United States.[16] The *moralistic culture* is a product of the Puritan era and is strongest in New England. The *traditionalistic culture* comes to us via the plantation society of the Deep South, and the *individualistic culture* was born in the commercial centers of the Middle Atlantic states, moving west and south along the Ohio River and its tributaries. It is the mix as well as the isolation of these cultures that gives American politics its flavor.

Important to students of electoral politics is that "the degree of political participation (i.e., voter turnout and suffrage regulations) is the most consistent indicator of political culture."[17] The moralistic culture perceives the discussion of public issues and voting as not only a right but also an opportunity that is beneficial to the citizen and society alike. In contrast, the traditionalistic culture views politics as the special preserve of the social and economic elite and a process of maintaining the existing order. Highly personal, it views political participation as a privilege and uses social pressure as well as restrictive election laws to limit voting. The individualistic culture blurs the distinction between economic and political life. Here business and politics are both viewed as appropriate avenues by which an individual can advance his or her interests, and conflicts of interest are fairly common. In this culture, business interests can play a very strong role, and running for office is difficult without their support.

Low voter turnout in Texas may be due in part to the state's political culture, which is a mix of the traditionalistic and the individualistic. The traditionalistic aspect is especially characteristic of East Texas, settled primarily by immigrants from the Deep South in the years prior to the Civil War. The individualistic aspect predominates throughout the rest of the state. As a result, participation in politics is not as highly regarded as it is in other states, particularly those with a moralistic culture, and politics in Texas is largely the domain of business interests. People may be less likely to vote in Texas because they do not value political participation itself and because they tend to think that they play a little role in politics.

Elections in Texas

Winning an office is typically a two-stage process. First, the candidate must win the Democratic or Republican Party nomination in the primary election. Second, the candidate must win the general election against the other party's nominee. It is possible for a candidate to get on the general-election ballot without winning a primary election (as will be discussed shortly), but this is rare. As in most other states, elections in Texas are dominated by the Democratic and Republican parties.

PRIMARY ELECTIONS

Three successive devices for selecting political party nominees have been used in the history of this country, each perceived as a cure for the ills of a previously corrupt, inefficient, or inadequate system. The first was the caucus, consisting of the elected political party members serving in the legislature. The "insider" politics of the caucus room motivated the reformers of the Jacksonian era to throw out "King Caucus" and to institute the party convention system by 1828. In this system, ordinary party members select delegates to a party convention, and these delegates then nominate the party's candidates for office and write a party platform. The

---

[16]Daniel J. Elazar, *American Federalism: A View from the States*, 3rd ed. (New York: Harper & Row, 1984).
[17]David C. Saffel, *State Politics* (Reading, MA: Addison-Wesley, 1984), p. 8.

convention system was hailed as a surefire method of ending party nominations by the legislative bosses. By 1890, the backroom politics of the convention halls again moved reformers to action, and the result was the **direct primary**, adopted by most states between 1890 and 1920. Texas's first direct primary was held in 1906, under the Terrell Election Law passed in 1903. It enables party members to participate directly in their party's selection of a candidate to represent them in the general election.

Traditionally regarded as private activities, primaries were at one time largely beyond the concern of legislatures and courts. Costs of party activities, including primaries, were paid for through donations and by assessing each candidate who sought a party's nomination. Judges attempted to avoid suits between warring factions of the parties as much as they did those involving church squabbles over the division of church property. This was the perception on which the U.S. Supreme Court upheld in 1935 the Texas Democratic Party convention's decision barring African Americans from participating in the party primary.[18] Because political party activities were increasingly circumscribed by law, the Court reversed itself in 1944 and recognized the primary as an integral part of the election process.[19]

It argued that in a one-party state, which Texas was at the time, the party primary may be the only election in which any meaningful choice is possible. Since the Democratic Party seldom had any real opposition in the general election, winning the nomination was, for all practical purposes, winning the office. The party balance in Texas has changed quite a lot in recent years, however. The Republicans have overtaken the Democrats and now hold every statewide elected office.

Who Must Hold a Primary? Like most other states, for decades Texas has required that "major" political parties—those whose candidates for governor received a fixed minimum number of votes in the last general election—select their nominees through the primary. Other parties, however, were at one time allowed to nominate by primary or convention, whichever they chose. In 1973, the legislature amended the Texas Election Code to provide that any party receiving 20 percent of the gubernatorial vote must hold a primary and that all other parties must use the convention system.[20]

Moreover, all new parties must meet additional requirements if their nominees are to be on the general-election ballot. In addition to holding a convention, these parties must file with the secretary of state a list of supporters equal to one percent of the total vote for governor in the last general election. The list may consist of the names of those whom participated in the party's convention, a nominating petition, or a combination of the two. Persons named as supporters must be registered voters who have not participated in the activities (primaries or conventions) of either of the two major parties. Each page (although not each name) on the nominating petition must be notarized. Such a requirement is, as intended, difficult to meet and therefore inhibits the creation of new political parties.

Financing Primaries From their beginning in 1906 through 1970, the Texas political party primaries were financed under the benefit-user theory, in which the user paid for the cost through fees or assessments. The beneficiaries were those who sought to become their party's nominees for public office. Consequently, a system of filing fees was instituted. For all statewide and a few local offices, nominal fixed-dollar amounts were assessed. The major costs of the primaries were borne by assessments on candidates for district, county, and precinct

---

[18]*Grovey* v. *Townsend*, 295 U.S. 45 (1935).

[19]*Smith* v. *Allwright*, 321 U.S. 649 (1944).

[20]The La Raza Unida Party challenged this limitation. The Justice Department and federal courts sustained the challenge, but only as it applied to La Raza Unida, which was permitted to conduct a primary in 1978. Otherwise, the law stands as written.

TABLE 3.3 FEES FOR LISTING ON THE PARTY PRIMARY BALLOT IN TEXAS, SELECTED OFFICES

Office	Fee
U.S. Senator	$5,000
U.S. Representative	$3,125
Texas Statewide Officers	$3,750
State Senator	$1,250
State Representative	$750
County Commissioner	$750–$1,250
District Judge	$1,500–$2,500
Justice of the Peace, Constable	$375–$1,000
County Surveyor	$75

How much do filing fees limit candidates' access to the state ballot? Should election laws attempt to discourage frivolous candidates?

offices. The county executive committees assessed candidates based on the estimated cost of the primaries in their respective counties.

Since 1971, however, primary elections have been funded primarily from the state treasury. State and county executive committees initially make the expenditures, but the secretary of state reimburses each committee for the difference between the filing fees collected and the actual cost of the primary. To get on the party primary ballot, a candidate needs only to file an application with the state or county party chair and pay the prescribed fee. The categories of fees, applicable also for special elections, are summarized in Table 3.3.

So that no person is forced to bear an unreasonable expense when running for political office, the legislature (prodded by the federal courts) provided an alternative to the filing fee. A petition is required bearing the names of 5,000 voters for candidates seeking nomination to statewide office. For district and lesser offices, the petition must bear the signatures of voters equal to two percent of the vote for the party's candidate for governor in the last election, up to a maximum of 500 required signatures. A sample primary ballot is reproduced in Figure 3.3.

Administering Primaries In the county primaries, the chair and county executive committee of each party receive applications and filing fees and hold drawings to determine the order of names on the ballot for both party and government offices. They then certify the ballot, select an election judge for each voting precinct (usually the precinct chair), select the voting devices (paper ballots, voting machines, or punch cards), and arrange for polling places and printing. After the primary, the county chair and executive committee canvass the votes and certify the results of their respective state executive committees.

In the state primary, the state party chair and the state executive committee of each political party receive applications of candidates for state offices, conduct drawings to determine the order of names, certify the ballot to the county-level officials, and canvass the election returns after the primary.

The Majority Rule In Texas, as in other southern states (except for Tennessee and Virginia) that were once predominantly Democratic, nominations are by a majority (50% plus 1) of the popular vote. If no candidate receives a majority of votes cast for a particular office in the first primary, a **runoff primary** is required in which the two candidates receiving the greatest number of votes are pitted against each other. Outside the South, where the balance between

Runoff primary

A second primary election that pits the two top vote-getters from the first primary, where the winner in that primary did not receive a majority. The runoff primary is used in states such as Texas that have a majority election rule in party primaries.

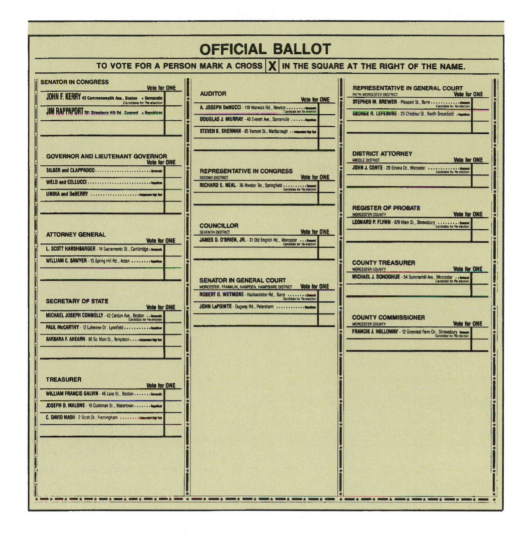

Figure 3.3

Example of the Office-Block Ballot Used in Massachusetts. In contrast with the party-column ballot, which lists candidates of each party in parallel columns, the office-block ballot lists candidates in rows underneath each office. Notice also that voters cannot easily vote a straight-party ticket.

Compared to the party-column ballot, how would this office-block arrangement encourage ticket-splitting?

the two major parties has traditionally been more equal, only a plurality of the votes (more votes than for anyone else) is required, and consequently no runoff is necessary.

Primary elections in Texas are held on the second Tuesday in March of even-numbered years. The runoff primary is scheduled for the second Tuesday in April or a month after the initial party primary election. Although there are earlier presidential primaries, no other state schedules primaries to nominate candidates for state offices so far in advance of the general election in November.

Until 1960, the primaries were held much later in the year, on the fourth Saturday in July and the fourth Saturday in August. The dates were moved up to the first Saturday in May so that presidential aspirant Senator Lyndon B. Johnson could "lock up" his renomination to the U.S. Senate before the convening of the Democratic national convention in Los Angeles.

The presidential ambitions of another Texan, Vice President George H. W. Bush, contributed to the adoption of an even earlier primary. Believing an early primary victory in Texas would benefit their candidate, Bush's Republican supporters joined conservative Democrats in urging Texas to join most other southern states holding a regional primary on "Super Tuesday." In a special session in 1986, the Texas legislature rescheduled the primary to nominate all state officials on the second Tuesday in March in both presidential and nonpresidential election years. In 1996, the southern regional presidential primary included Texas, Florida, Louisiana, Mississippi, Oklahoma, and Tennessee. Oregon also held its primary that day. (In later years, several states made further changes to their primary schedules, and these changes broke up the Super Tuesday primary.) By 2008, most states already had their primaries before March, but Texas (and Ohio, which held its primary on the same day) may have had a bigger impact on the process than in previous years. Both Texas and Ohio went for Hillary Clinton, temporarily disrupting Barack Obama's path to the Democratic nomination. The states also sealed the nomination for Republican presidential candidate John McCain.

Turnout in Texas primaries is much lower than in general elections. Take 2002 for example: although 4.5 million Texans voted in the general election, only 1.6 million participated in the Democratic and Republican primaries—that is, approximately 12 percent of the voting-age population. Matters were even worse in 2006, when 1.2 million people voted in either primary, less than 10 percent of the population. Turnout in presidential election years is higher but still averages below 30 percent. Participation was up a little in 2008, especially for the Democrats, as 2.9 million citizens turned out to support Obama or Clinton. Another 1.4 million voted in the much less competitive Republican primary in that year. In 2010, despite competitive gubernatorial nomination contests, particularly in the Republican primary, only 2.1 million Texans voted, approximately 12 percent of the 18 million people who were 18 years of age or older. The people who do vote in primary elections are hardly representative of the population—they tend to be better educated, more affluent, and more ideologically extreme.

Closed Primary Party primaries are defined as either *open* or *closed*. These terms relate to whether or not participation is limited to party members. Because the purpose of a primary is to choose the party's nominee, it is logical to exclude anyone who is not a party member. However, not every state recognizes the strength of that logic. Alaska and Washington used to have a "blanket primary," in which the voters could pick one party's candidate for one office and another party's candidate for another office, but the U.S. Supreme Court declared it unconstitutional in 2004. Seven states have an **open primary** in which voters decide at the polls (on election day) in which primary they will participate.

Texas and the remaining 40 states use what is legally called a **closed primary**. In practice, however, Texas operates as an open-primary state. As is true in some other closed-primary states, the primary voter is morally—but not legally—bound to vote only in elections for his or her own party. This means that people can participate in either the Democratic or the Republican primary whether they are members or not. Only two minor legal restrictions make Texas technically a closed-primary state:

1. A person is forbidden to vote in more than one primary on election day.
2. A person who has voted in the first primary cannot switch parties and participate in the runoff election or convention of any other party.

In contrast, the typical closed primary requires that a person specify a party preference when registering to vote. The party's name is then stamped on the registration card at the time of issuance. Each voter may change a party affiliation at any time up to 30 days (usually) before participating in a primary or a convention. Voters are limited, however, to the activities of the party they have formally declared as their preference. If the individual registers as an "independent" (no party preference), that person is excluded from the primaries and conventions of *all* parties. Note that how a person votes (or fails to vote) in any type of primary does not limit in any way the choice available in the general election in November.

Open primary

A type of party primary where a voter can choose on election day in which primary they will participate.

Closed primary

A type of primary where a voter only can participate in the primary for the party of which they are a member.

Crossover Voting   The opportunity always exists in Texas for members of one political party to invade the other party's primary. This is called **crossover voting**. It is designed to increase the chances that the nominee from the other party will be someone whose philosophy is like that of the invader's own party. For example, if Republicans can ensure the nomination of a strong conservative in the Democratic primary, either of the two major party candidates may be quite acceptable in November. It has been "institutionalized" by the Republican Party through the practice of some Republican Party county executive committees opting not to hold a primary. In those counties, Republicans have no place to go except to the Democratic primary.

It should not be assumed that the decision to forgo the primary is based on the lack of Republican voters. Although that is true in some counties, it is not true of all. Of the 22 counties that did not hold a Republican primary in 1980, President Reagan carried 10; in 1984, he carried 18 of 26. This was due to the fact that a large number of Democrats voted for Reagan in the general election.

Crossover voting has long been the liberal Democrat's nemesis in Texas because many persons who will vote for the Republicans in the general election cross over to support conservatives in the Democratic primary. The candidacy of Lloyd Bentsen for the U.S. Senate in 1970 illustrates the point. In the Democratic primary, Bentsen outpolled incumbent Senator Ralph Yarborough in 87 voting precincts in Dallas County, the great majority of which were located in the affluent areas of north Dallas. In the general election, however, Bentsen received far fewer votes and lost most of these precincts to the Republican candidate for the U.S. Senate, George H. W. Bush. There is some evidence that Republicans in other parts of the state voted for Yarborough because he would be easier to defeat.

Crossover voting is a double-edged sword, as the Republicans learned in 1976 when Texas Democrats apparently crossed over in many areas to vote for Reagan. The result was that President Gerald Ford was shut out. With the help of conservative Democrats, the Reaganites captured all 100 delegates to the Republican national convention. Many were startled that this could happen to an incumbent president. Mindful thereafter of the hazards of permitting crossover voting, many Republicans have supported a party purity law that would require the voter to register his or her party affiliation and be limited to participating in the primaries of that party.

Crossover voting

When members of one political party vote in the other party's primary to influence the nominee that is selected.

GENERAL ELECTIONS

The purpose of party primaries is to nominate the party's candidates from the competing intraparty factions. General elections, in contrast, are held to allow the voters to choose from among the competing political party nominees and write-in candidates—the people who will actually serve in national, state, and county offices. General elections differ from primaries in at least two other important ways. First, general elections are the official public elections to

HOW DOES TEXAS COMPARE?
TERM LIMITS

Twenty-one states have instituted term limits for state legislative offices since 1990, though six of these states later repealed the limits. Thirty-six states have gubernatorial limits. Texas does not limit the terms of either legislators or the governor, but most neighboring states limit both, including Arkansas, Colorado, Louisiana, and Oklahoma. The remaining neighbor, New Mexico, only has gubernatorial term limits.

Plurality vote

An election rule in which the candidate with the most votes wins regardless of whether it is a majority.

determine who will take office; thus, they are administered completely by public (as opposed to party) officials of state and county governments.[21] Second, unlike the primaries, in which a majority (50% plus 1) of the vote is required, the general election is decided by a **plurality vote**, whereby the winning candidate needs to receive only the largest number of the votes cast for all the candidates for that office.

General elections in Texas are held every other year on the same day as national elections—the first Tuesday after the first Monday in November of even-numbered years. In years divisible by four, we elect the president, vice president, all U.S. representatives, and one-third of the U.S. senators. In Texas, we elect all 150 members of the state house during these years and roughly half (15 or 16) of the 31 senators. We also elect some board and court positions at the state level, as well as about half of the county positions. However, most major state executive positions (governor, lieutenant governor, attorney general, and so forth) are not filled until the midterm national election, when the U.S. representatives and one-third of U.S. senators (but not the president) again face the voters. Of course, all state house representatives and half of the senators are elected in these years. Some board members, judges, and county officers are too.

Holding simultaneous national and state elections has important political ramifications. During the administration of Andrew Jackson, parties first began to tie the states and the national government together politically. A strong presidential candidate and an effective candidate for state office can benefit significantly by cooperating and campaigning under the party label. This usually works best, of course, if the candidates are in substantial agreement with respect to political philosophy and the issues.

In Texas, which is more politically conservative than the "average" American state, fundamental agreement is often lacking. This has been especially true for Democratic candidates. Popular Democrats in the state often disassociate themselves from the more liberal presidential nominees of the party. One incumbent Democratic governor, Allan Shivers, openly endorsed and worked for the election of the Republican candidate for president in 1952 and again in 1956. In 1980, four former governors (all Democrats) joined Republican Governor Bill Clements in endorsing Ronald Reagan for president. State leaders are often hesitant to be identified with a presidential nominee who may "drag them down" because the presidential candidate is less popular with the voters than they are.

When the Texas Constitution was amended in 1972 to extend the terms (from two years to four years) for the governor and other major administrative officials, the elections for these offices were set for November of midterm election years. This change had two main effects. First, although candidates are also running for Congress in midterm elections, separation of presidential and state campaigns insulates public officials from the ebb and flow of presidential politics and allows them to further disassociate themselves from the national political parties. Elections for statewide office now largely reflect Texas issues and interests. Second, the separation reduces voting in statewide elections and makes the outcomes much more predictable. As was shown earlier, turnout in midterm elections is much lower than in presidential election years, when many people are lured to the polls by the importance of the office and the visibility of the campaign. The independent and the marginal voters are active, and election results for congressional and state-level offices are less predictable. In midterm election years, however, the less informed and the less predictable voters are more likely to stay home, and the contest is largely confined to political party regulars. Most incumbent state politicians prefer to cast their lot with this more limited and predictable midterm electorate.

---

[21]County officials help administer general elections on behalf of the state.

SPECIAL ELECTIONS

As the name implies, special elections are designed to meet special or emergency needs, such as ratification of constitutional amendments or filling vacant offices. Special elections are held to fill vacancies only in legislative bodies that have general (rather than limited) lawmaking power. Typical legislative bodies with general power are the U.S. Senate and U.S. House of Representatives, state legislatures, and city councils from home-rule cities. (All other vacancies, including judgeships and county commissioners, are filled by appointment.) Runoffs are held when necessary. The elections provide for the filling of a vacancy only until the end of the regular term or until the next general election, whichever comes first.

Because special elections are not partisan, the process of getting on the ballot is relatively easy and does not involve a primary.[22] All that is required is the filing of the application form in a timely and appropriate manner and the payment of the designated filing fee. Unlike general elections, the winner of a special election must receive a majority of the votes. Thus a runoff special election may be necessary when no candidate wins outright the first time around. The runoff requirements have been enacted in piecemeal fashion—an illustration of how public policy is often enacted only for political advantage.

SHOULD TEXAS REQUIRE VOTER IDENTIFICATION?

In 2007, the Texas Senate narrowly rejected a bill that would have required every voter to present photo identification (ID) in addition to his or her voter registration card. Similar bills have passed in other states, including Florida, Georgia, and Indiana. Texas probably would have passed its version had the Democrats not resisted in a party-line vote, with Senator Mario Gallegos of Houston being brought in from a make-shift hospital room in the senate sergeant's office to cast the deciding vote against consideration. Since the Texas vote in 2007, the U.S. Supreme Court (in January 2008) heard a case challenging the Indiana voter ID law and decided to uphold it. Then, in 2009, Republican legislators in Texas introduced a new voter ID bill requiring photo identification. Although the senate passed the bill this time, the house did not, as Democrats staged a five-day slowdown that prevented a vote on voter ID and hundreds of other bills. There is reason to think that the issue will be back on the agenda.

VOTER ID WOULD PREVENT VOTER FRAUD

Reformers argue that under the current system, voter fraud is possible. Specifically, it is possible for people to go to the polls and pass themselves off as eligible voters. Proponents maintain that such fraud erodes voter confidence in the process, which already is low in the wake of the 2000 presidential election mess in Florida.

By requiring voters to present a photo identification card, such as a driver's license, the reformers argue, the possibility of fraud would be removed and voter confidence restored.

VOTER ID WOULD ONLY DISENFRANCHISE ELIGIBLE VOTERS

Those who defend the existing system argue that voter ID is a solution to a problem that does not exist—that there is no real evidence of people impersonating other voters in Texas or elsewhere. Although it would not solve a real problem, according to opponents of voter ID, it would have a big impact on legitimate voters who do not have a driver's license or some other government ID. Those with low levels of education and income, minorities, and young voters are most likely to be in this group. They also already are less likely to vote than the rest of the population.

FOR DEBATE

Is voter fraud a big problem in Texas? Would requiring voter identification solve the problem? Would it be worth the cost of turning away eligible voters?

GOING ONLINE

Attempts to change voting rules are usually about political advantage, and voter ID is not the exception. For an analysis of the party politics involved, read "Partisan Colors Fly in Voter ID case," on the **stateline .org** website at **http://www.stateline.org/live/details/ story?contentId=269702**

---

[22]The nonpartisan nature relates only to the fact that the party label does not appear on the ballot and certification by the party is not necessary. Special elections are in fact often partisan because regular party supporters work for "their" candidates.

Before 1957, all special elections required only a plurality vote, but when candidates identified as "liberals" began to win elections under the plurality requirement, the legislature acted quickly to require a majority. During the special election in 1957, the liberal candidate, Ralph Yarborough, appeared likely to win, so the Texas House (controlled by conservative Democrats) quickly passed a bill requiring a runoff in any election to fill a vacated U.S. Senate seat. However, a few liberal legislators were able to delay the bill in the state senate until after the election, in which Yarborough led the field of 23 candidates. Because he received only 38 percent of the popular vote, it is possible that Yarborough would have lost in a runoff. Sixteen days later, the senate passed the bill, and it was signed into law by the governor—too late to affect Yarborough's election. Once in office, Senator Yarborough was able to capitalize on his incumbency and served for 13 years.

In 1993, after U.S. Senator Lloyd Bentsen was nominated to serve as secretary of the treasury by President Bill Clinton, a special election was held to fill his vacancy. Even though the Democratic governor, Ann Richards, appointed a Democratic former congressman and ambassador-at-large, Robert Krueger, to fill in until the special election, the Republican candidate, Kay Bailey Hutchison, ultimately won, becoming the first woman elected to represent Texas in the U.S. Senate.

THE CONDUCT AND ADMINISTRATION OF ELECTIONS

Texas has entered a new era in the administration of elections. Gone are the days of almost complete decentralization of responsibility for elections. In the past, some Texas counties have not included certain contests on their ballot or have refused to hold elections at all (in an election for U.S. senator, no less). Trying to administer elections by statute was very difficult, and in 1967, the Texas legislature designated the secretary of state as the chief election officer of Texas. In this capacity, the secretary of state interprets legislation and issues guidelines. Because under the Voting Rights Act, the U.S. Department of Justice must approve these decisions, they appear to carry the weight of federal authority.

Since 1973, the secretary of state has had the responsibility of disbursing funds to the state and county executive committees to pay for the primary elections and is the keeper of election records, both party and governmental. The secretary of state also receives certificates of nomination from parties that have conducted primaries and conventions and uses these certificates to prepare the ballot for statewide offices. Along with the governor and a gubernatorial appointee, the secretary of state sits on the three-member board that canvasses election returns for state and district offices.

County-Level Administration Except for the preparation of the statewide portion of the ballot, county-level officials actually conduct general elections. In 1977, the legislature created three options from which the counties are free to choose for the administration of general elections. The first option is to maintain the decentralized system that the counties have used for decades. Under this system, the major portion of responsibility rests with the county clerk. By the time the clerk receives the state portion of the ballot from the secretary of state, he or she will have constructed the county- and precinct-level portion by having received applications and certified the candidates' names. The board of elections (consisting of the county judge, sheriff, clerk, and chair of the two major county executive committees) arranges for polling places and for printing ballots. The county tax assessor–collector processes all voter applications and updates the voting rolls. The county commissioners' court draws precinct voting lines, appoints election judges, selects voting devices, canvasses votes, and authorizes payment of all election expenses from the county treasury.

The two other options available are designed to promote efficiency. One is for the county commissioners' court to transfer the voter registration function from the tax assessor–collector's

GETTING OFF THE BALLOT IS NOT EASY!

Getting off a ballot can be as difficult as getting on. Take the case of Tom DeLay, the former member of the U.S. House of Representatives. After he resigned from Congress in June of 2006, the Republican Party tried to have him replaced on the general-election ballot. U.S. District Judge Sam Sparks ruled that he must remain on the ballot, and the Fifth Circuit Court of Appeals upheld the decision. The Texas Republican Party asked U.S. Supreme Court Justice Antonin Scalia to block the ruling, but he denied the request. DeLay ultimately withdrew from the race, leaving no Republican candidate on the ballot for the 22nd District. Would-be Republican contender Shelley Sekula-Gibbs ran as an independent write-in candidate and, despite campaign visits from President George W. Bush and Vice President Dick Cheney, could muster only 42 percent of the vote. Democrat Nick Lampson won the traditionally Republican district with 52 percent of the vote, which illustrates the difficulty of winning as a write-in candidate even when a candidate has the "partisan" advantage.

office to that of the county clerk, thus removing the assessor–collector from the electoral process. The other option, available for the first time in 1979, is more extensive and is believed to represent the direction of reform. It calls for all election-related duties of both the assessor–collector and the county clerk to be transferred to a county election administrator. This officer is appointed for a term of two years by the County Elections Commission, which, in those counties that choose the election administrator option, replaces the board of elections. (Membership is the same, except that in the use of the commission, the county clerk serves instead of the sheriff.)

Ballot Construction   Like so many other features of an election system, ballot construction reflects both practical and political considerations. Two basic types of general-election ballots are available—the party-column ballot and the office-block ballot. On the **party-column ballot**, the names of all the candidates of each party are listed in parallel columns. This type traditionally has been used in Texas. The ballot itemizes the offices as prescribed by law in descending order of importance, and the candidates are listed in each row. Beside each name is a box (on paper ballots) or a lever (on voting machines) that the voter must mark or pull if the voter wishes to vote a split ticket. At the top of each column is the party's name and a box or lever. To vote a straight-party ticket, the voter need only mark the box or pull the lever for the party of his or her choice.

On the **office-block ballot**, the names of the candidates are listed in rows underneath each office (Figure 3.4). To vote a straight-party ticket, the voter must pick that party's candidates in each of the columns. Several states use the office-block ballot, which is also called the "Massachusetts ballot" because it originated there. Minor parties in Texas (which once included the Republican Party) and independent voters advocate the use of this ballot type because it makes straight-ticket voting for the major parties more difficult.

The Politics of Ballot Construction   Understandably, supporters of the major Texas political parties strongly support the use of the party column ballot. It enables lesser-known candidates to ride on the coattails of the party label or a popular candidate running for major office. There may also be an extra payoff in the use of this type of ballot when a party is listed in the first column. Because there may be an advantage, candidates of the once dominant Democratic Party were always listed first, and the practice was accepted without challenge. In 1963, however, the legislature enacted a requirement that the parties be slated from left to right on the ballot according to the proportion of votes that each party's candidate for

Party–column ballot

A type of ballot used in a general election where all of the candidates from each party are listed in parallel columns.

Office-block ballot

A type of ballot used in a general election where the offices are listed across the top, in separate columns.

Figure 3.4

A Typical Texas Ballot from Bexar County. Recall from the text that Republican candidates were listed first in 2006 because their candidate (Rick Perry) received the most votes in the previous gubernatorial election.

Notice that voters are able to vote for all of the candidates of a single party—that is, vote a "straight ticket"—by making a single mark on the ballot. Why would party leaders prefer such a ballot arrangement?

OFFICIAL BALLOT   Joint General, Special and Bond Election
(BOLETA OFICIAL)   *(Elección Conjunto General, Especial y Elección De Bonos)*

(Condado de) **Bexar County, Texas**
November 7, 2006*(7 de Noviembre de 2006)*

General Election
(Elección General)

INSTRUCTION NOTE:
1. Vote for the candidate / statement of your choice in each race by darkening in the oval provided to the left of the name of the candidate / statement.
2. You may cast a straight-party vote (that is, cast a vote for all the nominees of one party) by darkening in the oval provided to the left of the name of the party. If you cast a straight-party vote for all the nominees of one party and also cast a vote for an opponent of one of that party's nominees, your vote for the opponent will be counted as well as your vote for all the other nominees of the party for which the straight-party vote was cast.
3. You may vote for a write-in candidate by writing in the name of the candidate on the line provided and darkening in the oval provided to the left of the line.
4. Use a #2 pencil.

NOTA DE INSTRUCCIÓN:
1. *(Vote por el candidato / declaración de su preferencia en cada carrera llenando completamente el espacio ovalado a la izquierda del nombre del candidato / declaración.*
2. *Usted podrá votar por todos los candidatos de un solo partido político (es decir, votar por todos los candidatos nombrados del mismo partido político) llenando completamente el espacio ovalado a la izquierda del nombre de dicho partido político. Si usted vota por un solo partido político ("straight-ticket") y también vota por el contrincante de uno de los candidatos de dicho partido político, se computara su voto por el contrincante tanto como su voto por todos los demás candidatos del partido político de su preferencia.*
3. *Usted podra votar por inserción escrita escribiendo el nombre del candidato en la linea provista y llenando completamente el espacio ovalado a la izquierda de la linea.*
4. *Solamente use un lápiz de #2.)*

Straight Party
(Partido Completo)

○ **REPUBLICAN PARTY**
(Partido Republicano)
○ **DEMOCRATIC PARTY**
(Partido Demócrata)
○ **LIBERTARIAN PARTY**
(Partido Libertario)

United States Senator
(Senador de los Estados Unidos)

○ Kay Bailey Hutchison (REP)
○ Barbara Ann Radnofsky (DEM)
○ Scott Lanier Jameson (LIB)

United States Representative, District 20
(Representante de los Estados Unidos, Distrito Núm. 20)

○ Charles A. Gonzalez (DEM)
○ Michael Idrogo (LIB)

Governor
(Gobernador)

○ Rick Perry (REP)
○ Chris Bell (DEM)
○ James Werner (LIB)
○ Carole Keeton Strayhorn (IND)
○ Richard "Kinky" Friedman (IND)
○ _____
Write-in *(Voto Escrito)*

Lieutenant Governor
(Gobernador Teniente)

○ David Dewhurst (REP)
○ Maria Luisa Alvarado (DEM)
○ Judy Baker (LIB)

Attorney General
(Procurador General)

○ Greg Abbott (REP)
○ David Van Os (DEM)
○ Jon Roland (LIB)

Comptroller of Public Accounts
(Contralor de Cuentas Públicas)

○ Susan Combs (REP)
○ Fred Head (DEM)
○ Mike Burris (LIB)

Commissioner of General Land Office
(Comisionado de la Oficina General de Tierras)

○ Jerry Patterson (REP)
○ VaLinda Hathcox (DEM)
○ Michael A. French (LIB)

Commissioner of Agriculture
(Comisionado de Agricultura)

○ Todd Staples (REP)
○ Hank Gilbert (DEM)
○ Clay Woolam (LIB)

Railroad Commissioner
(Comisionado de Ferrocarriles)

○ Elizabeth Ames Jones (REP)
○ Dale Henry (DEM)
○ Tabitha Serrano (LIB)

Chief Justice, Supreme Court, Unexpired Term
(Juez Presidente, Corte Suprema, Duración Restante del Cargo)

○ Wallace Jefferson (REP)
○ Tom Oxford (LIB)
○ _____
Write-in *(Voto Escrito)*

Justice, Supreme Court, Place 2
(Juez, Corte Suprema, Lugar Núm. 2)

○ Don Willett (REP)
○ William E. "Bill" Moody (DEM)
○ Wade Wilson (LIB)

Justice, Supreme Court, Place 4
(Juez, Corte Suprema, Lugar Núm. 4)

○ David M. Medina (REP)
○ Jerry Adkins (LIB)

Justice, Supreme Court, Place 6
(Juez, Corte Suprema, Lugar Núm. 6)

○ Nathan Hecht (REP)
○ Todd Phillippi (LIB)

Justice, Supreme Court, Place 8, Unexpired Term
(Juez, Corte Suprema, Lugar Núm. 8, Duración Restante del Cargo)

○ Phil Johnson (REP)
○ Jay H. Cookingham (LIB)

Presiding Judge, Court of Criminal Appeals
(Juez Presidente, Corte de Apelaciones Criminales)

○ Sharon Keller (REP)
○ J.R. Molina (DEM)

Judge, Court of Criminal Appeals, Place 7
(Juez, Corte de Apelaciones Criminales, Lugar Núm. 7)

○ Barbara Parker Hervey (REP)
○ Quanah Parker (LIB)

Judge, Court of Criminal Appeals, Place 8
(Juez, Corte de Apelaciones Criminales, Lugar Núm. 8)

○ Charles Holcomb (REP)
○ Dave Howard (LIB)

Member, State Board of Education, District 3
(Miembro de la Junta Estatal de Educación Pública, Distrito Núm. 3)

○ Tony Cunningham (REP)
○ Rick Agosto (DEM)

State Representative, District 116
(Representante Estatal, Distrito Núm. 116)

○ Trey Martinez Fischer (DEM)
○ John T. Tennison (LIB)

Justice, 4th Court of Appeals District, Place 2
(Juez, Corte de Apelaciones, Distrito Núm. 4, Lugar 2)

○ Catherine Stone (DEM)

Justice, 4th Court of Appeals District, Place 3
(Juez, Corte de Apelaciones, Distrito Núm. 4, Lugar 3)

○ Rebecca Simmons (REP)
○ Richard Garcia, Jr. (DEM)

Justice, 4th Court of Appeals District, Place 4
(Juez, Corte de Apelaciones, Distrito Núm. 4, Lugar 4)

○ Steve Hilbig (REP)
○ Dan Pozza (DEM)

Justice, 4th Court of Appeals District, Place 5
(Juez, Corte de Apelaciones, Distrito Núm. 4, Lugar 5)

○ Karen Angelini (REP)
○ Lauro A. Bustamante (DEM)

Justice, 4th Court of Appeals District, Place 7
(Juez, Corte de Apelaciones, Distrito Núm. 4, Lugar 7)

○ Phylis Speedlin (REP)
○ Eddie DeLaGarza (DEM)

District Judge, 45th Judicial District
(Juez del Distrito, Distrito Judicial Núm. 45)

○ Diane M. Rivera (REP)
○ Barbara Hanson Nellermoe (DEM)

Typ:01 Seq:0033 Spl:01
7.1.0.0 / 011002

Ballot Style #33

governor received in the most recent gubernatorial election. Next come candidates of parties that were not on the ballot in the last election, and last come the independents. After the election of Governor Bill Clements in 1979, the Republicans finally achieved the favored ballot position.

Beginning with the 2002 election, many Texas counties moved away from a strict party-column ballot. Partly because of the adoption of electronic voting systems (discussed later in this chapter), ballots in these counties combine features of both the office block and party-column designs (Figure 3.5). As with the office-block ballot, candidates are listed underneath each office. As with the party-column ballot, however, one can vote a straight-party ticket with a single mark; that is, before turning to specific offices, voters are first given the option to vote a straight ticket.

Getting on the Ballot   For a name to be placed on the general-election ballot, the candidate must be either a party nominee or an independent. For any party that received at least five percent of the vote for any statewide office in the previous general election, the full slate of candidates is placed on the ballot automatically. Thus, the Democrat and Republican parties have no problem submitting candidate names, and certification by the appropriate party officials for primary or convention winners is routine.

Minor parties have a more difficult time. For instance, neither the Libertarian Party nor the Green Party received the necessary votes in 2002, and had to petition to get their candidates on the ballot in 2004 (this time, the Libertarians succeeded; the Greens did not). Independent candidates for president have the most difficult challenge, for they must present a petition signed by one percent of the total state vote for president in the last election. For Congressman John Anderson in 1980, that meant a minimum of 40,719 names on the petition. In 1992, Ross Perot's supporters presented 54,275 signatures, which qualified him to appear on the ballot.

For all other offices except president, the total vote for governor is the basis for determining the required number of signatures for both independents and third-party candidates. For statewide office, signatures equaling one percent of the total gubernatorial vote are needed; for multicounty district offices, three percent; and for all other district and local offices, five percent. Although the number of signatures is relatively small for some offices (a maximum of 500 at the local level), the process of gaining access to the ballot by petition is difficult.[23]

As a general rule, candidates using the petition route seek twice the required number to ensure the petition's certifiability. For example, in 1980, the Libertarian Party submitted 55,000 signatures and the Socialist Workers Party (SWP) turned in 30,000 to ensure that each had 23,698 persons who were legally qualified to sign. Only the Libertarians succeeded; the SWP fell short of the minimum when almost half the submitted signatures were found to belong to persons not qualified to sign.[24]

Write-In Candidates   Write-in candidates are not listed on the ballot—voters must write them on the ballot. These candidates often are individuals who have entered and lost in a party primary. A different type of write-in candidacy developed in 1976 when Charles W.

---

[23]Signers must be registered voters and cannot have participated in the selection of a nominee for that office in another party's primary.

[24]The necessity of notarizing the pages increases the difficulty. The application of technical aspects of the law and adverse interpretations are but a part of the harassment that minor parties and independents have traditionally encountered in their quest for a place on the ballot. For example, in 1976, the secretary of state interpreted the law as requiring that each signature must be notarized. The next year, the legislature specified that a notary need sign only each part of the petition. See Richard H. Kraemer, Ernest Crain, and William Earl Maxwell, *Understanding Texas Politics* (St. Paul, MN: West, 1975), pp. 155, 157.

Figure 3.5

An English-Vietnamese Ballot Used in Harris County for the 2008 General Election. This ballot lists a special election first before offering the straight-party option and then the candidates for the separate offices.

Source: Harris County Clerk's Office, Texas, November 4, 2008.

What are the arguments for and against bilingual ballots such as the one shown here?

SAMPLE BALLOT   **LÁ PHIẾU MẪU**

Official Ballot   Phiếu Bầu Chính Thức
General and Special Elections
Các Cuộc Tổng Tuyển Cử và Bầu Cử Đặc Biệt
Harris County, Texas
Quận Harris, Texas
November 04, 2008 - Ngày 4 tháng Mười Một, 2008   Precinct Phân Khu Bầu Cử   All

Sample Ballot

Instruction Text:
TO VOTE: Mark the ballot by placing an "X" in the square beside the candidate of your choice. You may vote for a write-in candidate by placing an "X" in the square beside the write-in choice and writing the name of the write-in candidate of your choice. You may vote straight-party (that is, cast a vote for all the candidates of one party), by placing an "X" by the party of your choice. Voting straight-party automatically cast a vote for all of that party's candidates. If you change a vote to an opposing party candidate, your vote for the opposing party candidate will be counted as well as your vote for all other candidates of the party of the straight-party vote which was cast.

Ghi chú hướng dẫn:
BỎ PHIẾU: Điền lá phiếu bằng cách đánh dấu "X" vào ô vuông bên cạnh tên ứng cử viên mà quý vị lựa chọn. Quý vị có thể bỏ phiếu cho một ứng cử viên ghi thêm bằng cách đánh dấu "X" vào ô vuông của lựa chọn ghi thêm và ghi vào tên của ứng cử viên mà quý vị muốn bầu chọn. Quý vị có thể bỏ phiếu bầu cho một chính đảng [nghĩa là, bầu cho tất cả ứng cử viên của cùng một đảng] bằng cách đánh dấu "X" vào ô vuông bên cạnh tên của đảng mà quý vị muốn bầu chọn. Bỏ phiếu theo cách bầu đảng thì tất cả các ứng cử viên của đảng đó sẽ tự động được bầu. Nếu quý vị đổi để bỏ phiếu cho đối thủ của một ứng cử viên của đảng đó, lá phiếu bầu cho đối thủ kia sẽ được tính cũng như lá phiếu bầu cho tất cả các ứng cử viên khác của một đảng mà quý vị bầu chọn.

SPECIAL ELECTION
CUỘC BẦU CỬ ĐẶC BIỆT

State Senator, District 17, Unexpired Term
Thượng Nghị Sĩ Tiểu Bang, Khu Vực 17,
Nhiệm Kỳ Vô Thời Hạn

☐ Austen Furse
   Republican Party
   Đảng Cộng Hòa

☒ Ken Sherman
   Republican Party
   Đảng Cộng Hòa

☐ Stephanie E. Simmons
   Democratic Party
   Đảng Dân Chủ

☐ Grant Harpold
   Republican Party
   Đảng Cộng Hòa

☐ Joan Huffman
   Republican Party
   Đảng Cộng Hòa

☐ Chris Bell
   Democratic Party
   Đảng Dân Chủ

GENERAL ELECTION
CUỘC TỔNG TUYỂN CỬ

Straight Party
Bỏ phiếu cho các ứng cử viên của cùng một đảng

☐ Republican Party
   Đảng Cộng Hòa

☐ Democratic Party
   Đảng Dân Chủ

☐ Libertarian Party
   Đảng Tự Do

President and Vice President
Tổng Thống và Phó Tổng Thống

☐ John McCain / Sarah Palin
   Republican Party
   Đảng Cộng Hòa

☒ Barack Obama / Joe Biden
   Democratic Party
   Đảng Dân Chủ

☐ Bob Barr / Wayne A. Root
   Libertarian Party
   Đảng Tự Do

☐ Write-in
   Bầu chọn ứng cử viên không có tên trong lá phiếu

United States Senator
Thượng Nghị Sĩ Hoa Kỳ

☐ John Cornyn
   Republican Party
   Đảng Cộng Hòa

☐ Richard J. (Rick) Noriega
   Democratic Party
   Đảng Dân Chủ

☐ Yvonne Adams Schick
   Libertarian Party
   Đảng Tự Do

United States Representative, District 2
Dân Biểu Hoa Kỳ,
Khu vực số 2

☐ Ted Poe
   Republican Party
   Đảng Cộng Hòa

☐ Craig Wolfe
   Libertarian Party
   Đảng Tự Do

United States Representative, District 7
Dân Biểu Hoa Kỳ,
Khu vực số 7

☐ John Culberson
   Republican Party
   Đảng Cộng Hòa

☐ Michael Skelly
   Democratic Party
   Đảng Dân Chủ

☐ Drew Parks
   Libertarian Party
   Đảng Tự Do

United States Representative, District 9
Dân Biểu Hoa Kỳ,
Khu vực số 9

☐ Al Green
   Democratic Party
   Đảng Dân Chủ

☐ Brad Walters
   Libertarian Party
   Đảng Tự Do

United States Representative, District 10
Dân Biểu Hoa Kỳ,
Khu vực số 10

☐ Michael T. McCaul
   Republican Party
   Đảng Cộng Hòa

☐ Larry Joe Doherty
   Democratic Party
   Đảng Dân Chủ

☐ Matt Finkel
   Libertarian Party
   Đảng Tự Do

United States Representative, District 18
Dân Biểu Hoa Kỳ,
Khu vực số 18

☐ John Faulk
   Republican Party
   Đảng Cộng Hòa

☐ Sheila Jackson Lee
   Democratic Party
   Đảng Dân Chủ

☐ Mike Taylor
   Libertarian Party
   Đảng Tự Do

United States Representative, District 22
Dân Biểu Hoa Kỳ,
Khu vực số 22

☐ Pete Olson
   Republican Party
   Đảng Cộng Hòa

☐ Nick Lampson
   Democratic Party
   Đảng Dân Chủ

☐ John Wieder
   Libertarian Party
   Đảng Tự Do

United States Representative, District 29
Dân Biểu Hoa Kỳ,
Khu vực số 29

☐ Eric Story
   Republican Party
   Đảng Cộng Hòa

☐ Gene Green
   Democratic Party
   Đảng Dân Chủ

☐ Joel Grace
   Libertarian Party
   Đảng Tự Do

Railroad Commissioner
Ủy Viên Ngành Hỏa Xa

☐ Michael L. Williams
   Republican Party
   Đảng Cộng Hòa

☐ Mark Thompson
   Democratic Party
   Đảng Dân Chủ

☐ David Floyd
   Libertarian Party
   Đảng Tự Do

Chief Justice, Supreme Court
Chánh Thẩm, Tối Cao Pháp Viện

☐ Wallace B. Jefferson
   Republican Party
   Đảng Cộng Hòa

☐ Jim Jordan
   Democratic Party
   Đảng Dân Chủ

☐ Tom Oxford
   Libertarian Party
   Đảng Tự Do

Justice, Supreme Court, Place 7
Chánh Án, Tối Cao Pháp Viện, Vị Trí số 7

☐ Dale Wainwright
   Republican Party
   Đảng Cộng Hòa

☐ Sam Houston
   Democratic Party
   Đảng Dân Chủ

☐ David G. Smith
   Libertarian Party
   Đảng Tự Do

Justice, Supreme Court, Place 8
Chánh Án, Tối Cao Pháp Viện, Vị Trí số 8

☐ Phil Johnson
   Republican Party
   Đảng Cộng Hòa

☐ Linda Reyna Yanez
   Democratic Party
   Đảng Dân Chủ

☐ Drew Shirley
   Libertarian Party
   Đảng Tự Do

Judge, Court of Criminal Appeals, Place 3
Chánh Án, Tòa Kháng Án Hình Sự, Vị Trí số 3

☐ Tom Price
   Republican Party
   Đảng Cộng Hòa

☐ Susan Strawn
   Democratic Party
   Đảng Dân Chủ

☐ Matthew E. Eilers
   Libertarian Party
   Đảng Tự Do

Judge, Court of Criminal Appeals, Place 4
Chánh Án, Tòa Kháng Án Hình Sự, Vị Trí số 4

☐ Paul Womack
   Republican Party
   Đảng Cộng Hòa

☐ J.R. Molina
   Democratic Party
   Đảng Dân Chủ

☐ Dave Howard
   Libertarian Party
   Đảng Tự Do

Sample Ballot

Barrow, Chief Justice of the Fourth Court of Civil Appeals in San Antonio, was thought to be virtually unopposed for the Democratic nomination for associate justice of the Texas Supreme Court. The legal establishment was stunned when Don Yarbrough, a young Houston attorney involved in a number of legal entanglements, upset Barrow in the quest for the Democratic nomination. Apparently, the voters had confused the young attorney's name with former gubernatorial candidate Don Yarborough. No one had filed in the Republican primary.

Embarrassed, the legal establishment sought to have the primary winner disqualified from the ballot. Failing that, they mounted a write-in campaign supported strongly by the leaders of both political parties. Playing the name game themselves, they chose as their candidate District Judge Sam Houston Jones. The write-in campaign failed miserably. Don Yarbrough's victory was short-lived, however. Under threat of removal by the legislature, he resigned after serving approximately six months. He was replaced through gubernatorial appointment by Judge Charles W. Barrow, his opponent in the Democratic primary.

Write-in candidates have had an easier time as a result of a law subsequently passed by the legislature. It requires a candidate to register with the secretary of state before the beginning of absentee voting in general elections and 45 days before a primary election. The names of write-in candidates must be posted at the election site, possibly in the election booth. A candidate not properly registered cannot win, regardless of the votes he or she receives. Even when registered, write-in candidates are seldom successful—recall the earlier discussion ("Getting Off the Ballot Is Not Easy!") of the race to replace Tom DeLay in 2006, when circumstances for the write-in seemed unusually favorable.

The Secret Ballot and the Integrity of Elections

The essence of the right to vote is generally viewed as the right to cast a ballot in secret, have the election conducted fairly, and have the ballots counted correctly. The **Australian ballot**, adopted by Texas in 1892, includes names of the candidates of all political parties on a single ballot printed at the public's expense and available only at the voting place.[25] Given a reasonably private area in which to mark the ballot, the voter was offered a secret ballot for the first time.

Australian ballot

A ballot printed by the government (as opposed to the political parties) that allows people to vote in secret.

Although there are legal remedies such as the issuance of injunctions and the threat of criminal penalties, Texas has looked primarily to "political" remedies in its effort to protect the integrity of the electoral process. Minor parties have reason to be concerned that irregularities in elections administered by members of the majority party may not be observed or, if observed, may not be reported. Even in the absence of wrongdoing, the testimony of the correctness of an election by individuals with opposing interests helps ensure public faith in the process.

Traditional practice has been that in general and special elections, the county board of elections routinely appoints as election judges the precinct chair of the political party whose members constitute a majority on the elections board. Since 1967, each election judge has been required to select at least one election clerk from a list submitted by the county chair of each political party. Moreover, law now recognizes the status of "poll watchers," and both primary candidates and county chairs are authorized to appoint them.

Candidates can ask for either a recheck or a recount of the ballots. A recheck applies primarily to voting machines, relates to counting errors, and costs $3 per precinct. The loser of an election may also ask for a recount (this will be discussed in greater detail shortly). The candidate who requests a recount must put up a deposit and is liable for the entire cost unless he or she wins or ties in the recount. Moreover, the recount (but not the recheck) must be for all precincts. In a large county, the cost of a recount can be prohibitive. Despite drawbacks, these options in the supervision of elections mark a real improvement over the days when often ineffective judicial remedies were the only recourse.

---

[25]Optional at first, the Australian ballot was made mandatory in 1903.

Multilingualism Ballots in most Texas counties are printed in English. In more than 100 counties, the ballot is printed in both English and Spanish. In 2002, the U.S. Department of Justice ordered Harris County, which includes Houston, to provide ballots (and voting material) in Vietnamese as well (Figure 3.5). It is the only county in Texas to be included in the order and the only county outside of California to do so. In some parts of the country, other languages are required, including Chinese, Eskimo, Filipino, Japanese, and Korean. In Los Angeles County alone, ballots are printed in seven different languages. This all is due to the Voting Rights Act of 1965 and its subsequent amendment in 1992. According to Section 203 of the act, a political subdivision (typically, a county) must provide language assistance to voters if significant numbers of voting-age citizens are members of a single-language minority group and do not speak or understand English "well enough to participate in the electoral process." Specifically, the legal requirement is triggered when more than five percent of the voting-age citizens or else 10,000 of these citizens meet the criteria. The 2000 Census shows that more than 55,000 people living in Harris County identify themselves as Vietnamese, and the U.S. Department of Justice determined that at least 10,000 of them are old enough to vote but are not sufficiently proficient in English, thereby triggering the requirement. Given the levels of immigration into the United States, the number of ballot languages is almost certain to increase.

Absentee Voting All states allow members of the U.S. armed forces to vote absentee, and Texas, along with 40 other states, also permits absentee voting for reasons such as illness or anticipated absence from the county. Previously, absentee voting in Texas was mostly a convenience for the middle class and served as a booster for conservative candidates. In 1987, however, the legislature made changes that appear to have far-ranging effects. First, to vote absentee in person (rather than by mail), one need not swear that one intends to be out of the city or county in order to qualify. Second, the new law legitimated the practice of allowing such votes to be cast in substations in the urban counties. Third, in 1989, the legislature extended the absentee voting period so that it now begins 22 days before the election and ends on the sixth day before the election. Moreover, substation voting places remain open 12 hours a day during the week, with shorter hours on Saturdays and Sundays. As a result, absentee voting has increased tremendously. Whether cast by mail or in person, on paper ballots or by punch card or on electronic machines, absentee votes are not counted until election day.

Early voting

The practice of voting before election day at more traditional voting locations, such as schools, and other locations, such as grocery and convenience stores.

Early Voting In 1991, the Texas legislature instituted **early voting**.[26] All Texas voters can now vote before election day. Unlike absentee voting, early voting is available to any registered voter. In addition to traditional election day voting sites, such as schools and fire stations, there are a number of other more familiar places to vote early, including grocery and convenience stores. This innovation has clearly made voting easier in Texas, and people are using it. In 1992, approximately 25 percent of the votes were cast before election day; in 1996, approximately 33 percent of the votes were cast early; and in 2000, the number was just less than 39 percent. In 2004, more than 50 percent voted early and in 2008 two out of every three did so. Although people are voting earlier, they are not voting in greater numbers, as we noted earlier in the chapter. The growing tendency toward early voting may still have important implications for when and how politicians campaign.

Counting and Recounting Ballots We take for granted that when we vote, our votes count. As we learned in Florida in the 2000 presidential election, this is not true. The first machine count

---

[26]For a nice description of early voting and a preliminary assessment of its effects, see Robert M. Stein and Patricia A. Garcia-Monet, "Voting Early But Not Often," *Social Science Quarterly* 78 (December 1997), pp. 657–671. For a more recent review and assessment, see Paul Gronke, Eva Galanes-Rosenbaum, and Peter A. Miller, "Early Voting and Turnout," *PS: Political Science and Politics* 40 (December 2007), pp. 639–645.

HOW DOES TEXAS COMPARE?
EARLY VOTING

Early voting *without any excuse* is allowed in 35 states, three of which permit it only by mail. In Texas and four other states—Indiana, Louisiana, Maryland, and Tennessee—voters may only vote early in person. In 27 states, voters can choose whether to vote early in person or by mail. At least 30 percent of all votes nationwide in 2008 were cast before election day. In 11 states, more than half were cast early: Arizona, Colorado, Florida, Georgia, Nevada, New Mexico, North Carolina, Oregon, Tennessee, Texas, and Washington.[27]

of ballots in Florida showed George W. Bush with a 1,725-vote lead. In a mandatory machine recount of the same ballots, the same machines cut his lead to 327. We were also told that some two to three percent of the ballots were not counted at all. How could this happen? What does this mean? The answer is simple: Machines make mistakes. Some ballots are not counted. Some may even be counted for the wrong candidate. This shocked most Americans.

Experts have known for a long time that vote counting contains a good amount of error. By most accounts, the error rate averages one to two percent, although it can be higher depending on the ballot and the machines themselves. The error rate is largest for punch-card ballots, which have been commonly used in big cities in Texas and other states. To vote, one inserts the ballot into a slot in the voting booth and then uses a stylus to punch holes corresponding to candidates' names that are printed on separate lists, usually in the form of a booklet. There are two sources of error associated with these ballots. First, some voters do not fully punch out the pieces of paper from the perforated holes. That is, these pieces of paper, which are called **chad**, remain attached to the ballot. Second, even where the chad are completely detached, machines do not read each and every ballot. This is of importance to voters. It is typically of little consequence for election outcomes, however. Counting errors tend to cancel out, meaning that no candidate gains a much greater number of votes. Thus, the errors are important only when elections are very close, within a half percentage point, which is not very common. When it does happen, the losing candidate can request a recount.

In Texas, there are fairly specific laws about recounts. A candidate can request a recount if he or she loses by less than 10 percent. This is a fairly generous rule compared to other states. The candidate who requests the recount does have to pay for it, however, which means that most candidates do not request a recount unless the margin is much closer, say, one percentage point or less. As for the recount itself, the Texas Election Code states that "only one method may be used in the recount" and "a manual recount shall be conducted in preference to an electronic recount." The procedures are fairly detailed. What may be most interesting is the set of rules for how chad should be interpreted. Indeed, canvassing authorities are allowed to determine whether "an indentation on the chad from the stylus or other object is present" and whether "the chad reflects by other means a clearly ascertainable intent of the voter to vote."[28] This leaves a lot of room for discretion on the part of canvassing authorities in the various Texas counties.

Electronic Voting Partly in response to the events in Florida—and the seeming potential for similar problems in Texas—a number of counties introduced **electronic voting** in the 2002 midterm elections. Instead of punching holes in ballots or filling in bubbles

Chad
The small pieces of paper produced in punching data cards, such as punch-card ballots.

Electronic voting
Voting using video screens similar to e-ticket check-ins at most airports.

[27]National Council of State Legislatures, http://www.ncsl.org/default.aspx?tabid=16604; United States Election Project, http://elections.gmu.edu/Early_Voting_2008_Final.html; Election Reform Information Project, www.electionline.org

[28]Texas Code 127.130. Also see Carlos Guerra, "Texas Is Far Friendlier to *All* Our Chad," *San Antonio Express-News,* November 25, 2000, p. B-1.

Texas election law provides that incompletely detached chad can be counted as votes during hand recounts, at the discretion of county authorities. ☞

Are the problems with paper ballots really that serious?

AP Photo

Bush Vote   **Gore Vote**   **Under Vote**

on scannable sheets, voters in Dallas, Houston, and San Antonio voted by touching screens.

The technology is similar to what is used in automated teller machines (ATMs) and electronic-ticket check-ins at many airports and promises an exact count of votes. It is now used for voting throughout much of Texas and the United States. As with the introduction of any new technology, problems have occurred.[29]

ELECTION CAMPAIGNS IN TEXAS

The ultimate aim of party activity is to nominate candidates in the party primary or convention and get them elected in the general election. The pattern in Texas before 1978 was for Republicans and other minor parties to run only token, poorly financed candidates for most contested offices so that the real choices were made in the Democratic primary. These days in Texas, the battle has moved from the Democratic nomination process to the general election itself.

WHO GETS ELECTED

It is useful to think of elected offices in Texas as a pyramid. At the bottom of the pyramid are the most local of offices; at the top is the governor. Moving from bottom to top, the importance of the office increases and the number of officeholders decreases. It thus gets more and more difficult for politicians to ascend the pyramid, and only the best politicians rise to the top. This tells us a lot about candidates and elections in Texas and elsewhere.

In local elections, the pool of candidates is diverse in many ways, including educational background, income, and profession. As we move up the pyramid, however, candidates become much more homogeneous. For statewide office, the typical candidate is middle- or upper-class, from an urban area, and has strong ties to business and professional interests in the state. Most elected state officers in Texas, including the governor, lieutenant governor, and attorney general, must be acceptable to the state's major financial and corporate interests and to its top law firms. These interests help statewide candidates raise the large amounts of money that are critical to a successful race.

Successful candidates for statewide office in Texas have traditionally been white Protestant males. Prior to 1986, when Raul Gonzalez was elected to the state supreme court, no Latino or African American had been elected to statewide office, though these two ethnic groups

---

[29]Rachel Konrad, "Reports of Electronic Voting Trouble Top 1,000," *USA Today,* November 4, 2004.

Voters cast their votes electronically by touching screens.

Does electronic voting solve the problems with paper ballots? How can we tell?

Bob Daemmrich/The Image Works

combined represent one-half of the state's population. The only female governor was Miriam A. "Ma" Ferguson, who in the 1920s served as surrogate for her husband, Jim. In 1982, Ann Richards was elected state treasurer, becoming the second woman ever to be elected to state-wide office in Texas.

Women and minorities have made substantial gains in statewide offices. Ann Richards became the first woman elected governor in her own right. Kay Bailey Hutchison captured the state treasurer's office and in 1993 won a special election to become the first woman from Texas elected to the U.S. Senate. Dan Morales was the first Latino to win a state executive office, when he captured the attorney general's office. More history was made when Morris Overstreet of Amarillo won a seat on the Texas Court of Criminal Appeals and became the first African American elected to a statewide office.

Women and ethnic groups are starting to make inroads in other elected offices in Texas. In the 79th Legislature (2005–2006), 32 women were elected to the 150-member house and four to the 31-member senate. Women have also held the post of mayor in five of the state's largest cities: Houston, Dallas, San Antonio, El Paso, and Austin. Latinos hold 35 seats in the state legislature, and African Americans occupy 16. Among the state's 32 U.S. congressional representatives, there are three women, six Latinos, and two African Americans. Clearly, Texas politics has changed a lot over a short time.

THE GENERAL ELECTION CAMPAIGN

To a large extent, election outcomes are predictable. Despite all the media attention paid to the conventions, the debates, the advertising, and everything else involved in political campaigns, there are certain things that powerfully structure the vote in national and state elections.[30] In state elections, two factors predominate: party identification and incumbency.

---

[30]Most of the research has focused on presidential elections. See Christopher Wlezien, "On Forecasting the Presidential Vote," *PS: Political Science and Politics* 34 (March 2001), pp. 25–31. Some research has also been done on state gubernatorial and legislative elections. See, for example, Mark E. Tompkins, "The Electoral Fortunes of Gubernatorial Incumbents," *Journal of Politics* 46 (May 1984), pp. 520–543; Ronald E. Weber, Harvey J. Tucker, and Paul Brace, "Vanishing Marginals in State Legislative Elections," *Legislative Studies Quarterly* 16 (February 1991), pp. 29–47.

First, where more people in a state identify with one political party than with the other, the candidates of the preferred party have an advantage in general elections. For instance, when most Texans identified with the Democratic Party, Democratic candidates dominated elected offices throughout the state. As Texans have become more Republican in their identification, Republican candidates have done very well; indeed, as was mentioned earlier, Republicans now hold every statewide elected office. Identification with the political parties varies a lot within Texas, however, and this has implications for state legislative elections. In some parts of the state, particularly in the big cities, more people identify with the Democratic Party, and Democratic candidates typically represent those areas in the state house and senate. Thus party identification in the state and in districts themselves tells us a lot about which candidates win general elections.

Second, incumbent candidates—those already in office who are up for reelection—are more likely to win in general elections. This is particularly true in state legislative elections, where the districts are fairly homogeneous and the campaigns are not very visible, but incumbency is also important in elections for statewide office. Incumbents have a number of advantages over challengers, the most important of which is that they have won before. To become an incumbent, a candidate has to beat an incumbent or else win in an open-seat election, which usually involves a contest among a number of strong candidates. By definition, therefore, incumbents are good candidates. In addition, incumbents have the advantage of office. They are in a position to do things for their constituents and thus increase their support among voters.

Although party identification and incumbency are important in Texas elections, they are not the whole story. What they really tell us is the degree to which candidates are advantaged or disadvantaged as they embark on their campaigns. Other factors ultimately matter on election day.[31]

Mobilizing Groups Groups play an important role in elections for any office. A fundamental part of campaigns is getting out the vote among groups that strongly support the candidate. To a large extent, candidates focus on groups aligned with the political parties.[32] At the state level, business interests and teachers are particularly important. Republican candidates tend to focus their efforts on the former and Democratic candidates on the latter. Candidates also mobilize other groups, including African Americans and Latinos. Traditionally, Democratic candidates emphasized these minority groups, though Governor Bush broke somewhat with this tradition and focused substantial attention on the Latino community in Texas. Mobilizing groups does not necessarily involve taking strong public stands on their behalf, especially those that are less mainstream. Indeed, the mobilization of such groups is typically conducted very quietly, often through targeted mailings and phone calls.

Choosing Issues Issues are important in any campaign. In campaigns for state offices, taxes, education, and crime are very salient, and abortion matters a lot in many states. As for groups, the issues candidates select tend to reflect their party affiliations, but the tendency is not as clear. Very few candidates, after all, are in favor of higher taxes and less money for education and crime. Where candidates do differ is in their emphasis on

---

[31]For a detailed analysis of election campaigns in Texas in a single election year, see Richard Murray, "The 1996 Elections in Texas," in Kent L. Tedin, Donald S. Lutz, and Edward P. Fuchs (eds.), *Perspectives on American and Texas Politics*, 5th ed. (Dubuque, IA: Kendall/Hunt, 1998), pp. 247–286.

[32]For an analysis of how membership in various demographic groups influences voting behavior, see Robert S. Erikson, Thomas B. Lancaster, and David W. Romero, "Group Components of the Presidential Vote, 1952–1984," *Journal of Politics* 50 (May 1988), pp. 337–346. For an analysis of how identification with various social groups influences voting behavior, see Christopher Wlezien and Arthur H. Miller, "Social Groups and Political Judgments," *Social Science Quarterly* 78 (December 1997), pp. 625–640.

particular issues and their policy proposals. These choices depend heavily on carefully crafted opinion polls. Through polls, candidates attempt to identify the issues that the public considers to be important and then craft policy positions to address those issues. The process is ongoing, and candidates pay close attention to changes in opinion and, perhaps most important, to the public's response to the candidates' own positions. Polling is fundamental in modern political campaigns in America.

The Campaign Trail Deciding where and how to campaign are critical elements in campaign strategy. Candidates spend countless hours "on the stump," traveling about the state or district to speak before diverse groups. In a state as large as Texas, candidates for statewide office must pick and choose areas so as to maximize their exposure. Unfortunately for rural voters, this means that candidates spend most of their time in urban areas.

Nowadays, no candidate gets elected by stumping alone. The most direct route to the voters is through the media. There are 17 media markets in Texas. These include approximately 200 television and cable stations and more than 500 radio stations. In addition, there are 79 daily and 403 weekly newspapers dispersed throughout the state's 254 counties.[33] Candidates hire public relations firms and media consultants, and advertising plays a big role. These days, a successful campaign often relies on **negative campaigning**, in which candidates attack opponents' issue positions or character. As one campaign consultant said, "Campaigns are about definition. Either you define yourself and your opponent or [the other candidates do]. . . . Victory goes to the aggressor."[34] Although often considered an unfortunate development in American politics, it is important to keep in mind that negative campaigning can serve to provide voters with information about the candidates and their issue positions.

Negative campaigning

A strategy used in political campaigns in which candidates attack opponents' issue positions or character.

Timing The timing of the campaign effort can be very important. Unlike presidential elections, campaigns for state offices, including the governorship, begin fairly late in the election cycle. Indeed, it is common to hear little from gubernatorial candidates until after Labor Day and from candidates for the legislature until a month before the election.

Candidates often reserve a large proportion of their campaign advertising budget for a last-minute media "blitz." However, early voting may affect this strategy somewhat. Recall that in 2008, approximately 66 percent of the votes in Texas were cast early, during the weeks leading up to the election, which means that the final campaign blitz came too late to have any effect on more than half of all voters. Consequently, candidates in the future may be less likely to concentrate their efforts so tightly on the final days of the campaign.

MONEY IN POLITICAL CAMPAIGNS

Political campaigns are expensive, which means that candidates need to raise a lot of money to be competitive. Indeed, the amount of money a candidate raises can be the deciding factor in the campaign. Just how much a candidate needs depends on the level of the campaign and the competitiveness of the race. High-level campaigns for statewide office are usually multimillion-dollar affairs.

In recent years, the race for governor has become especially expensive. In 1990, Republican Clayton Williams spent a reported $20 million but lost to Democrat Ann Richards, who spent almost $12 million. Governor George W. Bush spent almost $15 million to defeat Ann Richards in 1994. In 2002, Tony Sanchez spent nearly $70 million, a striking sum and

---

[33] *Gale Directory of Publications and Broadcast Media*, Vol. 2, 129th ed. (Detroit, MI: Gale Research, 1997).
[34] Quoted in Dave McNeely, "Campaign Strategists Preparing Spin Systems," *Austin American-Statesman*, October 21, 1993, p. A11.

Latino businessman and Democratic gubernatorial candidate Tony Sanchez spent $70 million during his gubernatorial campaign in 2002 but lost to Rick Perry, who spent $30 million. ☛

What does this tell us about the influence of money in election campaigns?

AP Photo/Tony Gutierrez

mostly his own funds, but lost handily to incumbent Governor Rick Perry, who spent just less than $30 million. In 2006, the four candidates vying spent about $46 million, with Perry leading the way at $23 million.[35]

Although lower-level races in Texas are not usually million-dollar affairs, they can be expensive as well. This is certainly true if a contested office is an open seat, where the incumbent is not running for reelection, or if an incumbent is from a marginal district—one in which the incumbent won office with less than 55 percent of the vote. It is not unusual for a candidate in a competitive race for the state house to spend between $100,000 and $200,000.

Where does this money come from? Candidates often try to solicit small individual contributions through direct-mail campaigns. However, to raise the millions required for a high-level state race, they must solicit "big money" from wealthy friends or business and professional interests that have a stake in the outcome of the campaign. Banks, corporations, law firms, and professional associations, such as those representing doctors, real estate agents, or teachers, organize and register their **political action committees (PACs)** with the secretary of state's office. PACs serve as the vehicle through which interest groups collect money and then contribute it to political candidates. Another source of big money is loans—candidates often borrow heavily from banks, wealthy friends, or even themselves.[36]

Political action committees (PACs)

Organizations that raise and then contribute money to political candidates.

Where Does the Money Go? In today's political campaigns, there are many ways to spend money. Newspaper ads, billboards, radio messages, bumper stickers, yard signs, and phone banks are all staples in traditional campaigns. Candidates for statewide and urban races must rely on media advertising, particularly television, to get the maximum exposure they need in the three- or four-month campaign period. Campaigns are becoming professionalized, with candidates likely to hire consulting firms to manage their campaigns. Consultants contract with public opinion pollsters, arrange advertising, and organize direct-mail campaigns that can "target" certain areas of the state.

We can get some idea about spending in campaigns from what candidates pay for advertising and political consultants in Harris County, which includes Houston:[37]

★ A 30-second TV "spot" costs about $1,500 for a daytime ad, $2,000 to $5,000 for an ad during the evening news, and $5,000 to $20,000 during prime time (8:00 P.M. to 11:00 P.M.), depending on the show's popularity rating; for some very popular programs such as CSI, the cost can be as much as $25,000.

---

[35] http://www.statesman.com/news/content/region/legislature/stories/04/06/0406perryrga.html

[36] For a comprehensive treatment of money in political campaigns, see Frank J. Sorauf, *Inside Campaign Finance: Myths and Realities* (New Haven, CT: Yale University Press, 1992).

[37] Nancy Sims of Pierpont Communications, with offices in Austin and Houston, graciously provided this information.

WHAT KINDS OF PACS?

The number and variety of PACs in the United States is surprising. Consider a small sampling of the PACs that various organizations have established: AQUAPAC (set up by the Water Quality Association), BEEF-PAC (Texas Cattle Feeders Association), NUTPAC (Nut Processors Association), SIX-PAC (National Beer Wholesalers Association), WAFFLEPAC (Waffle House, Inc.), and WHATAPAC (Whataburger Corporation of Texas).[38]

★ Prime time for most radio broadcasting is "drive time" (5:00 A.M. to 10 A.M. and 3:00 P.M. to 8:00 P.M.), when most people are driving to or from work. Drive time rates range from $250 to $2,000 per 60-second spot.

★ Billboards can run from $600 to $15,000 a month, depending on the location (billboards on busy highways are the most expensive).

★ Newspaper ads cost around $250 per column inch ($300 to $500 on Sunday). In 2004, a half-page ad in the *Houston Chronicle* run on the day before the election cost about $15,000. Advertising rates for political campaigns are actually higher than standard rates, as political advertisers do not qualify for the discounts that regular advertisers receive.

★ Hiring a professional polling organization to conduct a poll in Harris County costs $15,000 to $30,000.

★ Hiring a political consulting firm to manage a campaign in Harris County runs up to $50,000 plus a percentage of media buys. (Technically, the percentage is paid by the television and radio stations.) Most firms also get a bonus ranging from $5,000 to $25,000 if the candidate wins.

Clearly, money is important in political campaigns. Although the candidate who spends the most money does not always win, a certain amount of money is necessary for a candidate to be competitive. Speaking with his tongue partly in his cheek, one prominent politician noted, in regard to high-level statewide races in Texas, that, even if "you don't have to raise $10 million, you have to raise $8 million."[39]

Control over Money in Campaigns   Prompted by the increasing use of television in campaigns and the increasing amount of money needed to buy it, the federal government and most state governments passed laws regulating the use of money in the early 1970s. The Federal Elections Campaign Act of 1972 (substantially amended in 1974) established regulations that apply only to federal elections: president, vice president, and members of Congress. It provided for public financing of presidential campaigns with tax dollars, limited the amount of money that individuals and PACs could contribute to campaigns, and required disclosure of campaign donations. In 1976, the Supreme Court declared that it was unconstitutional to set spending limits for campaigns that were not publicly funded; this means there are no spending limits for congressional races.[40]

Not surprisingly, expenditures in election campaigns continue to increase. The Federal Election Commission reported that $211.8 million was spent in the 1976 election of the president and members of Congress, with $122.8 million spent in the presidential race alone.

---

[38]Federal Election Commission, http://www.fec.gov
[39]"The Senate Can Wait," interview with Jim Hightower, *Texas Observer*, January 27, 1989, p. 6.
[40]*Buckley* v. *Valeo*, 424 U.S. 1 (1976).

Of the $60.9 million spent in the elections of the 435 House members, more money was spent on behalf of the candidates in Texas ($4.5 million) than on those of any other state except California. Such expenditure levels appear modest by today's standards. In 1998, outlays for all congressional races (House and Senate combined) totaled $740 million.[41] In the same year, candidates for Texas's 30 U.S. House seats spent $27 million in their election efforts, an average of just less than $1 million per seat. In 2002, spending totaled over $40 million, more than $1.25 million on average for the 32 seats that Texas holds. In 2006 the average ballooned again to over $1.75 million per seat and the level of campaign spending is likely to continue to rise. Costs of campaigns for state offices in Texas are at least proportionate in size, and Texas has joined other states in enacting legislation designed to control the flow of money.

The most important provisions of Texas law regarding money in campaigns are as follows:

★ Candidates may not raise or spend money until an official campaign treasurer is appointed.
★ Candidates and PACs may not accept cash contributions for more than an aggregate of $100.
★ Direct contributions from corporations and labor unions are prohibited, though this may change in the wake of a recent Supreme Court decision, as discussed below.
★ Candidates and treasurers of campaign committees are required to file sworn statements listing all contributions and expenditures for a designated reporting period to the Texas secretary of state's office.
★ Both criminal and civil penalties are imposed on anyone who violates the law's provisions.
★ Primary enforcement of campaign regulations is the responsibility of the Texas Ethics Commission.

Although these provisions may sound imposing, the fact is that raising and spending money on Texas campaigns still is pretty much wide open. For example, corporations and labor unions may not give directly to a candidate, but they may give via their PACs. Note also that there are no limits on the amount a candidate may spend. Probably the most important effect of the campaign finance law in Texas comes from the requirement of disclosure. How much money a candidate raises, who makes contributions, and how campaign funds are spent are matters of public record. This information may be newsworthy to reporters or other individuals motivated to inform the public.

Soft money

Money spent by political parties on behalf of political candidates, especially for the purposes of increasing voter registration and turnout.

Independent expenditures

Money individuals and organizations spend to promote a candidate without working or communicating directly with the candidate's campaign organization.

In 1979, amendments to the Federal Elections Campaign Act made it legal for political parties to raise and spend unlimited amounts of **soft money**, funds spent by political parties on behalf of political candidates. Party funds could be used to help candidates in a variety of ways, especially through voter registration and get-out-the-vote drives. The U.S. Supreme Court further opened up spending in 1985 by deciding that **independent expenditures** could not be limited.[42] As a result, individuals and organizations could spend as much as they want to promote a candidate as long as they were not working or communicating directly with the candidate's campaign organization. The 2002 Campaign Reform Act limited independent expenditures by corporations and labor unions, but this was overturned by the Supreme Court in its 2010 decision in *Citizens United* v. *Federal Election Commission*.[43] This may have implications for state and local races that have bans on corporate spending, including Texas. The 2002 Act also deprived the parties of their soft money resources, but activists simply set up nonparty organizations to collect and disperse such funds. Understandably, it has been difficult to effectively control money in political campaigns.

---

[41]*Congressional Quarterly Almanac, 1977* (Washington, DC: CQ Press, 1977), p. 35A; *Congressional Quarterly Weekly Report*, March 5, 1989, p. 478. Since 1976, the federal government has actually expanded the role of money in elections.

[42]Federal Election Commission, http://www.fec.gov

[43]*Citizens United* v. *Federal Election Commission*, 130 S.Ct. 876 (2010).

CHAPTER SUMMARY

★ Elections are the defining characteristic of representative democracy. It is through our votes that we hold elected officials accountable.

★ A small number of demographic and political variables are important in predicting who will vote. The most important demographic variables are education, income, and age. Certain political factors also influence the likelihood of voting, especially a person's level of interest in politics and intensity of identification with a political party. Other factors are important as well, but with this small set of demographic and political variables, we can make a good prediction as to whether a person will vote in a particular election.

★ Voting in Texas (and most other states) is a two-stage process. Before you can vote, you must first register. Traditionally, a barrier for women and minorities, the registration procedure today is as simple as voting itself—perhaps even simpler. Since the passage of federal "motor voter" legislation, a person can register when renewing a driver's license.

★ National turnout in presidential elections has fluctuated between 50 and 55 percent in recent years. In midterm elections, turnout is around 40 percent. These numbers are lower than what we find in most other advanced democracies. Voter turnout in Texas is even below the U.S. national average.

★ Low voter turnout in Texas may be due in part to the state's socioeconomic characteristics. A comparatively large percentage of the population lives below the poverty level. An even larger percentage has not graduated from high school, and these people are not very likely to vote. Income and education levels are low for African Americans and Latinos, so turnout is particularly low for these groups. Political factors, such as political structure and political culture, may also play a role in low turnout.

★ In Texas, as in other southern states that once were predominantly Democratic, a majority rule is used in primary elections. If no candidate receives a majority of the votes cast for a particular office in the first primary, a second, runoff primary is used to determine the winner. Outside the South, only a plurality of the votes is typically required.

★ Ballot design is an important factor in elections. Texas traditionally has used the party-column ballot, in which the names of all the candidates of each party are listed in parallel columns. The main alternative is the office-block ballot, in which the names of candidates are listed underneath each office. Beginning with the 2002 election, many Texas counties adopted electronic voting systems, which combine features of the office-block and party-column designs.

★ Texas is a diverse state, and the pool of candidates for local offices reflects this diversity. As we move up the pyramid of elected offices, however, the candidates become much more homogeneous—successful candidates for statewide office traditionally have been white males. While this remains true today, women and minorities have made substantial gains, and these gains are likely to continue as more women and minorities enter politics.

★ In a state as large as Texas, media advertising, political consultants, and polling are required for any candidate seeking to win statewide office or the most competitive state legislative and local elections. These services are expensive.

★ Without a certain amount of funding, it is impossible to be competitive in Texas elections. The high and rising costs of campaigns means that serious candidates must collect contributions from a variety of sources. Most candidates must rely on PACs and wealthy individuals. Although the Texas legislature has passed laws regulating campaign finance in state races, raising and spending funds is still fairly wide open.

HOW TEXAS COMPARES

★ Texas traditionally has had very restrictive voting rules, and voter turnout has been among the lowest of the 50 states. In the last two national elections, only one state posted a lower turnout rate.

★ It now is much easier to register and vote in the state. Texas was among the first states to institute early voting, and turnout has since come more in line with what we see in other states, though it still is below average.

★ Turnout in Texas has a lot to do with the state's education and income levels, which are well below the national average.

KEY TERMS

Australian ballot
chad
closed primary
crossover voting
direct primary

early voting
electronic voting
independent expenditures
negative campaigning
office-block ballot

open primary
participation paradox
party-column ballot
plurality vote
political action committees (PACs)

political culture
runoff primary
soft money
voter turnout
voting-age population

REVIEW QUESTIONS

1. What explains why some people are more likely to vote than others?

2. Why has voter turnout declined in the United States?

3. Why is voter turnout in Texas lower than it is in most other states?

4. What is the majority election rule, and why do we use it in Texas primaries?

5. Why are some candidates more likely than others to win elections in Texas?

6. What have elected officials in the United States and Texas done to control money in election campaigns? Have these measures been effective?

LOGGING ON

There are many websites related to voting, elections, and campaigns. The political parties have websites, as do most political candidates, and there are a lot of independent sites. For a wide-ranging list of political resources on the Web, try the American Political Science Association site at **http://www.apsanet .org/content_2775.cfm?navID=9**. For a virtual warehouse of national and state public opinion data, go to **http://www .pollingreport.com**. For current election polling data go to **http://www.pollster.com**. For specific information about U.S. voting behavior in every national election year, go to the National Election Studies home page at **http://www.electionstudies.org**. For specific information about voting and elections in Texas, go to the secretary of state's election page at **http://www.sos.state .tx.us/elections**

For information about particular issues, go to the League of Women Voters at **http://www.lwvtexas.org**. To find out more about youth voter turnout, visit CIRCLE at **http://www .civicyouth.org**. CIRCLE has conducted research on civic and political engagement by youth since 2001. At this site you can find information specifically about Texas voting.

One of the critical issues discussed in this chapter is money in elections. To do some research on this issue, go to **http://www.fec .gov**, the Federal Election Commission (FEC) site. Click on "Campaign Finance Reports and Data" and then on "Search the Disclosure Database." This gives you access to the campaign spending data collected by the FEC. For instance, you can see how much candidates received and spent and where the contributions came from. To start, follow the link "Candidate and PAC/Party Summaries." Once there, pick "Texas" in the state list and then "Send Query" and you will see what different candidates spent. You will also see what different PACs contributed. The names and numbers may surprise you!

The New Media and Texas Politics

Laura K. De La Cruz
El Paso Community College

INTRODUCTION

The media have played an important role in politics since our nation's birth, but the system is shifting from the "news" media to the "new" media. In the early 1800s, politicians campaigned via letter writing and newspaper articles, reaching hundreds. In the early 1900s, politicians campaigned via train tours and press coverage, reaching thousands. In the early 2000s, politicians campaigned via the new media of viral politics and social networking sites, reaching millions. Texas is becoming a leader in new media politics.

TRADITIONAL MEDIA

Historically, political news coverage was dominated by broadcast television and daily newspapers. Throughout Texas's quest for independence and statehood, newspapers were used to promote those goals and solicit support from the United States. William Travis's letter of appeal for support from February 24, 1836, was published in newspapers across the United States, garnering American support for the Texas War of Independence (**http:// www.lsjunction.com/docs/appeal.htm**).

The *Galveston County Daily News* is Texas's oldest continuously published newspaper and debuted on April 11, 1842. It is not, however, the first newspaper published in Texas. That honor goes to the *Gaceta de Texas,* which was published on May 25,

1813 in Nacogdoches. However, the reach of newspapers was fairly limited, and print media remained the primary source of Texas political news until the advent of radio.

In 1911, radio broadcasting began at The University of Texas (UT) and Texas A&M campuses and by the 1920s radio stations were broadcasting across Texas. Radios played an important role in Texas politics by offering news reports, covering campaigns, and broadcasting inaugurations. Like other radio stations across the nation, Texas stations were regulated by the Federal Communications Commission (FCC) and were required to offer equal time to candidates from different parties to present their views. After 1949, they were also required to comply with the FCC's Fairness Doctrine and avoid promoting a particular party or viewpoint over another.

Television appeared in Texas on September 27, 1948, when a Fort Worth station broadcast a speech by President Harry Truman. In 1954, Spanish television debuted in the El Paso–Juarez, Mexico area. Television quickly supplanted both radio and newspapers as people's primary source of political news with its ability to broadcast live events in dramatic fashion.

NEW MEDIA

During the past 30 years, and particularly the last 10, attention has shifted to new forms of media such as cable programs, talk radio/podcasts, websites/social networking sites, blogs/RSS feeds, and phone applications.

An event instrumental to this shift was the FCC's elimination of the Fairness Doctrine in the 1980s. Like radio stations, television stations initially were required to comply with the Fairness Doctrine. The advent of cable television and the increasing number of television channels convinced the FCC that there was no longer limited access to news and therefore, no longer a need for the Fairness Doctrine. Television and radio both responded to this change by creating programming specifically tailored to liberal and conservative audiences.

Cable Television Cable television channels have provided viewers with a growing variety of news programs—programs that have become increasingly partisan during the past 10 years. Many, such as Fox News and MSNBC, purposely slant their news toward their viewers' political ideologies and only cover items their viewers want to hear about.

The future: Webcams are allowing viewers to create their own television programming, with ready access by millions via YouTube and other video sites. Organizations such as Texas Tech (**http://www.youtube.com/texastech**) have already created their own channels on YouTube, with politicians soon to follow. Politicians will create their own programming for the Internet and YouTube in order to reach larger audiences.

Talk Radio/Podcasts There are dozens of talk radio stations in Texas, broadcasting in both English and Spanish. They cover a diverse range of topics from local events, tourism, entertainment, and politics. Talk radio stations, like cable television channels, are providing partisan political news targeting specific audiences.

The future: Online talk radio programs are cheap and easy for individuals to create and provide via the Internet. Sites like **http://www.blogtalkradio.com** give people the opportunity to offer their own version of the news, particularly local news. Conservative programs such as "Conservative Latino Talk

Radio" and progressive programs such as "Capitol Annex Radio" broadcast regularly.

Websites Websites are used by almost every government agency in Texas, from state to local. Politicians too have adopted websites, both incumbents and challengers. The Texas governor's office, for example, provides the incumbent with a site sponsored and maintained by the state of Texas (**http://www.governor.state .tx.us/**). This is an added benefit for the incumbent, who can use the site to promote his/her agenda and enhance their image. Personal websites allow politicians and candidates the opportunity to campaign, find volunteers, and fund-raise. For example, when Governor Rick Perry was running for reelection in 2010 he had the double benefit of his personal website (**http://www.rickperry .org/**) and the state's website as vehicles to highlight his successes.

The future: Politicians will continue to use websites but these will remain a fairly passive vehicle for politics. Their potential is limited as politicians look for more active ways to reach voters and to target specific audiences. In many ways, websites are becoming like newspapers. They can offer personalized videos, blogs and minute-by-minute news, but these are politician-driven. Nevertheless, their potential for fund-raising remains strong.

Blogs Anyone with an Internet connection can start a blog and thousands have on topics ranging from cooking to politics. Technology allows for RSS feeds whereby readers subscribe and blog posts are automatically delivered to their email. Phone applications now allow blog posting to be delivered via cell phone.

Blogs in Texas range from grassroots such as Burnt Orange (**http://www.burntorangereport.com**), started by students from UT Austin in 2004 to blogs such as the *Houston Chronicle's* Texas Politics blog (**http://blogs.chron.com/texaspolitics/**).

The future: Blogs are a time-consuming method of presenting a message and politicians are looking for media that get their message out faster. These methods tend to require a message that is brief and direct. Nevertheless, blogs will continue to be used by politicians who want to provide more extensive coverage of an issue.

Tweeting. Some observers think that the new media is changing American politics in important ways.

In what ways are new media changing election campaigns?

Social Networking Sites Social networking sites such as Facebook, MySpace, Twitter, and MeetUp can be credited with changing politics in 2008 when President Obama used social networking sites to campaign and fund-raise in unprecedented ways. These sites have been used to stream video, solicit feedback via like/dislike selections, and to provide postings in real time.

These sites are being used in 2010 by Texas politicians such as Governor Rick Perry (**http://www.twitter.com/governorperry** and **http://www.facebook.com/GovernorPerry**), candidates for the Texas Senate such as Wendy Davis (**http://www.myspace .com/wendydavisforsenate**), and political groups looking for potential members (**http://conservative-and-libertarian-politics.meetup.com/**).

The future: As social networking sites themselves network with each other (Facebook links with Flickr, Digg, Delicious, Technorati, YouTube, and others), more information about users becomes available in order to target their message. This will be particularly helpful for politicians who can then reach voters quickly and efficiently.

Phones Cell phones have opened up a whole new way of connecting with potential voters and supporters. Text messages about running mate selection, video streaming of press events and video capture of news events via phone cameras has changed politics in ways unheard of prior to 2005. Universities such as UT Austin already have phone applications or "apps" (**http:// www.utexas.edu/iphoneapp/**) so students, alumni, and supporters can keep up with the latest news.

The future: Phone apps will change politics in ways unimaginable today. Already apps exist that provide conservative talking points, offer *New York Times* opinion pieces, or copies of various political books and documents from throughout history. Potential uses include locator apps that allow users to find others who share a similar ideology—a "liberal or conservative finder" type application, bill-tracking applications, video streaming of legislative meetings, and GPS tracking of politicians and candidates.

Pros and Cons of the New Media The new media is a change from the traditional media in that it is viewer-driven (or voter-driven) as opposed to media-driven (or politician-driven). In many ways, it is democracy at its best. Voters can pick and choose what they see and hear, as well as provide instant feedback to express their views. Ultimately, however, voices may get lost in the din, creating mob rule online.

Another bonus of the new media is that viewers and readers now have a greater selection of news from which to choose and can share news with others. News becomes viral and spreads quickly across the world. It is the ultimate in free speech but may cause information overload (resulting in too much free speech, if there is such a thing!).

The new media also creates more points of history as individuals can now save history via technology. Pictures, video, and recordings will preserve larger and larger amounts of history, thus preserving politics for posterity—or will they? The sheer amount of material may keep relevant history from being recorded. Politicians may be haunted by videos that are decades old and no longer relevant. Furthermore, history could potentially be deleted. For example, Twitter postings maybe deleted if someone later regrets their posting, thus depriving historians of important artifacts.

Ultimately, the most significant consequence of the new media is that distance becomes irrelevant and as a result, national and international news now becomes Texas news and vice versa. The old saying, "All politics is local" now becomes "All political news is local."

JOIN THE DEBATE

1. How do consumers of the new media evaluate their sources? Will a highly competitive, worldwide new media environment replace traditional journalistic standards and editorial review?

2. How will the new media finance costly fact gathering and investigative journalism? Will advocacy journalism replace fact-based reporting?

3. In what ways does the development of the new media enhance democracy? Is there a danger that the fragmentation of the media will cause voters to become more polarized into hostile political camps?

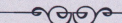

Chapter 4

Political Parties

CONTENTS

LEARNING OBJECTIVES

* Describe the features that characterize American political parties.
* Explain why Texas politics was dominated by the Democratic Party until the early 1990s.
* Describe the differences between liberal and conservative views.
* Name the types of people and groups who generally support Texas Republicans and Texas Democrats.
* Name the geographical areas of Texas that generally support the GOP and those areas where the Democratic Party is stronger.
* Explain the difference in temporary versus permanent party organization in Texas and give an example of each.
* Define realignment and describe the reasons a majority of Texas voters have gradually come to identify with the Republican Party.

Decide where you stand on the ideological spectrum. Sample conservative, liberal, and libertarian opinion:

Liberal/Progressive Groups

★ Check out the *Progressive* online magazine at **http://www.progressive.org**

★ Link up with the *Texas Observer* at **http://www.texasobserver.org/**

★ Plug into **http://www.offthekuff.com/** and **www.texaskaos.com/**

★ Nose around the *Capitol Annex* at **http://www.capitolannex.com**

★ Track "conservative bias" in the media with *Media Matters* at **http://mediamatters.org/**

Conservative Groups

★ Nose around *National Review Online* at **http://www.nationalreview.com/** and the *Weekly Standard* at **http://www.weeklystandard.com**

★ Tune into the *Austin Political Report* at **http://www.burntorangereport.com/diary/10723/the-texas-political-report-a-joint-project-of-burnt-orange-report-and-annies-list**

★ Connect with the *Lone Star Times* at **http://lonestartimes.com/**

★ Sound out the *Texas Conservative Review* at **http://www.texasconservativereview.com/index.html**

★ Track "liberal bias" in the media with the Media Research Center at **http://www.mediaresearch.org/**

Libertarian Groups

★ Get a feel for libertarian views at **http://www.reason.com/** and **http://www.nolanchart.com/**. The *Libertarian* website is at Texas Libertarian Party **http://www.tx.lp.org/**

Team up with your political party. On-campus organizations usually include the Young Democrats (**http://www.texasyds.com**) and Young Republicans (**http://www.tyrf.org/**)

Help select your party's nominee. Register and vote in your party's primary election. To vote in the primary you must be registered at least 30 days in advance. In Texas, you simply decide which party you prefer and vote to select that party's nominee. The only real restriction is that you must choose one party or the other.

Go to your party's precinct convention or caucus. If you vote in your party's primary, you are eligible to attend your party's precinct convention (or caucus as it is referred to in presidential election years). The convention begins a few minutes after the polls close, and is usually in the same location of the primary. Attendance is often sparse (the exception was Democratic caucuses in March 2008). This means you have a good chance of being heard and even being elected as a delegate.

Attend your party's county- or district-level convention. Delegates selected at the precinct level go on to attend their party's county or district. Delegates to these conventions pass resolutions and elect candidates to the state convention, which is held every two years in June. If you are selected as a delegate to the state convention, you have become a serious party activist.

★ For more information on the Texas party conventions and events, leaders, rules, and issue positions, check the websites of the state political parties, listed in "Logging On."

Keep your eye on breaking political events in Texas in the Quorum Report Daily Buzz (**http://www.quorum report.com/buzz/buzz.cfm**) and *Texas Monthly* political blog at **http://www.texasmonthly.com/blogs/burkablog/ index.php**. Of course, local daily newspapers also cover political developments, and most of them have extensive coverage online.

The Founders created our complicated system of federal government and provided for the election of a president and Congress. However, the U.S. Constitution makes no mention of political parties. Indeed, these early leaders held negative attitudes about parties. George Washington warned of the "baneful effects of the spirit of party" in his farewell address. James Madison, in Federalist Paper 10, criticized parties or "factions" as divisive but admitted that they were inevitable. Madison and others thought that parties would encourage conflict and undermine consensus on public policy. Yet despite their condemnation of parties, these early American politicians engaged in partisan politics and initiated a competitive two-party system.

Parties, then, are apparently something we should live neither with nor without. They have been with us from the start of this country and will be with us for the foreseeable future, influencing our government and public policy. It is important, therefore, to gain an understanding of what they are all about.

What is a political party? This question conjures up various stereotypes: smoke-filled rooms where party leaders or bosses make important behind-the-scenes decisions; activists or regulars who give time, money, and enthusiastic support to their candidates; or voters who proudly identify themselves as Democrats or Republicans. Essentially though, a political party is simply a broad-based coalition of interests whose primary purpose is to win elections. Gaining control of government through popular elections is the most important goal for political parties, and most of the activities parties pursue are directed toward this purpose. Parties recruit and nominate their members for public office. They form coalitions of different groups and interests to build majorities so that they can elect their candidates.

Political parties are vital to democracy in that they provide a link between the people and the government. Parties make it possible for the ordinary citizen and voter to participate in the political system; they provide the means for organizing support for particular candidates. In organizing this support, parties unify various groups and interests and mobilize them behind the candidate that supports their preferred positions.

Functions of Political Parties

Political parties developed and survived because they perform important functions. The first function of parties is to nominate and elect their members to public office. Except for local elections, in which parties are forbidden by law to participate, candidates are nominated by political parties, and parties run the election process. The second function of political parties is to simplify the issues for voters so that people understand the alternative positions on questions of public policy. In other words, parties educate the public. They help make sense of the issues and provide voters with cues on how to vote.

The third function of parties is to mobilize voters by encouraging participation in the electoral process. Citizens are persuaded to become active in support of party candidates. Contributing money to campaigns, telephoning, and door-to-door canvassing are all examples of how parties mobilize supporters. The more organized the party, the more effective it becomes in getting out the vote for its candidates.

Finally, the fourth function of parties is to run the government at whatever level they are active. The president, members of Congress, governors, state representatives, and Texas state judges are all elected to public office under the party label. Once elected, these officials try to push forward the positions of their party. However, in our political system, it is often difficult for parties to manage government because separate branches of government may not be under the control of the same party.

Characteristics of American Political Parties

American political parties have three distinct characteristics not always found in parties elsewhere in the world: (1) pragmatism, (2) decentralization, and (3) the two-party system.

PRAGMATISM

Pragmatism in politics means that ideas should be judged on the basis of their practical results rather than on an ideological basis.[1] In other words, a pragmatist is interested in what works on a practical basis. American parties are sometimes willing to compromise principles to appeal successfully to a majority of voters and gain public office. They willingly bargain with most organized groups and take stands that appeal to a large number of interests to build a winning coalition. In other words, American parties are much less programmatic than many Western European parties. The latter possess a consistent commitment to a particular ideology and their supporters are firmly committed to programmatic goals.

Pragmatism often means taking clear-cut positions only on issues where there is broad agreement. A campaign strategy designed to attract all groups and to repel none fails to bring the party's ideology into sharp focus. But taking clear stands on controversial issues may alienate potential members of the party's electoral coalition. Political parties and their candidates, including those in Texas, therefore, prefer to deemphasize issues and instead attempt to project a positive but vague image. Broad, fuzzy campaign themes that stress leadership potential, statesmanship, activities, family life, and personality often take precedence over issues.

Although the broad electoral coalitions that comprise American parties make it difficult for them to achieve ideological consistence, it would be a mistake to assume that parties in America do not differ from one another. Indeed, many observers feel that American parties have become more programmatic in recent years. To succeed, they must satisfy their traditional supporters: voters, public opinion leaders, interest groups, and campaign contributors. The candidates are not blank slates but have their own beliefs, prejudices, biases, and opinions. In most elections, broad ideological differences are apparent. Voters in Texas who participated in the presidential election of 2008 could easily differentiate between the conservative orientation of John McCain and the more liberal philosophy of his opponent, Barack Obama.

DECENTRALIZATION

At first glance, American party organizations may appear to be neatly ordered and hierarchical, with power flowing from the national to state to local parties. In reality, however, American parties are not nearly so hierarchical. They reflect the American federal system, with its **decentralization** of power to national, state, and local levels. Political party organizations operate at the precinct, or "**grassroots**," level; the local government level (city, county, or district); the state level (especially in elections for governor); and the national level (especially in elections for president).

Figure 4.1 illustrates the nature of power in American political parties. State and local party organizations are semi-independent actors who exercise considerable discretion on most party matters. The practices that state and local parties follow, the candidates they recruit, the campaign money they raise, the innovations they introduce, the organized interests to which they respond, the campaign strategies they create, and most important, the policy

Pragmatism

The philosophy that ideas should be judged on the basis of their practical results rather than on an ideological basis. American political parties are pragmatic because they are more concerned with winning elections than with taking clear uncompromising stands on issues.

Decentralization

Exercise of power in political parties by state and local party organizations rather than by national party institutions.

Grassroots

The lowest level of party organization. In Texas, the grassroots level is the precinct level of organization.

---

[1]Gail Kennedy, *Pragmatism and American Culture* (Boston: Heath, 1966), p. 13.

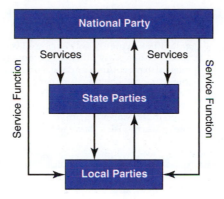

Figure 4.1
The Decentralized Nature of American Political Parties and the Importance of the National Party's Service Function. The diagram shows the semi-independent relationship that exists between national, state, and local party organizations and the increasingly important services and funds provided by the national party organization.

As national party organizations grow stronger, how much influence should they have over state and local parties and candidates? Should the latter pay close attention to the positions of the national party platform? Should voters hold state and local candidates accountable for the performance of national leaders?

orientations of the candidates who run under their label are all influenced by local and state political cultures, leaders, traditions, and interests.[2]

Compared with party systems in other countries, the American party system is quite decentralized. However, Figure 4.1 also illustrates how power has shifted to the national party organizations in recent years. Both the Democratic and Republican national parties have become stronger and more involved in state and local party activities through various service functions. By using new campaign technologies—computer-based mailing lists, direct-mail solicitations, and the Internet—the national parties have raised millions of dollars. Thus, the national party organizations have assumed a greater role by providing unprecedented levels of assistance to state parties and candidates. This assistance includes a variety of services—candidate recruitment, research, public opinion polling, computer networking, production of radio and television commercials, direct mailing, consultation on redistricting issues, and the transfer of millions of dollars worth of campaign funding. Not surprisingly, as national parties provide more money and services to state and local parties, they exercise more influence over state and local organizations, issues and candidates.[3]

TWO-PARTY SYSTEM

In a majority of states, political competition usually comes down to competition between the two major parties, the Democrats and the Republicans. Third parties have tried to gain office but with little success, primarily because the pragmatic major parties make a conscientious effort to absorb them by adopting their issues (for example, the Populist Party of the 1890s was absorbed by the Democratic Party). Voters, potential campaign contributors, and political activists also behave pragmatically; they tend to avoid supporting a losing cause. Our electoral system, the **single-member district system**, encourages this pragmatic behavior. If only one representative can be elected in a district, voters will cast their ballots for the candidates that have the best chance of winning.

Third parties also face the problem of historical inertia. Voters usually vote for the major parties because they have always done so. The national campaign for the presidency in 1992 by Texas billionaire Ross Perot illustrates the difficulty faced by third-party or independent candidates in American politics. Perot was able to appear on the ballot of all 50 states only because Perot supporters organized mass petition drives state by state. In the November 3,

Single-member district system

A system in which one candidate is elected to a legislative body in each election district.

---

[2]Norman J. Ornstein, Andrew Kohut, and Larry McCarthy, *The People, the Press, and Politics: The Times Mirror Study of the American Electorate* (Washington, DC: Times Mirror Center for the People and the Press, 1988).
[3]Margaret Hershey, *Party Politics in America*, 13th ed. (New York: HarperCollins, 2009), pp. 70–71.

1992, presidential election, Perot received 19 percent of the national vote and 22 percent of the vote in his home state of Texas. However, both nationally and in Texas, Perot's support was diffuse. It was not concentrated enough in any one state to win a state's electoral votes, the votes needed to actually win the presidency.

Development of the Texas Party System

Two-party system

A political system characterized by two dominant parties competing for political offices. In such systems, minor or third parties have little chance of winning.

Although for most of its existence, the United States has had a **two-party system**, many states and localities—including Texas—have been dominated by just one party at various times in history. Texas was formerly a one-party Democratic state, but in recent years the state parties have become competitive in congressional and state-level races. To understand political parties in Texas, it is necessary to examine the historical predominance of the Democratic Party, the emergence of two-party competition in the state, and the reality of Republican Party domination at present.

THE ONE-PARTY TRADITION IN TEXAS

Under the Republic of Texas, there was little party activity. Political divisions were usually oriented around support of, or opposition to, Sam Houston, a leading founder of the Republic. After Texas became a state, however, the Democratic Party dominated Texas politics until the 1990s. This legacy of dominance was firmly established by the Civil War and the era of Reconstruction, when "Yankee" troops, under the direction of a Republican Congress, occupied the South. From the time that the Republican and former Union soldier Edmund J. Davis's single term as governor ended in 1873 until the surprising victory of the Republican gubernatorial candidate Bill Clements in 1978, the Democrats exercised almost complete control over Texas politics.

The Democratic Party was at times challenged by the emergence of more liberal third parties. The most serious of these challenges came in the late 19th century with the Populist revolt. The Populist Party grew out of the dissatisfaction of small farmers who demanded government regulation of rates charged by banks and railroads. These farmers—joined by sharecroppers, laborers, and African Americans—mounted a serious election bid in 1896 by taking 44.3 percent of the vote for governor. Eventually, however, the Democratic Party defused the threat of the Populists by co-opting many of the issues of the new party. The Democrats also effectively disenfranchised African Americans and poor whites in 1902 with the passage of the poll tax.

Two events in the early 20th century solidified the position of the Democrats in Texas politics. The first was the institution of party primary "reforms" in 1906. For the first time, voters could choose the party's nominees by a direct vote in the party primary. Hence, the Democratic primary became the substitute for the two-party contest: the general election. In the absence of Republican competition, the Democratic primary was the only game in town, and it provided a competitive arena for political differences within the state.

The second event to help the Democrats was the Depression. Although the Republican presidential candidate, Herbert Hoover, carried Texas in 1928, Republicans were closely associated with the Great Depression of the 1930s. The cumulative effect of this association, the Civil War, and Reconstruction ensured Democratic dominance in state government until the early 1990s.

IDEOLOGICAL BASIS OF FACTIONALISM: CONSERVATIVES AND LIBERALS

Although members of a political party may be similar in their views, factions or divisions within the party inevitably develop. These conflicts may involve a variety of personalities and issues, but the most important basis for division is ideology.

To understand the ideological basis for factionalism in political parties in Texas, it is necessary to define the terms **conservative** and **liberal**—a difficult task, since the meanings change with time and may mean different things to different people.

Conservatives Conservatives believe that individuals should be left alone to compete in a free market unfettered by government control; they prefer that government regulation of the economy be kept to a minimum. However, conservatives support government involvement and funding to promote business. They favor construction of highways, tax incentives for investment, and other government aids to business. The theory is that these aids will encourage economic development and hence prosperity for the whole society (the trickle-down theory). On the other hand, conservatives are likely to oppose government programs

WHAT IS THE LIBERTARIAN PARTY?

If you have voted in a Texas election, chances are you have seen many Libertarian candidates on the ballot. In recent years, the Libertarian Party has become an active, if not always influential, force in Texas politics. The Libertarian Party has a "hands-off" philosophy of government that appeals to many Texas conservatives. The party's general philosophy is one of individual liberty and personal responsibility. Applying their doctrine to the issues, Libertarians would oppose Social Security, campaign finance reform, gun control, and many foreign policies. They consider programs like Social Security to be "state-provided welfare" and believe that regulating campaigns promotes too much government involvement. They also oppose U.S. intervention in world affairs. The Libertarian Party faces the same hurdles as other third parties: poor financing, a lack of media coverage, and in some states, getting access to the ballot. It has managed, however, to elect more than 300 Libertarians to public office at the local and state levels throughout the country.

that involve large-scale redistribution of wealth such as welfare, health-care aid, or unemployment compensation.

Some conservatives view change suspiciously; they tend to favor the status quo—things as they are now and as they have been. They emphasize traditional values associated with the family and close communities, and they often favor government action to preserve what they see as the proper moral values of society. Because conservatives hold a more skeptical view of human nature than liberals do, they are more likely to be tougher on perceived threats to personal safety and the public order. For example, conservatives are more likely to favor stiffer penalties for criminals, including capital punishment. Conservatives may combine support for the free market with support for traditional values, or they may adopt only one of these views.

Liberals Liberals believe that it is often necessary for government to regulate the economy. They point to great concentrations of wealth and power that have threatened to control government, destroy economic competition, and weaken individual freedom. Government power, they believe, should be used to protect the disadvantaged and to promote equality. Consequently, liberals are generally supportive of the social welfare programs that conservatives oppose. They are also more likely to favor progressive taxes, which increase as incomes increase. The best example of a progressive tax is an individual income tax.

Liberals possess a more optimistic view of human nature than conservatives. They believe that individuals are essentially rational and therefore that change will ultimately bring improvement in the human condition. Liberals want government to protect the civil rights and liberties of individuals and are critical of interference with any exercise of the constitutional rights of free speech, press, religion, assembly, association, and privacy. They are often suspicious of conservatives' attempts to "legislate morality" because of the potential for interference with individual rights.

CONSERVATIVE AND LIBERAL FACTIONS IN THE DEMOCRATIC PARTY

For many years, factions within the Texas Democratic Party resembled a two-party system, and the election to select the Democratic Party's nominees—the primary—was the most important election in Texas. Until the 1990s, conservative Democrats were much more successful than their liberal counterparts in these primaries, in part because Republican voters, facing no significant primary race of their own, regularly "crossed over" and supported conservative Democratic candidates. Voters in the general elections, facing a choice between a conservative Democrat and a conservative Republican, usually went with the traditional party—the Democrats. These Republican crossover votes enabled conservative Democrats, with few exceptions, to control the party and state government until 1978, when, as noted earlier, Bill Clements was elected the first Republican governor of Texas in 105 years.

Conservative Democrats in Texas provided a very good example of the semi-independent relationship of national, state, and local party organizations illustrated in Figure 4.1. Texas conservatives traditionally voted Democratic in state and local races but often refused to support the national Democratic candidates for president. Indeed, the development of the conservative Democratic faction in Texas was an outgrowth of conservative dissatisfaction with many New Deal proposals of Franklin D. Roosevelt in the 1930s and Fair Deal proposals of Harry Truman in the 1940s. Conservative Democrats in Texas continued their cool relationship with the national party when many of them supported Republican presidential candidates: Dwight Eisenhower in 1952 and 1956, Richard Nixon in 1968 and 1972, Ronald Reagan in 1980 and 1984.

In the past, the conservative wing of the Democratic Party enjoyed almost continuous success in Texas politics. Nearly every governor elected from the mid-1930s to the 1970s was supported by this faction. These governors included Allan Shivers (1949–1957), John Connally (1963–1969), and Preston Smith (1969–1973), all of whom later switched to the Republican Party. It also included governors Dolph Briscoe (1973–1979) and Mark White (1983–1987). Until recently, conservative Democrats held almost all of the state's congressional seats; they also dominated both chambers of the Texas legislature.

Several factors accounted for this success, but the most important was the power and resources of the conservative constituency. Conservatives have traditionally made up the state's "power elite," representing such interests as the oil, gas, and sulfur industries; other large corporations; bigger farms and ranches ("agribusiness"); owners and publishers of most of the state's major daily newspapers; and veterans. In other words, the most affluent people in the state are able and willing to contribute their considerable resources to the campaign of like-minded politicians. And these segments of the population are the most likely to turn out and vote in elections. This was a significant advantage to conservative Democrats competing in the party primary, in which turnout in the past has been particularly low.

Liberals in the Texas Democratic Party consist of groups who have supported the national party ticket and its presidents (Roosevelt, Truman, Kennedy, Johnson, Carter, Clinton, and Obama). These groups include the following:

★ Organized labor, in particular the American Federation of Labor–Congress of Industrial Organizations (AFL-CIO);
★ African-American groups, such as the National Association for the Advancement of Colored People (NAACP);
★ Latino groups, such as the American G.I. Forum, League of Latin American Citizens (LULAC), Mexican American Democrats (MAD), and Mexican American Legal Defense and Educational Fund (MALDEF);
★ Various professionals, teachers, and intellectuals;
★ Small farmers and ranchers, sometimes belonging to the Texas Farmers Union;
★ Environmental groups, such as the Sierra Club;
★ Abortion rights groups, such as the Texas Abortion Rights Action League; and
★ Trial lawyers—that is, lawyers who represent plaintiffs in civil suits and defendants in criminal cases.

ALLAN SHIVERS: CONSERVATIVE DEMOCRAT

Governor Allan Shivers, assuming office in 1949, did more than any individual to establish the dominance of the conservative faction of the Democratic Party. The Shivers faction (dubbed "Shivercrats" by liberals; see Chapter 1) officially announced its support for the 1952 Republican presidential nominee, Dwight D. Eisenhower, and urged Texas Democrats to vote Republican for president and Democratic for state offices. That same year, Shivers, along with all other Democratic state officeholders at the time (with the exception of State Agriculture Commissioner John White), was nominated by both the Democratic and Republican parties for the same offices. This circumstance of dual nomination was a unique situation in Texas politics.

This cartoon highlights the underdog status of the Democratic Party in Texas in recent years. What strategies should the Democrats employ to become more competitive in state elections?

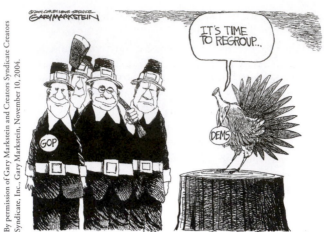

By permission of Gary Markstein and Creators Syndicate Creators Syndicate, Inc., Gary Markstein, November 10, 2004.

The success of liberal Democratic politicians in Texas was infrequent and rarely persisted for more than a few years. The heyday of Texas liberalism came in the 19th century and lasted through the 1930s with the election of several progressive governors, including James Hogg, "Pa" and "Ma" Ferguson, Dan Moody, and James V. Allred. Since the 1930s, liberals were able to capture a U.S. Senate seat only in 1957 with the election of Ralph Yarborough, but Yarborough was defeated in 1970 by the moderate-to-conservative Lloyd Bentsen, who held the seat until he became President Clinton's treasury secretary in 1992.

In recent years, liberal Texas Democrats have had more success in capturing their party's nomination, largely because conservatives are voting in the Republican primary. Lately, liberal or moderate Democrats have been routinely nominated for all the statewide races. This last point illustrates the irony for liberal Democrats: Although they have gained strength from the defection of conservatives, this very defection has propelled the Republicans to dominate Texas politics.

RISE OF THE REPUBLICAN PARTY

Before the presidential election of November 1988, only three contemporary Republicans had won statewide races in Texas: Senator John Tower (1961–1985), Governor Bill Clements (1979–1983 and 1987–1991), and Senator Phil Gramm (1985–2003). Why had the Republican Party failed to compete in Texas in the past? The most important reason is the bitter memory left by Texas's experience in the Civil War and during Reconstruction. The Republican administration of Governor E. J. Davis under the Texas Constitution of 1869 was considered the most corrupt and abusive period of Texas history. Only in the past few years has the Republican Party been able to shake its image as the "party of Reconstruction."

The Republicans become Competitive   The revival of the Republican Party was foreshadowed in the 1950s by the development of the so-called presidential Republicans (people who vote Republican for national office but Democratic for state and local office). Conservative Democrats objected to the obvious policy differences of the state and national Democratic parties and often voted for Republican presidential candidates.

The first major step in the rejuvenation of the Republican Party in Texas came in 1961, when John Tower, a Republican, was elected to the U.S. Senate. Tower won a special nonpartisan election held when Lyndon Johnson gave up his Senate seat to assume the vice presidency. Tower initially won with the help of many liberal Democrats and was reelected until he retired in 1984. His seat was retained by the Republicans with the election to the Senate of former Representative Phil Gramm over his liberal Democratic opponent Lloyd Doggett in 1984. In November 2002, John Cornyn, a Republican and the state's former attorney general, was elected to replace Gramm.

In November 1978, the Republicans achieved their most stunning breakthrough when Bill Clements defeated John Hill in the race for governor. After losing the governor's seat to moderate-conservative Mark White in 1982, Republicans regained their momentum in 1986, when Clements turned the tables on White and recaptured the governor's chair.

TABLE 4.1 CHANGES IN THE NUMBER OF REPUBLICAN AND DEMOCRATIC OFFICEHOLDERS IN TEXAS

Body	1973		2011	
	Democrats	Republicans	Democrats	Republicans
Texas House of Representatives	132	17	51	99
Texas Senate	28	3	12	19
U.S. House of Representatives	20	4	9	23
U.S. Senate	1	1	0	2

How do you think these numbers will change over the next ten years?

Developments in the 1990s and early 2000s transformed Texas into "Republican country." With the election in 1992 of U.S. Senator Kay Bailey Hutchison, Republicans held both U.S. Senate seats for the first time since Reconstruction. In 1994, Republican George W. Bush defeated incumbent Democratic governor Ann Richards.

By far the most impressive gains for the GOP came in the November 1998 elections, when incumbent Governor George W. Bush led a sweep of Republicans to victory in every statewide election. For the first time in living memory, no Democrats occupied any statewide executive or judicial office. Republicans have continued to maintain their monopoly on statewide offices. In 2004, after a successful effort at congressional redistricting, the GOP captured a majority in Texas's congressional delegation.

The Republican Party is also extremely competitive in lower-level offices in the state, where Democrats have been most firmly entrenched. In 1974, the GOP held only 53 offices at the county level; they now hold over 2000 county offices. In 1996, the GOP gained a majority of seats in the state senate, the first time in 126 years that Republicans held a majority in either house of the legislature, and in 2002, they captured the state house of representatives.

Table 4.1 shows the dramatic increases by Republicans in the Texas legislature and the Texas delegation to the U.S. House of Representatives. The extent to which these gains signal a Republican-dominated party system in Texas is discussed later in this chapter.

Sources of Republican Strengths and Weaknesses Republican voting strength in recent years has been concentrated in several clusters of counties (see Figure 4.2):

★ Houston area
★ Dallas–Fort Worth area
★ Midland–Odessa area
★ Northern Panhandle
★ East Texas oil field counties of Smith, Rusk, and Gregg
★ Hill Country–Edwards Plateau area

Results from the 2006 Agricultural Commissioner's race reveal that the Republican Party is weaker in the following areas:

★ South and South Central Texas
★ Pockets of Northwest Texas
★ Far West Texas
★ Far pockets of East Texas

Figure 4.2

Results of the 2008 Presidential Election. The map shows the 28 counties won by the Democratic candidate Barack Obama. Note that Obama carried the most populous counties in Texas (Bexar, Dallas, Harris, and Travis).

Source: Texas Almanac 2010–2011.

What does this mean for the future of the Democratic Party in Texas? Speculate on the electoral strategy that the Republicans should adopt for the future.

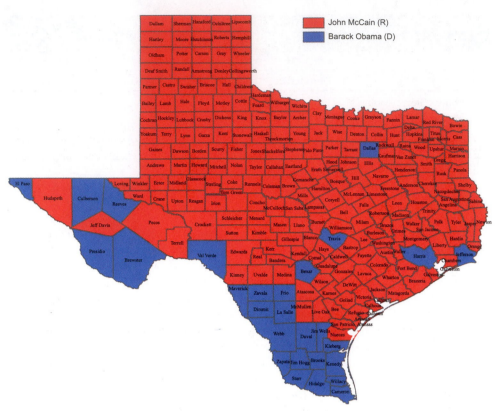

The Republican Party seems to appeal primarily to the following groups:

★ Middle- and upper-class individuals in urban and suburban communities;
★ Rural, high-income ranchers;
★ White Anglo-Saxon Protestants;
★ German Americans whose ancestors were strong supporters of the Union during the Civil War;
★ Active and retired military officers; and
★ Traditional conservatives who find themselves in a new urban setting.

The party has benefited from the economic growth and prosperity that occurred in Texas from the end of World War II to the early 1980s. During this period, newcomers from more Republican parts of the country were lured to the state by a sympathetic business climate or by the promise of jobs. These transplanted Texans joined more prosperous native Texans to provide a political climate more conducive to Republican Party politics.

AN EARLIER ERA

"We only had two or three laws [in Texas], such as against murder before witnesses, and being caught stealing horses, and voting the Republican ticket."—O. Henry (William S. Porter), "Law and Order," 1910.

CONSERVATIVE AND MODERATE FACTIONS WITHIN THE REPUBLICAN PARTY

As the Republican Party becomes more prominent in Texas politics, it is beginning to experience some of the factional differences that characterized the Democratic Party in Texas for years. For example, a bloc of conservative Christians, sometimes loosely referred to as **evangelical** or **fundamentalist Christians**, have increasingly dominated the Texas Republican Party. This group is concerned with such issues as family, religion, and community morals, and it has been effective in influencing the **party platform**. Associated with a broad spectrum of Protestant Christianity that emphasizes salvation and traditional values, evangelical voters are likely to support culturally conservative politics.

In 1992, the evangelical right wing of the Texas Republican Party easily controlled the GOP state convention and strengthened the antiabortion and antihomosexuality planks in the party's platform. They also captured more than half the seats on the Republican State Executive Committee. Since 1994, the state party chair and a majority of the members of the state executive committee have been conservative Christians. This dominance of leadership positions has given the conservative Christians a degree of control of the party machinery that continues today.

The control of the state's Republican Party by the conservative, or right, wing is opposed by the more moderate, or centrist, wing. Many of these moderates fear that the radicalism of the right will interfere with the party's ability to win elections. Many moderates represent business interests and are more concerned with keeping taxes low and limiting the government's interference in business decision making than with moral issues. The conservative faction of the Republican Party scored a major victory in the 2010 GOP primary when incumbent Governor Rick Perry received his party's nomination with more than 50 percent of the vote over incumbent U.S. Senator Kay Bailey Hutchison. Perry campaigned vigorously against President Obama's health care and other federal government initiatives and avoided a run off with his opponent.

In general, the Republican Party has failed to generate much support among the state's minority voters. African-American identification with the GOP consistently hovers around five percent. And party strategists have made no great effort to attract African Americans, since they are unlikely to switch parties.

Organizational Basis of Party Machinery in Texas

To better understand how political parties are organized in Texas, we can divide the party machinery into two parts: the temporary, consisting of a series of short-lived conventions at various levels; and the permanent, consisting of people elected to continuing leadership positions in the party (see Figure 4.3).

TEMPORARY-PARTY ORGANIZATION

Precinct Convention The voting precinct is the starting point of party activity, for it is the scene of the **precinct convention**, a gathering of the faithful that is open to all who voted earlier in the day in that party's **primary**. It is also the key to getting involved in politics. (See "Get Active!") On an early Tuesday in March in even-numbered years, both the Democratic and Republican parties hold conventions in almost all the voting precincts in the state. The ticket of admission is usually a voter registration card stamped to indicate that one has voted in the party's primary earlier in the day. The agenda of the precinct convention includes

Evangelical (fundamentalist) Christians

A number of Christians, often conservative supporters of the Republican Party, who are concerned with such issues as family, religion, abortion, gay rights, and community morals.

Party platform

The formal issue positions of a political party; specifics are often referred to as *planks* in the party's platform.

Precinct convention

A gathering of party members who voted in the party's primary for the purpose of electing delegates to the county or district convention.

Primary

An election held by a political party to nominate its candidates. Texas party primary elections are usually held in the spring.

Figure 4.3

Texas Political Party Organization. The chart shows the three levels of state party organization in Texas and the ties of the state organization to the national party organization.

Describe how voters are involved in both the temporary and permanent state organizations. How does the process of selecting delegates ensure that many of the delegates who attend the national convention have been "grassroots" supporters of the party?

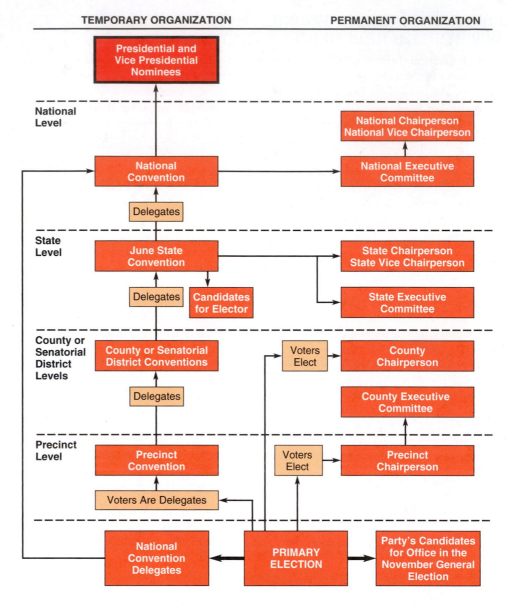

adoption of resolutions to be passed on to the county or senatorial district convention and selection of delegates to the county or senatorial district convention.

Although eligibility for participation in this grassroots level of democracy is open to all who vote in the first primary election, attendance is minimal—usually only two percent to three percent of those who vote. This low attendance makes it possible for a small, determined minority of the electorate to assume control of the precinct convention and dominate its affairs.

A precinct convention normally starts with the signing in of those present and certifying that they voted in the party's primary. In presidential years, those signing in also indicate their preference for a presidential candidate; in nonpresidential years, other designations may be used, such as "conservative caucus" or "moderate-progressive caucus." The preferences are used to evaluate the relative strength of support for each candidate or caucus.

THE EMERGING LATINO VOTE

Both Democratic and Republican party strategists in Texas and in the nation are aware of the growing importance of the Latino vote. This voting bloc is growing in numbers and power. For example, according to the Pew Hispanic Center, Latinos comprised nine percent of nationwide electorate in the 2008 presidential election and more than 20 percent of the electorate in Texas.

In 2004, George W. Bush received almost half of the "Tejano" vote in Texas (49 percent). This unprecedented support for a presidential candidate gave hope to Republicans. The GOP feels it is more in tune with Latino voters' support for conservative social positions such as abortion and family values. Democrats, on the other hand, still believe that Latinos will be attracted to the party for its traditional support for social welfare programs and civil rights. Both parties can be expected to pay close attention to the emerging Latino vote, sometimes referred to as the "sleeping giant."

Despite former President Bush's significant Latino support in Texas in the 2004 election, Latinos in Texas have traditionally identified strongly with the Democratic Party. Indeed, in 2008 Barack Obama captured 63 percent of the Latino vote in Texas. Democrats typically capture elections in heavily Latino counties such as those in the southern and southwestern areas of the state. Nevertheless, observers note that a substantial number of Latino voters are **swing voters** not bound by party identification.[1] The Democratic Party cannot afford to take this portion of the electorate for granted, and the GOP cannot assume that Latino party identification will trend its way.

Swing voters

People who cast their ballots on the basis of personality and other factors rather than strictly on the basis of party affiliation.

[1] National Council of La Raza, "How Did Latinos *Really* Vote in 2004?" (Memorandum), November 16, 2004, http://www.nclr.org/files/28218_file_NCLR_HOW_DID_LATINOS_REALLY_VOTE_IN_2004.pdf

---

The factions with the largest numbers present dominate the selection of delegates to the county convention.

If contending factions in a precinct are evenly divided, a walkout is possible if one side or the other loses a key vote and claims that a grave injustice was done. Such a group will conduct its own convention, called a "rump convention," going through the same procedures; then both precinct groups will appeal to a credentials committee appointed by the county executive committee. The credentials committee will decide which set of rival delegates is officially seated at the county convention. Although fairness and justice sometimes intervene, the decision on which group to seat usually depends on which faction is in the majority on the credentials committee.

County and Senatorial District Conventions In the weeks after the primary and the precinct conventions, county and state senatorial district conventions are held. In the most populous counties, the county convention has given way to state senatorial district conventions within those counties. Delegates vote on adoption of resolutions to be considered at the state convention and select delegates and alternates to attend that convention.

As with the precinct convention, liberal or conservative factions or those representing different presidential candidates will seek to dominate the selection of delegates. Walkouts followed by rump conventions may occur at the county or even the state level. In Texas, bitter intraparty conflict has historically characterized the Democratic Party more than the Republican Party, but that has changed as Republican primaries and conventions have grown in importance.

State Convention Both the Democratic and Republican parties in Texas hold state conventions in June of even-numbered years. The major functions of these biennial state conventions are to:

★ Elect state party officers;
★ Elect the 62 members of the state executive committee from their senatorial districts;

TABLE 4.2 EXCERPTS FROM THE TEXAS DEMOCRATIC AND REPUBLIC PARTY PLATFORMS

Texas Democrats	Texas Republicans
Believe a democratic government exists to help us achieve as a community, state, and nation, what we cannot achieve as individuals, and that it must not serve only a powerful few.	Believe that good government is based on the individual, and each person's ability, dignity, freedom, and responsibility must be honored and recognized.
Believe government should "provide multi-language instruction, beginning in elementary school, to make all students fluent in English and at least one other language…"	Demand "abolition of bilingual education. The best method is an 'English Immersion Program.'"
Oppose economic policies that "cut essential services and investments in our future [that] reward only the wealthiest Americans with tax cuts…"	Oppose the income tax at all levels of government and "urge that the Internal Revenue Service (IRS) be abolished and the Sixteenth Amendment to the U.S. Constitution be repealed."
Support abortion by trusting "the women of Texas to make personal and responsible decisions about when and whether to bear children . . . rather than having these personal decisions made by politicians."	Oppose abortion because "all innocent human life must be respected and safeguarded from fertilization to natural death; therefore, the unborn child has a fundamental individual right to life…"
Support "the establishment of a Texas Capital Punishment Commission to study the Texas Death Penalty system and a moratorium on executions pending action on the Commission's findings."	Believe "that properly applied capital punishment is legitimate, is an effective deterrent, and should be swift and unencumbered."
Believe the federal government should "fully fund all federal education mandates and should reform and fully fund No Child Left Behind."	Believe "the Federal Government has no constitutional jurisdiction over education . . . and call for the abolition of the U.S. Department of Education. . . ."
Support "the creation of a policy that would establish a path to citizenship for the majority of [illegal immigrants] currently here . . . with priority for those who have lived and worked here the longest."	Oppose "illegal immigration, amnesty in any form, or legal status for illegal immigrants."

Sources: Texas Democratic Party, http://www.txdemocrats.org/; Republican Party of Texas, http://www.texasgop.org/

What do these excerpts tell us about the attitudes of Democrats and Republicans toward government action and involvement?

★ Adopt a party platform (see Table 4.2 for examples of recent Texas party platform planks); and

★ Certify to the secretary of state the candidates nominated by the party in its March primary.

In addition, in presidential election years, the state convention:

★ Elects the party's nominees from Texas to the national committee of the party;

★ Selects the state's 34 potential presidential electors; and

★ Elects some delegates to the party's national nominating convention, held in July or August (the number of delegates selected is determined by national party rules).

The role of state convention delegates in selecting delegates to the national convention has diminished in recent years. Most of the delegates for both parties are now selected on the basis of the party's presidential preference primary. A **presidential preference primary** allows voters in the party primary to vote directly on the party's presidential nominee.

In 2008, Texas held its presidential primary on March 4. Both Democrats and Republicans, voting in their separate primaries, indicated their selections for presidential candidates, as well as candidates for state and local offices. Texas Democrats followed up the primary election with caucuses that helped determine a share of the delegates to the national Democratic convention. Democrats were allocated 228 delegates to the Democratic national convention, 126 of which were chosen by the primaries, 67 by precinct conventions or caucuses, and 35 by unpledged superdelegates or party leaders. Texas Republicans were allocated 140, all but three of which were determined by the primary vote. The rules for selecting delegates to the

Presidential preference primary

A primary election that allows voters in the party to vote directly for candidates seeking their party's presidential nomination.

PRESIDENTIAL CAUCUSES IN 2008: TOO MUCH DEMOCRACY?

In the past, the precinct conventions had very few attendees, even in presidential election years. In March 2008, however, the intensely competitive primary battle between Hillary Clinton and Barack Obama drew an estimated 1.1 million people to the precinct convention-caucuses, four times what party officials were expecting.

The unprecedented numbers caused a myriad of problems. Hundreds of people were squeezed into child-sized cafeterias or other small spaces. Some even caucused outside. Voters who arrived at 7:15 P.M. were kept waiting for hours while party officials tried to figure out obtuse procedures. Some left because of the time it took to sign in, figure out the rules, and find a place to caucus. In some polling places, the police were called to address clashes between highly charged supporters of both candidates. The confusion drew the attention of the national media and complaints from the candidates, particularly the Clinton campaign, who threatened to file suit over irregularities. It took weeks to finalize the final results.

Those who defended the caucuses claimed that the process energized the party, and attracted those who had never participated in the past. Still, the negative publicity had many party activists calling for changes in the system. See the second essay, "Presidential Primaries or Caucuses? Texas's Choices and the Outcomes," at the end of this chapter.

respective parties' national conventions are somewhat complex; each state party organization describes these rules in detail on their websites.

PERMANENT-PARTY ORGANIZATION

The permanent structure of the party machinery consists of people selected to lead the party organization and provide continuity between election campaigns.

Precinct-Level Organization At the lowest, or grassroots, level of the party structure is the precinct chair, who is chosen by the precinct's voters in the primary for a two-year term. Often the position is uncontested, and in some precincts, the person can be elected by write-in vote. The chair role serves as party organizer in the precinct, contacting known and potential party members. The chair may help organize party activities in the neighborhood, such as voter registration drives. The precinct chair is also responsible for arranging and presiding over the precinct convention and serving as a member of the county executive committee.

County-Level Organization A much more active and important role is that of the county chair. The voters choose who will hold this office for a two-year term in the party primary. The chair presides over the county executive committee, which is composed of all precinct chairs. With the later concurrence of the county commissioners' court, the county chair determines where the voting places will be for the primary and appoints all primary election judges. Accepting candidates for places on the primary ballot, the printing of paper ballots, and the renting of voting machines are also the chair's responsibilities. Finally, the chair, along with the county executive committee, must certify the names of official nominees of the party to the secretary of state's office.

The county executive committee has three major functions: assemble the temporary roll of delegates to the county convention, canvass the returns from the primary for local offices, and help the county chair prepare the primary ballot, accept filing fees, and determine the order of candidates' names on the ballot. This is an important consideration if "blind voting" may be a problem (in that ill-informed voters tend to opt for the first name they come to on the ballot).

State-Level Organization Delegates to the state convention choose the state chair— the titular head of the party—at the state convention for a two-year term. The duties of the chair are to preside over the state executive committee's meetings, call the state convention to order, handle the requests of statewide candidates on the ballot, and certify the election runoff primary winners to the state convention.

The 64-member state executive committee has a chair and a vice chair of the opposite sex. In addition, the Democratic and Republican state convention delegates choose one man and one woman from each of the 31 state senate districts. The main legal duties of the state executive committee are to determine the site of the next state convention—sometimes a crucial factor in determining whose loyal supporters can attend, since the party does not pay delegates' expenses—canvass statewide primary returns, and certify the nomination of party candidates.

The state executive committee also has some political duties, including producing and disseminating press releases and other publicity, encouraging organizational work in precincts and counties, raising money, and coordinating special projects. The state committee may work closely with the national party. These political chores are so numerous that the executive committees of both parties now employ full-time executive directors and staff assistants.

A New Era of Republican Dominance

Even with a national political climate that led to Democratic Party control of both houses of Congress and the presidency in 2006 and 2008, the Republican Party continues its dominance in Texas state politics (see Figure 4.4). Republicans hold 77 of the 150 seats in the Texas House and 19 of the 31 seats in the Texas Senate. In 1978, the GOP held just 92 elected offices in Texas. Today, the total is more than 2,000. Clearly, the old pattern of Texans voting Republican at the top of the ticket and Democratic at the bottom of the ticket is no longer true.

Most observers now agree that Texas has experienced **party realignment**, the transition from one stable party system to another. After more than a century of Democratic Party domination after the Civil War, the pendulum has swung to the Republican Party. Realignment involves more than just casting a vote for a Republican Party candidate; it refers to a shift in **partisan identification**. Evidence that Texas is becoming a two-party or even a Republican-dominated state comes from public opinion polls that show that more Texans are identifying with the Republican Party than in the past. As Table 4.3 indicates, in 1952, an overwhelming percentage of Texans who identified with a political party were Democrats. Fifty years later, polls show that identification with the Republican Party now exceeds that of the Democratic Party.

There are several reasons for the rise of Republican Party dominance in Texas. The first is the shift among existing voters as conservative middle- and upper-class white Democrats slowly but surely switch their allegiance to the Republican Party. After years of voting Republican in presidential elections but identifying themselves as Democrats, these conservatives began thinking of themselves as Republicans. Many white voters defected to the Republican Party because they were alienated by the national Democratic Party's emphasis on civil rights in the 1960s and 1970s. The existence of popular and powerful Democratic leaders from Texas such as President Lyndon B. Johnson (1963–1968) may have slowed the transition briefly but could not stop it.

This shift in partisan identification was also spurred, in part, by the election of an extremely popular Republican president. Ronald Reagan, elected in 1980 and reelected in 1984, combined clear conservative positions with a charismatic personality that attracted

Party realignment

The transition from one dominant-party system to another. In Texas politics, it refers to the rise and possible dominance of the Republican party in recent years.

Partisan identification

A person's attachment to one political party or the other.

HOW DOES TEXAS COMPARE?
PARTY COMPETITION

Research in political science has shown that states with higher levels of party competition for control of government tend to spend more on social programs and have higher levels of voter turnout. Although all 50 states have some competition between the two parties, some states are much more competitive than others. The map below indicates states in which the Democratic or Republican parties are dominant and states that are more evenly matched; it emphasizes voting patterns in state elections and does not necessarily reflect familiar electoral college maps for presidential elections.

Figure 4.4

Party Competition in the 50 States: How Texas Compares. The map illustrates the level of party competition in the American states.

Sources: Thomas M. Holbrook and Raymond J. La Raja, "Parties and Elections," in Virginia Gray and Russell L. Hanson (eds.), *Politics in the American States*, 9th ed. (Washington, DC: CQ Press, 2008). The authors recalculate a measure of interparty competition, the Ranney Index, developed by Austin Ranney, "Parties in State Politics," in Herbert Jacob and Kenneth Vines (eds.), *Parties in the American States*, 3rd ed. (Boston: Little, Brown, 1976).

Why does the lowest level of two-party competition occur in the South?

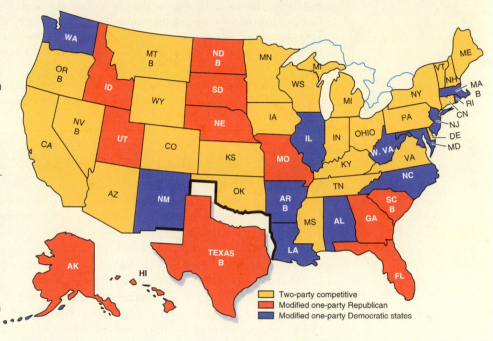

Legend:
- Two-party competitive
- Modified one-party Republican
- Modified one-party Democratic states

TABLE 4.3 PERCENTAGE OF VOTERS INDICATING A MAJOR PARTY

Year	Democrats	Republicans	Total
1952	66	6	72
1972	57	14	71
1990	34	30	64
2002	25	37	62
2008	35	36	71

Sources: Polls conducted by Belden Associates (1952 and 1972), Harte-Hanks Communications (1990), and American National Election Studies (2002), The University of Texas Austin/*Texas Tribune* Poll (2008).

The long term trend indicates fewer party identifiers in Texas. However, 2008 was an exception to this trend. Discuss why you think this occurred.

conservative Democrats into the Republican camp. The impact of Reagan's leadership was reinforced by the election of George W. Bush to the presidency in 2000 and 2004. Bush had been a very popular governor, and his election to the presidency helped solidify the Republican realignment in Texas.

Party switching by native Texans has not been the only cause of realignment. Another factor involves newcomers to the state. A majority of recent migrants to Texas from other states have been Republicans or independents. These newcomers, who came to Texas in large numbers in the 1970s and 1980s, have helped break down traditional partisan patterns.

Finally, long-term economic trends have provided opportunities for political change. Texas has slowly become an industrialized and urbanized state—a pattern that accelerated after the 1940s. Industrialization, urbanization, and the rise of an affluent middle class have created a new environment for many Texans, who have adopted a new party as part and parcel of their new lives. In some parts of the country, urbanization and affluence have been associated with support for the Democratic Party, but in Texas these phenomena may have benefited the Republicans.

CAN THE DEMOCRATS STILL BE COMPETITIVE?

Some observers believe that Texas will emerge as a competitive two-party state. They note that Democrats still have considerable resources in many local governments, especially in some central cities and South and Southwest Texas. For example, in 2006, Democrats swept every contested countywide race in Dallas county. Democrats also seem poised to make significant inroads in Houston. In 2006, they won back six legislative seats to bring them much closer in number to Republicans in the Texas House of Representatives.

Democratic strategists are also encouraged by the state's growing population of ethnic minorities, particularly Latinos. These voters tend to support Democratic candidates. In spring 2008, many Latinos and African Americans were energized by the race for the Democratic presidential nominee, and turned out in record numbers. Ethnic minorities now make up a majority of the state's population. The growing number of Latinos could cause the phenomenon of **tipping**, that is, growing numbers of a demographically significant group cause significant changes in the electorate. If Latino voters' energy and commitment to politics continues, a significant Democratic resurgence would probably occur.

DEALIGNMENT

There is some speculation that what is occurring in Texas is not realignment but **dealignment**, meaning that the voters are refusing to identify with either political party and are more inclined to call themselves "independents." Table 4.3 shows a realignment occurring as the number of Democrats decreased and the number of Republican identifiers increased. But there is also evidence for dealignment as the number of independent voters increased in the 1990s. Dealignment comes from evaluating the percentage of **ticket splitters**, who are willing to vote for candidates of both parties in the general election, and straight-ticket voters. Increased numbers of ticket splitters indicates that dealignment is occurring. In 2008, perhaps in part because of the hotly contested presidential election between Barack Obama and John McCain, party identification increases. These figures could indicate that although some voters are becoming more independent, others are closely identifying with one party or the other.

Tipping

A phenomenon that occurs when a group that is becoming more numerous over time grows large enough to change the political balance in a district, state, or county.

Dealignment

The situation that arises when large numbers of voters refuse to identify with either of the two parties and become increasingly independent of party affiliation.

Ticket splitters

People who vote for candidates of more than one party in a given election.

CHAPTER SUMMARY

★ Despite the hostility of the founders, political parties have become an important part of American political life. Parties perform critically important functions in a democracy. They nominate and elect their members to public office, educate and mobilize voters, and provide them with cues on how to vote and run the government at whatever level (local, state, or national) they are active.

★ In discussing political parties in the United States, we must look at three fundamental characteristics: (1) pragmatism, (2) decentralization, and (3) the effects of the two-party system. Pragmatism follows from the major goal of American parties, which is to build majority coalitions and win elections. This means that both Republican and Democratic party candidates are sometimes fuzzy on issues. Recently, however, American parties (including those in Texas) have become more programmatic. That is, Democrats and Republicans have become easier to distinguish.

★ Parties are relatively decentralized, with much of the control of the nominating process (the primary) and party machinery in the hands of state and local voters and their leaders. In the recent past, however, both the Democratic and Republican national party organizations have increased their control over state and local parties because of their capacity to raise large amounts of money and provide various services.

★ For much of its history, Texas was a one-party Democratic state. Until recently, one-party dominance meant that the election to select the Democratic Party's nominees—the

Democratic primary—was the most important election in Texas. Moderate and conservative factions within the Democratic Party became the key political players.

★ After years of domination by the Democratic Party, Texas began to experience a strong two-party competition. As a result, both parties strengthened their party machinery and made aggressive appeals to their traditional constituencies. By the late 1990s, the Republicans had become the dominant party in Texas. The transition from a party system in which the Democrats were overwhelmingly dominant to a new system in which the Republicans have a clear edge can be described as a political realignment. After the 1960s, the Republicans slowly but surely gained strength at the state level. In 1978, they gained the governorship. By 2002, they controlled both chambers of the state legislature, and in 2004 captured a majority in the state's congressional delegation. The Republicans will no doubt remain dominant in the near future.

★ Republicans have attracted voters in the expanding suburban areas of the state and have increased their appeal to white voters in rural areas. Democrats have attracted votes in inner cities and among ethnic minorities. The state's increasing ethnic diversity could thus augur well for the Democratic Party in the long run.

★ A second political mechanism that may be at work, in addition to realignment, is political dealignment. In this process, voters become detached from both political parties and begin to see themselves as independents.

HOW TEXAS COMPARES

★ Although Texas has a unique and colorful political history, its broad outlines parallel the pattern of other southern states. As in many other southern states, conservatives within the Democratic Party dominated state politics between the Reconstruction era and the 1960s. And like many other southern states, Texas underwent a general partisan realignment toward the Republican Party during the latter part of the 20th century.

★ Today, Texas has become one of the most reliably conservative Republican states in the nation in both state and national elections. In fact, Texas's loyalty to the Republican Party stands out as unique among the largest states. In recent presidential elections, such large diverse states as New York, Illinois, Ohio, Pennsylvania, Michigan, and Florida have been "swing states" in which the Democrats and Republicans are competitive.

Among the most populated states, only Texas has consistently supported the Republican nominee in all of the last eight presidential elections.

★ While Texas's historic and current politics reflect political dynamics similar to other southern states, its future is likely to follow the patterns of the southwestern states along the Mexican border. Like California, New Mexico, Arizona, and Nevada, Texas has a large and increasing Latino population. Already, Texas has the second largest Latino population among the 50 states, and Texas Latinos are projected to become the majority within the next 20 years. This growing minority has given heavy support to the Democratic Party in most states (except Florida), and it has the potential to change the future direction of politics in Texas and many other states as well.

KEY TERMS

conservative
dealignment
decentralization
evangelical (fundamentalist)
    Christians

grassroots
liberal
partisan identification
party platform
party realignment

pragmatism
precinct convention
presidential preference
    primary
primary

single-member district system
swing voters
ticket splitters
tipping
two-party system

REVIEW QUESTIONS

1. Explain why the Democratic Party dominated Texas politics until the 1970s.

2. Discuss what it means to be a conservative or a liberal.

3. Describe the development of conservative and liberal factions within the Democratic Party and later within the Republican party.

4. Discuss the reasons for and describe the events that led to the rise of the Republican Party in Texas.

5. Define *realignment*. Analyze to what extent realignment has occurred in Texas politics. Has Texas become a state that is dominated by the Republican Party, or is competition between the parties to be the norm in the future?

LOGGING ON

The two major political parties have websites both in Texas and nationally:

Democrats in Texas at **http://www.txdemocrats.org**

Democrats nationally at **http://www.democrats.org**

Republicans in Texas at **http://www.texasgop.org**

Republicans nationally at **http://www.rnc.org**

The website for the Texas Ethics Commission has information about campaign finance, forms to be filed for office seekers, and reports on expenditures of the two political parties. Visit it at **http://www.ethics.state.tx.us/index.html**

Who Killed the Texas Yellow Dog Democrat?

Robert Glen Findley
Odessa College

INTRODUCTION

This article highlights the dramatic party realignment that has reshaped the Texas political landscape. It traces the life cycle of the legendary "Yellow Dog" Democrat from birth, through a vigorous life, and finally death and reincarnation as a modern day Republican or "Blue Dog" Democrat.

In 1995, then agriculture commissioner (now governor) of Texas, Rick Perry pronounced the Yellow Dog Democrats in Texas dead. If they were indeed dead, how did they die? And who were they?

THE BIRTH OF TEXAS'S YELLOW DOG

"I'd vote for a yellow dog if he ran on the Democratic ticket." This line became popular during the 1928 presidential election between Republican candidate Herbert Clark Hoover, originally from Iowa, and Democratic candidate Alfred Emanuel Smith of New York. It indicated fierce loyalty to the Democratic Party, especially among southern Democrats despite the fact that Smith was not only a New York native, but also a Catholic who opposed Prohibition. However, Hoover carried Texas in the 1928 election, so a better story about Yellow Dog Democrats in Texas might be told regarding one of Lyndon Johnson's congressional campaigns. While courting a potential voter, Johnson was said to have proclaimed, "You're a Democrat, I'm a Democrat, why, hell, even that old yellow dog over there is a Democrat." Although the story is unverifiable, it is certainly more colorful and, quite possibly, more descriptive of one-party (yellow dog) rule in Texas.

The Texas Yellow Dog Democrat grew out of the period immediately after the Civil War historically known as the Reconstruction. Although the impact of Reconstruction on Texas was not that severe when compared with the rest of the Confederacy, for many old-line Texans, it was a world turned upside down. Union troops occupied the state, Union loyalist and Republican Edmund Jackson Davis was governor and, as per the Fourteenth and Fifteenth Amendments to the U.S. Constitution, the freedmen could now vote . . . and they voted Republican. On the other hand, many Texans who had served as Confederate officials were forbidden from voting by virtue of having served in the Confederacy. Once Congress passed a general amnesty law in 1872, allowing almost all of the former Confederates to vote, it became the duty of many of these "unreconstructed" Texans to try and reestablish the antebellum social order as closely as possible. This meant voting "early and often" while preventing certain groups (blacks, scalawags, and white Republicans from the North) from participating in the political process. This meant voting Democratic. With the election of former secessionist Richard Coke as governor of the state in 1873, the Democratic Party took hold of politics in Texas with a grip that it would not relinquish for a century.

THE YELLOW DOG BEGINS TO STUMBLE

Yet, the grip *was* broken. What happened? What led Rick Perry to pronounce the Yellow Dogs dead? In a one-party state, political competition is between factions rather than parties. This competition was the closest thing that Texas had to a two-party system. The Democratic Party in Texas was made up of a liberal wing and a moderate-to-conservative wing with the moderates in control of the majority of the time. However, one can begin to see the grip weakening as early as 1940, when Vice President John Nance "Cactus-Jack" Garner of Uvalde broke with President Franklin D. Roosevelt (FDR) by choosing not to run with or endorse FDR's unprecedented attempt for a third term in the White House. Garner, and many Texas Democrats were also disillusioned with many of the New Deal programs and what was seen as FDR's coziness with northern labor unions and African Americans. However, Garner did consult with and support the Democratic Party until his death in 1967.

As the state moved into the 1950s, the discontent that many Texas Democrats had with FDR, the New Deal, and the party's shift to the left at the national level began to make its presence felt. After Governor Beauford Jester died of a heart attack in 1949, 41-year-old Allan Shivers became the governor of Texas. He moved quickly to purge the party leadership of "liberals" and then proceeded to endorse the Republican nominee for president in 1952, Dwight David Eisenhower. Although Eisenhower was indeed born in Texas, he was hardly a native. His family had moved to Kansas shortly after his birth, and he had spent most of his adult life in the U.S. Army and the military outposts to which he was assigned. Nonetheless, this did not stop Shivers from supporting Eisenhower in his bid for the presidency with the slogan, "Texans for a Texan" and giving those Texas Democrats that supported the GOP at the national level a nickname, "Shivercrats." Although many conservative Texas Democrats were concerned with the sitting president's (Truman) stand on civil rights and what seemed to be a no-win war in Korea, it was Truman's veto (twice) of congressional legislation reaffirming the state's claim to the coastal tidelands that would alienate them. The state of Texas argued that control of these underwater seabeds extended 10.5 miles from the shoreline while the federal government argued that anything beyond a 3-mile limit belonged to the nation. This dispute became even more critical when it was determined that these tidelands held rich deposits of oil and gas. When the Democratic nominee for president in 1952, Adlai Stevenson, refused to support the state's tidelands claim, the Yellow Dogs became Shivercrats . . . at least, for the time being . . . though the Democrats carried all of the statewide races in 1952 and 1956.

The 1960s produced a Texas Democratic president and a first for Republicans in Texas as well as the South. Lyndon Johnson actively campaigned for the Democratic presidential slot in 1960. However, he was defeated at the Democratic National Convention on the first ballot by John F. Kennedy of Massachusetts. Nonetheless, much to the surprise of many and to the chagrin of others, he accepted an offer to run on the Kennedy ticket as the vice presidential nominee while also running for reelection to the U.S. Senate.

In 1959, Johnson convinced the Texas legislature to move the primary date so that he could campaign for both offices. This did not sit well with either liberals or conservatives. It did, however, create a possibility for Republicans in Texas. John Tower, an economics instructor at Midwestern University in Wichita Falls, had run a vigorous campaign against Johnson for the senate seat. Even though Johnson won reelection, his election as vice president superseded that and opened the door for a nonpartisan special election to replace him. The 1961 special election to replace Johnson in the U.S. Senate was entered by more than 60 candidates. Tower emerged as victor in a runoff election between himself and conservative Democrat William Blakley. Many liberal Democrats either voted for Tower in this particular election or "went fishing" (meaning they stayed home and/or did not vote) in an effort to rid the party of conservatives. The Yellow Dog was beginning to suffer from an identity crisis.

The election of Tower to the U.S. Senate was significant for a number of reasons: (1) he was the first Republican to win a statewide election in Texas since Reconstruction, and (2) he was the first Republican from the Old Confederacy to win a popular election since Reconstruction. His coattails did not go down very far in 1961, but his victory (followed by three additional terms in the U.S. Senate) did provide Texas Republicans with visibility and credibility. It is also important to note that as Democratic liberals in Texas tried to purge the party of conservatives, many of those conservatives began to see the Republican Party as a viable option.

THE YELLOW DOG SHOWS SIGNS OF RECOVERY

However, the Republicans in Texas did suffer a temporary setback with the Kennedy assassination. Not only did Kennedy's death propel Johnson into the White House (and to election in his own right in 1964), it also took place in Dallas. Dallas was the most Republican city in Texas at the time, but it was also home to many members of the John Birch Society, the red-baiting (anticommunist) radio program Life Line, and Lee Harvey Oswald's first target, ultraconservative General Edwin Walker. Dallas and Texas Republicans were perceived nationally as racists and right-wing extremists. With Johnson in the White House and John Connally as governor, the Democratic Party in Texas appeared as the epitome of unity, albeit temporary.

A SICK PUPPY

The 1970s presented a number of problems. Among them were the collapse of the American effort in Vietnam (severely tainting Johnson's presidency and contributing to his decision not to seek another term), the Watergate scandal and, notably for Texas, the Sharpstown banking scandal. However, the decade began well for the Yellow Dogs as the conservatives seemed to regain control of the party with the election of Preston Smith as governor and Lloyd Bentsen, Jr. to the U.S. Senate. However, this began to quickly unravel with the breaking of the story of the Sharpstown scandal by the left/liberal *Texas Observer* (founded in 1954 in response, to a large extent, to the emergence of Shivercrats). The scandal, which involved bribes in the form of stock to a number of Texas legislators and the governor in an effort to get legislation passed that favored Sharp's bank, really shook the foundations of the Democratic Party and subsequently, the Yellow Dogs. The scandal tainted a number of Democratic leaders both directly and indirectly as in the case of Lt. Governor Ben Barnes, an heir apparent to the Johnson/Connally crown. The impact of the scandal was felt in the 1972 elections as a significant number of incumbents, were not reelected. Uvalde rancher Dolph Briscoe won the Democratic primary and the general election, but just barely (by about 100,000 votes). The scandal decimated the Democratic ranks and continued the shift to the GOP.

The elections of 1978 witnessed one of the biggest upsets in Texas's political history. Briscoe had decided to run for a third term as governor, but was defeated in the Democratic primary by moderately liberal John Hill, who had been serving as the state's attorney general. The Republicans nominated Dallas oilman William Clements. To everyone's surprise, Clements won the election. Conservative Democrats voted for Clements rather than John Hill giving Clements the distinction of being the first Republican elected to the governor's office since 1869. Was this the beginning of a permanent place for the GOP in Texas or would Clements simply be a footnote in Texas's political history? Subsequent elections seemed to indicate the former as Texas appeared to be maturing into a two-party state with the election of Democrat Mark White in 1982, the reelection of Clements in 1986, and the election of Ann Richards (Democrat [D]) in 1990. However, while the elections seemed to indicate the permanent presence of the Republican Party in Texas, it now appears that what the state witnessed was a change in party label rather than a change in ideology.

The 1994 gubernatorial election indicated that the end was near for the Yellow Dogs, at least as Democrats. Richards, a very popular governor, ran for reelection against upstart George W. Bush and lost. Many argue that she ran a very poor campaign, and that may be true, but if one examines the voting patterns, it becomes obvious that the Yellow Dogs were changing labels. Nowhere was this more obvious than in the counties of East Texas, the last stronghold of the Old Confederacy and the Yellow Dogs. In 1994, Bush, with the help of his campaign manager Karl Rove, managed to carry five East Texas counties that had never voted Republican in a governor's race. In 1998, he carried all of the counties in East Texas. As now Governor Perry has said, the Yellow Dogs may be dead. However, closer examination seems to indicate that they are not dead, but have just simply changed colors. Depending on one's perspective, they are now either known as Blue Dog Democrats or, better yet, Yellow Pup Republicans.

JOIN THE DEBATE

1. After Ronald Reagan left the Democratic Party and became a Republican, he once said "I didn't leave the Democratic Party. The party left me." Would Reagan's sentiments accurately reflect Texas's changing political dynamics? Do you agree that Texans' fundamentally conservative political philosophy has not changed, but that the Republican Party now better represents that philosophy?

2. Democratic Vice President Lyndon Johnson urged President John F. Kennedy to support federal civil rights legislation, but warned "we might lose the South" as a result. How much does the success of Texas political parties depend on their opposition to federal civil rights legislation?

3. Which party positions best explain why Texans have gravitated toward the Republican Party in modern times? Can population changes, such as Republicans migrating from other states, help explain Texans' recent affinity for the GOP? Was the historical shift to the Republican Party in Texas inevitable? Or, are there strategies that the Texas Democrats can employ to keep the support of "Blue Dog" conservative Democrats or attract the support of "Yellow Pup" moderate Republicans?

Presidential Primaries or Caucuses? Texas's Choices and the Outcomes

Lynn Salas
El Paso Community College

INTRODUCTION

In Texas, presidential preference primaries are the way in which political parties choose most of their delegates to the national conventions and nominate their presidential candidate. In other states, most notably Iowa, caucuses are the preferred mode of delegate selection and candidate nomination. The following is a look at the essential differences between Texas's primaries and Iowa's caucuses. Voter registration restrictions, voter participation, and state influence in the presidential nomination process are just a few of the issues that help to contrast these two ways of choosing the nominee for president.

Essential to the nominating process for presidential candidates in a presidential election year are the primary and caucus elections. Presidential nominees from the two major parties who can run in the November general election must gain a majority of national convention delegate votes to receive their party's nomination. Many months before the national convention, primary voters are asked to choose their favorite candidate within their party by a popular vote. Caucus-goers are asked to participate in open meetings and choose their candidate by a raised-hand vote or an acclamation vote. Either way, the process of all 50 states completing their primaries and caucuses is a long and arduous trek for any potential participant.

DELEGATE SELECTION PROCESS

The excitement of the delegate selection process begins well before the summer scheduled national conventions. Initially, Iowa begins the season in January with the state's caucus meetings, leading off the next three months of primaries and caucuses where all 50 states engage in the frenzy known as the primary/caucus season. At the end of the process, each state's political parties have chosen its delegates, either through the primary vote or the caucus conventions, to the national convention.

Delegates to the Republican and Democratic national conventions are charged with the duty of selecting their party's nominee for president. For both parties, the delegate selection process always revolves around a combination of delegates that are committed to one particular candidate, other delegates that are uncommitted, and still others known as "superdelegates." The latter are elected officials, party officers, and others who are automatically made delegates because of their positions, and who are free to vote for any candidate.[1] For the Democratic Party, only a portion of the national convention delegates are selected in the state primaries and caucuses because a significant number of "superdelegates" are also seated at their national convention. The Republican Party chooses almost all of its convention delegates in the primaries and caucuses.

In most presidential election years, the choice of the nominee is all but officially decided before the national convention takes place. In 2004, John Kerry (D) and George W. Bush (R), had already gained enough delegates in the primary/caucus season to clinch their respective party's nominations before the end of the summer conventions. However, the nomination process is rarely as clear-cut as 2004. In 2008, the voting public was faced with a plethora of candidates from both parties since George W. Bush had met his two-term limit as president. With both parties needing a first-time nominee, no candidate had a popular vote mandate until toward the end of the primary/caucus season. Texas played a major role because it was among the last of the large states to hold a primary.

TIMING TEXAS PRIMARIES

The complexity and high cost of running a primary race in the state has lawmakers in a quandary of trying to figure out how to stay abreast of scheduling changes on the national scene, while maintaining a balance of the "open/closed" type of primary that Texans enjoy.[2] But, in early 2008, Texans missed out on the Super Tuesday primary because lawmakers had a difficult time trying to figure out how to work with the restriction of voter registration and state campaign laws for candidates.

The controversy over whether Texas should join the 24 other states holding primaries and caucuses on Super Tuesday had its origins in the fact that Texas helped to create Super Tuesday more than 20 years ago. It was dubbed the first Super Tuesday on March 9, 1988, and included Alabama, Arkansas, Florida, Georgia, Louisiana, Mississippi, North Carolina, Kentucky, Oklahoma, Tennessee, Maryland, Virginia, and Texas.[3,4] Interestingly, most of those states which are credited with creating the original

Super Tuesday schedule were now either in front of Texas or a part of the new 2008 Super Tuesday of February 5, a full four weeks before the Texas primary date of March 4.

Attempting to avoid being an afterthought in the presidential primary season, Texas lawmakers introduced HB 2017 and SB 1843 in the 2007 legislative session, which, if passed, would have moved the state's primary to February 5. Although the House bill passed, the Senate version died in committee. Objections included problems created by the holiday season (which could have delayed campaign starts for challengers), delayed filing dates, and the possibility that voter registration cards would not reach new registrants in time.[5]

In 2000, when George W. Bush won the Republican nomination, Texas's primaries came one week behind Super Tuesday. Thus the Texas GOP was only able to add its delegates to the already burgeoning delegate pool for Bush. Many Texans were disappointed that Texas primary voters were not decisively included in the choosing of their native son early in the season. And, in 2008, states seemed to be leapfrogging one another to be *the state* whose primaries or caucuses got the most notoriety, challenging the dominance of Iowa and New Hampshire. States like Wisconsin, Florida, and Michigan even risked being barred from voting at the national conventions for holding their primaries or caucuses earlier than the national party rules dictated.

THE CASE FOR AND AGAINST PRESIDENTIAL PRIMARIES

Voting is the most basic form of political participation, and voting in primary elections gives voters direct influence in choosing party nominees. However, restrictions in voting temper this participation. Voter registration laws in the last half-century have stripped many early restrictions and made suffrage wide open for minorities, women, and younger Americans. Although in Texas, any 18-year-old citizen can register to vote, early registration requirements continue to cause problems when an individual is late in becoming interested in voting, learns late about the process, or just does not know the rules and has not registered to vote in time for a primary or general election. The Texas deadline to register and be eligible to vote in any primary or other election is a full four weeks before the election. An individual who has moved may show up to a new polling place and be told that his or her name is not on that particular list. Moreover, many potential voters do not know that they are not registered.[6] Once those rules and restrictions are navigated, then potential voters are asked to remember registration deadlines, wade through the confusion over the differences between primaries and general elections, nonpartisan elections, special elections, and the myriad other elections held throughout any given year.

Most of each party's delegates are chosen by presidential primary in Texas. On the day of the Texas primary, voters are asked to go to their precinct and cast their vote for their favorite Democratic or Republican nominee. This popular vote begins the choosing of

[1]Texas Democratic Party, http://www.txdemocrats.org/ (Article 7 of the Party Rules); Texas Republican Party, http://www.texasgop.org/ (Rule No. 23A).

[2]Texas Politics: Voting, Campaigns and Elections, 2006, Liberal Arts Instructional Technology Services, The University of Texas at Austin, http://texaspolitics. laits.utexas.edu

[3]Time Magazine, "Will Super Tuesday Rope in Texas?" Tuesday, March 27, 2007, http://www.time.com/time/nation/article/0,8599,1603730,00.html

[4]Online Newshour, "The First Super Tuesday," March 9, 1988, http://www.pbs.org/newshour/retro/super_tuesday_88.html

[5]Eric M. Appleman. Democracy in Action: P2008, 2005, 2006, 2007, http://www.gwu.edu/~action/2008/chrnothp08.html

[6]The Texas Secretary of State: Frequently Asked Questions, at http://www.sos.state.tx.us/elections/pamphlets/faqs.shtml

convention delegates and the state's preferred presidential nominee. By the time of the primary vote in Texas, the candidates running in local partisan races have had a full eight weeks to run their campaigns. There has also been two full weeks of early voting and, as mentioned above, voter registration has to be completed at least four weeks prior to the primary election date.[7]

Texas primaries are a combination of an "open/closed" primary system. It is "open" because each voter may decide which party's primary to participate in on election day; it is "closed" because Texas says that once the voter has chosen to vote in one party's primary, that voter cannot later participate in conventions or runoffs for another party. Voters choose which party to vote in on the day of the primary.

Early voting booths have to be opened daily at 7:00 A.M. and closed at 7:00 P.M. Roving voting machines make the rounds throughout cities at community centers, malls, and other high-traffic areas. By the time the actual day hits, the candidates have spent millions of dollars in campaign funds, and the state has spent millions more.

On the evening of the primary popular vote, voters who voted that day are then asked to show up to a precinct convention to begin the convention season that will ultimately end in a presidential nominee for the party.

THE CASE FOR AND AGAINST CAUCUSES

Iowa, which calls itself "The First in the Nation," has set the standard in the caucus nomination processes. Its extensive nomination process is collectively called the caucus system. Promptly at 7:00 P.M. on January 3, 2008, 1,784 precincts' caucus participants met in homes, schools, community centers, or other places around the state. At the caucus meeting, the parties began their process of selecting delegates to their county, state, and national elections.

Iowa requires citizens to register to vote at least 10 days before a statewide or primary election. Iowa even provides a calendar on the Secretary of State's website to inform its voters and potential voters when to register. Iowa spends state money on education campaigns to inform its citizens of the caucus process. Speakers' bureaus, newspaper and TV advertising, and Internet sites are just a few of the ways that the state gets the message out. Caucus goers also choose down-ticket races the same evening by signing petitions for the candidates they support. The candidates who receive the most petition signatures in each race face the opposing party's candidate in the November election.[8]

Although the Iowa caucuses are more than a century old, Iowa has boasted a tremendous increase in citizen participation in the caucus process since its evolution began in 1972, when it moved its date up from April to January. Many caucus participants will have met the candidates in person and spoken to them directly about issues they consider important. And, since 1972, no candidate who has finished worse than third in Iowa has gone on to win a major party presidential nomination.[9]

Limitations to participating in the Iowa caucus include the restriction that the participants be registered in the party in which they wish to caucus. However, this requirement is not overly burdensome because voters may change their party registration at the caucus site when they show up to participate. Another restriction is that caucus goers do not get to directly choose their national delegates. Instead they choose delegates to county conventions, which in turn send delegates to district, state, and finally national conventions. However, the registration limitation imposed on Texas primary voters is eliminated by allowing Iowa's registered voters who show up on the caucus evening to register in the party of their choice just before the caucus begins.

CONCLUSION

Which is best, primaries or caucuses? On the face of it, caucuses seem to run more smoothly and quickly, allow for faster results, and involve more direct input from citizens. As Iowa caucuses consistently show, participants are more involved, interested, and informed. Participation is portrayed as fun and interesting with exciting outcomes. At first glance, changing from a primary state to a caucus state may seem like the way to go to make the Texas delegate selection process more flexible and responsive to the changing national election climate. Caucuses are much less expensive than primaries because there is no need for early voting and no paid poll workers. Voter registration laws tend to be more relaxed, voters can be allowed to register later in the process, and voters can make last minute decisions to become involved in the process.

Perhaps the most compelling case for caucuses is that they are easier to schedule than primary elections. When Iowa was confronted with the possibility of other states leapfrogging in 2008, the Iowa legislature simply moved the date for its caucuses from January 19 to January 4. It proved to be a decisive move, because it began the landslide of states moving up their primaries and caucuses. This, in turn, caused Super Tuesday in 2008 to be almost a month earlier than in 2004.

However, there are also advantages to primary elections. Simply walking into a polling place, touching a computer screen, and walking out, is personal, simple, and private. There are no complicated formulas to remember. In Iowa, the only way for voters to express their preference for presidential nominees is to attend their precinct caucuses to cast their votes. For the elderly, sick, single mothers, and others who may not be able to make it on the *one night* of the caucus, early voting, the roving voting booths, mail-in ballots, and all of the other methods of easy access make primaries seem like the best remedy.

And, Texas's strategy of holding on to the late primary date in 2008 paid off. Along with a few other large states, Texas played a significant role in the national Democratic Party's nomination contest. Nevertheless, voter restrictions and costly campaigns are still the bane of legislators who want to make Texas a viable player in the presidential nomination process.

Ultimately, the job of selecting the presidential nominee is a party decision. The delegates, selected either through the primary or caucus method, end up at the national convention, where the front-runners make their final case to be selected as the nominee.

[7]Texas Secretary of State: Elections Division, at http://www.sos.state.tx.us/elections/

[8]Iowa Secretary of State: Guide to Registered Voters, at http://www.sos.state.ia.us/pdfs/elections/GuidRegVoters.pdf

[9]University of Iowa: Election 2008, 2007, at http://www.uiowa.edu/election/history/index.html

So whether Texas keeps its current system or changes its voter registration laws or becomes a caucus state or has a combination of laws and voting requirements that ease the current restrictions, involving voters in party affairs is the only way of participating in the selection of the presidential nominee.

JOIN THE DEBATE

1. Which are better: primaries or caucuses? What are the advantages of primaries? What are the advantages of caucuses?

2. Are voter registration laws too restrictive? How would Texas benefit from more relaxed voting laws? What are the dangers of relaxing voter registration laws?

3. Should Texas replace its presidential primaries with caucuses to select all of its delegates to national party conventions? Besides monetary cost savings, what are the advantages that could be gained from Texas becoming a caucus state? Which groups in the electorate might be at a disadvantage if caucuses were instituted?

Chapter 5

Interest Groups

CONTENTS

LEARNING OBJECTIVES

- ★ Explain the role of the First Amendment in protecting the rights of interest groups.
- ★ Define *interest group.*
- ★ Know the difference between types of interest groups.
- ★ Describe what lobbyists must report as well as what they do not report.
- ★ Describe the work of lobbyists.
- ★ Know the different actors that lobbyists attempt to influence.
- ★ Differentiate between iron triangles and issue networks.

★ GET ACTIVE ★

Go to the Texas Ethics Commission's website to discover which people, corporations, labor unions, and nonprofit organizations are lobbying Texas state government. The address is **http://www.ethics.state.tx.us**

For a good discussion of how to lobby, go to the Texas State Teachers Association website at **http://www.tsta.org/**. Click on *Legislative,* then click on *Guide to Lobbying.*

Identify a state or local interest group related to your career or professional ambitions. Research this group—an easy way to start is to type the name of the group into a search engine such as Yahoo! or Google—and identify the officers, membership dues, size of membership, issues being promoted, and name and frequency of any publications. To go further, consult the Texas Ethics

Commission's reports on campaign contributions or lobbyists at **http://www.ethics.state .tx.us** to see how active the group is in Texas.

Other sites of interest include those of the Texas House and Senate: **http://www.house .state.tx.us** and **http://www.senate.state .tx.us**. Identify your state representative and senator and explore his or her background.

Using a search engine such as Yahoo! or Google, type in the name of a major corporation, a labor union, a professional organization, a nonprofit organization, or a public interest group. See what public policy issues each is promoting in Texas and in the nation.

You can find out which lobbies are giving the most money to politicians at **http://www .tpj.org/reports/Austin soldest06/clients .html**

When visiting Austin, it is impossible to overlook the number of buildings that are headquarters for countless trade associations, lobbying firms, and other interest groups. These groups are in Austin to defend the interests of the members of their organizations. They will appear before members of the legislature, governor's office, or some of the countless government agencies that have jurisdiction over the interests they exist to protect. These interest groups are so prevalent in Austin because Texas is a powerful political and economic actor determining "who gets what, when, how."[1] The state of Texas is important to policy making for several reasons. Texas has a large number of resources, and interest groups would like to have access to a small portion of those resources. Texas also has one of the most diverse populations in the country, and this diversity produces a diversity of special needs and interests. Because of its size, Texas is an important policy-making actor that can create public policy that impacts the rest of the country. As goes Texas, so goes the country.

The state of Texas has one of the most productive economies in the world. Texas has an annual gross state product worth more than 1.2 trillion dollars.[2] The state's budget exceeds 182 billion dollars.[3] Special interest groups that depend on government spending lobby policy makers for a piece of the government largess. Book publishers that want public schools to adopt their books can lobby the Texas Education Agency. Road construction companies can

---

[1]Harold Lasswell first defined politics as who gets what, when, and how. See Harold D. Lasswell, *Politics: Who Gets What, When and How* (New York: Whittlesey House, 1936).

[2]Texas Comptroller of Public Accounts, *Gross State Product and Income,* 2009, http://www.texasahead.org/ economy/indicators/ecoind/ecoind5.html#product

[3]Legislative Budget Board, *2010: Texas Fact Book,* p. 37 at *http://www.lbb.state.tx.us/Fact_Book/Texas_Fact-Book_2010.pdf*

HOW DOES TEXAS COMPARE?
STATES WITH TOP GROSS DOMESTIC PRODUCT IN 2008

Despite the recent economic downturn, Texas has one of the most productive economies in the country. In 2008, the value of Texas's gross domestic product exceeded that of every other state except for California. Although much of its success can be attributed to recent energy prices, Texas has a very productive economy because it has a productive workforce. Having a large and productive workforce contributes greatly to the state's gross domestic product. States with large economies, like the one that Texas has, attract interest groups attempting to either protect their market share or to gain a larger share.

STATES WITH TOP GROSS DOMESTIC PRODUCT IN 2008

State	GDP in Millions
California	1,846,757
Texas	1,223,511
New York	1,144,481
Florida	744,120

Source: Bureau of Economic Analysis: Regional Economic Accounts, *Gross Domestic Product by State*, 2008, http://www.bea.gov/regional/gdpmap/GDPMap.aspx

FOR DEBATE

Should we expect to see a decrease in the number of interest groups in Texas when the economy takes a turn for the worse? Why or why not?

ask the governor for support to increase spending on infrastructure projects. And universities can lobby the legislature for legislation deregulating tuition. Because the state spends so much money on the many public goods it provides, interest groups want to capitalize on these government expenditures. Many interest groups lobby the government to either spend more, or, if under threat from cutbacks, maintain current spending levels.

Although agriculture and energy make up a large sector of the Texas economy, the state has diversified its economy significantly since the mid-1980s. The state's population exceeds 24 million people and is growing fast, and the racial and ethnic makeup of the state is one of the most diverse in the country. The state attracts people from a variety of religious backgrounds, it has a highly dispersed age demographic, and Texas is becoming more tolerant of gay and lesbian populations. The state has both a large poor and middle-income population. Texas is diverse in a variety of ways, and this diversity brings with it a greater variety of special interest groups. Citizens with special interests organize around their concerns, **lobbying** the government for fair and equal treatment, for protections from more powerful groups, and for protection of liberties.

Some states have such huge markets that they are in a position to enact legislation that dictates to whole industries what and how it manufactures things. Texas is such a state. By setting requirements, the state can dictate to manufacturers what to produce. Manufacturers wanting to sell in Texas amend their products to meet the specifications set by the state. Smaller states, with a smaller purchasing power, would simply be ignored by manufacturers if they enacted regulations that dictated to manufacturers what they should produce and how they should produce those products. But large states like Texas, barring federal action, are in a position to have precisely such influence. The huge purchasing power of these states makes it difficult for manufacturers to ignore the policy created by these states. As a result, special interest groups will lobby Texas in one direction or another to try to get the state to either lead the rest of the country, or to preserve the status quo.

Lobbying

Direct contact between an interest group representative and an officer of government.

When citizens organize into interest groups, they increase their ability to protect the interests of the groups. The structure of our state government, like that of the federal government, encourages citizens to organize and petition the government. The structure of the government is such that it provides groups with many different avenues that can be followed to influence the government. Not only can special interest groups lobby the 150 members of the Texas House and 31 members of the Texas Senate, special interest groups can petition members of the Texas executive branch, the thousands of executive branch appointees and bureaucrats. Special interest groups can bring lawsuits before the courts. Special interest groups can also influence the public, rallying their support. When citizens organize, they can influence policy by lobbying the government and the public to support their position.

Constitutional Guarantees

The constitutions of the United States and of the state of Texas guarantee citizens the right to political participation through voting, speaking, writing, and petitioning government "for redress of grievances." To peaceably assemble *for political expression* is likewise clearly encouraged. The Texas Constitution says it very well:

> The citizens shall have the right . . . to . . . apply to those invested with the powers of government for redress of grievances or other purposes, by petition, address or remonstrance. (Article 1, Section 27)

The First Amendment to the United States Constitution makes our liberty even more clear:

> Congress shall make no law . . . abridging the freedom of speech, or of the press; or the right of the people peaceably to assemble, and to petition government for redress of grievances. In these constitutional expressions, free speech, a free press, and the right to join together in political parties and interest groups are guaranteed.

These guarantees and the right to vote are essential to having a democracy, *but representative democracy also creates dangers*. The liberty that comes with representative democracy requires that citizens who care for state and community must sufficiently inform themselves about political issues and involve themselves in the choices to be made. Extreme behaviors in either direction—zealousness or apathy—can endanger democracy. Highly organized and active groups can threaten the well-being of the unorganized majority. The organized and zealous can be expected to triumph over the apathetic or unorganized. Hence small factions of the population at odds with the majority may control selected policy areas. Let us examine the role of interest groups in democracy and in Texas.

What Is an Interest Group?

Citizens may act alone to influence government, and millions do. When citizens join with others in an organizational structure designed to express their preferences to government, they act as an **interest group**. The media frequently speak of the interests of women, minorities, employers, Texans, and others, but interests must unite in a cooperative effort to promote some policy objective before they may be thought of as interest groups.

Interest groups are private entities. Interest groups are not governmental bodies, but they seek to influence government. They are not political parties because they do not nominate candidates for office. Interest groups seek to influence the outputs of government. They must work with members of both parties to secure their goals.

Interest group

An organization that expresses the policy desires of its members to officers and institutions of government; also known as a *pressure group*.

Lobbying is direct face-to-face contact between interest group representatives and public officials. ☜

What is the difference between an interest group and a political party?

Bob Daemmrich/The Image Works

In summary, interest groups are collections of citizens with shared interests who have organized to influence government decision makers. Interest groups are private institutions pursuing public policy goals on behalf of their members. Their interests are narrower than those of political parties. Unlike parties, they do not nominate candidates for office, but because the individual who holds office affects what government does, interest groups often endorse and support candidates favorable to their cause.

Pressure group

See *interest group*.

Interest groups are also called **pressure groups**. This second name derives from the fact that interest groups apply pressure on decision makers when seeking favorable policy outputs. Pressure is inherent in any situation in which one is asked to take a particular course of action and there are several choices. Pressure on officeholders also comes from their knowing the voting power of the group and the value of its endorsement, campaign contributions, and volunteer help in the next election. Groups employ **lobbyists** to express their values to public officials.

Lobbyist

In state law, a person who directly contacts public officials to influence their decisions. Registered lobbyists are paid to represent the interests of their employers.

What Do Interest Groups Do?

The primary goal of interest groups is to influence all branches of government at all levels to produce policies favorable to their members. They also seek to block policies that might be harmful to their members. Interest groups are instrumental in drawing *selected* citizens into political participation to influence public policies, most often in a way that encourages the promotion of narrow, selfish interests. Indeed, interest groups can be viewed either positively or negatively. Their critics focus on the harm that can result from powerful groups demanding that public policy reflect their values.

Private meetings with public officials present no opportunity for rebuttal. An illustration of this criticism came to light in January 2003. Texas Senator Jeff Wentworth, representing the 400-member law firm of Locke, Liddell, and Sapp, met with top officials of the Houston Community College System at a private luncheon to discuss a lobbying contract between the law firm and the community college. No public or media were invited. The discovery of this event raised questions about spending taxpayers' money to lobby and the apparent conflict of interest inherent when a state senator attempts to secure a lobbying contract for the law firm for which he works.[4]

Critics of the system of influence also worry about corruption and intimidation of public officials by what they call "special interests." The need for campaign contributions, they believe, makes elected officials especially vulnerable to pressure. The bottom line for critics is their concern that special interests will prevail over the desires of the general public. In the words of Professor Bob Stein, "Long before the legislature sits down and writes a bill, the lobbyists are there."[5]

Interest groups, however, have the ability to draw citizens into the political processes. Democracy calls for politically attentive and active citizens. From this perspective, interest groups educate their members about issues and mobilize them to participate in constitutionally

[4]Ron Nissimov, "HCCS Hires Firm after Closed Lunch," *Houston Chronicle*, January 3, 2003, p. A29.
[5]Quoted in Clay Robison, "Weak State Government Paved Way for Lobbyists," *Houston Chronicle*, December 29, 2002, p. A1.

TABLE 5 .1 POSITIVE AND NEGATIVE ASPECTS OF INTEREST GROUPS	
Positive	**Negative**
Increased political representation	Narrow interests
Political participation and mobilization	Secret communications with officials
Education of their members	Corruption or intimidation of public officials
Shared information and data	
Reduced cost to taxpayers	

approved ways. Simultaneously, interest groups inform and educate public officials. Table 5.1 summarizes the positive and negative views of interest groups.

Interest groups serve the purpose of providing policy makers with valuable information. This information is often provided in the form of testimony before committees. Because state law makes it a crime to share knowingly false information with state lawmakers,[6] most special interest groups are careful to provide truthful, albeit one-sided, information. The information provided by interest groups can be costly to gather both in terms of time and money. However, because interest groups provide the information free of cost, taxpayers are spared the expense.

The number and variety of interest groups also ensures that no one group will be dominant. States like Texas, which have a diverse and complex economic system, tend to produce a greater diversity of interest groups. The diversity of interest groups that exist in Texas makes it difficult for any one special interest group to dominate Texas politics. As a result, the public is protected from public policy that benefits one group at the expense of the many. The agricultural, energy, legal, banking, medical, religious, racial, ethnic, and educational interest groups are just a few organized interests in Texas, and all compete with one another for favorable legislation. Because there are so many interest groups in Texas, no one group is the sole recipient of public goods.

There are direct and indirect ways to influence outcomes. Lobbying, filing suit in a court of law, serving on state boards and commissions, and holding demonstrations are direct means of influencing government decisions. Electioneering, making campaign contributions, educating the public, and socializing with public officials are indirect methods of influencing state decisions.

Direct Means of Influencing Government

LOBBYING THE LEGISLATIVE AND EXECUTIVE BRANCHES

Lobbying is direct contact between an interest group representative and a legislative or executive branch official or employee for the purpose of influencing a specific public policy outcome.[7] Most people seem to understand that legislatures create, finance, and change government programs. Therefore, individuals and groups affected by these decisions participate in the lawmaking process. The enormous sums of money, privilege, and prestige at stake in the executive decision-making process following the lawmaking are not so obvious.

---

[6]Texas Government Code, 305.021.
[7]Texas Government Code, 305.003a.

Do interest groups hinder or promote democracy?

The executive branch or administration is charged with the **implementation** (carrying out) of legislative policy. The legislature delegates a great deal of **discretion** to executive agencies, both directly and indirectly. This freedom to select the means to carry out law is the **delegation** of power from the legislative branch to the executive branch. The administrative agencies finish the policy-making process by promulgating rules or regulations that specify how the law shall be applied to actual situations. Organized interest groups have a real interest in shaping the regulations that will apply to them. In short, because what government does is not simply a function of legislative decisions, lobbyists must actively monitor and seek to influence executive-branch rule making and enforcement. The importance of this is revealed in the average number of registered lobbyists in Austin. In 2009, there were 1,861 registered lobbyists at work.[8]

FILING SUIT IN COURT

There are several reasons why organized interests use the courts to further their cause. One is that a lack of funds or public support dictates that their resources be spent on litigation. Lawsuits are less expensive than trying to influence the legislature, and public opinion has little relevance to judicial outcomes. A second reason for using the courts is to seek a more favorable interpretation of the law than that given by the enforcing agency. More favorable means less costly to the profession, occupation, or activity that must obey the rules set by the overseeing agency. A third purpose is to delay the implementation of the law or rules. Courts often stay implementation of the law or rule while a case is pending. The members of the group can continue to operate as before, in a more profitable and unrestrained manner. Filing suit, even when one expects to lose, serves to delay application of costly rules. If one does prevail in court, two good outcomes for the special interests are possible: The previous way of doing things is restored, and the state must wait until the next session of the legislature to take action again. Finally, an interest group that has lost the political struggle may be able to challenge the constitutionality of the law or the means of enforcement selected by the administering agency.

ADVISING AND SERVING THE STATE

State law in Texas generally requires that appointed boards be composed of members, a majority of whom come from the profession, occupation, business, or activity the state agency is regulating. The mere existence of such laws is testimony to the power of special interest groups to shape government decisions. These board members and commissioners are part-time officials and full-time practitioners of the activity that they have the power to regulate. They personally exercise power as state officials and as members of a special interest group that testifies and presents information to the agency. This blurring of the line between the state

---

Implementation

The carrying out by members of the executive branch of policy made by the legislature and judiciary.

Discretion

The power to make decisions on the basis of personal judgment rather than specific legal requirements.

Delegation

The legal transfer of authority from an official or institution to another official or institution.

---

[8]The Texas Ethics Commission listed 1,561 registered lobbyists in 1999. In 2009, the number of registered lobbyists had increased to 1,861. See Texas Ethics Commission, "Lobby Lists and Reports," http://www.ethics.state .tx.us/dfs/loblists.htm

and the special interest is called **co-optation**. The **public interest** is endangered when state officials act as agents for the group the agency regulates. A **conflict of interest** exists when the decision maker is personally affected by the decision being made.

ORGANIZING PUBLIC DEMONSTRATIONS

Marches and demonstrations are used periodically to obtain publicity for a cause. Press coverage is all but guaranteed. This sort of "theater" is especially suited for the television news. When the legislature is in session, demonstrations are plentiful. Witness the pro-school voucher demonstration of February 4, 2007, and the protest against more coal-fired generating plants seven days later.[9] The challenge for interest groups using this method of pressuring the state is to enlist enough members to be impressive and to keep control of the activity. One solution to the challenge has been found in the development of **astroturf lobbying**—or the fabrication of public support for issues supported by industry and special interest groups, but which give the impression of widespread public support. Violating the law, forging signatures on letters sent to lawmakers, blocking traffic, damaging property, and using obscenities do not win support from fellow citizens or the public officials with the power to change the conditions one is protesting.

Indirect Means of Influencing Government

ELECTIONEERING

Although interest groups do not nominate candidates for office, one candidate for an office may be more favorable to their cause than another. The organization may decide to endorse and recommend that its members vote for the candidate more disposed to support their values.

The organization's newsletter or magazine will be used to carry this message. A second means of helping candidates who are favorable to the group's interests is to create a political action committee (PAC). As explained in Chapter 3, the sole purpose of a PAC, which is legally separate from the interest group, is the funneling of money to candidates for office.

Special interest groups are powerful enough to influence the outcome of elections. Interest groups are in a position to make significant campaign contributions that will elect candidates that hold positions that are favorable to their interests. In some cases, interest groups are powerful enough to have their own employees selected for public office. Several of the state's major law firms, which also have powerful lobbying arms in the Texas government, boast members of the Texas legislature and executive branch as current or former members. Similarly, senior administrators with powerful corporations or special interest groups tend to be successful in being selected to serve on government boards and commissions.

EDUCATING THE PUBLIC

There is wisdom in providing the general public with messages that build a positive image. Interest groups that are well-funded employ the services of public relations people to build reputations for honesty, good products and services, concern for the well-being of the

Co-optation

The "capturing" of an institution by members of an interest group. In effect, in such a situation, state power comes to be exercised by the members of the private interest.

Public interest

The good of the whole society, without bias for or against any particular segment of the society.

Conflict of interest

The situation that exists when a legislator, bureaucrat, executive, official, or judge is in a position to make a decision that might result in personal economic benefit or advantage.

Astroturf lobbying

The fabrication of public support for issues supported by industry and special interest groups, but which give the impression of widespread public support.

---

[9]Gary Scharrer, "Thousands Rally for School Vouchers," at http://www.chron.com/disp/story.mpl/special/07/legislature/4535600.html; Eric Berger, "Politics of Global Warming Heating Up in Texas," at http:blogs.chron.com/sciguy/archives/2007/02/politics_of_glo.html

customers, and good citizenship. Organizational magazines, annual reports for stockholders, and press releases to newspapers are vehicles for building reputations and educating the public about the wisdom of policy proposals supported by the organization. Occasionally, print and broadcast advertisements are purchased to shape and mobilize public opinion on behalf of the interest or to neutralize opposition to what the interest wants to do.

It is very important for a group or individuals that want government to take action to articulate the need or problem in exactly the right language to evoke a favorable response and stay in control of the definition. It is best to educate public officials before the issue becomes public. Once an issue becomes public, every opponent will try to change the favorable characterization to something unacceptable by redefining the issue in a negative light. For example, people who want to promote school vouchers that may be used in religious schools must emphasize the responsibility of the state to assist all children to learn. Opponents will seek to convince the majority that such aid is a violation of the "separation of church and state." Words are the weapons of political battle, and most new political struggles are group-against-group battles.

SOCIALIZING

Interest groups know that friendships can be formed at social functions. Informal occasions allow people to interact in comfortable settings. A lobbyist may invite a public official to lunch or to a party to establish a positive relationship. Formal occasions designed to honor a person can also serve to build positive relationships. Invitations to speak before a group are also a way to cultivate friendships. The purpose of all social invitations is to establish an impression that pays off in favorable votes or other kinds of friendly decisions by public officials. Thus, socializing is seen as a good "investment" for interest groups, whether or not there is an immediate need for the public official's support.

Access to public officials is the prerequisite for influencing public decisions. Getting in the door to discuss a matter of concern in time to shape the public policy outcome is the goal. Indirect means of influencing government often pave the road to the direct lobbying event. Groups that have established good reputations with public officials do not have to engage in demonstrations, but even the most successful groups can expect to lose sometimes. Resorting to the courts is frequently the next strategy in this event.

Why People Join Interest Groups

People join interest groups for many reasons. To influence government, one needs to become a joiner. Most individuals lack the status, knowledge, political skills, and money to succeed on their own. Joining together creates a network of like-minded people who can pool their talents and other resources to pursue their political end. Furthermore, work and family obligations leave little time for one to become an expert on the complexities of policy issues. The solution is to create or "hire" an **advocacy** organization to protect one's economic, recreational, social, or political interests. The organization can monitor activities in the capitol and alert its members to the need to call or write public officials and influence the decisions relevant to them. Working as a group with many members contacting officials at the same time increases the organization's chances of obtaining favorable results.

Joining groups also advances career and social goals. Certainly, to belong to a collectivity that gets together periodically is to increase one's circle of friends and business contacts. Getting to know others in your trade or profession can certainly lead to job offers, exchanges of knowledge, and enjoyment of others who share your interests. Hence, active membership leads to networking that has economic, social, and political benefits.

The culture of a profession may require membership; that is, it is regarded as unprofessional not to be a member. People are expected to stay current in their field. All organizations exist

Advocacy

Promotion of a particular public policy position.

to disseminate information or knowledge, but an organization may also have other tangible benefits that make the dues very reasonable. For example, malpractice insurance is available to teachers, attorneys, and medical professionals through memberships. A monthly or quarterly magazine or newsletter may be the factor that attracts membership. Publications of nature and conservation groups are invariably so beautiful that one might join simply to enjoy the magazine. Whatever the principal reason for joining, one should not be surprised to learn that these groups actively engage in the practice of influencing government. After all, the government regulates our occupations and professions. It decides who pays how much in taxes and who receives the benefits of those tax dollars through public-spending programs. There is no aspect of life untouched by the political system. Those who do not pay attention to what is going on in Washington and Austin and their local city hall sooner or later feel the effect of what occurs there.

> Government is too important to be a spectator sport.
> —Barbara Jordan

> Politics is a struggle to gain power to determine the policies that affect the members of society. Those who don't enter the political arena stand to be victimized by those who do participate. Victimization results from the fact that policy represents the imposition of one set of values on society over all other value choices.
>
> Nonparticipants forfeit their influence.
> —Edwin S. Davis

Types of Interest Groups

Interest groups can be classified in a multitude of ways. The simplest is to categorize them according to their primary purpose—economic, noneconomic, or both.

ECONOMIC INTEREST GROUPS

The traditional categories of economic interests operating at the state level are business and professions in education, local government, agriculture, and labor. Each group in each category seeks financial advantages for its members. Business and agriculture are always interested in keeping their taxes low, securing benefits called subsidies, avoiding regulation, and receiving government contracts to increase profits. Education and local government groups want greater state support for their governments and increased salaries and benefits for their public employees. In addition, blocking unfunded state mandates and obtaining more local control or less state control over their affairs is often an objective. Labor unions seek legislation to make it easier to organize (unionize) labor and to obtain generous workers' compensation and workplace safety packages.

State employees such as these teachers can become an interest group when they attempt to affect policy by calling publicity to their jobs and the services they provide.

Are interest groups that benefit more people more or less effective at organizing? Why or why not?

Levels and branches of government also lobby. They are not generally recognized as interest groups, but they are affected by what other political institutions and jurisdictions decide. Governors have staff that promotes their political agenda in the legislature. Cities, school districts, and other local governments are seriously affected by legislative decisions on finances and local government authority. They are also affected by rules set by state executive branch agencies. Therefore, they must protect and/or promote their interests by employing lobbyists or reassigning employees to be lobbyists as needed.

In recent years, the public has been critical of governmental agencies for hiring lobbyists. Critics argue that the public elects representatives, not lobbyists, to represent their interests. The hiring of lobbyists is simply an added cost to taxpayers. But cities, universities, and other public agencies respond that they are at a tremendous disadvantage when they do not have the additional assistance of lobbyists. When the Texas Department of Transportation hired a lobbyist, Robert Black, a spokesman for Governor Rick Perry defended the action by saying, "The fact of the matter is the transportation bureaucracy in Washington, D.C., is incredibly extensive and to have people on the ground who can traverse that bureaucratic maze is highly valuable."[10] Cities and other local government that do not hire lobbyists to represent their interests can find themselves at a disadvantage.

NONECONOMIC INTEREST GROUPS

Noneconomic groups seek the betterment of society as a whole or the reform of the political, social, or economic systems in ways that do not directly affect their members' pockets. Such groups are difficult to form because the groups work for goods that everyone benefits from. This creates an incentive for individuals who will benefit from the work of a noneconomic interest group to become what Mancur Olson calls a *free rider*.[11] A free rider is an individual who benefits from the work of an interest group but who does not participate in the collective actions that made the benefits possible. Environmental and political reformers maintain that the beneficiaries of their programs are the members of society. Clean air, water, and elections are said to promote the well-being of all. Many individuals who join noneconomic interest groups are motivated to participate by two or three things—intense passion, selective incentives, and social pressures. Individuals who join the Texas Right to Life movement are motivated by strong beliefs about conception and when life begins. The intensity of passion that a citizen possesses motivates him or her to join. Other organizations recruit members by offering selective incentives like T-shirts, coffee mugs, and newsletters as a way of attracting members.

Still, other noneconomic interest groups rely on social pressure to attract members to join. Neighborhood organizations can pressure neighbors to join the local civic association. Failing to join a neighborhood group makes one auspiciously absent from civic life in the community. The threat of ostracism leads many to join such groups. Noneconomic interest groups benefit from large memberships because they translate into greater political clout in the Texas legislature. Group members can write letters, call, and even vote for or against members of the Texas legislature. What some noneconomic interest groups lack in financial resources they make up for in group membership.

MIXED-INTEREST GROUPS

Many groups do not fit neatly into the economic or noneconomic classification because they pursue social goals that have clear economic effects. Discrimination in any form—on the basis of age, disability, ethnicity, gender, or native language—is a social problem that has negative consequences on wages and promotion in the workplace. Groups pursuing social equality and economic goals are classified as mixed or hybrid organizations. Few, if any, demands on the political system affect all classes of citizens equally. Some benefit, some suffer inconvenience, and others experience economic loss from any policy adopted. Table 5.2 gives some examples of Texas interest groups in all three categories.

---

[10]Michelle Mittelstadt, "Democrats Rip State Agency for Hiring D.C. Lobbyists," *Houston Chronicle*, February 2, 2007, Section A, 1.

[11]Olson, Mancur, *The Logic of Collective Action: Public Goods and the Theory of Groups* (Revised edition, Boston: Harvard University Press, 1971).

TABLE 5. 2 INTEREST GROUP CLASSIFICATIONS AND REPRESENTATIVE EXAMPLES

Classification	Sector	Examples
Economic	Agriculture	Texas Farm Bureau
	Business	Texan Association of Business and Chambers of Commerce
	Labor	Texas AFL-CIO; American Federation of State and County Municipal Employees
	Occupations and professions	Texas Association of Realtors; Texas Trial Lawyers
Noneconomic	Patriotic	American Legion
	Public interest	Texas Common Cause; Texans for Public Justice
	Religious	Texas Christian Life Commission
Mixed	Education	Texas State Teachers Association
	Environment and recreation	Texas Nature Conservancy; Texas Committee on Natural Resources
	Race and gender	League of United Latin American Citizens; NAACP
	Local government	Texas Municipal League; Texas County Judges and Commissioners Association

Factors That Affect Interest Group Power

CULTURE OF NONPARTICIPATION

One hundred and fifty years of one-partyism (see Chapters 2 and 3) created less incentive for average Texans to participate in political affairs than citizens living in states with competitive parties. The absence of two parties also helped establish a history of elitist rule and strong special interests. Indeed, the conservative Texas political elites used their control of state government to enact laws that discouraged mass political participation, including the poll tax, annual voter registration, and the white primary. These barriers to participation promoted "acceptable conservative" interests and a culture of nonparticipation for the masses that has not been undone in one or two generations.

PARTY COMPETITION

Studies of the power of interest groups consistently show that where political parties are weak, interest groups are strong. States with a long history of two-party competition have weaker interest groups than states in the early stages of party development.[12] Parties in competitive states must appeal to the majority of the population to have a chance of winning elections. They cannot focus on a single issue or a limited number of issues, as interest groups do, and win a majority of the vote. The 1990 election convinced many skeptics that Texas had become a two-party state, but since 2002, elections have shown that Texas has transitioned from one-party Democratic to one-party Republican and that two-partyism in Texas was just a passing phase. As of the summer of 2010, Republican Party control in Texas encompassed the two highest courts in the state, both houses of the legislature, and all elected officers in the executive branch. A one-party Republican state is as vulnerable to interest group domination as a one-party Democratic state. Time will reveal the level of party competition and its effect on interest group power in Texas.

---

[12]Ronald Hrebenar and Clive Thomas, "Who's Got Clout? Interest Group Power in the States," *State Legislatures*, April 1999, pp. 30–34.

THE PART-TIME NATURE OF THE TEXAS LEGISLATURE

State legislatures are often described as either part-time or full-time legislative bodies. Although the Texas legislature does not always fit neatly in either one of the two categories,[13] it does share some characteristics that are found in part-time legislatures. Part-time legislatures tend to meet for shorter periods of time, its members tend to be paid less for their service than the members of full-time legislatures, and they tend to have smaller legislative staffs.

For its part, the Texas legislature meets for 140 days on odd-numbered years, unless the governor calls a special session. Members of the Texas legislature are paid $7,200 per year plus a *per diem* (daily allowance) for days when the legislature is in session. Members of the Texas House average a staff of about three people, whereas senators average a staff of a little more than seven. By most accounts the Texas legislature is considered a part-time legislative body.

Texas legislators must often depend on outside sources of income to earn a living, making them vulnerable to the temptations of special interest groups. Some lawmakers will work in areas in which their clients are the very interests groups that also lobby these lawmakers when the legislature is in session.[14] Legislators who are not paid adequately are also more likely to leave their posts after a short period of service, leading to greater instability in the legislative body.[15] As lawmakers leave the legislature, they take with them policy and political expertise that is necessary to adequately represent the public.

Some have argued that a part-time legislature is better because it governs less, but in Texas, this is not always the case. In the 140 days of the 81st Legislative Session, more than 1,459 bills became law.[16] The 110th Congress, by contrast, produced 460 laws in twice as many days. With fewer resources and less time, the Texas legislature produces many more pieces of legislation than the U.S. Congress. Although the Texas legislature is certainly not governing less (as measured by legislative activity), some have speculated about the quality of so much legislation produced in such a short period of time.

As it stands, legislators rely on lobbyists to write bills that lawmakers then introduce. Because of time constraints, it is difficult for lawmakers to properly vet bills. As a result, legislators are often not familiar with the legislation on which they are asked to vote. A full-time legislative body would provide lawmakers with the necessary resources to better represent the public.

It is unlikely that the Texas legislature will be reformed any time soon. Current lawmakers have been successful under this system and are unlikely to want to change the legislature to a system that would bring uncertainty into their lives. The public is also unlikely to want to go along with such a change because of assumptions that the public has about lawmakers and lawmaking. The public assumes that Texas legislators are compensated more than adequately. Or, when the public is familiar with the part-time nature of the Texas legislature, the public assumes that the Texas legislature governs best when it governs least. Such assumptions from the public, and concerns about the future from legislators, make it unlikely that the legislature will be reformed any time soon.

PART-TIME LEGISLATURE

Texas, with a population of more than 23 million, is the second largest state in the Union. It is the only large state with limited legislative sessions and infrequent meetings. In addition, legislative pay is below poverty level, and legislator turnover is fairly high. Professor Cal Jillson put it this way: "If you meet only occasionally, get paid little and have weak staffs, you are at the disposal of the [lobbyists] because you have to go to them to get information."[17] The result is a legislative body that is easily influenced by special interest groups.

DECENTRALIZATION OF EXECUTIVE BRANCH POWER

Texas has a plural executive. Power is divided among numerous independently elected executives: governor, lieutenant governor, attorney general, comptroller, agricultural commissioner,

---

[13]NCSL, 2008, "NCSL Backgrounder: Full- and Part-Time Legislatures," January 2008, http://www.ncsl.org/programs/press/2004/backgrounder_fullandpart.htm

[14]Center for Public Integrity, 2008, "Low-Paid Texas Lawmakers Tops in Connections to Lobbyists," http://www.public-i.org/Content.aspx?id=489

[15]Peverill Squire, "Career Opportunities and Membership Stability in Legislatures," *Legislative Studies Quarterly* 13 (February 1988), pp. 65–82.

[16]House Research Organization, 2009, "Focus Report: Major Issues of the 81st Legislature, Regular Session and First Session Called," http://www.hro.house.state.tx.us/framer1.htm

[17]Quoted in Robison, "Weak State Government," p. A24.

land commissioner, and the multimember Railroad Commission and State Board of Education. The **fragmentation**, or division of power, within the executive branch is expanded further by the preference for independent boards and commissions as the structures for implementing the law. The governor appoints all members of nearly every unelected board and commission, usually one-third of the members every two years, but has little power to remove those appointed. If each agency were headed by a single executive, appointed and removable by the governor, agencies would theoretically be more responsive to the broader values represented by the governor than those of the specific clientele they serve.

The plural executive and structure of fragmentation mean that there is no strong central executive authority with the legal power to control this branch of government. This arrangement increases the vulnerability of each executive agency to the power of interest group influence. This can result in policies with little regard for the public interest.

Increasing this likelihood are state laws that require many boards and commissions to be composed of a majority of people engaged in the profession, business occupation, or activity that the board regulates. Critics would say that this arrangement leaves the fox to guard the henhouse. At a minimum, it raises the question of conflicts of interest and balancing the public interest with the need for expertise in board membership.

LAW

Laws to regulate the relationship between public officials and private parties who seek special favors from government have long been advocated. Texas, as we will see later, has laws that define lobbying and require reporting of information about the lobbyist, the lobbyist's employer, and the expenses associated with trying to influence government decisions. Everyone can access this information via the **Texas Ethics Commission**. The press has a special obligation to examine this information and report it to the public in a usable form. The public has a responsibility to act on it.

THE MEDIA

One of the institutions essential to the survival of democracy is the media. Radio, television, and print journalists serve as watchdogs of government. Public officials and bureaucrats know that every decision they make, as well as their general conduct, is fair game for the news media. The public has a right to know what its public servants are doing, and the media are committed to telling it. But the media communicate in two directions: They not only relay the activities of government to the people but also transmit the people's moods and messages to the halls of state. The media are thus a link between people and government—but not a neutral one.

The media are allies of the people in their demands that the government's business be conducted in public view. They work to promote open meetings, open records, and recorded votes on policy decisions in the legislature and in administrative boards and commissions. Openness is the enemy of corruption, bribery, conflicts of interest, and other forms of unethical conduct, and the press delights in exposing such to the public. Thus the interaction of lobbyists and public officials is a matter of interest to the media.

The self-imposed restraints on reporting what the state of Texas is doing remind us that newspapers, newsmagazines, and radio and television stations are businesses that are concerned with making a profit. Austin, the state capital, is not home to the major newspapers or broadcasting channels in the state. It is expensive to employ journalists and station them in Austin for your hometown news industry. Most Texas media outlets subscribe to wire services (Associated Press and Reuters) to get the news from Austin, even when the legislature is in session. Many newspapers are parts of a chain of information companies that keep an office in Austin and feed all their papers and radio and TV stations in the state. Cox, Knight-Ridder, Scripps Howard,

Fragmentation

Division of power among separately elected executive officers. A plural executive is a fragmented executive.

Texas Ethics Commission

A constitutionally authorized agency charged with accepting reports of candidates and lobbyists and making them public. It also establishes standards of conduct for officeholders, candidates, and lobbyists.

Hearst, and A. H. Belo each maintain staffs in Austin. In addition, hundreds of Texas radio stations subscribe to the Texas State Network, which maintains an office in the capital city.

Clearly, media presence in Austin keeps the government honest and responsive to the public. However, there is much duplication of reporting efforts among members of the different news organizations. Separation of the journal staffs appears to leave each too understaffed to ensure thorough reporting. If the media combined their staffs and worked cooperatively, there would be sufficient press personnel to cover many more aspects of state government. Breadth and depth of reporting would be vastly improved by pooling staffs without any increase in cost to the individual media companies.

CONSTITUENT INFLUENCE

The constant forces affecting interest group strength on any policy issue are constituent values, attitudes, and beliefs. No elected official can consistently ignore the "folks back home." Most state representatives and senators have lived in their district for a long time; many were born and raised there. They know the culture of the region. On many issues before the legislature, they know what the voters would have them do. In other words, even in the absence of public input, legislators may know the preferences of their constituents. Texas has a part-time legislature; it is in regular session for only 140 days every odd-numbered year. Hence, members are in their home district 590 days of the 730 days every two years—in other words, 80 percent of the time. Furthermore, they are home almost every weekend during the four and a half months of the 140-day session. It is almost impossible for members *not* to know what their constituents want.

The question remains, however, would an elected representative vote contrary to clear-cut constituent desires to please a special interest? The answer is probably not. An experienced interest group, knowing that the voters in the district disagree with its position, would probably not punish the legislator by withholding campaign funds in the next election. However, when the voters back home have no expressed consensus on an issue, interest groups, fellow legislators, the governor, and the party struggle for influence.

As noted earlier in this chapter, the most fundamentally important activity of political citizenship is voting. Residents who continually fail to register and vote do not see the connection between their fate and that of the larger society. Such people also tend not to join civic clubs, work in political campaigns, or participate in other organizations such as the Chamber of Commerce, the Community Betterment Association, or the Nature Conservancy. To influence government or almost anything else, one has to be informed and involved. Membership in an interest group reduces some of the hard work of citizenship. The organization provides information to its members about issues of concern to them in concise and effective ways.

INTEREST GROUPS AS CHECKS ON INTEREST GROUPS

On issues of major public importance, one interest group is likely to be confronted by one or more others that do not want the same outcome. In such circumstances, they offset each other's influence. On more obscure issues, one group may happily find itself without opposition. Whether there are many special interests involved in the policy-making process or only one, the status, resources, size, reputation, and lobbying skills of any group affect its access to agency heads and legislators. These factors, plus the substance of what the group is seeking and state finances, shape policy outcomes.

When a special interest seeks a very narrow or specific outcome, the general public and other interest groups may not know of it or, if they do, may not participate. The matter is simply of no concern to them. The participating interest under such circumstances must persuade only a few key people, such as legislative committee chairs and presiding officers. If the committee approves, the vote on the floor will most likely be favorable. When a special interest is seeking a change in policy that affects the balance of power in the political, social, or economic system, there will be much greater participation and conflict. Group will be pitted against group, and the general public will get the opportunity to participate because the media will transmit stories of conflict to their readers, listeners, and viewers.

Many groups and many types of people take an interest in broad issues concerning tax policy, education, campaign finance reform, gun control, and abortion; conflict may become intense on such issues. The challenge for the public officials involved is to lead the warring groups to a compromise. Without that, no policy output will occur. Needless to say, as the number of participants in any political debate increases, conflict increases and the influence of each interest group diminishes.

CAMPAIGN CONTRIBUTIONS

Money in politics is the "hot" topic of the day. There has been a startling increase in the amount of money raised and spent by candidates for elective office at all levels. A candidate for state representative in a metropolitan area may well spend more than $200,000 to win an office that pays $7,200 a year! Most campaign contributions for the state legislature and the statewide offices come from large donors. These donors represent banks, insurance companies, the petrochemical industry, physicians, trial lawyers, real estate agents, teachers, and others who, through political action committees, funnel money to candidates. Why? Because the state legislature, the governor, the Railroad Commission, and other agencies and officers make decisions that affect these donors' economic well-being. Donors contribute in order to gain **access** to public officials, which means getting in the door to sit down and talk about their needs. A substantial contribution seems to create an obligation on the part of an elected official to listen when a contributor calls. Ordinary citizens find access more difficult.

According to Texans for Public Justice, legislative candidates raised $95 million in the 2008 election cycle. An estimated $70 million was raised by the 281 major candidates vying for a seat in the Texas House, and an estimated $25 million was raised by the 31 candidates vying for seats on the Texas Senate.[18] Sixty-five percent of the dollars raised by house candidates went to incumbents, and 58 percent of money raised by senate candidates went to incumbent senators.[19]

Texans for Public Justice report that 126 individual donors contributed over $100,000 in 2008. These 126 donors contributed $45.5 million. The top 143 institutional donors that contributed over $150,000 gave $89.8 million during the 2008 election cycle.[20] PACs and businesses contributed $51.9 million. Individuals contributed $43 million.[21] Even when candidates face little or no opposition, they raise large amounts of money. Their success in raising campaign contributions is indicative of the state's economic and political importance.

One of the biennial rituals in Austin occurs after each election, when special interest groups hold fund-raising events to honor selected legislators. State law forbids giving and accepting campaign contributions 30 days before the start of a legislative session and throughout the session, causing a rush of fund-raising activity during the five weeks after election day. These lobbyist fund-raising parties occur after the election, not before. The reason, as one lobbyist said, is to "pay the price of admission" or to obtain good access to legislators. These so-called **late train contributions** are commonly given to the winning candidates in the executive branch as well. Losers are rarely the beneficiaries of such largess.

Access

The ability to contact an official either in person or by phone. Campaign contributions are often used to gain access.

Late train contributions

Campaign funds given to the winning candidate after the election up to 30 days before the legislature comes into session. Such contributions are designed to curry favor with individuals whom the donors may not have supported originally.

HOW DOES TEXAS COMPARE?
CAMPAIGN CONTRIBUTIONS FOR MEMBERS OF THE TEXAS LEGISLATURE

Candidates for the Texas legislature, on average, raise some of the largest amounts of money to run their campaigns. In 2008, the 281 candidates for the 150 member Texas House of Representatives raised an average of $250,057 in campaign contributions. Only the 80-member California Assembly, and the 118-member Illinois House of Representatives raised more campaign contributions, on average. The 31 candidates for the Texas Senate, by comparison, raised $798,349 on average. Candidates for the Texas Senate raised more money in 2008 than the state senate candidates of most other states. The table below lists the total dollar amounts raised by the five states to raise the most money for state house and state senate races in 2008. The Texas Senate, with 31 senate candidates running for office, comes in fifth place in total dollar contributions. New York's 142 candidates for the state senate raised the most money, followed by California, with its 79 candidates running for office. Illinois with 93 candidates running for the state senate, and Pennsylvania with 90 candidates, also raised more money than the 31 Texas state senate candidates.

2008 CAMPAIGN CONTRIBUTIONS FOR STATE HOUSE AND SENATE CANDIDATES

State	Total House Contributions	State	Total Senate Contributions
California	$84,390,298	New York	$47,019,720
Texas	$71,266,729	California	$45,351,422
Pennsylvania	$45,787,518	Illinois	$30,470,315
Illinois	$42,866,912	Pennsylvania	$29,456,144
Ohio	$34,867,032	Texas	$25,941,340

Source: Data from the National Institute on Money in State Politics, http://www.followthemoney.org/

JOIN THE DEBATE

1. Should Texas set limits on the amount of money that interest groups can contribute to political campaigns? Or, is reporting the contribution sufficient?

2. Would Texans be better off or worse off with more interest groups, rather than fewer interest groups, making campaign contributions?

3. Try this exercise: Divide the total campaign contributions for the senate candidates by the total number of candidates running for office. How does Texas compare now?

Does money buy sponsorship of bills and special favors? The public and the press think it does. Lobbyists and legislators claim it does not.[22] The increasing amounts of campaign contributions and the 16 percent increase in the number of lobbyists from 1998 to 2009 hardly leads to any other conclusion.[23] Records of the 2009 session of the legislature show lobbyists spending as much as $344 million trying to influence decisions of the Texas House and Senate.[24] In 2009, there were 10.3 lobbyists for every legislator.[25]

---

[22]James Gibbons, "Officials Come and Go; the Lobby Rules," *Houston Chronicle*, January 27, 2003.

[23]The Texas Ethics Commission lists 1,561 registered lobbyists in 1999. In 2009, the number of registered lobbyists increased to 1,861. See: Texas Ethics Commission, "Lobby Lists and Reports," http://www.ethics.state .tx.us/dfs/loblists.htm; *Austin American-Statesman*, May 5, 1999, p. B2; Michael Holmes, "Lobbyists Paying Plenty for Attention, Study Finds," *Austin American-Statesman*, May 24, 1999, p. B2; Texans for Public Justice, "Austin's Oldest Profession: Top Lobby Clients and Those Who Service Them," 2005, at www.tpj.org/reports/ austinsoldest06/facts.html

[24]*Texans for Public Justice*, "Austin's Oldest Profession: Texas's Top Lobby Clients and Those Who Support Them," 2010 Edition, available at http://info.tpj.org/reports/austinsoldest09/facts.html

[25]The ratio of lobbyists to lawmakers is calculated by dividing the number of registered lobbyists in 2009 (1,861) by 181—the number of legislators in the Texas House and Senate.

Anecdotal evidence that contributions buy public policy is mixed, but cases have been identified, which leave the casual observer with the perception that **conflicts of interest** do arise. An example of such a case occurred on February 2, 2007, when Governor Rick Perry issued an executive order to vaccinate preteen girls against the sexually transmitted human papillomavirus, which causes cervical cancer in women. Fearing opposition from members of his own party, Governor Perry, with his executive order, circumvented the Texas legislature completely. He expected opposition from conservative groups that believe such a vaccine would give young girls tacit consent to have sex.

Shortly after he issued the executive order, it was revealed that Governor Perry's Chief of Staff Deirdre Delisi met with other members of the governor's team for an "HPV Vaccine for Children Briefing," October 16, 2006.[26] That same day, Merck and Company's political action committee contributed $5,000 to the Perry campaign. Merck is the only manufacturer of Gardasil, the vaccine that is believed to fend off the virus. One of Merck's lobbyists at the time was Mike Toomey, Rick Perry's former chief of staff and Deirdre Delisi's predecessor.

In early March of 2007, the Texas legislature passed a bill rescinding the executive order, which Governor Perry grudgingly allowed to become law without his signature.

Although the governor's office claims that the connection between the campaign contribution and the meeting held by his chief of staff was merely a coincidence, critics contend that the coincidence, at the very least, sheds light on the conflicts of interest that can occur between elected officials in need of raising campaign contributions, and the need of special interest groups for public policy that provides them direct benefits.

Conflicts of interest

The situation that exists when a legislator, bureaucrat, executive, official, or judge is in a position to make a decision that might result in personal economic benefit or advantage.

Conclusions about Balance in the Political System

Do interest groups dominate the state's political system? Contemporary wisdom says they do. Look at the money poured into the system by corporate Texas and other special interests. The average person cannot compete. Every attempt to secure campaign finance reform has failed. Voting and political attentiveness is so low in Texas that the public is easily fooled. The press is conservative in Texas; the most powerful interests are conservative. Is it bad economics for the press, which is itself a business, to expose the elites who control the state? There are numerous examples of economic interests, such as insurance companies, oil and gas companies, and certain utilities, having their way with the state.

Indeed, sitting members of the legislature are known to represent special interests before the state or have economic ties with enterprises that have interests in pending legislation. Governor Rick Perry, Texas Senators David Sibley and Jeff Wentworth, former House Speaker Tom Craddick, and Texas Representative Linda Harper-Brown provide recent examples of legislators arranging special benefits for their employers and campaign contributors.[27]

[26]Liz Austin Peterson, "Perry's Staff Discussed Vaccine on Day Merck Donated to Campaign," *Associated Press*, February 22, 2007.
[27]*Texans for Public Justice*, "How Politicians Got Fat on a Risky Weight-Loss Stimulant," October 21, 2002, www.tpj.org/ page_view.jsp?pageid5240&pubid5121; "Revolving-Door Lobbyist Adopts So-Craddick Method," November 21, 2002, http://www.tpj.org/page_view.jsp?pageid5238&pubid5119; "Companies Paid Craddick a Big Income While Claiming His 1999 Energy Tax Cut," November 14, 2002, http://www.tpj.org/ page_view. jsp?pageid5236&pubid5117; Formby, Brandon, and Gromer Jeffers, Jr., "Questions Raised About Rep. Linda Harper-Brown's Use of a Mercedes," *The Dallas Morning News*, June 18, 2010, http://www.dallasnews.com/ sharedcontent/dws/news/politics/local/stories/061710dnmetharperbrown.b2379636.html

The counterargument focuses on the structure of government, which is designed to make it hard for any group to dominate the state. The structure of government is characterized by (1) the separation of powers, (2) checks and balances, (3) elected officials responsible to different constituencies at the ballot box at different times, (4) appointed officials with fixed terms, and (5) career bureaucrats. These structures make the political system difficult to capture by any one interest. The house and senate and the governor must agree to create law. The implementation of that law is placed in the hands of elected and appointed executive officers and the unelected bureaucrats below them. Texas is too pluralistic or diverse for the whole governmental enterprise to be dominated by one interest, but one interest may control the policy outcomes of the legislature and executive agencies in the area of its concern.

Perhaps the biggest change affecting existing power relationships in the state is the increasing use of the computer as a political tool. Contacting public officials has never been easier. Interest groups starved for economic resources now have a medium that connects them to their members and state decision makers. The computer does not overcome disadvantages deriving from lack of money and other resources, but it does facilitate the input of under-represented and new voices.

Special interests do, of course, sometimes come into conflict with each other. Matters involving large amounts of money or important changes in existing policy invite crowds. In such situations, for anything to happen, some compromising among competing interests must occur, resulting in a mix of values incorporated into the policy decision.

The general public is critical, if not cynical, of the current political process. Many Texans believe that special interests control government and perceive that as bad. The prevailing view of the "average" man or woman is that the little guy has no chance of being heard or heeded. These same Texans may not realize that if they belong to a rod or gun club, teach school, drive a truck, or practice carpentry, they are members of a group that lobbies the legislature and executive agencies in Austin. Cynicism seems to be encouraged by the media, which is driven by bad news. Good news just cannot compete. A story about a lobbyist helping a legislator by supplying needed information or assisting in the actual writing of a bill useful to the people back home does not make the news. Two comical but cynical characterizations of lobbyists convey the reputation of those who practice the craft: "Please don't tell my mother I'm a lobbyist; she thinks I'm a piano player in a bordello," and "Dear Senator, Meet Me in the Lobby . . . The Second Oldest Profession."

The Regulation of Lobbying

WHO MUST REGISTER AND REPORT LOBBYING COSTS?

Not all lobbyists are required by state law to register and report their activities. Lobbyists not paid wages or reimbursed for their expenses are not required to register with the state. But individuals and organizations that spend more than a specified amount of money attempting to shape public decisions are required to register and file reports with the Texas Ethics Commission. The behavior of both lobbyists and public officials is spelled out in Chapter 305 of the Government Code of Texas.

Classes of lobbyists not required to register and report include state officials and state employees who lobby, even as their principal function. Also exempt are citizens from the private sector who are not paid for their services and do not directly spend any money to influence legislative or administrative action. Those who do have to register and report are private-sector lobbyists who cross through the "compensation threshold" of $1,000 salary per calendar quarter or the "expenditure threshold" of $500 per quarter. That these people should have to register and report seems simple and straightforward, but an examination of the law reveals that not all compensation and expenditures are counted as lobbying. Exempted from reporting are (1) compensation received to prepare for lobbying; (2) office expenses including telephone, fax, copying, office supplies, postage, dues and subscriptions, transportation, and the costs of clerical help; and (3) costs associated with events to which all members of the legislature are invited.[28] These and other exemptions in the law mean that a very incomplete picture of the "investment" in lobbying is made available to the people.

WHAT DOES A LOBBYIST REPORT?

The registration form requires the lobbyist to reveal (1) for whom the person lobbies, (2) information about these clients and employers, (3) the policy areas of concern, (4) the compensation category into which the salary or reimbursement received falls, and (5) the identity of and information about anyone who assists the principal lobbyist through direct contact with public officials. Activity reports must be filed by the 10th day of each month for any lobbyist who foresees expending more than $1,000 per year. Those who spend less need file only annually.[29]

Very often a firm or entity represents multiple clients before the state legislature or administrative agencies. The reporting law requires that the lobbyist working for a lobbying firm report who pays the firm to represent its interests to the government. Without such a requirement, those who wanted to influence legislative and executive officials anonymously could simply hire someone else to lobby on their behalf. For many years, this loophole was in the law. Some critics of the law maintain that there remain provisions that leave the public ill-informed about the investment made in lobbying in this state. They believe that reporting the lobbyist's compensation and expenditures in broad categories rather than in actual amounts understates the influence of money in policy making. An example of the reporting method was illustrated by the report filed with the Texas Ethics Commission by Electronic Data Systems Corporation (EDS) of Dallas in 1995. Forty-two lobbyists were identified: 31 were paid from $0.00 to $9,999.99; two received $50,000 to $99,999.99; seven obtained $150,000 to $199,999.99; and one was paid $200,000 to $999,999.99. Merely reporting by category indeed leaves a lot unsaid! EDS, in other words, spent somewhere between $1,400,000 and $3,008,990, but the exact amount is unknown.[30] In 1999, EDS reported using 28 lobbyists and paying them between $1.8 and $2.5 million.[31] Why the difference? Issues in the legislature were less salient four years later. In 2005, Southwestern Bell (now renamed AT&T) reported having 129 paid lobbyists. The payroll for the session was between $4 and $7 million.[32]

Reporting on which policy area a lobbyist seeks to influence is similarly accomplished. The lobbyist need only check the appropriate box on the form. Such requirements hide as much as they reveal. Disclosing the actual compensation and expenditures of a lobbyist would require no more effort than checking a box does, because one must have the actual figures to know which category to mark on the form. To reveal what one lobbied about would enable the public to see where corporations, trade associations, labor unions, and individuals were spending their political capital. To provide a clear picture of lobby activity would require the listing of the bill numbers that one lobbies for or the rule-making hearings before executive agencies at

---

[28] *Texas Ethics Commission*, "Lobbying in Texas," pt. IIIA.

[29] Ibid.

[30] *Texas Ethics Commission*, "List of Employers and Clients," 1995, pp. 63–65.

[31] *Texas Ethics Commission*, "List of Employers/Clients with Lobbyists Sorted by Employer/Client Name," 1999, pp. 59–60.

[32] *Texans for Public Justice*, "Austin's Oldest Profession: Texas's Top Lobby Clients and Those Who Service Them," 2005, at http://www.tpj.org/reports/austinsoldest06/clients.html

TABLE 5.3 NUMBER AND MAXIMUM VALUE OF CONTRACTS SIGNED BY SELECTED LOBBY INDUSTRY GROUPS: 2009

Industry Group	Contracts	Maximum Value of Contracts
Energy/Natural Res./Waste	1,228	$62,315,000
Ideological/Single Issue	1,768	$55,221,570
Health	986	$41,770,000
Miscellaneous Business	830	$37,600,000
Communications	378	$20,380,000
Lawyers and Lobbyists	341	$19,365,000
Real Estate	461	$18,735,000
Finance	413	$16,177,000
Construction	293	$13,341,000
Insurance	260	$12,495,000
Computers and Electronics	283	$12,485,000
Transportation	349	$12,385,000
Other	176	$6,640,000
Agriculture	142	$6,335,000
Labor	123	$5,760,000
Unknown	94	$2,635,000
TOTALS:	**8,125**	**$343,639,570**

Source: Texans for Public Justice, "Austin's Oldest Profession: Texas's Top Lobby Clients and Those Who Service Them," June 20, 2010, http://info.tpj.org/reports/austinsoldest09/clients.html

which one testifies. This would require more time and expense in filling out the activity forms. The reason these additional pieces of information are not required is that special interests have sufficient power in Texas to avoid reporting what they do not want the public to know. That is to say, special interests have successfully lobbied the legislature to have a weaker lobby law than might otherwise be advocated.

Thanks to the research of Texans for Public Justice and the Texas Ethics Commission, several interesting facts about the lobby industry in Texas are clear: Special interests entered into 8,125 lobby contracts with 1,690 lobbyists in 2009.[33] These contracts are estimated to be worth between $167 and $343 million.[34] Thirty-six lobbyists earned more than $1.5 million for their services; fourteen identifiable "industry" groupings spent more than $5 million each to have their interests protected or advanced; and most lobbyists are affiliated with law firms in Texas.[35] Table 5.3 provides details of the 14 identifiable interests spending the most money to influence Texas state government and the number of contracts each entered into.

There is one category of expenditures that does require detailed reporting. Expenditures on members of the state legislature in excess of $50 a day on food, drink, transportation, or lodging or in the form of a gift must be reported by name, date, place, and purpose.[36] Expenditures for broadcast or print advertisements, mass mailings, and other communications

---

[33]*Texans for Public Justice*, "Austin's Oldest Profession: Texas's Top Lobby Clients and Those Who Service Them," 2010, at http://info.tpj.org/reports/austinsoldest09/index.html
[34]Ibid.
[35]Ibid.
[36]*Texas Ethics Commission*, "Lobbying in Texas," pt. IVB.

designed to support or oppose legislation or administrative actions must also be identified.

WHAT IS NOT REPORTED AS LOBBYING THAT AFFECTS LOBBYING?

Campaign and "late train" contributions to public officials are not lobbying expenses as defined by law even though the state recognizes their potential influence on policy making. As noted earlier, such contributions cannot be made during a legislative session or the 30 days before it begins. This is to prevent corruption or the appearance of corruption. Campaign contributions are reported to the Texas Ethics Commission at different times from what the law recognizes as lobbying expenses.

Rep. Sylvester Turner, D-Houston, center, is approached by lobbyists outside the Texas House of Representatives.

What evidence is there that campaign contributions influence policy making?

AP Photo/Harry Cabluck

ACCESS TO THE REPORTS OF LOBBYISTS

The members of the Texas legislature are provided with a list of registered lobbyists and their clients by February 1 of each legislative (odd-numbered) year. The public may obtain copies of registration and activity reports from the Ethics Commission. Much of this information is available at **http://www.ethics.state.tx.us**

REPORTING TO CLIENTS

There is much evidence that regulation of lobbying remains—in the public's mind— "unfinished business" and controversial. The legislature "tweaks" the laws frequently in response to suspected or verifiable scandal. In 2001, for example, a new conflict-of-interest statute directed the Ethics Commission to write rules requiring lobbyists to provide written notice to the commission and to their clients when they represent more than one client that may have incompatible legislative goals. It is a common practice for a lobbyist in Texas to represent multiple clients. Because many firms represent many clients, the question remains as to whether a conflict exists when different people in the firm represent clients with opposing legislative objectives.

The Craft of Lobbying
BEFORE THE LEGISLATURE

It is obvious that anyone who directly contacts public officials to influence their behavior should be extroverted and enjoy socializing. The lobbyist's first job is to become known and recognized by members of the legislature and any executive officials relevant to the interest he or she represents. Before a legislative session begins, a lobbyist must have successfully completed several tasks: (1) learn who is predisposed to support the cause, who is on the other side, and which members can be swayed; (2) memorize the faces of the members, their non-legislative occupation, the counties they represent, and a little about their family; (3) establish rapport through contact with the members of the legislature; (4) get to know the staffs of legislators because through them the member can be influenced; and (5) know the legislative issues, including the arguments of opponents. To maintain a relationship, the lobbyist must provide the legislator with sound, accurate information about the legislation that the lobbyist's group is supporting or opposing. This includes "off-the-record" admission of the pluses and minuses of the legislation. Honesty is, in fact, the best policy for a lobbyist when dealing with a public official.

A lobbyist can befriend a legislator in several ways that may eventually pay off. Lobbyists have information that may be valuable to a legislator, and they may be able to help draft an important piece of legislation for the official. Providing an occasional free meal or acknowledging a helpful legislator at a banquet in the legislator's honor also has merit from the lobbying perspective. All these actions are necessary to create and maintain goodwill, without which nothing is possible.

How does a lobbyist approach a member of the legislature or the leadership? How do you get in the door, and what do you say when you get in? How important is the staff of a legislator to a lobbyist? Is it necessary to see all 181 members of the legislature, the lieutenant governor, and the governor? Because there are only 140 days in a session, it should be clear that lobbying must precede the convening of the legislature. The 18-month period between regular sessions leaves ample time to work on relationships, learn what proposals have a chance of receiving favorable response, draft legislation, and line up sponsors to introduce bills in the house and senate at the beginning of the next session. Not all members of the legislature are equal. Establishing rapport and obtaining feedback from the very powerful presiding officers—the speaker of the house and lieutenant governor—is especially useful. There is no endorsement more important to an interest group than that of the presiding officers. If an endorsement for the group's legislative proposal is not forthcoming, the lobbyist must persuade the presiding officers to be neutral in the legislative struggle. Securing the endorsement of the chair of each committee through which the legislation must pass before it can go to the floor for a vote is an advantage second only to that of securing the support of the presiding officers. Legislation sought by local governments must have the endorsement of the members representing that community, or it is doomed to fail.

BEFORE ADMINISTRATIVE AGENCIES

Both administrators and interest group representatives seek each other out to provide and obtain information. For example, if the Texas Educational Diagnosticians Association and colleges of education wish to know whether the examination for certification is scheduled for revision, they would contact the State Board for Educator Certification to find out. The issue is important to the Texas Educational Diagnosticians Association because the content and difficulty of the examination affect the number of recruits to the profession. The faculties of education know that changes in the examination by the state mean changes in the curriculum. The inquiry about the examination also allows the interest groups to communicate their professional opinion about the current examination and make suggestions about any changes.

Administrators seek to discover the impact of their programs and rules on the clientele they serve. They may seek input from those they serve about current and planned programs. Thus, they surrender some of their power to the profession to maintain the political support for their agency that is necessary to retain support from the legislature and governor.

An agency's clients are especially interested in influencing the rules and guidelines that control how they do business because the rules of doing business directly affect profits. Guidelines are issued by agencies to govern the actions of their employees (bureaucrats) in applying the law. The agency also issues formal rules that prescribe the standards of conduct followed by citizens subject to the law. The rule-making process in Texas gives all interested parties an opportunity to influence the agency's decision. Notice of intent to make a rule is required to be published in the ***Texas Register***. A time for written public comment on the proposed rule is established. At the close of the comment period, the agency analyzes the public's views. It then publishes a "final rule" having the same force as law.

Although all citizens have the right to participate in the rule-making process, it is obvious that only those who are aware of and interested in the proposed rule participate. Ordinary citizens do not subscribe to the *Texas Register*. Corporations, labor unions, law firms, and interest groups do. Hence, they know when to mobilize their members to influence decision making. Interest groups contact members by mail, email, or phone and ask them to call or write the agency about the rule. Sometimes preaddressed cards with the desired message are distributed to members to sign and mail to the agency.

There is a natural linkage from agency to clientele and clientele to agency. Most state agencies are headed by boards and commissions drawn from the industry, trade, profession, or activity that the agency regulates. Those who govern and those who are governed know each other because of their concern and participation in the same activity. Movement from being a citizen engaged in a particular economic activity to serving on the state board or commission regulating that activity and then later returning to the private sector as a citizen again engaged in the activity for profit is the norm. The age-old question is, can the interests of the larger society be protected when there is such a blurring of roles? Can someone regulating an economic activity that he or she has been engaged in and to which he or she intends to return be an objective public servant? Is there a built-in bias in a system in which the regulators are chosen from the ranks of the regulated? One might argue that such arrangements endanger the public interest and benefit only special interests. At least one observer has concluded that "The state's business and political elites are hopelessly intertwined."[37] "Crony capitalism" has for generations characterized the relationship between major industries in Texas and the political leadership.

BEFORE THE COURTS

Filing suit is not lobbying or pressure politics. It is using a long-established set of legal procedures to challenge the substance of law, administrative rules, or other government action. Only persons licensed to practice law can handle cases in the state's major trial courts.

Anyone negatively affected by a law, administrative rule, or government action may seek relief from the courts. The challenge may be that the agency failed to follow proper procedures in making the rule or that it misinterpreted the law in writing guidelines or rules. Applying the law or rules unfairly is another basis for suit. The use of the courts is the last resort. Major corporations, labor unions, and interest groups employ attorneys on their staffs to protect their interests. Small and less wealthy organizations may keep attorneys on retainer or use any attorneys on their board of directors to represent their interests as needed. As with everything else in life, money makes a difference in what one can do.

In a state that elects judges, the question arises as to whether wealthy corporations, interest groups, and unions can influence judicial decisions through campaign contributions. Twice in the past 15 years, CBS has run programs about "justice for sale" on *60 Minutes* alleging that the Texas Supreme Court overwhelmingly identifies with specific interests. These reports have led to demands for campaign finance regulations to reduce any possible conflicts of interest caused by justices accepting campaign contributions. In the 2008 elections for the Texas Supreme Court, the incumbents and their challengers "took

Texas Register

The official publication of the state that gives the public notice of proposed actions and adopted policies of executive branch agencies.

---

[37]"The Future Is Texas," *Economist*, December 19, 2002, p. 29.

approximately two-thirds of their political funds from contributors with business before the court."[38] Thus far, the legislature has resisted enactment of anything but voluntary compliance standards for judicial campaigns.[39] The U.S. Supreme Court steered clear of restricting campaign contributions in the 2009 *Caperton* v. *A. T. Massey Coal Company* case. In this case, the Supreme Court ruled:

> We conclude that there is a serious risk of actual bias—based on objective and reasonable perceptions—when a person with a personal stake in a particular case had a significant and disproportionate influence in placing the judge on the case by raising funds or directing the judge's election campaign when the case was pending or imminent. The inquiry centers on the contribution's relative size in comparison to the total amount of money contributed to the campaign, the total amount spent in the election, and the apparent effect such contribution had on the outcome of the election.[40]

Although the decision begins to set parameters for the most egregious examples of conflicts of interest, *Caperton* v. *A. T. Massey* does not ban campaign contributions made by litigants or attorneys. If greater restrictions are to be established, it will be up to the Texas legislature to set those restrictions.

Large campaign contributions to judicial candidates are newsworthy because judges are held to a higher standard than elected legislators and executives. Legislators and elected executives are expected to be highly partisan. Judges must be as impartial as human imperfection allows. Texas is one of 15 states that elects its judges in partisan elections. Although most voters do not know who the judicial candidates are, they prefer to elect their judges rather than allow an independent commission or some other body to nominate nonpartisan judges. Political parties and campaign consultants also have a vested interest in maintaining the status quo. Reformers, however, will continue to seek changes in the method of selecting judges, even when they do not advocate changes in the other branches of government.

Which Interests Are Powerful?

Twenty-five years ago, business and the professions tended to be the most powerful interests in the states. They still are, despite a mushrooming of a number of groups. Generally speaking, the newer interests, such as the environmentalists, have not supplanted the old. In conservative pro-business Texas, that is not surprising. For many corporations, the power of interest groups waxes and wanes depending on the political environment. If an industry believes that it stands to gain or lose from government action, it will lobby the legislature. Although it is not the best measure of the strength of an interest group, one can gauge the strength of a lobbying effort by the amount of money spent to lobby.

Table 5.4 lists the 27 groups that spent up to $1 million or more on lobbying in 2009. Note the frequency of times that groups from the energy and natural resources sector appear. Eighteen percent (or up to $62 million) of all lobbying contracts in 2009 were made on behalf of the energy and natural resources sector of the economy.[41] In 2009, the energy sector, led by Energy Future's Holding Corporation lobbied for a piece of the $5 billion Texas Public Utility Commission bid request to build power lines that would move wind power energy from north

---

[38]Texans for Public Justice, "Courtroom Contributions Stain Supreme Court Campaigns," October 2008, http://info.tpj.org/reports/courtroomcontributions/index.html

[39]Clay Robison, "Campaign '96: 'Justice for Sale' Charges Leveled Anew," *Houston Chronicle*, September 22, 1996, p. 1A.

[40]*Caperton* v. *A. T. Massey*, 129 U.S. 2264 (2009).

[41]Texans for Public Justice, "Austin's Oldest Profession: Texas's Top Lobby Clients and Those Who Support Them," 2010 Edition, available at http://info.tpj.org/reports/austinsoldest09/facts.html

TABLE 5.4 THE BIGGEST SPENDERS ON LOBBYISTS IN TEXAS

Client	Maximum Value of Lobbying Contract	Industry
AT&T Corp.	$9,250,000	Communications
Energy Future Holdings Corp.	$3,240,000	Energy/Natural Resources
Reliant Energy, Inc.	$2,540,000	Energy/Natural Resources
McGinnis, Lochridge & Kilgore	$ 2,175,000	Lawyers/Lobbyists
TX Trial Lawyers Assn.	$1,850,000	Lawyers/Lobbyists
American Electric Power	$1,800,000	Energy/Natural Resources
TX Assn. of Realtors	$ 1,770,000	Real Estate
TX Medical Assn.	$ 1,720,000	Health
TXU Energy Retail Co.	$ 1,495,000	Energy/Natural Resources
CenterPoint Energy	$ 1,485,000	Energy/Natural Resources
Oncor Electric Delivery Co.	$ 1,470,000	Energy/Natural Resources
Assn. of Electric Companies of TX	$ 1,425,000	Energy/Natural Resources
City of Houston	$ 1,315,000	Ideological/Single Issue
Wholesale Beer Distributors of TX	$ 1,305,000	Misc. Business
Baker Botts	$ 1,285,000	Lawyers/Lobbyists
ExxonMobil Corp.	$ 1,260,000	Energy/Natural Resources
El Paso County	$ 1,250,000	Ideological/Single Issue
TX Cable & Telecom. Assn.	$ 1,245,000	Communications
Linebarger Heard Goggan Blair	$ 1,200,000	Lawyers/Lobbyists
Verizon	$ 1,115,000	Communications
Luminant Holding Co.	$ 1,110,000	Energy/Natural Resources
RRI Energy, Inc.	$ 1,050,000	Energy/Natural Resources
City of Austin	$ 1,045,000	Ideological/Single Issue
Atmos Energy Corp.	$ 1,015,000	Energy/Natural Resources
Henderson Global Investors	$ 1,002,000	Finance
Locke Lord Bissell & Liddell	$1,000,000	Lawyers/Lobbyists
UnitedHealth Group	$1,000,000	Health

Source: Texans for Public Justice, "Austin's Oldest Profession: Texas's Top Lobby Clients and Those Who Support Them," 2010 Edition, available at http://info.tpj.org/reports/austinsoldest09/facts.html

and west Texas to the urban centers.[42] Such a huge energy contract brought a lot of energy sector lobbyists to the capitol. Oncor, which is a subsidiary of Energy Future's Holding Corporation, and American Electric Power, received the biggest awards.[43] The power of interest groups is in part a function of the lobbying campaigns they organize.

That said, politicians in the past have identified the most powerful interests in Texas as the Texas Trial Lawyers Association, Texas Medical Association, Texas Realtors Association, and the Texas State Teachers Association. Other groups with more than average influence are the Texas Motor Truck Association, Texas AFL-CIO, Independent Oil and Gas Producers Association, Texas Association of Business and Chambers of Commerce, and the Texas Municipal

[42]Ibid.
[43]Ibid.

League.[44] These groups have the money to maintain permanent headquarters in Austin and employ the clerical and research staffs as well as lobbyists to make their prominence known. These resources, when competently managed, literally allow some interest groups to create a need for themselves within the halls of government. Research shows that the number one element determining the political power of a group is how much public officials need the group. This need may be for the expertise that the group has that can help the state solve problems. It may be dependence on the group for campaign contributions. Perhaps it is dependence on the economic health of the sector of the economy the group represents. There are many explanations of the need that a public official may have for a particular interest.[45]

Most registered lobbyists represent business. Business is a huge category, encompassing both the powerful and the weak. Not everyone in business shares the same viewpoint. Independent and small businesses frequently seek policy outcomes opposed by larger enterprises. Business should not be thought of as monolithic.

Unfortunately, unraveling the lobbyist registration report to determine the number of lobbyists representing a trade group, business association, or other interest is challenging. There may be a number of organizations listed, supported by the same benefactors, representing the same industry, business, or activity. It is easier to identify the lobbyists representing a particular company, profession, union, or employee association. Fifty-seven percent of the business interests are associated with an identifiable company. However, many companies are also represented in **umbrella organizations**, in which industries, wholesalers, producers, retailers, and others join together to promote their collective interests. In other words, one may employ lobbyists directly through the firm and also through these umbrella organizations.

Whether the interest is one of the elite and powerful or one of the relatively unknown groups, they all attempt to inform their membership through newsletters or other means about important matters likely to come before the legislature and executive agencies. They also seek to organize their membership into telephone or mail chains. When a "hot" issue is about to come to a vote, an "action alert" is dispatched and members are asked to contact public officials and express the group's position on the issue. The intent is to apply outside (grassroots) pressure while the lobbyist works inside with the public officials in Austin.

What seems logical is that special interests having full-time staffs, multiple lobbyists, and the ability to disburse sizable campaign contributions achieve more than resource-poor groups. There are, however, additional factors involved. The media can sway the opinion of the people and public officials on many issues. The governor may intervene in affairs before executive agencies or in legislative issues and change the outcome. Access and goodwill "bought" by campaign contributions can be nullified by media exposure, public opinion, and the countervailing power of rival interest groups. Thus, the so-called powerful groups may win more than they lose, but they do not own the government and are not guaranteed success.

Interest Group Dynamics and Power

Ernest Griffin observed in the 1930s that the relationships and interactions among members of the legislature are generally weaker than the relationships between the legislators and lobbyists, academics, and high-ranking bureaucrats who interact to address specific needs and solve specific problems.[46] When these participants are active, they become a subsystem of the legislative or administrative decision-making process. In the literature of political science, the stable interaction patterns among legislative committee members, high-ranking bureaucrats, and representatives of

Umbrella organization

An organization created by interest groups to promote common goals. A number of interest groups may choose to coordinate their efforts to influence government when they share the same policy goal. The organization may be temporary or permanent.

---

[44]Hrebenar and Thomas, "Who's Got Clout?" in Ronald Hrebenar and Clive Thomas (eds.), *Interest Group Politics in the Southern States* (Tuscaloosa: University of Alabama Press, 1992), pp. 58–162.
[45]Ibid.
[46]Ernest Griffin, *The Impasse of Democracy* (New York: Harrison-Hilton Books, 1939), p. 182.

special interests are called "**iron triangles**." This cooperative set of actors is very powerful when operating out of public view. Indeed, the group may control the policy choice. This is especially likely if the policy issue is very narrow and affects only a small segment of society.

The iron triangle arrangement does not describe the environment of all or even most decision making. Another kind of arrangement called "**issue networks**" is less solid. Actors are interested in general policy areas such as health, transportation, or rural economic development, but as the specific topics change, the participants, individuals, and groups change too. For example, some actors concerned about health care focus on cost and access to services, whereas others are concerned more with professionalism and supply of health-care providers. Thus, people representing organizations (and occasionally themselves) move into and out of the subsystem as specific issues change.[47] There are more participants in issue networks than in iron triangles because opposing networks exist.

Iron triangles are most likely to control rather routine decisions. Economic concerns dominate their agenda. What motivates the actors are subsidies in the form of cash grants or tax deductions that favor their economic interests. Issue networks are broader in their interests and hence have more participants. Their focus may be economic, social, or both. The participants may be members of professional and social organizations that are connected through the exchange of information via newsletters and other publications. They strive to bring legislative and bureaucratic actors together in agreement to solve problems. This is because bureaucrats make rules regulating individual and corporate business behavior under authority given by the legislature.

Although issue networks have more participants than iron triangles, the numbers are still small. The general public is absent from most public policy-making and policy-implementing events.

In November 2004, after the special session failed to solve the school finance/property tax problem, a state district court in Austin declared the property tax system as constituted, a violation of the state constitution. The court gave the state a deadline to rectify the problem, giving time for the 2005 regular session of the legislature to act.[48] A deal appeared to be in the making at the end of the 140-day session, but disagreement between the speaker of the house and the lieutenant governor, the presiding officer of the senate, killed the measure. The governor decided that a cooling-off period and time for quiet bargaining among the key players was in order. Therefore, he did not call a special session again until June 2006. In the interim, he appointed a commission headed by well-respected Democrat and former state comptroller, John Sharp, to make recommendations on how to fund public education and reduce property taxes at the same time. Key business leaders of the state made up the majority of members on the commission. Expansion of gambling and gambling taxes was never heard of again. Instead, the focus turned to the expansion of business and excise taxes and reduction of property taxes. The end result, however, had to yield an additional $1.5 billion state dollars for education in Texas.[49]

After the party primaries nominated candidates for office including Governor Perry, the special session was called. Success! With little apparent conflict, the house and senate promptly processed five bills encompassing the key recommendations of the Sharp Commission. What made the difference in 2006 were five conditions: (1) the court deadline imposed for legislative action; (2) the exhaustion of the state's ability to appeal the decision; (3) the ability of state public and private elites to come together and negotiate an agreement; (4) disparagement of the state political leadership for previously failing to solve the problem; and (5) the forthcoming election for governor and other offices.

Iron triangle

A working coalition among administrative agencies, clientele interest groups, and legislative committees that share a common interest in seeing either the implementation or the defeat of certain policies and proposals.

Issue network

Collections of individuals in organizations who are interested in a policy area and get involved in policy making as topics affect their interests. They are not consistently in alliance or opposition with other groups or networks. Internet "blogs" are an example.

---

[47]Hugh Heclo, "Issue Networks and the Executive Establishment," in Anthony King (ed.), *The New American Political System* (Washington, DC: American Enterprise Institute, 1978), pp. 87–124.

[48]See *Neeley v. West Orange-Cove Consolidated Independent School District*, 176 S.W.3d 746 (2005).

[49]Clay Robison, "Some School Funding Fixes Aren't All That Wonderful," *Houston Chronicle*, May 20, 2006, at http://www.chron.com/disp/stoy.mpl/editorial/robison/3876407.html

THE REVOLVING DOOR AND THE TEXAS LEGISLATURE

In recent years, a peculiar practice has developed among many former members of state legislative bodies. Many ex-lawmakers are becoming lobbyists for the very interest groups they once regulated. To be certain, few people would be better suited to serve as lobbyists than ex-lawmakers. Former legislators are intricately familiar with the legislative process, many are policy experts, and they often have friendships with lawmakers who are still in office. Their familiarity with the policy-making process, their policy expertise, and their kinship with other lawmakers make them very attractive candidates for the lobbying profession.

Despite their fitness to serve as lobbyists, there are some dangers to permitting former lawmakers to serve as lobbyists. *Ex*-lawmakers, after all, were once *lawmakers*. That is to say, they were once in the position of creating legislation, regulating industry, and providing oversight of government agencies. Lawmakers, planning their next career move, might feel compelled to reward their future employers with favorable public policy. Ex-lawmakers might author bills that help the industries on whose behalf they hope to lobby, once they leave office. Ex-lawmakers might remove onerous legislation, or be less diligent in their oversight responsibilities when they plan to become lobbyists.

Unlike the federal government and many other states, Texas does not ban former lawmakers from becoming lobbyists. Although 26 other states have some ban on lobbying immediately after leaving office, Texas has no such restrictions. Furthermore, Texas pays its citizen legislators a mere $7,200 per year. A legislator's poor pay does not compare to the salaries of successful lobbyists. In a recent study conducted by the Center for Public Integrity, 70 former members of the Texas legislature were working as lobbyists—the largest number of any state. California and New York, which have full-time legislative bodies, only reported 35 and 19 ex-lawmakers-turned-lobbyists, respectively.[*]

If ex-lawmakers were banned from lobbying, the legislator's freedom to choose a career path would be denied for the sake of assumed improved representation. Many ex-lawmakers leave public office with financial obligations. They have mortgage payments, their kids' college tuition, and many other expenses to which they must attend. As former lawmakers, these individuals have developed skills that can be parlayed into a lobbying career that could allow them to address the personal needs that they were unable to fully address as public servants. As it stands, Texas lawmakers are poorly compensated for their public service. The public expects legislators to represent them fully. When a legislator does so, that legislator compromises personal finances for public service.

Unfortunately, the risk of affording lawmakers the freedom to choose lobbying careers upon leaving office creates a more sinister outcome. Lawmakers are in a position to exploit their positions for the sake of future returns. Unscrupulous lawmakers can sponsor legislation that rewards those interest groups that will provide such lawmakers employment upon leaving the legislature. Although

difficult to gauge the extent to which *quid pro quo* occurs, the coincidences can be troubling. In 2003, Texas Representative Jamie Capelo coauthored a bill that capped medical liability lawsuits. Shortly after leaving office, Capelo was a lobbyist for interest groups that benefited from his earlier legislation. Such connections between public policy and the interest group beneficiaries that would later employ the sponsors of the public policy are common.

Others are critical that the use of public service as a stepping-stone to a more lucrative career as a lobbyist is simply unseemly. "[P]eople rightfully wonder when did they stop being a lawmaker and when did they start to become a special-interest lobbyist," states Andrew Wheat, with Texans for Public Justice.[**] Public service should be its own reward. Most public servants do not enter public service because it is lucrative, but because they care about creating good public policy.

A ban on lobbying would lead to many public servants having limited freedom to choose career paths. It would also ensure that ex-lawmakers do not seek personal gain from their positions, upon leaving office.

A compromise that many state legislative bodies have arrived at, and one that the federal government relies on, is a one- or two-year ban on lobbying. Ex-lawmakers must wait either one or two years before they can lobby their former colleagues. This still does not get around the aforementioned problems, but some believe that a one- or two-year ban reduces the number of ex-lawmakers who become lobbyists. Relying on the Center for Public Integrity's data for 2005, one can gauge the effectiveness of these programs. Whereas states with no ban on lobbying produced an average of 29 ex-lawmakers who became lobbyists, states with a one-year ban averaged 22 lawmakers who became lobbyists, and the six states with a two-year ban averaged 28 lawmakers who became lobbyists. The differences among the states are even smaller when one takes into account that some states have much smaller legislative bodies, thus producing fewer ex-lawmakers.

Further contributing to the number of former lawmakers who become lobbyists is the number of states that have set term limits for lawmakers. Term limits help produce more ex-lawmakers in need of employment—employment that ex-lawmakers tend to find as lobbyists.

A complete ban on postlegislative service would ensure that ex-lawmakers do not use their public service as a stepping stone to a more lucrative lobbying career. Such a ban, however, would deny the ex-lawmaker the liberty to choose a career after public service.

FOR DEBATE

What other factors might explain why ex-lawmakers become lobbyists? Is the cost of denying a lawmaker the freedom to choose a lobbying career outweighed by the public's expectation for good public policy?

---

[*]Center for Public Integrity, "Ex-Legislators Registered to Lobby 2005," October 12, 2006, http://www.publicintegrity.org/hiredguns/reg.aspx
[**]Grissom, Brandi, "Ex-Lawmaker's Lobbying Looks Bad, Group Says," *El Paso Times*, May 21, 2009.

The fourth time the legislature met to solve the problem left no time for issue avoidance. Failure, so close to an election, would be worse for state political leaders than changing the tax code. State private elites were anxious to resolve the dilemma, as the problem was negatively affecting the Texas business climate. The governor, experiencing opposition from two write-in candidates for his job as well as a Democratic and Libertarian Party candidate, had to secure a solution to remain in office. The Sharp Commission succeeded in melding the most powerful special interests into a unified force that agreed on the key provisions of policy. A review of press coverage before and during the special session reveals very few references to conflict among the key interests.

CHAPTER SUMMARY

* Interest groups are organizations of people who agree on policy issues that affect their members. Interest groups do not nominate candidates for office but do care about the ideologies of those who stand for election. They therefore may form political action committees to support candidates favorable to their causes.

* The constitutions of the United States and Texas promote political expression. The right to organize to petition officials is explicit. This right recognizes that representatives of the people can represent their constituents only when they are informed of their wishes. Interest groups are therefore constitutionally protected.

* Groups with sufficient resources employ staff to monitor the government. They proactively bring issues before decision makers and reactively move into the political process to stop or alter proposals that negatively affect their membership.

* Business groups are among the strongest interests. Large corporations lobby decision makers both through umbrella organizations and directly. It is not uncommon for large interests to have more than 20 paid lobbyists working for them during a legislative session. Between sessions, groups conduct research, draft proposed legislation for the next session, and monitor and influence the executive branch, which writes the rules to carry out laws.

* Interest groups have been powerful in Texas due to the historical absence of competitive two-party politics, restrictive election laws, low voter turnout, and the below-average educational attainment of many citizens.

* As happens at the national level, "iron triangles" often form in Texas. These triangles unite interest groups that represent a particular industry or activity with the bureaucracy that regulates the activity and with the members of the legislative committee that oversees the bureaucracy. Iron triangles are especially potent in Texas because regulatory boards and commissions are required to have members who actively participate in the regulated activity. This requirement almost guarantees conflicts of interest. Looser alliances called issue networks also form. These may consist of legislators, legislative staff members, interest group leaders, bureaucrats, journalists, scholars, and others who support a particular policy position on a given issue.

* The media, a few nonprofit and officially nonpartisan special interests, and the Texas Ethics Commission are the sources of most of the information we have about the relationship between interest groups and public officials in Texas. Most lobbyists are required to file reports with the Ethics Commission, which in turn publishes the names, addresses, employers, expenditures, and salaries (in broad categorical ranges) of lobbyists. The media and the nonpartisan interests "blow the whistle" about conflicts of interest and official behavior that is suspect.

KEY TERMS

access
advocacy
astroturf lobbying
conflict of interest
co-optation

delegation
discretion
fragmentation
implementation
interest group

iron triangles
issue networks
late train contributions
lobbying
lobbyist

pressure group
public interest
Texas Ethics Commission
Texas Register
umbrella organization

REVIEW QUESTIONS

1. What are interest groups? What do they do? How do they do what they do?

2. Interest groups are not political parties. What is the difference between these two political institutions in scope and purpose?

3. What are the two major classifications of interest groups? What are the subcategories? Identify an interest group in each subcategory.

4. What characteristics of the people of Texas affect the influence of interest groups?

5. Where political party competition is strong, interest group power is weakened. Why?

6. Interest groups attempt to influence the decisions of all three branches of government, but not by the same methods. Explain.

7. What is lobbying? What does a lobbyist do?

8. Which interests are the most powerful in Texas? Why?

9. Define *conflict of interest*. Cite some hypothetical instances of such conflicts. How can the state regulate legislators and groups to minimize them? Can the public interest be balanced with the need for expertise on the boards and commissions of Texas?

10. Reformers are seriously concerned about the methods of financing judicial elections. What kinds of interest groups are involved in this issue? Specifically, what groups favor and oppose change? What are the stated and real reasons?

LOGGING ON

To access the websites of some of the leading economic interest groups in Texas, go to the following addresses:

Texas Trial Lawyers Association: **http://www.ttla.com/tx**
Texas Farm Bureau: **http://www.txfb.org**
Texas AFL-CIO: **http://www.texasaflcio.org**
Texas State Teachers Association: **http://www.tsta.org**
Texas Association of School Boards: **http://www.tasb.org**

To access the websites of some leading noneconomic interest groups in Texas, go to the following addresses:

National Organization for Women: **http://www.now.org**
NAACP: **http://www.naacp.org**

Center for Public Integrity: **http://www.publicintegrity.org**
Texans for Public Justice: **http://www.tpj.org**
Texas Common Cause: **http://www.commoncause.org**

To access the websites of some think tanks in Texas, go to the following addresses:

Center for Public Policy Priorities: **http://www.cppp.org**
Center for Responsive Politics: **http://www.opensecrets.org**
FreedomWorks: **http://www.freedomworks.org**
Texas Public Policy Foundation: **http://www.texaspolicy.com**

God, Gays, Guns, and Immigration in Texas

John Osterman
San Jacinto College

INTRODUCTION

This article offers a sampling of interest groups that have engaged in the so-called "culture wars" over social issues embodying such fundamental personal values that they are difficult to compromise. Unlike economic issues, which can be settled with compromises that "split the differences" between competing interest groups, social issues are often so deeply embedded in social group identity that their interest group demands tend to be more nearly absolute. As a result, interest groups organized around basic cultural divisions have pushed polarizing political agendas.

Interest groups seek to influence the government at the national, state, and local levels. Unlike political parties, they do not seek to control the government. Interest groups are the product of a pluralistic society, and society is the aggregate of the ideals, values, and beliefs of the individuals that comprise it. Given these truths, a study of interest groups is also a study of the ideology that is the foundation of society. The source of these beliefs is found in families and institutions, and the process of adopting them is called socialization. What makes Texas different from other states in terms of ideology is what is taught or practiced in homes and institutions throughout the state.

There are at least four issues that garner a lot of attention in Texas; God, gays, guns, and immigration. There may not be specific groups organized for just these issues; however, there are plenty of interests competing to influence the government at all levels as well as society as a whole. Organized interests typically lobby elected and unelected government officials for changes in the law, policy, or constitutional interpretation. They also mobilize voters through email campaigns and get media attention with marches and demonstrations. Of course, a changing culture can bring about policy changes as well, and the issues that impact Texas also impact the nation.

GOD

When one thinks of Texas, one often thinks of tradition and religion; they go hand-in-hand. From "one nation under God" to "God bless Texas," from the Texas pledge to the moment of silence, God is alive and well in Texas. This can be witnessed by looking at the many mega-churches in Texas such as Lakewood Church in Houston led by Joel Osteen, which boasts the largest average attendance in the nation. Osteen's message reaches far and wide. He has preached at both Dodger and Yankee stadiums to sold-out crowds. The Second Baptist Church of Houston led by Ed Young is another example and is ranked as the fifth-largest church in the country. The Catholic Church also has an enormous presence in Texas, with two archdioceses. More than 1.5 million Catholics live within archdiocesan boundaries of the Archdiocese of Galveston–Houston, the largest in the state of Texas and the 11th largest in the United States. These institutions and the families that frequent them shape the values that define the culture.

Recently, the Texas State Board of Education (SBOE) debated the issue of God in textbooks among other things. For example, changes were proposed to remove Christmas from the Texas Essential Knowledge and Skills examination. In addition, recommendations were made to require classroom analysis of the Founding Fathers' intent in the First Amendment rather than merely use the expression "separation of church and state." The 15-member SBOE chooses the next generation of history textbooks for Texas children. The board has ten Republicans and five Democrats, many of which are social conservatives. The board writes the curriculum standards for subject areas such as English, science, and social studies. This has been a controversy in part because liberals and conservatives have different ideas about history and the influence of religion in history. On the liberal side are such groups as American Atheists, Americans United for Separation of Church and State, and the American Civil Liberties Union. On the conservative side is the Liberty Institute.

GAYS

Houston recently elected its first openly gay mayor, Anise Parker. Many were shocked and surprised that such a conservative city in a conservative state could elect someone from the gay, lesbian, bisexual, transgender (GLBT) community to the highest political position in the fourth-largest city in the nation. However, it was no surprise to many in Houston. Parker, a Rice University graduate, had been the comptroller for the city and a city council member while never hiding her sexual preferences. She was recently named to *Time*'s list of the "World's Most Influential People." That influence includes the power to appoint judges who are also from the GLBT community. She recently named Municipal Court Judge Barbara E.

Hartle to be the chief presiding judge of the municipal courts in Houston.

Another aspect of sexual preference that has received attention is same-sex marriage. In 2004, Texas Baptists passed a resolution affirming that marriage is between a man and a woman. Such groups mobilized voters to support an amendment to the Texas Constitution defining marriage in the same way, and this is a result of the culture. This view was reinforced when the SBOE asked publishers to rewrite textbooks to reflect the same language when defining marriage. However, in 2010, a same-sex couple from Massachusetts filed for divorce in Texas, and it was granted by an Austin judge. Texas Attorney General Greg Abbott argued against granting the divorce because there is no recognition of same-sex marriage in the state.

GUNS

Texas is no stranger to guns. Recently, the legislature voted to give every college student and their teachers the right to carry weapons on campus. The bill was ultimately defeated; however, it shows the degree to which Texans believe in the Second Amendment. In a related story, a person was detained at the state capitol after discharging a weapon outside. After such an event it is natural to think there would be an immediate call for changes in security policy; however, no such call came. It seems like just another day in the Lone Star State. On another typical day in Texas, Governor Rick Perry shot and killed a coyote while jogging by using a .308 laser-sighted Ruger pistol with hollow point bullets. From the classroom to the capitol, guns are a way of life in Texas.

Texas is a right-to-carry state, which requires a concealed weapon permit. With that right in mind, the school board in the Harrold Independent School District voted to allow teachers and staff to carry weapons on campus. Along the same lines, the Castle Doctrine in Texas is also a product of the culture. It states that Texans have a legal right to defend themselves with deadly force in their homes, cars, and workplace if a person unlawfully enters or attempts to enter, and there is no duty to retreat on the part of the property owner. Although the Second Amendment to the U.S. Constitution guarantees every American the right to keep and bear arms, the battle to preserve the right wages on in Texas. Obviously, the National Rifle Association plays a role in Texas and across the nation.

IMMIGRATION

In light of Arizona's recent law allowing state and local law enforcement to ask for proof of citizenship or residence when detaining someone for allegedly committing a crime, Texas became the focus of attention advocating that it adopt a similar law. In 2008, Texas Representative Debbie Riddle (R-District 150) filed a bill allowing state and local law enforcement officers to arrest those who are in the country illegally. Although the bill did not pass, it is likely to be reconsidered as a result of the passage of the Arizona law.

Clearly, the League of Latin American Citizens and the Mexican American Legal Defense and Educational Fund are the most prominent interest groups supporting illegal immigrants in Texas, followed closely by the Roman Catholic Church; however, there does not appear to be a single significant group opposed to illegal immigration. The Minuteman Project received abundant media attention for several years during the Bush administration and has not been covered very much since. The project describes itself as a multi-ethnic immigration law enforcement advocacy group, and law enforcement appears to be the driving concern of conservative groups. One factor contributing to the lack of border security groups in Texas might be the size of the Latino population. Latinos comprise more than 30 percent of the population in Texas, and there is an ongoing socialization due to the integration of Latinos and non-Latinos in public schools and other social institutions. There is unmeasured influence from groups that disseminate information pertaining to these issues via websites and blogs, which provide readers with an opportunity to educate themselves in the absence of such coverage by the mainstream media. (e.g., the *Texas Insider* and the Texas Public Policy Foundation, a nonpartisan research institute or think tank).

CONCLUSION

Interestingly, each of these issues and the groups that debate these issues coincide on many levels. For instance, many immigrants in Texas are Latino and Catholic. Immigrants to Texas bring their culture with them. Texas holds true to the death penalty while Catholics do not, and the Catholic Church does not support gay marriage; however, Mexico recently allowed gay marriages. The conflict between groups over law and order issues as well as religious and privacy issues is often described as a culture war. This war is witnessed in the public square where cultures meet. Moreover, families, schools, and churches teach their culture to new generations. The future of interest groups and the policies they promote are found in the ever-changing culture.

JOIN THE DEBATE

1. Why are Texans more familiar with these issues than with economic issues?

2. Should these disparate groups be afforded the same treatment under the law? Why or why not?

3. Examine your own ideals, values, and beliefs. Discuss whether or not you would have these views if you had been raised differently or in a state other than Texas.

4. Underlying each of these issues is a concern for freedom. How might your freedom be challenged by groups that have views different from your own?

5. Is there a danger that, as interest groups fight the culture wars, tribalism will disintegrate society? Today, how much are churches, neighborhoods, schools, media, and even professions segregated into competing cultural groups?

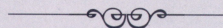

Chapter 6

The Legislature: Organization and Structure

CONTENTS

LEARNING OBJECTIVES

* Become familiar with the factors that contribute to legislative districting.
* Describe the significance of *Reynolds* v. *Sims*.
* Describe the differences between formal and informal qualifications.
* Define *descriptive representation* and assess extent to which minority populations have achieved it.
* Know who the presiding officers of the Texas House and Texas Senate are and what they do.
* Differentiate between the different types of committees.
* Determine the significance of legislative staff sizes.
* Know the consequences of poor compensation, short legislative sessions, and small staffs.

★ GET ACTIVE ★

Volunteer on a political campaign or intern for a member of the Texas House or Texas Senate. Here's how to identify candidates running for public office:

★ Visit the Texas Secretary of State's website at **http://www.sos.state.tx.us/** and click on the Elections and Voter Information.

★ View the list of candidates on the Texas Democratic and Republican parties websites at **http://www.txdemocrats.org/** and **http://www.texasgop.org/**

★ Try the League of Women Voters of Texas (**http://www.lwvtexas.org/**) for a source of valuable information on candidates.

You also might explore these internship opportunities for Texas students:

★ Investigate the Texas Legislative Internship Program, at **http://www.rodneyellis.com/tlip/**

★ Try the Moreno Rangel Legislative Leadership Program (**http://www.mallfoundation.org/program.html**), which provides internship opportunities to Latino/Latina undergraduate and graduate students.

★ Or, try Senator Gregory Luna Legislative Scholar Fellows Program (**http://www.tshrc.org/program.html**).

★ Check with your own university. Many universities have their own legislative internship programs.

★ Call your representative in the Texas House or Senate for additional internship opportunities. For a listing of members of the Texas House, check **http://www.house.state.tx.us/welcome.php**, and for a listing of members of the Texas Senate, check **http://www.senate.state.tx.us/**

★ Local political campaigns for city council and county governments also offer great opportunities for political involvement.

You can have a meaningful impact in Texas politics by participating in your community's precinct convention. Precinct conventions perform two main functions. They select delegates to attend the county convention (in counties with large populations, senatorial district conventions are held instead of county conventions). Precinct convention delegates also propose, discuss, and vote on resolutions that are then submitted to the county or senatorial district convention. Precinct conventions are usually held in the voting precinct, and the meeting begins shortly after the polls close on primary election night. Primary elections are held on even-numbered years, the first Tuesday in March. If you voted in the Democratic primary, you are eligible to participate in the Democratic precinct convention. If you voted in the Republican primary, you are eligible to participate in the Republican precinct convention. If you did not vote in the primary, you are not eligible to participate in the precinct convention. Generally, few people attend the primary convention, so bring a friend and maximize your impact.

 In 2009, Texas Monthly *named Wendy Davis the "Rookie of the Year," for her service in the Texas House.* Texas Monthly *would write, "[S]he tackled substantive subjects like oil and gas drilling, electric utility regulation, and consumer debt in her debut session. That old rule that freshmen are supposed to stay quiet? She proved it can be ignored if you're smart, tough, and well prepared."[1] Senator Davis defeated incumbent Kim Brimer to become one of 42 women to serve in the 81st Legislature—36 in the Texas House and 6 in the Texas Senate.*

---

[1]Paul Burka and Patricia Kilday Hart, "The Best and Worst Legislators 2009," *Texas Monthly,* July 2009, http://www.texasmonthly.com/2009-07-01/feature2-4.php

Hillary Clinton, Sarah Palin, Nancy Pelosi, Sonia Sotomayor, and Elena Kagan are just a few examples of women making history at the national level, but Texas women are making their own history in the state legislature. Women now account for 19 percent of the Texas Senate and 24 percent of the Texas House. Although these figures are far less than the 50 percent of the population that is female, women are nevertheless, increasing their representation in the legislature.

More importantly, however, women are bringing their voices to the table, contributing to the creation of public policy and influencing decisions that are informed by their own personal experiences. Senator Davis describes her mother and grandmother's life:

> They were poor their entire lives. They tenant-farmed, share-cropped, and raised and sold pigs. They grew all of their own food, canned vegetables, and, when they had them, killed one cow and one pig each fall to sustain them through winter. My mother recalls a time when they moved to Muleshoe, Texas, looking for work and living on "water gravy" and "water biscuits." It was like eating glue, my mom says, as she recalls what it was like to live for weeks on end in a state of unabating hunger.[2]

Senator Davis would go on to have opportunities that her mother and grandmother would not have. She graduated from Texas Christian University and Harvard Law School before becoming a senator. But her experiences as a woman, and her connection to other women, guide her politics. After describing the plight of women with breast cancer or the suffering that other women have endured she writes, "None of these women would allow the difficulty of a tough battle to dissuade them from their cause. Neither should I."[3] Statements like this suggest that the gender of lawmakers influences their decisions, bringing greater diversity and representation to legislative institutions. This chapter will describe representation and the organizational structure of the legislature, beginning with a discussion of legislative districts.

Geographic Districts

In 2010, the U.S. Census Bureau attempted to count every person in the United States. In Texas, like in other states, these data are used to draw the geographic boundaries for the districts of the Texas House, Texas Senate, and other elected positions. The Texas House of Representatives is composed of 150 members, and the Texas Senate is composed of 31 members. The members of the Texas House of Representatives, like the members of the Texas Senate, are elected from single-member districts. The Texas House and Senate districts for the 82nd Legislative Session are found in Figures 6.1 and 6.2, respectively. These districts all have approximately equal populations as required by the U.S. Supreme Court decision in *Reynolds* v. *Sims*. In this case, the Supreme Court ruled, "Simply stated, an individual's right to vote for state legislators is unconstitutionally impaired when its weight is in a substantial fashion diluted when compared with votes of citizens living in other parts of the State."[4] Known as "one person, one vote," this decision mandated **reapportionment**, or the requirement that each legislator should represent approximately the same number of people. Redistricting or redrawing the district lines is required following each census to maintain equal representation.

Reapportionment

The redrawing of district and precinct lines following the national census to reflect population changes.

---

[2]Wendy R. Davis, "Getting up on My Pink Tractor," *Connection with Senator Wendy R. Davis*, Vol. 4, 2010, http://www.senate.state.tx.us/75r/Senate/members/dist10/pdf/D10NL_Vol04.pdf
[3]Ibid.
[4]*Reynolds* v. *Sims*, 377 U.S. 533 (1964).

The Capitol Building in Austin ☛

Elena Yakusheva, 2010/Used under license from Shutterstock.com

Should the Texas legislature fail to redistrict, the state constitution provides for the function to be performed by the Legislative Redistricting Board. The board is **ex officio**, which means that its members hold other offices. It is made up of the lieutenant governor, the speaker of the house, the attorney general, the comptroller, and the commissioner of the General Land Office.

Ex officio

Holding a position automatically because one also holds some other office.

The average population of an electoral district for the Texas House of Representatives in 2010 exceeds 160,000. House members now represent more than 40,000 more people than they did a decade ago. Representing approximately 800,000 residents, Texas senators serve an estimated 150,000 more people in 2010 than they did in 2000. Members of the Texas Senate represent more people than the Texas delegation to the U.S. House of Representatives. These house and senate seats must be drawn to be as evenly matched as possible. Legislative districts can deviate plus or minus five percent from the mean, but not much more. In instances in which districts deviate too much from the mean, the state of Texas must justify these deviations to the U.S. Justice Department. The once-per-decade redistricting ritual goes more or less unnoticed by the casual observer of politics. For the political practitioner and the political activist, however, it may resemble a life-or-death struggle.

Drawing district lines for partisan political advantage got the name *gerrymandering* in 1812 when the legislature of Massachusetts and Governor Elbridge Gerry, wishing to preserve a Republican majority, redrew a district in such a convoluted shape that a political cartoonist portrayed it as a salamander and dubbed it the "Gerry-mander." The shapes of several current Texas congressional districts exceed the oddity of the original gerrymander.

The way districts are drawn at any level of government determines to a large extent the political, ideological, and ethnic makeup of the legislative body. With redistricting, political careers may be made or broken, public policy determined for at least a decade, and the power of ethnic or political minorities neutralized. A district drawn in such a way as to give candidates from a certain party, ethnic group, or faction

Gerrymander

A district or precinct that is drawn specifically to favor some political party, candidate, or ethnic group.

an advantage is known as a **gerrymander**. Because gerrymandering decreases or increases the political power of specific groups of voters, it has a very powerful effect on politics and public policy. The relative influence of political parties, ethnic groups, ideological combatants, and individual politicians in the political process is at stake. (See Figure 6.3.)

Texas has had to contend with a spate of gerrymandering issues during the past two decades. A special session of the Texas legislature, 11 lawsuits, and various other legal actions in both state and federal court from 1990 through 1994 were necessary before the drawing of district boundaries after the 1990 Census was settled. Republican membership in the senate immediately increased from 9 in 1991 to 13 in 1993. And, by 1996, Republicans were in control of the Texas Senate, although Democrats continued to be the majority in the house. Legislative Republicans refused to accept the legislative redistricting that followed the 2000 Census and forced the redistricting effort into the Legislative Redistricting Board, on which Republicans enjoyed a 4-to-1 majority. After redistricting, the 2002 election increased the senate Republican majority to 19 and gave Republicans a majority in the Texas House for the first time since Reconstruction.

Although the congressional districts were redrawn by a panel of U.S. district judges (one Democrat and two Republicans), Democrats still maintained a 17-to-15 majority in

Figure 6.1

Texas House of Representatives Districts, 82nd Legislature, 2011–2013

Source: Texas Legislative Council.

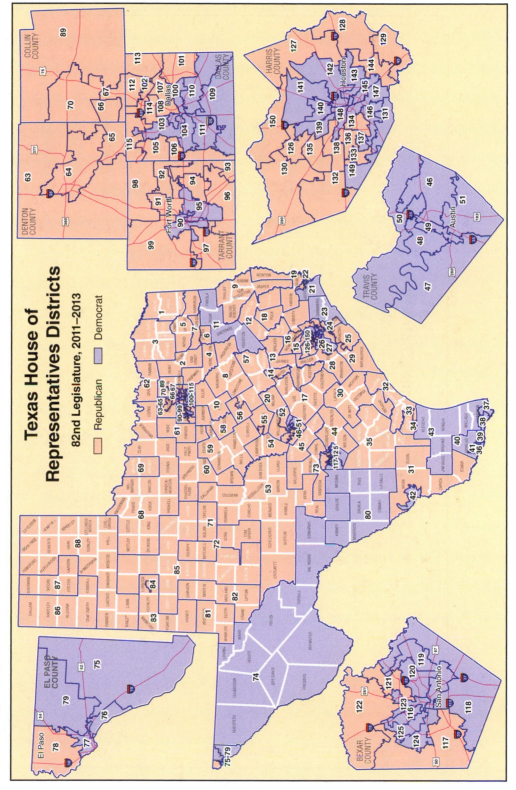

Texas House of
Representatives Districts
82nd Legislature, 2011–2013

Republican
Democrat

Figure 6.2
Texas Senate Districts, 82nd Legislature, 2011–2013

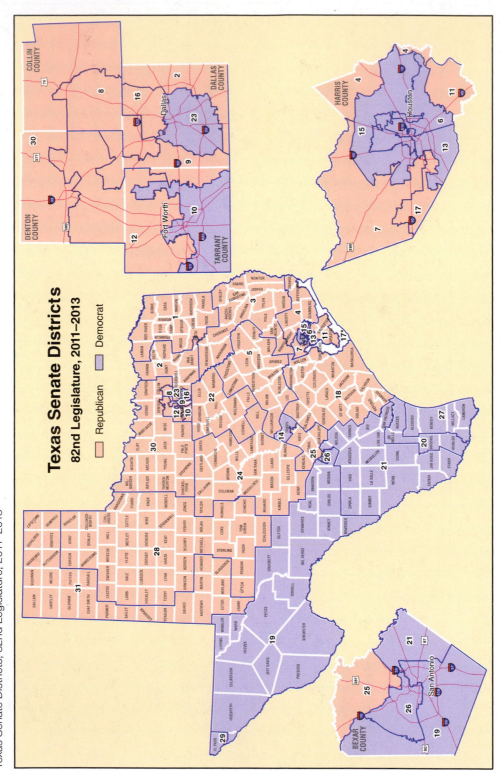

Texas Senate Districts
82nd Legislature, 2011–2013

Republican
Democrat

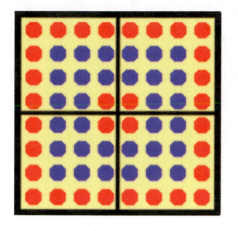 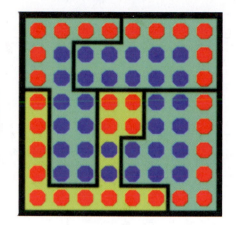

Figure 6.3

Redrawing the boundaries in the balanced electoral districts in this example creates a guaranteed 3-to-1 advantage in representation for the blue voters. The districts were gerrymandered.

Texas's congressional delegation. Because U.S. House Majority Leader Tom DeLay feared that the 2004 election might give Democrats control of the U.S. House of Representatives, he encouraged Republican-controlled legislatures in Texas, Colorado, and other states to redraw congressional districts before the 2010 Census to favor Republican candidates. This tactic was successful and contributed to the continued Republican control of the U.S. House.

In Texas, Governor Rick Perry called three special sessions to redo the 2000 congressional redistricting. The first two special sessions failed to enact redistricting because house Democrats in the first special session and senate Democrats in the second left the state, thereby denying the Republican majority a quorum, which is necessary for the legislature to conduct business. The third attempt for a redistricting special session was successful, as Democratic senators were unable to muster the necessary 11 members to deny the quorum, and the congressional districts were gerrymandered. After the 2004 election, the Texas congressional delegation changed from a 17-to-15 Democratic majority to a 21-to-11 Republican majority. This new redistricting plan hurt Anglo-American Democratic congressmen and rural constituents, whereas suburban cities came out ahead. By the 110th Congress (2007–2009), Democrats would pick up a few more of those seats, but the election of 2010 would give the Republican congressional delegation a 20 to 12 seat advantage. Figure 6.4 shows the congressional districts for the 112th Congress. The redistricting battles will continue during the 82nd Legislative Session, as the legislature addresses the state's population growth, new congressional seats, and a growing Latino population. The redistricting generated numerous lawsuits challenging its legality. The U.S. Supreme Court combined four of the cases and in March 2006 considered four legal questions:

1. Can the legislature, on its own initiative, undertake mid-decade redistricting?
2. Did the redistricting of the 23rd and 24th Districts diminish the rights of minority voters under the Voting Rights Act?
3. Is the state obligated to create additional Latino districts in South and West Texas?
4. Is the Republican redistricting plan a legitimate use of the political process to correct past redistricting injustices, or is it an unconstitutional "partisan gerrymander?"

On June 28, 2006, the Court upheld most of the actions of the Texas legislature, ruling that unless prohibited by law, states could redistrict more than once each decade and that Texas's partisan redistricting was constitutional. The only ruling that favored the plaintiffs was that the new boundaries of the 23rd District discriminated against Latino voters and

Figure 6.4

Texas Congressional Districts, 112th Congress, 2011–2013

Source: Texas Legislative Council.

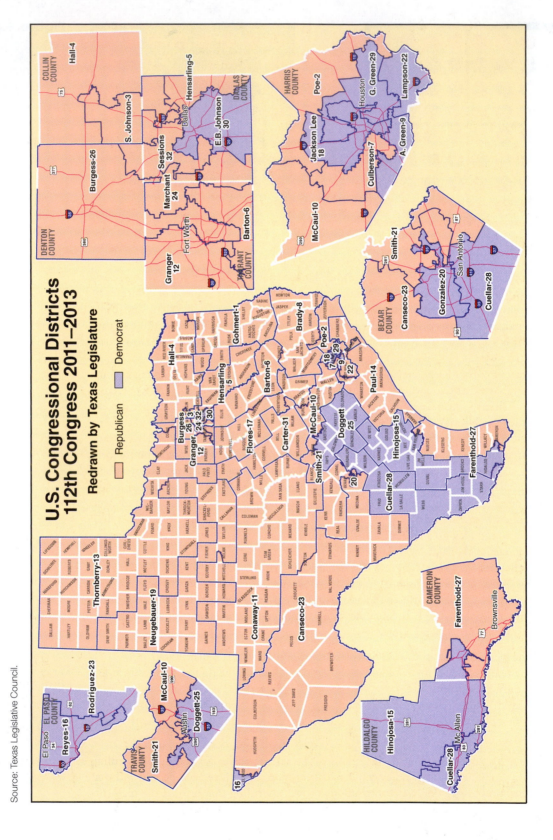

HOW DOES TEXAS COMPARE?
FEMALE REPRESENTATION IN STATE LEGISLATURES

Increasingly, more women are running for office, and one place in which their success manifests itself is in state legislatures. Texas is no exception. The Texas legislature has experienced an increase in the number of women holding seats, but it falls below the average among the 50 states. Although the average percentage of female state lawmakers is 23.4 across the 50 states, during the 82nd Legislative Session, 21 percent of Texas lawmakers were female. Texas ranks 33rd in the percentage of female lawmakers. The table below lists the 32 states with greater percentages of female lawmakers than Texas.

THE STATES WITH THE GREATEST PERCENTAGE OF FEMALE LAWMAKERS

State	Percent	State	Percent
Colorado	39.0	Oregon	25.6
Vermont	38.3	Florida	25.6
Arizona	34.4	New Hampshire	24.5
Hawaii	32.9	Wisconsin	23.5
Washington	31.3	Massachusetts	23.5
Minnesota	31.3	Missouri	23.4
Maryland	30.9	Montana	23.3
Connecticut	29.4	Georgia	23.3
Nevada	28.6	Alaska	23.3
New Mexico	28.6	New York	22.6
New Jersey	28.3	Nebraska	22.4
Illinois	28.2	North Carolina	22.4
Kansas	27.9	Arkansas	22.2
California	27.5	Iowa	22.0
Idaho	26.7	Ohio	21.2
Delaware	25.8	Texas	21.0
Rhode Island	25.7		

Source: National Conference of State Legislatures: Women's Legislative Network of NCSL; Women in State Legislatures: 2011 Legislative Session, http://www.ncsl.org/LegislaturesElections/WomensNetwork/WomeninStateLegislatures2011/tabid/21606/Default.aspx

therefore violated the Voting Rights Act. The new district boundaries were redrawn by a district court and accepted.[5] The political and legal fallout from the election preceding the gerrymander forced Congressman Tom DeLay to leave Congress.

Three basic gerrymander techniques are generally used. One is to diffuse a concentrated political or ethnic minority among several districts so that its votes in any one district are negligible. A second tactic is used if the minority's numbers are great enough when diffused to affect the outcome of elections in several districts: the minority is concentrated in one district, thereby ensuring that it will influence only one election and that its influence in the whole legislature will be minimal. A third tactic is a **pairing** technique that redistricts two or more **incumbent** legislators' residences or political bases so that both are in the same district, thereby ensuring that one will be defeated. Pairing can be used to punish legislators who have fallen from grace with the legislative leadership.

Gerrymandering is also used to protect the "right kind" of incumbents, those who support the legislative leadership or the agenda of powerful special interests. Although the federal courts prohibit racial gerrymandering, they are reluctant to become involved in political gerrymandering.

Pairing

Placing two incumbent officeholders in the same elective district through redistricting. This is usually done to eliminate political enemies.

Incumbent

The current holder of an office.

[5]*League of United Latin American Citizens* v. *Perry*, No. 05-204 (U.S. 2006).

Qualifications for Membership

FORMAL QUALIFICATIONS

Although legal, or formal, qualifications must be met before anyone can serve in the state legislature, rarely do these requirements prohibit serious candidates from seeking legislative seats. In fact, the criteria are broad enough to allow millions of Texas residents to run for the legislature.

> The archaic language of the Texas Constitution refers to officeholders as *he* and *his*, as in, "No person shall be a Senator, unless *he* be a citizen of the United States, and, at the time of *his* election a qualified voter of this State, and shall have been a resident of this State five years next preceding *his* election, and the last year thereof a resident of the district for which *he* shall be chosen, and shall have attained the age of twenty-six years."[6]

To be a Texas state senator, an individual must be a U.S. citizen, a qualified voter, at least 26 years of age, and must have lived for the previous five years in the state, with the most recent year having been lived in the district in which he or she seeks election. Qualifications for house membership are even more easily met. A candidate must be a U.S. citizen, a qualified voter of the state, at least 21 years of age, and have lived in Texas for the two previous years and in the district for one year prior to being elected.

INFORMAL QUALIFICATIONS

The most important requirements for holding legislative office in Texas are not the legal limitations but the informal ones. Certain political, social, and economic criteria determine who is elected not just to the state legislature but to offices at all levels of government—national, state, county, city, and special district.

Party and Race Until the 1990s, the Democratic Party was the dominant legislative party in Texas. However, the resurgence of the Republican Party has made Texas a strongly Republican state. By the end of 2004, Republicans had established dominance over all three branches of state government, with two Republican U.S. senators and a Republican majority in the U.S. House of Representatives. It is increasingly advantageous to be a Republican candidate in Texas electoral politics. Although not a majority, the plurality of Texans are Anglo American and Protestant, they elect legislators who share these characteristics, just as a predominantly Latino district usually elects a Latino legislator and members of an African-American district usually elects an African-American representative.

When the people in legislative districts elect representatives that "look like" the people they represent, the legislative body is said to achieve *descriptive representation*. The state of Texas has one of the most diverse populations in the United States. It is one of the few states with a majority–minority population, meaning that the majority of the population is a member of a minority group.[7] Currently, 46 percent of the population is non-Latino white, 37 percent is Latino, 12 percent is African American, 4 percent is Asian American, and the remaining 1 percent is of some other racial or ethnic group. Much of this diversity is also found in the Texas House, although there are differences among the makeup of the various racial and ethnic groups in the state and the makeup of the representatives in the Texas House and Texas Senate.

Minority populations in Texas have experienced significant improvements in their respective levels of descriptive representation. In the 82nd Legislative Session, 20 percent of the members of the Texas House were Latino, 11 percent were African American, and 0.01

---

[6]Texas Constitution, Article III, Section 6.
[7]Robert Bernstein. "Texas becomes Nation's Newest 'Majority–Minority' State, Census Bureau Announces," U.S. *Census Bureau News*, August 11, 2005, http://www.census.gov/Press-Release/www/releases/archives/population/005514.html

percent (or 2 representatives) were Asian American. Women, who account for slightly more than one-half of the state's population, account for 21 percent of the representatives in the Texas House.[8] The differences between the makeup of the state's population and the members of the Texas House vary for each group but are major improvements from the recent past.

The Texas Senate, by contrast, is 71 percent non-Latino white, 23 percent Latino, 6 percent African American, and 19 percent female. Although the non-Latino white population accounts for 46 percent of the state's population, 71 percent of the senators are non-Latino white. These discrepancies are in part a function of gerrymandering, and in part a function of low voter turnout in minority communities.

The Latino population has grown significantly since the Voting Rights Act of 1965. As a result, Latino levels of representation in the Texas House and Senate have also increased. Figure 6.5 shows the percentage of the state's Latino population, as well as Latino members of the Texas House and Senate. As the state's Latino population has grown, so too have the share of house and senate seats held by Latinos. In recent years, the percentage of Latino senators has been greater than the percentage of Latino house members. All of the Latinos in the Texas Senate are Democrats, and 26 of the 30 Latinos in the Texas House are Democrats. In 2010, 4 Latino Republicans won seats to the Texas House of Representatives.

The percentage of African Americans in the Texas legislature also improved since the Voting Rights Act of 1965. Figure 6.6 shows the percentage of African Americans in Texas as well as the percentage of African-American Texas House and Senate members. The African-American population in Texas has remained at about 12 percent for the last several decades, whereas the proportion of house seats held by African Americans had remained relatively steady at 9 percent until 2010, when it rose to 11 percent. The percentage of African Americans in the senate, on the other hand, has leveled off at six percent, beginning in the early 1990s.

Of Latinos, African Americans, and women, women are by far the most under-represented group in the Texas legislature (see Figure 6.7). Although slightly more than one-half of the

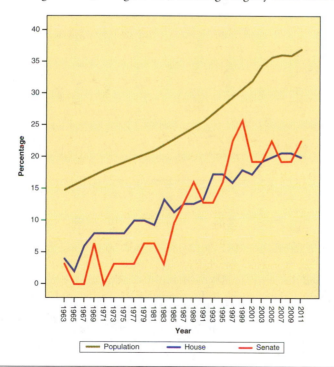

Figure 6.5

Latino Population and Latino Representation in the Texas House and Senate

---

[8]It should be noted that female legislators are counted twice, once as females and once as belonging to one of the racial or ethnic groups.

Figure 6.6

African-American Population and African-American Representation in the Texas House and Senate

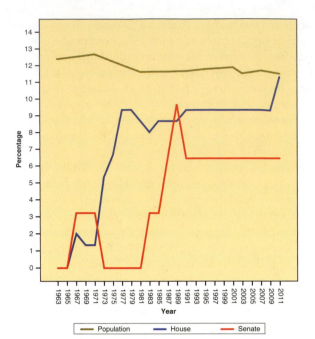

Figure 6.7

Female Population and Female Representation in the Texas House and Senate

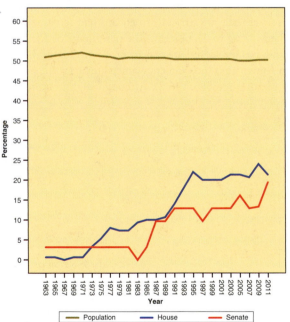

state's population is female, for 2011–2012 only 21 percent of house members and 19 percent of Texas senators are women. Women have been involved in Texas politics for quite some time. Texans elected their first female governor in 1925, and it has been sending women to the Texas legislature since the women's suffrage movement. In the mid-1970s, women began to win house seats with greater frequency, and in the senate a similar pattern was seen beginning in the mid-1980s. In recent years, women have continued to make improvements.

Asian Americans account for a little more than three percent of the state's population.[9] Nevertheless, two Asian-American members of the Texas House served in the 82nd Legislative

---

[9]U.S. Census Bureau, Estimates of the Resident Population by Race and Hispanic Origin for the United States and States: July 1, 2009 (SC-EST2009-04), http://www.census.gov/popest/states/asrh/SC-EST2009-04.html

Session—Republican Angie Chen Button from Dallas and Democrat Hubert Vo from Houston.

Latinos, African Americans, Asian Americans, and women are underrepresented in the Texas legislature relative to their percentages in the general population. The numerical representation of these groups in the legislature should increase dramatically during the next decade. As women and minority groups grow and become more active in the legislative process, it is expected that these groups will experience greater descriptive representation in the Texas House and Senate. However, because the Anglo-American ethnic group is currently overrepresented, where the legislative lines are drawn will determine how equitable the representation will be following the 2010 Census.

Lawyers Law is the most frequently represented profession in U.S. legislative bodies. In other democratic countries, the percentage of lawyers in legislative bodies is far smaller, and lawyers are viewed as just another professional group that might seek to advance its own interests. In the United States, however, the expectation that politicians be lawyers is so woven into our political fabric that people who want political careers often become lawyers as a step toward that goal.

Increasingly, however, legislative bodies are becoming more diverse in the occupations and training of their members. The number of lawyers serving in state legislative bodies has decreased, somewhat. There are several reasons for this, including the professionalized nature of state legislative assemblies. One study has determined that as legislative bodies enact ethics reform, the number of lawyers in the legislature diminishes.[10] Others report that lawyers are much more common in southern states.[11] In Texas, lawyers account for less than one-half of the lawmakers. In the 81st Texas Legislative Session, 29 percent of house members and 39 percent of senators were lawyers.[12] Lawyers are increasingly being replaced by lawmakers from other occupations. This diversity of elected officials further contributes to descriptive representation. Lawmakers are not only looking more like their constituents in their race, ethnicity, and gender, they are also representing a greater diversity of occupations.

> In the 2008 election cycle, the 361 candidates for seats to the Texas House of Representatives raised $71,266,729. In 2006, the 426 candidates raised $65,478,865.[13]

Money The primary qualification for winning legislative office is access to money. Many competent, motivated citizens who want to serve are excluded because they are unable to raise the money necessary to finance an adequate campaign. Thus, the voters' pool of potential candidates is initially reduced by the economic special interests that make most campaign contributions. Securing office space, printing campaign literature, buying postage stamps, building a campaign organization, and purchasing advertisements are all among the necessary ingredients for a successful campaign. In 2008, the National Institute on Money in State Politics found that the 361 candidates who ran for the Texas House raised an average $197,415 for their campaigns. In 2006, the candidates raised an average of $153,706 for the campaign. In two years, the average amount raised increased by more than $43,000. The

---

[10]Beth A. Rosenson, "The Impact of Ethics Laws on Legislative Recruitment and the Occupational Composition of State Legislatures," *Political Research Quarterly* 59 (2006), p. 626.

[11]Peverill Squire, "Legislative Professionalization and Membership Diversity in State Legislatures," *Legislative Studies Quarterly* 17, no. 1 (February 1992), p. 75.

[12]Data for the Texas House was obtained from the Chief Clerk's Office, Joe Straus, Speaker, *Biographical Data House of Representatives 81st Legislature* (June 1, 2010), http://www.house.state.tx.us/members/pdf/biodata.pdf. The data for the Texas Senate were obtained from the Texas Senate website, http://www.senate.state.tx.us/75r/senate/members.htm#members

[13]See http://www.followthemoney.org for comprehensive information on Texas campaign contributions.

Texas Senate candidates raised an average $478,530 for their campaigns.[14] Candidates raised more than $95 million for their campaigns in the house and senate races.[15] The key ingredient in Texas politics is money![16]

Organization of the Texas Legislature

PRESIDING OFFICERS

The most visible individuals in the Texas legislature are the two presiding officers: the lieutenant governor in the Texas Senate and the speaker of the Texas House of Representatives. Each exercises tremendous power.

Lieutenant Governor The presiding officer in the Texas Senate is the lieutenant governor, who serves as the senate president. Although not a senator, the lieutenant governor is in the unique position of being a member of both the legislative branch and the executive branch.

> In 2006, David Dewhurst (R) raised $10,204,273 in the winning campaign for lieutenant governor. The Democratic candidate, Chris Bell raised $7,359,018. The independent candidates Carole Keeton Strayhorn and Richard "Kinky" Friedman raised $9,084,635 and $6,288,113, respectively.[17]

The lieutenant governor is elected in a statewide, partisan election, and can have a party affiliation that is different from that of the governor or other members of the Texas executive branch. In the event that the office becomes vacant through death, disability, or resignation, the senate elects one of its members to serve as lieutenant governor until the next regular election. The senators have adopted rules that grant the lieutenant governor extensive legislative, organizational, procedural, administrative, and planning authority.

This statewide election, for a four-year term, attracts far less public attention than the power of the office merits; the lieutenant governor is one of the most powerful officials in Texas government. Organized interests are aware of the importance of the office, however, and contribute sizable sums to influence the election.

Lieutenant governors in most other states, like the vice president in the federal government, are neither strong executives nor strong legislative officials. Some states have either eliminated the office or have the governor and lieutenant governor run as a team. In other states, the governor and other executives monopolize the executive function, and the upper house, where the lieutenant governor usually presides, is often too protective of its legislative powers to include him or her in the real power structure. Although many lieutenant governors exercise a hybrid executive–legislative function, their actual powers do not approach those enjoyed by the lieutenant governor of Texas.

Speaker of the House The Texas House of Representatives, in a recorded majority vote of its members, chooses one of them to serve as its presiding officer. The campaign for this post can be very competitive and may attract candidates from all parts of the ideological spectrum. Since the vote for speaker is not secret and punitive action by the successful candidate against opponents and their supporters is common, incumbent speakers had, until the 2002 election, faced almost no opposition. In 2002, Republicans gained a majority in the Texas House,

---

[14]National Institute on Money in State Politics, "Election Summary," http://www.followthemoney.org/

[15]*Texans for Public Justice*, "Money in PoliTex: A Guide to Money in the 2008 Texas Elections," September 29, 2009, at http://info.tpj.org/reports/politex08/index08.html

[16]See http://www.followthemoney.org for comprehensive information on Texas campaign contributions.

[17]National Institute on Money in State Politics, http://www.followthemoney.org

and with it came the ousting of the Democratic incumbent and the election of its first Republican speaker since Reconstruction, Tom Craddick. Since that time, the speaker has experienced challenges from the left and right.

During the 80th Legislative Session, Speaker Craddick faced an open challenge from members of his own party who were critical of Craddick's autocratic style. House Republicans attempted to oust the speaker, but the speaker refused to recognize motions

Texas Lieutenant Governor David Dewhurst (center)

What other factors would contribute to challenges to the legislative leadership?

that would lead to him being unseated. In legislative bodies, when majority parties hold a significant majority over the minority party, party leaders like Tom Craddick enjoy centralized party control. Under centralized party control, the party leadership maintains strong control over the activities of the chamber. When the majority party loses seats, however, the party leadership loses control of the legislative agenda, that is, the legislative body becomes decentralized. When the Republicans took control of the Texas House, they enjoyed an 88 to 62 majority. In 2008, the Republicans lost an additional four seats in the house, giving Republicans a 76 to 74 majority over Democrats. In 2010, however, a national Republican sweep gave the Republicans 65 percent of the house seats. Figure 6.8 shows the percentage of Democratic and Republican officeholders in the Texas House since the Republicans took control of the chamber. In 2009, Republicans and Democrats joined together to elect Joe Straus as their new speaker. Conservatives have continued to challenge the more moderate Joe Straus for the speakership. Joe Straus is a more moderate Republican from San Antonio,

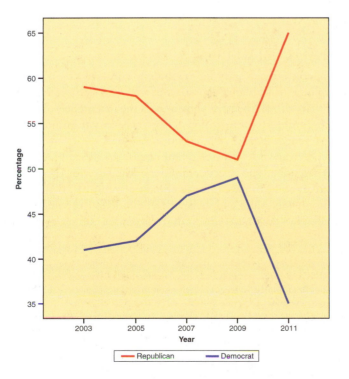

Figure 6.8

Percentage of Texas Democrat and Republican House Members Since 2003 (the year Republicans won control of the House)

who some members of his own party have called a RINO (Republican in Name Only).[18] Although speakers generally do not attract a lot of opposition, Speaker Straus's moderate views have continued to attract opponents from within his own party. After the 2010 Republican state convention, Speaker Straus was challenged by several more conservative members of the Republican Party for being too cozy with Democrats.[19]

House members or candidates who support the winning candidate can become a part of the speaker's "team," even if they are a member of the opposition party. Team status may include membership on a prestigious committee or even a committee chair or vice chair appointment. During the 81st Legislative Session, Republican Speaker Joe Straus relied on Democrats to chair or vice chair committees. Of the 34 **standing committees** in the Texas House, 18 were chaired by Democrats, and another 15 were vice chairs. Under Speaker Craddick, Democrats held 25 percent of chairs and 38 percent as vice chairs. Under Speaker Straus, Democrats experienced an improvement in fortunes. In 2009, Democrats chaired 53 percent of the standing committees, and 44 percent of the vice chair positions. The declining majority of the Republican Party has contributed to an increase in the strength of the Democratic Party. Team members also may attract campaign contributions and other assistance for their own political campaigns and may gain lobby support for legislative programs. This team policy is known as the "no-party" philosophy. Representatives are elected as party members but achieve leadership status by supporting the winning candidate for speaker. In an attempt to curtail abuses of power, candidates who use threats or promises of important appointments are guilty of "legislative bribery." The law is difficult to enforce though, and the speaker's supporters are usually appointed to important committees.

Funds raised and spent for this campaign are part of the public record. Candidates for speaker are required to file a complete statement of loans, campaign contributions, and expenditures with the secretary of state. No corporation, labor union, or organization may contribute, and individual contributions are limited to $100. All expenditures greater than $10 must be reported. These requirements are an attempt to reduce the influence of lobbyists and interest groups on the speaker's race by limiting and making public their campaign contributions. However, the support of "**The Lobby**" (major Texas economic interests) is necessary for a representative to become speaker.

LEGISLATIVE COMMITTEES

Legislative committees are necessary for any orderly consideration of proposed legislation. Because of the volume of legislative proposals offered each session, legislators cannot possibly become familiar with all the bills—not even all the major ones. They therefore organize themselves into committees for the division of labor necessary to ensure that at least someone knows something about each piece of proposed legislation.

There are several types of legislative committees in the Texas House and Texas Senate: standing, conference, joint, and select committees. The latter of these are also referred to as special committees and can have features of joint committees. Committees are classified based on function, membership, and longevity. The function of some committees, such as standing and conference committees, is to draft legislation. Other committees are charged

Standing committees

Permanent committees that function throughout the legislative session.

The Lobby

The collective characterization of the most politically and economically powerful special interest groups in the state.

---

[18]Leo Berman, in a television interview claimed that the Republican Party had been "taken over by 11 people last session that we call RINOs, Republicans in Name Only." Representative Berman counts Speaker Straus as one of the 11 RINOs. Watson, Brad, *Inside Texas Politics* [Television Broadcast] (Dallas/Fort Worth, TX: WFAA News 8, June 20, 2010), http://www.wfaa.com/video?id=96754954&sec=552937

[19]Jason Embry, "Former Party Leader Tries to Rally Republican against Straus," *Austin American-Statesman*, (June 12, 2010), http://www.statesman.com/blogs/content/shared-gen/blogs/austin/politics/entries/2010/06/12/former_party_leader_tries_to_r.html?cxntfid=blogs_postcards

THE TEXAS ETHICS COMMISSION AND REPORTING THE VALUE OF CHECKS

The eight-member Texas Ethics Commission enforces state ethics and campaign finance law and may propose legislative salary increases, subject to voter approval. The governor, lieutenant governor, and speaker appoint the commission from a list (which cannot include legislators) provided by the Democratic and Republican legislative caucuses. The commission has never completed a thorough audit, subpoenaed a single document, or ever met in person with a witness.

Bill Ceverha, a lobbyist and former Texas legislator, was treasurer of the Republican Majority Political Action Committee (TRMPAC), a major contributor to the Republican candidates, who successfully gained control of the Texas House of Representatives in 2002. TRMPAC received hundreds of thousands of dollars in corporate contributions, which, unfortunately for Ceverha, are illegal under Texas law. In May 2005, a district court ordered Ceverha to personally pay $197,000 to house Democrats defeated in the 2002 election. Ceverha declared bankruptcy to avoid paying the judgment.

Speaker Craddick then appointed Ceverha to the board of the Employees Retirement System of Texas, which oversees the state employees' $20 billion pension fund. While in this capacity Ceverha was given a gift of money by Bob Perry, a Houston home builder and major contributor to Republican causes. Ceverha, as a state official, is required by law to report any gift greater than $250 to the Texas Ethics Commission, describe the gift, and identify the giver. Using the precedent established by a 1999 Ethics Commission ruling that the value of the gift need not be reported, Ceverha described the gift only

as a "check." A public watchdog organization, Texans for Public Justice (TPJ), asked that the Ethics Commission overturn the prior ruling and require Ceverha to divulge the size of the gift. TPJ argued that the description was not adequate, because in this instance the gift was not an item like a shotgun or an automobile but money—and the public had the right to know how much. Attorneys for Ceverha argued that the size of the gift need not be public, since Bob Perry had no business with the Employees Retirement System.[20]

On a 5-to-3 vote, the Texas Ethics Commission ruled that simply describing the gift as a check was sufficient. In the fall of 2006 the commission ruled, "the legislative intent as discerned from the plain reading of the words in the statute is that the description of a gift is not required to include the value of the gift."[21] The commission went on to say:

> In our opinion, the requirement to describe a gift of cash or cash equivalent may be satisfied by including in the description the following: "currency," or a description of the gift, such as "check" or "money order," as appropriate. In our opinion, a description consisting of "pieces of paper" or "envelope" is not sufficient.[22]

The decision created an uproar among some members of the Texas legislature. Representative Jim Dunnam responded, "This opinion assaults common sense requirements for full and open disclosure."[23]

The 80th Texas Legislature quickly remedied the problem posed by the Texas Ethics Commission by passing Senate Bill 129. The law now requires state officers to report the value of gifts provided in the form of a check.

with a specific purpose such as studying a problem or making recommendations. The Select Committee on Federal Legislation, created by Speaker Joe Straus to monitor the activities of the federal government in January 2010, is an example of this type of committee. The membership of standing and select committees may include members of one chamber, whereas conference and joint committees may consist of members from both chambers. Some special committees may even include members of the public. Conference and select committees tend to be temporary or **ad-hoc committees**, whereas others are more long-lasting (standing and joint committees). Table 6.1 summarizes the charactcristics that each type of committee has.

There are two types of standing committees, substantive and procedural. Substantive standing committees are permanent committees that consider bills and monitor

Ad-hoc committee

A temporary committee.

---

[20]Rick Casey, "Ethics in Wonderland," *Houston Chronicle*, March 28, 2006; Lisa Sandberg and Kelly Guckian, "Lobbyists' Money Talks—Softly But It's Heard," *San Antonio Express News*, April 12, 2006.

[21]Texas Ethics Commission, November 27, 2006, Ethics Advisory Opinion No. 473, http://www.ethics.state. tx.us/opinions/473.htm

[22]Ibid.

[23]Jim Dunnam as quoted by Christy Hoppe in "Cash Gifts Sums Can Stay Secret: Ethics Panel Rules Public Officials Don't Have to Tell Their Value," *Dallas Morning News,* November 27, 2006, http://www.dallasnews.com/sharedcontent/dws/news/texassouthwest/stories/112806d ntexethics.2cc223e.html

A bipartisan coalition in the Texas House of Representatives elected Republican Joe Straus as its speaker in January 2009. Straus, however, had to deal with new political realities as the 2010 election boosted the Republican majority to an unprecedented level. ☞

How is the speaker's bargaining position affected by the need to win a majority vote of representatives to be reelected?

Subcommittees
Divisions of a committee that consider specific subtopics of a committee's primary jurisdiction.

Conference committees
Ad hoc committees that meet to resolve differences between senate and house versions of the same legislation.

Interim committees
Committees that meet between legislative sessions.

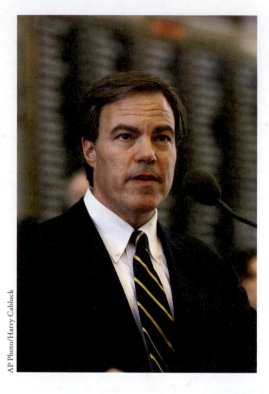

AP Photo/Harry Cabluck

administrative behavior on a specific subject matter such as taxing, education, and agriculture. The Texas House also has several *procedural* standing committees that influence the flow of legislation, passage of resolutions, investigations, and so forth.

★ **Subcommittees** are divisions of standing committees. They consider bills within their areas of specialization.

★ Ad-hoc committees are temporary committees appointed to consider specific issues or problems.

★ **Conference committees** are ad-hoc committees appointed to compromise house and senate versions of a bill. A separate conference committee is appointed to resolve differences between each bill passed by the two houses in different form.

★ **Interim committees** meet when the legislature is not in session to consider proposed legislation for the next legislative

session or to study a particular problem that has arisen since the last session. A chair and a vice chair head every committee. Each legislator serves on at least one committee, and some serve on several. A committee's membership is further divided into subcommittees, which have their own chairs and vice chairs. The subcommittees are usually the first to become familiar with a bill.

LEGISLATIVE STAFF

The legislature provides only minimal funds for hiring competent staff. Monthly staff allotments are $13,250 for house members and $35,623 for senators, who are also reimbursed for other "reasonable and necessary" office expenses. This money is for staff salaries and office expenses, not personal use. House members have about three or four staff people, whereas in

TABLE 6.1 TYPES OF COMMITTEES IN TEXAS LEGISLATURE

	Type of Committees			
	Standing	**Conference**	**Joint**	**Select**
Function	Lawmaking authority	Lawmaking authority	Advisory	Advisory
Longevity	Permanent	Temporary	Permanent	Temporary
Membership	From one chamber only	From both the house and senate	From both the house and senate	May include members of one chamber, members of both chambers, or members of the legislature and nonlegislators
Examples	House: Agriculture and Livestock Committee; Senate: Criminal Justice Committee		Legislative Budget Board	House Select Committee, Emergency Preparedness

CHALLENGES TO SPEAKER OF THE HOUSE

Democratic Speaker Gib Lewis received only one dissenting vote in 1991 for his fifth consecutive term, despite the fact that he was under indictment by the Travis County grand jury on misdemeanor ethics charges involving an alleged gift from a law firm that had opposed legislation before the house. His predecessor, Billy Clayton, was elected speaker four times, and the most recent ex-speaker, Pete Laney, served five terms in the office. Supported by a newly won Republican majority in the house, Tom Craddick (R-Midland) ousted Democrat Laney in 2003. Craddick easily won a second term in 2005.

Intraparty opposition to Craddick emerged in 2006, primarily because of his leadership style, which was viewed by some Republicans as authoritarian and punitive. This precipitated a challenge by moderate Republican Brian McCall of Plano. But some Republicans who were sympathetic to change characterized McCall as "the Democratic nominee" because of his strong support among Democrats. McCall then withdrew in favor of the more acceptable conservative Representative Jim Pitts (R-Waxahachie). Pitts's campaign gained traction, although many supporters remained tentative unless he could gain a procedural change in house rules to provide temporary confidentiality of individual votes. Legislators' fear of Craddick and his financial supporters cast a long and unrelenting shadow over Pitts's campaign from the beginning.

The 2007 election for speaker began immediately after the swearing-in ceremony. Proponents on both Craddick and Pitts agreed on basic procedure and style of the balloting but disagreed over the important issue of confidentiality. Craddick supporters wanted the results of each representative's vote to be made public immediately after the vote tally. Pitts's floor managers proposed an amendment to change the rules so that the vote of the membership would be made public only after assignments to committees and designations of committee chairs were complete.

A long afternoon of procedural debate on Pitts's amendment followed with points of order concerning both house rules and constitutional questions. Procedural wrangling ended when presiding chair (Secretary of State Roger Williams) made a final ruling that the members of the house could legally have a secret ballot if they chose. Speaker Craddick's supporters then moved to table (kill) the proposed amendment to the house rules. However, this "vote to table" was a public electronic vote and proved to be the test vote that would determine the outcome of the 2007 campaign for speaker. The move to table was successful by an 81-to-68 vote, thereby denying a "yes" or "no" vote on the amendment. Sensing failure and to protect his supporters from retribution, Representative Pitts withdrew his candidacy, announced his support for Craddick and urged conciliation between the factions and parties. Craddick was then elected to his third term as Speaker.

By the end of the 80th Legislative Session, Speaker Craddick had barely fended off Republican opponents. He succeeded in staying in power by refusing to recognize opponents who tried to make a motion to remove him. But the next year would not help Speaker Craddick. His party would lose another four seats in 2008, whereas some of the few Craddick Democrats would find themselves in tight races, or falling to defeat.

Even before the start of the 81st Legislative Session, it was clear that Tom Craddick was on his way out. Days before the start of the new session, Republican Joe Straus reported having the 76 votes needed to win the speakership, leading Tom Craddick to pull his name from the running. Joe Straus, who had only served in one full session before being elected speaker, was chosen from among 11 candidates who were vying for the position.

Speaker Straus was chosen, in part, because he would be able to garner support from Democrats. Because of his support from the left, some have called Speaker Straus a RINO (Republican in Name Only). As this book was being prepared for publication, Speaker Straus had already attracted opponents from the right wing of the Republican Party. Representative Leo Berman filed to challenge Speaker Straus for the speakership. And, as the Tea Party moves the Republican Party further to the right, house Republicans may feel pressure to move to the right. The difficult budget challenges the state is facing, plus continued losses in house races will impact the speaker's ability to hold the Republican caucus together as Straus attempts to lead from the center.

---

the senate, the average staff size is slightly more than seven. Some senators have as many as 14 staff members, while others have as few as four.[24]

Neither individual legislators nor legislative committees have professional staff comparable with that of special interest groups. With minimal staff support, "expert" testimony and arguments of interest group lobbyists and agency liaisons can mislead ill-informed legislators and committees. Powerful interests and administrative agencies have a distinct advantage when they monopolize the available information and expertise and thus force legislators to remain dependent on them for research data, advice, and other services.

Both legislative houses have established nonpartisan institutions to provide information to legislators. Former House Speaker Laney created the House Bill Analysis Department as

---

[24]The data was calculated using the following report of the House Research Organization: "Legislative Staff: 80th Legislature," *Focus Report No. 80-4,* 1, March 2007, at http://www.hro.house.state.tx.us/focus/staff80.pdf

Is democracy compromised for efficiency when the number of legislative staff increases?

part of legislative operations. Continued and renamed the House Research Organization by Speaker Craddick, it provides bill analyses, floor reports, issue focus reports, and interim news to legislators and the public.[25]

The Senate Research Center was formed in 1979 as the Senate Independent Research Group. It currently provides research and bill analysis to the Texas Senate and the lieutenant governor's office. The center's staff also attend meetings and conferences of other governmental entities and report to the senators on their content.

Whenever the legislature considers increasing appropriations to hire competent staff for individual legislators and, even more important, for committees, both the general public and special interests voice strong opposition: the former out of ignorance, the latter out of self-interest.

Ironically, legislators who report a surplus in their expense accounts are acclaimed by the press and their constituents as conscientious guardians of the public treasury, whereas in fact their ignorance of proposed legislation may cost taxpayers millions of dollars in wasted revenues. By contrast, legislators who use their allotted money to become informed about pending legislation are often suspected of wasting the money—or stealing it.

Texas legislative committees lack year-round professional staffs, which could give the legislators sources of information and services independent of those provided by interest groups, administrators, and the legislative leadership. Texas senators have enough staff to research some legislation each session, but house members are not as fortunate. Texas spends less than 0.3 percent of total state expenditures on legislative staff salaries, services, and accommodations.

CITIZEN LEGISLATORS

Texas has "citizen legislators" who meet for only 140 days every other year and receive most of their income from outside sources. It is only reasonable to expect them to be more focused on their full-time careers and outside sources of income than on the public interest.

TERMS

Texas senators are elected for four-year staggered terms and representatives are elected for two-year terms. That means that the entire house and half the senate are elected every two years. All senators were elected in the first election following redistricting (2002). At the beginning of the session, the senators draw lots to determine which senators will serve a

---

[25]The public can access much of the House Research Organization data by visiting its website, at http://www.hro .house.state.tx.us/; the Senate Research Center can be found at http://www.senate.state.tx.us/SRC/Index.htm

two-year term. The unlucky senators had to run for reelection in 2004, whereas the lucky senators did not face another reelection campaign until 2006. All senators then serve four-year terms until the 2012 election.

The relative competitiveness of the senators' districts determines whether the decision of the lottery is only an inconvenience or an incident of major significance. Texas legislators experience a more rapid turnover than their counterparts in the U.S. Congress, where seniority brings political power.

Low salaries, short sessions, heavy workloads, and inadequate staff and clerical assistance all diminish the Texas legislator's effectiveness. Frustrated by the inability to achieve legislative goals not supported by "The Lobby" or the presiding officers, many legislators leave office to pursue full-time careers or to seek higher political office. The generally more prestigious senators tend to serve longer than their house counterparts.

The argument in favor of retaining experienced legislators conflicts with growing public opinion for limiting the number of terms that legislators may serve. Legally mandated **term limits** reflect an increasing frustration with government, especially the legislative branch, which seems more and more to be the captive of organized special interests. Supporters of term-limit legislation assume that the election of new legislators will disrupt established working relationships between legislators and interest groups. However, the new legislators would be immediate "lame ducks" with legally mandated tenure and be even more vulnerable to influence by expert lobbyists and career bureaucrats.

Term limits

Restrictions on the number of times that a politician can be reelected to an office or the number of years that a person may hold a particular office.

COMPENSATION

Legislators receive an annual salary of $7,200 plus $132 per day for expenses for both regular and special sessions. They also have a travel allowance on a reimbursement basis when the legislature is in session. The Texas Ethics Commission is constitutionally empowered to propose a salary increase to be approved by the voters for both legislators and the lieutenant governor. Lawmakers have not received a pay increase since 1975, when Texas voters approved a pay raise for lawmakers. An attempt to increase their salaries failed in 1991. As a result, lawmakers often rely on campaign contributions to offset the cost of public service. Texas lawmakers are among the worst paid legislators in the country, but the law allows them to rely on campaign contributors to offset their living expenses.

There is little motivation for a legislator to seek or keep the position solely for the salary. Present legislative salaries are so low that legislators must obtain their primary income from other sources. Texans thus oblige their legislators to seek additional income, yet ask few questions about the nature or sources of this income. People tend to be loyal to those who pay them, and it is not the public that furnishes most of the legislators' incomes.

The potential for conflict between the public interest and the interests of a lawmaker's business or employer is obvious. Some legislators recognize the dilemma. For example, Bob Bullock faced it in 1991, when he left the comptroller's office, which paid $74,698 per year, and became the lieutenant governor for a salary of $7,200. Although many employers were eager to hire the lieutenant governor, the appearance of a conflict of interest concerned Bullock enough that he rejected several lucrative offers and accepted employment as a counselor and consultant with View Point Recovery Centers, a network of alcohol rehabilitation hospitals. His salary from View Point, his state employee retirement income, and his salary as lieutenant governor gave Bullock approximately the same income he had received as comptroller. Many Texas officials have not shared Bullock's desire to avoid even the appearance of impropriety. (Bullock retired in 1998 and died in 1999. The Texas State History Museum is named in his honor.) Higher pay would not guarantee honest legislators, but it would enable the conscientious ones to perform their legislative duties without turning to other vocations.

Retainership system
A special interest group or organization's placing lawyers who are also legislators on retainer with the intent of legally purchasing their support as legislators.

Perhaps then, **retainer** fees, legal fees for lawsuits against state agencies, and consulting fees would not be necessary for subsistence and could be made illegal.

THE LIMITED SESSION

The Texas legislature meets on the second Tuesday in January in odd-numbered years for a 140-day session. It is the only legislature in the ten most populous states to meet only every two years. In these short, infrequent sessions, the volume of legislation can be overwhelming. Most bills are passed or killed with little consideration, but they still consume valuable time that could be used for more practical purposes. Conversely, many very important bills are never granted a legislative hearing.

The short biennial sessions and the increasingly complex problems of a modern society make 30-day special sessions, which can be called only by the governor, more probable. They are, however, unpopular with both the general public and the legislators. The public views their $1.2 million price tag as wasteful, and legislators are put out by being called away from their homes, families, and primary occupations. Furthermore, the interests that kill the legislation by intentional neglect in the regular session will strongly oppose a special session to reconsider its corpse.

Because most of the legislative work is performed during the regular session, time becomes critical. Legislators find it increasingly difficult to maintain even rudimentary knowledge of the content of much of the legislation that must be considered, whether in committee or on the floor. These time constraints dictated by the limited session, combined with inadequate staff support and the lack of legislative institutions like the Office of House Bill Analysis, serve to isolate individual legislators and deepen their reliance on the information provided by lobbyists, administrators, and the legislative leadership.

Bills of limited scope or on trivial matters are a further drain on legislative time. For example, bills regulating the size of melon containers or minnow seining in a specific county do affect public policy, but they could easily be delegated to the department or agency responsible for their administration.

Other bills are introduced as a favor to an interested constituent or interest group by a friendly legislator. When these bills lack legislative, interest group, or administrative support, they have no chance of passage or even serious committee consideration.

The limited biennial session tends to work against deliberative, orderly legislative practice and ultimately against the public interest. Texas legislators cannot possibly acquaint themselves in only 140 days with the immense volume of legislation presented to them. Few legislators have personal knowledge of any particular subject under consideration unless they are employed, retained, or hold investment interests in the particular field.

The Texas Senate Floor ☛

Are part-time legislatures more or less legislatively active than full-time legislatures?

Bob Daemmrich Photography

Although 43 states have annual sessions to conduct state business, Texans refuse to accept annual regular sessions. Texans' general belief is that the legislature does more harm than good when it is in session and that a longer session will simply give legislators more time for legislative mischief. Unfortunately, there is evidence to support this position. Historically, much of the most odious legislation is passed in the final days of the session. Because of the

THE GROWING NUMBER OF TEXAS SYMBOLS

Various legislatures have chosen at least 50 official Texas symbols. A partial list includes the bluebonnet (flower), friendship (motto), pecan (tree), mockingbird (bird), petrified palmwood (stone), blue topaz (gem), sideoats grama (flora: grass), "Texas, Our Texas" (song), Lone Star (flag), chili (dish), lightning whelk (mollusk), square dance (dance), the Commemorative (formerly Confederate) Air Force (armed services), Guadalupe bass (fish), Texas red grapefruit (fruit), Mexican free-tailed bat (fauna: flying mammal), longhorn (fauna: large mammal), armadillo (fauna: small mammal), "Honor the Texas flag, I pledge allegiance to thee, Texas, one and indivisible" (pledge), "The Lone Star State" (license plate slogan), rodeo (sport), sweet onion (vegetable), and Brachiosaur sauropod, Pleurocoelus (archeological history: dinosaur).[26]

shortness of the session and procrastination and delaying tactics by legislators, the end-of-session flow of legislation became a deluge. Under these conditions, legislators simply did not have time for even the most rudimentary review of important last-minute legislation.

In 1993, the house adopted new rules to deal with the end-of-session legislative crunch. During the last 17 days, the house may consider only bills that originated in the senate or that had received previous house approval. The new rules also gave house members 24 hours to study major legislation before floor action. These reforms diminished the volume of last-minute legislation and gave legislators time to become better acquainted with bills.

Resolutions by legislators to congratulate a distinguished constituent, a winning sports team, or a scout troop for some success or other are common. Legislators usually pay little attention to this legislation, but it is important to the recipients. Demonstrating the lack of legislative scrutiny, one such resolution passed unanimously by the Texas House on April Fools' Day 1971—a congratulatory recognition of Albert DeSalvo for his "noted activities and unconventional techniques involving population control and applied psychology." The house later withdrew this recognition when it discovered that DeSalvo was in fact the "Boston Strangler," an infamous serial murderer.

CHAPTER SUMMARY

★ The Texas legislature meets on odd-numbered years for 140 days. Only Texas, among the large states, has such a restricted period of time in which to conduct legislative business. The Texas legislator tends to be a white male Protestant businessperson or lawyer with enough personal wealth or interest group support to adequately finance a campaign.

★ There are 31 senators and 150 representatives. The Texas two-chamber legislature is presided over by the lieutenant governor in the senate and the speaker in the house of representatives. Actual power in the legislative process rests with these presiding officers. Through appointive, jurisdictional, and other procedural powers, they are able to strongly influence state policy.

★ Historically, Texas government has been dominated by a coalition of conservative Democrats and Republicans. This coalition dominated the legislature through ideology rather than using party membership as the basis for control. Under Republican control of the legislature, the no-party system of legislative organization remains superficially intact, and Democrats continue to be appointed to chair committees under Republican leadership. The viability of the no-party system may be nearing its end as state politics becomes more partisan.

★ Legislative action is based on the committee system. The presiding officers appoint the committee chairs and many of the committee members. The officers assign bills to committees and have discretion over which committee to use. If a committee does not report on a bill (but instead pigeonholes or tables it), the measure is most likely dead for the session.

---

[26]Texas Legislature Online, "State Symbols," at http://www.capitol.state.tx.us/Resources/StateSymbols.aspx

HOW TEXAS COMPARES

★ Women have had the right to vote since the ratification of the Seventeenth Amendment to the U.S. Constitution, in 1920. Nevertheless, female political participation in the state of Texas ranks well below that of female participation in other states.

★ In the 2008 presidential election, only one other state—Hawaii (47%)—had a lower female voting rate than Texas, where 52 percent of females 18 years of age and older voted.[27]

When controlling for citizenship, Texas female participation is still among the worst in the country. In the 2008 presidential election, only 58.4 percent of citizen females in the state of Texas voted. Hawaii with 52.2 percent, West Virginia with 54.6 percent, Arkansas with 57.1 percent, and Utah with 58 percent were the only states with a lower participation rate among their female citizen population.[28]

KEY TERMS

ad-hoc committees
conference committees
ex officio
gerrymander

incumbent
interim committees
pairing

reapportionment
retainership system
standing committees

subcommittees
term limits
The Lobby

REVIEW QUESTIONS

1. What are the formal and informal qualifications for holding office in the Texas legislature?

2. What are geographic single-member districts? What are some of the advantages and disadvantages of this system?

3. Who are the presiding officers of the Texas legislature, and how are they each chosen? What are their duties and powers?

4. What is legislative amateurism, and how does it affect the legislative process?

5. Describe the several types of legislative committees. What is the function of each?

LOGGING ON

The *Texas Legislature Online* has all the information on the Texas legislature at **http://www.capitol.state.tx.us**. Be sure to check out the "Presiding Officer" pages. The lieutenant governor is at **http://www.senate.state.tx.us/75r/ltgov/ltgov.htm**. The speaker of the house is at **http://www.house.state.tx.us/speaker/welcome.htm**. The Legislative Budget Board, which helps the legislature prepare the budget, is at **http://www.lbb.state.tx.us**.

The Texas State Library is a source for legislative, administrative, and judicial research as well as general information about many political, economic, and social aspects of Texas. The library can be accessed at **http://www.tsl.state.tx.us**

The Legislative Reference Library of Texas is another good source of information about the Texas legislature. The address is **http://www.lrl.state.tx.us**

There are a number of citizen and consumer lobbies. Texas Common Cause works to make government more responsive to citizens. Its site is **http://www.commoncause.org**. To follow the money in state politics, the Center for Public Integrity provides

details of campaign financing at **http://www.publicintegrity.org**. Texans for Public Justice is a nonpartisan, nonprofit policy and research organization that tracks the influence of money in politics. It is located at **http://www.tpj.org**. The Texas Public Policy Foundation is the premier think tank for conservative political policies and initiatives. Find it at **http://www.texaspolicy.org**

There are many good sites to visit to find out about civil rights. Go to the Senate Hispanic Research Council Inc. site at **http://www.tshrc.org**. You may also want to visit the Texas Civil Rights Project at **http://www.texascivilrightsproject.org**. To learn about Latino civil rights and advocacy organizations in Texas, visit the National Council of La Raza, at **http://www.nclr.org**, and click on NCLR Affiliates.

Other sources of political information that researchers may find interesting include **http://www.selectsmart.com**, **http://www.votesmart.com**, **http://www.opensecrets.org**, **http://www.speakout.com**, and the Texas Public Interest Research Group at **http://www.texpirg.org**

[27]U.S. Census, "Table 4b. Reported Voting and Registration of the Total Voting-Age Population, by Sex, Race and Hispanic Origin, for States: November 2008" in *Voting and Registration in the Election of November 2008*, February 2009, http://www.census.gov/hhes/www/socdemo/voting/publications/p20/2008/tables.html
[28]Ibid.

Texas State Senator Judith Zaffirini: A Texas Service Pioneer

David Branham, Sr.
University of Houston–Downtown

INTRODUCTION

This article examines the legislative career of one of the state's most respected and powerful political leaders. Students should consider which factors contribute to a legislator's lifetime success and the importance of leadership style in a collective body such as the Texas Senate.

Judith Zaffirini is a pioneer in Texas politics. Elected in 1986, she was the first Hispanic woman to enter the Texas Senate and she is currently the highest ranking woman and the highest ranking Hispanic in the institution. That said, "pioneer" may be misleading. Such a description suggests that major accomplishments in one's life have been completed, that high-energy levels are a thing of the past, and that retirement is at hand. Zaffirini shows no sign that any of this will occur in the near future. In nearly a quarter of a century of service, she has yet to miss a single vote or be absent for a session of the senate in quorum. When *Texas Monthly* named her one of the ten best legislators in the state in 2005, the publication said "Zaffirini arrives before dawn to pursue her goals of improving health care for the poor and enhancing higher education opportunities with the relentlessness of a robot; session after session, she is at the top of the list of lawmakers who do the most good."[1] As a result she has sponsored 581 successful bills and cosponsored 278 others.[2]

Her resume is not exactly typical for a state senator. She was a stellar student, receiving three degrees from the University of Texas, including her Ph.D. in communications. She attended UT with her friend and husband, Carlos Zaffirini. Both were involved in politics and education. While UT students working with then Texas Senator Wayne Connally, they together worked to bring higher education to her hometown of Laredo. In 1984, she become vice chair of the Texas Democratic Party and in 1986, threw her hat in the ring to make a run for the Texas Senate. That year she took on and was victorious against popular Texas House Representative Billy Hall, Jr. in the Democratic

runoff. She then defeated Republican attorney and businessman Bennie Walter Bock of New Braunfels, 52 to 48 percent, in the general election to take her seat.

As a senator, a large amount of her energy has been devoted to protecting families and children. One might attribute her calling to her own situation. Her son Carlos, Jr., was just starting school when she took office in 1987. Being the mother of a young child may have been a constant reminder of the importance of taking care of children. But if that was true, the fire did not go out after he reached adulthood. Carlos, Jr. is now a successful attorney and business owner, and her commitment continues. In May 2010, the Amerigroup Foundation honored her as a "Champion for Children" citing her long-time leadership in the Texas Senate on issues of importance to children.[3] The merits she receives for her commitment to children have been well earned. She served on the Senate Education Committee for two decades and in 2009, was appointed as chair of the Senate Higher Education Committee. "Improving access to early and higher education is my greatest passion and highest priority. There is no better way to prepare for the challenges ahead than to equip our children with the educational tools needed for a better future."[4] In 1993, she would see the dream of her and her husband become a reality when as senator she would push through legislation creating Texas A&M International University in Laredo.

Yet, although education may be her greatest passion, other issues are not ignored. She also served as the chair of the Senate Health and Human Services Committee and has had long service on the Appropriations Conference Committee and the Senate Committee on Finance. "Serving on the Senate Health and Human Services Committee and the Senate Finance Committee has given me valuable opportunities to pass legislation and secure funding that improves the lives of Texans, especially the very young, the very old, and persons with disabilities," Senator Zaffirini said.

Upon entering office, Zaffirini had a professional style that was unique in Texas politics. In 1997, *Texas Monthly* said "Zaffirini is not out to win Miss Congeniality awards. She is out to pass bills—and she passes them by the truckload. Her legislative program will touch millions of lives on subjects that really matter."[5] There is evidence that her style is not only effective in getting things done, it has also changed the way things are done. Confirmation of this came in 1993, when Lieutenant Governor

Texas Senator Judith Zaffirini

[1] "Best and Worst Legislators of 2005," *Texas Monthly, July 2, 2005,* http://www.texasmonthly.com/2005-07-01/feature17.php

[2] "State Symbols," *Texas Legislature Online,* at http://www.capitol.state.tx.us/Resources/StateSymbols.aspx

[3] "Amerigroup Foundation Honors Texas Sen. Judith Zaffirini as a 'Champion for Children.'" *Earth Times.* May 11, 2010, http://www.earthtimes.org/articles/show/amerigroup-foundation-honors-texas-sen,1294143.shtml

[4] "Senator Judith Zaffirini Reports to the Families of District 21, 2006–2007," http://www.senate.state.tx.us/75r/senate/members/dist21/pdf/Z-NL06.pdf

[5] "Best and Worst Legislators of 1997," *Texas Monthly,* http://www.texasmonthly.com/1997-07-01/feature15.php

Bob Bullock joked inappropriately about the way Zaffirini went about her business, saying that she could pass any legislation "if she'll cut her skirts off about six inches and put on some high heels." Although Bullock was chastised in the media for the comment, Zaffirini never seemed insulted. She had a productive working relationship with the Lieutenant Governor that even outside observers could see.[6] Perhaps she understood that the comment was not so much to insult her, but an expression of chauvinistic attitudes about how women could be effective legislators. "My immediate response was that I would rather suffer Bullock's humor than his wrath," Zaffirini said. "He had just appointed me to serve as Chair of the Senate Health and Human Services Committee and a member of the Senate Finance Committee. Accordingly, I judged his attitude by his actions, not by his words." With astuteness and patience she was changing the traditional good ol' boy way of doing things.

Outside public office, Zaffirini spends a significant amount of her time as a consultant in her area of expertise, communications. It is unusual for Texas legislators not to have extensive outside employment. Texas senators receive $600 monthly salaries, with additional per diem pay during special sessions. This is not to say that representatives in Texas are part-time legislators. Most Texas legislators spend more than 30 hours a week on legislative duties and minority, female, and Democratic legislators spend even more time on these duties than their colleagues.[7]

Another important part of being a state senator is the need to provide service to the constituents of the district. Senate districts in Texas have approximately 700,000 people, which makes personal service for all constituents quite difficult, especially with limited staff resources. Districts in the Texas House of Representatives are approximately five times smaller in population than senate districts. As a result, one-on-one constituent service is better suited for house members and their staffs. However, as a member of an institution that has only 31 members, it is quite important that the state senator take the lead and work closely with other house members within the senate district to craft legislation that is important to the area. Zaffirini's district has special needs that other senate districts do not. Per capita income is far lower in the district than in the rest of the state and 25 percent of the population in the district is below the poverty level in comparison to 15 percent in the rest of the state.[8]

In the 2009 session alone she collaborated with house members to pass 66 bills, including 14 separate pieces of legislation designed to help her district. The legislation allowed Starr County Hospital in Rio Grande City to borrow funds; helped farmers and ranchers by requiring Bee Groundwater Conservation District directors to own land in their single-member districts; authorized Starr County to create a drainage district; permitted Webb County to obtain a Texas Department of Public Safety building and sell mineral rights on land held for the permanent school fund; allowed area commissioners to remove appointed directors for failure to submit required financial reports; and empowered the Zapata County Commissioners Court to regulate development around Falcon Lake's tributaries.[9]

Figure 6.9

Judith Zaffirini's Texas Senate District 21 (in blue shaded area) encompasses 17 counties and stretches from San Antonio to the Rio Grande Valley. She has offices in both her hometown of Laredo and San Antonio.

Zaffirini's tenure in the Texas State Senate has truly been remarkable. She was the first Hispanic woman to take a seat in the institution and she has done what every first-timer dreams of doing. She has set a standard of excellence in service and dedication that will probably never be matched by anyone. She has changed the way politics are conducted in the institution by taking integrity to a new level. And she has refuted all misconceptions that Hispanic women could not be effective legislators. A great story, indeed. However, it appears that the story is not close to being finished.

JOIN THE DEBATE

1. How important is ethnic and gender diversity in the Texas legislature? Does the presence of diverse members bring different perspectives to the legislative process? Should the concept of representation mean that the make-up of legislature look like the general population as a whole? How important is it that traditionally underrepresented minorities have role models to inspire a younger generation of leaders?

2. Should Texas consider increasing the number of state senators so that they do not have to represent so many constituents? Does long tenure in office contribute to a legislator's experience and influence?

[6]Peggy Fikac, "Harassment Accusations Can Strike a Chord with Women Lawmakers." *San Antonio News*, May 10, 2009, http://www.mysanantonio.com/news/Harassment_accusations_can_strike_a_chord_with_women_lawmakers.html

[7]Kathleen A. Bratton, "The Behavior and Success of Latino Legislators: Evidence from the States," *Social Science Quarterly* 87(5), (2006). pp. 1136–1157.

[8]Texas Legislative Council, "Income and Housing Profile," http://www.fyi.legis.state.tx.us/fyiwebdocs/HTML/senate/dist21/r3.htm

[9]"Senator Judith Zaffirini Reports to the Families of District 21, 2009–2010," http://www.senate.state.tx.us/75r/senate/members/dist21/pdf/Z-NL09.pdf

Chapter 7

The Legislative Process

CONTENTS

LEARNING OBJECTIVES

* Identify the presiding officers of the Texas House and Senate and identify their powers.
* Assess the role of committees in the Texas legislature.
* Define the different types of committees and know their functions.
* Explain the impact of the calendars on bill passage.
* Explain the two-thirds rule in the Texas Senate.
* Know the difference between a *recorded vote* and a *voice vote*.
* Identify procedural tools at the disposal of senators in their efforts to block or pass bills.
* Describe how a bill becomes a law.
* Identify and describe the various legislative boards and committees at the disposal of the legislative leadership.

Adopt a bill of your own on a topic in which you have an interest. (Or, visit the website of an organization that you support or admire and choose a bill that they support.)

Find out which interest groups favored and opposed your bill. Why did they take the positions they took?

Use the Internet to follow the bill through the legislative process. Did your bill pass, or was it killed in the process? If it was killed, where did it die?

What action did the governor take on the bill?

If your bill became law, which agency is responsible for its administration?

★ Your best place to start the exercise is *Texas Legislature Online* at **http://www.capitol.state.tx.us/**. To get legislative process information, click on "Legislation." Information about the governor's role and other topics can be found at **http://www.governor.state.tx.us/**. Information on state agencies can be found at **http://www.state.tx.us/category.jsp?language5eng&categoryId56.9**

Legislative Budget Board

The body responsible for proposing the legislature's version of the proposed biennial budget. The governor also proposes a budget to the legislature.

Legislative Council

The body that provides research support, information, and bill drafting assistance to legislators.

Legislative Audit Committee

The body that performs audits of state agencies and departments for the legislature.

Sunset Advisory Commission

A body that systematically evaluates most government agencies and departments and may recommend restructuring, abolishing, or altering the jurisdiction of an agency.

Lieutenant Governor David Dewhurst and House Speaker Joe Straus look over the House calendar. ☞

How might the calendar be used as a tool of power?

An understanding of power exercised by the lieutenant governor in the Texas Senate and the speaker in the Texas House of Representatives is necessary to understand how the Texas legislature works. The powers of the two presiding officers can be roughly divided into two general categories: procedural powers, which are directly related to the legislative process, and institutional powers, which are used to affect administrative policy and management of Texas government.

Powers of the Presiding Officers

The rules of each house, formal and informal, give the presiding officers the procedural power to appoint most committee members and committee chairs, assign bills to committees, schedule legislation for floor action, recognize members on the floor for amendments and points of order, interpret the procedural rules when conflict arises, and appoint the chairs and members of the conference committees. Laws or legislative rules grant the presiding officers nonprocedural, institutional power to appoint the members and serve as joint chairs

AP Photo/Harry Cabluck

of the **Legislative Budget Board** and **Legislative Council** and determine the members of the **Legislative Audit Committee** and the **Sunset Advisory Commission**. Power in the Texas legislature is thus concentrated in the offices of the lieutenant governor and the speaker of the house.

PROCEDURAL TOOLS OF LEADERSHIP

Committee Membership The committee is of great importance in the legislative process. Therefore, those who determine membership of a committee are able to exercise considerable influence on its policy decisions. In Texas, this power belongs to the lieutenant governor and the speaker.

PROCEDURAL COMMITTEES	
Committee on Calendars	General Investigating and Ethics Committee
Committee on Local and Consent Calendars	Committee on House Administration
Committee on Rules and Resolutions	Committee on Redistricting

The speaker appoints the total membership as well as the chair and vice chair of all house *procedural committees.* One such committee, the House Calendars Committee, controls the flow of legislation from the committees to the house floor. The speaker uses his or her influence with this procedural committee to determine when or whether bills are heard on the house floor.

The speaker also appoints the total membership as well as the chair and vice chair of the powerful 27-member Appropriations Committee, whose members serve as chairs of the subcommittees for budget and oversight of the substantive committees with such budget and oversight subcommittees. Thus, the speaker's appointees to the Appropriations Committee also control the budget requests of the other committees and serve as liaisons between the two. The Appropriations Committee strongly influences the expenditure of funds for all divisions of state government.

For all substantive committees other than appropriations, a limited seniority system in the house determines up to one-half of a committee's membership; the speaker appoints the other half. The speaker also appoints the committee's chair and vice chair, which ensures that the committee leadership as well as a numerical majority of each substantive committee will be speaker appointees. The standing committee chairs appoint the membership and the chairs and vice chairs of the subcommittees.

The lieutenant governor officially appoints the total membership as well as the chairs and vice chairs of all senate committees and permanent subcommittees. In practice, an informal seniority system allows senators to choose their preferred committee until one-third of the committee's positions are filled. This ensures that senior senators will serve on the more powerful committees. The chairs of the standing committees, at their discretion, may appoint subcommittees from the committee membership.

The appointive power of the presiding officers means that the action of a committee on specific legislation is usually predictable. The presiding officers can also use the power of appointment to reward friends and supporters as well as to punish opponents. Interest groups often attempt to influence the presiding officer's decision to their advantage. (It is of vital importance to interest groups to have sympathetic members on a committee that reviews legislation important to their interests.)

Because the relative power of a committee varies, a legislator's committee assignment directly affects the legislator's influence in the legislature. Membership on an important committee gives a legislator a strengthened bargaining position with administrators, lobbyists, and other legislators. Of course, the legislator's influence is further expanded if the appointment is as the committee's chair. There is no way to determine precisely all the coalitions, compromises, and bargains that can relate to a desirable committee appointment. Negotiations for committee positions are intense, and all legislative bodies have conflicts over

> It is generally accepted that among the most powerful committees in the house are Appropriations; Ways and Means; and State Affairs. The most powerful senate committees are Finance; Jurisprudence; and State Affairs.

committee appointments. Concentrating the power over committee selection in the presiding officers is one way to resolve such conflicts.

Selection of Committee Chairs

Because the chairs of legislative committees play an extremely important role in determining the ultimate success or failure of legislation, conflict over their selection must be resolved. In some states, the majority of the committee selects committee chairs; in others, a seniority system is used. In Texas, the presiding officers make these decisions.

Owing to the power of the chair over each committee's organization, procedure, and the jurisdiction of its subcommittees, the fate of much public policy is determined when the chair is selected.

The presiding officers, by virtue of their power to appoint the chairs of all committees, have a tool that works like a magnet to attract legislators to their team. If legislators want to "get along," they "go along" with the presiding officers. Their influence over other legislators also increases the bargaining position of the presiding officers relative to interest groups. The lobbyist who can help get a sympathetic legislator appointed as chair of an important committee has earned the salary paid by the interest group employer. At the same time, the lobbyist owes the presiding officer a real favor for appointing the "right" committee chair.

The appointive power of the presiding officers, although significant, is not absolute; they often appoint as chairs key committee people who have political power in their own right, such as members with close ties to a powerful special interest group. The presiding officers may then have the support of some of the more powerful members of the legislature in a reciprocally beneficial relationship. The presiding officers can usually count on the loyalty of the chairs, who can in turn, usually depend on the presiding officer's support. They are all looking after the interests of the same groups.

The No-Party System

The Texas legislature has historically been organized on the basis of ideology, rather than political party, with a coalition of conservative-to-moderate Democrats and Republicans usually in control. Under this no-party system, party affiliation has less significance than ideology and interest group ties, and conservative Democratic speakers and lieutenant governors appointed mostly Democrats but also some Republicans to committee chair positions. The no-party system has been modified and continued under conservative Republican leadership. In 2009, for example, under a Republican-controlled house, 53 percent of standing committees were chaired by Democrats, and 44 percent were vice-chaired by Democrats. The chairs of the most powerful committees are usually, but not always, appointed from the presiding officer's party.

It is important to understand that with Texas's no-party organization, the political party caucuses do not fill positions of power as they do in the U.S. Congress, and members of the minority party may join the presiding officers' teams, serve on important committees, and become committee chairs. However, differences on public policy issues are sometimes intense and are becoming increasingly more partisan.

Committee Jurisdiction

The presiding officers in the Texas legislature are responsible for assigning bills to particular committees. Because committee jurisdiction in the Texas legislature is often poorly defined, they have considerable discretion when making these assignments. The speaker may even reconsider a bill's assignment and change committees. Texas's presiding officers do not hesitate to assign a bill they oppose to a committee they know will report unfavorably on the bill—and likewise assign a bill they favor to a committee that will report on it favorably. Because the presiding officers can stack the committees to their liking, this is simple to do.

There are several reasons why the presiding officers may oppose a specific bill:

★ The backers and financial supporters of the presiding officer may view the bill as a threat to their economic or political well-being.

★ The presiding officer and his or her team may feel that supporters of the bill and the special interest group that it favors have been uncooperative in the past and should be punished.

★ The supporters of the bill may either refuse or be unable to match the bargaining level of the bill's opponents.

★ The presiding officer and his or her supporters may feel that the bill, if it became law, would take funds away from programs that they favor.

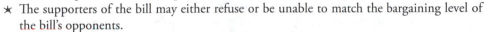

AP Photo/Harry Cabluck

🖋 *Standing committees do much of the legislative work ignoring or pigeonholing bills lacking significant support, gathering information in public hearings, and rewriting or marking up legislation to make essential political compromises that make a bill's passage possible.*

Legislators' negotiations with the leadership may include such things as promising substantial changes in the bill, supporting legislation favored by the leadership team, or opposing legislation that the leadership wants to defeat. A politically knowledgeable leadership that astutely uses this power can help consolidate support for its policies.

Committee Powers and Functions Committees are often called "**little legislatures**" because they normally conduct the real legislative business of compromise and accommodation. It is the committees that most often change the content of a bill or kill the bill. This is especially true in the Texas legislature, where they are seen as extensions of the presiding officers. In the committees, bills may be totally rewritten, **pigeonholed** (buried in the committee), or substantially altered (portions may be added or deleted). When a bill is reported out of committee, it is seldom in its original form.

Division of Labor Because several thousand bills are introduced into the Texas legislature each session, a division of labor is necessary. Each bill brought before the Texas legislature is assigned to a committee, which holds public hearings where witnesses—both for and against—may be heard, debates held, and **bills marked up** (rewritten, amended, and so forth).

Because standing committees do the basic legislative work, the general membership relies heavily on them for guidance in deciding how to vote on a bill being considered on the floor. In fact, attempting to amend some bills, or even to question the work of the committee, violates the norms of the Texas Senate.

Competency Where a seniority system is used, committee members and chairs are usually returned to the same committee posts each session, and legislators can thus become reasonably informed, if not expert, in a given subject. This expertise is important because committee members must first hear interest group representatives and administrative officials and evaluate their arguments concerning the merits of proposed legislation.

Because Texas legislators operate under only a limited seniority system, the expertise of committee members may be gained outside the formal structures of government. State legislators are seldom politicians to the exclusion of other occupations, and these other endeavors can result in conflicts of interest for committee members. For example, if the primary occupation of a legislator is banking, that particular lawmaker may be more sensitive to interests of the banking industry

Little legislatures

Another name for standing committees because most of the work of legislation occurs in committees.

Pigeonholed

Eliminated from consideration by committee vote. If the committee considering a bill votes to table the bill, it has been pigeonholed and is effectively killed.

Bills marked up

Bills that have been amended or otherwise changed while in a legislative committee.

than to those of the public interest. The same problem arises with regard to any occupation—oil, real estate, the law, insurance, and so on.

Although legislators may not be initially involved in an occupation that benefits from their committee activity, they often become investors, employees, or attorneys for related business interests. Such "expertise" is common on Texas legislative committees.

The Pigeonhole Another important function of committees in the Texas legislature is to serve as a burying ground for bills. A legislator may introduce a bill as a favor to some group or constituent who feels very strongly about something, knowing full well that it will be killed in committee (and that the committee will take the blame). Other bills may be assigned to a hostile committee with the intent that they will be totally rewritten if not pigeonholed.

When legislators who do not serve on the committee oppose a bill, these legislators may bargain with the members of the committee to pigeonhole it. There may be several reasons for this. The most obvious is that their ideology or the interest they represent may be opposed to the substance of the bill. Also, a legislator may want to kill a bill on which his or her political supporters are evenly divided, for no matter how the legislator voted, he or she would lose political support and face political or economic repercussions from angered interest groups or constituents.

All legislative bodies have some procedure whereby bills can be extracted from reluctant committees, but it is usually difficult to accomplish. Legislators, even though they may support a bill that is buried in a committee, are reluctant to vote to discharge it. They see the **discharge petition** as a threat to the privileges of the whole committee system— privileges that they too enjoy.

The Texas Senate rules allow **tagging**, which permits a single senator to delay committee hearings for up to 48 hours on a specific bill. The process works like this: A senator notifies the chair of a senate committee that he or she wants 48 hours' advance notice before hearings are held on Senate Bill 246. Any committee action on the bill within the 48-hour period is void. This delays the legislative progress on the bill and is effective only because of the short legislative session. Tagging enables a single senator to kill or modify a bill late in the session, but if the bill's sponsors can get the senator to remove the tag, the bill can be immediately cleared for committee hearings. Each senator is allowed one tag for a given legislative session, and use of the tagging tactic is not debatable.

Bureaucratic Oversight In a parliamentary form of government, legislators actually serve as administrators; in the United States, legislatures have a watchdog function over the executive branch—that is, the legislature "oversees" the administrative **bureaucracy** as it executes the law and public programs. The vehicle for **bureaucratic oversight** is usually the legislative committee. Legislators are interested in determining whether the bureaucrats are administering the laws the way that the legislature intended. They must also determine whether new or revised legislation is needed. Accordingly, committees hold hearings and ask bureaucrats under their jurisdiction about the laws and programs that are being implemented.

Although the committees are ostensibly watching out for the public good by checking on whether the bureaucrats perform their duties in ways consistent with the public interest, more often than not the committees serve as the legislative advocates for the bureaucrats and their interests and viewpoints. In effect, critical scrutiny of agencies by committees is minimal. Because each committee usually provides the same service for the agency involved in its subject-matter jurisdiction, conflicts occur between the various coalitions of legislative committees, agencies, and interest groups for the spoils from public policy. This competition disappears if a bill is proposed that is viewed as a threat to an entire class of interests. The affected coalitions of interests then close ranks and present a united front against the common enemy.

Discharge petition
A legislative process for rescuing a pigeonholed bill from a committee. It is seldom used.

Tagging
A senate rule that allows a senator to stop consideration of a bill by the standing committee for 48 hours.

Bureaucracy
The system of nonelected officials administering government policies and programs.

Bureaucratic oversight
The legislative function of monitoring administrators to make sure they are administering the laws according to legislative intent.

The importance of the roles played by each of these forces within the political system varies from government to government. In Texas, legislative committee activity is proportionately less, and the power of the bureaucracy and special interests is proportionately more, than in some other jurisdictions. The reasons for the lack of strong legislative participation may include the short legislative session—committees seldom meet and are unable to provide effective oversight due to the time limitations—the mobility of members from one committee to another, which limits expertise and lengthy association; and the relatively short periods of service for Texas legislators compared to top administrators and lobbyists.

The Calendar The instrument for controlling the flow of legislation from the committees to the floor of the houses is the **calendar**. With the calendar schedules, as with other important aspects of the legislative process, power in the Texas legislature is centralized in the offices of the presiding officers.

Because timing a bill for consideration on the floor is crucial to its eventual passage or defeat, control of this stage in the life of a bill is a powerful weapon that can be used to aid or hinder legislation and to reward allies or punish enemies. For example, any of the following situations may occur:

★ Supporters may want floor consideration of a bill delayed until they can muster the necessary votes to get it passed. (Opponents may think they have the necessary votes to defeat the bill but feel that the votes could erode if the supporters are given time to consolidate their forces.)

★ Conversely, supporters may want an early consideration of a bill because the opposition appears to be gaining strength. (Opponents would want a delay under these circumstances.) Legislative opponents of a bill may use various tactics to delay and thereby kill the legislation. One such tactic is the **filibuster**, a prolonged debate on the senate floor conducted by a senator who opposes the bill. Individual senators may also delay a bill in committee for 48 hours by tagging it. Members of both houses may use various other parliamentary maneuvers to delay and thereby kill a bill that has been placed far down on the calendar.

Control of the calendar of bills is important in any legislative body. In Texas, it is paramount because the Texas legislature has short biennial sessions, giving great power to the forces that control the calendar.

House Calendars Unlike most of the organizational and procedural powers that are inherent in the offices, the control of the speaker and the lieutenant governor over scheduling in the Texas legislature is determined as much by their influence with other legislators as by the formal powers of the offices. For example, the speaker exercises no formal control over house calendars.

The two calendars committees perform this function. This apparent decentralization of power is more fiction than fact, however. The members and the chairs of these committees are all appointed by the speaker and can usually be persuaded to accommodate the speaker's wishes.

There are several calendars for different kinds of bills; unimportant or trivial bills are placed on special schedules and are usually disposed of promptly with little debate by the body of the house. However, the process is not so automatic for major or controversial legislation. In fact, the speaker and the committee chair often use the House Calendars Committee as a "black hole" into which bills simply disappear. In a

Calendar

The list of bills reported out of committee and ready for consideration by the house or the senate.

Filibuster

An attempt by a senator to delay a bill by unlimited debate. The speaker hopes to focus attention on the bill, elicit a compromise on some point, or force the withdrawal of the bill from consideration. Unlike a U.S. senator, a Texas senator may not surrender the floor to another sympathetic senator in order to continue the filibuster.

The Texas House legislative calendars are as follows: Emergency, Major State, Constitutional Amendments, General State, Local, Consent, Resolutions, and Congratulatory and Memorial Resolutions. The two calendars committees are the Local and Consent Calendars Committee and the far more important Calendars Committee.

Suspension of the rule

The setting aside of the rules of the legislative body so that another set of rules can be used.

Blocking bill

A bill placed early on the senate calendar that will never be considered by the full senate. Its purpose is to require two-thirds of the senators to vote to suspend the senate rule that requires bills to be taken off the calendar in chronological order. The effect is that any bill appearing later on the calendar must have the support of two-thirds of the senate if it is to be allowed to come up for debate and passage.

Floor

The part of the capitol building where the senate or the house meets. The term can also be applied to the senate or house acting as a whole to debate, amend, vote on, enact, pass, or defeat proposed legislation.

much applauded action, the 1993 house under Speaker Pete Laney adopted rules making the process more open to the general house membership.

Senate Calendar   Officially, the senate has a calendar system that advances bills systematically. A senate rule requires that bills be placed on the calendar and then considered on the senate floor in the same chronological order in which they were reported from the committees. In practice, bills are taken off the calendar for senate floor consideration by a **suspension of the rule**, which requires a two-thirds majority vote of the entire membership of the senate. The process goes something like this: The first bill placed on the senate calendar each session is called a **blocking bill**. It is usually a bill dealing with a proposed horticultural change somewhere around the state capitol or in the state park system. It will never be taken off the calendar. It does, however, "block" the consideration of all other bills' access to the floor except by the two-thirds vote to suspend the rule that requires chronological consideration of bills.

This senate practice affects the senate's entire legislative process. The irony is that although only a simple majority is necessary for final passage in the senate, a two-thirds majority is necessary to get the bill to the **floor** for consideration. It can be said that this process protects the minority from the majority.

The two-thirds rule is also a means whereby the senate can kill a bill without having a floor vote for or against—it just fails to reach the floor and thus dies on the calendar. Although lobbyists are keenly interested in this action, the general public is usually unaware that a vote even occurred or where the individual senators stood on the issue. It is also a tool that can be used to enhance the powers of the presiding officer. By using this two-thirds vote requirement, the lieutenant governor may keep a bill from reaching the floor of the senate by simply persuading 11 members to vote against it. The bill would then lack the necessary two-thirds majority and could not advance to the floor. Any coalition of 11 senators can, of course, achieve the same result—occasionally against the wishes of the lieutenant governor.

At least two-thirds of the senators (21) must be present to conduct business. The absence of 11 or more senators brings all senate action to a halt, as in the 1979 "Killer Bee," 1993 "Killer WASP," and 2004 "Killer D" incidents (see box).

During the 81st Legislative Session, the senate changes its rules for one bill and one bill only. In 2009, Republicans in the state legislature, fearing voter fraud, wanted to pass a bill that would require voters to show a picture identification card when voters cast their votes. Democrats, fearing that the bill would prevent low-income and elderly populations from voting (because they are less likely to have a picture identification card) objected to such a law. The senate Democrats held 12 of the 31 seats (or 39% of the seats). These 12 votes effectively prevented the senate from moving the Voter ID Bill to the senate floor. Because of the two-thirds rule, Republicans needed 21 votes, or two-thirds of the votes, to pass the Voter ID Bill. To permit this, they changed the rules for this one bill, allowing the Voter ID Bill to come up for a floor vote with a simple majority, rather than the two-thirds votes typically needed.

The bill would eventually die in the house, however, but only after Democrats in the Texas House slowed down the work of the chamber to such an extent that the session would end before the house would get to the Voter ID Bill. The house Democrats used a tactic known as *chubbing*, in which house members pepper bill sponsors with questions on seemingly innocuous bills for 9 minutes and 30 seconds, having the effect of delaying the legislative process, and essentially killing bills that the chamber does not get to because the session has ended.

The Floor   In several ways, the presiding officers in the Texas legislature can influence a bill's progress at each crucial step from the committee to the floor. They can kill legislation, strongly influence its content, or accumulate political credits from legislators that can be cashed in at some future date.

The Texas Constitution requires that bills must be "read on three consecutive days in each house." The purpose of the requirement was to ensure that laws would not be passed without adequate opportunity for debate and understanding. Bills are read once upon being introduced prior to being assigned to a committee by the presiding officer. In practice, though, the entire bill is seldom read at this time. Instead, a caption or a brief summary is read to acquaint the members of the legislature with the subject of the bill. The bill is read the second time before floor debate in each house, and if an entire bill is to be read, it is usually on this second reading. The third reading occurs at least one day after floor passage.

The constitution allows bills that are "cases of imperative public necessity" as so stated in the bill, to be read for the third time on the same day as floor passage, as long as four-fifths of the membership agrees. All bills now routinely contain this provision and usually pass the third reading immediately following floor passage. A simple majority is required for passage on the third reading, but amendments must have a two-thirds majority.

Floor of the House   As bills reach the floor of the house of representatives, a loudspeaker system allows the members and visitors to follow the debate on the floor. The **floor leaders** are representatives who are attempting to get the bill passed. They usually stand at the front of the chamber, answer questions, and speak in favor of the bill. Microphones located elsewhere in the house chamber serve either the opponents of the bill or other concerned lawmakers as they speak against the bill, speak in favor of the bill, or simply ask questions.

The consideration of bills on the floor of the house would seem to be a study in confusion and inattention. Throughout the process, members of the house may be laughing, talking, reading papers, or sleeping at their desks. Often, however, because many members may know very little about the bill under consideration, this is an excellent opportunity for both proponents and opponents of the legislation to seek support for their positions. Many members

Floor leader

The legislators who are responsible for getting legislation passed or defeated. Their job is to negotiate, bargain, and compromise because they are in the center of political communication.

KILLER BEES, KILLER WASPs, AND KILLER Ds

THE "KILLER BEES"

A proposed presidential primary bill that would have benefited conservative Democrats was opposed by at least 12 of the 31 state senators. These 12 senators, dubbed the "Killer Bees," had taken a "blood oath" to refuse to allow the split primary bill to be considered on the floor of the senate. When it became clear that the Killer Bees could stop floor action, Lieutenant Governor W. P. Hobby removed the two-thirds requirement for consideration of the presidential primary bill. Conservative Democrats were thereby assured both a floor hearing and, as they had a majority in the senate, passage of the bill. However, 21 senators must be present to constitute a quorum, which is the minimum number present to conduct business. The 12 Killer Bees simply refused to meet, thus denying the senate a quorum.

Because the presiding officer has the authority to order the senate sergeant at arms and law enforcement officials to compel absent senators to attend sessions unless they are excused, the Killer Bees were forced to go into hiding. Lieutenant Governor Hobby ordered the Texas Rangers to find them. The Rangers proved to be particularly inept in implementing the order and in fact arrested the brother of one of the Bees in Houston and forcibly transported him to Austin, where he was correctly identified by a legislative assistant as the brother.

The Bees were not found but ultimately were returned to the senate chamber to complete the important business of the session, following the assurance of Lieutenant Governor Hobby that the usual senate rules would be followed.

THE "KILLER WASPs"

In the 1993 regular session, the "Killer WASPs" (the senate's 13 Republican members) briefly denied the senate a quorum. They instituted a one-day walkout to protest a resolution calling for the settlement of a lawsuit to elect urban state district judges by single-member districts rather than by the present county at-large system. Mexican Americans and African Americans originated the suit to foster the election of more minorities to the state judiciary. The U.S. Fifth Circuit Court of Appeals eventually rejected the settlement, leaving the at-large system in place.

THE "KILLER Ds"

The gerrymandering fight in 2004 produced the "Killer Ds," legislative Democrats who opposed redrawing Texas's 32 U.S. Congressional District lines for a second time following the 2000 Census. Regarding the action as a power grab by the majority Republicans but easily outvoted by them, the Ds denied a quorum, first to the house and then to the senate. The senate action followed Lieutenant Governor David Dewhurst's removal of the two-thirds requirement for consideration of the redistricting bill. The Ds were required to leave the state to escape the jurisdiction of Texas law officers, who were instructed to forcibly bring them to their respective chambers. The conflict even reached the halls of Congress when U.S. Majority Leader Tom DeLay (R-Texas) requested the Federal Aviation Administration's assistance in returning the house Democrats from Oklahoma, an action that resulted in his being "admonished" by the U.S. House Ethics Committee. The redistricting bill passed during the third special session when one of the Democratic senators refused to continue his absence from the session.

Source: Portions adapted from Ernest Crain, Charles Deaton, and William Earl Maxwell, *The Challenge of Texas Politics* (Saint Paul, MN: West, 1980), pp. 94–95.

may already have a well-defined position on the bill under consideration but may know little of its content. Eloquent speeches seldom change votes. In fact, many members vote for or against legislation based on who is supporting it or who is against it and only then ask what the bill was about. This practice is especially true of specialized bills that have generated little statewide interest. Voting time usually brings both supporters and opponents of the bill up and down the aisles pleading with either one finger (vote "yes") or two fingers (vote "no").

House members then insert cards that allow them to push buttons to record a "yes," "no," or "present" vote on a large electronic scoreboard by means of green, red, and white bulbs next to each legislator's name. Until recently, the votes cast by lawmakers were by **voice vote** only, which meant that the votes cast by lawmakers were not recorded. As a result, voters had no way of knowing whether their representatives supported or opposed particular legislation. With the passage of Proposition 11 in November 2007, the Texas Constitution now requires that all final votes cast be **recorded votes**.

The matter of recorded votes, which became a political issue in the 79th (2005) and 80th (2007) Legislative Sessions, can be viewed from several legitimate perspectives. The most important argument is that voting records are necessary for constituents to know how their representatives and senators voted on the issues. Without this information, voters cannot make informed decisions on election day—and democracy itself can become reduced to choosing political leaders on the basis of television image, mudslinging, and trivialities.

On the other hand, recorded votes can become political weapons wielded unfairly against legislators in campaigns. A legislator may be strongly opposed to one provision in an important bill and may unsuccessfully work, lobby, and argue against this measure in committee and on the floor of the chamber. Yet if the bill contains other provisions that the legislator views as important and worthwhile, he or she may vote for the entire bill despite the objectionable provision. Political opponents may then pluck this provision from the total bill and use it as a campaign issue to defeat the legislator. These rivals know that the legislator cannot deny having voted for the objectionable provision, but they conveniently fail to point out that it was a small part of a much larger bill. This is an unfair but effective campaign tactic.

Also, the final recorded vote may or may not be a measure of the legislator's efforts for or against the legislation. Test votes on amendments or procedural issues are often more

Voice vote

Vote cast by lawmaker but that is not recorded in the official record as that lawmaker's vote.

Recorded vote

Votes in which the names of those who cast the vote are recorded in the house journal.

LAWMAKERS MAKE IT EASIER FOR THE PUBLIC TO KNOW HOW THEY VOTED

In the recent past, lobbyists had gone to unusual lengths to find out how individual legislators voted. For example, a high-stakes "tort reform" bill that limited the damages that injured people could collect from manufacturers and sellers of defective products was being voted on in the house. Business lobbies were strongly in favor of the limitation, whereas plaintiffs' lawyers and consumer advocates were just as strongly opposed. House Speaker Gib Lewis ordered cameras removed from the house gallery when an employee of a business lobby was seen using a video camera to record the individual votes on the electronic scoreboard.*

Also, without a record vote, ghosts occasionally participate in the legislative process. On August 7, 1991, State Representative Larry Evans (D-Houston) died but continued to perform his legislative functions by casting three votes on the house electronic voting machine!**

In another instance, supporters suspected that the defeat of a 1993 bill to increase the penalties for having drugs or weapons near schools was the result of ghost voting. The bill's supporters requested a "verification," or roll-call vote, whereupon the bill passed, 65 to 58. Apparently, only the spirits of ten members, eight of whom had voted against the bill, were present that day.***

It is believed that Proposition 11 will bring an end to these practices. The law went into effect November 2007, and the Texas Constitution now requires that all final votes cast be recorded votes.

*Clay Robison, "Politicians Get Creative to Conceal Voting Records," *Houston Chronicle,* December 4, 2004, p. B6.
**W. Gardner Selby, "Legislators Sometimes Push Each Other's Buttons," *San Antonio Express-News,* December 5, 2004, p. 1. For a news report of lawmakers casting ghost votes, see Nanci Wilson, "One Lawmaker, Many Votes?" *CBS 42 Investigates,* May 14, 2007. The video can be seen on *YouTube* under "Texas Politicians' Multiple Voting Breaks Legislature Rules."
***Austin American-Statesman,* May 30, 1993, p. B7.

important and more informative regarding where legislators actually stand. Under Proposition 11, these more important votes, which occur in the second reading, may continue to be obfuscated with voice votes unless the chamber provides exceptions to the rules. Throughout the floor voting process, the speaker presides by recognizing members from the floor, ruling on points of order, and so forth. A **point of order** is an objection to a bill on the floor of the chamber by a member who believes that a procedural error was made during the committee process. If the point is sustained late in the session, there may not be time to correct the error, and the bill dies.

Although not uncommon, the point-of-order rule has rarely had the impact that it did during the 1997 legislative session. Representative Debra Danburg (D-Houston) raised a successful point of order on a bill that required parental notification before a minor could have an abortion. In return, Representative Arlene Wohlgemuth (R-Burleson) raised points of order on some 80 pending bills, many of which were supported by Governor George W. Bush and other Republican legislators. The bills were all killed.

Floor of the Senate The senate scene may be similar to that in the house in one sense—usually few members are paying attention to the debate. Debates on even important bills are usually much shorter in the senate than they are in the house, primarily because of the all important two-thirds rule that requires suspension of the senate rule before a bill can be brought to the floor out of its calendar sequence. Because the suspension of the rule is standard procedure and requires the cooperation of the lieutenant governor and at least 21 senators, it can be assumed that the major compromises have been reached before the legislation reaches the floor.

The filibuster is still a threat to bills in the Texas Senate, just as it is in the U.S. Senate. The difference in the Texas Senate is that a member may not yield the floor to another senator who wants to continue the filibuster. In the Texas Senate, the floor is controlled by the lieutenant governor, so only one senator may filibuster as long as he or she can physically last, and then the vote is taken. **Cloture**, or limiting debate by senatorial vote, is not an option available to Texas senators.

The purpose of the filibuster in the Texas Senate is either to attract public attention to a bill that is sure to pass without the filibuster or to delay legislation in the closing days of the session. In fact, just the *threat* of a filibuster may be enough to compel a bill's supporters to change the content of the bill to reach a compromise with the dissatisfied senator. If a filibuster does occur, it means that it was impossible to reach a compromise, usually because a sufficient number of senators strongly favor the bill and refuse to be intimidated by the threat of a filibuster.

After the debate, the vote in the senate is taken without the benefit of an electronic scoreboard. Senators plead for votes by holding up a single finger for a "yes" vote and two fingers for a "no" vote. A clerk records the vote, and only a simple majority is necessary for passage.

Conference Committee A unique byproduct of bicameralism is the necessity of resolving differences in similar bills passed by the two houses. A temporary or ad-hoc committee

---

A bill's general subject and its supporters may determine how legislators vote. In 1965, for example, 22 members of the Texas House of Representatives voted against the U.S. Bill of Rights when it was introduced as "an act to protect our fundamental liberties" by Representative Jake Johnson, a liberal from San Antonio.*

Antonio Light, May 2, 1965.

Point of order

A formal question concerning the legitimacy of a legislative process. A successful point of order can result in the postponement or defeat of legislation.

Cloture

A parliamentary move to stop legislative debate and force a floor vote; also known as *closure*.

Former Texas Senator Bill Meier set the world record for a filibuster in May 1977 by talking for 43 hours. This feat broke the old record of 42 hours and 33 minutes set in June 1972 by former Texas Senator Mike McKool. There have been a number of other notable filibusters in the Texas Senate. In 1993, Senator Gonzalo Barrientos filibustered for 17 hours and 50 minutes in an attempt to kill legislation that negated an Austin ordinance designed to protect the Barton Springs watershed from development. During the filibuster, Barrientos was required to stand and was restricted to a 3-square-foot area. The bill eventually passed, 22 to 7.*

*Diana R. *Fuentes, San Antonio Express-News*, May 1, 1993, p. 17A.

Conference committee

An ad-hoc committee that meets to resolve differences between senate and house versions of the same legislation.

known as a **conference committee** is appointed for each bill to resolve these differences. To determine the acceptability of proposed compromises, the members of this committee remain in contact with interested legislators, lobbyists, administrators, and the presiding officers as they deliberate.

In Texas, conference committees are composed of five members from each house, appointed by the respective presiding officer. The compromise proposal must win the support of a majority of the committee members from each house to be reported out of the committee. Because the members of the conference committee may strengthen, weaken, or even kill a bill, the attitudes of the legislators appointed to the committee are of crucial concern to the various interests involved. This affords the presiding officers, as well as the conference committee members, enviable bargaining positions. Bargaining before the selection of the committee is common, and it continues within the committee during deliberations.

After a bill has been reported from the conference committee, it may not be amended by either house but must be accepted or rejected as it is written or sent back to the conference committee for further work. In practice, due to the volume of legislation that must be considered in the limited time available, the Texas legislature tends to accept **conference committee reports** on most legislation.

Conference committee report

A compromise between the house and senate versions of a bill reached by a conference committee. It may not be amended by either house but must either be rejected, accepted, or sent back to the committee for more work.

How a Bill Becomes a Law Bills may be introduced in either house or, to speed the process, in both houses at the same time. Let us consider the example of a bill that is introduced in the senate before it is sent to the house of representatives. The numbers in Figure 7.1 correspond to the numbers in the following discussion.

Figure 7.1

How a Bill Becomes a Law

As a bill works its way through the legislative process, what other factors also influence how a bill becomes a law?

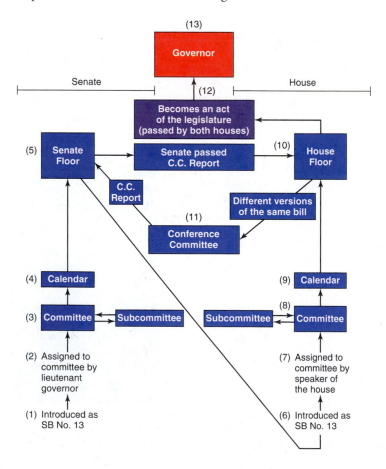

HOW DOES TEXAS COMPARE?
TEXTING WHILE DRIVING AND STATE REGULATIONS

As technology changes, society is presented with new challenges that lawmakers must address. In recent years, the use of cell phones, and in particular, the practice of texting while driving has forced lawmakers to take action. Lawmakers are presented with two major challenges—ensuring public safety while at the same time not interfering with an individual's right to freedom of speech. In recent years, some states have taken steps to address the perceived dangers associated with driving and texting. Nine states have banned the use of hand-held devices. Some states have banned the use of hand-held devices among younger drivers, whereas others have left it to local governments to set their own restrictions. Other states have simply restricted the use of hand-held devices around school zones. As of 2010, Texas only partially limits the use of hand-held devices, banning their use in school zones.

The National Highway Traffic Safety Administration reports the total number of traffic fatalities for 2007 and 2008, showing that traffic fatalities were down in most states.* The biggest reductions, however, came from states that banned using hand-held devices while driving. Those states experienced an average 11.67 percent reduction in traffic fatalities from 2007 to 2008, whereas states with no bans on hand-held devices experienced a 9.45 percent reduction in traffic fatalities from 2007 to 2008. Although most states experienced significant reductions from 2007 to 2008, Texas experienced a modest two percent reduction from 2007 to 2008. Below are the states that experienced the worst changes from 2007 to 2008. Note that the first four experienced increases in fatalities. Although Texas did not experience an increase, its modest 2.4 percent change ranks it with the seventh worst change from 2007 to 2008.

STATES THAT EXPERIENCED THE WORST PERCENT CHANGE IN TRAFFIC FATALITIES FROM 2007 TO 2008

State	Percent Change from 2007 to 2008
Vermont	11
New Hampshire	8
Wyoming	6
Delaware	3
Colorado	−1
Oklahoma	−2.2
Texas	−2.4

*National Highway Traffic Safety Administration, "2008 Traffic Fatalities by State and Percent Change from 2007," http://www-fars.nhtsa.dot.gov/States/StatesCrashesAndAllVictims.aspx

1. *Introduction to the senate.* Only a senator may introduce a bill in the senate, and only a representative may do so in the house. It is not difficult to find a legislator who is willing to perform this somewhat clerical function. More difficult is finding a sponsor who will devote political skill and bargaining prowess to help get the bill through the intricacies of the legislative process. Upon introduction, the bill is assigned a number, for example, Senate Bill 13 (SB 13). The first bill introduced in the house of representatives would be styled as HB 1.

2. *Assignment to a committee.* The lieutenant governor assigns bills to committees in the senate and will for many bills have a choice between two or more committees. It is very important to proponents of the bill that the committee chosen not oppose the spirit of the bill. If possible, proponents of the bill and their allies will gain the lieutenant governor's support and get a friendly committee assignment in exchange for their support of or opposition to a bill of particular interest to the lieutenant governor.

3. *Senate committee action.* As noted earlier, committees are often called "little legislatures" because of the power they have over bills. In both the committee and the subcommittee, the supporters and the opponents of the bill are allowed to testify. Witnesses are often lobbyists or concerned bureaucrats affected by the bill. The subcommittee then

marks up the bill (makes changes) and sends it to the committee, where it may be further marked up. Some senate committees do not have subcommittees; in that case, the entire committee initially hears testimony and marks up the bill. The committee may then report on the bill favorably or unfavorably or may refuse to report on it at all.

4. *Senate calendar.* As described earlier, the senate has only one calendar of bills, and it is rarely followed. In the usual procedure, a senator makes a motion to suspend the regular calendar order and consider a proposed bill out of sequence. For this parliamentary maneuver to succeed, prior arrangements must be made for the lieutenant governor to recognize the senator who will make the motion. If two-thirds of the senators agree to the motion, the bill, with the blessings of the lieutenant governor, is ready for action on the senate floor.

5. *Senate floor.* The president of the senate (the lieutenant governor) has the power to recognize senators who wish to speak, to vote in the event of a tie, and to interpret rules and points of order. Rarely do members of the senate overrule these interpretations.

    Unlimited debate is the rule in the Texas Senate. This is not meant to imply that the Texas Senate is a deliberative body, for it is not; such a luxury is prevented by the short legislative session. Unlimited debate could, however, lead to a filibuster—an attempt to "talk the bill to death" or force a compromise. If a bill is successful in reaching the senate floor, it has already cleared its major obstacle (the two-thirds majority necessary for senate consideration) and will usually be passed in some form. Only a simple majority is necessary for a bill to pass. The lieutenant governor may vote only to break ties.

    The senate may also form itself into a **committee of the whole**, at which time the lieutenant governor appoints a senator to preside. Only a simple majority rather than the usual two-thirds is necessary to consider legislation, and the lieutenant governor may debate and vote on all questions, but otherwise the senate rules are observed. No journal is kept of the proceedings.

6. *Introduction to the house.* After the senate passes a bill, the bill is sent to the house of representatives. A procedure similar to that in the senate is followed there.

7. *Assignment to a committee.* It is the responsibility of the speaker of the house to assign each bill to a committee. The speaker, like the lieutenant governor, has some freedom of choice because the jurisdiction of house committees over specific kinds of legislation is vague.

8. *House committee action.* Committee action in the house of representatives is similar to that in the senate. Each bill is assigned to a committee and then to a subcommittee, which may want to hold public hearings. The subcommittee as well as the committee may amend, totally rewrite, pigeonhole, or report favorably or unfavorably on a bill.

9. *House calendars.* A bill that is either reported favorably by the committee or receives a favorable minority report by the required number of committee members is placed on one of the eight house legislative calendars by one of the committees on calendars.

    This establishes the approximate order in which the whole house will consider the legislation. If the calendars committees fail to assign the bill to a calendar, it may be forced to do so by the action of a simple majority of the house. However, if a bill has the blessing of the speaker, it is sure to be promptly placed on the appropriate calendar.

10. *House floor.* The speaker of the house has the power to recognize representatives on the house floor and also to interpret the rules and points of order. Although the speaker may be overruled, he or she seldom is. The size of the house necessitates that debate be more limited than in the senate—usually 10 minutes for each member. Bills may be amended, tabled (which usually kills the measure), killed outright, or sent back to committee. "Yes" votes of only a simple majority of members present and voting are necessary for a bill to be passed.

11. *Conference committee.* If the house of representatives make a change in the senate-passed version of a bill, a conference committee is necessary to resolve the differences between the two houses. The lieutenant governor appoints five senators, and the speaker appoints

Committee of the whole

The entire senate acting as a committee. Its purpose is to allow the senate to relax its rules and thereby expedite legislation.

five representatives to sit on the committee. The compromise bill must be approved by a majority of both the senators and the representatives before it can be reported out of the conference committee.

12. *Final passage.* The bill is sent first to the chamber where it originated and then to the other chamber for final approval. Neither one may amend the reported bill but rather must accept it, reject it, or send it back to the conference committee. The conference report is sent to the governor after it passes both houses.

13. *The governor.* The governor has several options concerning an act arriving on his or her desk. First, the governor may sign it into law. Second, the governor may choose not to sign, in which case it becomes law in 10 days if the legislature is in session or in 20 days if the legislature is not in session. Third, the governor may choose to veto the act, but the veto can be overridden by a two-thirds vote in each house. The governor must either accept or veto the complete act if it does not contain provisions for appropriating funds. In appropriations acts the governor may strike out an item of appropriation, but the governor does not have a reduction veto to reduce spending for an item. Also, the governor may not veto riders on appropriations bills that do not appropriate.

The governor may use the veto late in the legislative session without fear of the legislature's overriding it because a veto cannot be overridden in a subsequent session. If the governor signs an act of the legislature, it will become law in 90 days—or sooner if it appropriates funds or the legislature has designated it as emergency legislation. If the act requires the expenditure of funds, the comptroller of public accounts must certify that adequate revenue is available for its implementation. If revenue is lacking, the act goes back to the legislature, where either adequate funds are provided or it is approved by a four-fifths majority in each house. If neither option is successful, it cannot be implemented.

INSTITUTIONAL TOOLS OF LEADERSHIP

Taken as a whole, the procedural tools of leadership give the presiding officers enough authority, both formal and informal, to exercise fundamental control over the legislative process. Complementing their procedural powers, the institutional powers given the offices of lieutenant governor and speaker ensure influence over the actual policy implementation and governing processes of Texas government, which further enhances their bargaining position with the economic and political players who seek to influence the state's public policy.

Legislative Budget Board Most states, the U.S. government, and most countries have only one budget. Texas has two. Each agency in state government presents its budget requests to both the governor's office and the Legislative Budget Board. The board then provides to the governor and the legislature the draft of the appropriations bill. The Legislative Budget Board has also been given broad authority concerning strategic planning for the state, bill analyses, and policy and impact analyses affecting education, criminal justice, and other policy areas. Its influence on state government is significant.

The Legislative Budget Board operates continuously, even when the legislature is not in session. It comprises ten members, including the lieutenant governor and the speaker, who serve as joint chairs. The remainder of the board is composed of the chairs of the Senate Finance Committee and the House Ways and Means and Appropriations Committees, who serve as automatic members and two house members and three senate members appointed by their respective presiding officer. The administrative director is appointed by the board.

Clearly, control of the board is in the hands of the two presiding officers, who are in a position to strongly influence state government from the budgeting stage through the final appropriating stage. The board staff assists appropriating committees and their chairs and also has the watchdog function of overseeing to some extent the expenditures of the executive agencies and departments. Thus, in this critical area of finance, the concentration of power in the hands of the presiding officers is even greater than in other legislative areas.

Legislative Council Another instrument of influence is the 14-member Legislative Council, made up of 6 senators, the chair of the House Administration Committee, 5 other representatives, and the lieutenant governor and speaker, who serve as joint chairs. The lieutenant governor appoints the senate members, and the speaker appoints the house members. A director and staff serve at the pleasure of the council to do the administrative work. With the exception of the speaker and lieutenant governor, the terms of the appointees end with the beginning of the regular legislative session. The presiding officers govern the council during the regular session.

The Legislative Council functions as a source of information and support to the legislature, state agencies, and other governmental institutions. It also provides research, computing, and printing support for legislators and helps them draft legislative proposals.

Legislative Audit Committee The function of the Legislative Audit Committee is to appoint and govern the state auditor, who with the consent of the senate, heads the State Auditor's Office and serves at the pleasure of the committee. Appointed by the presiding officers, the committee is comprised of four senators and four representatives with equal representation from the two major political parties.

The authority of the Office of the State Auditor is both broad and deep. Under the direction of the committee, state agencies and departments, including colleges and universities as well as any entity receiving funds from the state can be audited. Also, a variety of audits, including financial, compliance, economy and efficiency, effectiveness and special, may be conducted. The management of the fiscal affairs of the Texas government is under the firmly entrenched influence of the presiding officers.

Sunset Advisory Commission The Texas Sunset Act requires that most statutory state agencies undergo a reevaluation, usually on a 12-year cycle, to determine the need for their continuance. Because they are automatically terminated, the "sun sets" on those agencies not specifically renewed by the legislature, and many of those that are reauthorized by legislation are given altered scope and authority.

Representative Jim Keffer urges an "aye" vote on the floor of the Texas House of Representatives. ☞

Given the number of institutional tools of leadership, are lawmakers shirking their legislative responsibilities to the leadership, or are they constrained by the part-time nature of the Texas legislature?

AP Images/Harry Cabluck

The 12-member Sunset Advisory Commission enforces the act. The lieutenant governor appoints five senators and one public member, and the speaker appoints five representatives and one public member to the commission. Public members are appointed for two-year terms and the legislators for four-year staggered terms. The commission chair is appointed by the presiding officers and alternates between senate and house members. The agency's chief executive officer is appointed by the commission.

In the Sunset Advisory Commission's more than 30-year history, the commission has abolished more than 52 state agencies, saving taxpayers hundreds of millions of dollars. In recent years, however, abolishing state agencies has proven politically unpopular. As a result, the Sunset Advisory Commission has worked to improve state agencies, rather than attempt to abolish them.

Restraints on the Powers of the Presiding Officers

Although the aggregate of the organizational, procedural, and institutional powers of the speaker and the lieutenant governor seems to be—and at times is—overwhelming, there are certain restraints that curtail arbitrary and absolute use of these powers.

PERSONALITY

The personalities of the individual presiding officers and the way they view the role of their offices determine their approach to legislative leadership. They may use their powers to develop strong, aggressive leadership, ruthlessly overpowering opposition, or they may be accommodating and compromising, accomplishing the desired results with only the implied threat of reprisal.

THE TEAM

The presiding officers require a strong coalition of legislative support to accomplish their aims despite the concentration of powers they enjoy. Support from other legislators may come because of friendship or ideological agreement. More likely, legislators may feel that it is in the best interest of their constituents and supporters for them to be "team players" and back the presiding officers. The speaker and the lieutenant governor are usually able to build and add cohesiveness to this support through the use of their powers to reward or punish.

THE LOBBY AND BUREAUCRACY

The relationship between the presiding officers, the Lobby, and their bureaucratic allies is of great importance in determining the chance of success for specific legislation. When the lieutenant governor, speaker, bureaucrats, and Lobby all agree and work together toward a common goal, legislative victory is almost assured.

In the event of conflict between the Lobby–bureaucracy coalition and the speaker or the lieutenant governor, the program of the presiding officer may be either diluted or defeated, depending on such complex factors as the amount of support that can be mustered from the governor, interest groups, and legislators.

Against a strong coalition between an interest group and the bureaucracy, all of a presiding officer's formal and informal powers may not be enough to control the legislation. The officer would simply be confronted by too much combined political power. A conflict of this nature is unusual. Generally, the presiding officers are in basic agreement with the more powerful interests, which have often given political and financial support to their campaigns.

THE GOVERNOR

Among the most important powers given the governor in the Texas Constitution are those concerning legislation. They include the veto and the item veto over appropriations. These formal powers place the governor in a strong bargaining position, and the governor's support for or opposition to specific programs is an important factor. The governor's influence with The Lobby and the threat to veto constitute the most useful instruments to achieve changes in the substance of a bill while it is still in the legislature.

The governor also has the support of friendly interest groups that can often be enlisted to exert pressure on the presiding officers and other legislators. This complements the governor's formal legislative power and enhances his or her influence. A governor who tends toward activism can exercise substantial influence over legislation and thereby diminish the powers of the presiding officers. In fact, a coalition of the governor, the lieutenant governor, and the speaker is the norm, with each affecting the content of legislation. Of course, the governor has lost a battle with the legislative leadership if forced to veto a bill after attempting to influence it. If the governor chooses a passive legislative role, however, his or her influence is significantly decreased; inaction or restraint affects public policy as profoundly as activist leadership does.

POLITICAL CLIMATE

The general public is seldom aware of events in Austin. Rare exceptions are when a climate of scandal spreads over the state, as in the veterans' land scandals of the 1950s, the Sharpstown Bank scandal of the 1970s, or the delinquent property tax scandal of the 1990s. Although public interest is stimulated by a scandal, it seems confined to finding guilty parties rather than making serious inquiries into the need for reform of basic government procedures. Scandal does have the benefit of making the presiding officers aware of public scrutiny and therefore more responsive to criticism. In fact, the political climate following the Sharpstown and delinquent property tax scandals both resulted in ethics reform legislation. Without scandal, the legislative leadership is all but freed from public attention, with only interest groups, administrators, a few concerned citizens, some members of the press, and the governor exhibiting awareness of legislative activity.

Should Texas achieve true two-party government, the authority of the presiding officers, especially the lieutenant governor, could be weakened. Although the house majority party would simply choose a member of that party as speaker and in all likelihood retain the somewhat authoritarian house rules, the facade of nonpartisan legislative policy would be removed, and policy proposals of the opposition could be openly debated by politicians, the press, and the general public. On the other hand, a senate majority of a different political party than the lieutenant governor could bring about rule changes to drastically reduce the lieutenant governor's influence. In this event, the senate majority would have to institute other mechanisms to broker power and resolve conflict.

POLITICAL OR ECONOMIC AMBITION

Through effective management of the press, accumulation of political credits to be collected at some future date, and consolidation of interest group support, the offices of the speaker and lieutenant governor can serve as stepping-stones for both advancement in politics and future economic comfort. Because interest group support, campaign finances, and the support of established politicians are all necessary, the presiding officers must play their political cards right if they want to build an economic and political base solid enough to attain future political or economic success. The presiding officers must not, therefore, antagonize powerful economic and political forces in the process. Consequently, political and economic ambition can serve as a very real restraint on their independence.

OTHER LEGISLATORS

Many committee chairs and other legislators exercise a great deal of influence in their own right through their mastery of the intricacies of legislative rules and procedures, strong support of powerful interest groups, and the respect or fear they can generate in other legislators.

Because of the ties that these individuals have built over the years with administrators, interest groups, and other legislators, the presiding officers may need to solicit their support on key legislation. Generally, however, these individuals are the exception in an environment heavily influenced by the lieutenant governor or speaker.

CHAPTER SUMMARY

★ To reach the floor of the house, a bill must also be placed on a calendar by one of the two calendar committees. These committees are firmly under the control of the speaker. A bill that does not receive a calendar assignment is probably out of the running.

★ The senate calendar is an artificial device. The first item on the calendar is a "blocking bill," which is never brought to the floor. Actually bringing a bill other than the "blocking bill" to the floor requires a vote by two-thirds of the senators to "suspend the rule" and vote on the bill out of its calendar order. Given that two-thirds of the senate must vote in the affirmative even to bring a measure to the floor, most bills that reach the floor are approved.

★ To become an act of the legislature, a bill must pass both chambers with identical language. To iron out any differences, bills are sent to a conference committee, a special joint committee with members from both chambers. The presiding officers appoint these committees. Once a conference committee report is accepted by both chambers, the bill is sent to the governor.

★ The governor can sign or refuse to sign a bill (in which circumstance it eventually becomes law without the governor's signature). The governor can also veto a bill. If the bill contains an appropriations clause, the governor can strike it out with an item veto. In theory, the legislature could override a veto, but by the time the veto is issued, the legislature is usually no longer in session.

★ The institutional powers of the presiding officers include control over legislative boards and commissions that manage the budgeting function of state government (the Legislative Budget Board), the auditing function (the Legislative Audit Committee), and policy research (the Legislative Council).

HOW TEXAS COMPARES

In recent years the Texas legislature has attempted to reduce the property tax burden on Texans.

★ In 2008, Texans paid a median property tax rate of $2,232, putting Texas in 14th place for highest property taxes. New Jersey ranked first, with a median property tax burden of $6,320. Louisiana was in last place, with a median property tax burden of $188.

★ As a percentage of the value of the home, Texas ranks first.

★ As a percentage of median income, Texas ranks 14th, with 3.5 percent of income going to pay property taxes. New Jersey residents pay 7.02 percent of their median income to property taxes.

★ Texas is one of seven states that does not collect a state income tax.

Source: Tax Foundation, "Property Taxes on Owner-Occupied Housing by State, 2008," 2009, **http://www.taxfoundation.org/research/show/1913.html**

KEY TERMS

bills marked up	committee of the whole	Legislative Audit Committee	Sunset Advisory Commission
blocking bill	conference committee	Legislative Budget Board	suspension of the rule
bureaucracy	conference committee reports	Legislative Council	tagging
bureaucratic oversight	discharge petition	little legislatures	voice vote
calendar	filibuster	pigeonholed	
cloture	floor	point of order	
commission	floor leaders	recorded votes	

REVIEW QUESTIONS

1. Describe the procedural tools of leadership. Explain why each increases the powers of the presiding officers.

2. Describe the institutional tools of leadership. Explain why each increases the powers of the presiding officers.

3. Describe the process for a bill to become a law.

4. List the restraints on the powers of the presiding officers.

LOGGING ON

A complete summary of the legislative process in Texas is available at **http://www.tlc.state.tx.us/gtli/legproc/process.html**

You can research legislation pending before the legislature. Go to the legislature online at **http://www.tlc.state.tx.us/gtli/legproc/process.html**. Click on "Legislation," then scroll to and click on "Bill Lookup." Type in what you are searching for.

More information about the Legislative Budget Board can be found at **http://www.lbb.state.tx.us/**, on the Legislative Council at **http://www.tlc.state.tx.us/**, on the State Auditor's Office at **http://www.sao.state.tx.us**, and on the Sunset Advisory Commission at **http://www.sunset.state.tx.us/**

The Texas State Library is a source for legislative, administrative, and judicial research, as well as general information about many political, economic, and social aspects of Texas. The library can be accessed at **http://www.tsl.state.tx.us/**

The Legislative Reference Library is another source of information about the Texas legislature. The address is **http://www.lrl.state.tx.us/**

Other sources of political information, issues, and information about campaign contributions that student researchers may find interesting include **http://www.followthemoney.org/**, **http://www.opensecrets.org/**, and **http://www.speakout.com/**

The Texas Public Policy Foundation is a prominent and influential conservative think tank that plays an important part in issue initiative and policy formulation, especially now that Republicans control all branches of state government. Go to **http://www.texaspolicy.com/**

Texans for Public Justice is a nonpartisan, nonprofit policy and research organization that tracks the influence of money in politics: **http://www.tpj.org/**

Treehuggers is a cornucopia of websites for liberal, environmental, consumer, and other issues: **http://www.afn.org/~afn49740/**

The Texas Hispanic Research Council at **http://www.tshrc.org/** is a good source for a number of links on state and national government as well as for legislative information. This site also has other resource and organizational links relating to civil rights and civil liberties.

News information from any state newspaper can be found through **http://www.refdesk.com/paper.html**. The *Dallas Morning News* at **http://www.dallasnews.com/** and the *Houston Chronicle* at **http://www.chron.com/** are two excellent sources for state political news.

The Politics of Legislative Procedure

John David Rausch, Jr.
Teel Bivins Professor of Political Science, West Texas A&M University

INTRODUCTION

Many citizens fail to understand that the intricacies of legislative procedure have a direct impact on the kinds of policies that have a chance to become law. Like the filibuster in the U.S. Senate, the two-thirds rule in the Texas Senate protects the minority against abuse by an overbearing majority, but it also allows the minority to thwart the will of the majority with uncompromising obstructionism. Balancing minority rights and majority rule is a difficult problem in a representative democracy.

The Texas legislature experienced something of a role reversal during the opening days of the 81st Legislature in January 2009. Usually, legislative watchers expect to see raucous partisan debate over the rules in the house of representatives. This time it was partisan division in the Texas Senate that was on display. The *Austin American-Statesman* described the senate as "an upper chamber long known for its decorum and reluctance to publicly air its dirty laundry." To start the new legislative session, the paper opened with an article describing the debate over the rules as "a dramatic display of partisan bloodletting."[1] The *Dallas Morning News* reported, "The usually harmonious Senate began its year with discord."[2] The cause of the discord was the senate's "two-thirds" rule and the way Republicans in the senate wanted to alter the rule to allow for a vote on proposals to advance voter identification legislation.

The rule is officially known as the "two-thirds" rule and it is unique among the legislative procedures used by state legislatures in the United States. I will consider below the various other names applied to the rule such as the "blocker" bill and the "rosebush" bill. Most properly, it is the two-thirds rule. Under the rules of the Texas Senate, "senators are required to take up bills and resolutions for debate according to the 'regular order or business.'" The regular order of business in the Texas Senate is governed by Rules 5.09 through 5.12. "Bills and resolutions shall be considered on second reading and shall be listed on the Daily Calendar and Resolutions on the President's table in the order in which the committee report was received by the Secretary of the Senate."[3] Bills and resolutions on third reading are considered

[1] Mike Ward, "Texas Senate Adopts Rules Chance to Allow Voter ID Vote," *Austin American-Statesmen*, January 15, 2009.
[2] Terrence Stutz, "Texas Senate at Odds over Voter ID Legislation, Two-Thirds Rule," *Dallas Morning News*, January 14, 2009.
[3] Legislative Reference Library, "The Two-Thirds Rule," http://www.lrl.state.tx.us/citizenResources/twoThirds.html

in the order in which they received the second reading. Rule 5.13 establishes a procedure for getting around the regular order of business requirement: "A bill, joint resolution, or resolution affecting a state policy may be considered out of its regular calendar order if two-thirds of the members present vote to suspend the regular order of business."[4] The two-thirds rule has been a part of legislative procedure in the Texas Senate since the 1870s.

A little clarification is in order. One term often used in a discussion of the politics of the two-thirds rule is the "blocker bill" or "blocking bill." A "blocker bill" is that piece of legislation that is reported out of committee first to require suspension of the rules. Usually, this piece of legislation is a minor bill. In the 81st Legislature, the blocker bills were SB 621 relating to the creation, purpose, implementation, and funding of the County Park Beautification and Improvement Program; and SJR 19, authorizing the state to accept gifts of historical value. Both measures died in the senate. Sometimes one reads about the "Rosebush" bill, specifically in Republican opinion pieces critical of the practice.[5] I have not been able to identify the origin of the "Rosebush" bill.

This two-thirds rule seems to violate the idea of majority rule because 11 senators working together can defeat any piece of legislation by blocking the bill from reaching the senate calendar. Writing in the *Temple Daily Telegram* in January 1956, reporter Stuart Long documented the history of the two-thirds rule and how procedures developed to use the rule to defeat legislation. Following the rules, each morning the calendar clerk prepared the list of bills to be considered that day in the order specified by the rules. However, near the middle of the 20th century, senate leadership changed the procedure making the calendar meaningless. Long writes, "For, in the last eight years, there has been a gradual abandonment of the use of the calendar, as called for in the rules. The abandonment became complete in the 1951 session."[6]

Instead of following the calendar, all important bills are brought up for consideration by a "motion to suspend the regular order in order to take up Senate Bill xxx." The motion requires a two-thirds majority of the senators present to carry, in legislative parlance. Since the senate has 31 members, 11 senators can vote "no" on the motion to suspend the rules, and, therefore, prevent a bill from being considered on the floor.[7]

According to Long's research, the lieutenant governor determined the order of business, a practice in effect today. The lieutenant governor chooses to recognize a senator to make a motion to suspend the rules. If the motion is successful, then that senator is allowed to "run" with his or her bill. If the motion is defeated because it did not have the support of 21 senators, then that senator must wait for another opportunity to bring up his or her legislation. The practice began gradually while Governor Allan Shivers was lieutenant governor

(1947–1949) and expanded under the leadership of Lieutenant Governor Ben Ramsey (1951–1963; the post was vacant from 1949 to 1951).[8]

Commentators and senators have decried the practice as undemocratic because it places significant power in the hands of the lieutenant governor, acting as president of the senate. If a senator is not on the lieutenant governor's favored list, the senator could find that he or she is not recognized to make a motion to suspend. A small minority working together could prevent important legislation from being enacted by banding together and voting not to accept the motion to suspend the rules. In 1956, Senator A. M. Aiken, Jr., Democrat of Paris, announced that he was running for lieutenant governor, telling his senate colleagues that he would return to using the senate calendar if elected.[9]

Why did the two-thirds rule spur such heated partisan conflict in the Texas Senate at the beginning of the 81st Legislature? It would appear as though many senators would find the procedural tradition hurts their ability to represent their constituents especially if they are not part of the lieutenant governor's team. The Legislative Reference Library offers the following justification for the maintenance of the tradition: "Among other things, it is generally acknowledged that the senate's two-thirds rule fosters civility, a willingness to compromise, and a spirit of bipartisanship."[10]

The Republican Party of Texas wants the senate to end the use of the blocker rule. The party's 2008 platform clearly states, "Rosebush–Blocker Rule—We oppose the Rosebush–Blocker Rule in the Texas Senate."[11] Many Republicans argue that conservative legislation has to be "watered down" in order to pass a bill. Opponents of the blocker bill point out that legislation important to conservatives in Texas was killed by the blocker bill. These bills include a Voter Photo ID Bill in 2007 and a 2003 bill calling for a reduction in the property tax appraisal cap. Senator Dan Patrick, a Republican from Houston, emphasizes the elimination of the blocker bill in his campaign materials and public speeches. If the senate must maintain a super-majority requirement, Senator Patrick would prefer a three-fifths majority, or at least 19 senators.[12] In 2009, there were 19 Republicans serving in the Texas Senate.

Not all Texas Republicans agree that the two-thirds rule has outlived its usefulness. Senator Robert Duncan, a Republican from Lubbock, argued in January 2009, "The conservative position should be to protect the two-thirds rule." The rule prevents "bad legislation and too much government in the state of Texas." "Only in very rare and specific situations, such as voter identification laws that are being prevented from passing based on pure partisan grounds, should we consider exceptions to the two-thirds rule."[13]

---

[4]Legislative Reference Library.

[5]Jared Woodfill, "Time to Kill the Blocker Bill," *Harris County Republican Party Online Newsletter*, January 10, 2009, http://www.harriscountygop.com/eblast/eb011009.asp

[6]Stuart Long, "With 11 Senators for You, Kill Any Bill You Want To," *Temple Daily Telegram*, January 21, 1956.

[7]Ibid.

[8]Ibid.

[9]Ibid.

[10]Legislative Reference Library, http://www.lrl.state.tx.us/citizenResources/twoThirds.html

[11]Woodfill, "Time to Kill the Blocker Bill."

[12]Stutz, "Texas Senate at Odds over Voter ID Legislation, Two-Thirds Rule."

[13]Senator Robert Duncan, "Rare Amendment to the Senate's Two-Thirds Rule," January 22, 2009, http://www.duncan.senate.state.tx.us/pdf/012209.Duncan.pdf

Texas Republican Party Chair Cathie Adams also spoke out in support of the theory behind the two-thirds rule. She did not want to see the two-thirds rule abolished completely for all senate issues. Getting rid of the two-thirds rule might make it easier to enact pro-gambling measures, for example.[14]

The partisan rancor that marked the start of the Texas Senate's regular session in January 2009 was settled by a rules change. The change provided that an exemption from the two-thirds rule be allowed for the voter ID legislation. The passage of this bill would require that voters present photo identification before voting at a polling place. Democratic senators argued that other important pieces of legislation also be exempted from the rule. Senator Kirk Watson, a Democrat from Austin, wanted to include children's health care, affordable college tuition, relief from rising utility costs and insurance bills, environmental protection, and job creation, on the list of bills exempt from the two-thirds rule. According to Watson, the only bills worthy of being in the special class of exempt legislation were "the most political, partisan bills that protect the powerful."[15] None of Watson's proposed bills were exempted.

The rule change, with the exemption, was adopted by a vote of 18 to 13. Senator John Carona, a Republican from Dallas, was the only Republican to vote against the change.

JOIN THE DEBATE

1. Should the two-thirds rule be abolished? Is the rule a useful tradition or an obstacle that can kill legislation important to all Texans? Should it be replaced with a lower threshold for having legislation considered and voted on in the senate? If so, what should that lower threshold be?

2. Does the two-thirds rule grant too much power to a political minority?

3. Is Senator Watson correct in arguing that the senate's list of bills worthy of exempting from the two-thirds rule do not include those that would help the greatest number of Texans?

4. Does the two-thirds rule work?

---

[14]Ward, "Texas Senate Adopts Rules Change to Allow Voter ID Vote."
[15]Kirk Watson, "Watson Wire: Two-Thirds of a Wrong Isn't Right," January 19, 2009, http://www.kirkwatson.com/watson-wire/two-thirds-of-a-wrong-isnt-right

---

Politics and Climate Change: The Texas Legislature Grapples with the Environment

Adolfo Santos
University of Houston–Downtown

INTRODUCTION

The Texas legislature has the potential to create public policy that can have a broad impact on the country. Because of the size of Texas's economy, population, and geography,

policy makers can create public policy that leads the rest of the country. Texas can take the lead on climate change legislation, making dramatic improvements in the environment. The focus of this essay is on what Texas has done to combat global warming and environmental degradation.

Perhaps the single most important issue facing every human being on this planet is the issue of climate change. As the earth warms and sea levels rise, Texans will certainly not be immune to the problems brought on by climate change. Already, Texas has experienced warmer temperatures, "extreme rainfall events have become more frequent," and sea levels along the Texas coast have risen eight inches."[1] Texas is not only impacted by the effects of climate change, its industries are major contributors to it. The state's petrochemical industry not only produces billions of dollars in revenue for the state, its residents, and the industry, it also produces more than 650 million metric tons of carbon dioxide annually.[2] Given its propensity to pollute, "if Texas were a country, it would rank seventh in the world of greenhouse gas emissions."[3] The seriousness of the problem, coupled with the state's role in contributing to greenhouse gas emissions places the Texas legislature in the difficult position of choosing between the petrochemical industry, on the one hand, and the long-term health of the

---

[1]Union of Concerned Scientists, "Gulf Coast's Ecological Heritage at Risk, the Gulf States: Texas," August 2, 2005, http://www.ucsusa.org/gulf/gcstatetex_cli.html
[2]U.S. Energy Information Administration, U.S. Emissions Data, January 2008, www.eia.doe.gov/environment.html
[3]Ibid.

environment, on the other. In making these choices, the Texas legislature is in the unique position of shepherding the energy sector into new ventures that will preserve the state's role as the energy capital of the world. Currently, the state has attempted to address the problem with incentives that coax individuals and industry to cut down on the amount of pollution they produce. The question remains whether Texas can solve the problem with incentives, or whether more forceful government action is necessary.

During the 80th Legislative Session, the Texas legislature addressed seven major bills dealing with environmental issues.[4] Of these seven bills, four became law. This was an improvement over the 79th Legislative Session, when the legislature only enacted one environmental bill. This is not to say that the Texas legislature has not taken action. The Texas legislature has taken important steps to improve air quality. During the 78th Session, the Texas legislature created the Texas Emissions Reduction Plan (TERP), which was implemented by the Texas Commission on Environmental Quality (TCEQ). TERP is a model program that is expected to help bring the state of Texas into air quality compliance with the Environmental Protection Agency (EPA). Currently, the region is under an EPA order to improve its air quality or else run the risk of losing federal transportation dollars.

In 1999, The Texas legislature took steps that would make it one of the leaders in wind energy. In deregulating the electric utility companies, the Texas legislature provided incentives for companies to become more efficient and increase the use of renewable sources of energy. As a result, Texas produces more watts of energy from wind than any other state, and only three countries produce more wind energy than Texas. In 2007, the Texas legislature went further; requiring utility companies to cut energy demand by 20 percent through energy savings measures. It also required local governments, public schools, and universities to use energy more efficiently. University students at public universities can expect to see their campuses take steps to become more energy efficient.

In Texas, the primary concern has been with improving air quality. Although improving air quality can sometimes have the added benefit of reducing greenhouse gases, Texas has been most concerned with reducing ground-level ozone, a pollutant formed by a chemical reaction between pollution from combustion engines and other chemicals in the presence of sunlight. The Texas legislature has failed to tackle the problem of greenhouse gases directly. Large states like Texas are in a position to take the lead in the fight against greenhouse gases. With its large economic clout, as Texas goes, so goes the country.

In 2006, another big state took the lead on greenhouse gases. California enacted legislation (AB32) that aimed to cut greenhouse gases in a significant way. Governor Arnold Schwarzenegger described the aim of AB32, "Using market-based incentives, we will reduce carbon emissions to 1990 levels by the year 2020. That's a 25 percent reduction. And by 2050, we will reduce emissions to 80 percent below 1990 levels. We simply must do everything in our power to slow down global warming before it's too late."[5] Among other things, the law would require the auto industry to curtail emissions. This legislation made California, if for a very brief period, the country's leaders in cutting greenhouse gases. The Environmental Protection Agency quickly rejected the California plan, claiming that the Energy Independence and Security Act that President Bush signed into law was a better alternative to having states create their own laws. Oddly, neither the Environmental Protection Agency nor the Energy Independence and Security Act regulate greenhouse gas emissions.

Texas, like California, has the economic clout to lead the rest of the country in cutting greenhouse gases. In Texas, however, the Texas legislature has attempted to remedy the state's air quality problems with incentives for industry and residents alike. While California is *pushing* industry and its citizens to combat the emission of greenhouse gases, Texas is *pulling* its industry and citizens to do so. Texas has offered numerous incentives to industry and consumers, coaxing them to be more energy efficient and to pollute less. Only time will tell if the Texas incentives model will work better than the mixed incentives/regulatory model followed by California.

JOIN THE DEBATE

Should the Texas legislature require or encourage citizens and industries to produce fewer greenhouse gases?

---

[4]House Research Organization, 2007, "Focus Report: Major Issues of the 80th Legislature, Regular Session," http://www.hro.house.state.tx.us/focus/major80.pdf
[5]"Gov. Schwarzenegger Signs Landmark Legislation to Reduce Greenhouse Gas Emissions," Press Release, September 27, 2006, http://gov.ca.gov/index.php?/_press-release/4111

Chapter 8

The Governor

CONTENTS

LEARNING OBJECTIVES

⋆ Discuss the reasons for decentralization in Texas's administration.

⋆ List and describe the informal requirements for the Texas governor.

⋆ Describe the process, other than election, for removing a Texas governor from office. What is the order of succession?

⋆ What are the governor's formal and informal legislative tools of persuasion?

⋆ What is the item veto and what is its purpose?

⋆ Describe the importance of bargaining to the governor. What powers does the governor bring to the bargaining table? What are some of his limitations?

⋆ Why are appointments one of the most important administrative powers of the governor?

⋆ Describe the governor's administrative tools for persuasion. How are they weaker than other governors and the president?

⋆ What is the chief of state function and how is it important for the governor's political influence?

*A*lthough the Texas Constitution designates the governor as chief executive, the executive branch is splintered into various offices and agencies that are often beyond the governor's effective control. The division of Texas executive power is largely based on the Jacksonian democratic theory that most major officeholders should be elected. The authors of the current Texas Constitution also were reacting negatively to the centralization of power in the hands of Reconstruction Governor E. J. Davis. Although the legislature has recently strengthened the governor's administrative influence over several agencies, the continued preference for decentralized government by powerful special interest groups, bureaucrats, the legislative leadership, and the general public ensures the continuation of the weak governor administrative structure for Texas. As a result, Texas government has evolved into a hodgepodge of administratively independent entities, with no single official responsible for either policy initiation or implementation.

The lack of administrative authority does not mean that the office lacks the potential for significant political power. The governor's legislative powers, media access, party influence, and appointive powers to boards, commissions, and the judiciary provides enough political muscle for an astute, savvy officeholder to exert meaningful influence on both legislative and administrative policy.

Governor Rick Perry delivers the State of the State Address to the Texas legislature.

What is the purpose of the State of the State Address?

Bob Daemmrich/The Image Works

Qualifications, Tenure, and Staff

FORMAL QUALIFICATIONS

As is usual with elective offices, the legal requirements for becoming governor are minimal: One must be 30 years of age, an American citizen, and a citizen of Texas for five years before running for election.

INFORMAL CRITERIA

Whereas the formal qualifications for governor are easily met, the informal criteria are more restrictive.

Elected state treasurer in 1982, Ann Richards was the first woman to win a statewide election in Texas since Governor Miriam "Ma" Ferguson. Richards won the governor's office in 1990 after hard-fought and bitter primaries and general election contests, disproving the assumption that Texans will not support an assertive politician who also happens to be a woman. As a moderate-to-liberal single divorcee and a recovering alcoholic, Richards was also an exception to several other informal criteria for becoming Texas's governor. Ann Richards died September 13, 2006, and is buried in the Texas State Cemetery in Austin.

WASP Since the Texas Revolution, governors have all been WASPs (i.e., white Anglo-Saxon Protestants). They have been white Protestants, usually Methodist or Baptist, and also Anglo American, with family names originating in the British Isles.

Male The governor is historically male. The only female governor of Texas before Ann Richards (1991–1995) was Miriam A. Ferguson, who served for two nonconsecutive terms (1925–1927 and 1933–1935). As noted in Chapter 1, she ran on the slogan "Two Governors for the Price of One" and did not really represent a deviation from male dominance in Texas politics, for it was clear that her husband, former governor James E. Ferguson, exercised the power of the office. In reality, Governor Richards was the first woman to serve as the governing Texas chief executive.

Middle-Aged Businessperson or Attorney The governor will be successful in business or law; in fact, more than one-half of the governors who have served since 1900 have been lawyers. The governor will probably be between 40 and 60 years of age, have a record of elective public service in state government or some other source of name recognition, and be a participant in service, social, and occupational organizations.

Conservative to Moderate Texas was a two-party state for top-of-the-ticket elections for president, U.S. senator, and governor for more than two decades but was basically Democratic for most other offices. It became an authentic two-party state with the 1990 election of two Republicans to the down-ticket offices of state treasurer and commissioner of agriculture.

However, it seems that Texans are uncomfortable with effective two-party politics for in only 14 years, Texas completed its evolution into a strong Republican one-party state. Republicans first swept statewide offices in 1998, electing the governor, lieutenant governor, and all elected down-ticket administrators including the Texas Railroad Commission. The down-ticket Republican victories have additional political significance. Statewide elective offices can provide political experience and name recognition and can serve as a springboard to higher office, as Kay Bailey Hutchison demonstrated by her promotion from state treasurer to U.S. senator. In 1998, Rick Perry moved from Commissioner of Agriculture to lieutenant governor, and in 2002, he was elected governor. That same year, Attorney General John Cornyn was elected to the U.S. Senate. As evidenced by the 2002 and 2004 general elections, the state's electorate strongly favors Republican candidates for public office.

The Democratic gubernatorial primary is usually a match between conservative-to-moderate and moderate-to-liberal candidates. The Democratic nominee must forge a slippery coalition of business leaders, ethnic minorities, unions, intellectuals, teachers, conservationists, and consumer advocates in order to win the general election.

In an attempt to energize this coalition in the 2002 general election, Democrats nominated a Mexican American for governor, an African American for the U.S. Senate, and an Anglo American for lieutenant governor. The tactic failed, and none of these candidates was successful.

The Republican primary is a joust between conservative-to-moderate candidates, with the more conservative candidate usually being the winner. Republican gubernatorial candidates usually have the campaign funds to outspend their Democratic opponents, thereby purchasing the all important political image and name recognition and being able to identify and define the issues of the campaign.

Money Money is a critical factor in any serious campaign for Texas governor. Although the candidate who spends the most does not always win the office, a hefty bankroll is necessary for serious consideration. Challengers usually must spend more than incumbents to buy name recognition. Paul Taylor, executive director of the Alliance for Better Campaigns, commented that "the legacy is a political culture in which we auction off the right to free speech 30 seconds at a time to the highest political bidder."[1]

TENURE, REMOVAL, AND SUCCESSION

As in 47 other states, Texas governors serve a four-year term. Unlike most states, however, there is no limit on the number of terms that a governor may serve. The governor may be removed from office only by **impeachment** by the house of representatives and conviction by the senate. Impeachment is the legislative equivalent of indictment and requires only a simple majority of members present. Conviction by the senate requires a two-thirds majority. If the office is vacated, the lieutenant governor becomes governor; the next in the line of succession is the president pro tempore of the senate.

If the governor is removed or vacates the office, the lieutenant governor becomes governor for the remainder of the elected term. The Texas Senate then elects a senator as acting lieutenant governor, who serves in both positions until the next general election.

Impeachment
Officially charging an office holder with improper conduct in office.

COMPENSATION

The governor's salary is set by the legislature. At present, it is $150,000 yearly and stands in marked contrast to the low salaries paid to legislators. Although the governor's salary is among the highest in the nation, several other Texas state officials earn more.

In addition to the governor's mansion, there is an expense account to keep it maintained and staffed, along with a professional staff with offices in the capitol. This is important because the modern chief executive depends heavily on staff to carry out the duties of office.

STAFF

The governor's greater involvement in legislative affairs and appointments and increasing demands on government by the general public have placed intensified pressure on the time and resources of the executive. The Texas governor, like all executives in modern government, depends on others for advice, information, and assistance before making decisions and recommendations. A good staff is a key ingredient for a successful chief executive.

Among the most important concerns of the governor's staff are political appointments. Each year, the governor makes several hundred appointments to various boards, commissions, and executive agencies. The executive also fills newly created judicial offices and those vacated because of death or resignation. Staff evaluation of

AP Images/Harry Cabluck

The governor congratulates the president of Zachry Construction on receiving the Trans-Texas Corridor contract. Federal and state highway administrators and the chairman of Group Ferrovial also participate. Public policy formulation is often a group project including the governor, bureaucrats, and special interest groups.

Why are so many people involved in making public policy?

---

[1]Colleen McCain Nelson, *The Dallas Morning News*, November 7, 2002.

Consumer groups expressed fear of excessive corporate influence on the office of the governor when in 2002, Governor Perry appointed Mike Toomey, a prominent lobbyist for corporate interests, as his chief of staff. Governor Perry said that Texans should not worry because "Texas leaders have a long tradition of turning to lobbyists to fill high-level state jobs." In disagreement, the director of Texas Public Citizen, Tom "Smitty" Smith, said that Toomey's "clients sort of form a who's who of those who cost consumers significant money in Texas." Toomey's selection came only days after soon-to-be-elected Speaker of the House Tom Craddick (R-Midland) announced that his transition team included several corporate lobbyists.[2]

potential appointees is necessary because the governor may not personally know many of the individuals under consideration.

Legislative assistants provide liaison between the office of the governor and the legislature. Their job is to stay in contact with key legislators, committee chairs, and the legislative leadership. These assistants are, in fact, the governor's lobbyists. They keep legislators informed and attempt to persuade them to support the governor's position on legislation. Often the success of the governor's legislative program rests on the staff's abilities and political expertise.

Some administrative assistants head executive offices that compile and write budget recommendations and manage and coordinate activities within the governor's office. Staff

DIVISIONS OF THE OFFICE OF THE GOVERNOR

The office of the governor provides direct support for the governor's staff, including accounting, internal budget, human resources, computer services, operations, and mailroom. Administrative divisions of the office of the governor provide more specialized support.

★ **Advisory Council on Physical Fitness**: Concentrates on improving the state's overall fitness through sports, health, exercise, and nutrition education.
★ **Appointments**: Recommends individuals for appointment to boards, commissions, and advisory committees.
★ **Budget, Planning, and Policy**: Prepares the governor's biennial budget and provides financial information and analysis relating to the state's fiscal policies.
★ **Commission for Women**: Promotes opportunities for Texas women through outreach, education, research, and referral services.
★ **Committee on People with Disabilities**: Helps people with disabilities enjoy full and equal access to lives of independence, productivity, and self-determination.
★ **Constituent Communication**: Maintains a two-way conversation with Texans and provides the link between the governor and the people of Texas by responding to letters, faxes, emails, and phone calls.
★ **Criminal Justice**: Administers and allocates state and federal grants for local, regional, and statewide criminal justice projects.
★ **Economic Development and Tourism**: Coordinates and promotes tourism and business relocation. This office manages the Enterprise Fund, the Emerging Technology Fund, and Texas Economic Development Bank.
★ **Financial Services**: Ensures that financial transactions in the governor's office set the highest standard for the state.
★ **General Counsel**: Provides legal advice to the governor and his team.

★ **Homeland Security**: Protects Texas citizens, infrastructure, and key resources from natural and human-caused disasters.
★ **Human Resources (HR)**: Assists applicants seeking employment, students pursuing the Texas governor's fellowship program, and employees in need of HR support.
★ **Press Office**: Serves as the primary conduit between the governor and the people of Texas.
★ **Scheduling and Advance**: Creates a clear, concise schedule for the governor on a daily basis.
★ **State Grants Team**: Monitors federal, state, and private funding information sources and alerts state agencies, nonprofit organizations, units of local government, and other entities to funding opportunities.
★ **Texas Criminal Justice Statistical Analysis Center**: Collects, analyzes, and reports statewide criminal justice statistics; evaluates the effectiveness of state-funded initiatives; and disseminates analysis results to interested parties and institutions.
★ **Texas Film Commission**: Assists the various elements of the entertainment industry in finding Texas locations, talent, and services.
★ **Texas Health Care Policy Council**: Recommends informed improvements to the health-care system in Texas.
★ **Texas Military Preparedness Commission**: Works to curb military base closures and coordinates with Defense Department communities to provide state support for future Defense Department needs.
★ **Texas Music Office**: Promotes the Texas music industry.
★ **Texas Workforce Investment Council**: Advises the governor and the legislature on strategic direction for and evaluation of the state's workforce development.[3]

The office also assists in developing and passing the governor's legislative initiatives, provides information and analysis on state policy and policy proposals, and coordinates with state agencies and boards. Scheduling and managing the governor's official out-of-office activities is also a function.

[2]*The Dallas Morning News*, December 4, 2002.
[3]Office of the Governor, http://governor.state.tx.us/organization/

HOW DOES TEXAS COMPARE?
THE GOVERNOR'S POWER

The Texas governor's office ranks below the average of other state governors in authority to actually see that the laws are administered. In fact, the Texas governor's combined administrative and legislative power ranking is 34th among the 50 states. By comparison, Utah's governor ranks 1st and Vermont's ranks 50th.[4]

Using a 1- to 5-point scale with 5 having the greatest power in a 2007 study, Thad Beyle ranked the various institutional powers of U.S. governors on several important categories. With a Governor's Institutional Powers (GIP) rating of 3.2, the Texas governor ranked above only 10 other state governors and slightly below the GIP average of 3.5. Beyle also ranked the governors on personal power, awarding Texas's governor a Governor Personal Power (GPP) index ranking of 3.8, above the governors in 12 other states but slightly below the GPP index average of 3.9. Both the *Congressional Quarterly* and Beyle ranked the powers of the Texas governorship as slightly below average, but above the even lower rankings often associated with the Texas governor's office.[5]

members also exercise administrative control over the governor's schedule of ceremonial and official duties.

The governor is the official planning officer for the state, although coordination and participation by affected state agencies is voluntary. The planning divisions also help coordinate local and regional planning between the councils of governments in an effort to bring the work of these jurisdictions into harmony with state goals. In addition, national and state funds are available through the governor's office to local units of government for comprehensive planning (master planning).

The governor's staff, although primarily responsible for assisting with the everyday duties of the office, also attempt to persuade legislators, administrators, and the representatives of various local governments to follow the governor's leadership in solving common problems.

Tools of Persuasion

The governor's ability to influence the making and executing of government policy depends on his or her bargaining skills, persuasiveness, and ability to broker effectively between competing interests—the tools of persuasion. Thus the **informal, or extralegal, powers** of the office are as important as its formal or legal powers (those granted by the constitution or by law). The governor's ability to use informal power is largely determined by the extent of the **formal, or legal, powers**. Compared to governors of other states (especially other populous, industrialized states), the governor of Texas has weak formal administrative powers. However, some Texas governors have been able to exert significant influence on policy formulation and even on policy execution when the formal and informal powers are enhanced by a fortunate blending of other conditions such as a strong personality, political expertise, prestige, a knack for public relations and political drama, good relations with the press, supporters with political and economic strength, a favorable political climate, and simple good luck.

LEGISLATIVE TOOLS OF PERSUASION

Ironically, the most influential bargaining tools that the Texas governor has are legislative. How these tools are used largely determines the governor's effectiveness.

Informal (extralegal) powers

Powers that are not stated in rules, a law, or a constitution but are usually derived from these legal powers.

Formal (legal) powers

Powers stated in rules, a law, or a constitution.

---

[4]Kendra A. Hovey and Harold A. Hovey, *CQ's State Fact Finder 2003: Rankings across America* (Washington, DC: CQ Press/Congressional Quarterly, 2003), p. 406.

[5]Thad Beyle, *The Institutional Power Ratings for the 50 Governors of the United States,* University of North Carolina at Chapel Hill, 2007, http://www.unc.edu/~beyle/gubnewpwr.htm

The Veto One of the governor's most powerful formal legislative tools is the veto. After a bill has passed both houses of the legislature in identical form, it is sent to the governor. If signed, the bill becomes law; if vetoed, the bill is sent back to the legislature with a message stating the reasons for opposition. The legislature has the constitutional power to override the governor's **veto** by a two-thirds vote, but in practice vetoes are usually final.

Because legislative sessions in Texas are short, the vast majority of important bills are passed and sent to the governor in the final days of the session. The governor need take no action on the legislation for 10 days when the legislature is in session (20 days when it is not in session), so he can often wait until the legislature has adjourned and thereby ensure that a veto will not be overridden. In fact, it is so difficult to override a veto that it has happened only once since World War II. Thus the veto gives the Texas governor a strong bargaining position with legislators.

The Texas governor, however, lacks the *pocket veto* that is available to many other chief executives, including the president of the United States. The pocket veto provides that if the executive chooses to ignore legislation passed at the end of a session, it dies without ever taking effect. By contrast, if the Texas governor neither signs nor vetoes a bill, it becomes law. By not signing a bill and allowing it to become law, the governor may register a protest against the bill or some of its provisions.

The Item Veto Probably the most important single piece of legislation enacted in a legislative session is the appropriations bill. If it should be vetoed in its entirety, funds for the operation of the government would be cut off, and a special session would be necessary. Thus Texas, like most other states, permits the governor an item veto, which allows the governor to veto funds for specific items or projects without killing the entire bill.

If used to its fullest potential, the item veto is a very effective negative legislative tool. Money is necessary to administer laws; therefore, by vetoing an item or a category of items, the governor can in effect kill programs or whole classes of programs. The governor cannot, however, reduce the appropriation for a budgetary item, as some governors may. Because the appropriations bill is usually passed at the end of the session, the item veto is virtually absolute.

Threat of Veto An informal legislative power of the governor not mentioned in the constitution or the law is the **threat of veto**. Nevertheless, it is a very real and effective tool for the governor, but like all informal power, its effectiveness depends on existing formal powers.

Both the veto and the item veto are negative tools that simply kill bills or programs; they do not let the governor shape legislation. However, by threatening to use these formal powers, the governor can often persuade the legislative supporters of a bill to change its content or face the probability of a veto. In this way, a compromise can often be negotiated. Although the veto itself is negative, the threat of veto can be used to positively affect the content of bills during the legislative process.

The governor can also use this powerful informal tool of persuasion to influence bureaucrats. Bureaucrats are very active in the legislative process, often seeking increased funding for favorite programs and projects or seeking authorization to administer new programs. Because of this, the

---

Veto

The executive power to reject a proposed law unless an unusual majority of the legislature (usually two-thirds) votes to override the governor's opposition. This is almost an absolute power in Texas because the legislature is seldom in session when the governor issues the veto.

Threat of veto

An informal power of the Texas governor. Threatening in advance to veto legislation enhances the governor's bargaining power with legislators, enabling the governor to shape the content of legislation while it is still in the legislature.

Governor Rick Perry signs a bill authorizing the creation of the Tejano Monument on the south lawn of the Texas Capitol to honor the contributions of people of Latino heritage. ☞

What human need do monuments fulfill?

Bob Daemmrich/PhotoEdit

HOW DOES TEXAS COMPARE?
THE POLITICS OF THE ITEM VETO

Forty-three governors have the item veto (or line-item veto), and some reformers have long advocated that the U.S. president should also be given this tool as a way to reduce federal budget deficits and help eliminate "earmarks" or "pork barrel"—wasteful special spending projects included in spending bills at the request of individual members of Congress to benefit a few of their constituents or campaign supporters.

However, at the state level, there is little evidence that chief executives have the political courage to use the tool to confront special interests, nor has it been an effective tool for responsible fiscal management. State legislatures have avoided the threat of the item veto by simply passing broad categories of spending that include funding for essential services that the governor is unwilling to veto. States with governors who have the item veto have about the same level of per capita state spending as those without. In Texas, Governor Rick Perry item-vetoed only $289 million of state appropriations in 2009, most for legislation that failed to pass the legislature.[6] Although there is little evidence that the item veto is an effective tool for financial discipline, governors can use the item veto as a bargaining chip with legislators. For example, in 2005, when Texas Governor Perry item-vetoed the entire $35.3 billion appropriation for the Texas Education Agency (one-fourth of state spending), he put pressure on the state legislature to pass his own version of educational spending in a 30-day special session. Without a compromise between the governor and the legislature, Texas public schools would have closed.

governor may be able to influence the administration of existing programs by threatening to withhold funds or veto bills actively supported by an agency. The agency's legislative liaison personnel (its lobbyists) may also be encouraged to support the governor's legislative program in exchange for support (or neutrality) with respect to agency-supported bills.

The threat of veto can also be used to consolidate lobby support for the governor's legislative proposals. Lobbyists may offer to support the governor's position on legislation if the governor will agree not to veto a particular bill that is considered vital to the interests of their employers. The governor can thus bargain with both supporters and opponents of legislation in order to gain political allies.

Bargaining   The governor's bargaining with legislators, lobbyists, and administrators is often intense as other political forces attempt to gain gubernatorial neutrality, support, or opposition for legislation. If the governor or political and financial supporters have not made particular legislation an explicit part of their legislative program, avenues are left open for political bartering to gain hard political support for the governor's legislative program or equally firm resistance to proposals that the governor opposes. Whoever seeks the governor's support must be willing to give something of real political value in return. All sides of the negotiation want to gain as much as possible and give as little as possible. There is, of course, a vast difference in political resources among politicians, just as among interest groups.

> In 2001, Governor Perry frustrated and surprised many lawmakers by vetoing 78 bills on one day without voicing prior concern. Dubbing the event the "Father's Day Veto Massacre," disgruntled legislators claimed that Perry had played unfairly. In all, Perry vetoed 82 bills in 2001, which is only 9 fewer in one session than Governor Bush had cast in three sessions and 22 more than Governor Richards had vetoed in two sessions. Governor Perry vetoed 52 bills in 2003 and 37 in 2009.[7]

The flexibility and intensity that the governor brings to the bargaining table depend on several very real political factors:

1. The depth of the governor's commitment to the bill is a factor. If the governor is committed to a position, because of either a political debt or ideological belief, this support or opposition may not be open to negotiation.

[6] The Associated Press, Governor Vetoes 37 Bills, *The Bryan-College Station Eagle*, http://www.theeagle.com/Governor-vetos-37-bills

[7] Texas Politics, "The Executive Branch Limits of the Veto," http://texaspolitics.laits.utexas.edu/html/exec/0502.html and The Associated Press, Governor Vetoes 37 Bills, *The Bryan-College Station Eagle*, http://www.theeagle.com/governor-vetos-37 bills

2. Timing is also important. Politicians often try to be the ones to tip the scales for the winning side.

3. The political and financial support given the governor during a campaign may determine his or her flexibility. This does not mean that *all* campaign contributions buy political decisions, but they do increase the chances that contributors will get a favorable hearing.

4. Future campaign support is another major factor. Bargaining may involve financial or political support for the reelection or advancement of an ambitious politician.

5. Who supports and who opposes the bill? For political reasons, the governor may not want to align with a political group that is unpopular with either financial supporters or the general electorate—for example, advocates for the legalization of marijuana or a graduated state income tax.

6. The amount of firm legislative support for or opposition to the proposal is important. Even if the chief executive is inclined to a particular position, backing a losing cause could mean a loss of prestige.

7. The political benefits to be gained must be carefully considered. Some groups may be more willing or more able than others to pay a high price for the governor's support. Thus, an important consideration is the relative strength of the supporters and the opponents of a bill and their ability to pay their political and financial debts. For example, because medical patients in Texas have no organization and few political allies, their interests are not as well represented as those of the Texas Medical Association, health maintenance organizations, or insurance companies, which have strong organizations and ample political and financial resources.

8. Some governors may be hesitant to alienate interests that could provide postgubernatorial economic opportunities or political assistance. Other governors may have extensive investments and are unlikely as governor to make political decisions that could mean personal financial loss.

Presession Bargaining   If, before the legislative session begins, the governor, the legislative leadership, concerned administrators, and special interest groups can arrive at successful bargains and compromises, through **presession bargaining**, the prospect for passage of a proposal is greatly enhanced.

Presession bargaining seeks compromises, but harmonious relationships seldom develop immediately. Powerful and often competing political forces may continue bargaining throughout the legislative session. Failure to reach an amicable settlement usually means either defeat of a bill in the legislature or a veto by the governor.

There are several advantages if advance agreement can be reached on a given bill:

1. The advocates of the bill are assured that both the legislative leadership and the governor are friendly to the legislation.

2. The governor need not threaten a veto to influence the content of the bill. This keeps the chief executive on better terms with the legislature.

3. The legislative leaders can guide the bill through their respective houses, secure in the knowledge that the legislation will not be opposed or vetoed by the governor.

Presession bargaining

Negotiations that let the governor and the legislative leaders reach the necessary compromises prior to the start of the legislative session. This usually ensures passage of the legislation.

The fourth special session in 2004 was an attempt to reform education funding. Although the governor, speaker, and lieutenant governor met at the lieutenant governor's ranch, presession bargaining was unsuccessful, and the legislature was unable to reach a consensus on the reform.

Special Sessions   The constitution gives the governor exclusive power to call the legislature into special session and to determine the *legislative* subjects to be considered by the session. The legislature may, however, consider any *nonlegislative subject*, such as confirmation of appointments, resolutions, impeachment, and constitutional amendments, even if the governor does not include it in the call. Special sessions are limited to a 30-day duration, but the governor may call them as often as he or she wants.

Often when coalitions of legislators and lobbyists request a special session so that a "critical issue" can be brought before the legislature, other coalitions of legislators and interests oppose consideration of the issue and therefore oppose calling the special session. Because there is seldom any legislation that does not hurt some and help others, the governor has an opportunity to use the special session as a valuable bargaining tool. The governor may or may not call a special session on the basis of some concession or support to be delivered in the future. The supporters and opponents of legislation may also have to bargain with the governor over the inclusion or exclusion of specific policy proposals for the special session. Of course, this position may not be open to negotiation if the governor has strong feelings about the proposal and is determined to call (or not to call) a special session. If the governor does think that an issue is critical, the attention of the entire state can be focused on the proposal during the special session much more effectively than during the regular session.

Message Power As a constitutional requirement, the governor must deliver a state-of-the-state message at the beginning of each legislative session. This message includes the outline for the governor's legislative program. Throughout the session, the governor may also submit messages calling for action on individual items of legislation. The receptiveness of the legislature to the various messages is influenced by the governor's popularity, the amount of favorable public opinion generated for the proposals, and the governor's political expertise.

The **message power** of the governor is a formal power and is enhanced by the visibility of the office. Through the judicious use of the mass media (an informal power), the governor can focus public attention on a bill when it might otherwise be buried in the legislative maze. He or she must not overuse the mass media, however, for too many attempts to urge legislative action can result in public apathy for all gubernatorial appeals. An effective governor "goes to the people" only for the legislation considered vital to the interest of the state or to the governor's political and financial supporters.

Fact-Finding Commissions Governors also appoint **blue-ribbon commissions** consisting of influential citizens, politicians, and members of concerned special interest groups. Commissions can serve either as trial balloons to measure public acceptance of the proposal or as a means to inform and increase public and interest group support. Blue-ribbon commissions are also commonly used to delay the actual consideration of a political hot potato until it has cooled. Politicians know that the attention span of the public is short and that other personally important issues, such as jobs, families, and favorite soap operas or sports teams, easily distract people. Once the public becomes distracted, meaningful action may become unnecessary.

EXECUTIVE TOOLS OF PERSUASION

The Texas Constitution charges the governor, as the chief executive, with broad responsibilities. However, it systematically denies the governor the power to meet these responsibilities through direct executive action. In fact, four other important elective executive offices—lieutenant governor, comptroller of public accounts, attorney general, and commissioner of the General Land Office—are established in the same section of the constitution and are legally independent of the governor, thus undermining the governor's executive authority (see Figure 8.1).

Other provisions in the constitution further fragment executive power. For example, the constitution establishes the elective Railroad Commission of Texas and states that the Board of Education can be either elected or appointed. (It is elected.) Moreover, the Texas legislature, by statute, has systematically continued to assume executive functions such as

Message power

The influence a person gains merely by being in the public eye. For example, message power allows the governor to focus the attention of the press, legislators, and citizens on legislative proposals that he or she considers important. The visibility of high office draws instant public attention for the officeholder's proposals, a power that led Teddy Roosevelt to refer to the presidency as the "bully pulpit."

Blue-ribbon commission

A group assembled by the governor (or legislature) that may have both fact-finding and recommending authority. It often contains public personages or authorities on the subject that is being considered. Such commissions can help measure public reaction to proposals and may also let the governor delay consideration of issues that may be politically uncomfortable.

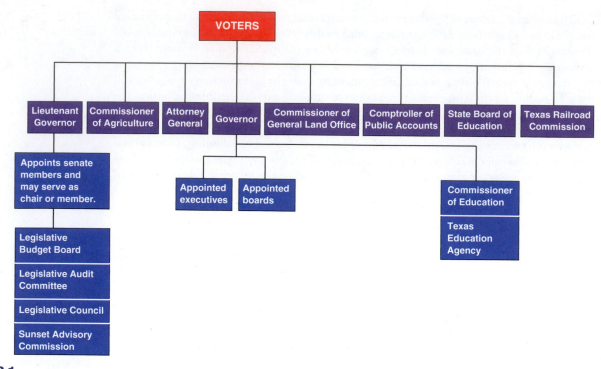

Figure 8.1

Texas's Elected Officials

What are the arguments for and against electing so many state administrators?

budgeting and auditing. It has also created the Department of Agriculture and a multitude of boards and commissions to administer state laws that are independent of direct gubernatorial control. Although these commissions are usually gubernatorial appointees, their terms are staggered, and it may be several years before one governor's appointees constitute a majority of a board or commission. Boards and commissions perform a function similar to that of the independent school district board, such as hiring and firing executives and establishing general agency policy.

Given the present fragmented executive branch of the Texas government, few executive bargaining tools are available to the governor, making that officer one of the weakest state chief executives in the nation.

Appointive Powers An effective governor will use the power of appointment to the maximum. Probably the most important appointments that the governor makes are to the independent boards and commissions. The members of these boards establish general administrative and regulatory policy for state agencies or institutions and choose the top administrators to carry out these policies (see Figure 8.2).

The governor's ability to affect board policy through appointments is not immediate, however, as the boards are usually appointed for fixed, six-year staggered terms. Because only one-third of these positions become vacant every two years, the governor will only have appointed a majority of most boards in the second half of his or her term.

Interest groups in Texas are vitally concerned with seeing that the "right kinds" of appointees are selected to serve on these boards and commissions. In the present age of consumerism, industry interest groups are particularly anxious to have an industry advocate (often an ex-lobbyist or industry executive) appointed to the board that oversees and sets

Proposals by the 1984 blue-ribbon commission appointed by former governor Mark White and headed by Ross Perot resulted in several public education reforms by the 1985 legislature. Governor George W. Bush appointed a similar commission to make proposed property tax reforms to the 1997 legislature. His recommendations were not adopted by the legislature.

policy for "their" agency. Appointment of a consumer advocate could disorient the close relationship that usually exists between an industry and its agency (see Chapter 9, "The Bureaucracy"). There may also be competing interest groups within one industry that may bargain individually with the governor for an appointee who is favorable to their particular viewpoint. Thus, an appointment to important boards often results in intense lobbying by special interest groups, which conversely gives the governor opportunities to develop support for policies and to help secure funds for future political campaigns.

Senators also have some influence over appointments from their districts as the result of **senatorial courtesy**. Senators will usually refuse to vote for confirmation if a senator announces that an appointee from his or her district is "personally obnoxious." The senators thereby show courtesy to the disgruntled senator by refusing to confirm a political enemy.

Administrators also want commissioners appointed to their agency who are sympathetic to their problems and who share their goals. Appointments that are friendly to their interests can strengthen a governor's influence with these administrators.

The governor can exert a great deal of influence on the state's judiciary. It is common for judges to retire or resign prior to the end of their terms. The governor is empowered to fill these vacancies until the next general election. The result is that the governor is able to repay political supporters with judicial appointments, and the appointees enjoy the advantage of incumbency in the general election.

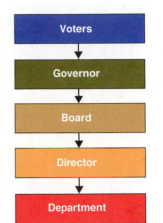

Figure 8.2

The Board and Commission System

What is the political reason for using this structural organization? Is it successful?

Legislative sources revealed that Governor Rick Perry, newly elected Lieutenant Governor David Dewhurst, and soon-to-be-elected Speaker Tom Craddick were negotiating the extent of influence that the governor's office would have on the 2003 to 2004 state budget. Past budgets were largely written by the Legislative Budget Board, which is controlled by the lieutenant governor and speaker. Perry's argument was that since all are Republicans, the governor should have more input into the process. The specific decision made in these negotiations is not known, but Governor Perry either declined or was denied the opportunity to contribute to the budget process and submitted a budget with no monetary recommendations.[8]

Removal Powers Although the governor possesses broad appointive power to boards and commissions, the powers of removal are limited. He or she may remove members of the executive office and a few minor administrators. The governor may also remove, for cause and with the consent of two-thirds of the senate, his or her own appointments to boards and commissions. If the governor decides that an elected administrator is administering a law so as to violate its spirit, there is no official way to force a revision of such administrative interpretation or procedures. In general, the governor cannot issue directives or orders to state agencies or remove executive officials who do not abide by his or her wishes. Only by focusing public attention on the agency and garnering public support can the governor force an administrator to change positions or resign.

Planning Powers The office of the governor has become a focal point for planning activities at all levels of government in the state of Texas. This increase in the governor's planning authority is a first step toward comprehensive coordination of the planning, policy formulation, and administrative activities of local units of government and of the various independent agencies in the state government. But again, the governor's office has been granted

Senatorial courtesy

The tradition of allowing a senator to reject the governor's appointment of a political enemy from the senator's district. The senator declares the appointee "personally obnoxious," and the other senators vote to reject the appointee.

---

[8]W. Gardner Selby, *San Antonio Express-News*, December 18, 2002, p. 5b; John Mortz, *Fort Worth Star-Telegram*, January 18, 2003.

responsibility without the necessary enforcement powers. The governor has no power to enforce compliance from the various local governments and state agencies involved.

The power that does exist in the governor's office to encourage compliance is derived from a requirement of the federal government that the state undertake some planning prior to the issuance of federal grants. This requirement was necessary because previously there had been little comprehensive planning to coordinate the goals of the various local governments with those of the state government. In fact, very little coordination of any kind existed for city, county, or even special district governments, between these local governments and state government, or between different departments in the state government. The federal government attempted to help (that is, to force) Texas to develop some kind of overall plan for program development. Thus encouraged, the state government designed rudimentary coordination and cooperation between the various government units and subunits in the state. The natural center for such statewide planning is the governor's office, which has the scope to determine whether grant requests are in accord with statewide plans. The result is a centralization of planning in the office of the Texas governor.

The 2003 inauguration of Governor Perry and Lieutenant Governor Dewhurst was paid for primarily by large corporations, including AT&T, Philip Morris, SBC Communications, and Sprint; insurance companies; and the state's primary Medicaid contractor. Consumer lobbyists voiced concern, considering the pending slate of insurance, health care, and other legislation facing the 2003 legislature. The festivities cost about $1.5 million, of which $500,000 was raised by ticket sales to the event.[9]

Chief of State The governor, as the first citizen of Texas, serves as a symbol of Texas as surely as the bluebonnet or the pecan tree. A significant part of the governor's job is related to the pomp and ceremony of the office. These ceremonial duties include throwing out the first baseball of the season, greeting Boy Scout troops at the state capitol, visiting disaster areas, and riding in parades for peanut festivals, county fairs, or cow chip-throwing contests.

This ceremonial role is important because it can contribute indirectly to the governor's leadership effectiveness through increased popularity and prestige. The governor also broadens the image as first citizen to that of the first family of Texas whenever possible; voters identify with the governor's family, and so the governor's spouse is often included in the visual enactment of the office—particularly if the spouse is attractive and articulate.

Chief of state

The governor, who serves as the symbol of Texas and who performs ceremonial duties and represents the state at meetings with foreign officials and other governors.

Three notable facets to the role of **chief of state** that supplement the other formal and informal powers discussed here can be summarized as follows:

1. The governor serves as a member of (or appoints representatives to) numerous multistate organizations and conferences that work to coordinate relations between Texas and other state governments. These conferences deal with oil, civil defense, nuclear energy, and other important matters. It is also the governor's responsibility to ask other states to extradite fugitives from Texas law and to grant or refuse like requests from other states.

2. To facilitate the governor's job of coordinating the activities of state agencies and local governments with the national grant-in-aid programs, the Texas government has established an office in the nation's capital, the Office of State–Federal Relations (OSFR). The governor appoints (and may remove) the director of this office, who serves as a representative from Texas to the federal bureaucracy. "Our person in Washington" tries to keep current on the numerous federal aid programs and grants that might be available to either state agencies

---

[9]*The Dallas Morning News*, January 2, 2003; J. Taylor Rushing, *Fort Worth Star-Telegram*, January 21, 2003.

or local governments. The director also serves as spokesperson for state agencies and local governments when their ideas and points of view differ from those held by the federal government.

3. The governor may request federal aid when the state has suffered a disaster, a drought, or an economic calamity. As chief of state, the governor often flys over or visits a disaster area to make a personal assessment of the damage—and also to show the victims that the governor is concerned for their welfare. Then, as a "voice of the people," the governor may make a highly publicized request for federal aid to the area.

Budget Powers The governor is designated as the chief budget officer of the state. Every other year, the various agencies and institutions submit their appropriation requests to the governor's staff and to the staff of the Legislative Budget Board. Working from these estimates, the governor and staff prepare a budget that is determined by both the state's estimated income and the estimated cost of program proposals. When completed, the budget is submitted to the legislature. However, the governor's proposals are usually not as influential as those prepared by the Legislative Budget Board.

Law Enforcement Powers The governor has little law enforcement power. Following Texas tradition, the state's law enforcement power is decentralized at both the state and local levels.

At the state level, the Texas Rangers and the Highway Patrol are responsible for law enforcement. Both agencies are under the direction of the director of public safety, who is chosen by the Public Safety Commission. The three members of the Public Safety Commission are appointed by the governor for six-year staggered terms.

At the local level, police functions are under the jurisdiction of county sheriffs and constables (who are elected) and city chiefs of police (who are appointed by city officials). Criminal acts are prosecuted either by elected district or county attorneys or by appointed city attorneys.

The judiciary, which tries and sentences criminals, is elective (except for municipal judges, who are appointed by city officials).

Military Powers The governor is commander in chief of the state militia, which consists of the Texas National Guard and the Texas State Guard. The governor appoints (and can remove) an adjutant general who exercises administrative control over both units.

The governor may declare an area under martial law (usually after a riot or a natural disaster) and send units of the militia to keep the peace and protect public property. The governor may also employ the militia, according to Article 4, Section 7, of the Texas Constitution, "to execute the laws of the state, to suppress insurrection, and to repel invasions." The Texas National Guard has both army and air force components and is financed

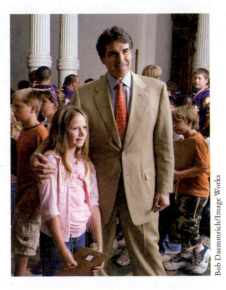

High School Champions Day at the state capitol: Governor Perry poses for photos with members of championship teams.

What role is the governor playing in this photo?

Bob Daemmrich/Image Works

Facing greater deficit projections during the 2003 legislative session, Governor Perry submitted a proposed budget with no spending recommendations, passing the whole budget "hot potato" to the legislature. The number "0" filled all the spaces of the proposed budget.[10]

[10]R. G. Ratcliffe, "Perry Targeted Schools Health," *Houston Chronicle*, April 23, 2003.

by the U.S. government. It is required to meet federal standards and may be called to active duty by the president. In the event the Guard is nationalized, command passes from the governor to the president.

The Texas State Guard was established during World War II and serves as a backup organization in the event that the National Guard is called to active duty by the president. It cannot be called into active duty by the federal government, and its members receive no pay unless mobilized by the governor.

Clemency Powers The 1876 Texas Constitution granted the governor virtually unlimited power to pardon, parole, and grant reprieves to convicted criminals; these are known as **clemency powers**. Several governors were very generous with these powers, resulting in a 1936 constitutional amendment that established the Board of Pardons and Paroles. Many of the powers that had been held by the governor were transferred to the board, which grants, revokes, and determines the conditions for parole and makes clemency recommendations to the governor. However, the governor appoints the board's members and can grant less clemency than recommended by the board but not more. Nor can the governor any longer interfere in the parole process by blocking early releases from prison. The governor can postpone executions, but only for 30 days (see Chapter 11, "Law and Due Process").

Clemency powers

Executive authority to grant relief from criminal punishment; Texas's governor's clemency powers are very limited.

GOVERNOR AS PARTY CHIEF

Although there are varying degrees of competition from other elected officials and from political activists, the governor usually maintains the leadership of his or her party by controlling the membership of its executive committee. Although formally elected at the party's state convention, the chair and a majority of the executive committee are typically selected by the governor.

Party control is a useful channel of influence for a governor, and it permits what is often considered one of the most effective tools of persuasion of the governor's office: rewarding supporters with political patronage. Influential party members who support the governor's party choices and proposals and contribute to his or her election may influence the several hundred appointments that the governor makes each year.

The Texas governor can also be a major player in national politics if so inclined. Unless the Texas governor experiences serious public relations problems, any candidate from the governor's party who seeks the nomination for president would want the support of the governor of the nation's second most populous state. Texas's number of electoral votes also makes the governor an attractive candidate for president or vice president. A governor's support for a winning presidential candidate provides influence over the political patronage that flows from Washington into the state. Of course, patronage to the state can be dramatically increased if the Texas governor becomes president.

National politics also affords the governor an opportunity to build a firm, clear image for the people back home. The governor can take positions on political issues that do not involve the Texas government and over which, as governor, he or she has no control but with which people can easily identify (such as foreign aid or national defense). Issues of state government are often hazy and indistinct (attributable to either the complexities of the issues or inadequate reporting by the mass media), so the electorate can more easily make political identifications through national issues.

CHAPTER SUMMARY

★ The government of Texas was conceived in the post-Reconstruction era, after an unfortunate and unhappy experience with a centralized, alien, and unpopular state government.

★ The state government has been systematically weakened and decentralized by both the constitution and statutes as voters exhibit a basic distrust in government in general and in the executive branch in particular. This distrust is reflected in a governor's office with extensive appointive powers to boards and commissions but without meaningful removal or direct administrative powers.

★ The governor is, however, given relatively strong legislative prerogatives with the veto and the item veto. These formal powers, together with the astute use of the informal powers inherent in the office, enable the governor to exert a significant influence on the direction and to some degree on the operation of the state's government.

★ The office of the governor in Texas is administratively weak when compared to the office in other states and also with other political forces in Texas.

★ This denial of power to the governor (and the legislature) has created a power vacuum in government that has been willingly filled by interest groups and administrative agencies. Thus, nonelective institutions may supersede elected officials, especially in the area of policy formulation and initiation.

★ Because much of the real power in Texas government rests with these institutions, the legislature and governor are frequently placed in the position of merely ratifying, as public policy, the proposals advocated by dominant economic and other interest groups and their allies in the administrative agencies.

HOW TEXAS COMPARES

★ Like 48 governors and the U.S. President, Texas's chief executive is elected to a four-year term. However, unlike 38 states and the national government, there are no limits on the number of terms the chief executive may serve.

★ The Texas governor's institutional powers are somewhat weaker than the typical state governor. The Texas governor has especially weak administrative powers because he or she shares power with numerous other elected executives in a plural executive system, and unlike most governors, the Texas governor does not have a cabinet. The Texas governor appoints supervisory boards and commissions, but directly appoints only some agency directors. The Texas governor has relatively limited powers to remove state officers. Unique to Texas is a budget system in which the governor's budget proposals are largely ignored in favor of the recommendations of the Legislative Budget Board.

★ As in most states, the Texas governor has the power to call special sessions and line-item veto spending bills. Of course, the governor also wields considerable influence within his or her political power and commands greater access to publicity than any other state politician. Still more than most chief executives, the Texas governor must develop leadership power through informal personal relationships, manipulation of publicity, and vigorous bargaining among special interests.

KEY TERMS

blue-ribbon commissions	formal (legal) powers	message power	threat of veto
chief of state	impeachment	presession bargaining	veto
clemency powers	informal (extralegal) powers	senatorial courtesy	

REVIEW QUESTIONS

1. Contrast the formal qualifications for governor with the informal criteria for being elected to the office. What are the informal criteria? What do you think of this? Do you foresee a change in the future? Why or why not?

2. Discuss the various functions of the governor's staff. Why is a competent staff important for a successful administration?

3. Describe the governor's legislative tools of persuasion. What are informal powers, and how can they be more important than formal powers?

4. Describe the executive tools of persuasion. Why are they weaker powers than the governor's legislative powers?

5. How did Jacksonian Democracy and the Reconstruction period following the Civil War affect the creation of the Texas governor's office?

LOGGING ON

★ To check out the governor's appointive power, go to **http://www.governor.state.tx.us/division/appointments**

★ To learn about the governor's powers as commander in chief of the militia, check out the Texas Adjutant General at **http://www.agd.state.tx.us**

★ To send an email to Governor Rick Perry about an issue of concern to you, go to the governor's page at **http://www.governor.state.tx.us/priorities**

★ Select one of the priority issues for Governor Perry. The Texas State Library is an excellent source of state information at **http://www.tsl.state.tx.us/**

★ Texans for Public Justice, a nonpartisan, nonprofit policy and research organization that tracks the influence of money in politics, can be reached at **http://www.tpj.org**

★ The Texas Public Policy Foundation at **http://www.tppf.org** is the premier think tank for conservative political policies and initiatives. This organization has considerable influence in policy initiatives and planning, as conservative Republicans hold all the major state offices.

★ Texas Common Cause works to make government more responsive to citizens and to make citizens more active in public issues. Its site is **http://www.commoncause.org**

★ To follow the money in state politics, go to the Texas Public Interest Research Group site at **http://www.texpirg.org** and to the Campaign Finance Information Center at **http://www.campaignfinance.org/states/tx/**

Governor Perry: Leadership by Appointments

Richard Huckaby
North Central Texas College

INTRODUCTION

Fear of executive power has been a prominent feature of Texas's political culture, and its constitution and statutes have been written to limit the power of the governor in almost every imaginable way. The chief executive's appointive power is limited by the fact that the governor usually does not directly appoint agency heads. Instead, the governor appoints multimember supervisory boards that serve for fixed, staggered terms and must wait for these terms to expire before filling vacancies. A further weakness is that the governor generally lacks the power to issue direct binding orders to many agencies or to fire state officers except under very limited circumstances. This article shows how Governor Perry's long tenure in office and his astute use of political skills have made his appointive powers a formidable tool of political influence.

The familiar warning "Don't Mess with Texas" seems to capture the character of Texas and Texans. The phrase had its origins in the 1980s as an antilitter campaign slogan to encourage Texans not to toss their trash onto the landscape, but it has become much more. It may well describe the feelings of many Texans after the Civil War and Reconstruction, to include their dissatisfaction with the then Republican Governor E. J. Davis.

The Texas Constitution of 1869, formulated under pressure from Washington,[1] was disputed by a large constituency of Texans. They might well have described this document as Washington, "Messing with Texas." Under this constitution, Governor Davis enjoyed substantial power as the chief executive.[2]

By 1875, Reconstruction had come to an end, and Democrats had regained power in Texas. One of their first acts was to call a constitutional convention to undo the hated 1869 Constitution.[3] The new 1876 Constitution reflected the lack of faith in government that the delegates had formed over the Reconstruction years and slashed the power of officials including the governor. It is this 1876 Constitution and the structurally weak executive it established, that all subsequent Texas governors have had to deal with. Some have fared better than others.

The current Texas Constitution provides Texas governors precious few formal leadership tools. Nevertheless, Governor Perry has successfully spread his influence throughout the state by exercising his authority to make governmental appointments.

[1] *Handbook of Texas Online*, http://www.tshaonline.org/handbook/online/articles/CC/mhc6.html

[2] Texas Governor Edumnd J. Davis, "An Inventory of Records at the Texas State Archives," 1869–1874, *Handbook of Texas Online*, http://www.tshaonline.org/handbook/online/articles/CC/mhc6.html

[3] *Texas Constitution of 1876*, Texas State Library and Archives Commission, http://www.tsl.state.tx.us/treasures/constitution/index.html

During a four-year term, a governor will make approximately 3,000 appointments. The majority of these appointments are volunteer positions, representative of our citizen government. Most appointments include[4]:

★ State officials and members of state boards, commissions, and councils that carry out the laws and direct the policies of state government activities;

★ Members of task forces that advise the governor or executive agencies on specific issues and policies; and

★ State elected and judicial offices when vacancies occur by resignation or death of the officeholder.

Most boards and commissions have six-year staggered terms, with one-third of the members' terms expiring every two years.[5] Governor Perry's longevity in office has a significant impact on his influence on the make up of Texas boards and commissions. If you do the math, since becoming governor in 2000, Governor Perry has appointed literally thousands of Texans to the various boards and commissions that operate our state agencies. Given the average length of a board or commission member's term of office, Governor Perry can be credited or blamed with having appointed or reappointed most members now serving. This relationship, with few exceptions, can provide the governor with loyalty and a support system unmatched in our history. No previous governor has been in office long enough to achieve this end. Some appointments can garner positive public recognition, while others may expose the governor to criticism by political opponents.

Some of Governor Perry's appointments have made history and generated a very positive public reaction to the governor. For example, in March 2001, Governor Perry appointed the first African American, Wallace Jefferson, to the Texas Supreme Court to fill a vacancy. As required by Texas law, Justice Jefferson had to run for the position in the next scheduled election, but he did so as the incumbent and was elected in his own right in November 2002. Governor Perry subsequently appointed Justice Wallace to Chief Justice of the Court in September 2004.[6]

Likewise, in October 2009, Governor Perry appointed the first Hispanic woman, Eva Guzman, to serve on the Texas Supreme Court, also to fill a vacancy.[7] Similar to Chief Justice Wallace, Justice Guzman successfully ran for the position in her own right in the March 2010 Republican primary as the incumbent.[8] As the Republican nominee she will face Blake Bailey, the Democratic candidate, for Place 9 on the court in the November 2, 2010 general election. Justice Guzman's appointment was well received by the public, but was not without some criticism.

During the contested Republican primary, in which Justice Guzman successfully defeated her Republican opponent and Governor Perry succeeded in defeating Senator Kay

Bailey Hutchinson for the Republican nomination to run in the November 2010 general election, pejorative comments of "favored candidate" (Guzman) and accusations of "cronyism" (Perry) were leveled by the opposition.

Another example, with more serious political implications to Governor Perry in seeking yet another term as governor is the controversy over appointments to the Texas Forensic Science Commission. The Texas Forensic Science Commission was created by the Texas Legislature in 2005 to investigate complaints that alleged professional negligence or misconduct by a laboratory, facility, or entity that had been accredited by the Director of the Texas Department of Public Safety that would substantially affect the integrity of the results of a forensic analysis.[9]

In 2006, the *Innocence Project* (founded in 1992 to assist prisoners who could be proven innocent through DNA testing)[10] requested that the Texas Forensic Science Commission launch a full investigation into the *Cameron Todd Willingham* case. Willingham was executed in 2004 for the 1991 arson-related death of his three children at his home in Corsicana, Texas. In 2008, the Texas Forensic Science Commission agreed to investigate the case.[11]

The Texas Forensic Science Commission hired the noted fire scientist Craig Beyler to investigate the case and scheduled a hearing for October 2, 2009, to review his report. Beyler reportedly concluded that a finding of arson could not be sustained based on a "standard of care" grounded in science. If Beyler was correct, there was no arson and there was no murder for which to try or execute Willingham. Other experts and Texas officials dispute the Beyler findings. Numerous judicial, legal, criminal, and scientific experts have investigated this case and expressed contrary opinions.[12]

Two days before the scheduled hearing, Governor Perry removed three of the nine members. The three members' terms had officially expired, and Governor Perry told reporters that it would be better to replace them during the "start" of any investigation rather than after it had begun. Critics suggest that both the firings of the commission members and the now inevitable delay in the release of the commission's final report—probably until after the then upcoming Texas primary gubernatorial election in which Governor Perry was a candidate—were politically motivated. Governor Perry strongly denied both suggestions and maintained that the execution of Willingham was appropriate and that Texas did not execute an innocent man. He called the controversy "nothing more than propaganda from the anti-death penalty people across the country."[12]

An editorial in the *Austin American-Statesman* on October 25, 2009, put the controversy into perspective and demonstrates the contentiousness of almost any decision made in a political environment. Supporters and critics lined up to have their

[4]Office of the Governor, http://governor.state.tx.us/appointments/

[5]Ibid., http://governor.state.tx.us/appointments/process/

[6]The Supreme Court of Texas, http://www.supreme.courts.state.tx.us/court/justice_wjefferson.asp

[7]Ibid., http://www.supreme.courts.state.tx.us/court/justice_eguzman.asp

[8]Office of the Secretary of State, http://enr.sos.state.tx.us/enr/results/mar02_148_race31.htm

[9]Texas Forensic Commission, http://www.fsc.state.tx.us/

[10]Innocence Project, 100 Fifth Avenue, 3rd Floor, New York, NY 10011, http://www.innocenceproject.org/about/Contact-Us.php

[11]Ibid., http://www.innocenceproject.org/Content/2170.php

[12]*The Austin Chronicle*, http://www.austinchronicle.com/gyrobase/Issue/story?oid=oid%3A891716

say. "There's no doubt that Gov. Rick Perry has the authority to appoint Texas Forensic Science Commission members. And there's no doubt that some members' terms ended recently.... When Perry recently shuffled the board and—two days before a crucial meeting about a controversial execution—put a tough-on-crime prosecutor in charge of the panel, we supported his right to do so. And in the face of cries of protest, we counseled patience and expressed confidence the commission would do the right thing."[13]

The *Statesmen* continued to scold the Governor, "Perry, in the face of unavoidably important new input about the case, either reacted politically or, perhaps worse, evidenced an inability or unwillingness to think his way through the new material." The *Statesman* added, "Perhaps because it is campaign season, Perry doesn't seem to have it in him to do anything other than act and react as a candidate. It is unattractive and invites discredit upon Texas and its death penalty."[14]

Despite the potential for criticism for particularly visible and/or controversial appointments, most of the appointments and reappointments made by the governor go virtually unnoticed. Likewise, the work of these appointees is virtually invisible to the general public. However, their continuing presence on state

boards and commissions significantly enhances the governor's influence in every aspect of state operations. For the most part, they remain loyal to the governor's agenda and programs, provide a network of supporters throughout the various state agencies, and provide a solid political base among centers of influence throughout the state.

JOIN THE DEBATE

1. How has Governor Perry's long tenure in office given him control over members of virtually every board and commission member? How can appointing loyalists to these boards give the governor control over state agencies despite his limited power to fire state officers or to issue orders to state agencies?

2. What political implications can you see in Governor Perry's appointment of Jefferson and Guzman to the Texas Supreme Court? What would have been the likely political consequences if it were determined that Texas executed an innocent man during Governor Perry's tenure?

[13]*Austin American-Statesman,* http://www.statesman.com/opinion/content/editorial/stories/2009/10/25/1025perry_edit.html
[14]Ibid.

Chapter 9

The Bureaucracy

CONTENTS

LEARNING OBJECTIVES

* Understand the civil law and criminal law functions of the Texas Attorney General. Be able to explain how the attorney general's opinion is an important function in both the formulation and the administration of Texas's public policy.

* Understand the comptroller's function in the formulation public policy.

* Be able to explain the concept of bureaucratic neutrality and the various ways that Texas governments have been organized to accomplish it.

* Be able to describe the principal of hierarchy and explain how the principal is evident in the Texas bureaucracy. In what way is it not evident?

* Be able to describe the interconnecting web of support and interests that comprise the Iron Texas Star. Explain how each political player could benefit both personally and professionally from a system like this. Explain how economic interests benefit.

* Understand how the powers that are inherent in the bureaucracy, such as expertise, information, and administrative review, are also a source of power within the political system.

* Be able to describe the various approaches that are used to hold administrators accountable. Why is administrative accountability important?

The executive branch is the part of government that administers the law and implements public policy. When a highway is built, when a police officer writes a ticket, when taxes are collected, or when a public school teacher conducts a class, an executive (or administrative) function is being performed. Executive branch employees check gas pumps and meat scales for accuracy; they license morticians, insurance agents, and doctors; they check food for purity; and they arrest poachers for illegal hunting. The executive branch of government enforces public policies and is responsible for the day-to-day management of the government. It is the operational branch of the government and basically does what government does. Almost all of a citizen's contacts with the government are with the executive branch.

The Texas Administration

The most distinctive characteristic of the Texas administration is that no one is really in charge of the administrative apparatus.[1] As in many other states, the administration of laws in Texas is fragmented into several elective and numerous appointive positions. Although the principle of hierarchy exists within each department, the formal organization of the Texas **bureaucracy** follows the basic administrative principle of hierarchy only as far as the elected administrator or an appointed board. *There is no single official in the Texas government who bears ultimate responsibility for the actions of the Texas bureaucracy.* And there is no single official who can coordinate either planning or program implementation among the many agencies, commissions, and departments. The Texas bureaucracy can be visualized as some 220 separate entities, each following its own path of endeavor, often oblivious to the goals and ambitions of other (often companion) agencies.

Various divisions of the executive branch of government can be grouped according to whether their top policy maker is a single-elected administrator, a single-appointed executive, or a multimember board or commission, which may be elected, ex officio, or appointed.

Bureaucracy

The system of nonelected officials administering government policies and programs.

---

[1]Information in this section is drawn from the *Guide to Texas State Agencies*, 11th ed. (Austin: Office of Publications, Lyndon B. Johnson School of Public Affairs, The University of Texas at Austin, 2001); Legislative Budget Board, *Texas Fact Book 2009–2010* (Austin: Legislative Budget Board, 2009–2010), http://www.lbb.state.tx.us/ Fact_Book/Texas_Factbook_2010.pdf; and *Texas Online*, http://www.state.tx.us

ELECTED EXECUTIVES

The constitutional and statutory requirement that several administrators (in addition to the governor) be elected was a deliberate effort to decentralize administrative power and prevent any one official from gaining control of the government. Thus, Texas has a plural executive, meaning that the governor shares executive power with several other independently elected executives and boards. These elected officials are directly responsible to the people rather than to the governor. The fact that few Texans can name the individuals in these offices, much less judge their competence or honesty, tends to contradict the democratic theory of the popular election of administrators.

Texas Attorney General Greg Abbott and Luis Carlos Treviño Berchelmann, the Attorney General of Nuevo León, Mexico, after signing a memorandum of understanding commemorating the two border states' commitment to combat transnational crime.

Why is cooperation between the two states important?

AP Photo/Harry Cabluck

Attorney General The attorney general is elected for a four-year term, with no limit on the number of terms that may be served. Holding one of the four most powerful offices in Texas government, the attorney general is the lawyer for all officials, boards, and agencies in state government. The office is authorized to employ more than 4,150 persons, many of them lawyers. The legal functions of the office range from assisting in child support enforcement, antitrust actions, Medicaid fraud investigation, crime victim compensation, consumer protection, and other civil actions concerning insurance, banking, and securities. A broad spectrum of the state's business—oil and gas, law enforcement, environmental protection, highways, transportation, and charitable trusts, to name only a few—is included under the overall jurisdiction of the attorney general.

The attorney general performs two major functions for the state. One is to give an **attorney general's opinion**. As the state's chief lawyer, the attorney general advises his or her client. In the absence of a prior judicial interpretation, the attorney general has the power to interpret law or to give an opinion that a law or practice does or does not violate other laws or the Texas or U.S. constitutions. Although these advisory opinions are technically not legally binding, they carry great weight in the Texas government. If an official ignores the opinions, the attorney general will not defend the action in court.

The attorney general's opinion is usually requested only after the legal staff of another agency or official has been unable to reach a decision. The requests usually concern difficult questions, and several staff attorneys general consider each question. Only agencies and officials may request these opinions, and then only for official business. Occasionally a legislator will request an attorney general's opinion during the legislative session (sometimes merely to delay and thus help kill the legislation). The vagueness of laws and, particularly, the ambiguity of the Texas Constitution require the attorney general to give numerous opinions.

The second major function of the attorney general is to represent the state and its government in both civil and criminal litigation. This includes conflicts with the national government, such as the tidelands dispute in the 1950s; the defense of Texas's poll tax, abortion, segregation, and obscenity laws; and challenges to state legislative districts, judicial at-large elections, and affirmative action programs. The attorney general also represents Texas

Attorney general's opinion

Interpretation of the constitution, statutory laws, or administrative laws by Texas's attorney general. Government officials may request opinions, and although they are not legally binding, government officials usually follow them.

Many state executives use their contacts and access to publicity as resources to run for higher office. Former Attorney General John Cornyn was elected U.S. senator in 2002.

in legal conflicts with the governments of other states, as with Louisiana and Oklahoma over the exact boundary between the two states. The attorney general initiates suits against corporations for antitrust violations or consumer protection. However, the attorney general's criminal power is relatively narrow because the primary responsibility for criminal prosecution in Texas lies with the locally elected district and county attorneys.

Part of the importance of the office is that it is viewed as a stepping-stone to the governor's chair, even though only 4 of the 21 governors since 1900 have served as attorney general. Political as well as legal considerations must therefore be taken into account. When opinions are handed down and litigation is conducted, the ambitious attorney general must not sever connections to campaign funds and political support if he or she hopes for higher office.

Former Comptroller Carole Keeton Strayhorn was defeated as an independent candidate for governor in 2006.

Texas Comptroller Susan Combs explains how mortgage foreclosures will drop Texas' revenue about $9 billion for the 2010–2011 fiscal cycle. ☞

What is the role of the comptroller concerning Texas legislative appropriations?

AP Photo/Harry Cabluck

Comptroller of Public Accounts The comptroller is elected for a term of four years, with no limit on the number of terms that may be served. The functions of the comptroller's office encompass either directly or indirectly almost all financial activities of state government. The comptroller is the chief tax collector and the chief pre-audit accounting officer in the Texas government. The comptroller manages state deposits and investments and pays warrants on state accounts.

The comptroller's most important constitutional duty is to certify the state's approximate biennial revenue. The constitution requires a balanced budget, and the state legislature may not appropriate more funds than are anticipated as income for any two-year period. The comptroller also certifies the financial condition of the state at the close of each fiscal year. Any surplus funds can give the governor and legislature fiscal flexibility for tax cuts or increased appropriations without increasing taxes.

Commissioner of the General Land Office The commissioner of the General Land Office is elected for a term of four years. The office has more than 600 employees. Principal duties of the commissioner are managing and collecting rentals and leases for state-owned lands; awarding oil, gas, sulfur, and other hard-mineral leases for exploration and production on state lands; and leasing mineral interests in the state's riverbeds and tidelands, including bays, inlets, and the marginal sea areas. (Out-of-state oil and gas leases require Railroad Commission review.)

As is the case with many officials, the land commissioner serves ex officio on several boards and chairs the important Veterans Land and the School Land boards, whose programs are administered by the General Land office. (Ex officio members hold their positions because they hold some other elective or appointed office.) The Veterans Land Board was established by a grateful state after World War II. The board loans money to veterans for land purchases and home purchases or improvements.

The School Land Board oversees approximately 20 million acres of public land and mineral rights properties, of which 4 million are submerged tidelands along the Gulf Coast. The

SUPERAGENCIES

Following a recommendation for extensive administrative reorganization by Comptroller John Sharp, the legislature in 1991, consolidated several existing programs and agencies into three "superagencies": the Texas Natural Resources Conservation Commission, the Department of Transportation, and the Health and Human Services Commission. The governor appoints the director of the Health and Human Services Commission for a two-year term and the boards of the others for six-year staggered terms.

lease and mineral income from these public lands varies with the production and price of oil and gas, but revenues from the management of public lands (recently about $500 million per year) are dedicated to the **Permanent School Fund**, which benefits the state's public schools.

Commissioner of Agriculture The commissioner of agriculture is elected for four years to oversee the Texas Department of Agriculture, which has more than 500 employees and is responsible for the administration of all laws as well as research, educational, and regulatory activities relating to agriculture. The duties of the department range from checking the accuracy of scales in meat markets and gas pumps at service stations to determining labeling procedures for pesticides and promoting Texas agricultural products in national and world markets. The commissioner also administers the Texas Agricultural Finance Authority, which provides grants and low-interest loans to businesses that produce, process, market, and export Texas agricultural products.

Like the U.S. Department of Agriculture, the Texas Department of Agriculture is charged with administering laws for both consumer and labor protection, as well as the other laws related to the agribusiness industry. The possibility of a conflict of interest between these potentially incompatible groups is likely, especially if the department begins to protect consumers to the perceived disadvantage of the more powerful economic interests. Just such a conflict emerged in 1984, when Agriculture Commissioner Jim Hightower issued regulations concerning pesticide use with the intent of protecting agricultural workers and consumers from the physical dangers of contamination. As a result, agribusiness interests tried to limit the department's budget, reduce its authority to regulate pesticides, and make the office appointive. This conflict resulted in the creation of a new commission, the Agriculture Resources Protection Authority, which coordinates pesticide management policies and programs for the Department of Agriculture and several other state agencies. The authority is currently comprised of six appointed and nine ex officio members, including the commissioner of agriculture.

This is an almost classic example of an agency with two contradictory constituencies with conflicting interests being given the function of protecting each interest from the other. The threat perceived by agribusiness interests was resolved when, with agribusiness support, Rick Perry was elected commissioner. He became the first Republican to ever hold the office. Former Commissioner Hightower's political error was that his attempt to protect the aggregate, largely unorganized consumers and farm workers was perceived as a threat to the interests of agribusiness, which sees itself as the principal constituency of the agency.

Lieutenant Governor Although technically part of the executive branch, the source of executive powers for the office of lieutenant governor comes from the legislative branch. The lieutenant governor, as

🔊 *With a wind energy classification map in the background, Texas Land Commissioner Jerry Patterson announces the search for companies to lease state land, both inland and in the Gulf of Mexico, to build and operate windmills to generate energy.*

Why does the land commissioner have anything to do with leasing land in the Gulf of Mexico?

AP Photo/Harry Cabluck

Permanent School Fund

A small source of funding for the Texas public school system. Leases, rents, and royalties from designated public school land are deposited into the fund. The school system uses the interest and dividend income from this fund for public education.

Former Agriculture Commissioner Susan Combs was elected Comptroller of Public Accounts in 2006 and former Agriculture Commissioner Rick Perry was elected lieutenant governor and then governor in 2002, 2006, and 2010.

🔊 *Agriculture Commissioner Todd Staples discusses the accuracy of Texas gasoline pumps, a function of the Texas Agriculture Department.*

What are some of the other functions of the agriculture commissioner?

AP Photo/Harry Cabluck

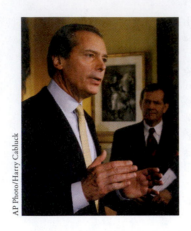

Lt. Governor David Dewhurst answers questions about the plan to restructure Texas's struggling Medicaid program as U.S. Department of Health and Human Services Secretary Michael Leavitt, looks on. ☞

What are the major administrative responsibilities of the lieutenant governor?

president of the senate, is an ex officio chair of the Legislative Budget Board, the Legislative Council, and the Legislative Audit Board and, if he or she desires, can exercise considerable personal influence on the Sunset Advisory Commission and the Legislative Criminal Justice Board. These legislative boards and commissions are not part of the bureaucracy, but they conduct continuing studies of administrative policies and make recommendations to the legislature.

APPOINTED EXECUTIVES

Secretary of State Appointed by the governor, with confirmation by the senate, the secretary of state serves at the pleasure of the governor. The secretary is keeper of the Seal of the State and also serves as the chief election officer for Texas, administers Texas's election laws, maintains voter registration records, and receives election results. The secretary of state's office also serves as a repository for official, business, and commercial records filed with the office.

The secretary publishes government rules and regulations and commissions notaries public. By executive orders, Governor Rick Perry has also directed the secretary of state to serve as his liaison for Texas border and Mexican affairs, and to represent him and the state at international and diplomatic events.

Adjutant General Also appointed by the governor with the consent of the senate for a two-year term, the adjutant general is the state's top-ranking military officer and exercises administrative jurisdiction over the Texas National Guard and Texas State Guard. It is one of the few state agencies under the direct administrative control of the governor.

Health and Human Services Commissioner The executive director of the Health and Human Services Commission is appointed by the governor with the advice and consent of the senate. The commissioner heads the Consolidated Texas Health and Human Services System, an umbrella or superagency that oversees and manages four major health and welfare departments.

The director of the commission is also granted extensive administrative and policy-making authority over the departments. The power within the commission clearly rests with the director, who reports directly to the governor. The powers of the governor's office were significantly increased by the 78th Legislature, moving in the direction of a cabinet-type administrative format.

Insurance Commissioner The commissioner of the Texas Department of Insurance is directly appointed by the governor for a two-year fixed term, subject to senate confirmation. The department monitors and regulates the Texas insurance industry. It provides consumer information; monitors corporate solvency; prosecutes violators of insurance law; licenses agents and investigates complaints against them; develops statistics for rate determination; and regulates specific insurance lines such as property, liability, and life.

BOARDS AND COMMISSIONS

Boards and commissions, which number about 220, are elective, appointive, ex officio, or some combination of these. Members may be salaried or serve only for expenses. There are also considerable differences in their political power. Generally speaking, the most important boards are those concerned with chartering or regulating the business, industrial, and financial powers within the state. Power is also measured by the number of people affected by the board's decisions or the size of its agency's appropriations.

These measures are general, however, because a relatively minor licensing board such as the Real Estate Board could be the most important agency in state government to a real estate broker whose license was about to be revoked.

Elective Boards Elective boards include the Texas Railroad Commission and the Texas Education Agency.

Texas Railroad Commission One of the most important state regulatory boards in the United States is the Railroad Commission, a constitutionally authorized elective board whose three members serve for overlapping six-year terms. The governor fills vacancies on the board, and these appointees serve until the first election, at which time they may win election to the board in their own right.

The board is politically partisan, and its members must first win their party's nomination before being elected. The chair position is rotated so that each member becomes the chair during the last two years of his or her term. This forces any candidate who is challenging an incumbent commissioner to run against the chair of the commission.

The commission's duties include the regulation of gas utilities, oil and gas pipelines, oil and gas drilling and pumping activities, and intrastate railroad transportation. It is also responsible for regulation of waste disposal by the oil and gas industry and the protection of both surface and subsurface water supplies from oil- or gas-related residues.

The Railroad Commission had regulated intrastate motor carriers until 1994, when the U.S. Congress deregulated Texas's trucking industry because the state's rules were an "obstacle to free commerce among the states." The 74th Legislature (1995) transferred the commission's remaining motor carrier responsibilities to the Departments of Transportation and Public Safety.

Texas Education Agency The Texas Education Agency (TEA) has the State Board of Education (SBOE) as its policy-making body, and the commissioner of education serves as its chief executive. The agency oversees and regulates the Texas public school system below the college level and administers national and state education law and SBOE rules and regulations. The SBOE is elected in partisan elections for four-year staggered terms from fifteen single-member districts. The governor appoints the chair

STRANGE HAPPENINGS . . . !

Incumbent Texas Railroad Commission Chair Victor Carillo was defeated in the Republican primary by politically unknown David Porter who won a resounding 60 percent of the vote. The incumbent outspent the challenger $600,000 to $30,000, and had the backing of the Texas Republican establishment.

Bob Daemmrich/Image Works

Harry Cabluck/AP Photo

Harry Cabluck/AP Photo

◥ *Newly elected David Porter (R), Michael Williams (R), and Elizabeth Ames-Jones (R) serve as the Texas Railroad Commissioners.*

What does the Railroad Commission do other than regulate railroads?

for a two-year term from the SBOE membership. The SBOE establishes policy, implements policy established by law, and oversees the TEA. The board also recommends three nominees for commissioner of education, who is appointed by the governor, with the senate's consent, to a four-year term.

Texas has historically had a decentralized school system in which most educational and administrative policy was established by local school boards. Recently, however, the legislature, the courts, and the TEA began mandating more educational policy. The TEA writes regulations for and compels local compliance with legislative and judicial mandates and reforms; dispenses state funds; serves as a conduit for some funds from the national government to the local schools; and selects the textbooks to be purchased at state expense for use by local districts.

Ex Officio Boards Numerous boards have memberships that are completely or partly ex officio, that is, boards whose members are automatically assigned due to their holding some other position. There are two basic reasons for creating such boards. One is that when travel to Austin was expensive and time-consuming, it seemed logical to establish a board with its members already in Austin. Another reason is that subject-matter expertise on the part of the ex officio members is assumed.

The Texas Bond Review Board is an example of an ex officio board. It has four ex officio members—the governor, lieutenant governor, speaker, and comptroller of public accounts. It reviews and approves all bonds and other long-term debt of state agencies and universities. It also engages in various other functions pertaining to state and local long-term debt.

McCarthyism

A false or unproven attack on the character, integrity, or patriotism of a political opponent.

The State Board of Education (SBOE) is one of those relatively invisible government bodies that wield considerable impact on Texans' lives. However, the SBOE attracted national attention as well as internal conflict in 2010, while in the process of establishing what Texas schoolchildren would be taught about U.S. history and other social studies for the next 10 years. These curriculum standards determined content and emphasis for both textbook and achievement test criteria.

Republicans currently enjoy a two-to-one majority on the Board. The Democratic minority charged the Republican majority with interjecting its religious and political philosophies into the curriculum by minimizing the contributions of ethnic minorities and liberals while exaggerating the political contributions of conservatives, Anglo Americans and Christianity. Democratic board members also charged that the advice and recommendations of Texas's history teachers were largely ignored.

U.S. Secretary of Education Arne Duncan (Obama) and Former Secretary Ron Page (George W. Bush) were also critical of the Board's actions.

Some controversial Board actions required:

★ That the First Amendment concept of "separation between church and state" be compared with the actual words in the Constitution. Social conservatives charge that separation of church and state was not intended by the Founding Fathers but was the result of actions by activist judges and lawmakers.

★ That U.S. history students learn about leading conservative groups and individuals but did not require a comparable study of liberal or minority individuals or groups.

★ A more positive portrayal of former U.S. Senator Joseph McCarthy, who during the 1950s period known as the "second red scare" and with scant real evidence, charged numerous academic, literary, entertainment, and government personages as being communists, subversives, or fellow travelers. The careers of these individuals were usually ruined by a practice known as blacklisting. His tactics are rejected by most historians. Today, the practice of charging dissenting people with treason or disloyalty without adequate evidence is known as **McCarthyism**.

★ Inclusion of C.S.A. President Jefferson Davis's inaugural address with the study of U.S. President Abraham Lincoln's political philosophy.

★ That the names of the eight Latinos who died at the Alamo fighting for Texas independence be omitted, while requiring that the names of Jim Bowie, Davy Crockett, and William B. Travis be included.

★ That economic studies be about the "'benefits' of the free enterprise system" instead of about the "effects" of the free enterprise system.

Source: Terrence Stutz, "Texas State Board of Education Approves New Curriculum Standards, *The Dallas Morning News*, May 22, 2010.

STATE AND FEDERAL AGENCIES BATTLE OVER HOW TO ENFORCE THE CLEAN AIR ACT

The Texas Commission on Environmental Quality (TCEQ) operates under three commissioners who are appointed by the governor for 6-year staggered terms. The commissioners appoint a director who oversees the approximately 3,000 employees.

The TCEQ is the primary environmental regulator for the state. It oversees cleanups, licensing, permits, registration, and writes the rules and policies that govern all areas of the Texas environment.

In 2010, the TCEQ policy called the "flexible permit system" ran afoul of the U.S. Environmental Protection Agency (EPA). Flexible permit rules issued by the TCEQ allow one part of a plant to pollute more than the federal Clean Air Act allows so long as another part of the plant pollutes less than the maximum and as long as the total plant emissions do not violate federal air standards. The EPA argues that this policy violates the Clean Air Act and that Texas's flexible permits must be invalidated, requiring reapplication and possibly plant upgrades in order to be granted the more demanding EPA permits. Industry shutdowns are not expected during the process.

Governor Perry called the action "irresponsible and heavy-handed ... and threatens thousands of Texas jobs, families, businesses, and communities." Whether the state or the federal view is correct, it is clear that different agencies have different views on how to implement the same law. The actual impact of a law depends on bureaucratic interpretation and rule-making.

Source: R. G. Ratcliffe, "Flexible Emissions Disallowed," *San Antonio Express-News*, July 1, 2010, p. 1B.

A number of agency boards have some ex officio members. The Texas Appraiser Licensing and Certification Board (nine members, one ex officio) and the Texas Racing Commission (nine members, two ex officio) are examples of such boards.

Appointed Boards Appointed boards vary greatly in terms of importance, administrative power, and salary. The members of these boards, who are usually unsalaried, set the policies for their agencies and appoint their own chief administrators. The governor, with the consent of the senate, usually appoints board members, but there are many mixed boards whose members are appointed by the governor or by some other official or have partly ex officio membership. Because of the usual practice of appointing members to staggered terms, six years may lapse before a governor can appoint a complete board.

Board appointees are often representatives of groups that have an economic interest in the rules and policies of the board. Appointments may be either a reward for political support or an attempt to balance competing interest groups whose economic well-being is affected by board rules and policies.

ADVISORY BOARDS

There are also advisory committees and boards that do not make official government decisions but study special issues or make recommendations to operating agencies. Texas has hundreds of advisory boards with their total membership in the thousands.

Characteristics of Bureaucracy

Although bureaucracy is often thought of as exclusive to government, it is also common to corporations, universities, churches, and foundations.[2] Bureaucracies develop wherever human beings organize themselves to systematically accomplish goals and in the process lose some of their flexibility and efficiency. This discussion concentrates on government bureaucracies, especially those in Texas government.

---

[2]The characteristics of bureaucracy are described in detail in Max Weber, *Theory of Social and Economic Organization*, ed. Talcott Parsons (New York: Oxford University Press, 1974). Weber's book was originally published in 1920.

HOW DOES TEXAS COMPARE?

As shown in Table 9.1, the largest number of government employees work for local governments; the U.S. government actually hires fewer civilian employees than either state or local governments. The fact that it is the largest single government, however, results in its being criticized as excessive "big government."

SIZE

The complexities of 21st century society, together with increased demands on government at all levels, have resulted in a dramatic increase in the number of people employed by public administrations, and large numbers of employees mean large bureaucracies. Much of the harshest current criticism of **government bureaucracy** comes either from those who have simply lost confidence in our federal system or from propagandist demagogues in economic, political, and religious special interest groups who, for their own reasons, attack public employees as a means of discrediting specific government programs.

Various public officials, from time to time, attempt to systematically streamline both national and state bureaucracies and to make them more efficient and receptive to the wishes of policy makers. These attempts may or may not have positive results, but their level of success varies widely and is based largely on the expectations, perceptions, and political ideology of the reviewer.

Attacking "the bureaucracy" remains an effective political strategy. It is unfair, however, to compare only the bureaucracies of the state governments. Each state has its own organizational system, and great variations may relate to whether a specific service is provided by the state or by one of its political subdivisions. A reduction in public bureaucracy almost invariably results in either reducing services, government contracting with private firms, or requiring the administration of specific services or programs by lower governments.

Since the 1980s, there has been an increase in privatization as governments have turned to the private sector for services ranging from police to garbage collecting. Texas has privatized some of its prisons and state jails and has experimented with privatizing determining eligibility for social service programs, and plans a privately operated highway system. The Trans-Texas Corridor is controversial because the state proposes using powers of eminent domain to take private property away from its owners to make way for a "for profit" system of highways, railways, and pipelines.

The national government has also increasingly mandated policies and regulations but has left the burden for funding and implementation to state and local governments, often

Which single government employs the most Texans?

TABLE 9.1	CIVILIAN GOVERNMENT EMPLOYEES IN 2007 FOR THE UNITED STATES AND TEXAS (IN THOUSANDS)			
	All Governments	**U.S.**	**State**	**Local**
United States	18,266	1,812	4,307	12,147
Texas	1,468	124	290	1,054

Source: U.S. Bureau of the Census, Federal Government Finances and Employment, 2007 Employment by Geographic Area (December 2009), www.opm.gov/feddate/

forcing them to increase taxes or decrease services (or both). The state of Texas has also shifted much responsibility for public services to local governments through unfunded mandates.

NEUTRALITY

Administration of the laws in a "neutral" fashion—the separation of politics and administration—has long been an aim of reformists in American government. Ideally, elected public officials should establish and define a program's priorities, goals, or services. Administrators should then administer the law the "best way" and equally to all, rich or poor, black or white, powerful or weak, male or female.

The national government took the lead in bureaucratic reform when it established a strong **civil service (merit) system** with competitive examinations or objective measures of qualifications for hiring and promoting employees. The employee spoils system—government employment and promotion based on political support—was replaced by a merit system.

Many other states also adopted a merit system of public employment. However, Texas never implemented systematic statewide civil service reform; it still depends on a spoils or patronage system of public employment. Elected officials in Texas appoint major campaign supporters to top-level positions. Some of Texas local governments use a merit system.

Conservative, pro-business supporters of privatization argue that contracting with private businesses to provide traditional public services both increases efficiency and reduces the size and power of government. They contend that government agencies lack the powerful forces of the profit motive and competition that energize the private marketplace. In short, they have faith that that private enterprise is inherently more effective than the public sector.

Privatization's skeptics argue that private businesses are profiteering at the public expense because they are likely to "cut corners" on services to improve their "bottom line." Opponents also contend that private businesses are not as accountable to the public because the internal operations of private businesses are not as well publicized as government activities.

They suspect that political contacts and campaign contributions "grease the wheels" for contractors. Critics also see a new kind of **spoils system** developing. Unlike the historic spoils system in which elected officials hired campaign workers as public employees, today's new spoils system is based on a network of **contract spoils**, or contract patronage, in which politicians now award contracts to their political supporters in the business community. Although the contract patronage system is not new, critics believe that it has become a major political reason for support of the privatization movement.

Figure 9.1 shows how Texas attempted a different way to depoliticize the state bureaucracy—establishing the independent board and commission system, which tries to insulate the bureaucracy from the legislature and the governor, who are elected and hence

Civil service (merit) system

An employment system used by governments that takes merit into account in hiring and promotions.

PRIVATIZATION AND THE "REVOLVING DOOR"

Both sides in the debate over **privatization** may have valid points.

Privatization

The hiring of private contractors to perform government services and functions.

Spoils system

A system that gives elected officials considerable discretion in employment and promotion decisions.

Contract spoils

The practice by which public officials award government contracts to benefit their campaign contributors, supporters, and allies. Also referred to as *contract patronage*.

Why would politics be involved in awarding some of the state's contracts?

Figure 9.1

The Board and Commission System

Why is the structural organization of the board and commission system so popular in Texas?

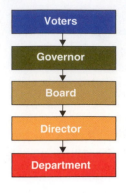

political by definition. Both agency policy and administrative oversight are the responsibility of boards, usually appointed by the governor with approval by the senate. Their terms are fixed, usually for six years, and are staggered so that it takes two years or more before a new governor can appoint a majority.

Board members cannot be removed until the expiration of their terms unless they have been appointed by the sitting governor, and then only with the concurrence of two-thirds of the senate. However, the governor may "encourage" board members to resign by publicly criticizing the board members or the board's policies. The board appoints a chief executive officer to manage the department and see to the administration of public policy. Administrative power is thus "removed from politics" and excludes the governor from direct executive control over the state bureaucracy. This system also placates the basic Texas fear of power concentrated in the chief executive.

Local governments in Texas have attempted to accomplish similar goals by such devices as nonpartisan elections for city officials and special district boards. As shown in Figures 9.2 and 9.3, many cities have also adopted the council–manager form of government in which an unelected "professional" manager supervises city departments and in school districts a "professional" superintendent administers the public schools.

With these safeguards, reformers believed that administrators could and would treat everyone equally and fairly, simply carrying out the policies of the elected officials. However, the theory of executive neutrality is naive, for public administration cannot be separated from politics—it *is* politics!

HIERARCHY

Hierarchy

A pyramid-shaped administrative organization in which several employees report to a single higher administrator until there remains only one person with ultimate authority at the top.

All bureaucracies are formally characterized as **hierarchical** structures, with formal authority and control exercised at successive levels from the top to the bottom. Theoretically, formal authority and directives flow down through the chain of command to lower levels, and information filters up through channels to the top from lower-level employees in the field. A framework of rigid rules and regulations formally assigns authority to various levels and defines the relationship between those individual bureaucrats who are of near equal rank.

An ideal *hierarchy* looks like the military chain of command for the U.S. Army, where the president as the commander in chief outranks the secretary of defense, who outranks the secretary of the army, who outranks all the generals, who in turn outrank all the colonels, and so on, down to the new private E-1, who is outranked by everybody. Actually, a hierarchy seldom functions according to its organizational chart. Usually, it can be influenced at all levels by legislators, the chief executive, interest groups, and other bureaucrats regardless of the formal lines of authority.

Department of Criminal Justice Although the formal theory of hierarchy is evident in each administrative unit, the Texas government as a whole is not arranged hierarchically because authority is not centralized in a single executive. For example, the Texas Department of Criminal Justice is not under the direct administrative control of the governor, and the direct lines of authority and communication stop abruptly when they reach the Texas Board of Criminal Justice.

Ironically, the governor is elected by the people to be the chief executive but has little direct authority over most administrators. However, the authority to appoint the membership of most of the boards and commissions, together with close personal ties to powerful special interest groups, makes the governor an important player in shaping the direction of Texas administrative policy.

EXPERTISE

To function smoothly, individual bureaucrats should have an understanding of their jobs and the effects of their decisions on others. Students of administration have concluded that this can be accomplished by clearly defining the duties of the job and the limit of its authority. Thus individual bureaucrats, through training and experience in specific job classifications, become experts in specialized areas of administration. This results in better, more efficient administration and is a major source of bureaucratic power.

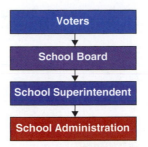

Figure 9.2

Independent School District

The Bureaucracy and Public Policy

Each attempt to depoliticize the bureaucracy simply meant that one kind of politics was substituted for another. Most political observers today agree that the Texas bureaucracy is deeply engaged in politics, that politics strongly affects public policy, and that policy formulation cannot, in fact, be separated from policy administration. Public administration is "in politics" because it operates in a political environment and must seek political support from somewhere if it is to accomplish goals, gain appropriations, or even survive. The result of strong political support for an agency is increased size, jurisdiction, influence, and prestige. The less successful agency may experience reduced appropriations, static or reduced employment, narrowed administrative jurisdiction, and possibly extinction. Where then, does a unit of the bureaucracy look for the political support so necessary for its bureaucratic well-being? It may look to clientele interest groups, the legislature, the chief executive, and the public. Political power also comes from factors within the bureaucracy, such as expertise, control of information, and discretion in the interpretation and administration of laws.

Figure 9.3

Council–Manager System

What is the usual assumption for choosing this structural organization for public schools and municipal governments?

CLIENTELE GROUPS

The most natural allies for an agency are its constituent or **clientele interest groups**—the groups that benefit directly from agency programs. The agency reciprocates by protecting its clients within the administration. At the national level, examples of such a close-knit alliance of an interest group and agency are defense contractors and the Department of Defense; agribusiness and the Department of Agriculture; and drug manufacturers and the Food and Drug Administration. In Texas, some of the closer bedfellows are the Texas Good Roads and Transportation Association and the Texas Department of Transportation; oil, gas, and transportation industries and the Texas Railroad Commission; the banking industry and the Department of Banking; and the Texas Medical Association and the State Department of Health. Agitation by such groups often leads to the establishment of a state agency, and its power and importance are usually directly related to the power and influence of its clientele groups and the intensity of their support.

The agency and its clientele groups are usually allied from the very beginning, and this alliance continues to grow and mature as mutual convenience, power, and prosperity increase. Economic and political ties are cemented by mutual self-interest. Agencies and clients share information, have common attitudes and goals, exchange employees, and lobby

Clientele interest groups

The groups most concerned with the laws and policies being administered by a government agency.

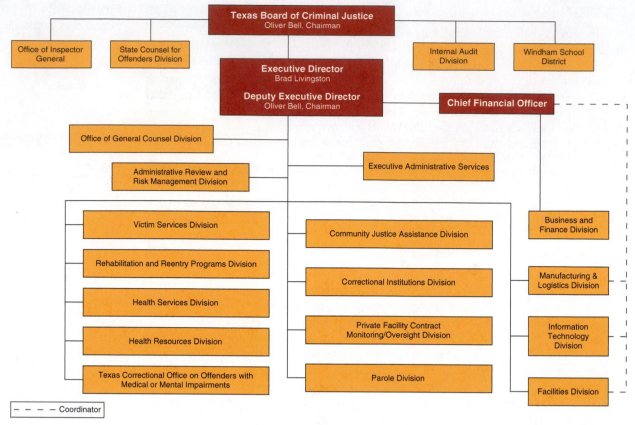

Figure 9.4

Texas Department
of Criminal Justice
Organizational Structure

Source: http://www.tdcj.state.
tx.us/orgchart

How would you describe this
organizational structure?

the legislature together for both agency appropriations and government policies that favor the interest groups. Mutual accommodation has become so accepted that the clientele groups often speak of "our agency" and spend considerable time and money lobbying for it. The agency reciprocates by protecting its clients within the administration.

Because neither the bureaucracy nor the special interests are single entities, there is often competition among the various special interests and the agencies for appropriations, so both seek allies in the legislative branch.

THE LEGISLATURE, THE LIEUTENANT GOVERNOR, AND THE SPEAKER

Bureaucratic power is enhanced by the support of powerful legislators, often including the chair of the committee that exercises legislative oversight over the agency. The agency is dependent on legislative allies for laws that expand its powers, increase the scope of its duties, protect it from unfriendly interests, and appropriate the funds for its operation. Therefore, administrators seek the favor of influential lawmakers.

Although the committee chairs are important in the Texas legislature, the short session and the power of the presiding officers limit their influence. For this reason, an agency seeks the support of the lieutenant governor and the speaker of the house, as well as members of the finance and appropriations committees, the Legislative Budget Board, and the Legislative Council.

The importance of legislative support explains the intense lobbying activity that surrounds the appointment of legislators to powerful committees and the campaign activity that precedes election to positions of legislative leadership. If the interest group and its agency are unable to get allies appointed or elected to positions of influence in the legislature, they are forced to try to win support after the influential legislators are chosen—a more difficult endeavor.

The "revolving door" practices of special interest groups help them gain influence over public policy. Corporations employ ex-administrators and ex-legislators as executives, lobbyists, or consultants. The practice of government employees resigning and accepting lucrative employment with a corporation, an organization, or an individual that has profited financially by that employee's actions casts a shadow of doubt over the whole public policy-making process. Unfortunately, this "sleaze factor" negatively affects public perception of all public servants and prompts cynicism toward all government.

In this environment, legislators, administrators, and regulators often become promoters of the regulated industry, formulating increasingly suspicious public policy. Increased cynicism and declining public respect and confidence in all government and its employees are the inevitable result.

THE REVOLVING DOOR

The **revolving door** between special interests and government officials is a permanent fixture in Texas. Literally hundreds of former administrators and legislators work for special interests as lobbyists, consultants, and executives.[3]

"Revolving door"

The interchange of employees between government agencies and the private businesses with which they have dealings.

THE GOVERNOR

The need of administrative agencies for the governor's support depends on the extent of the governor's formal and informal powers and how successful the agency has been in finding other powerful political allies.

Even when an executive has extensive administrative powers (as the U.S. president does), most agencies have considerable independence. In Texas, where the executive is decentralized and the governor has few direct administrative powers, administrative autonomy is enhanced. Agencies still need the support of the governor, however, for a governor can influence the legislature when it considers appropriations bills and other matters important to the agency. The governor's item veto can also seriously affect an agency's funding.

The governor's cooperation is also important because of his or her appointive power to policy-making boards and commissions. Agency employees develop shared attitudes, esprit de corps, and a sense of communality with the employees of the agency's constituency interest groups. Since an agency's interests are usually similar to those of its constituency, both want the governor to appoint board members who will advance their mutual political goals.

Moreover, the governor's support gives the agency greater bargaining power with legislators and interest groups in achieving its goals. Although the Texas governor has few direct administrative powers, she or he can influence and shape agency programs and success through veto power and appointments to policy-making boards and commissions.

PUBLIC POLICY AND THE IRON TEXAS STAR

The explanation of how public policy is made and implemented is a complex endeavor. Teachers and writers often use models as a means of simplification to explain the process. A model is a simplification of reality in order to explain reality.

---

[3]Texans for Public Justice, "Million-Dollar Clients," *Austin's Oldest Profession: Texas's Top Lobby Clients and Those Who Service Them* (Austin, TX: Texans for Public Justice, 2002), http://www.tpj.org/reports/lobby02/page4.html

Iron Texas Star
A model depicting policy making in Texas by a coalition of interests that includes interest groups, the lieutenant governor, the speaker, standing committees, the governor, administrators, and boards and commissions.

One such model, the **Iron Texas Star**, is depicted in Figure 9.5. This model attempts to explain the relationships between the political actors in Texas government that make legislative and administrative public policy happen.

Texas has weak legislative committees when compared with their counterparts in the U.S. Congress. This is attributable to the hands-on authority of the lieutenant governor and the speaker of the Texas House of Representatives, who select most of the members and all of the chairs of the standing committees, conference committees, and legislative boards and commissions. Their exercise of this power includes them in the iron star coalitions that formulate and implement public policy in Texas. The governor is also included, as a result of the item veto power and the power to appoint members of state policy-making boards and commissions. The virtual absence of a civil service for Texas government employees makes them more vulnerable to influence by the appointed boards. Finally, economic interest groups provide the mortar that builds and holds together this five-pointed coalition of administrators, legislators, presiding officers, the governor, and clientele interests.

All economic interests want friendly government policies. Some industries, such as insurance and oil and gas, have little need for direct appropriations and basically want only to be free of government interference. This class of interests may, however, want to use the powers of government for favorable regulations and protection from consumers and competitors. Other interests, such as the Texas State Teachers Association and the Texas Good Roads and Transportation Association, literally survive on government appropriations.

The basic goal of special interests is to accumulate "friends" in the policy-making and regulatory areas of government. It is equally critical for political operatives to acquire friends among economically powerful individuals and special interest groups. The members of the coalition also support the friends of their friends at the other points of the iron star and thereby develop a mutual support group from which all can benefit.

Legislators, administrators, the governor, and the presiding officers rely to varying degrees on the support of their interest group friends for campaign contributions, supplemental income, political advancement, financial advice and opportunity, and after-office employment and income. As time passes and members of the coalition become more interdependent, each looks to the other for support. Legislators bargain for the interest of the coalition in the legislature. Administrators issue favorable regulations and support their friends' viewpoints in administrative decisions. The presiding officers may shepherd the proposals of their friends

Figure 9.5

The Iron Texas Star Model

What are the bargaining chips that each of the entities at the five points of the Iron Texas Star bring to the table when engaging in the formulation of Texas public policy?

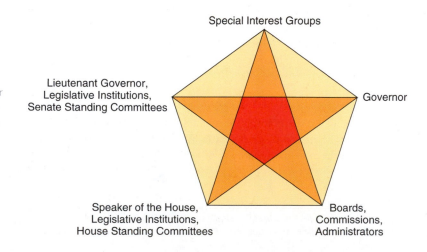

through the legislative process and also place the friends of economic special interests on powerful legislative committees and legislative boards and commissions. Also, the governor appoints friends and friends of friends to various boards and commissions that make policy affecting these same friends. Other government officials may also broker with political operatives for decisions favorable to their friends and to the friends of their friends inside the iron star coalition.

PUBLIC SUPPORT

Good public relations with the electorate are usually beneficial for any agency, both in its appropriations requests and in its battles with other agencies over areas of jurisdiction. Favorable propaganda combined with myth and literature have created broadly based public support for such agencies as the Texas Department of Criminal Justice, the Texas Rangers, and to some extent the Texas Highway Patrol.

EXPERTISE

A kind of power inherent in any professional bureaucracy stems from administrators' ability to shape public policy because of their knowledge of a given subject. Policy-making officials such as the legislature and governor can seldom be as well-versed in all policy-making areas as the administrative personnel, who have often made a lifetime career of administration in a single area of government activity. Policy-making officials, whether appointed or elected, frequently find themselves forced to rely on longtime government employees for advice concerning both content and procedural matters. Persons whom the public may see as only the administrators of the law are often important players in its conception, promotion, and enactment.

> An excellent example of positive public relations is the Texas Rangers baseball team being named after the state law enforcement agency.

INFORMATION

Because the bureaucracy is the branch of government that works most directly with constituent interest groups and the general public, administrative agencies gather the information used by these groups or the general public to determine what laws are needed or wanted. Information of this nature is valuable to legislators as well as to elected or appointed administrators but may be available only at the discretion of top government administrators. In other words, these administrators may dispense or interpret information in a way that benefits their agency or constituency interests, thus affecting the formation of public policy.

ADMINISTRATION OF THE LAW

Just as judges use judicial review to interpret the meaning of the law and to write case law for its implementation, bureaucrats use what might be termed **administrative review** in the process of administering the law. When administrators interpret the law and write the rules and regulations for its enforcement, they are making law that is known as **administrative law**. Administrative law defines the meaning of the law and determines its effect on both special interests and the public.

Either written or unwritten decisions by administrators to enforce a dog leash, speed limit, pure food, or underage smoking law either leniently or not at all alters the spirit of the law and dilutes its impact. Although the law may remain on the books indefinitely, its effect is

Administrative review

Administrators' study and interpretation of a law and writing the rules and regulations to implement the law's enforcement. All laws undergo administrative review, whereas relatively few undergo *judicial review*, which is the courts' interpretation of the law.

Administrative law

The rules and regulations written by administrators to administer a law. The effectiveness of a law is often determined by how administrative law is written.

diminished with lax or selective enforcement. In this way, administrators establish public policies that not only affect the lives of the general public but can also, to an extent, modify the decisions of the state's elected policy makers. Although administrative decisions can be overturned by the courts and statutory law can be rewritten by legislatures, administrative review is the first and usually the last determination of the meaning of a law and how rigidly it will be enforced.

ACCOUNTABILITY

Throughout the history of the United States, people have tried to hold government responsible for its policies. The rise of the bureaucratic state is the most recent challenge to responsible government. The size and political power of modern bureaucracy make the problem of administrative accountability ever more acute. Various organizational arrangements and legal restrictions have been used in attempts to make the bureaucracy accountable to the citizenry, or at least to someone whom the citizens can hold responsible.

Elective Accountability The simplest approach has been to make the bureaucracy directly accountable to the people through the democratic process—the theory of **elective accountability**. In Texas, this goal was to be accomplished through the election of the governor, lieutenant governor, attorney general, treasurer, comptroller of public accounts, commissioner of the General Land office, commissioner of agriculture, Railroad Commission, and State Board of Education. The reasoning was that the public, if given an opportunity, would keep a close watch on elected administrators and refuse to reelect those who were incompetent or dishonest. Administrators would therefore be sensitive to the wishes of the voters and would administer the laws only in the interest of the general public.

Several problems have developed with the application of this theory. The most obvious is the difficulty of determining the will of the people or even of determining the public interest. Texas is a mixture of many divergent groups with many often incompatible public interests—to please one group frequently means displeasing another.

A further problem is the relative invisibility of elected executives. As shown in Figure 9.6, the list of elected executives is so long that very few voters are even aware of the names of many officeholders, much less their administrative competence. Common everyday ineptitude, inefficiency, corruption, or incompetence goes unnoticed by the public and an apathetic press. Administrators, once elected, are usually returned to office until they die, retire, anger powerful client special interests, or commit an act so flagrant that the voters finally "throw the rascals out." Although elective accountability for local offices may be more practical in rural areas, in an increasingly urban society, accountability to the general public seems an ineffective method of either influencing administrative behavior or enforcing accountability.

Legislative Accountability Some advocates of administrative reform argue that the bureaucracy should be accountable to the legislature, since many view the legislature as the branch of government "closest" to the people. Because it is elected to protect constituent interests and because legislators establish policies, many argue that these elected representatives should determine whether those policies are being administered according to legislative intent. This principle has been implemented in Texas by establishing various auditing, budgeting, and oversight boards as well as legislative committees to try to hold administrators accountable. For example, the Texas legislature established the Sunset Advisory Commission to make recommendations as to the alteration, termination, or continuation of more than 200 state boards, commissions, and agencies. Agencies and their operations are reviewed

Elective accountability

The obligation of officials to be directly answerable to the voters for their actions. This allows elected administrators to ignore the wishes of the chief executive.

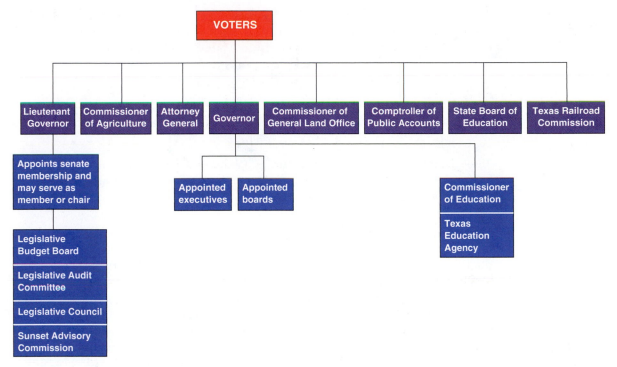

Figure 9.6

Texts's Elected Executives and Boards

Why do you think that Texas elects so many people? Would a simpler process be better or worse for Texas?

periodically, usually in 12-year cycles, and cease to exist without specific legislative action to renew. Functions may be expanded, diminished, or reassigned to other agencies by legislative action. If renewed, the Sunset Commission evaluates agency compliance with legislative directives. The state auditor also evaluates any management changes recommended by the commission. It is reasoned that periodic legislative evaluation, together with agency self-evaluation, should result in better, more efficient administration.

The principle of accountability to the legislature is questionable, however. Not only is the ability of any government to separate policy formulation from policy administration in doubt, but the assumption that the legislative branch best represents the people is debatable. Legislators' independent judgments may be compromised by financial conflicts of interest, campaign contributions from special interest groups, and political ambition. Although interests of the individual legislators and special interests might well be served, the general public may or may not.

Another problem is the invisibility of the committee hearings and the decision-making processes in the legislature; the public is just not aware of many policy decisions made in its name by the legislature.

Finally, because the Texas legislature is seldom in session, permanent legislative institutions such as the Legislative Budget Board and the Legislative Council are given the task of overseeing the administration. These institutions are incapable of enforcing accountability by the autonomous agencies in Texas government; they also lack the visibility necessary for effective operation in the public interest. Accordingly, a major problem of responsible government is knowing who is watching the watchers.

Accountability to the Chief Executive Some reformers advocate a Texas administration patterned after the **cabinet system** of the federal government. As shown in Figure 9.7, this would entail a reorganization and consolidation of the executive branch into larger subject-matter departments, with the governor being given power to appoint and remove top administrators

Cabinet system

A system that allows the chief executive to appoint and remove top-level administrators, thereby giving the chief executive more control over the administration.

and to control the budget. Administrative authority would be concentrated at the top. (Advocates argue that this is only proper, as the governor usually receives the blame for administrative blunders anyway.) Furthermore, a governor who had these powers could hold the appointed bureaucrats accountable for their actions.

Theoretically, several benefits could result from accountability to the governor. The office is visible to the general public, so the problem of who watches the watchers would be solved. There would be no question regarding final responsibility for any corruption or incompetence in the administration. Administrative control could be simplified, resulting in coordinated planning and policy implementation. Waste and duplication could be reduced.

Consolidation and reorganization of the Texas administration is, without a doubt, necessary for an orderly, modern executive branch. Analysis of the national government demonstrates that although no person can control the dozens of agencies, their chiefs, and the thousands of government employees who work in these agencies, one means by which the president can hold this bureaucracy accountable is through the executive office. If public administration was reorganized according to the federal model, the governor would need a similar executive office. This executive staff, although relatively invisible to the public, would nevertheless be accountable to the governor.

This chain of accountability—administrative agency to appointed executive to staff to governor to the people—is weakened by the close ties usually found between administrators, constituent interest groups, and legislators. Interest groups would continue to influence administrative appointments and removals in "their agencies" just as they now influence appointments to the boards and commissions under the present system. Even under a cabinet system, the governor would have problems enforcing the accountability of agencies that have allies among powerful interest groups and legislators.

Bureaucratic Accountability To whom is the Texas administrator really accountable? The answer is, in all probability, to the interest groups that benefit from the service programs the administrator provides (clientele groups). Politics works on the basic principles of mutual accommodation between allies and conflict between opponents, coalition building, and compromise. Agency officials are often obligated to administer the law and make policy decisions in ways that are favorable to the goals and aspirations of their political allies among private economic interests. Appointees to boards and administrative positions are usually chosen from the industry concerned, and the policy decision they make tends to benefit the most influential operatives in the industry. In turn, when government employees leave government service, many find jobs in the industry where their expertise lies. Thus, because the success of their agency, their government career, and possible after-government employment often depend on their actions while in the bureaucracy, it is understandable that many administrators feel more directly accountable to the economic powers they affect than to the public at large.

How then, can the Texas administration be made more accountable to the public? There is no single answer. One possibility could be more openness. A basic concept of democratic government is that policy made in the name of the public should be made in full view of the public. Texas has made great strides in this area. **Open-meetings laws** require that meetings of government bodies at all levels of government be open to the general public except when personnel, land acquisition, or litigation matters are being discussed. The laws further prohibit unannounced sessions and splitting up to avoid a quorum, and they require that public notice be posted for both open and closed sessions. However, these laws are continuously being tested by policy makers, who feel more comfortable operating in secret.

Openness is further encouraged by the state's **open-records law**, which requires that the records of all government proceedings be available to the public for only the expense involved in assembling and reproducing them.

Another source of openness is **whistle-blowers**—government employees who expose bureaucratic excesses, blunders, corruption, or favoritism. These employees could be commended and protected from retribution, but too often they are instead exiled to the bureaucratic equivalent of Siberia or fired for their efforts. To its credit, Texas's whistle-blowers law prohibits governments from acting against employees who report law violations. But enforcement is difficult and time-consuming, and whistle-blowers often suffer.

An ombudsman is an official who takes, investigates, and mediates complaints about government bureaucrats from private individuals. The office originated in Sweden in 1819, and is presently used by some state and local governments in the United States. Texas Governor Ann Richards established an ombudsman in the governor's office in 1991.

The appointment of **ombudsmen** at every level of government would give each individual increased access to the bureaucracy regarding real or imagined administrative injustices. In this way, administrative error, injustice, or oversight could be rectified, allowing individual citizens to have a more positive attitude toward government. Any lack of public accountability by Texas administrators cannot wholly be blamed on poor structural organization or the lack of consumer- or citizen-oriented agencies. No amount of reorganization and no number of consumer agencies can overcome the willingness of an apathetic or indifferent public to accept bureaucratic errors, inefficiency, excesses, favoritism, or corruption.

Open-meetings laws

With some exceptions, laws that require meetings of government bodies that make decisions concerning the public interest to be open to public scrutiny.

Open-records laws

Laws that require most records kept by government to be open for the examination of the parties involved.

> Three corporate whistle-blowers were honored on the cover of *Time* magazine as "Persons of the Year" in 2002. They were Cynthia Cooper (of WorldCom), Sherron Watkins (of Enron), and Coleen Rowley (of the FBI).

Whistle-blowers

Government employees who expose corruption, incompetence, and criminal acts by other government employees.

Ombudsman

An official who hears complaints of employees and citizens concerning government administrators or policy administration. Ombudsmen usually lack authority to force administrative compliance, but they can bring the complaints to the proper authorities and represent the interests of the complaining individual within the administration.

CHAPTER SUMMARY

★ Public administration can be seen as a government activity that applies the power of government to enforce its policies. Size, hierarchy, expertise, and neutrality characterize all bureaucracies. The size of the bureaucracy has increased dramatically in the past century as demands for government action, assistance, and regulation have increased. Government bureaucracies in the United States are large and may seem overwhelming to individuals or small businesses that must deal with them. This leads many people to conclude that we live in an "administrative state" ruled by bureaucrats who are largely independent and lack real accountability to any politically responsible official. Thus, "big government," which is really big bureaucracy, is increasingly criticized by people on both sides of the political spectrum.

★ Bureaucracies are usually organized into hierarchies with centralized control and accountability at the top. The lines of authority and communication are clearly established, although in practice they may not be followed. In contrast, the most notable characteristic of the Texas administration is that no single official is responsible for the execution of policy. Numerous elected and appointed officials sit atop a multitude of little hierarchies and are normally responsible to no one in particular except their clientele interest groups.

★ Bureaucrats develop extensive specialization and experience in particular job classifications. Ideally, this results in increased job efficiency, but it is also a major source of bureaucratic power.

★ Although administrative neutrality is a goal long pursued by reformists, it remains a myth because politics cannot be separated from administration. All attempts to develop neutrality, such as the civil service and independent boards and commissions, have simply substituted one kind of politics for another.

★ Elected officials and public interest groups have devised various techniques to hold Texas administrations accountable, but real administrative accountability will ultimately rest with the agency's clientele interest group.

HOW TEXAS COMPARES

★ Texas's bureaucracy is less controlled by its chief executive than in most states. Texas governor is part of a plural executive system in which more independently elected officers share executive power than is typical. Texas is among the few states that lack a cabinet system to coordinate programs, to supervise agencies, and to advise the governor. The governor's power to appoint, remove and direct agency heads is more limited than in most states. In no state is the chief executive's influence over agency budgets limited by the dominant influence of the competing Legislative Budget Board.

★ State and local employees in Texas outnumber federal government employees almost eight to one. Most public services are provided by state and local governments rather than by federal agencies.

KEY TERMS

administrative law	civil service (merit) system	Iron Texas Star	Permanent School Fund
administrative review	clientele interest groups	McCarthyism	privatization
attorney general's opinion	contract spoils or patronage	ombudsman	"revolving door"
bureaucracy	elective accountability	open-meetings laws	spoils system
cabinet system	hierarchy	open-records law	whistle-blowers

REVIEW QUESTIONS

1. Define and explain the characteristics of a bureaucracy. What are the characteristics of the Texas bureaucracy? How does the Texas bureaucracy differ from the hierarchy model of Max Weber?

2. Discuss the importance of the Texas bureaucracy in policy formation, development, and implementation.

3. Describe the Iron Texas Star model. How does it differ from the iron triangle?

4. Discuss the various methods used to hold the bureaucracy accountable to the people. Which methods are used in Texas government? Which method do you believe is most effective?

5. How do the open-records and open-meetings laws affect bureaucratic behavior? Why are these laws important?

6. Become familiar with Texas's elected executives and elected boards. To whom are they responsible? How do they affect the governor's ability to serve as the "chief executive" of Texas?

7. What is the structural organization of Texas's appointed and ex officio boards and commissions? What role do they play in Texas government? To whom are they responsible?

LOGGING ON

Each member of the statewide elected executives has a separate website:

★ Governor: **http://www.governor.state.tx.us**

★ Attorney general: **http://www.oag.state.tx.us**
Comptroller of public accounts: **http://www.cpa.state.tx.us**

★ Commissioner of the General Land office: **http://www.glo.state.tx.us**

★ Commissioner of agriculture: **http://www.agr.state.tx.us**

★ Lieutenant governor: **http://www.ltgov.state.tx.us/**

The key appointed executives also have websites:

✴ Secretary of state: **http://www.sos.state.tx.us**

✴ Adjutant general: **http://www.agd.state.tx.us**

The key elected boards in Texas have the following sites:

✴ Railroad Commission: **http://www.rrc.state.tx.us**

✴ Texas Education Agency: **http://www.tea.state.tx.us**

✴ State Board of Education: **http://www.tea.state.tx.us/sboe/**

Research the Texas bureaucracy. Select one of the lesser-known Texas agencies or commissions to research. Go to

http://www.government.texasonline.state.tx.us/category. jsp?categoryId=6.9 for a list of all the state agencies. Select one, and go to that site to find out all you can. Does the agency have an email address where you can request additional information?

For information on Texas government and numerous other subjects, go to the Texas State Library site at **http://www.tsl.state .tx.us/**

To follow money in politics, try OpenSecrets.org at **http://www.opensecrets.org**, Public Citizen of Texas at **http:// www.citizen.org/texas**, and Texans for Public Justice at **http://www.tpj.org**

The State of E-Government in Texas

Neal Coates
Abilene Christian University

INTRODUCTION

In addition to the academic questions that this chapter covers, we offer this essay so you can sample the main reason that state agencies exist—to provide you and every Texan with important state services. We have tried to write a textbook that you can use in practical ways; we want to make state government accessible to you through the media that you use most often, and we want you to become an intelligent consumer of state services. We offer this article to engage you with some of the state's main websites and to put its Internet access efforts into perspective.

Many college students in Texas are aware that their counterparts in China are forbidden by government firewalls from accessing Google, Facebook, Twitter, or YouTube. Because of Americans' high use of these sites, we sympathize with persons in the People's Republic of China when reading in media and textbooks that freedom on the Internet is extremely limited there.[1] What we do not realize is that e-government is also restricted in China, nor do we really appreciate this unless we see the vast amount of information and services available at the state of Texas home page, **http://www.texasonline.com**, and understand that openness also fosters government accountability.

For young adults, the Internet is an integral part of daily life, whether it is for talking with friends, listening to music, checking sports or news, playing games, making purchases, or banking online. At Abilene Christian University, an iPhone or iTouch is distributed to each student and is used for in-class assignments and course work.[2] Many of the 25 million Texans use the Internet, including the 1.3 million persons enrolled in higher education.[3] But college students in the Lone Star State are just now beginning to understand that the Internet has also become an integral part of "delivering" government.

Many states and counties in the United States now maintain an extensive electronic presence, providing invaluable access to economic and quality-of-life information. E-government is the use of information technologies by government agencies to provide a wide range of services and programs via the Internet, wide area networks, and mobile computing.[4] These initiatives have transformed relations among citizens, businesses, and the various arms of government, and have saved costs because of fewer in-person transactions. E-government also allows citizens to hold officials more accountable by increasing transparency—one example is the ability of offices to publish policies on the Internet, helping set uniform and known regulations.

E-KNOWLEDGE, E-SERVICE, AND E-GOVERNANCE

Several years of research show that e-government can be evaluated by examining the strength of its basic elements,

---

[1] Miguel Helft and David Barboza, "Google Shuts China Site in Dispute over Censorship," *New York Times,* March 22, 2010, http://www.nytimes.com/2010/03/23/technology/23google.html?hp

[2] "ACU First University in Nation to Provide iPhone or iPod Touch to All Incoming Freshmen," Abilene Christian University press release, February 25, 2008, http://www.acu.edu/news/2008/080225_iphone.html

[3] As of 2007, 68 Percent of Texas Households Had an Internet Connection, *Networked Nation: Broadband in America 2007*, U.S. Department of Commerce (2008).

[4] See the World Bank's e-government website, a repository of best practices and case studies, http://go.worldbank.org/6WT3UPVG80

e-knowledge, e-service, and e-governance—and the good news for Texans is that their state government, 254 counties, and thousands of cities rank high in these elements. E-knowledge is the easiest to implement and includes governmental rules, required documents, officials' duties, and information about trading markets. E-service involves aiding citizens or businesses in carrying out activities by providing interactive sites for subjects such as weather, local maps, job information, and instructions on procedures such as vehicle registration and business operation guides. Finally, e-governance creates government-to-citizen connections through links to websites and emails of officials and policy-making bodies, online forums and polls, surveys, chat rooms, and complaint forms. This facilitates civic engagement and builds trust, and increases efficiency and accountability by officials.

TEXAS'S BUREAUCRACIES: THE EXECUTIVE BRANCH

Do you need to renew your driver license? Find a job? Plan your Spring Break? Pay your school tuition and fees? (This has been set up for Texas A&M University students.) Apply for a fishing license or concealed handgun license? Even donate to the restoration of the Governor's Mansion? One day you will be interested in filing for a "vital record" (marriage, birth, and death certificates).

TexasOnline divides e-services into 18 categories, organized alphabetically. These categories include searchable license records databases, commonly used government forms, access to vital records, renewable vehicle registrations and driver licenses, industry permits, and the filing of court documents. An emergency preparedness portal gives information for hurricane season and other natural disasters and provides weather updates and evacuation routes.[5] A business portal breaks down the process of starting a business in Texas into four easy steps. In addition, a majority of the sites feature audio and video clips, and there is a Spanish version of nearly every page. Twenty-four hour customer assistance is available. An online service that generates a significant amount of online revenue collection for the state is the WebFile program, which enables businesses to file and pay sales tax returns via the Internet. Other notable sections of the home page include the Governor's site, Department of Public Safety, Department of Family and Protective Services, and the Texas Film Commission.[6]

TRAVEL

When getting ready for vacation during Spring Break or the summer, planning a trip in Texas is extremely easy with aid from the home page's link to traveltex.com. Whether it is lake levels or types of fish, all the information anglers can dream about is available. Whether it is fees or weather or the location of state parks with mountains, hikers have the best source of information (130 pages of selections!). Order a free travel guide to be mailed to you, or check out the calendar of special events across Texas. Attractions are organized by topics such as arts and culture, beaches, golf, historic, music, outdoor, rodeos, shopping, and sports. There is truly something for everyone, right at their fingertips.

EMPLOYMENT

Another important reason that college students should use TexasOnline is to find work, including obtaining occupational licenses. For state government jobs, the "Work in Texas" website (formerly called the Governor's Job Bank) is the most comprehensive resource—the "Job Search" section allows for various criteria such as region, title, salary, and so forth.[7] For other types of jobs, persons can go to the Texas Workforce Commission home page and its searchable job base.[8] Another reason exists for students to check out job information through the state of Texas home page—a significant number are interested in teaching careers. The State Board for Educator Certification issues credentials for use in the public schools, and its site lists information about certification, application procedures, and fees.[9] The Texas Education Agency, at **http://www.tea.state.tx.us**, has a "School District Locator" interactive map, which shows school district and education service center region boundaries, school locations, contact information for district staff, district accountability ratings, and enrollment.

LOCAL GOVERNMENT

Are you from a Texas city? Look at your hometown's website, and your home county's site, and you should see that local government is also "in" on e-government. County governments such Bexar or Harris provide links to their Commissioners Court with agendas. Election information, such as registration and polling places, for state and local races is posted, even sample ballots. Perhaps it will not be long before the legislature allows online voting! Even many district courts and county courts-at-law have courtroom rules and dockets posted online. One of the most interesting and money-saving sites are those for the appraisal districts—there persons can search a database for properties in the various counties providing information such as property value, tax bills, structure size, deed history, dimensions, and even the ability to file a tax protest online.[10]

Every major city in Texas, and most of the midsized and smaller cities have web pages. Whether it is **http://www. dallascityhall.com** or **http://www.abilenetx.com**, there is a large amount of helpful information. When selecting the maps feature on Dallas' home page, you can find parks, libraries, even an overlay with aerial views. Flood zones and school districts and

---

[5]See http://www.texasonline.com/portal/tol/en/emergency

[6]Respectively, their websites are http://www.governor.state.tx.us; http://www.txdps.state.tx.us, www.tdprs.state.tx.us; http://www.governor.state.tx.us/film. The legislature and its members also have a link on the home page, http://www.capitol.state.tx.us

[7]See http://www.twc.state.tx.us/jobs/gvjb/sota.html

[8]See http://www.twc.state.tx.us

[9]See for example, "How to Become a Teacher in Teacher in Texas" at http://www.sbec.state.tx.us/SBECOnline/certinfo/becometeacher.asp?width=1024&height=768

[10]See Tarrant Appraisal District, http://www.tad.org/

other features can be added. Persons can also pay utility bills and parking tickets—a common feature of many cities' home pages. Whether a homeowner or businessperson, all benefit when they can read their city's laws posted online (they are called the Code of Ordinances). The City of Abilene site has this feature, and even the watering schedule for residential and business lawns, promotional videos to draw applicants for the police and fire departments, and a feature to adopt stray pets (and see their picture)![11]

MAINTENANCE OF TEXAS HOME PAGE

Texas's official portal provides quick access to about 850 state and local government services and has been recognized as the best state government site in the United States.[12] It has even been used as an example of how to create and run e-government in research to better developing countries' systems.[13] But how is TexasOnline run? In 2000, a company called BearingPoint began operating TexasOnline with oversight by the Texas Department of Information Resources. It is a contractual public/private partnership—in other words, the state's home page is partially privatized. BearingPoint provided management for web applications, payment processing, a call center, and intrusion-detection monitoring. All project expenses were paid by BearingPoint, which was reimbursed via project revenue from convenience and subscription fees; in 2006, the company began to make a profit.[14] In 2009, the contract was rebid and won by Texas NICUSA.

An example of how online fees are charged is demonstrated by the Texas vehicle registration system. If a person processes by mail instead of visiting their local county tax office, there is a $1 fee. For online transactions, customers use a credit card, and those companies charge TexasOnline a retail merchant fee. This averages about 2.25 percent of total dollars charged plus 25 cents for other fees, bringing the processing cost to $1.83. This convenience fee is rounded to $2 to compensate the contractor for running the home page.

It should be noted Texas's e-government did not come about because of healthy revenues or because political institutions provided an easy path. In 2004, Texas was spending roughly $2 billion on information technology but was in deficit. The chief information officer for Pennsylvania, who helped that state save $270 million by consolidating data centers, putting telecommunications services under one contract, and building a common email platform, was hired by Texas. But as director, Larry Olson faced a difficult structure for making change—Texas has a governor with no cabinet, a strong legislature, and about 250 independent agencies. DIR faced enormous hurdles convincing the legislature and the multiple bureaucracies to cooperate in a strategic plan to accomplish cost savings.[15] It has worked. Persons access TexasOnline at no cost, and every month the home page receives more than 2 million visitors and conducts 1.5 million financial transactions involving $300 million. Since its beginning, the home page has had over 198 million visits, processed 116 million financial transactions, collected more than $13 billion, and contributed $60 million to the State Treasury.[16]

CONCLUSION

In Texas, millions of persons know that freedom of speech on the Internet is alive and well, and they do not fear the loss of search engines or social networking from government decrees. In addition, more and more persons are finding that our state and local officials have worked hard to create excellent e-government. College students, who almost universally use the Internet, are awakening to the opportunities that TexasOnline provides for entertainment, jobs, travel, interacting with their elected officials, and so much more. Join the crowd!

JOIN THE DEBATE

1. Sample TexasOnline and other state websites suggested in this article and inside the back cover of this text. How could the state make its services more efficient and available through its websites? Browse other states and discuss how the quality of Texas's websites compares.

2. Describe ways that your instructor and this textbook could make the study of Texas government and accessing its services easier through the Internet or other media.

3. How can the Internet be used to make state government more accountable to ordinary citizens?

---

[11]See the Abilene Animal Control Department, http://www.abilenetx.com/Animal/index.htm

[12]"TexasOnline.com Named Best State E-government Site in the Nation," Texas Department of Information Resources press release, August 28, 2006, http://www.dir.state.tx.us/dir_overview/pressreleases/20060825txo/index.htm. TexasOnline earned the award in 2006 in the Seventh Annual Study of State and Federal E-government conducted by the Taubman Center for Public Policy at Brown University. Researchers evaluated various features including the number of online services, online publications, language translation, disability access, privacy policies, and security.

[13]Neal Coates and Lisa Nikolaus, "Zambia and E-Government: An Assessment and Recommendations," in Blessing Maumbe and Vesper Owei (eds.), *E-Agriculture and E-Government for Global Policy Development: Implications and Future Directions* (IGI Global, 2009).

[14]"Texas Web Site Surpasses $1 Billion in State Revenue Collection," *Government Technology*, April 27, 2004, http://www.govtech.com/gt/articles/90060

[15]William Welsh, "Texas-Size Opportunity: Hard-Charging CTO Larry Olson Aims to Make the Lone Star State a National Leader in IT Innovation," *Washington Technology* 19(18) (2004), http://washingtontechnology.com/articles/2004/12/10/texassize-opportunity.aspx

[16]See the DIR home page, "What Is TexasOnline?", http://www2.dir.state.tx.us/texasonline/Pages/texasonline.aspx

Education: State Bureaucracy versus Federal Bureaucracy

Sherri Mora and Pam Tise, Texas State University—San Marcos

INTRODUCTION

One of the most contentious political issues surrounding bureaucracy in years has been whether the availability of federal funding has given national government agencies too much influence over state decisions. This essay shows how Texas responded to federal attempts to influence state education policies through the federal "Race to the Top" awards. Texas rejected participation in the competition and instead relied on its own ongoing state strategies.

Under the U.S. Constitution's "Commerce" and "General Welfare" clauses, Congress has the power to pass legislation that affects public education. Congressional education legislation normally falls into two categories: general legislation concerning areas such as civil rights and specific legislation that applies only to education. In 2009, Congress included such specific legislation as part of the American Recovery and Reinvestment Act. In the *Race to the Top Assessment Program*, Congress authorized funding for states to develop assessments "that are valid, support and inform instruction, provide accurate information about what students know and can do, and measure student achievement against standards designed to ensure that all students gain the knowledge and skills needed to succeed in college and the workplace."[1] The U.S. Department of Education's *Race to the Top* program requests that states enact reforms around four specific areas:

✴ Adopt standards and assessments that prepare students to succeed in college and the workplace and to compete in the global economy;

✴ Build data systems that measure student growth and success, and inform teachers and principals about how they can improve instruction;

✴ Recruit, develop, reward, and retain effective teachers and principals, especially where they are needed most; and

✴ Turn around our lowest-achieving schools.

Race to the Top funds will be given to states that lead the way with "ambitious yet achievable plans for implementing coherent, compelling, and comprehensive education reform. *Race to the Top* winners will help trail-blaze effective reforms and provide examples for states and local school districts throughout the country to follow as they too are hard at work on reforms that can transform our schools for decades to come"[2]; and address the growing problem of ill-prepared, entry-level college students and the lack in foundational knowledge necessary to engage successfully in postsecondary education.

A CONCERT TO TEXAS

College readiness has long been of interest to the Texas legislature. In 1987, the legislature passed the Texas Academic Skills Program (TASP). TASP required that entry-level college students take proficiency exams in mathematics, reading, and writing. Developmental education programs were created on public college campuses to carry out the mandate using standardized assessment for placement purposes. Those students that failed the assessments were required to enroll in remedial classes.[3] In 2003, the 78th Texas Legislature replaced TASP with the Texas Success Initiative Program (TSIP), again focusing on assessing college readiness and mandating remediation for those students deemed unprepared for entry-level university courses.[4]

In response to the increasing numbers of underprepared students, the third special session of the 79th Texas Legislature enacted House Bill 1 to "ensure that students are able to perform college-level work at institutions of higher education" (HB 1, 2006, Art. 5, Sect 28.008 [a]).[5] The bill required the creation of vertical teams composed of secondary and postsecondary faculty, tasked to identify "college readiness standards" that focus on key knowledge and skills that facilitate academic success.

CREATING COLLEGE READINESS STANDARDS (CRS)

In a joint effort, commissioners of the TEA and the Texas Higher Education Coordinating Board (THECB) established vertical teams composed of high school teachers and college faculty in the content areas of mathematics, science, language arts, and social studies. The teams were charged with developing standards that would "serve equally well those students heading to college and those to the workforce."[6] In addition, Governor Rick Perry appointed a Commission for a College Ready Texas (CCRT) to provide support and guidance to the

[1] U.S. Department of Education, Race to the Top Assessment Program, http://www2.ed.gov/programs/racetothetop-assessment/index.html
[2] Ibid.
[3] Texas Education Agency and Texas Higher Education Coordinating Board, *Texas Academic Skills Program. TASP Test: Information Summary, 1988,* http://www.eric.ed.gov/ERICWebPortal/custom/portlets/recordDetails/detailmini.jsp?_nfpb=true&_&ERICExtSearch_SearchValue_0=ED305853&ERICExtSearch_SearchType_0=no&accno=ED305853
[4] Texas Higher Education Coordinating Board, "Texas Success Initiative Information," *Developmental Education* (2010), http://www.thecb.state.tx.us/index.cfm?objectid=18555FEC-AF44-3B38-21A9F804FDBD3516
[5] House Bill 1, 2006, http://www.capitol.state.tx.us/tlodocs/793/billtext/html/HB00001F.htm
[6] Educational Policy Improvement Center, *Texas College Readiness Standards* (Seattle, WA: Author, 2008), p. 5.

state board of education and the vertical teams, noting "every student deserves to receive the necessary groundwork to be academically equipped for college. With the guidance of the Commission for a College Ready Texas, students will have access to improved college preparation tools."[7] In January 2008, the standards crafted by the vertical teams were adopted by THEBC and incorporation into the Texas Essential Knowledge and Skills (TEKS).[8] The Education Policy Improvement Center (EPIC) concluded that the College Readiness Standards (CRS) accurately reflected "expectations for readiness in a cross-section of representative entry-level college courses from all levels of the state's postsecondary system."[9]

WHAT ABOUT ACCOUNTABILITY?

Although it is clear that Texas has mandated that students meet certain criteria to be considered college-ready, the process was based on collaborative inquiry. The Texas legislature continues to monitor whether students are meeting specified learning objectives. The purpose of House Bill 1 was to establish a set of standards that would improve alignment between secondary and postsecondary education. With the adoption of CRS by THECB and the incorporation of these standards into TEKS, the requirements of Texas Legislature's House Bill 1 have been largely fulfilled.

To address the issue of accountability, the 81st Texas Legislature passed House Bill 3, which changed high school graduation criteria and requires THECB and TEA to set performance standards for admission to public institutions of higher education. Performance standards are defined as the level of proficiency required for a student to succeed in entry-level college courses. End-of-course (EOC) exams will be used to assess proficiency levels for high school students. Students passing EOC exams are therefore deemed college-ready and exempt from any developmental education requirements.[10]

TEXAS AND RACE TO THE TOP

In a January 13, 2010 letter to U.S. Secretary of Education Arne Duncan, Governor Rick Perry explained the success of the Texas College and Career-Ready Standards and Assessments program. The goals of this program include strong school accountability and focus on education development, with the intent of creating an "education system that prepares our students for success after graduation."[11]

Yet, despite the accomplishment of the Texas College and Career-Ready Standards and Assessments program, the U.S. Department of Education prefers that Texas adhere to the National Race to the Top program. To do so, Texas taxpayers would need to commit to "unfunded obligations or to the adoption of unproven cost-prohibitive national curriculum standards and tests."[12] Governor Perry refused to commit Texas to the estimated $3 billion that the Race to the Top Program would cost the state.

As one of the first states to adopt college-and-career ready standards and assessment, Texas "efforts ensure our curriculum standards are vertically aligned, starting in kindergarten and progressing through graduation."[13] Many of the national Race to the Top program requirements mirror the Texas state educational requirements, created to improve the future of Texans rather than to meet federal mandates. Since the enactment of the College and Career-Ready Standards and Assessments program, Texas education outcomes have been on the rise. For example, the 2009 mathematics National Assessment of Educational Progress exams results for eighth-grade African American students confirmed that Texas preformed the best in the nation. "The drop-out rates have declined for students in every demographic, and graduation and completion rates have improved."[14]

Regardless of federal mandates, the state of Texas, Governor Rick Perry, and the Texas legislature are committed to improving public schools and to building a successful future through education. The Texas Constitution states that it is "the duty of the Legislature … to establish and make suitable provision for the support and maintenance of an efficient system of public free schools."[15] The Texas legislature has carried out this charge in creating the Texas Higher Education Coordinating Board and the Texas Commissioner of Higher Education. And Texas citizens address the standards of education through state representatives and local school boards. In his letter to Secretary Duncan, Governor Perry's closing statement sums up the governor's opinions on education polices, "We believe that education polices, curriculum and standards should be determined in Texas, not in Washington, D.C."[16]

JOIN THE DEBATE

1. Should Texas have participated in the "Race to the Top" competition when doing so may have changed state practices to meet the goals of federal decision makers?

2. From your experience, how could Texas improve coordination between public schools and institutions of higher learning?

[7]Donna Garner, "The Texas College Readiness Process," *Education News*, http://www.ednews.org/articles/the-texas-college-readiness-process.html

[8]Texas Essential Knowledge and Skills are high school competencies mandated by law and measured in state-administered standardized exams called Texas Assessment of Knowledge and Skills (TAKS).

[9]Educational Policy Improvement Center, *Texas College Readiness Standards* (Seattle, WA: Author, 2008), p. 3.

[10]Texas Education Agency, Text of House Bill 3, *House Bill 3 Graduation Requirements* (2009), http://www.tea.state.tx.us/graduation.aspx

[11]Letter from Governor Rick Perry, January 13, 2010, http://governor.state.tx.us/files/press-office/O-DuncanArne201001130344.pdf

[12]Ibid.

[13]Ibid.

[14]Ibid.

[15]HCR 280, 78th Legislature, Regular Session, August 6, 2003, Texas Legislative Reference Library of Texas Legislative Reports, http://www.lrl.state.tx.us/research/interim/chargesDisplay.cfm?CmteID=8992

[16]Perry, 2010.

Chapter 10

Texas Judiciary

CONTENTS

LEARNING OBJECTIVES

* Distinguish the differences between criminal and civil cases.
* Know the difference between original and appellate jurisdiction.
* Describe the jurisdiction of major Texas courts.
* Distinguish the types of cases handled by the Texas Supreme Court from those decided by the Texas Court of Criminal Appeals.
* Distinguish between grand juries and trial juries.
* Identify the most common methods of judicial selection in the United States.
* Explain Texas's system of selecting judges and its advantages and disadvantages.
* Explain the role of campaign contributions in selecting Texas judges.

Support independent courts at **http://www.justiceatstake.org/**. On the state drop down, click on "'Your State' National Map."

Fight for the independence, ethics, and unbiased selection of judges with the American Judicature Society at **http://www.ajs.org/**

Track money and corporate influence in Texas politics at Texans for Public Justice at **http://www.tpj.org/**

Connect to groups with various views of the courts:

Conservative Groups

★ Connect with the conservative Texas Civil Justice League at **http://www.tcjl.com/** for the pro-business view of court business.

★ Fight frivolous and abusive lawsuits with Texans for Lawsuit Reform at **http://www.tortreform.com/**

★ Plug into another conservative organization, Judicial Watch, at **http://www.judicialwatch.org/**. Search "Texas" for breaking news about court rulings, ethics laws, government transparency, and illegal immigration.

Liberal/Progressive Groups

★ Link up with the progressive Texas Watch at **http://www.texaswatch.org/**. This watchdog organization is keeping tabs on Texas Supreme Court cases dealing with insurance company excesses, environmental abuses, and the rights of consumers, workers, and patients.

★ Team up with groups that advocate using the courts to protect consumers, workers, and patients, such as the American Association for Justice **http://www.atla.org/** and its associated state organization, the Texas Trial Lawyers Association **http://www.ttla.com/tx**

★ Fight for the personal privacy, religious liberty, reproductive rights, and freedom from discrimination with the Texas Civil Liberties Union at **http://www.aclutx.org**

Be an intelligent juror. Check out the jury selection system in your county at **http://www.juryduty.org/JuryDuty.htm**

★ Investigate state constitutional provisions for juries at **http://www.constitution.legis.state.tx.us/** (Articles 5 and 16). From there, click on "Texas Statutes" and investigate the law about juries. Browse the Civil Practice and Remedies Code, Chapter 23, and Code of Criminal Procedure, Chapters 35, 36, and 104.

American society has increasingly turned to the judiciary to find answers to personal, economic, social, and political problems. Courts are often asked to determine our rights, and important legal questions touch almost every aspect of our lives. For example, what level of privacy should we expect in our cars, offices, and homes? What treatment should people of different racial, gender, or age groups expect? In a divorce proceeding, with which parent should the children live? Should an accused person go to jail, and if so, for how long? Should a woman be allowed to terminate her

Bob Daemmrich Photography

🖝 *An attorney addresses the jury in a civil trial.*

Why have civil suits become so common in Texas? Explain the differences between civil and criminal law.

pregnancy? Should a patient be allowed to refuse potential lifesaving treatment? These are among the thousands of questions asked and answered daily by courts in the United States.

In fact, we are considered the most litigious society in the world. We have approximately one-quarter of the world's lawyers.[1] There are more than 1 million attorneys in the United States today.[2] Whereas 1 out of approximately every 700 people was a lawyer in 1951, that figure is now 1 out of approximately 260 people.[3] As a comparison, there are almost 27,000 lawyers in Japan, or 1 for every 4,700 people.[4] Cases in U.S. courts have included such issues as blaming McDonald's food for causing obesity in children, a lawsuit by parents against school officials for disciplining their children for cheating, a wife who sued her husband for not shoveling the snow in front of their home, and a woman who asked for $12 million because she was "pawed" and "humiliated" when a fur-costumed actor interacted with her during a Broadway performance of the musical Cats.[5]

Texas clearly fits into this general pattern of using the courts often. Texas has been found to rank 18th among the states in terms of litigation.[6] In recent years, it was found to have 337 people per attorney.[7] Texas also has more than 2,700 courts and approximately 3,300 justices or judges.[8] These courts dealt with more than 12 million cases in 2009, or on average about one case for every two residents of the state.[9] In recent years, Texas courts have heard important or controversial cases involving topics such as flag burning, the death penalty, school desegregation, school finance, sexual orientation, the welfare of children in a polygamist sect, and a case involving two large oil companies where one was found liable for more than $10 billion.

In this chapter, our focus will be the Texas judicial system and general attributes of American legal procedure and process. What will quickly become clear is the sheer size and complexity of the Texas court system. Furthermore, courts are undeniably important because they affect our lives. This is due to the subject matter they consider, which determines our legal rights and often shapes public policy. What should also become clear is that various controversies surround the selection of Texas judges and the politics connected to these courts.

> We simply have too many courts.
>
> —Former Texas Chief Justice Tom Phillips.[10]

---

[1]G. Alan Tarr, *Judicial Process and Judicial Policymaking*, 5th ed. (Belmont, CA: Wadsworth, 2009), p. 97.

[2]American Bar Association, *National Lawyer Population by State, 2009*, http://www.abanet.org/marketresearch/2007_Natl_Lawyer_FINALonepage.pdf

[3]G. Alan Tarr, *Judicial Process and Judicial Policymaking*, 5th ed. (Belmont, CA: Wadsworth, 2009), p. 98.

[4]Robert Carp, Ronald Stidham, and Kenneth L. Manning, *Judicial Process in America*, 8th ed. (Washington, DC: CQ Press, 2009), p. 111; Japan Federation of Bar Association, 2009 Fiscal Year Country Report, http://www.nichibenren.or.jp/en/activities/statements/data/2009CountryReport_JFBA.pdf

[5]*Newsweek*, December 15, 2003, p. 45; *The Dallas Morning News*, January 23, 2003, p. 4A; *The Dallas Morning News*, February 8, 1997, p. C6.

[6]*Forbes*, January 17, 1994, p. 70.

[7] *The Dallas Morning News*, "Number of Attorneys in Texas Growing," November 30, 1997; American Bar Association, *National Lawyer Population by State, 2009,* http://www.abanet.org/marketresearch/2007_Natl_Lawyer_FINALonepage.pdf

[8]*Annual Statistical Report for the Texas Judiciary, Fiscal Year 2009* (Austin: Office of Court Administration, Texas Judicial Council, 2009), p. 3, http://www.courts.state.tx.us/pubs/AR2009/AR09.pdf

[9]*Annual Statistical Report for the Texas Judiciary, Fiscal Year 2009* (Austin: Office of Court Administration, Texas Judicial Council, 2009), pp. 31, 34, 37.

[10]Quoted in the *Dallas Times Herald*, June 7, 1991, p. A13.

CIVIL CASES

★ Deal primarily with individual or property rights and involve the concept of responsibility but not guilt.
★ Plaintiff, or petitioner, is often a private party, as is the defendant, or respondent.
★ Dispute is usually set out in a petition.
★ A somewhat more relaxed procedure is used to balance or weigh the evidence; the side with *the preponderance of the evidence* wins the suit.
★ Final court remedy is relief from or compensation for the violation of legal rights.

CRIMINAL CASES

★ Deal with public concepts of proper behavior and morality as defined in law. A plea of guilty or not guilty is entered.
★ Case is initiated by a government prosecutor on behalf of the public.
★ Specific charges of wrongdoing are spelled out in a grand jury indictment or a writ of information.
★ Strict rules of procedure are used to evaluate evidence. The standard of proof is guilt *beyond a reasonable doubt*.
★ Determination of guilt results in punishment.

Civil and Criminal Cases

In the American legal system, cases are generally classified as either civil or criminal. A civil case concerns private rights and remedies and usually involves private parties or organizations (*Smith* v. *Jones*), although the government may be involved. A personal injury suit, a divorce case, a child custody dispute, a breach-of-contract case, a challenge to utility rates, and a dispute over water rights are all examples of civil suits.

A *criminal case* involves a violation of penal law. If convicted, the lawbreaker may be punished by a fine, imprisonment, or both. The action is by the state against the accused (*State of Texas* v. *Smith*). Typical examples of criminal actions are arson, rape, murder, armed robbery, speeding, jaywalking, and embezzlement. With exceptions, the characteristics in the aforementioned box generally distinguish criminal and civil cases.

One of the most important distinctions between civil and criminal cases involves the issue of **burden of proof** (the duty and degree to which a party must prove its position). In civil cases, the standard used is a **preponderance of the evidence**. This means that whichever party has more evidence or proof on its side should win the case, no matter how slight the differential is. However, in a criminal case, the burden of proof falls heavily on the government or prosecution. The prosecution must prove that the defendant is guilty **beyond a reasonable doubt**. The evidence must overwhelmingly, without serious question or doubt, point to the defendant's guilt; otherwise, the defendant should be found "not guilty."

Burden of proof
The duty of a party in a court case to prove its position.

Preponderance of the evidence
The amount of evidence necessary for a party to win in a civil case; proof that outweighs the evidence offered in opposition to it.

Beyond a reasonable doubt
The standard used to determine the guilt or innocence of a person criminally charged. To prove a defendant guilty, the state must provide sufficient evidence of guilt such that jurors will have no doubt that might cause a reasonable person to question whether the accused was guilty.

Original and Appellate Jurisdiction

Original jurisdiction is the power to try a case being heard for the first time. It involves following legal rules of procedure in hearing witnesses, viewing material evidence, and examining other evidence (such as documentary evidence) to determine guilt in criminal cases or responsibility in civil cases. The judge oversees procedure, but evaluating evidence is the jury's job (unless the right to a jury trial has been waived, in which case the judge weighs the evidence also). The verdict or judgment is determined and the remedy set. A trial involves the determination of fact and the application of law.

Appellate jurisdiction refers to the power of an appellate court to review the decisions of a lower court. Such appeals do not involve a new trial but rather a review of the law as it was

Original jurisdiction
The authority of a court to consider a case in the first instance; the power to try a case as contrasted with appellate jurisdiction.

Appellate jurisdiction
The power vested in an appellate court to review and revise the judicial action of an inferior court.

Brief

A written argument prepared by the counsel arguing a case in court that summarizes the facts of the case, the pertinent laws, and the application of those laws to the facts supporting the counsel's position.

Double jeopardy

A second prosecution for the same offense after acquittal in the first trial.

applied in the original trial. Many appeals are decided by review of the record (transcript) of the case and the lawyers' **briefs** (written arguments); sometimes lawyers may appear and present oral arguments. Appellate proceedings are based on law (legal process), not fact (no witnesses or material or documentary evidence). A reversal does not necessarily mean that the individual who was convicted is innocent, only that the legal process was improper. Consequently, that person may be tried again, and questions of **double jeopardy** (being prosecuted twice for the same offense) are not involved because the individual waives the right against double jeopardy by appealing the case.

Sometimes an action may have both civil and criminal overtones. Suppose that in the course of an armed robbery, the thief shoots a clerk at a convenience store. The state could prosecute for the robbery (criminal action), and the clerk could sue for compensation for medical expenses, lost earning power, and other damages (civil action). This dual nature is not unusual.

Court Organization

Figure 10.1 shows the organizational structure of the Texas court system and the various types and levels of courts in the system. It is important to note that some courts within this rather large and complicated system have overlapping jurisdiction.

MUNICIPAL COURTS

Municipal courts in Texas were once known as *corporation courts*, but the name was changed to *municipal courts* in 1969. Although authorized by state statute, incorporated cities and towns set them up. Their status and organization are normally recognized in the city charter or municipal ordinances.

Legally, the municipal courts have exclusive jurisdiction to try violations of city ordinances. They also handle minor violations of state law—class C misdemeanors for which punishment is a fine of $500 or less and does not include a jail sentence. (Justice of the peace courts have overlapping jurisdiction to handle such minor violations.) Approximately 82 percent of the cases disposed in municipal courts involve traffic and parking violations (see Figure 10.2).[11]

The legislature has authorized the city governments to determine whether their municipal courts are *courts of record*. Normally they are not. However, when they are so designated, records from such courts are the basis of appeal to the appropriate county court. (Only slightly more than one percent of all cases are appealed from municipal courts.) Otherwise, where records are not kept, defendants may demand a completely new trial (trial *de novo*) in overworked county courts, where most such cases are simply dismissed. Where it is available, drivers frequently use this procedure to avoid traffic convictions and higher auto insurance rates.

De novo

Latin for "anew"; a *de novo* trial is a new trial conducted in a higher court (as opposed to an appeal). In *de novo* cases, higher courts completely retry cases. On appeal, higher courts simply review the law as decided by the lower courts.

People who favor the court-of-record concept point to the large amount of revenue lost because trials *de novo* usually result in dismissal. Opponents of the concept argue that municipal courts are too often operated as a means of raising revenue rather than for achieving justice. The fact that municipal courts collected $734 million in 2009, lends some support to the latter argument.[12]

Judges of the municipal courts meet whatever qualifications are set by the city charter or ordinances. Some cities require specific legal training or experience. Other charters say very little about qualifications. Judges may serve for one year or indefinitely. Most are appointed

---

[11]*Annual Statistical Report for the Texas Judiciary,* Fiscal Year 2009, p. 37.
[12]*Annual Statistical Report for the Texas Judiciary,* Fiscal Year 2009, p. 62.

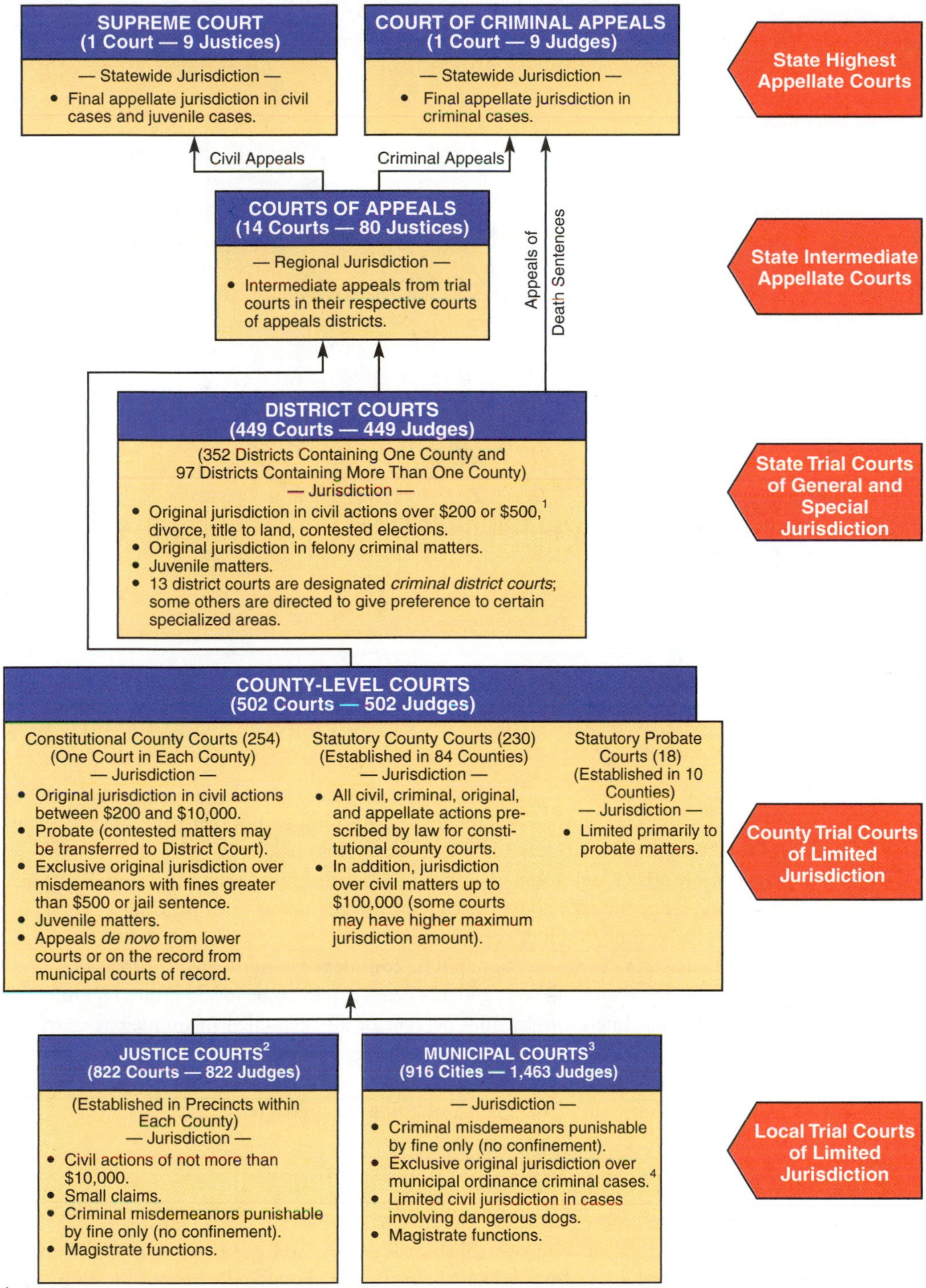

Figure 10.1

Court Structure of Texas. This court organizational chart arranges Texas courts from those that handle the least serious cases (bottom) to the highest appeals courts (top). As you read the text, look for ways to simplify and professionalize the state's court structure.

Source: Office of Court Administration, Texas Judicial Council, *Texas Judicial System Annual Report 2009*. http://www.courts.state.tx.us/pubs/AR2009/jud_branch/1-court-structure-chart-sept09.pdf

How can Texas voters intelligently choose between candidates for so many judicial positions?

[1] The dollar amount is currently unclear.
[2] All justice courts and most municipal courts are not courts of record. Appeals from these courts are by trial *de novo* in the county-level courts, and in some instances in the district courts.
[3] Some municipal courts are courts of record—appeals from those courts are taken on the record to the county-level courts.
[4] An offense that arises under a municipal ordinance is punishable by a fine not to exceed: (1) $2,000 for ordinances that govern fire safety, zoning, and public health, or (2) $500 for all others.

Figure 10.2

Municipal Courts, Categories of Cases Filed, Year Ending August 31, 2009. Notice that the largest slice of the pie chart labeled All Cases Added is for traffic cases. Should municipal courts serve as a major source of city revenue?

Source: *Texas Judicial System Annual Report,* 2009. Activity Report for Municipal Courts (Austin: Office of Court Administration, Texas Judicial Council, 2000) http://www.courts.state.tx.us/pubs/AR2009/mn/1-mn-court-case-types.pdf

What is the argument for making these courts of record?

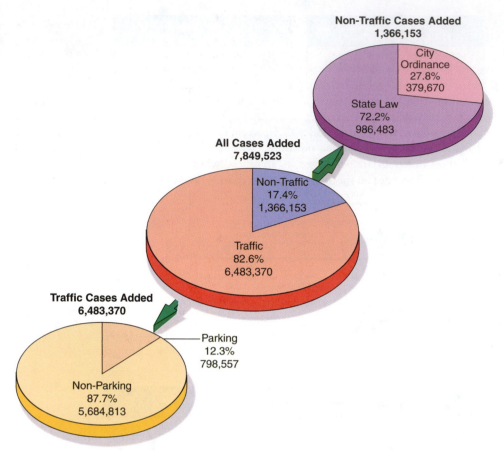

for two-year terms but serve at the pleasure of the governing bodies that have selected them. Furthermore, these judges' salaries are paid entirely by their respective cities and vary widely. Where statutes authorize them, some cities have established more than one municipal court or more than one judge for each court. In view of the volume of cases pending before these courts, the need for a number of judges is obvious.

As will be discussed in the next section, public confidence in municipal courts is low. Out-of-town, out-of-county, or out-of-state residents often expect to be found guilty regardless of the evidence presented. Interestingly, 36.4 percent of all cases filed in municipal courts in 2009 were settled before trial.[13] Such large percentages of settlement could indicate guilt or that many people fear that the legal process will not be fair. It could also indicate people's desire to avoid the inconvenience or expense of going through a trial.

JUSTICES OF THE PEACE

The *justice of the peace* courts in Texas are authorized by the Texas Constitution, which requires that county commissioners establish at least one and not more than eight justice precincts per county (the area from which the justice of the peace is elected for each four-year term). County commissioners determine how many justices of the peace shall be elected (determined by the population) and where their courts shall sit. Changes are made continuously, making it difficult to determine how many justices of the peace there are at any given

---

[13]Ibid., p. 61.

time. The Texas Judicial Council determined that there were more than 820 justices of the peace in 2009.[14]

The functions of the justice of the peace courts are varied. They have jurisdiction over criminal cases where the fine is less than $500. Original jurisdiction in civil matters extends to cases where the dispute involves less than $10,000. They may issue warrants for search and arrest, serve ex officio as notaries public, conduct preliminary hearings, perform marriages, serve as coroners in counties having no medical examiner, and serve as small claims courts. Figure 10.3 shows that approximately 87.5 percent of cases filed in justice courts were criminal and that most involved traffic violations.[15]

All these functions are performed by an official whose only qualification is to be a registered voter. There are no specific statutory or constitutional provisions that a justice of the

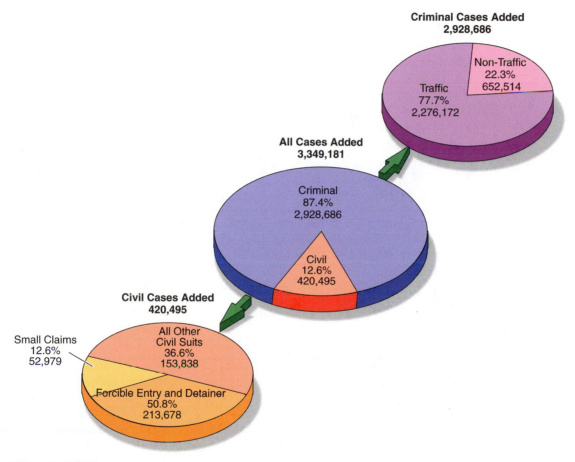

Criminal Cases Added
2,928,686

Non-Traffic
22.3%
652,514

Traffic
77.7%
2,276,172

All Cases Added
3,349,181

Criminal
87.4%
2,928,686

Civil
12.6%
420,495

Civil Cases Added
420,495

Small Claims
12.6%
52,979

All Other
Civil Suits
36.6%
153,838

Forcible Entry and Detainer
50.8%
213,678

Figure 10.3

Justice of the Peace Courts: Categories of Cases Filed, Year Ending August 31, 2009. The pie chart for All Cases Added shows most cases in justice of the peace courts are criminal, and the smaller breakdown chart shows most of these are traffic cases.

Source: *Texas Judicial System Annual Report,* 2009. Justice Courts, Overall Activity (Austin: Office of Court Administration, Texas Judicial Council, 2009) http://www.courts.state.tx.us/pubs/AR2009/justice/2-justice-courts-overall-activity-fy09.pdf

What problems might drivers experience as they seek justice in justice of the peace courts?

[14]Ibid., p. 13.
[15]Ibid., p. 58.

peace must be a lawyer. A justice of the peace who is not a licensed attorney is required by statute to take a 40-hour course in the performance of the duties of the office, plus a 20-hour course each year thereafter, at an accredited state-supported institution of higher education. There is a serious question as to the constitutionality of this provision, since it adds a qualification for the office not specified in the constitution.

For many years, counties in Texas varied widely as to whether they paid their justices of the peace a specific salary or designated them to be paid by fees based on services performed. Some counties had a mixed system whereby some justices were salaried while others were on a fee system. Since January 1973 (Article 16, Section 61, in the Texas Constitution as amended in November 1972), all justices of the peace have been paid a salary, but the salary may vary a great deal from county to county and from justice to justice within the same county.

The public's perception of justices of the peace is often not flattering with many justices regarded as biased individuals, untrained in the law, and incompetent to hold the office.

Skepticism about receiving a fair trial may be a major factor in the settlement of a high percentage of cases before trial (34% of criminal cases in 2009).[16] If a person appears before a justice of the peace in a county other than his or her home, the general assumption is that fairness and decency are the exception rather than the rule.

Justices of the peace who are conscientious, objective, and fair find it difficult to overcome the stereotype, and this negative image is reinforced by the activities of justices of the peace who act as coroners. Though the function of the coroner is to determine the cause of death in specified cases, for decades, stories have been told about such verdicts that left more questions than answers.

Thus, despite changes affecting the qualifications, salaries, and responsibilities of justices of the peace, they still do not inspire confidence in many people. Defenders traditionally refer to the justice courts as the "people's courts" and maintain that elimination of the justice courts would remove the close contact many treasure. To eliminate them, it is argued, would put judicial power in the hands of professionals and would ignore the amateur status of these courts, which depend to a considerable extent on "common-sense" law. This is consistent with the widely held view that government is best when it is closest to the people. Critics counter that incompetence, bias, and stupidity are not justified simply because these courts are close to the people.

COUNTY COURTS

Each of the 254 counties in Texas has a *county court* presided over by the county judge (sometimes referred to as the *constitutional county judge* and the court as the *constitutional county court*). The Texas Constitution requires that the county judge be elected by voters for a four-year term and be "well informed in the law of the state"—a rather ambiguous stipulation. Thus, the constitution does not require that a county judge possess a law degree. Salaries are paid by the county and vary greatly. County courts handle probate and other civil matters in which the dispute is between $200 and $10,000, and their criminal jurisdiction is confined to serious misdemeanors for which punishment is a fine greater than $500 or a jail sentence not to exceed one year.

Because the constitutional county judge also has administrative responsibilities as presiding officer of the commissioners' court (the governing body for Texas counties and not a judicial entity at all), he or she may have little time to handle judicial matters. The legislature has responded to this by establishing county courts-at-law in certain counties to act as auxiliary or supplemental courts. There are 230 of these statutory courts-at-law, with judges elected for four-year terms, in 84 Texas counties.[17] As determined by the legislative

---

[16]Ibid., p. 58.
[17]Ibid., p. 11.

act that established them, these courts have either civil or criminal jurisdiction or a combination of both. Their civil jurisdiction involves cases less than $100,000. Their criminal jurisdiction includes misdemeanors that are more serious than those tried by the justice of the peace and municipal courts or misdemeanors that include a jail sentence or a fine in excess of $500.

The qualifications of the judges of the statutory county courts-at-law vary according to the statute that established the particular court. In addition to residence in the county, a court-at-law judge usually must have four years experience as a practicing attorney or judge.

More than two-thirds of cases disposed in county-level courts are criminal (see Figure 10.4) with cases involving theft and driving while intoxicated or under the influence of drugs being the most common. Civil cases include probate matters and suits to collect debt.

Administration of justice is very uneven in Texas county courts. Although many of the judges are competent and run their courts in an orderly manner, others regard their courts

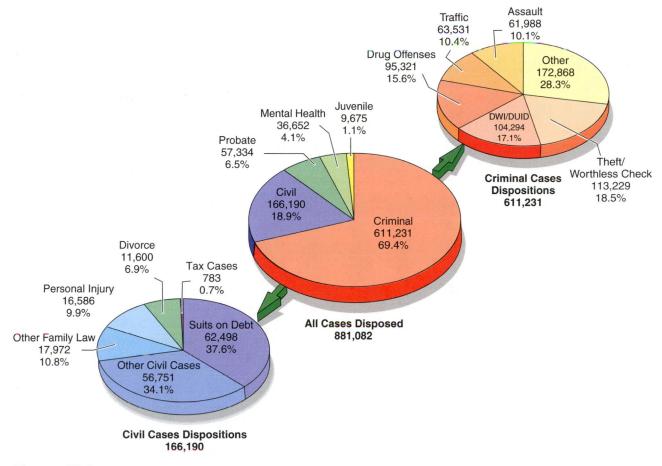

Figure 10.4

County-Level Courts: Categories of Cases Disposed, Year Ending August 31, 2009. The larger pie chart shows that county-level courts mostly handle criminal cases, and the smaller breakdown pie charts show that a wide range of cases are decided by these courts.

Source: *Texas Judicial System Annual Report,* 2009. County-Level Courts, Summary of Activity by Case Type (Austin: Office of Court Administration, Texas Judicial Council, 2009), http://www.courts.state.tx.us/pubs/AR2009/cc/4-co-activity-summary-by-case-type-fy09.pdf

What are the differences between constitutional county courts and statutory county courts-at-law?

and official jurisdictions as personal fiefdoms, paying little attention to the finer points of law or accepted procedures. Opportunities for arbitrary action are compounded if the county judge is performing as a judicial officer as well as the chief administrative officer of the county.

DISTRICT COURTS

District courts are often described as the *chief trial courts* of the state, and as a group, these courts are called the *general trial courts*. The names of these courts and their jurisdictions vary (e.g., constitutional district courts, civil district courts, criminal district courts, and so on, through more than 40 jurisdictions). Currently, there are 444 district courts, all of which function as single-judge courts. Each judge, elected for four-year terms by voters in their districts, must be at least 25 years of age, a resident of the district for two years, a citizen of the United States, and a licensed practicing lawyer or judge for a combined four years.

Texas pays $125,000 of the salary of each district judge, and although each county may supplement the salary, the total must be at least $1,000 less than that received by justices of the courts of appeals.

District courts possess jurisdiction in felony cases, which comprise approximately one-third of their caseload.[18] Civil cases in which the matter of controversy exceeds $200 may also be tried in district courts, and such cases constitute the greatest share of their workload (see Figure 10.5). In addition, juvenile cases are usually tried in district courts. Although most district courts exercise both criminal and civil jurisdiction, there is a tendency in metropolitan areas to specialize in criminal, civil, or family law matters.

It should also be mentioned that the caseload for these courts is so heavy that **plea bargaining** is often used to dispose of criminal cases. Plea bargaining refers to a situation in which the prosecutor and defense attorney negotiate an agreement whereby the accused pleads guilty to a less serious crime than originally charged or in return for a reduction in the sentence to be served. This process saves the state a tremendous amount of time and cost. For example, it is often estimated that approximately 90 percent of criminal cases are disposed of in this way. If plea bargaining were not used in many urban areas, court delays would be increased by months if not years. Although efficient, this practice raises many issues concerning equity and justice, for it often encourages innocent people to plead guilty and allows guilty people to escape with less punishment than provided for by the law.

Likewise, many civil lawsuits are resolved by negotiated settlements between the parties. At times this may be an appropriate and just recourse, yet in many urban areas, there is such a backlog of cases before the courts that it can take years for a matter to be heard and settled. As a result, litigants often choose to settle their case out of court for reasons other than justice.

COURTS OF APPEALS

Fourteen *courts of appeals* hear immediate appeals in both civil and criminal cases from district and county courts in their area. Actually, only a small percentage of trial court cases are appealed; for example, in 2009, the courts of appeals disposed of 11,286 cases, and the appeals courts reversed the decision of the trial court, in whole or in part, only 9.2 percent of the time.[19]

The state pays each chief justice $140,000 and each associate justice $137,500. Counties may pay a supplement to appeals judges, but the total salary must be at least $1,000 less than that of the supreme court judges, and the total supplement cannot exceed $7,500 per year.

Plea bargaining

Negotiations between the prosecution and the defense to obtain a lighter sentence or other benefits in exchange for a guilty plea by the accused.

---

[18]Ibid., p. 36.
[19]Ibid., p. 31.

Appeals judges are elected from their districts for six-year terms (see Figure 10.6) and must be at least 35 years of age, with a minimum of 10 years experience as a lawyer or judge.

COURT OF CRIMINAL APPEALS

An 1891 constitutional amendment established the present system of dual courts of last resort. The Texas Supreme Court is the highest state appellate court in civil matters, and the Texas Court of Criminal Appeals is the highest state appellate court in criminal matters. Only Oklahoma has a similar system.

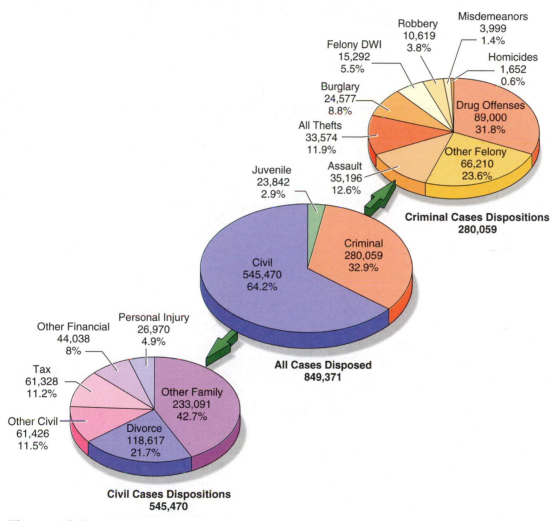

Criminal Cases Dispositions
280,059

Robbery 10,619 3.8%
Misdemeanors 3,999 1.4%
Felony DWI 15,292 5.5%
Homicides 1,652 0.6%
Burglary 24,577 8.8%
Drug Offenses 89,000 31.8%
All Thefts 33,574 11.9%
Other Felony 66,210 23.6%
Assault 35,196 12.6%

Juvenile 23,842 2.9%
Civil 545,470 64.2%
Criminal 280,059 32.9%

All Cases Disposed
849,371

Other Financial 44,038 8%
Personal Injury 26,970 4.9%
Tax 61,328 11.2%
Other Family 233,091 42.7%
Other Civil 61,426 11.5%
Divorce 118,617 21.7%

Civil Cases Dispositions
545,470

Figure 10.5

District Courts: Categories of Cases Disposed, Year Ending August 31, 2009. The pie charts show the kind of serious legal matters that district courts decide. Explain how many of these district court cases are settled by negotiated agreements between the parties.

Source: *Texas Judicial System Annual Report,* 2009. District Courts, Summary of Activity by Case Type. (Austin: Office of Court Administration, Texas Judicial Council, 2009), http://www.courts.state.tx.us/pubs/AR2009/dc/4-dc-summary-of-activity-by-case-type-fy09.pdf

What are the benefits and problems resulting from legal negotiations such as plea bargaining?

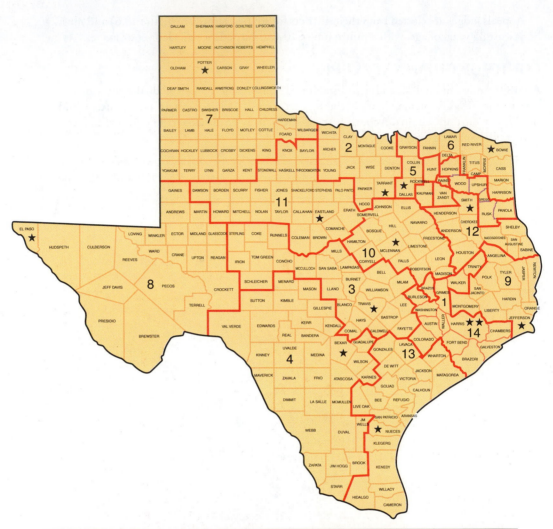

Court No.	Location	Number of Judges
1	Houston	9
2	Fort Worth	7
3	Austin	6
4	San Antonio	7
5	Dallas	13
6	Texarkana	3
7	Amarillo	4
8	El Paso	4
9	Beaumont	3
10	Waco	3
11	Eastland	3
12	Tyler	3
13	Corpus Christi	6
14	Houston	9

Figure 10.6

Appeals Court Districts. Fourteen courts of appeals serve the geographical areas shown on this map. These courts handle both criminal and civil appeals from district courts in their area.

Source: *Texas Judicial System Annual Report,* 2009. Appeals Court Districts (Austin: Office of Court Administration, Texas Judicial Council, 2009), http://www.courts.state.tx.us/pubs/AR2009/coas/1-counties-in-each-district-2009.pdf

How does appellate jurisdiction differ from original jurisdiction?

Although most criminal cases decided by the 14 courts of appeals do not advance further, some are heard by the court of criminal appeals, which consists of a presiding judge and eight judges. In 2009, criminal appeals court judges issued 447 opinions, of which more than 76 percent were "determinative opinions" that disposed of cases, and the remainder were dissents, concurrences, or opinions on rehearings.[20]

Criminal court judges are elected statewide in partisan elections for six-year overlapping terms. They must be at least 35 years of age and be lawyers or judges with 10 years of experience. The presiding judge of the court of criminal appeals receives a salary of $152,500; other judges receive $150,000.

Historically, the Texas Court of Criminal Appeals has generated a large measure of public controversy regarding its alleged "coddling" of criminals. Between 1900 and 1927, the court reversed 42 percent of all the cases it reviewed. As early as 1910, the court was cited by the American Institute of Criminal Law as "one of the foremost worshippers, among the American appellate courts, of the technicality."[21] In the 1940s, largely in response to both professional and public criticism, the reversal rate began to decrease, and by 1966 it was only three percent.

Thus, the nature of its work makes the court of criminal appeals a highly visible court, even if its individual members are not. When the court reverses convictions on the basis of inadmissible arguments by prosecutors or the introduction of unacceptable or tainted evidence, protests are sure to follow from prosecutors, newspaper editorial writers, and civic club luncheon speakers. Remarks concerning legal technicalities are frequent when a conviction is overturned, despite the fact that the real reason for the reversal might be an overly zealous prosecutor or other inappropriate behavior by the state. Ordinarily, a reversal means only that the case will be retried.

The court of criminal appeals has been involved in another controversy. Previously criticized for its "nitpicking" opinions, the court has also been accused of reading unfounded interpretations into the Texas Bill of Rights. For example, in the 1991 case of *William Randolph Heitman* v. *State* (815 S.W.2d 681), the court ruled that the Texas Constitution provided criminal defendants more protection against illegal searches and seizures than the U.S. Constitution. Critics argue that the court should be restricted to opinions that guarantee the accused no broader rights than those protected by the U.S. Constitution. Those supporting the court's decisions point out that the bill of rights in the Texas Constitution is not identical to the Bill of Rights in the U.S. Constitution and therefore lends itself to a different level of interpretation.

It should also be noted that the court of criminal appeals has exclusive jurisdiction over automatic appeals in death penalty cases. In 2009, death penalty appeals made up 6.3 percent of filed direct-appeal cases.[22] Since the U.S. Supreme Court restored the use of capital punishment in 1976, Texas has executed far more citizens than any other state. By 2007, the state had executed more than 400 people (quadruple the number of any other state). Since 1990, the average has been approximately 25 a year (including a record of 40 in 2000).[23] Death penalty cases have led to a number of headline stories, including controversies regarding the use of lethal injection, executing a woman, a 66-year-old man, persons who were juveniles at the time of their crime, individuals who are mentally challenged or mentally ill, those who receive poor legal counsel (including one whose attorney slept during the trial),

---

[20]Ibid., p. 29.

[21]Paul Burka, "Trial by Technicality," *Texas Monthly*, April 1982, p. 131.

[22]*Annual Statistical Report for the Texas Judiciary, Fiscal Year, 2009*, p. 24.

[23]"Retarded Man's Impending Execution Prompts Scrutiny of Death-Penalty Laws," *The Dallas Morning News*, February 15, 2000; "Who Really Deserves to Die?" *Fort Worth Star-Telegram*, January 14, 2001; "Man Set to Die for '92 Slaying," *The Dallas Morning News*, November 8, 2006.

The Texas Court of Criminal Appeals is the final court for criminal appeals in Texas and automatically reviews death penalty cases. In the text, find what percentage of trial court verdicts result in appeal. ☞

How likely is it that a conviction will be reversed on appeal?

Black/Gold Photography

or persons who might actually be innocent of the crime.[24] A heated debate occurred in September 2007, when the presiding judge on the Texas Court of Court of Criminal Appeals, Sharon Keller, refused to keep the clerk's office open 20 minutes late to allow a last-minute death penalty appeal to be filed. Without his appeal, accused murderer Michael Richard was put to death later that night.[25]

SUPREME COURT

The Texas Supreme Court is the final court of appeals in civil and juvenile cases. Original jurisdiction of the court extends to the issuance of writs and the conduct of proceedings for involuntary retirement or removal of judges. All other cases are in appellate jurisdiction. The court also has the power to establish rules for the administration of justice—rules of civil practice and procedure for courts having civil jurisdiction. In addition, it makes rules governing licensing of members of the state bar.

The supreme court consists of one chief justice and eight associate justices—all elected statewide after their nominations in party primaries. Three of the nine justices are elected every two years for six-year terms. The Texas Constitution specifies that a supreme court justice must be at least 35 years of age, a citizen of the United States and resident of Texas, and a lawyer or judge of a court of record for at least 10 years. The salary of the chief justice is $152,500, and the salary of associate justices is $150,000.

During 2009, the court disposed of 787 petitions for review.[26] The justices issued 165 opinions, of which approximately 82 percent were deciding opinions that disposed of cases. The court also reversed, in whole or in part, approximately 67 percent of the cases that came to it from the 14 courts of appeals on petitions for review (formerly known as "applications for writs of error").[27]

The Texas Supreme Court spends much of its time deciding which petitions for review will be granted because not all appeals are heard. Generally, it only takes cases it views as presenting the most significant legal issues. It should also be noted that the supreme court at times plays a policy-making role in the state. For example, in 1989, the court unanimously declared, in *Edgewood* v. *Kirby* (777 S.W.2d 391), that the huge disparities between rich and poor school districts were unacceptable and ordered changes in the financing of Texas's public schools.

---

[24]"Ruling Reopens Door to Injection," *The Dallas Morning News*, April 17, 2008; "Karla Faye Tucker Executed," *The Dallas Morning News*, February 4, 1998; "Questions of Competence Arise in Death Row Appeal," *The Dallas Morning News*, September 11, 2000; "Man Denied New Trial Despite Sleeping Lawyer," *Fort Worth Star-Telegram*, October 28, 2000; "Death-Penalty Trials Rife with Errors, Study Finds," *The Dallas Morning News*, June 12, 2000; "Man Executed for 1988 Revenge Killing," *Fort Worth Star-Telegram*, November 21, 2002; "Death Penalty Debate Reopens," *Fort Worth Star-Telegram*, November 8, 2002; "At Last Name Is Cleared," *The Dallas Morning News*, October 6, 2004; "Old Enough to Kill, Too Young to Die," *The Dallas Morning News*, October 10, 2004; "Trial by Fire: Did Texas Execute an Innocent Man?" *The New Yorker*, September 7, 2009.
[25]"Sharon Keller is Texas' Judge Dread," *Dallas Observer*, January 17, 2008.
[26]*Annual Statistical Report for the Texas Judiciary, Fiscal Year* 2009, p. 31.
[27]Ibid., p. 31.

Juries

Juries are an important and controversial aspect of the American judicial system. Some people argue that juries are beneficial because they allow for community input and the use of "common sense" in the legal system. Others claim that they often do not fairly represent the community and that their reasons for their decisions are often inappropriate or suspect. What is certain is that while millions of Americans serve on juries every year, the frequency of their use is declining, and the overwhelming number of cases in our legal system are not decided by them.[28] The use of juries also varies widely by state and location. For example, the frequency of jury trials in criminal cases ranges from only 11 per 100,000 in Wisconsin to 153 per 100,000 in the District of Columbia.[29]

Supreme Court of Texas

The Texas Supreme Court is the final court of appeals only in civil cases. Such civil cases can have a broad impact on society, and they generate much attention from interest groups when they affect business regulation or corporate liability.

Why would corporations and plaintiffs' attorneys have an interest in making contributions to the campaigns of candidates for the Texas Supreme Court?

GRAND JURY

In Texas, when a person is accused of a crime, the matter is likely to be taken to a 12-member **grand jury**. (Some states do not have grand juries, but in those that do, the size ranges from 5 to 23 members.) An alternative to a grand jury indictment is the **information**, which is used for minor offenses not punishable in the state penitentiary. Filed by the prosecutor with the appropriate court, an information must be based on an investigation by the prosecutor after receiving a complaint and a sworn affidavit that a crime has been committed.

The grand jury does not determine the guilt or innocence of the accused but rather whether there is sufficient evidence to bring the accused to trial. If the evidence is determined to be sufficient, the accused is indicted. An **indictment** is sometimes referred to as a **true bill** by the grand jury, and the vote of at least 9 of the 12 grand jurors is needed to indict. If an indictment is not returned, the conclusion of the grand jury is a **no bill**.

At times, a grand jury may return indictments simply because the district attorney asks for them. In fact, grand juries return true bills in approximately 95 percent of the situations brought before them.[30] This high indictment rate is attributable at least in part to the fact that the accused cannot have an attorney in the room during questioning. Some grand juries, known as "runaway" grand juries, may consider matters independent of the district attorney's recommendation. In general, prosecutors do not like a grand jury to be so assertive and are likely to refer only routine matters to it. To bypass it, the prosecutor may refer cases to a second grand jury meeting simultaneously or postpone action for another, more favorable grand jury.

The process of selecting the grand jury has also come under criticism in recent years. Because it can be chosen by a grand jury commission (of three to five members) appointed by the district judge, the grand jury panel might not be truly representative of the county's citizenry. A total of 15 to 20 people are nominated by the commission, and 12 are selected to become the grand jury for the term of the court. In some counties, grand juries are chosen through a random selection by computer.

Grand jury

In Texas, 12 persons who sit in pretrial proceedings to determine whether sufficient evidence exists to try an individual and therefore return an indictment.

Information

A written accusation filed by the prosecutor against a party charged with a minor crime; it is an alternative to an indictment and does not involve a grand jury.

Indictment

A formal written accusation issued by a grand jury against a party charged with a crime when it has determined that there is sufficient evidence to bring the accused to trial.

True bill

An indictment returned by a grand jury.

No bill

A grand jury's refusal to return an indictment filed by the prosecutor.

---

[28]Henry Abraham, *The Judicial Process*, 7th ed. (New York: Oxford University Press, 1998), p. 119; Tarr, *The Judicial Process*, p. 151.
[29]Abraham, *The Judicial Process*, p. 119.
[30]Ibid., p. 111.

The district attorney may determine whether or not a person indicted for a crime will be prosecuted. Some district attorneys will prosecute only if the odds are high that a conviction can be secured. This improves their statistical record, which can be taken to the voters when reelection time comes. Other prosecutors may take most indicted persons to trial, even if the chances for conviction are low, but this may prove politically costly and can make the prosecutor appear ineffective.

PETIT (TRIAL) JURY

Petit jury
The jury for a civil or criminal trial.

A jury in a criminal or civil trial is known as a **petit jury**. Trial by jury in criminal cases is a right guaranteed by the Texas Constitution and the Sixth Amendment of the U.S. Constitution. Even if the accused waives the right to trial by jury, expecting to be tried by the judge, the state may demand a jury trial in felony cases. Although not required by the U.S. Constitution, in Texas, the parties to a civil case generally decide whether a jury trial will be held. If a jury is to be used in a civil case in district court, the party requesting it pays a nominal fee to see that a jury panel is called. After the panel is summoned, the per diem for each juror is paid from public funds, which can entail considerable expense to the public if a trial becomes lengthy. County courts have 6-person juries, whereas there are 12 people on juries at the district court level. However, only approximately one percent of the cases handled in the county and district courts of Texas involve jury trials.

The method of selecting a jury can be crucial and does not guarantee that a jury will be fair, unbiased, competent, or objective. As of January 1, 1992, the *venire*, a jury panel, is selected from driver's license lists. Texas statutes spell out in detail the qualifications for jurors. They are selected using a jury wheel (much like a lottery-drawing drum) in some counties and by sophisticated computer systems in the populous urban counties. No longer are telephone books, tax rolls, or city directories the basis for juror selection.

Exemptions for jury service, which once formed a long and interesting list, are now severely restricted. Persons older than 70 years of age, actively attending students, and women with custody of a child younger than the age of 10, are automatically exempt from jury service but may serve if they desire. Fathers have sought to claim the same exemption when they are legally responsible for children. Other excuses from jury service are at the discretion of the judge.

In cases that receive a great deal of publicity, a special venire may consist of several hundred persons. Jury selection (*voir dire*) may last days or weeks, sometimes even longer than the trial itself. If either side believes that a prospective juror has a preconceived opinion about guilt or innocence, the prosecutor or defense attorneys may bring a **challenge for cause**. Challenges for cause extend to any factor that might convince a judge that the juror could not render a fair and impartial decision. There are no limits to the number of challenges for cause, but the judge decides whether to grant the challenge.

Challenge for cause
A request to a judge that a certain prospective juror not be allowed to serve on the jury for a specific reason, such as bias or knowledge of the case.

Peremptory challenge
A challenge made to a prospective juror without being required to give a reason for removal; the number of such challenges allotted to the prosecution and defense are limited. Also called a *peremptory strike*.

Statutes also allow challenges of jurors without cause. Known as a **peremptory challenge** or *peremptory strike*, no reason needs to be provided to remove a juror. The possibility exists, therefore, that nothing other than intuition can cause an attorney in a case to ask that a juror be dismissed. The only limitations of this type of challenge occur when the judge believes that prospective jurors are being eliminated solely because of their race or sex. Although peremptory challenges provide lawyers with a great deal of freedom in deciding to remove jurors, each side is given only a limited number of these challenges in each case.

Many lawyers maintain that jury selection is more significant than the actual argument of a case. Some firms hire jury and trial consulting firms to assist in the selection process. Psychological profiles of ideal jurors may be used to try to avoid jurors who might be unfavorable to a client and identify those who might be favorable. For example, the prosecution would quite possibly want a grandparent or parent of young children on a jury dealing with child molestation, while the defense would wish to avoid such a juror. Many trial law firms and prosecutors also maintain a file on jurors from completed cases to help them select or avoid prospective jurors based on past behavior.

Whereas some states allow nonunanimous jury verdicts in both criminal and civil matters, juries in criminal cases in Texas must agree unanimously (this is not required, though, in civil cases). Even if only one juror disagrees, the result is a **hung jury**. In this event, the prosecutor must decide whether to try the case again with a different jury or drop the matter. (Because no verdict was reached with a hung jury, the accused person is not put in double jeopardy by a second trial.) Usually, in the event of a second hung jury, the prosecution will drop the case.

Hung jury

A jury that is unable to agree on a verdict after a suitable period of deliberation; the result is a mistrial.

Selection of Judges

States use several methods to select judges. In fact, some states use different methods for different types of courts. One principal variant is often called the **merit plan** or **Missouri plan**. This plan has been adopted by a number of states in recent years and will be described in more detail. A relatively large number of states elect judges; in some states, the elections are partisan (candidates are officially affiliated with a political party), and in the others they are nonpartisan. There are also some states that provide for the appointment of judges by governors and a few that allow the legislature to make the selections. Table 10.1 compares Texas's Supreme Court selection method with other states selection methods.

Reformers developed the merit plan in an attempt to make the selection of judges less political. This style of selection supposedly bases its choices on the merit or quality of the candidates as opposed to political considerations. Under this system, the governor fills court vacancies from a list of three nominees submitted by a judicial commission chaired by a judge and composed of both lawyers and laypersons. Individuals who are selected hold their posts for at least one year, until the next election. Their names are then put on a retention ballot, which simply asks whether a judge should be retained. It is a "yes" or "no" vote for the candidate with no other competition. Historically, more than 90 percent of such votes result in the candidate's election (or reelection). It is important to note that researchers have overwhelmingly found that this process is no less political than other selection methods and that there is no clear evidence that this process produces different or more meritorious judges.[31]

Officially, Texas elects its judges (although not municipal court judges) in partisan elections. However, such a statement oversimplifies the process and is somewhat misleading. Former Chief Justice Robert W. Calvert referred many times to the system as an "appointive–elective" one. It is quite common for judges to first assume office through appointment to fill vacancies to complete unexpired terms. These appointments between elections are made by the governor with the advice and consent of the senate. In the elections for judicial offices, the vast majority of all Texas judges are reelected unopposed. Furthermore, open competition for judicial posts between nonincumbents is uncommon.[32]

Merit plan

An attempt by reformers to institute a method of selecting judges on the basis of the merit or quality of the candidates and not on political considerations. Under this system, the governor fills court vacancies from a list of nominees submitted by a judicial commission, and these appointees later face retention elections. Also known as the *Missouri plan*.

Missouri plan

See *merit plan*.

[31]For example, see Bradley Canon, "The Impact of Formal Selection Process on the Characteristics of Judges, Reconsidered," *Law and Society Review* 6 (1972), pp. 579–593; Victor Flango and Craig Ducat, "What Difference Does the Method of Judicial Selection Make?" *Justice System Journal* 5 (1979), pp. 25–44; Henry Glick and Craig Emmert, "Selection Systems and Judicial Characteristics: The Recruitment of State Supreme Court Judges," *Judicature* 70 (1986), pp. 228–235.

[32]Anthony Champagne, "The Selection and Retention of Judges in Texas," *Southwestern Law Journal* 40 (May 1986), pp. 53–117; Charles Sheldon and Linda Maule, *Choosing Justice: The Recruitment of State and Federal Judges* (Pullman: Washington State University Press, 1997).

The Politics of Judicial Selection in Texas

The system of judicial selection in Texas, and practices related to it have been under attack. Some critics have alleged that Texas has the best justice that money can buy. In fact, the court system has received negative national exposure from the TV program *60 Minutes*. We shall examine why the courts and judges of Texas are criticized and in doing so will gain a clearer understanding of the political nature of the court system.

Because Texas elects judges, a natural question arises: How knowledgeable are voters in these judicial elections? In other words, are voters cognizant of the candidates and their records in office? Research on the U.S. Supreme Court has repeatedly shown that the vast majority of the public knows little about its rulings and actions.[33] Therefore, if most Americans know very little about the U.S. Supreme Court—the court that receives the most media attention in this country—how much do voters know about state and local courts? A voter in Texas could be asked to vote for candidates running for the Texas Supreme Court, the court of criminal appeals, the courts of appeal, district courts, county courts, and for justices of the peace. Not surprisingly, polls and research indicate that most voters enter the voting booth with scant knowledge of the candidates running for various judicial posts.[34] For example, a poll taken in Texas after a presidential general election found that only 14.5 percent of the voters could recall the name of even one of the candidates for either the Texas Supreme Court or the court of criminal appeals.[35]

In addition to the more systematic research conducted, there is also an abundance of anecdotal evidence indicating that most voters in Texas are unaware of candidates' qualifications or experience. Thus name recognition of any sort can lead people to cast their votes for a candidate. Consequently, candidates with names similar to those of movie stars, historical figures, or public personages are often candidates for judicial positions.[36] In 1976, for example, Don Yarbrough, an unknown attorney, was elected to the Texas Supreme Court. It is believed that many voters confused him with former Senator Ralph Yarborough or with Don Yarborough, who had run for governor. Soon after winning the seat on the supreme court, Yarbrough resigned because criminal charges were filed against him. He was later convicted of perjury and after fleeing the country was eventually apprehended and imprisoned in Texas.

In a similar vein, because voters know so little about individual candidates, they may use party identification as a cue to determine how to vote. In other words, a voter who has no knowledge of the views or backgrounds of the candidates on the ballot may make a choice based on the candidates' political party affiliation. In Texas, this appears to be a common approach for making selections in judicial elections. Historically, Texas was part of what was commonly called the "Solid South" (it was monopolized, like other southern states, by

---

[33]For example, see John Kessel, "Public Perceptions of the Supreme Court," *Midwest Journal of Political Science* 10 (1966), pp. 167–191; Kenneth Dolbeare, "The Public Views the Supreme Court," in Herbert Jacob (ed.), *Law, Politics, and the Federal Courts* (Boston: Little, Brown, 1967); Gregory Casey, "Popular Perceptions of Supreme Court Rulings," *American Politics Quarterly* 4 (1976), pp. 3–45; *Gallup Report* 264 (1987), pp. 29–30; Thomas Marshall, *Public Opinion and the Supreme Court* (New York: Longman, 1989); Lee Epstein et al., *The Supreme Court Compendium* (Washington, DC: CQ Press, 2003).

[34]For example, see Philip Du Bois, *Judicial Elections and the Quest for Accountability* (Austin: University of Texas Press, 1980); Anthony Champagne and Gregory Thielemann, "Awareness of Trial Court Judges," *Judicature* 74 (1991), pp. 271–276.

[35]Charles Sheldon and Nicholas Lovrich, "Voter Knowledge, Behavior, and Attitude in Primary and General Judicial Elections," *Judicature* 82 (1983), pp. 216–223.

[36]"Kelly's Swan Song?" *The Dallas Morning News*, March 2, 2008.

HOW DOES TEXAS COMPARE?
SELECTING JUDGES

There are different methods by which states choose judges. A few states allow their governor or legislature to make the choices. More commonly, states use elections to select their judges. There are three general types of judicial elections. Texas (along with 7 other states) holds partisan elections, whereas 13 other states do not include partisan designations on the ballot. The most popular method of selection is the merit, or Missouri, plan that claims to be less political and combines an initial appointment with retention elections.

TABLE 10.1 NUMBER OF STATE SUPREME COURTS SELECTED BY VARIOUS METHODS	
Merit plan	24
Nonpartisan election	13
Partisan election	8
Gubernatorial or legislative appointment	3
Combined merit selection and other methods	2

Source: American Judicature Society, *Judicial Selection in the States* (Des Moines, IA: American Judicature Society, 2009), http://www.ajs.org/selection/docs/Judicial%20Selection%20Charts.pdf

the Democratic party). This was also true of the makeup of judicial posts throughout the state. However, as Texas became a more competitive two-party state in the 1980s, many Republicans were suddenly elected judges. As one piece of research noted, "In one decade the Republican party moved from a position of being locked out of power in the courthouse to controlling 36 of 37 district seats" in the city of Dallas.[37] This dramatic change has impacted both the Texas Supreme Court and the court of criminal appeals, which, since the elections of 1996, have had a vast majority of Republican members. At the end of 2009, both high courts had 100 percent Republican membership (in fact, only two Democrats ran for the eight seats voted on in 2006). This trend led to a considerable amount of party switching by incumbent judges to the Republican Party.[38]

However, Democrats have had some success at the local level in some counties; they swept all judicial positions in Dallas County in 2006, and surged in Harris County in 2008. Whether the Democratic Party's success in these largest urban counties can be repeated elsewhere in the state remains to be seen.[39]

> "He's got the 'R,'" she said, referring to Republican affiliation, "and he's got a good ballot name. Most voters don't have a clue in these races and his name is a real factor."
>
> —Democrat Margaret Mirabal, describing her Republican opponent, Steven Wayne Smith, in a race for the Texas Supreme Court.[40]

It has been argued that because judges, especially at the appellate level, make significant policy decisions, it is reasonable for voters to select judges on the basis of political party affiliation.[41] Party affiliation may provide accurate information concerning the general ideology and thus the decision-making pattern of judges. However, even if this is true, voting based solely on a candidate's political party can lead to controversial results. Some critics point to the 1994 election of Steve Mansfield to the Texas Court of Criminal Appeals as evidence of

---

[37]Champagne and Thielemann, "Awareness of Trial Court Judges."
[38]Champagne, "Selection and Retention of Judges," pp. 79–80.
[39]"Dallas County Judges Lose Seats in Democratic Deluge," *The Dallas Morning News*, November 8, 2006; "Sweep Revives Debate on Election of Judges," *Houston Chronicle*, November 8, 2008.
[40]"Maverick Spices Up Race, But Is It Too Hot?" *The Dallas Morning News*, October 2, 2002.
[41]Du Bois, *Judicial Elections*.

what can happen when voters do not educate themselves on the candidates' qualifications or background. During the campaign, it was revealed that Mansfield had very limited legal experience and lied in his campaign literature concerning his credentials and personal and political background. He won nonetheless in what many observers attribute to straight-ticket voting (casting all of one's votes for candidates of the same political party).

Because voters often look for simple voting cues (such as name familiarity or party identification), candidates often want to spend as much money as possible to make their name or candidacy well known. In recent years, spending in judicial races has increased dramatically. Candidates need to win two elections: their party's nomination and the general election. In modern politics, this can be an expensive endeavor, and for more than a decade, Republican candidates have dominated the race for campaign contributions. For example, in 2006, a Democratic challenge was outfunded 387 to 1 ($937,000 to $2,549) by the Republican justice[42]; and in 2008, the three Republican incumbents raised more than $2.8 million whereas their Democratic challengers raised just more than $1 million.[43] Not surprisingly, the Republican candidates were successful.

In addition to questions concerning fairness or the advantages of incumbency surrounding campaign finances, many critics (including *60 Minutes*) have also asked whether justice is for sale in Texas. More directly, individuals or organizations often appear before judges to whose election campaigns they have contributed. Do such contributions affect a judge's impartiality in deciding a case? If nothing else, such a system gives the appearance of possible impropriety or bias. An infamous example involves the 1987 case of *Pennzoil* v. *Texaco* (729 S.W.2d. 768). This lawsuit involved billions of dollars and was decided by justices on the Texas Supreme Court who had received hundreds of thousands of dollars in campaign contributions from the opposing attorneys and their respective law firms. In 1998, research indicated that 40 percent of campaign contributions to supreme court justices came from sources with cases before the court.[44] In 2008, Texas Supreme Court incumbents running for reelection received half their support from lawyers, law firms, and lobbyists.[45] More recently, a public advocacy group sued Texas over this system, claiming that it violates due process and the right to a fair trial. The group cited surveys indicating that 83 percent of the Texas public, 79 percent of Texas lawyers, and 48 percent of Texas judges believe that campaign contributions significantly affect judicial decisions.[46]

In 2009, the United States Supreme Court weighed in on the question of judicial bias where litigants significantly influenced the election of judges hearing their cases. In *Caperton* v. *A. T. Massey Coal Co., Inc.,* the U.S. Supreme Court held that the chairman of A. T. Massey Coal had created such a question by donating $3 million to help finance the successful election of a new justice to the Supreme Court of Appeals of West Virginia. The possible conflict of interest arose because A. T. Massey Coal Company had a $50 million civil suit appeal pending before the court at the time; it was later decided in their favor by a 3-to-2 vote with the new justice voting with the majority. A 5-to-4 U.S. Supreme Court majority reversed and remanded the case holding "there is a serious risk of actual bias . . . when a person with a personal stake in a particular case had a significant and disproportionate influence in placing the judge on the case."[47]

---

[42]"Judge Aims to Boot a Justice," *The Dallas Morning News*, August 4, 2006.

[43]"Interested Parties: Who Bankrolled Texas' High Court Justices in 2008?" *Texans for Public Justice*, October 2009.

[44]"Lawyers Give Most to High Court Hopefuls," *The Dallas Morning News*, February 28, 1998, p. A26.

[45]Texans for Public Justice, *Interested Parties: Who Bankrolled Texas' High-Court Justices in 2008?* October. 2009, http://info.tpj.org/reports/supremes08/InterestedParties.oct09.pdf

[46]"State Sued over Judicial Elections," *Fort Worth Star-Telegram*, April 4, 2000.

[47]*Caperton* v. *A. T. Massey Coal Co., Inc., 556 U.S.__2009.*

There is also the possibility that the issue of corporate campaign financing will need to be readdressed. In 2010, the United States Supreme Court decided the case of *Citizens United* v. *Federal Election Commission*. A divided court, in a 5-to-4 decision, ruled in favor of Citizens United. Although the ruling did uphold disclosure requirements for corporate campaign contributions, the majority ruling removed many financial restrictions on those contributions. The decision also seemed to expand first amendment rights of free speech to include political advocacy ads paid for by corporations and unions. This decision could impact campaign finance laws at the state level and begin a debate about whether corporations will have increased influence on elected officials.[48] Currently, Texas campaign finance laws ban corporations and unions from making contributions to candidates participating in statewide elections.[49]

> *Successful candidates for the state supreme court raise large amounts of campaign contributions.*
>
> Do campaign contributions compromise the independence of state judges?

Part of this debate of possible impropriety involves the battle between plaintiffs' attorneys and civil defense attorneys. Texas has traditionally been a conservative, pro-business state. This perspective was usually reflected in the decisions of the judiciary, which often favored big business and professional groups (such as the medical profession). Plaintiffs' lawyers and their related interest group, the Texas Trial Lawyers Association, have made a concerted effort in the past few decades to make the judiciary more open to consumer suits, often filed against businesses, doctors, and their insurance companies. The plaintiffs' lawyers poured millions of dollars into the political funds of candidates they believed would align more favorably with their perspective. Defense and business attorneys responded with millions of dollars of their own contributions. These lawyers, from both vantage points, then often appear before the very judges to whom they have given these large sums of money.

A final major criticism of the current partisan elective system involves questions concerning diversity and minority representation. In 1988, African American and Latino groups in federal court challenged the way that judges were elected in urban Texas, citing the Voting Rights Act of 1965, as amended. It was argued that the *at-large* (countywide) election of district and county court judges in Tarrant, Dallas, Harris, Bexar, Travis, Lubbock, Midland, Ector, and Jefferson counties made elections of minorities difficult because it diluted their voting strength. Attorney General Dan Morales pointed out that African Americans and Latinos made up 40 percent of Texas's population but held only 5 percent of state district judgeships. In August 1993,

> Texas has "the most expensive judicial races in the world and the most politicized judicial races in the world."[50]
>
> —Former Chief Justice Tom Phillips

> "I don't like the current system, and I'm opposed to all the alternatives."[51]
>
> —A Texas district court judge

---

[48] *Citizens United* v. *Federal Election Commission*, 558 U.S. ___ (2010).

[49] *Texas Politics: Voting, Campaigns, and Elections*, University of Texas Press, http://texaspolitics.laits.utexas.edu/6_7_2.html

[50] Quoted in *The Dallas Morning News*, February 10, 1995, p. A18.

[51] Quoted in *The Dallas Morning News*, March 9, 1997, p. A24.

after several movements up and down in the federal court system, the full court of appeals for the Fifth Circuit upheld the current system. In January 1994, the U.S. Supreme Court rejected the appeal of the decision without comment.

In recent years, high-profile victories for minority judges have occurred. For example, in 1984, Raul A. Gonzalez became the first Latino to serve on the Texas Supreme Court. In 1990, Morris Overstreet became the first African American to serve on the Texas Court of Criminal Appeals. In 2001, Governor Perry filled two vacancies on the Texas Supreme Court with minorities (one of these individuals, Wallace Jefferson, was appointed chief justice in 2004).[52]

Overall, however, minorities are still underrepresented as compared to the general population. In 2009, of the state's 98 appellate judges, only 12 were Latino and 4 were African American. In terms of the district courts, only 19.5 percent of 436 (including one vacant seat) judges were Latino or African American.[53] The system thus continues to be harshly criticized by representatives that are of minority groups.

Clearly, the current system is quite political, and many people oppose it for a number of distinct reasons. This has led to repeated attempts to reform the current selection style or change what is permissible in campaign fund-raising. Proposals for change have come from many sources, including chief justices of the state supreme court and a committee formed by the lieutenant governor. However, with such divergent interests involved and no clear alternatives that are acceptable to all groups, very little judicial reform has occurred.

CHAPTER SUMMARY

★ There are two classifications of cases in the legal system: (1) *Civil cases* deal primarily with individual or property rights, and (2) *criminal cases* deal with violations of penal law.

★ There are two types of jurisdiction: (1) *Original jurisdiction* is the basic power to try a case for the first time. Courts with original jurisdiction determine guilt in criminal cases or responsibility in civil cases. (2) *Appellate jurisdiction* is the ability to review the decisions of a lower court.

★ The Texas judiciary has many critics and perceived flaws. The Texas court system is often viewed as too big and complicated. Lines of jurisdiction sometimes overlap. Legislation dealing with court personnel, organization, and procedures is often a maze of confusion. Crowded court dockets usually result in new courts, not court

realignment. Reorganization of the courts along more simplified lines has been urged for decades.

★ Juries are an important aspect of the American judicial system. There are two primary types of juries in the judicial system: (1) A *grand jury* issues indictments that indicate whether there is sufficient evidence to bring the accused to trial. (2) A *petit jury* is a jury in a criminal or civil trial. Potential jury members can be excluded from service through either a challenge for cause or a peremptory challenge.

★ The judiciary performs a vital role in our society. Courts make life-altering decisions and often shape public policy. In Texas, where judges are chosen in partisan elections, the selection of judges is very politicized. The politics of the Texas court system has led to numerous controversies and suggested reforms. Judicial reform in Texas is difficult to achieve and continues to be unlikely to occur.

---

[52]"First Black Named to Texas High Court," *The Dallas Morning News*, March 15, 2001; "Perry Taps Jefferson as Chief Justice," *The Dallas Morning News*, September 15, 2004, p. A4.

[53]Texas Courts Online, *Profile of Appellate and Trial Judges (As of March 1, 2009)* (Austin, TX: State of Texas Office of Court Administration, 2009).

HOW TEXAS COMPARES

★ Many states use a *merit plan* for the selection of judges. Variations of this plan, sometimes called the "Missouri plan," include the nomination of judges by a judicial qualifying commission. After a short-term appointment by the governor, voters are allowed to decide whether to retain the judge. In some states with the merit plan, candidates are allowed to run against the incumbent judge, whereas in others, voters simply vote on the issue of whether to retain or remove the judge. Supporters argue that this judicial selection plan emphasizes qualifications and reduces the effects of campaigning and politics.

★ Some states use a system of *nonpartisan election* in which judges do not run as a party's nominee and their party affiliation does not appear on the ballot. Supporters of this judicial selection method argue that justice is not a partisan matter and that voters should not elect candidates simply because of their party membership.

★ Including Texas, fewer than 10 states use *partisan elections* to select judges. Supporters of partisan elections argue that judges are public officials and that voters should not be denied the right to elect them in the same way that they elect other public officials. Defenders argue that party labels are relevant because they give voters cues about a judicial candidate's political philosophy. Critics reason that campaigning for judicial positions introduces conflicts of interest due to campaign contributions from special interest groups with a stake in court decisions. They argue that party labels, ethnicity, personality, and organization overshadow judicial competence in political campaigns.

KEY TERMS

appellate jurisdiction	*de novo*	information	peremptory challenge
beyond a reasonable doubt	double jeopardy	merit plan	petit jury
brief	grand jury	Missouri plan	plea bargaining
burden of proof	hung jury	no bill	preponderance of the evidence
challenge for cause	indictment	original jurisdiction	true bill

REVIEW QUESTIONS

1. How do Americans rank in terms of lawyers and litigation? How do court decisions affect society?

2. Describe the characteristics that distinguish criminal and civil cases. What is the nature of the parties involved in both types of cases? What are the requisite standards of proof regarding evidence?

3. What is the difference between original and appellate jurisdiction? What types of issues and evidence are considered in each?

4. What types of jurisdiction do the various courts have? What basic elements of a case determine where the case is heard?

How do the qualifications of judges vary from court to court?

5. Compare and contrast grand juries and petit juries. How are jurors selected to serve on panels? How many are chosen? In what instances are exemptions from jury duty granted? What is the function of each type of jury?

6. What are some of the methods employed for selecting judges? How are judges chosen in Texas? Is the process of judicial selection a political one? How knowledgeable is the public in terms of making judicial selections? What are some criticisms of the manner in which judges are chosen?

LOGGING ON

★ The courts of the state of Texas can be accessed at the Texas Judicial Server located at **http://www.courts.state.tx.us/**

★ The 14 courts of appeals can be accessed at **http://www .courts.state.tx.us/courts/coa.asp**. You can access the court of criminal appeals at **http://www.cca.courts.state.tx.us**. The Texas Supreme Court is at **www.supreme.courts.state .tx.us/**

★ Find out who the municipal court judges are in your community. These are judges who will hear cases involving traffic tickets or violations of municipal ordinances. Go to **http:// www.courts.state.tx.us/courts/mn.asp** and click on the link to the Texas Judicial System Directory.

★ The Texans for Public Justice website, located at **http://www .tpj.org/**, has a section devoted to the judiciary branch.

New-Style Judicial Elections in Texas: Examining the Costs and Effects of Electing Judges

Brent Boyea
University of Texas–Arlington

INTRODUCTION

This article examines how the election of judges has evolved in recent years. It raises issues about how increasing campaign contributions and party politics might bias court decisions especially in tort litigation cases. Students should consider whether or how Texas could change its judicial selection methods to reduce the impression and the reality of conflict of interest in its courts.

Following the decision of the U.S. Supreme Court in *Republican Party of Minnesota* v. *White* (2002)[1] and the Court's subsequent decision in *Caperton* v. *A. T. Massey Co.* (2009),[2] attention to the practice of electing judges has increased as a salient concern affecting state courts. The recent decision of the U.S. Supreme Court in *Caperton* featured a question relating to bias when elected judges, like those in Texas, receive contributions and subsequently make decisions involving parties that have made contributions. The U.S. Supreme Court reasoned that elected judges are obligated to recuse themselves when "a risk of actual bias" presents itself, whether or not bias would actually occur.[3] The linkage between contributions and the decisions of judges and fear about the appearance of impropriety featured prominently in the opinion of the Court.

The question of whether judges should be accountable to their constituents or independent from political pressures makes elective state court systems subject to controversy.[4] Twenty-two states, including Texas, use elective methods of judicial selection for their highest appellate court, meaning voters are charged with selecting the jurists of their state courts.[5] Further, among states using elective court systems, Texas and six additional states use judicial election formats that designate the political party affiliation of judicial candidates.

EVOLVING JUDICIAL ELECTIONS IN TEXAS

One prominent yet understated reason for concern about judicial elections relates to the changing nature of judicial campaigns during the last quarter century. Although judicial elections were traditionally low-information and staid campaigns, the new style of judicial election resembles elections for alternative offices, including those for more political offices like the U.S. House of Representatives or a state's legislature.[6] A consequence of this new style transformation has been the development of more expensive and controversial judicial campaigns. For states that assign political parties a formal role in the selection and retention of judges, contemporary judicial elections cause apprehension about the correctness of having judges seek money to conduct their campaigns. Further, contemporary judicial elections are often qualified as mean-spirited affairs that are expensive to wage.[7] The result has caused increased criticism from a variety of opponents from former U.S. Supreme Court Justice Sandra Day O'Connor to advocacy groups such as the American Judicial Society and the American Bar Association.

Twenty-five years ago, opposition to judicial elections and descriptions of judicial elections as noisy, nasty, and costly affairs were unusual.[8] Today in Texas, these descriptions are increasingly accurate. Fitting neatly within the constraints imposed by partisan elections and competition between the two major parties (i.e., the Republican Party and the Democratic Party), plaintiffs' attorneys are often linked with the Democratic Party, whereas civil defense attorneys are conventionally tied to the Republican Party.[9] For the Democratic Party, this development has been challenging with the ascendency of the Republican Party in the modern two-party era in Texas. From 1999 through the 2008 judicial elections, judges serving in the Texas Supreme Court, the highest Texas court assigned to civil appeals, were universally affiliated with the Republican Party.

[1]*Republican Party of Minnesota v. White*, 536 U.S. 765 (2002).

[2]*Caperton v. A. T. Massey Co.*, 556 U.S. ___ (2009).

[3]*Id* at 2.

[4]*Id* at 1 (O'Connor concurring).

[5]Melinda Gann Hall, "State Courts: Politics and the Judicial Process," in Virginia Gray and Russell L. Hanson (eds.), *Politics in the American States: A Comparative Analysis*, 9th ed. (Washington, DC: CQ Press, 2008).

[6]Anthony Champagne, "Tort Reform and Judicial Selection," *Loyola of Los Angeles Law Review* 38 (2005), pp. 1483–1515.

[7]Chris W. Bonneau, "What Price Justice(s)? Understanding Campaign Spending in State Supreme Court Elections," *State Politics and Policy Quarterly* 5 (2005), pp. 107–125.

[8]*Id* at 6.

[9]Deborah Goldberg, "Interest Group Participation in Judicial Elections," in Matthew J. Streb (ed.), *Running for Judge: The Rising Political, Financial, and Legal Stakes of Judicial Elections* (New York: New York University Press, 2007).

EXPENDITURES AND CONTRIBUTIONS TO JUDICIAL CAMPAIGNS

As for the role of money, judicial races in Texas are now expensive affairs. Compared with spending in other states with judicial elections, Texas ranked ninth nationally from 1990 to 2004.[10] A judicial contest in 2006 and 2008 for seats on the Texas Supreme Court cost an average of $515,463, considering the amount spent by all major party candidates.[11] In 2008, when three elections were featured for seats on the Texas Supreme Court, including a race for the position of chief justice, an average election cost $723,426. Relating to the cost of running a campaign, candidates for judicial office from 2006 to 2008 collected an average of $619,659, and winning candidates collected an average of $755,251.[12] Without exception, the candidate who collected more money than his opponent was the victor. Republicans universally collected more contributions and spent more in their campaigns than their Democratic opposition, leading to Republican success in both 2006 and 2008. Although the costs of judicial races in Texas are milder than contests in states like Alabama or Pennsylvania, access to contributions and larger expenditures equates to success in these new style judicial elections.

CONSEQUENCES OF CAMPAIGN SPENDING

Despite the costs of judicial elections, the public in states with elective courts remain strongly in favor of their elective system.[13] Obscured by broad support for judicial elections is the impact of spending in judicial races on participation by voters and political competition. One method for exploring participation by voters is the roll-off vote, which reflects the percentage of voters that do not participate in the judicial office section of a state's election ballot. Spending appears related to decreased roll-off. From 1990 to 2004, roll-off in judicial races for the Texas Supreme Court and Texas Court of Criminal Appeals averaged 13.0 percent, or 9.9 percent less than the average among all state high court elections.[14] Questions about judicial elections also relate to the competitiveness of judicial races. Incumbent campaigns that spend more than their challengers are generally more successful, whereas contests between candidates with similar resources are more closely contested. In Texas, incumbent candidates received an average of 59.9 of the vote, compared to the cross-state average of 70.2 percent.[15] In addition to narrow elections where incumbents seek reelection, judicial races in Texas are nearly always contested (97.6 percent of races) and defeats among incumbent candidates are commonplace (26.9 percent of incumbent reelection bids).[16]

PARTY POLITICS, CONTRIBUTORS, AND TORT LITIGATION

With partisan elections as the device for selecting judges, different groups in the Texas legal environment use judicial elections to promote their causes. With the success of Republican candidates in judicial elections since 1996, voters have placed their support with pro-business candidates aligned with the Republican moniker. In both 2006 and 2008, when Republican candidates for the Texas Supreme Court swept aside their Democratic Party opposition, 13 of the top 20 contributors to high court candidates were law firms engaged largely in civil defense litigation.[17] For civil defense law firms and interest groups in Texas, a financial relationship between candidates and contributors is strengthened by the necessities of judicial elections. Of the remaining contributors in both 2006 and 2008, several were anti-lawsuit groups seeking tort reform.[18] In reviewing the civil docket of the Texas Supreme Court from 1995 to 1998, 50.8 percent of the docket applied to tort litigation.[19] Of those cases, only 46.2 percent were decided in favor of the original plaintiff.

The environment of the Texas court system is well-suited for concerns about judicial elections. With expensive elections that favor Republican candidates and pro-business interests, the Texas Supreme Court reflects a prominent display of the new style of judicial elections. To succeed, candidates for the Texas Supreme Court are required to raise and spend considerable sums of money. With the transformation of the Texas courts largely structured around the battle over tort reform, the influx of money could suggest the appearance of impropriety.[20] Although evidence exists of linkage between contributions and behavior,[21] an equally significant revelation is the utility of judicial elections in Texas for structuring electoral conflict. Judicial elections in Texas encourage a strong association between interests within the law and their representation on the courts; thereby affecting the costs of elections, democratic participation within the public, and judicial representation by pro-business and Republican judges.

---

[10]Chris W. Bonneau and Melinda Gann Hall, *In Defense of Judicial Elections* (New York: Routledge, 2009).

[11]Judicial expenditures data was obtained and is available through the Texas Ethics Commission, http://www.ethics.state.tx.us/

[12]Judicial contribution data were obtained and is available through the National Institute on Money in State Politics, http://www.followthemoney.org/

[13]*Id* at 10.

[14]*Id.*

[15]*Id.*

[16]*Id.*

[17]*Id* at 12.

[18]Torts represent a civil rather than criminal wrong, where "damages" are claimed by a plaintiff (or plaintiffs) seeking an award.

[19]Data obtained from the State Supreme Court Data Archive, http://www.ruf.rice.edu/~pbrace/statecourt/index.html

[20]Donald W. Jackson and James W. Riddlesperger, Jr., "Money and Politics in Judicial Elections: The 1988 Election of the Chief Justice of the Texas Supreme Court," *Judicature* 74 (1991), pp. 184–189.

[21]Madhavi M. McCall and Michael A. McCall, "Campaign Contributions, Judicial Decisions, and the Texas Supreme Court: Assessing the Appearance of Impropriety," *Judicature* 90 (2007), pp. 214–225.

JOIN THE DEBATE

1. Should Texas judges be elected? Why or why not?

2. Can elected judges set aside the interests of their largest campaign contributors when those contributors appear before them in court? Are there ways to hold judges accountable to the electorate without forcing judicial candidates to solicit campaign contributions?

3. How would justice in Texas be affected if Texas used alternative methods of judicial selection such as nonpartisan elections or appointment?

4. How would the Texas Supreme Court's inclination to rule for business in tort litigation be changed if Democrats controlled the court? Can litigants expect fair rulings when either party controls all seats on the court?

Chapter 11

Law and Due Process

CONTENTS

LEARNING OBJECTIVES

* Distinguish between criminal and civil law.
* Describe the important controversies in civil law.
* Identify the major types of crimes and the major factors contributing to them.
* Identify state and local law enforcement agencies and specify their jurisdictions.
* Describe groups most often victimized by crime.
* Explain major law enforcement functions.
* Define a prisoner's rights between arrest and trial.
* Explain the rights of the accused, step-by-step, between arrest and conviction.
* Explain the courts' role in the due process of law.
* Define and evaluate the functions of correctional institutions.

★ GET ACTIVE ★

Deal intelligently with your personal legal matters:

★ For tips on civil legal matters, browse **http://texaslawhelp.org** to get free legal advice, do-it-yourself, and low-cost legal strategies relating to bankruptcy, consumer complaints, divorce, identity theft, tenant rights, utility bills, and a wide range of other topics.

★ Take control of legal issues in your life—learn about family law, tenants' rights, and how to sue in small claims court at **http://www.texasbar.com**. Click on "News and Publications" and then on "Pamphlets."

★ Learn how to deal with identity theft from the Texas Department of Public Safety at **http://www.txdps.state.tx.us/**

Link up with the group that reflects your position on civil lawsuits:

★ Fight frivolous lawsuits that drive up the costs of doing business and support limits on civil judgments with Texans for Lawsuit Reform at **http://www.tortreform.com/**

★ Support workers, patients, and consumers right to compensation for negligence from businesses, medical providers, and insurance companies with Texas Watch at **http://www.texaswatch.org/**

Join with those who share your views on the death penalty:

★ Fight the death penalty by joining Texas Students Against the Death Penalty at **http://www.texasabolition .org/**, or the Texas Coalition to Abolish the Death Penalty at **http://www.tcadp .org/**

★ Support capital punishment by posting your views on Pro-Death Penalty.com, at **http://www.prodeathpenalty.com/**

Work with other student volunteers to free innocent prisoners at The Innocence Project of Texas at **http://www.innocenceprojectoftexas .org/**

Support a vigorous criminal justice system and victims rights with Justice for All at **http://www.jfa.net/**

Civil law
Nonpenal law dealing with private rights and responsibilities.

Criminal law
Law prosecuted by the state, seeking punishment for violations of public concepts of morality.

Most law enforcement is a local matter. Here a city police officer conducts a field sobriety test. Students can access alcohol related regulations at http://www.tabc .state.tx.us/ ☞

How much should the law regulate individual conduct when it impacts on society at large?

There are substantial differences between criminal and civil law. **Civil law** deals largely with private rights and individual relationships, obligations, and responsibilities. **Criminal law** is concerned with public morality—concepts of right and wrong as defined by government.

Yellow Dog Productions/Getty Images

Hence, criminal cases are prosecuted by public officials (usually county or district attorneys) in the name of the public. Civil suits are brought by **plaintiffs**, who are usually private citizens or corporations, although agents of government occasionally initiate civil suits when seeking to enforce antitrust laws, abate public nuisances, or pursue other noncriminal matters.

Perhaps the most important distinction between civil and criminal *law is the way each deals with court findings. In criminal law, the aim is punishment, but in civil law, the **remedy** (the means used to redress an injury) is relief or compensation. For example, criminal law might punish a thief, but the civil law remedy for the unlawful seizure of property might be the return of the property to its rightful owner. Juvenile proceedings, which are regarded as civil rather than criminal, are an interesting illustration of the difference between civil and criminal law. Assigning juveniles to the custody of reform schools is not intended as punishment but as an effort to correct their delinquency. Assigning an adult to the penitentiary, however, is considered punishment.*

Civil Law

TYPES OF CIVIL LAW

Civil law in the states today is based in large part on centuries-old English **common law**. Common law is judge-made law; whether written or unwritten, it is based on **precedents**, or previous cases. If the essential elements of a current case are like those of a case already decided, the judge makes the same decision as was made in the earlier case. The principle of following these precedents is called *stare decisis*, and over the years, these cumulative decisions have fallen into patterns that form the basis of common law. In contrast, statutory law is law that has been passed by legislative bodies and is written in codebooks. Legislatures have incorporated many common-law principles into civil statutes and thereby reduced the need to rely directly on common law.

The family is protected by civil law in Texas. For example, even if a man and a woman have not participated in a formal ceremony of marriage in the presence of authorized officers of religious organizations or judges, the law may nevertheless recognize the existence of a marriage. A man and a woman who live together, agree they are married, and publicly present themselves as husband and wife will have a **common-law marriage**, their children will be legitimate, and the marriage can be terminated through a legal divorce. However, divorce action must be taken within one year of separation, or the marriage will be treated as if it never existed.

Texas courts may require alimony between the filing and granting of a divorce or when one spouse is incapable of self-support and the marriage has existed at least 10 years. As a **community property** state, Texas requires that a couple divide property acquired during marriage, and one spouse is not usually responsible for the other's support after divorce. Children, however, have the right to be supported by their parents even if the parents are divorced. Either parent might be given legal custody of the children, but the other parent may be responsible for part of their support. State licenses, including driver's licenses, can now be revoked from parents who are delinquent in child support.

A person cannot lose title to a **homestead** in a civil suit except to satisfy tax liens, home-improvement loans, mortgage loans for initial purchase of the property, or home equity loans. The protected homestead includes the home and 200 acres of land in rural areas or 1 acre in the city and cemetery lots.

Even in death, property rights are protected because a person may control transfer of his or her estate through a will. If a will exists at the time of death, the function of the courts (usually the county courts) is to **probate** the will, which means to determine that it is the last and valid will of the deceased. If the deceased departed **intestate** (without leaving a will), civil law defines the right to inherit among various relatives; if there are no living relatives, the property passes to the state.

Title to **real property** (land and buildings) is registered in the office of the county clerk, and the legitimate use of any property by its owner is enforceable in the courts. State and

---

Plaintiff
The private person bringing a civil suit.

Remedy
The means to redress an injury, including relief from ongoing injury or compensation for past damages.

Common law
Customs upheld by courts and deriving from British tradition.

Precedent
A previously decided legal case used as a guiding principle for a current or future case.

Stare decisis
The principle of following precedents in deciding legal cases.

Common-law marriage
A marriage without an official ceremony made legally binding by mutual agreement and legally established conditions.

Community property
Property acquired during marriage and owned equally by both spouses.

Homestead
An owner-occupied property protected from forced sale under most circumstances.

Probate
The procedure for proving the validity of a will.

Intestate
Without leaving a will at the time of death.

Real property
Land and buildings.

Eminent domain

Government taking private property for public purposes with compensation.

Charter

The organizing document for a corporation or a municipality.

Writ of injunction

A court order to compel or restrain a particular action.

Right-to-work laws

Laws that prohibit union shop agreements requiring new employees to join a union.

Closed shop

A workplace in which management hires only labor union employees (illegal in Texas).

Union shop

A workplace in which management requires all new employees to join a union or pay dues as a condition for employment (illegal in Texas).

local governments may take private property for public purposes with the power of **eminent domain** but must provide compensation, and owners may sue state and local governments to invalidate certain policies that devalue their property by 25 percent or more. An individual may gain ownership of another's property through "adverse possession" by fencing it and using it for ten years without objection by the owner of record.

The right to inherit, bequeath, sell, lease, or transfer property is protected by law, but the rights of ownership do not include the privilege of misuse. The right to own a gun does not convey the right to use it as a weapon in murder; the privilege of opening an industrial plant does not include the right to pollute. The regulation of private property for public purposes is one of the oldest functions of law. To that end, Texas law includes thousands of provisions and establishes hundreds of courts and administrative agencies to elaborate, interpret, and enforce them. State regulatory agencies include the Texas Railroad Commission, the Commissioner of Insurance, the Texas Finance Commission, the Public Utilities Commission, and occupational licensing boards. Their administrative regulations (administrative law) have the same binding effect as civil law and are usually enforced by civil courts.

Corporations secure permission from the state to conduct business; the secretary of state issues them a **charter**, which defines their structure, purposes, and activities. For corporations chartered in other states ("foreign" corporations), the secretary of state also issues permits to operate in Texas. Civil law holds that upon the chartering of a corporation, a new legal person is created—one who can sue, be sued, or be fined for criminal activity. The attorney general is responsible for bringing civil suits to seek **writs of injunction** (court orders compelling or prohibiting specific actions) to end violations of the Texas antitrust and consumer protection laws.

When two parties enter into a valid contract, the courts will enforce the terms of the contract. However, certain kinds of contracts are not enforceable in the courts— for example, contracts with minors. Texas's **right-to-work laws** also forbid contracts between labor and management that establish a **closed shop** (in which management agrees to hire only labor union members) or a **union shop** (management agrees to require all new employees to join

THE EMINENT DOMAIN CONTROVERSY IN TEXAS

Since the time of the Republic, Texas constitutions, like the U.S. Constitution, have required that owners must be given "adequate" or "just" compensation when government takes their private property for public "use." Just compensation has long been interpreted to mean fair market value. Recently, however, the meaning of public "use" has become controversial. In *Kelo* v. *City of New London Connecticut*, 545 U.S. 469 (2005), the U.S. Supreme Court interpreted public use to include private commercial development so long as it benefits the community as a whole. In its ruling, the Court approved seizing private residences to make way for a resort hotel, office buildings, and posh apartments.

Although this is the interpretation of "use" that was used in Texas and many states, property rights advocates were outraged. They hoped that the Court would ban taking, or condemning, private property for the benefit of other investors. Property rights activists argued that

wealthy, politically well-connected buyers have the power to profit by influencing government to displace homeowners from property to use it for their own purposes.

In response, Texas joined several other states in limiting government's power of eminent domain. A 2005 special legislative session banned state and local governments from condemning private property for economic development projects except roads, parks, libraries, auditoriums, ports, and utilities. And in 2009, voters confirmed these property rights with a state constitutional amendment. However, some property rights advocates are disappointed that local governments are still allowed to transfer property from one owner to another for flood control and urban renewal projects.

FOR DEBATE

When, if ever, should government have the right to take away property legally belonging to a private citizen? Could government operate if property rights were absolute?

the union as a condition for their continued employment). Because of these restrictions, Texas is considered inhospitable to unions.

Civil law is also designed to protect a person's reputation against false and malicious statements. **Slander** (spoken defamation) or **libel** (published defamation) may result in a lawsuit to recover monetary compensation for damage to one's reputation and earning potential. The law effectively extends the protection against libel to vegetables in that farmers may sue people who make unfounded allegations against their products.

Negligence—failure to act with the prudence or care that an ordinary person would exercise—may result in someone's bodily harm or other injury, and negligent persons are liable for damages. If a personal injury suit results, it is a **tort** action (a case involving a private or civil wrong or injury other than a breach of contract).

These are only selected illustrations. Texas civil law fills volumes of printed matter. Much of it is contained in *Vernon's Annotated Civil Statutes* and elsewhere. It is impossible to discuss the state's civil laws in detail—even the most competent attorneys tend to specialize in specific fields of law. More valuable to the average Texas citizen is an understanding of the major political issues surrounding civil suits.

ISSUES IN CIVIL LAW

Tort Reform Insurance companies, corporations, medical practitioners, and others argue that society has become too litigious (inclined to go to court to settle differences). They assert that "frivolous" lawsuits have overcrowded court dockets, and excessive damage awards have unnecessarily driven up insurance premiums and other business costs. Governor Rick Perry and most Republican leaders have joined with groups representing defendants in civil actions, the Texas Civil Justice League, insurance companies, and a wide range of business and medical interest groups to urge **tort reform**.

As a result of this political alliance, Texas restricted lawsuits by prison inmates, reduced frivolous lawsuits, limited liability in civil cases involving multiple defendants, and capped jury awards for **punitive damages** (judgments in excess of actual damages that are intended to punish the defendant). Texans narrowly approved a constitutional amendment to allow the legislature to limit claims for pain and suffering and punitive damages.

Consumer and environmentalist groups, Public Citizen, Texas Watch, Texans for Public Justice, the Texas Trial Lawyers Association, and most Democratic Party leaders generally oppose sweeping tort reform of the type Texas enacted. They argue that isolated anecdotal instances of lawsuit abuse should not be used as a justification to restrict the fundamental right to trial by jury. They contend that only a jury hearing all evidence presented by both sides can make an appropriate judgment in cases of extreme negligence and abuse of an individual's rights. They view tort reform as a big business attack on the laws protecting consumers against defective products and deceptive trade practices and argue that the threat of meaningful civil action is the only way to hold manufacturers and professionals responsible for their actions and force companies to improve safety procedures. Tort reform makes lawyers reluctant to take on costly and time-consuming lawsuits against well-funded corporations.

Tort reform issues are becoming the primary driving force in judicial campaigns. Corporations, insurance companies, health professionals, and frequently sued business groups generally contribute money to Republican judicial candidates who are inclined to interpret the law to limit damages in civil lawsuits. Consumer groups, environmentalists, plaintiffs' lawyers,

Slander
Spoken falsehood defaming a person's character.

Libel
Published falsehood defaming a person's character.

Negligence
Failure to act with the prudence or care that an ordinary person would exercise.

Tort
A private or civil injury or wrong other than a breach of contract.

Tort reform
Efforts to limit liability in civil cases.

Punitive damages
Judgments in excess of actual damages intended to punish a defendant in a civil suit.

Failure to follow industry standards may have caused the April 2010 explosion of a deepwater drilling rig in the Gulf of Mexico, which then caused the costliest oil spill in U.S. history. BP's liability for economic and environmental damages to property, fisheries, wetlands, tourist businesses, and related losses in coastal states, including Texas, were estimated to be well in excess of $20 billion. Texans Against Lawsuit Abuse reported that within three weeks of the spill more than 200 lawyers had brought over 70 lawsuits against BP as a result of the incident.

What kinds of limits should Texas place on tort liability for negligence in such civil cases? What are the arguments for and against limiting corporate liability?

HOW DOES TEXAS COMPARE?
TEXAS'S LAWSUIT CLIMATE

Sponsored by insurance, tobacco, energy, and pharmaceutical industries, the pro-business Pacific Research Institute concluded that by 2008, Texas had the second toughest legal restraints on tort claims among the 50 states.

Go online to see how some tort reform advocates compare Texas's lawsuit climate with other states at the U.S. Chamber of Commerce's Institute for Legal Reform (**http://www .instituteforlegalreform.com/states**).

patient-rights groups, and workers' organizations usually rally around Democratic judicial candidates, who tend to be friendlier to their causes.

No-fault insurance

An insurance plan allowing the insured person to collect from the individual's own insurance company regardless of who is at fault in a vehicular accident.

Liability insurance

Insurance against negligence claims such as those arising from auto accidents.

Liability Insurance Automobile insurance is one area for tort reform that the Texas legislature has not seriously considered. A **no-fault insurance** plan would allow an insured person to collect damages from the individual's own insurance company regardless of who is at fault in an accident. Under Texas's **liability insurance** plan, an expensive and time-consuming legal effort is often required to determine which of the individuals involved in an accident is to blame and thus legally responsible for damages. With no-fault insurance, insurance company costs for court trials would be substantially reduced, and the resulting savings could presumably be passed on to policyholders. Although there have been some instances of insurance fraud, at least a dozen states have successfully used limited no-fault insurance programs. In Texas, major opposition to no-fault insurance, not surprisingly, has come from the Texas Trial Lawyers Association representing plaintiffs' lawyers.

The Elements of Crime
THE CRIME

Crime is a national issue, but despite the popularity of "law and order" as a campaign slogan in national elections, only five percent of crimes are prosecuted under federal law. The activities of the criminal justice system are primarily state, not federal, functions.

An act of Congress provides that federal offenses include crimes (1) committed on the high seas; (2) committed on federal property, territories, and reservations; (3) involving the crossing of state or national boundaries; (4) interfering with interstate commerce; or (5) committed against the national government or its employees while they are engaged in official duties. Otherwise, the vast majority of crimes are violations of state rather than federal law.

As commonly used, the word *crime* refers to an act that violates whatever an authorized body (usually a state legislature) defines as the law. Many obey the law simply because it is law; others obey out of fear of punishment. Nevertheless, it is people's basic attitudes and values that are most important in determining whether they will respect or disobey a law. If a law reflects the values of most of society, as the law against murder does, it is usually obeyed. However, if a large element of society does not accept the values protected by law, as was the case with Prohibition in the 1920s, violation becomes widespread.

Felony

In Texas, a serious crime punishable by state institutions.

Felonies (see Table 11.1) are serious crimes. Murder is the illegal, willful killing of another human being. Robbery is attempting to take something from a person by force or threat of force. It is inaccurate to say that "a house was robbed"—this implies that a masked bandit stood at the front door with a pistol drawn on the doorbell and demanded that the building deliver up all its valuables. Buildings are burglarized—unlawfully entered to commit a felony or theft.

TABLE 11.1 CRIME AND PUNISHMENT UNDER THE TEXAS PENAL CODE

Offense	Terms*	Maximum Fine
Capital murder: Including murder of a police officer, firefighter, prison guard, or child younger than the age of 6; murder for hire; murder committed with certain other felonies; mass murder.	Execution or life sentence without parole	n\a
First-degree felony: Including aggravated sexual assault, theft of money or property greater than $200,000, robbery, murder, sale of more than 4 grams of "hard" drugs such as heroin.	5 to 99 years	$10,000
Second-degree felony: Including theft of money or property greater than $100,000, burglary of a habitation.	2 to 20 years	$10,000
Third-degree felony: Including theft of money or property greater than $20,000, drive-by shootings, involuntary manslaughter.	2 to 10 years	$10,000
State jail felony: Including theft of money or property greater than $1,500, burglary of a building other than a habitation, sale of less than 1 gram of narcotics, auto theft, forgery.	180 days to 2 years	$10,000
Class A misdemeanor: Including theft of money or property greater than $500, driving while intoxicated, resisting arrest, stalking.	Up to 1 year	$4,000
Class B misdemeanor: Including theft of money or property greater than $50, possession of small amounts of marijuana, reckless conduct (such as pointing a gun at someone).	Up to 180 days	$2,000
Class C misdemeanor: Including theft of money or property less than $50, smoking on a public elevator, disorderly conduct (such as indecent exposure).	—	$500

* Punishments may be reduced for murder committed in "sudden passion" or enhanced to the next level for crimes involving gang activity (three or more persons), the use of deadly weapons, previous convictions or hate crimes (motivated by bias on the basis of ethnicity, religion, or sexual orientation).

Theft (larceny) is simply taking property from the rightful possession of another. Grand larceny—taking something valued more than $1,500—is a felony. Regardless of value, livestock rustling (including shoplifting a package of bologna) is a felony. It is also a felony for an adult to have sexual relations with a child less than 17 years of age.

In Texas, it is a crime to disturb game hunters or for a commercial fisherman to possess a flounder less than 12 inches in length. Possession of tobacco by minors is outlawed. Most traffic violations are crimes, and the resulting fine is a form of punishment. Such minor crimes are called **misdemeanors**, punishable by a sentence in county jail or a fine (or both).

Whether felonies or misdemeanors, some criminologists consider such crimes as prostitution, gambling, and illegal drug possession as being **victimless crimes** because their primary victims are the criminals themselves. However, the families of these criminals and society also pay a price for these activities, and they are often linked to more serious crimes.

Misdemeanor

A minor crime punishable by a county jail sentence or fine.

Victimless crime

A crime such as prostitution, gambling, or drug possession that primarily victimizes oneself rather than society at large.

HOW DOES TEXAS COMPARE?
WHEN STATES HAVE DECIDED "THERE OUGHT TO BE A LAW"

★ Tennessee makes it illegal for anyone other than a zoo to import skunks.
★ West Virginia makes it illegal to taunt someone fighting a duel.
★ Texas makes it a crime to disturb someone who is hunting.
★ Rhode Island requires that a driver must make a loud noise when passing on the left.
★ North Carolina limits bingo games to five hours.

★ New Jersey and Texas make it illegal to wear a bulletproof vest while committing murder.
★ In Wisconsin, it is a crime for restaurants to serve margarine unless requested by the customer.*

*Source: Lance S. Davidson, *Ludicrous Laws and Mindless Misdemeanors* (New York: Wiley, 1998); Dumb Network, "Dumb Laws," http://dumblaws.com; see also Barbara Seuling, *You Can't Eat Peanuts in Church and Other Little-Known Laws* (Garden City, NY: Doubleday, 1975).

What causes people to commit crimes? What leads them to adopt values different from those reflected in the laws of society?

THE CRIMINAL

Persons who become criminals vary across the broad spectrum of human personality and come from virtually any of the multitudes of social and economic classes. Yet persons who *typically* commit serious crimes are astonishingly similar. For one reason or another, they are unwilling to accept the **mores** (the beliefs about "right" and "wrong") of the people who write the law. Lawbreakers are disproportionately young, poor, and members of racial or ethnic minority groups; many have acute emotional and social problems. They have little stake in the values that lawmakers hold dear.

With the decline of traditional family life and the rise of single-parent households, many young people are inadequately socialized by adults and generally lack a useful and rewarding role in society. They lack the sense of responsibility that usually goes with a job or a family. The young person who has dropped out of school or who is unemployed has difficulty functioning in legitimate society.

In some neighborhoods, street gangs provide the sole opportunity for social life and capitalistic endeavor. Membership in a gang is a powerful source of approval and a sense of belonging—often a member's only source—and thus gangs become training grounds in crime for successive generations. Lessons not learned on the streets may be picked up from the thousands of demonstrations of crime seen in movies and on television.

Whether as gangs or individuals, persons younger than the age of 17 commit a disproportionate share of crime. In Texas in 2008, juveniles (<17 years) accounted for 17 percent of all arrests for theft, 20 percent for burglary, and 31 percent for arson.[1] Americans younger than the age of 18 accounted for 23 percent of all arrests nationwide for **FBI index crimes**.[2] Used as the barometer for the crime rate, FBI index crimes are murder and nonnegligent manslaughter, forcible rape, robbery, aggravated assault, burglary, theft, and motor vehicle theft.

Many people refuse to recognize that the young are major perpetrators of crime, and others are convinced that they will "grow out of it." The truth is that disproportionate numbers of young people commit crimes and, rather than growing out of it, graduate into more serious crime; yet little is done to rehabilitate juveniles early in their criminal careers. Juvenile courts in Texas provide only limited social services for delinquents, and many have no access to vocational training, employment placement, emergency shelter, foster homes, or halfway houses. Severely limited in resources and facilities, Texas juvenile facilities not only fail to correct but serve as breeding grounds for adult crime.

Far more men than women are arrested for crimes. In 2008, men accounted for 90 percent of Texans arrested for burglary, 87 percent for robbery, and 79 percent for aggravated assault.[3] Perhaps the man's social position and psychological attitudes make it difficult for him to accept certain mores of society. Aggression, violent sports, assertiveness, protectiveness, and earning money are often regarded as essentials of a boy's training for manhood. Apparently, many young men fail to learn the distinction between the kind of assertiveness that society approves and the kind it condemns.

Minority group members are arrested disproportionately for crime. In 2008, 44 percent of Texans arrested for robbery, 33 percent for murder, and 25 percent for rape were African

Mores

Society's strong beliefs about right and wrong.

FBI index crimes

Crimes used as a national barometer of the crime rate (murder and non-negligent manslaughter, forcible rape, robbery, aggravated assault, burglary, grand theft, and motor vehicle theft).

---

[1] Department of Public Safety, *Texas Crime Report for 2008* (Austin: Department of Public Safety, 2009), pp. 30–36.

[2] Calculated using data from the Federal Bureau of Investigation, *Uniform Crime Reports: Crime in the United States, 2008* (Washington, DC: U.S. Government Printing Office, 2009), Table 38.

[3] Department of Public Safety, *Texas Crime Report for 2008*, pp. 26–30.

American. Latinos accounted for 39 percent of arrests for murder, 40 percent for rape, and 36 percent for robbery.[4] Prejudice among law enforcement agencies may account for some disproportion in minority arrests, but it is also clear that the actual crime rate is greater among minorities.

Poverty is among the social injustices experienced disproportionately by ethnic minorities, but it is by no means unique to them. Poor education and substantial psychological problems are also caused by poverty. The poor, regardless of racial or ethnic background, are more likely to commit violent crimes than members of the middle and upper classes.

Crime is more likely in large metropolitan areas. More than three-fourths of all Texans live in densely populated metropolitan areas of more than 50,000 people (called *standard metropolitan statistical areas*). The character of urban life may contribute to crime in that cities are more anonymous, and social sanctions seem less effective there than in rural areas and small towns. Not only is there greater freedom in the city to act criminally, but there are also gangs and other organizations that openly encourage criminal activity. A majority of inmates in Texas prisons were from the San Antonio, Dallas, and Houston areas.

Addiction contributes to crime in a variety of ways. In 2008, some 144,953 Texans were arrested for narcotics violations,[5] and it is impossible to estimate what percentage of robberies, burglaries, and thefts are committed to finance illegal habits. Narcotics and alcohol also reduce inhibitions, and at least one-third of all crimes are committed under their influence.

Most violent crimes are committed by citizens who in one way or the other are on the fringes of society. In many instances, these perpetrators simply live in an environment that promotes despair, low self-esteem, and weak emotional ties to the "legitimate" society. Some criminals consciously identify themselves as victims and rationalize their conduct based on their victim psychology.

In contrast to street criminals, few people think of a successful business person or a college professor as being a criminal; yet these people may stretch the meaning and intent of federal income tax laws, keep fraudulent business accounts, and pollute the environment. But because they seldom rob, rape, murder, or commit other violent acts, they are often punished less severely. Crimes such as bribery, tax fraud, business fraud, price-fixing, and embezzlement are **white-collar crimes**, committed by people who have often benefited from the very best advantages that society has to offer.

The American people have paid the costs of white-collar crime for centuries, but the recent near collapse of the economy has focused the public's attention, as never before, on white-collar crime. High-profile cases of fraud such as that committed by Bernie Madoff, R. Allen Sanford, and officials at Enron and the resulting loss in confidence in the economy and stock values cost victims many times more than all robberies, burglaries, and thefts in recent years.

Despite these alarming statistics and frequent violence-centered news coverage, the crime rate has continued its general decline since 1991.[6] (See Figure 11.1.)

White-collar crime

Bribery, tax fraud, business fraud, embezzlement, and other nonviolent crimes usually committed by more prosperous individuals than those who commit street crime.

THE VICTIM

Although more affluent areas of the state and nation are sometimes victimized by perpetuators of street crime, police reports continue to demonstrate that the greatest rates of victimization remain in the poor sections of our cities. Crime is largely a neighborhood affair and is often committed against friends and families of the criminal. Acquaintance rape, or date

---

[4]Ibid., pp. 20–26.
[5]Ibid., p. 40.
[6]Department of Public Safety, *Texas Crime Report for 2008*, p. 13.

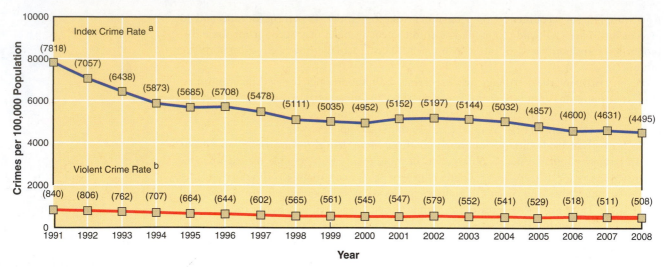

Figure 11.1

Texas Crime Rates Since 1991. This figure shows that the violent crime rate and total index crime rate per 100,000 citizens in Texas have decreased over most of the past two decades.

[a] Total of violent and property crimes (burglary, theft, and motor vehicle theft) per 100,000 population.
[b] Murder, rape, robbery, and aggravated assault.

Source: Department of Public Safety, *Crime in Texas, 2008* (Austin: Department of Public Safety 2009), p. 10.

Why do news media continue to focus on crime at a time when crime rates are declining?

rape, has been well publicized, and at least 46 percent of Texas killers were acquainted with their victims. In fact, 15 percent of all murder victims were killed by members of their own family. Minorities and young people suffered most from crime—39 percent of Texas murder victims were Latino and 35 percent were African American.[7]

Victims have the right to be informed of investigations and court proceedings against the accused and to have their victim impact statements taken into account during sentencing and parole action. The Texas Crime Victims' Compensation Fund is administered by the attorney general and financed by small fees collected from criminals when they are convicted. These meager funds are available to victims with extreme personal hardships resulting from physical injury during a crime. However, most victims are not eligible, nor is there compensation for the billions of dollars of property stolen each year.

TEXAS CRIME CLOCK, 2008

★ One major crime every 29 seconds
★ One murder every 6 hours and 23 minutes
★ One rape every 1 hour

★ One robbery every 14 minutes
★ One aggravated assault every 7 minutes
★ One burglary every 2 minutes
★ One theft every 48 seconds

---

[7]Ibid., p. 21.

Law Enforcement

Defining crime is primarily the function of the state legislature. Yet most of the responsibility for investigating and arresting violators of state law falls on local officials, particularly on sheriff and police departments.

The state system of law enforcement was not planned for efficiency and coordination but evolved slowly as state and local governments reacted haphazardly to changing conditions and circumstances. Lack of coordination makes it difficult to apprehend, try, and rehabilitate highly mobile criminals who may evade the maze of authorities and jurisdictions. Organized crime is particularly elusive and overlaps literally thousands of government jurisdictions. Yet the widespread fear of having a centralized police force has prevented a unified system of law enforcement by either the state or the national government.

STATE AGENCIES

As in most other states, the little law enforcement that is carried out by Texas state agencies is rather specialized. In Texas, the most important state law enforcement agency is the Department of Public Safety (DPS), whose employees are charged with functions such as handling emergency management, conducting driver examinations, collecting crime statistics, operating regional crime labs, and managing narcotics, intelligence, and motor vehicle theft sections. By far the largest single service in the department is the highway patrol, whose major function is the enforcement of traffic regulations along Texas highways, especially in rural areas. The most legendary division in the DPS is the Texas Rangers. Other state law enforcement agencies include the Alcoholic Beverage Commission that enforces state regulations regarding the manufacture, sale, and possession of alcoholic beverages. The Commission on Law Enforcement Officer Standards and Education sets minimum legal qualifications for peace officers and enforces basic training requirements before peace officers (police, sheriff's deputies, and DPS officers) may be licensed.

LOCAL AGENCIES

Large metropolitan cities and counties may spend as much as 30 percent of their total budgets on law enforcement, whereas the Texas state government spends only about 1 percent.

THE TEXAS RANGER LEGEND

Since 1936, the legendary Texas Rangers have also been a part of the Department of Public Safety. Soon after Stephen F. Austin established them in 1823 to defend the frontier, they got their name because they "ranged widely." During the 19th century, they grew from a band of 10 to a semimilitary force of nearly 1,000 Indian fighters. In their hall of fame in Waco, they honor the renowned Captain Jack Hays, "who left the land littered with victims of his fearless spirit." In the 20th century, the threat of Mexican bandits revived the Rangers, but in 1919, the legislature reduced their number to 60 because of findings of numerous indiscriminate killings of innocent Mexicans. They were directly involved in the violence of desegregation in the 1950s and the strike by farmworkers (mostly Mexican Americans) in the 1960s.

The Rangers' silver star-in-a-circle badge symbolizes racial repression to some people. In fact, the U.S. Civil Rights Commission once called for the abolition of the force. Not until Lee Roy Young, Jr. was appointed in 1988 had there been an African-American Ranger in its 165-year history.

In 1993, the first two women were promoted to the Ranger force, but by 1995, both had filed civil rights complaints for harassment and discrimination. After one of them, Cheryl Steadman, resigned, the Public Safety Commission declared her "incompatible" with the force.

The Rangers cling to the belief that "as long as there is a Texas, there will be a Texas Ranger." Their supporters point to Frank Hamer, who led the posse to capture the notorious bank robbers Bonnie Parker and Clyde Barrow. The Rangers also captured the outlaw Sam Bass and the bank robber and kidnapper George "Machine Gun" Kelly. Ranger John Armstrong brought the gunslinger John Wesley Hardin to justice, clubbing him with a Colt .44. When William J. McDonald was sent to quell a riot in a small East Texas town, the astonished mayor asked why the state sent only one Ranger. McDonald responded, "Well, you ain't got but one mob, have you?" Such legends inspired a TV series, *The Lone Ranger*.

Today, the Rangers' small force of detective-investigators is assigned to major felony cases. To some people, they represent the romantic glory of an era long past; to others, they embody the very essence of Texas racism.

Although state government provides certain specialized law enforcement services, the general responsibility of enforcing state laws belongs to local governments.

The major enforcer of law in the county is the sheriff, who is elected for a term of four years. Together with appointed deputies, the sheriff manages the county jail, executes court orders, and apprehends violators of state law in the county. In urban counties, the sheriff usually, by mutual agreement, leaves law enforcement within city limits to the police.

Because the major qualification for office is election by the voters, county sheriffs may be able to win what are sometimes hotly contested elections even though they may not be competent law enforcement officers. Once in office, many are able to combine political talents with large budgets and staffs to exert a powerful and independent influence in county politics. As a result, some sheriffs become almost immune to defeat at the polls and are independent of the county commissioners' courts that approve their budgets.

Constables, unlike sheriffs, are relatively minor county officials. They serve four-year terms and are each elected from the same one to eight precincts as the justices of the peace. Constables work closely with justices of the peace, maintaining court order and delivering legal papers. Constables may cooperate with county sheriffs and city police in general law enforcement and have the power to make arrests.

City police bear the greatest law enforcement burden. Supervised by a mayor or city manager, the police department usually responds to the problem of urban crime by developing a better-trained and more professional agency than the typical sheriff's department.

Some cities have placed their police department under statutory civil service standards; others have established their own merit system. However, charges of police ineffectiveness and corruption continue.

PREVENTION OF CRIME

Peacekeeping operations may settle family quarrels and other disputes that might erupt into violations of the law. However, patrolling streets and otherwise providing a physical presence has a marginal effect on would-be lawbreakers. Because arrest rates are low, the extent of obedience to the law depends far more on acceptance of society's mores than on effective law enforcement.

DETECTION OF CRIME

Detection of crime is often hampered by certain public attitudes. Individuals may believe that the police cannot or will not do anything about crime anyway, so there is no reason to get them involved. Many dislike or distrust authority, particularly that of the police. Others may be unwilling to report a friend or relative. Reporting a crime can itself be a painful process—as few as 1 in 20 rapes is reported. For whatever reason, the majority of serious

PRIVATIZING LAW ENFORCEMENT

Although Texas has not yet become a vigilante state, law enforcement has undergone considerable privatization. Privately financed "crime stoppers" offer informers rewards for evidence leading to arrest and conviction of criminals, and private security officers outnumber government agents almost three to one. They supplement and support public forces but often are not as well trained or subject to the same procedural restrictions to safeguard individual constitutional rights.

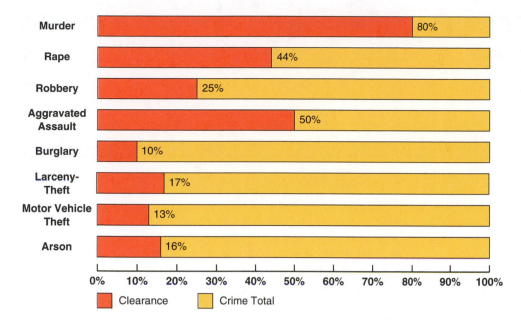

Figure 11.2

Clearance Rates for Major Texas Crimes. Violent crimes are more likely to be cleared by arrest than property crimes.

Source: Department of Public Safety, *Texas Crime Report for 2008* (Austin: Department of Public Safety 2009), p. 12.

Are the clearance rates for violent crimes better because law enforcement devotes more resources to solving them, or are arrests easier because such crimes are most likely to be committed by acquaintances or other apparent suspects and in the presence of witnesses?

crimes go unreported. Although there is a tendency to blame police, prisons, courts, or legal "technicalities" for the large numbers of unpunished criminals, *the most serious failure in the criminal justice system is citizens' unwillingness to report crime.*

ENFORCEMENT OF LAW

Even for crimes known to them, police have a poor record of solving crimes by arrest. Only about 18 percent of reported felonies in Texas result in an arrest (see Figure 11.2). Low rates of arrest result from the collection of inadequate evidence, and many of the individuals arrested are not convicted—due in part to limited funds, equipment, personnel, and training of police officers.

GATHERING EVIDENCE

At certain crucial points in the investigation and apprehension of suspected criminals, society has for centuries demanded various external checks and limits on law enforcement agencies. To protect the innocent and the presumption of innocence for individuals accused of crime, procedural and constitutional safeguards are essential. The Fourth Amendment to the U.S. Constitution prohibits "unreasonable" searches, but warrants are not always required. Warrantless searches of prisoners (to protect law enforcement personnel) and pedestrians (to protect the public safety) are permitted. Motor vehicles may be searched without warrants because it is simply impractical to require a warrant when evidence may be driven away.

For the most part, the reasonableness of a search is determined by supposedly neutral and independent courts, which supervise the law enforcement agencies that propose to intrude on private premises in search of evidence. In Texas, justices of the peace usually determine **probable cause**—whether the facts and circumstances are sufficient to lead a "reasonable person" to believe that evidence is probably contained on the premises and thus justify a warrant for the invasion of privacy.

To make the Fourth Amendment effective, the U.S. Supreme Court, in the 1914 case of *Weeks* v. *United States* (232 U.S. 383), established the **exclusionary rule**, under which

Probable cause

Sufficient information to convince a reasonably cautious person that a search or arrest is justified.

Exclusionary rule

The requirement that illegally obtained evidence not be used against the accused.

evidence acquired in violation of the Fourth Amendment could not be admitted in federal courts. The decision discouraged law enforcement agents in federal cases from engaging in illegal invasions of privacy because the evidence obtained could not be used against the accused. In the 1961 case of *Mapp* v. *Ohio* (367 U.S. 643), the U.S. Supreme Court held the exclusionary rule also to be essential to the "due process of law" that the Fourteenth Amendment requires states to respect.

ARREST

Like privacy, an individual's liberty is a particularly valued right. The mere fact that a person has been arrested may damage his or her reputation in the community. In short, arrest is in itself a form of punishment.

To prevent arrests for frivolous causes, the courts generally supervise police in the arrest of suspects. In Texas, magistrates issue a warrant to take a person into custody when they are presented with probable cause that the person has committed a crime. Warrants are also issued when a prosecutor files for a *writ of information* (usually charging a person for a misdemeanor) or when a *grand jury* issues an *indictment* (usually for a felony).

Police officers may make arrests without a warrant when they have probable cause and when circumstances do not permit their obtaining one. They may make arrests for crimes they witness or those that are reported directly to them by a witness. Although an arrest resulting from investigation is technically illegal without a warrant, police have considerable flexibility. By contrast, *citizens' arrests* are legal only for felonies or other offenses against the public peace committed in the citizens' presence.

DETENTION

The time between a person's arrest and appearance before a magistrate is critical. Historically, this period was a time of much police abuse, during which law enforcement officers sometimes used physical violence or "third degree" psychological tactics. Police would also delay taking a suspect before a magistrate, where probable cause for arrest would have to be shown and the suspect informed of certain constitutional rights. As a result, law enforcement agents were able to extract confessions or other evidence from the frightened and sometimes abused suspects. Confessions obtained in this manner are unreliable and violate the Fifth and Fourteenth Amendments of the U.S. Constitution.

In Arizona, the Phoenix police unknowingly set the stage for a far-reaching U.S. Supreme Court decision when they extracted a confession from Ernesto Miranda, a young Latino. Having only an eighth-grade education, the suspect could not possibly have been expected to know his constitutional right to remain silent, and his interrogators did not so inform him. The Court declared that confessions such as Miranda's could not be admitted as evidence. Its ruling established guidelines for informing a person of the following rights before a confession could be admitted as evidence:

1. The suspect has the right to remain silent.
2. Any statement made may be used against the suspect.
3. The suspect has the right to an attorney, whether or not he or she can afford one.

A suspect may knowingly waive these rights and agree to talk to police.

The decision of the U.S. Supreme Court in *Miranda* v. *Arizona* (384 U.S. 436, 1966) was one of its most controversial, and many people claimed that the Court was "coddling criminals." Others argued that no system worth preserving should have to fear an accused person's being aware of basic constitutional rights.

Despite the outcry and controversy, there is little evidence that conviction rates have declined as a result of the *Miranda* decision. It is less sweeping than has been assumed—its purpose is to ensure that confessions are voluntary when they result *from interrogation.* An interrogation occurs when police focus questioning on a primary suspect, expecting to extract a confession. Information resulting from unsolicited confessions or general questioning is admissible. Admitting an improper confession at trial does not automatically result in reversal of conviction—if other evidence is sufficient to convict.[8]

It is often justices of the peace, among the least qualified judges, who supervise law enforcement agencies at critical stages. They issue warrants and protect privacy, liberty, presumption of innocence, and the right to remain silent. Whatever the legal doctrine may provide, the quality of justice depends on the caliber of those who administer it.

STEPPING BACK FROM THE MIRANDA RULE

The U.S. Supreme Court has carved out many exceptions to strict adherence to the Miranda rule. Here are some examples:

★ When a confession given without the Miranda warning leads to witnesses, their testimony may be used.
★ A confession made without Miranda warnings may be used as evidence of perjury if later statements by the accused contradict it.
★ When the public's safety is endangered, Miranda warnings are unnecessary.[9]
★ When an attorney has been appointed, police may interrogate a suspect even before he has the opportunity to consult with his court-appointed attorney unless he specifically requests that his attorney be present *during* the interrogation.[10]
★ Suspects may not invoke the right to remain silent by simply remaining silent.[11]
★ Police do not need to honor a previous request for an attorney if a suspect is rearrested at least 14 days later as part of the same investigation.[12]
★ Police may ad lib the Miranda warnings without using the precise language provided in the 1966 decision.[13]

GO ONLINE

Learn how police work with and get around the Miranda decision at **http://www.prospect.org/cs/articles?article=the_assault_on_miranda** and **http://www.davekopel.org/CJ/OpEds/Miranda.htm**, originally published in the National Review Online.

[8]*Arizona* v. *Fulminante,* 499 U.S. 279 (1991).
[9]*New York* v. *Quarles,* 467 U.S. 649 (1984).
[10]*Montejo* v. *Louisiana,* 556 U.S. ___ (2009).
[11]*Berghuis* v. *Thompkins,* 560 U.S.___(2010), 08-1470.
[12]*Maryland* v. *Shatzer,* 559 U.S.___ (2010), 08-680.
[13]*Florida* v. *Powell,* 559 U.S.___(2010), 08-1175.

The Courts

It is in the courts that the most general concept of justice and the broadest norms of society are enforced against specific individuals. The courts must blend two conflicting goals of society: (1) to protect society according to the state's legal concepts of right and wrong and (2) to protect the rights of the individual charged with wrongdoing. As a result, elaborate traditions of court process and procedure have developed over the centuries, from a time long before the American states were colonies in the British Empire. Many of these traditional procedures came from the English experience; others were developed more recently in the American states. Some court procedures have been written into state and national constitutions and statutes; others are included in written and unwritten traditional codes of court process. Such procedures are designed to promote justice and protect the individual from the government, and together they constitute what is called **due process**.

Unfortunately, the guaranteed rights of the accused are very nearly meaningless unless courts, prosecutors, and law enforcement agents are careful to protect them. In practice, due process is frequently more an abstract philosophy of how things should be than how they really are.

PRETRIAL COURT ACTIVITIES

After arrest, the suspect is jailed while reports are completed and the district attorney's office decides whether or not to file charges and what bail to recommend. As soon as is practical, the accused is presented before a justice of the peace or other magistrate. This initial **arraignment** has four major purposes:

1. To explain the charges against the accused.
2. To remind the suspect of the rights to remain silent and to be represented by counsel and to request a written acknowledgment that the Miranda warning was given and understood.
3. To set bail.
4. To inform the accused of the right to an examining trial.

The suspect is usually told the charges multiple times—upon arrest, in the arraignment, and again in subsequent proceedings. Being told the nature of charges is one of the most fundamental aspects of due process. Because the states have governments of "laws and not men," a person should never be held in custody on whim but only for *legal* cause. In other words, there must be sufficient justification—probable cause—for being held. If the law no longer justifies imprisonment, counsel may secure release through a **writ of habeas corpus**, a court order requiring that the prisoner be presented in person and legal cause shown for imprisonment. The right to counsel is vital to the accused—an attorney should clearly understand the constitutional rights of the accused and be familiar with the intricacies of the law and the courts. So important is the assistance of counsel that many suspects will contact an attorney even before they first appear in front of a magistrate.

Yet this right to counsel has never been absolute. Guaranteed in both the U.S. and Texas constitutions, the right to counsel had traditionally been interpreted to mean that the accused has a right to counsel if he or she could afford one. In 1932, the U.S. Supreme Court ruled that the Sixth Amendment requires state courts to appoint counsel for the poor, but only in capital cases.[14] Later the Court extended an indigent's right to counsel in other felony cases and in serious misdemeanor cases in which imprisonment might be involved, but it does not extend to petty offenses such as traffic violations.[15] However, the right to court-appointed counsel does not necessarily guarantee equal justice for the poor.

Due process

The following of proper legal procedures. Due process is essential to guaranteeing fairness before the government may deprive a person of life, liberty, or property.

Arraignment

A prisoner's initial appearance before a magistrate in which the charges and basic rights (to an attorney and bail) are explained.

Writ of habeas corpus

A court order requiring that a prisoner be presented in person and that legal cause be shown for imprisonment; also used in some civil cases.

---

[14] *Powell* v. *Alabama*, 287 U.S. 45 (1932).

[15] *Gideon* v. *Wainwright*, 372 U.S. 335 (1963); *Argersinger* v. *Hamlin*, 407 U.S. 25 (1972).

QUALITY LEGAL REPRESENTATION

Some Texas counties still rely on an *assigned counsel system* in which private lawyers are selected and paid on a case-by-case basis or in which they work by contract to defend a group of indigent cases assigned to them. Paid by the county, some attorneys find that time spent defending poor people does not significantly advance either their practice or their income. Other attorneys have developed highly successful practices based on indigent defense, and some judges have been charged with cronyism for assigning cases to lawyers who have contributed to their political campaigns.

A number of states have established a system of salaried full-time public defenders to serve as advocates for indigents in serious criminal cases. Supporters of a *public defender system* have argued that it is more professional and less costly than the assigned counsel system. Texas recently gave counties the option of establishing a public defender system or continuing to use an assigned counsel system. Despite the reforms adopted in some counties, the quality of indigent representation varies tremendously from county to county and from defendant to defendant.

Nor does having privately paid counsel necessarily guarantee adequate representation. Death penalty opponents have begun to challenge the quality of legal representation and found that disbarred and suspended attorneys have represented clients in Texas murder cases. Some failed to present evidence of mental retardation or challenge racist assertions by a prosecution psychologist. The federal Fifth Circuit Court of Appeals reversed one conviction because the defendant's attorney repeatedly fell asleep during the trial.

FOR DEBATE

Why should taxpayers pay for the defense of accused criminals?

GO ONLINE

Search for indigent defense at **http://www.courts.state .tx.us**

Bail is the security deposit required for the release of a suspect awaiting trial. Some persons released on bail fail to appear in court, and their security deposit is forfeited. Others commit still more crimes while out on bail. However, the legal system presumes that an individual is innocent unless convicted, and bail supports this assumption by permitting the accused to resume a normal professional and social life while preparing a defense.

Although bail may be reset or denied following indictment, the Texas Constitution guarantees the right to bail immediately after arrest, except where proof is "evident" in capital cases or when the defendant is being charged with a third felony after two previous felony convictions. The state constitution allows bail to be denied if the defendant is charged with committing a felony while released on bail or under indictment for another felony.

In practice, the right to bail exists only for those who can afford it. Private licensed bonding companies may be willing to post bond for a fee (usually 10 to 50% of the bail as set by the court), which, unlike bail, is not refunded. Many defendants cannot afford even this fee, and unless released on **personal recognizance** (the defendant's personal promise to appear), the prisoner will await trial in jail. Bail was designed to free a person not yet found guilty of a crime, but some innocent people await trial in jail, unable to work, carry on their family life, or gather evidence for their own defense. In our criminal justice system, bail procedures, more than any other single practice, punish the poor for their poverty. Professional criminals released on bail often return to work. They may even commit more crimes to pay their attorneys' retainers and bonding fees.

Bail
The security required for release of a suspect awaiting trial.

Personal recognizance
A defendant's personal promise to appear; sometimes allowed instead of cash bail or bond.

One court-appointed attorney fell asleep during trial.

Can you think of arguments for or against using public defender systems?

Examining trial

An initial court hearing to determine if there is sufficient evidence to send a case to a grand jury.

Although few defendants request one, the accused has the right to an **examining trial** in felony cases. A justice of the peace reviews the facts and decides whether the case should be bound over to a grand jury. Or, if the facts warrant, the charges may be dismissed or bail adjusted.

FORMAL CHARGES

Although indictment sometimes precedes arrests, a felony case is usually bound over to a grand jury for indictment following arraignment. A grand jury should not be confused with a petit, or trial, jury. Grand juries do not determine a person's guilt or innocence as trial juries do; the accused may not even be asked to appear before the grand jury. Instead of hearing the defense, the grand jury primarily weighs the evidence in the hands of the prosecutor to determine whether there is a *prima facie* **case** (sufficient evidence to convict when the case is taken to trial). If it determines the existence of such evidence, the grand jury issues an indictment (a *true bill*), which constitutes formal charges that enable the case to go to trial (a *no-bill* is a refusal to indict).

Prima facie case

Sufficient evidence to convict if unchallenged at trial; the amount of evidence necessary to indict a defendant.

A *prima facie* case is necessary to bring formal charges because if the prosecutor does not have enough evidence to convict, there is no point in bringing the case to trial. Trying a case on flimsy evidence not only costs the taxpayers money but also causes the accused to suffer needless expense, lost time, and a damaged reputation. The right to a grand jury indictment is guaranteed in both the Texas and federal courts to protect the rights of innocent citizens against harassment on unjustified charges.

In practice, grand juries are usually made up of ordinary citizens who have never been trained to critically evaluate cases and so usually act as a rubber stamp for the prosecutors. Some states have abolished the grand jury in favor of writs of information in which a judge evaluates the evidence to determine if there is sufficient evidence to go to trial. Texas guarantees the right to indictment in all felony cases but uses the writ of information to charge people with misdemeanors.

PRETRIAL HEARINGS

After the indictment, the defendant has the right to yet another hearing, sometimes called the *second arraignment*. A district judge (rather than a justice of the peace) presides as the formal indictment is read, and the defendant enters a plea. If the plea is guilty, a later hearing is scheduled to set punishment. Most often the defendant pleads not guilty at this point, and the case is placed on the **docket** (schedule of court activity) for subsequent trial. A variety of motions may be presented, including a motion for delay (**continuance**) or for the suppression of certain evidence. Other subjects of pretrial hearings concern possible insanity or **change of venue** (change in the site of a trial). A person cannot be held morally and criminally responsible for a crime if at the time of the offense, mental illness made it impossible for the person to recognize that it was wrong. There is considerable controversy as to the effects of mental disorder, so professional testimony may be necessary to establish legal insanity, and psychiatric opinion is frequently divided. It is rare that the courts find a defendant not guilty by reason of insanity.

Docket

The schedule of court activity.

Continuance

Delay of a trial.

Change of venue

A change in the location of a trial.

A change of venue may be necessary when the news media have so publicized a case that it becomes impossible to select an unbiased jury locally or when inflamed public opinion may prevent a fair trial. A real tension exists between the rights of the free press and the rights of the accused, and in a modern society, the rights of the accused can be protected only with great vigilance by our courts.

PLEA BARGAINING

Ideally, the trial is the final step in society's elaborate guarantees of due process. Only through the deliberations in the courtroom can our system's genuine concern for justice emerge. Yet for most people who are accused of a crime, their final day in court never comes. In fact, the system is designed to discourage and even punish those who choose to exercise their right to trial. Most cases end in *plea bargaining*—a secret bargaining session with the prosecutor.

Facing overcrowded dockets and limited staff, prosecuting attorneys usually meet with the accused and offer a deal in exchange for a plea of guilty, which eliminates the need for a trial. The usual deal is to offer to drop some of the charges, to recommend probation or a lighter sentence, or to charge the accused with a lesser crime. The prosecutor may agree to delay prosecution (this is known as *deferred adjudication*) and later drop charges if the defendant agrees to meet conditions like those required under probation. Such plea agreements save tax money and court time and may be useful to law enforcement, as when certain defendants are given a lighter sentence in exchange for testifying against fellow criminals who have committed more serious crimes.

On the other hand, the guilty obviously benefit from plea bargaining because they are not punished for the full measure of their crimes. Justice is thus exchanged for a cheaper system that benefits the guilty. Defense attorneys frequently encourage their clients to accept the bargain in order to save them the effort of a courtroom trial, and some become as much agents for the prosecution as advocates for the defense. The innocent and those who are unwilling to trade their rights for a secret backroom bargain take the chance of being punished more severely for demanding a trial.

THE TRIAL

Unless the defense waives the right to a trial by jury, the first major step is the selection of a jury. The right to a trial by jury is often regarded as one of the most valuable rights available in the criminal justice system. In fact, every state provides for trial by jury in all but the most minor cases, and Texas goes even further, providing for the right to trial by jury in every criminal case.[16]

Nevertheless, the right to trial by jury in a criminal case is one of the most frequently waived rights, especially in cases where the defendant is an object of community prejudice (a member of an unpopular political group or ethnic minority) or if the alleged crime is particularly outrageous. If the right to a jury trial is waived, the presiding judge determines the verdict. Regardless of whether or not a person chooses to exercise it, the right to trial by jury remains a valuable alternative to decisions by possibly arbitrary judges.

During initial questioning of prospective jurors (***voir dire** questioning*), they may be asked about possible biases, their previous knowledge of the case, or any opinions they may have formed. Either the prosecution or the defense may challenge a prospective juror for reason of prejudice, and the presiding judge will evaluate that challenge. Furthermore, both the prosecution and the defense may dismiss a number of jurors by peremptory challenges (without cause), also called *strikes*, depending on the kind of case involved. Considering occupations, social status, and attitudes of possible jurors, experienced attorneys and prosecutors use peremptory challenges to select a friendly jury; some have been known to use psychologists to assist in the selection process, and lucrative consulting businesses have developed to assist attorneys in jury selection.

All English-speaking countries have developed an **adversary system**, in which two parties to the case (the prosecution and the defense in criminal cases) arm themselves with whatever evidence they can muster and battle in court, under the rules of law, to final judgment. An adversary system cannot operate fairly unless both the defense and the prosecution have an equal opportunity to influence the decision of the court. Hence procedural guarantees are designed to ensure that both sides have equal access to an understanding of the laws and the

Voir dire questioning
The initial questioning of jurors to determine possible biases.

Adversary system
The legal system used in English-speaking countries in which two contesting parties present opposing views and evidence in a court of law.

[16]The U.S. Supreme Court held in the case of *Duncan* v. *Louisiana,* 391 U.S. 145, 149 (1968), that trial by jury is an essential part of due process when state criminal proceedings involve more than petty offenses.

evidence. So that equal knowledge of the laws is guaranteed, the legal knowledge of the prosecution is balanced by the right of the defendant to have legal counsel. Since the government (in the person of the prosecutor) has the power to seize evidence and to force witnesses to testify under oath, the defense must be given that same power (called **compulsory process**).

Compulsory process

A procedure to subpoena witnesses in court.

In the adversary system, each side can challenge the material evidence and cross-examine witnesses who have been presented by the opposition. Only evidence that is presented in court can be evaluated. The fact that both parties to a case have opposite biases and intentions means that they have an interest in concealing evidence that could benefit the opposition.

Because it is the legal responsibility of the prosecutor to prove guilt beyond a reasonable doubt (the burden of proof lies with the state), the counsel for the defense has no responsibility to present evidence of the defendant's guilt, nor can the defendant be forced to take the stand to testify. On the other hand, since the responsibility of the prosecutor is to convict the guilty rather than the innocent, it is a violation of due process for the government to withhold evidence that could benefit the accused—but it happens. There is no way of knowing how many unjust verdicts have been decided because all the evidence was not presented.

In jury trials, once the evidence has been presented, the judge reads the charge to the jury—the judge's instructions about how the law applies in the case. The judge will instruct the jurors to ignore such things as hearsay testimony and other illegal evidence to which they may have been exposed during the course of the trial. (Realistically, however, it is difficult for jurors to erase from their minds the impact of illegal testimony.) The judge is supposedly neutral and cannot comment on the weight of the evidence that has been presented.

After the judge's charge to the jury, the prosecution and defense are each allowed to summarize the case. During their summary remarks, the prosecutor will comment that the evidence points toward guilt, and the defense will conclude that the evidence is insufficient to prove guilt beyond a reasonable doubt. The jury then retires to decide the verdict—guilty or not guilty. Texas law requires that all the jurors agree on the verdict in criminal cases. If the jury cannot agree, a *hung jury* exists, and the judge will declare a **mistrial**, but the defendant may be tried again.

Mistrial

A trial not completed for legal reasons, such as a hung jury; a new trial may be possible.

Regardless of whether the judge or the jury determines guilt, the judge may prescribe the sentence, unless the defendant requests that the jury do so. In considering the character of the defendant, any past criminal record, and the circumstances surrounding the crime, the judge may assess a penalty between the minimum and maximum provided by law. An offender may be given **probation**, which allows the person to serve the sentence in free society according to specific terms and restrictions and under the supervision of a probation officer. Similarly, deferred adjudication allows judges to postpone final sentencing in criminal cases, and after a satisfactory probationary period, the charges are dismissed.

Probation

A judge's sentence of an offender to serve outside a correctional institution but under specific restrictions and official supervision.

Judges have a great deal of latitude in assessing penalties, so the fate of a defendant will depend in large part on the attitudes of the presiding judge. Different judges sometimes assess vastly different penalties for the same crime committed under similar circumstances.

Upon sentencing, the prisoner will be sent to one of the state's penal institutions. Time served in jail before and during trial is usually deducted from the sentence of the guilty. (For the innocent, however, the time served awaiting trial is a casualty of an imperfect system of justice that underlines the necessity for care in accusing and trying our citizens.)

POST-TRIAL PROCEEDINGS

Acquitted

Found not guilty in a court of law.

To protect the accused from double jeopardy, a person who is **acquitted** (found not guilty) cannot be tried again for the same offense. However, protection from double jeopardy is much more limited than many citizens believe. In the event of a mistrial or an error in procedure in which a person is not acquitted, another trial may be held for the same offense on the theory that the defendant was never put in jeopardy by the first trial. A person found not guilty of one crime may be tried for other related offenses. For example, a person who is accused of driving 75 miles per hour through a school zone, going the wrong way on a one-way street, striking down a child in the crosswalk, and then leaving the scene of the accident has committed four crimes. Being acquitted for one of them does not free the defendant of possible charges for each of the other offenses. Likewise, such acts as bank robbery and kidnapping may violate both federal and state law, and the accused may be tried by both jurisdictions.

Although the state cannot appeal a not-guilty verdict, because doing so would constitute double jeopardy, prosecutors may appeal the *reversal* of a guilty verdict by a higher court, and the defendant may appeal a guilty verdict. Misdemeanor cases from justices of the peace and municipal courts may be either tried *de novo* (anew) or appealed in county courts. Appeals from county and district courts go to one of 14 courts of appeals and finally to the Texas Court of Criminal Appeals.

Appellate procedure is designed to review the law as applied by lower courts, not to evaluate evidence to determine guilt or innocence. Its major concern is procedure. Even if overruled, the antics of defense attorneys in raising frequent objections to court procedure may build a case for appeal. If serious procedural errors are found, the appellate courts may return the case to a lower court for retrial. Such a retrial does not constitute double jeopardy.

Having exhausted the rights of appeal in the Texas courts, a very few cases are appealed to the federal courts, which have jurisdiction in federal law. Thus, the grounds for appeal to federal courts are the assertion that the state courts have violated the U.S. Constitution or other federal law.

THE SPECIAL CASE OF JUVENILE COURTS

As the result of a reform effort in the 19th century, most states began to provide special treatment for children. In 1943, Texas followed the lead of other states in replacing all adult criminal procedures in juvenile cases with special civil procedures. Under the legal fiction that juveniles were not being punished for crimes, lax procedures were used that would never have been permitted in adult criminal courts. Court proceedings were secret, the rights to counsel and to trial by jury were ignored, standards of evidence were relaxed, and frequently charges were not specific.

As a result of federal court rulings, much of due process has since been restored to juvenile proceedings— except the rights to bail, a grand jury indictment, and a public trial. Juvenile proceedings remain civil, and juvenile records may be sealed from the public with the approval of the juve-

nile judge, who is usually appointed by the county's judges or juvenile board to have exclusive jurisdiction in such cases. The law allows juvenile felony arrest warrants to be entered into statewide computers, and police can gather information such as juvenile fingerprints and photographs. Children as young as 14 years of age arrested for serious crimes may be certified to stand trial as adults, but a majority of those arrested for lesser crimes are counseled and released without further proceedings.

UPPA/Photoshot

Children tried as adults seem to be more likely to commit crimes than those who are dealt with in the juvenile system, according to the U.S. Centers for Disease Control and Prevention. (See http://www.cdc.gov/mmwr/PDF/rr/rr5609.pdf.) Texas allows children to be tried as adults at age 14.

How should the legal rights and responsibilities of children differ from those of adults?

Rehabilitation and Punishment

Texas jails and penitentiaries are intended to have several functions:

1. Punishment (or social vengeance) is society's way of settling accounts with those who have violated its norms. By providing public institutions that extract justice, society offers an alternative to private revenge and the resulting feuds that plagued the early stages of Western civilization. Until the 18th century, punishment meant imposing physical or financial pain. But ideas of human dignity led to the development of prisons to deny a person liberty as a more humane way of punishing. Today, although some prisoners brutalize each other, the death penalty is the only remnant of formal physical punishment left in the law.

2. **Deterrence** of criminals is a major rationalization for the development of prison systems. Society uses punishment of convicted criminals as an example to discourage would-be lawbreakers.

3. Isolation of criminal elements from the law-abiding population is designed to protect society from future crimes. Yet for most crimes, society is unwilling to prescribe the permanent imprisonment of convicted criminals.

4. **Rehabilitation** of convicted criminals is supposed to allow those who are ultimately released to take useful and noncriminal roles in society.

Deterrence

Discouragement of an action, especially of criminal acts, by threat of punishment.

Rehabilitation

The effort to correct criminals' antisocial attitudes and behavior.

In practice, prisons and jails have performed none of these functions. Punishment and isolation are cut short because prisons are overcrowded, and criminals are released after having served only a fraction of the time assessed by judges and juries. Punishment is neither swift nor certain and cannot effectively deter crime. Texas has put a larger percentage of its population in prison than almost any other state, yet it still has one of the nation's highest crime rates. Texas has executed more people than any other state, yet it still has a murder rate greater than most other states in the nation.

TEXAS DEPARTMENT OF CRIMINAL JUSTICE

The Texas Department of Criminal Justice (DCJ) supervises the state's adult correctional functions—probation, prison, and parole. Probation, allows convicts to serve their sentences outside prisons, but under varying degrees of supervision—probationers may be required to report to probation officers, submit to electronic monitoring, undergo treatment for chemical dependency, or live in community residence or restitution centers. Approximately 260,000 Texans are currently under direct community supervision for felony violations. Although probation functions are largely the responsibilities of local community supervision and corrections departments, DCJ sets standards and provides funding, training, information, and technical assistance to local officers.

The criminal justice department also operates the prison units for those offenders not granted probation. Texas's prison population has tripled since the mid-1980s, and 52 prison facilities, 20 state jails, 14 transfer facilities, and other confinement units now accommodate more than 150,000 inmates.

One goal of a modern prison system is to turn convicted criminals into useful and functional citizens. A prison term begins with a stay at the diagnostic center, where a prisoner's personal attributes are assessed and an appropriate plan for rehabilitation is developed. According to age, health, and previous criminal record, the prisoner is assigned to one of the prison units. Medical, dental, and psychiatric services are available; problems requiring such treatment are far more common among criminals than among the general population. Personal and religious counseling are also significant elements in the correctional program. Because the vast majority of prison inmates have not finished high school, an educational

HOW DOES TEXAS COMPARE?
CRIME AND PUNISHMENT

Texas's crime rate is greater than that of 41 other states—it is nearly twice as high as those of New York and New Hampshire. The state's high crime rate is related to the high proportion of young, low-income, ethnic minority, poorly educated, urban population. Lack of family unity, high rates of addiction, and numerous other social factors also contribute to high crime rates. Figure 11.3 shows that the highest crime rates are generally in the southern and western states.

Texas's conservative political culture has been receptive to a "get-tough" approach to dealing with its high crime rates. Texas has officially imprisoned a far larger percentage of its population than authoritarian nations such as China, Cuba, Iran, and Russia. Among the 50 states, only 3 states have a larger number of prison inmates per 100,000 population than Texas. Table 11.2 shows that Texas also has a greater proportion of its population on parole and probation than most states.

Unfortunately, these facts do not answer the larger policy issue of whether high rates of imprisonment serve as a deterrent to crime. One might expect states, like Texas, with high rates of imprisonment would have a lower crime rate; yet ironically, Texas continues to have one of the highest crime rates in the United States.

Criminologists usually argue that *severity* of punishment is less important than the *certainty* of punishment. Many crimes are never reported, and police clear only a small share of known crimes with arrests. In fact, most criminals are never punished for the crimes they commit in Texas or in any other state.

Prisons are failures as institutions of rehabilitation. Far from being humane alternatives to corporal punishment, they are often brutal dens of violence, vice, and homosexual rape. Personal development is subordinated to personal degradation. Instead of rehabilitating prisoners, prisons have become publicly supported institutions of higher criminal learning. A large majority of those released from these human warehouses will again commit serious crime; as many as 80 percent of all felonies may be committed by repeaters (**recidivists**) who have had previous contact with the criminal justice system. A major factor in crime is thus the failure of our correctional systems to correct.

Recidivist

A criminal who commits another crime after having been incarcerated.

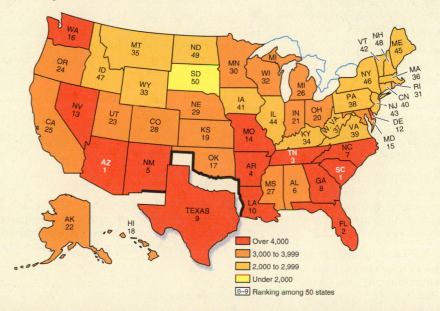

Figure 11.3

FBI Index Crime Rates per 100,000 Population, 2008.

Source: Federal Bureau of Investigation, Uniform Crime Reports: Crime in the United States, 2008 (Washington, DC: U.S. Government Printing Office, 2009), Table 5; http://www.fbi.gov/urc/2008cius/data/table_05.html

Why do crime rates vary so dramatically from one state to another?

TABLE 11.2 PERSONS IN PRISON, ON PROBATION, AND ON PAROLE PER 100,000 POPULATION*

	Federal	50 States	Texas	Texas Ranking among 50 States
Prisoners	60	445	639	4
On Probation	10	1,835	2,401	8
On Parole	43	315	579	5

*Prisoners reported per 100,000 residents; probationers and parolees reported per 100,000 adults on December 31, 2008.

Source: Bureau of Justice Statistics, Prisoners in 2008, December 2009, Appendix Table 10, p. 30 (http://bjs.ojp.usdoj.gov/index.cfm?ty=pbdetail&iid=1763) and Probation and Parole in the United States, 2008, December 2009, Appendix Tables 2 and 12, pp. 18 and 37 (http://bjs.ojp.usdoj.gov/index.cfm?ty=pbdetail&iid=1764).

HOW DOES TEXAS COMPARE?
THE DEATH PENALTY

States with the Death Penalty Three states (New York, New Jersey, and New Mexico) have abolished the death penalty within the past few years, leaving 35 states with death penalty laws on the books. However, many of them rarely, if ever, carry out executions.

The South is the region in which most executions take place. Between 1976 and 2009, Southern states performed more than 80 percent of all executions in the United States. Texas led the nation (437), and Virginia ranked second (103). By 2009, Texas accounted for 38 percent of all executions nationwide.

Explaining Texas's Reputation as a Death Penalty State Texas has a large population, but its population does not explain the state's large number of executions. Between 1976 and 2009, only Oklahoma had a greater execution rate (2.4 per 100,000 of the population) than Texas (1.8 per 100,000).

Surprisingly, Texas juries are no more likely to impose the death penalty in murder cases than juries in other states, but Texas does follow through to execute a larger share of its death row prisoners. In Texas, about 2 percent of murder cases result in a death sentence (about average in death penalty states), but Texas authorities executed 44.7 percent of those sentenced to death between 1977 and 2009—only Virginia executed a greater portion (66.2%) of its death row inmates.

Capital Punishment as a Deterrent Ironically, states with capital punishment have consistently had a *greater* murder rate than the states without it. For example, in 2008, the average murder rate was 5.2 per 100,000 in states with the death penalty while the murder rate in states without it was only 3.3. A historic pattern of such statistics has been interpreted to mean that death penalty laws do not act as a deterrent to murder. Perhaps states with a higher murder rate have been the most receptive to politicians willing to vigorously enforce the death penalty.

Alternatives to the Death Penalty Texas was the last state to allow life without parole as an alternative to the death penalty and initial evidence shows that prosecutors are less likely to seek the death sentence and juries are less likely to impose it when a secure and sufficiently punitive alternative is available.

Methods of Execution All 35 states with the death penalty use lethal injection as a primary method of execution, but several allow alternatives, including electrocution (9), the gas chamber (5), hanging (2), and firing squad (1).

FOR DEBATE

What is the best argument in favor of capital punishment? As an alternative, can life imprisonment serve justice as well as capital punishment? Why? Why not?

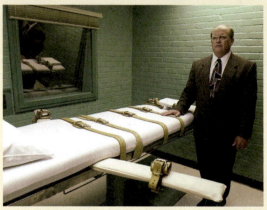

AP Images/Par Sullivan

👍 *Lethal-injection gurney. Texas was the first state to use lethal injection in executions. Today, it is an option for execution in all 35 states with the death penalty. Critics argue that the lethal drug cocktail can cause excruciating pain in still conscious subjects who show few signs of discomfort because of drug-induced paralysis. Despite these arguments, the U.S. Supreme Court ruled in 2008 that lethal injection does not violate the Eighth Amendment ban on cruel and unusual punishment.**

Can you think of ethical reasons to keep the death penalty or to abolish it?

GO ONLINE

Find a wealth of information about the death penalty at the Bureau of Justice Statistics **http://bjs.ojp.usdoj.gov/** *and at the Death Penalty Information Center* **http://deathpenaltyinfo .org/**. *Search for studies that show capital punishment as a deterrent to murder.*

**Baze et al.* v. *Rees et al.*, 553 U.S. 35 (2008).

program is vital to help the convicts become productive members of society. Academic education is available from elementary through college levels, and apprenticeship programs train inmates for jobs ranging from welder to computer operator. Some prison work may offer skills for use in later life, but it usually provides little practical training beyond the value of work itself.

A prerelease program is designed to ease the transition of the inmate from prison back into free society. Job-placement assistance, employment counseling, and psychological counseling assist the prisoner with personal adjustment and family problems. Unfortunately, such efforts toward rehabilitation have failed most inmates because most will again be arrested for criminal activities.

After an initial stay in prison, **parole** allows many inmates to serve the remainder of their sentences under supervision in the community. Whereas DCJ is responsible for their supervision after release, the Board of Pardons and Paroles decides which inmates will be granted parole.

Inmates serving life sentences for capital crimes are not eligible for parole, and those convicted of other violent offenses must serve at least one-half of their sentences before being considered for parole. Those convicted of other offenses must serve only one-fourth of their sentences or 15 years, whichever is less. However, additional time against the sentence is allowed for making a positive effort toward rehabilitation, good behavior, and providing various services such as serving as a prison trusty (an inmate assigned to assist prison staff). As a result, an inmate may become eligible for parole in fewer calendar years than the original sentence indicated.

The Board of Pardons and Paroles does not grant parole to prisoners automatically when they become eligible. Instead, the board examines each inmate's record for positive evidence of rehabilitation. When granted parole, the freed prisoner must abide by strict codes of conduct under the general supervision of parole officers. Parole, as the concept has developed, should not be forgiveness but a continuation of the process of correction.

Parole rehabilitation is based on the idea that the elimination of antisocial attitudes can be more effectively accomplished when the individual is not severed from society.

Parole is far less expensive than incarceration. Supervision of a prison inmate costs as much as 20 times that of a parolee. Because parolees are inadequately supervised and often run afoul of the law, parole revocations are frequent.

CLEMENCY

The Board of Pardons and Paroles takes the initiative to recommend executive clemency (leniency) to the governor. Three types of clemency are available: pardon, commutation of sentence, and reprieve. Since conviction for crime carries a legal condemnation as well as a possible sentence, a *full pardon* is designed to absolve a citizen from the legal consequences of his or her crime. A *commutation of sentence* is a reduction in punishment. A *reprieve* is temporary interruption of punishment. The governor may grant less, but not more, clemency than the board recommends. Without board approval, the governor may grant only one 30-day reprieve to delay execution in a capital case.

Parole

Early release from prison under official supervision.

PARDONS ARE RARE IN TEXAS

The governor does not commonly grant pardons. In 2003, however, the governor did pardon 35 Tulia residents who were convicted based on the fabricated testimony of Tom Coleman, a rogue undercover narcotics officer. Many of them were eligible under Texas law for compensation, now $80,000 for each year of false imprisonment.

TEXAS YOUTH COMMISSION

Most juvenile offenders are handled by county authorities. They are usually detained in county facilities before a disposition of the case. They are usually released (on probation) to the custody of parents or placed in county facilities.

For serious criminal acts or violations of probation, the juvenile may be placed in the custody of the Texas Youth Commission (TYC). The TYC operates training schools, boot camps, and halfway houses. After becoming notorious itself for child neglect and abuse, including widespread sexual assault by guards against children in their custody, TYC transferred many of its students to privately operated community child-care facilities, placed many on parole, and released others. Restructuring of the TYC is now under way to make its operations fit to accommodate violent and chronic offenders who cannot be transferred to state prisons until they reach adulthood.

JAILS

State government assumes the responsibility for some juvenile delinquents and convicted felons, but adults who are convicted of the misdemeanors for which confinement is prescribed will serve their terms in jails operated by local governments, usually counties. Jails also hold individuals awaiting trial who have not been released on bail and convicted felons awaiting transfer to DCJ prison facilities. Our jails are human warehouses and, like our prisons and reform schools, fail to rehabilitate. There are at least three probable reasons for this:

1. Jails are operated by county sheriffs, whose major qualification for office is their ability to get elected.
2. Jail staffs and physical facilities are designed to maintain custody rather than to rehabilitate. Many prisoners in county jails are either awaiting trial or being held for other agencies (federal or state). Those who are actually serving their sentences in the county jail will be there for only a short period of time, usually less than one year. This is insufficient time to correct criminal attitudes that the prisoner may have been forming for a lifetime.
3. Many of the people who serve their sentence in local jails have been convicted of habitual vices such as gambling, prostitution, and drunkenness, which are not amenable to rehabilitation in a jail setting.

A backlog of prisoners awaiting transfer to Texas state prisons forced several counties to construct new facilities. Other counties place prisoners in private-enterprise institutions. Many jails are still overcrowded and credit inmates with three days against their sentence for each day actually served.

CHILDREN'S LEGAL RIGHTS

The U.S. Supreme Court led the way in advancing minimum standards of due process for juveniles. *In re Gault* (387 U.S. 1, 1967) guaranteed juveniles reasonable notice of charges, the right to counsel, the right to confront witnesses, and the privilege against self-incrimination. *In re Winship* (397 U.S. 358, 1970) ruled that charges must be proved beyond reasonable doubt, and in *Breed* v. *Jones* (421 U.S. 519, 1975), the Court extended to juveniles protection against double jeopardy.

CHAPTER SUMMARY

★ In an attempt to impose their values on others, the dominant elements of society have turned to government with its power to define crime and punish it. Law reflects the values of the people who make and enforce it.

★ Within the American legal system, cases are classified as either civil or criminal. Civil cases primarily involve the rights of private parties or organizations. Resolution is based on the concept of responsibility rather than guilt.

★ Tort actions are common in civil law—a tort is a wrong suffered by a party. The Texas legislature, in an effort to lighten overcrowded court dockets and limit allegedly frivolous suits, has undertaken tort reform. At the urging of business, insurance companies, and medical professionals it has restricted lawsuits and limited awards for damages.

★ Criminal cases deal with public concepts of proper behavior and morality as defined by law. Punishment for a conviction ranges from a fine to imprisonment to a combination of both. More serious crimes are called felonies and minor crimes are called misdemeanors. Generally, younger, less educated members of ethnic minorities living in cities are more likely to be arrested for crime, but crime rates have been declining in recent years.

★ Although the Texas Department of Public Safety and a number of other state agencies enforce state law, law enforcement is primarily a local responsibility. The most serious failure in the criminal justice system is citizens' failure to report crime, but even among crimes known to police, the rate of clearance by arrest of a suspect is low, especially for property crimes such as burglary and theft.

★ The court procedures that constitute due process aim to promote justice and protect individuals from the government. These procedures are generally either written into state and national constitutions and statutes or included in traditional codes of court process.

★ It is largely through due process, though, that the courts aim to blend two conflicting goals of society: (1) to protect society according to the state's legal concepts of right and wrong, and (2) to protect the rights of the individual charged with wrongdoing. Unfortunately, the goal of due process is often an ideal rather than a reality. These careful guarantees of due process are often circumvented by the practice of plea bargaining.

★ Correctional institutions such as prisons and jails are intended to punish, deter, isolate, and rehabilitate. Unfortunately, they perform these functions poorly, and a majority of inmates will return to crime after their release.

HOW TEXAS COMPARES

★ Texas has a greater crime rate than most states, even though Texas has imprisoned a larger percentage of its population than China, Russia, and Iran. Texas has incarcerated a larger percentage of their populations than all but three other states, and has a larger proportion of its population on probation or parole than most states.

★ On the basis of comparison with other states, there is no conclusive evidence that incarcerating a large portion of the population effectively deters crime because punishment is neither swift nor certain in Texas or any other state.

★ Texas executes more death row inmates than any other state but still has a higher murder rate than most states.

★ The most likely explanation for why Texas has a higher crime rate than most states is that it has a high proportion of young, minority, urban, poorly educated, low-income residents among its population.

KEY TERMS

acquitted	deterrence	mores	rehabilitation
adversary system	docket	negligence	remedy
arraignment	due process	no-fault insurance	right-to-work laws
bail	eminent domain	parole	slander
change of venue	examining trial	personal recognizance	*stare decisis*
charter	exclusionary rule	plaintiff	tort
civil law	FBI index crimes	precedent	tort reform
closed shop	felony	*prima facie* case	union shop
common law	homestead	probable cause	victimless crime
common-law marriage	intestate	probate	*voir dire* questioning
community property	liability insurance	probation	white-collar crime
compulsory process	libel	punitive damages	writ of habeas corpus
continuance	misdemeanor	real property	writ of injunction
criminal law	mistrial	recidivist	

REVIEW QUESTIONS

1. What distinguishes criminal cases from civil cases? Give examples of each type.

2. Discuss the root causes of crime. What are the social characteristics of the typical criminal?

3. Outline the basic elements of the criminal justice system, including law enforcement, court procedure, punishment, and rehabilitation.

4. What are the major functions of jails and penitentiaries? Evaluate their effectiveness at preventing recidivism and deterring crime.

LOGGING ON

✶ The Texas Civil Justice League supports tort reform to limit civil court awards. Go to **http://www.tcjl.com** and click on "About." At the same site, click on "Membership" to note the kinds of business interests that the organization represents. On the other side of the issue are plaintiffs' attorneys represented by the Texas Trial Lawyers Association at **http://www.ttla .com**. At that site, click on "Debunking Myths" to learn about trial lawyers' views of lawsuit abuse.

✶ Renew driver's licenses, check latest state crime statistics, and identify registered sex offenders in your neighborhood through the online services of the Texas Department of Public Safety at **http://www.txdps.state.tx.us**

✶ To search for crime reports, click on "Crime in Texas." Compare that with the national index crime reports at the FBI page, **http://www.fbi.gov**. Click on "Reports and Publications," and scroll to "Crime in the United States."

✶ Visit the Bureau of Justice Statistics website, **http://www .ojp.usdoj.gov/bjs/**, for a rich source of national data about crime, victims, prosecution, prison, probation, and capital punishment.

✶ See criminal punishments in the Texas Penal Code at **http:// www.capitol.state.tx.us**. Click on "Penal Codes" and then on "Punishments."

✶ The attorney general at **http://oag.state.tx.us** has a Criminal Victims Services Division. Click on "Crime Victims' Compensation Program."

The Other War: Texas–Mexico Border Security

Ray Leal
St. Mary's University

INTRODUCTION

Providing border security between Texas and Mexico is yet another law enforcement issue that has gripped headlines and dominated political campaigns throughout the state and nation. Efforts to deal with the crime problems in this area have generated innumerable questions about the balance between personal liberty and security.

CNN reports that there have been 3,889 soldiers killed in Iraq as of December 12, 2007.[1] Most Americans have been focused on the number of soldiers killed or wounded in Iraq because of the constant media coverage and ongoing debate about the war. However, the number of deaths along the United States–Mexico border attributed to the drug cartels' war has exceeded the casualty figures for the Iraq War. According to Stratfor, an Austin-based private intelligence firm, from 2005 through January 2007 there have been 5,743 drug-related killings in Mexico during the last three years, and some of the more dramatic ones have occurred along the Texas–Mexico border, particularly in Nuevo Laredo.[2] Although many Americans are unaware of the border violence, criminal justice professionals such as Webb County Sheriff Rick Flores sum up the dangerousness of the current border situation like this: "It's a war zone. We've got level-three body armor. They've got level four. We've got cell phones. They've got

[1]"U.S. and Coalition Casualties," accessed December 12, 2007, at http://www.cnn.com/SPECIALS/2003/iraq/forces/casualties
[2]Strategic Forecasting, Inc., "Mexican Drug Cartels: The Evolution of Violence," October 15, 2007, Austin, TX, p. 3.v

satellite cell phones that we can't tap into."[3] The situation has become so dangerous that the Mexican drug cartels have even put up bounties of up to $200,000 against federal agents on both sides of the Texas–Mexico border.[4]

Although the drug cartels' border violence has created uneasiness in border communities and decreased tourism along the Texas–Mexico border, it has brought the issue of border security to the forefront of the national political debate. This debate has resulted in new legislation that includes the Real ID Act, passport and visa improvements, increased use of technology along the border, deployment of more personnel along the border, and the erection of border fencing in the Rio Grande Valley. The Real ID Act signed into law as P.L. 109-13 by President Bush on May 11, 2005, will require states to issue driver's licenses and identification cards approved by the federal government. These licenses and cards will be needed by U.S. citizens and permanent lawful residents to drive, collect Social Security, use bank or airline services, and other essential activities. It is an unfunded mandate and more than 600 organizations have opposed it.[5] Needless to say, these measures have not been met with overwhelming support by Texas border communities and raise serious questions about the federal government's interference into matters generally associated with state governmental powers.

The U.S. Customs and Border Protection agency planned construction of 70 miles of border fencing to consist of a 16-foot wall in 21 segments, ranging from 1 to 13 miles, along the border near Rio Grande City, McAllen, Mercedes, Harlingen, Brownsville, and Fort Brown.[6] So, like China, the former Soviet Union, and Israel, the United States is the latest nation to use a "wall" to defend itself. Unfortunately, history has shown that two of these three previous walls failed. Even Lou Dobbs has doubts about the Bush Administration's passage of the Secure Fence Act, the legal force behind the new border wall. Dobbs criticizes House Republicans who in 2006 had the president sign the Secure Fence Act during formal proceedings before the November 2006 midterm elections, elections that clearly changed the political balance in Washington.[7] He goes on to say that although funding one-half of a 700-mile fence along a nearly 2,000-mile border is a good beginning, it isn't enough to stem the tide of illegal immigration.

Border community leaders have made their opposition to the new border wall known to the federal government. The Texas Border Coalition composed of border mayors, county judges, and business leaders have urged the Bush Administration to keep the "border wall" out of the Lone Star State and use "smart technology," so that the border economy will not be disrupted and relations with Mexico not be damaged.[8] With regards to the federal government's border wall project, Chad Foster, mayor of Eagle Pass and chairman of the Texas Border

Scott Olson/Getty Images

Border Patrol agents detain undocumented immigrants apprehended near the Mexican border on May 28, 2010, near McAllen, Texas. About 25 immigrants were captured in the group about one mile north of the Rio Grande River. During fiscal year 2009, 540,865 undocumented immigrants were apprehended entering the United States along the Mexican border.

What policies should the state of Texas adopt to prevent drug-related violence from spilling across the Mexican border? What laws should the state adopt to deal with immigrants who have illegally crossed the border to find work?

Coalition, has stated, "They've never been open. They've never been above board. There's never a good time for a bad idea, but at least they're consistent about that."[9] El Paso Mayor John Cook recently received hate mail and a death threat after an Associated Press story mistakenly stated that Cook had denied federal employees building a border-fence access to city property.[10] Others have also fought the federal government's efforts to pay them for access to their lands after federal workers were denied access to conduct surveys for the border wall on their land. Brownsville Mayor Patricio M. Ahumada, Jr. has referred to proposed federal payments as "blood money, bribery."[11] The proposed federal payments were later dropped by the administration.

Another group that has concerns over current efforts by the U.S. Border Patrol's efforts along the Texas–Mexico border is the Border Land Association.[12] A letter from former Texas Governor Dolph Briscoe encourages border landowners to join this association in efforts to formulate efficient border security policies. However, the group also emphasizes its disagreement with the Border Patrol's policy of turning many ranches into "chasing

[3]Associated Press, Brownsville, Texas, December 2007.
[4]Associated Press, Brownsville, Texas, December 2007.
[5]A. Ramasastry, "Why the 'Real ID' Act Is a Mess," 2005, http://www.cnn.com/2005/LAW/08/12/ramasastry.ids/index.html
[6]A. Ustinova and H. Rozemberg, *San Antonio Express-News*, September 25, 2007.
[7]L. Dobbs, "Border Fence Will Leave Texas-Size Hole," http://cnn.com/2006/US/10/24/Dobbs.Oct 25/index.html?iref=newssearch
[8]"Texas Border Coalition Urges Feds to Scrap Border Wall in Favor of 'Smart' Technology," Eagle Pass, TX, October 16, 2007, http://www .texasbordercoalition.org
[9]Ibid.
[10]L. Gilot, "Mayor Receives Death Threat," *El Paso Times, October* 5, 2007, p. 1B.
[11]A. Caldwell, "Feds Scrap Plan to Pay Landowners for Border Access," *El Paso Times*, October 24, 2007.
[12]http://www.borderland.dus/

grounds," a tactic that they feel is inefficient. More efforts should be focused on apprehending illegal immigrants at the border. The Border Patrol is authorized to "enter private lands within twenty-five miles of the international border at any time, for any purpose and without any notice."[13] Some critics of this federal law see the Border Patrol's activities as a violation of their property rights and their Fourth Amendment rights.

Another border security concern is whether federal officials can perform their duties without additional assistance. In May 2007, President Bush pledged to send 6,000 reserve troops to the Mexican border until full-time Border Patrol agents can be hired to beef up security. This initiative is known as Operation Jump Start and it has allowed more Border Patrol agents to be used in the field.[14] Although these troops are now on duty at border checkpoints in Laredo, legal questions regarding their use based on the Posse Comitatus Act of 1876 have not been resolved.[15] This federal law[16] prohibits members of the national armed forces from exercising nominally state law enforcement or peace officer powers on nonfederal property. Additionally, citizen groups such as the Minutemen Project that have been active in the southwest generally have not been welcomed in Texas because of a large Latino presence along the border. Some have questioned the legality of such patrols and other view these patrols as vigilantism.[17] Another strategy employed by the U.S. Immigration and Customs Enforcement (ICE) agency has been to provide immigration cross training for local law enforcement agencies. However, few Texas border law enforcement agencies have shown an interest in this training.

Some oppose this initiative on the grounds that the federal government is asking local governments to do federal law enforcement, which raises jurisdictional concerns. Some border partnerships with ICE have resulted in some successes. ICE partnered with federal, state, and local law enforcement officials in Laredo in an initiative called Operation Black Jack in July 2005, which later evolved into the Border Enforcement and Security Task Force (BEST).[18] BEST has resulted in the arrest of individuals wanted for murder, weapons smuggling, and possession of illegal drugs and contraband. One individual arrested was wanted for his role in a May 2006 incident in which

he threw live grenades into a Monterrey nightclub resulting in four deaths.

Another border security issue has involved kidnapping for ransom. In recent years, Mexico has become known as the "kidnapping capital of the world," which has had a chilling effect on the tourism industry along the Texas–Mexico border. Wealthy businessmen are increasingly the victims of these crimes. Unfortunately, the drug-related killings and kidnappings have had disastrous results on the border economy on the Mexican side. Those Mexican nationals who are able to have moved to the Texas side of the border. The fencing projects, increased Border Patrol officers, the efforts by ICE, the Minutemen Project, and citizen patrols are a reaction to an unacceptable security situation on the Texas–Mexico border. Efforts must be taken by both governments to create economic opportunities in Mexico if we are ever to secure our border and reduce illegal immigration. Lack of legal economic opportunities causes personal and border insecurity along the Texas–Mexico border.

JOIN THE DEBATE

1. The Posse Comitatus Act was passed after Reconstruction in 1876 to prevent repetition of perceived abuse by the military and national guard when they were involved in domestic law enforcement. Is there any danger today in using the military and national guard to bring law and order to the Texas border?

2. Do citizen volunteer organizations such as the Minuteman Project help solve the problem of illegal immigration, or do they pose a threat of vigilantism?

3. What is the most promising approach to the problems of crime and illegal immigration on the Texas border? What procedural guarantees should be used to protect the rights of Texas citizens?

4. Research the controversy surrounding the Real ID Act. Why would states such as Maine and Utah oppose its implementation?

[13]8 U.S.C. § 1357 (a) (3).

[14]C. Reddick, "National Guard Troops Grow in Their Roles," *Laredo Morning Times,* July 21, 2006.

[15]G. Thomas, *Posse Comitatus and the Use of the Military in Denying Terrorist Access to the United States along the Border with Mexico* (Carlisle Barracks, PA: Army War College, 2005).

[16]18 U.S.C. § 1385.

[17]S. Vina and B. Nunez-Nieto, B., *Civilian Patrols along the Border: Legal and Policy Issues* (Congressional Research Service: Washington, DC, 2006).

[18]Department of Homeland Security, *ICE Initiatives to Combat Southwest Border Violence* (Washington, DC: Government Printing Office, 2006).

Chapter 12

Taxing and Budgeting

CONTENTS

LEARNING OBJECTIVES

* Explain why taxing and spending decisions are political.
* Describe major taxes used by federal, state, and local governments.
* Outline the political arguments for taxing different groups differently.
* Contrast progressive and regressive taxes and give examples.
* Explain why consumption taxes burden lower-income families and how business taxes can become consumer taxes.
* Identify Texas's non-tax revenues. including federal grants-in-aid and state borrowing.
* Describe the major decision-making steps in the budgeting and spending process and identify where the process can be reformed.

★ GET ✦ ACTIVE ★

Decide which side you are on. Browse progressive and conservative websites; then plug into the groups that best represent your views on taxes:

Conservative Groups

★ Get the conservative view on taxes and other policies at the Texas Public Policy Foundation at **http://www.texaspolicy.com**

Connect up with Texas Taxpayers and Research Association representing the conservative and business perspective on taxation at **http://www.ttara.org**. Click on "Documents" to examine the group's lobbying positions.

★ Monitor other pro-business, anti-tax arguments at the Tax Foundation website at **http://www.taxfoundation.org**. Click on "Research Areas" and select "State Tax and Spending Policy."

Liberal/Progressive Groups

★ Tune into the liberal and labor position on taxes, browse the Citizens for Tax Justice site at **http://www.ctj.org**. Select "State Tax Publications and News" and go to Texas.

★ Check out what your family pays in taxes at the Institute on Taxation and Economic Policy at **http://www.itepnet.org**. Click on "Who Pays?" and go to "State Specific Fact Sheets."

★ Engage Texas funding challenges with Texas's Center for Public Policy Priorities at **http://www.cppp.org**. Click on "Research" and sift through the latest studies on Texas's taxes.

★ Probe budget and fiscal policies in the 50 states with the Center on Budget and Policy Priorities at **http://www.cbpp .org**

Check out your family's tax burden compared with other Texas families in Exemptions and Tax Incidence, 2009, available at the Texas Comptroller of Public Accounts website, **http://www.window.state.tx.us**

Protest property tax appraisals and apply for tax exemptions at the tax appraisal authority in your county. Find your county appraisal authority at **http://www.txcounty-data.com**

The Texas legislature finally passed and sent to the governor the largest budget in the state's history—a total of almost $182.2 billion was approved for fiscal years 2010 and 2011. Counting one dollar every second without resting for weekends, holidays, and coffee breaks, it would take about 5,778 years to count these appropriations! Texas has the third-largest state budget, exceeded only by those of California and New York.

In a sense, however, the size of the most recent Texas budgets is not surprising. Each successive budget during the past several years has been larger than the preceding one, resulting in a long succession of record expenditures. Figure 12.1 shows that inflation and population increases explain much of the growth in state spending.

Inflation alone explains some of the increase in government spending; just as there has been an increase in the cost of what citizens and families buy, there has also been an increase in the cost of what government buys. However, inflation has also driven up salaries and profits with which residents pay their taxes.

Texas's population has grown more rapidly than that of most other states. Each new person must be served, protected, and educated. Of course, the demands of a larger population for increased state services are offset by the fact that more people also are paying taxes to support them. Adjusted for population and inflation, state spending has grown at an average annual rate of 1.6 percent since 1996.

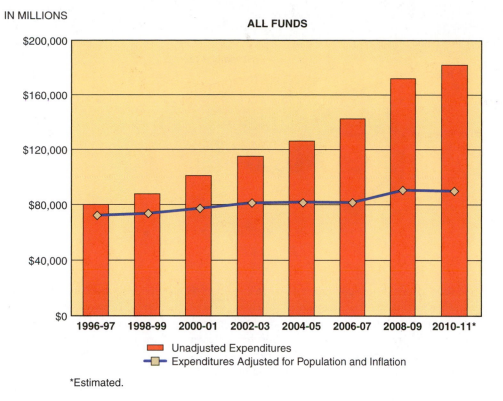

IN MILLIONS

ALL FUNDS

Unadjusted Expenditures
Expenditures Adjusted for Population and Inflation

*Estimated.

Figure 12.1
Trends in Texas State
Expenditures, All Funds,
by Biennial Budget Periods
1996–2011 (in millions of
dollars). The columns show
that state expenditures have
grown considerably, but
the line shows only modest
spending growth controlling
for inflation and population
growth.

Source: Legislative Budget Board,
Fiscal Size-Up, 2010–2011 (Austin:
Legislative Budget Board, 2009),
p. 9.

Why should measures of state
spending be adjusted for inflation and population growth?

So, from where do the funds for this spending come? Surprisingly, much state revenue comes from sources other than state taxes. During the 2010–2011 fiscal years, 43 percent of estimated Texas revenues are from state taxes, whereas federal funding—mostly grants in aid—accounts for 37 percent. The remainder comes from interest on investments, revenues from public lands, and licenses, fees, and other minor non-tax sources (such as the lottery, which accounts for only 1.8%). Figure 12.2 shows the major sources of Texas state revenues.

Taxation

Governments rely on a variety of tax sources, and each level of government—national, state, and local—tends to specialize in certain types of taxes.

NATIONAL TAXES

With ratification of the Sixteenth Amendment to the U.S. Constitution in 1913, the income tax became available to the national government. Individual and corporate income taxes immediately became the national government's major source of funding and today constitute approximately 60 percent of federal tax revenues, with most of the remainder coming from payroll taxes for Social Security and Medicare.

STATE TAXES

Property taxes were once the major source of state revenue, but property values collapsed during the Great Depression of the 1930s, and with them went the property tax revenues. At the

Figure 12.2

Sources of Estimated State Revenues, 2010–2011 Budget Period. This figure shows that Texas's largest single revenue source is federal funding and the largest state tax is the general sales tax.

Source: Legislative Budget Board, *Fiscal Size-Up, 2010–2011* (Austin: Legislative Budget Board, 2009), p. 21.

Besides the general sales tax, which of Texas's other taxes should be considered sales taxes? What are the arguments for and against consumer taxes?

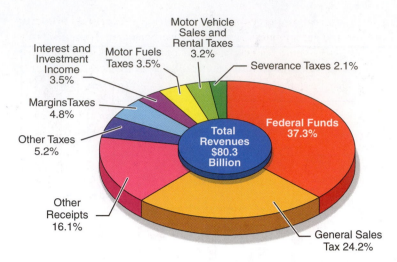

General sales tax

A broad-based tax collected on the retail price of most items.

Selective sales (excise) taxes

Taxes levied on specific items only; also known as *excise taxes*.

Hidden taxes

Taxes included in the retail prices of the goods and services.

Gross-receipts tax

A tax on the gross revenues of certain enterprises.

Severance tax

A tax on raw materials (such as oil and natural gas) when they are extracted from their natural state.

Ad valorem tax

A tax assessed according to value, such as the tax on *real property* and *personal property*.

same time, demands for economic assistance and other public services skyrocketed. Forced to seek other revenue sources, states came to rely on various sales taxes. Texas adopted a tax on cigarettes in 1931, on beer in 1933, and on distilled spirits in 1935. Additional selective sales taxes were adopted in the 1940s and 1950s, but it became apparent that a more general and more broadly based tax would be necessary to meet revenue needs. In 1961, Texas adopted a general sales tax on most items sold. At the same time, Texas, like most states, first drastically reduced its property taxes and then abandoned them for exclusive use by local governments. States have adopted several types of sales taxes:

1. **General sales taxes** are broadly based taxes collected on the retail price of most items.
2. **Selective sales taxes**, also known as *excise taxes*, are levied on the sale, manufacture, or use of particular items, such as liquor, cigarettes, and gasoline. Because these taxes are usually included in the item's purchase price, they are often **hidden taxes**.
3. **Gross-receipts taxes** are taxes on the total gross revenue (sales) of certain enterprises. A broad-based margins tax (also known as the *franchise tax*) applies to the gross sales of most corporations and limited partnerships after taking a deduction for cost of goods or personnel. Small companies, sole proprietorships, and general partnerships are exempt.

Most state tax revenue in 2010–2011 came from various sales tax collections. The general sales tax (6.25% on retail sales of most items) yielded 24.2 percent of the state's revenues; the margins tax, 4.8 percent; motor fuels taxes, 3.5 percent; and motor vehicle sales and rental taxes, 3.2 percent. Once a major source of state revenue, **severance taxes** (production taxes on oil and natural gas) now account for only 2.1 percent. Texas also collects special taxes on a range of items and activities, such as tobacco, alcohol, registration of motor vehicles, hotel and motel occupancy, and insurance company operations.

LOCAL TAXES

Many services financed by state governments in other states are left to local governments in Texas. State government also has imposed many mandates (required services) on local governments, especially school districts, without funding them. As a result, state taxes have remained low, but local taxes are greater than in many states.

Property taxes are the major source of revenue for virtually all local governments—cities, counties, and special districts. **Ad valorem** (according to value) **taxes** may be applied to two major types of property including **real property** (land and buildings) and **personal property** (possessions such as furniture and automobiles). Most local governments in Texas primarily tax real property. A central appraisal authority in each county determines property values for all taxing units in the county according to uniform state standards and procedures. The tax rate is set by local policy-making bodies—city councils, county commissioners' courts, and boards of trustees for special districts.

Local governments also impose other taxes. For operating expenses, most Texas cities have adopted a one percent city sales tax applied to items taxable under the state general sales tax. Cities in counties with more than 500,000 population may also collect an additional sales tax up to one percent for economic development projects. Mass transit authorities and other special districts also collect sales taxes, but total local sales taxes are capped at two percent. Other local revenue sources include miscellaneous taxes, user fees, and federal grants in aid.

The Politics of Taxation

Taxes cannot be evaluated objectively. As with all public policy, the state's tax policy is designed by elected politicians who make tax decisions on the basis of which groups will be most affected by different types of taxes. People tend to evaluate taxes according to their social and economic position. Although their arguments are usually about the "public interest," one must recognize that the millions of dollars in campaign funds, the millions of hours devoted to campaigning, the thousands of lobbyists who fill our state and national capitols— all of the resources of persuasion our political system can muster—are called into play not simply to settle some abstract academic argument. Politics, especially the politics of taxation, affects the way people live in real and concrete ways. Any evaluation of taxes must be based on the way particular taxes affect various groups in society.

THE TAX BASE: WHO SHOULD PAY?

What to Tax Not all taxes are equally effective in raising funds for the public till. **Tax rates** (the amount per unit on a given item or activity) may be raised or lowered, but simply raising the tax rate may not guarantee increased revenues because people may cut back on purchases of the taxed item.

Tax rates affect the **tax base** (the object taxed). Excessive property taxes discourage construction and repair of buildings. High income taxes can discourage general economic activity and individual initiative, undermining the tax base. To raise necessary revenue, a tax must not discourage too much of the activity that produces the revenue.

Most governments tax a wide variety of items and activities, having found that **broad-based taxes** (those paid by a large number of taxpayers), such as taxes on property, general sales taxes, and income taxes, are most effective at raising revenue. High tax rates on a narrow base tend to destroy the base and thus make the tax ineffective as a source of revenue.

In the battle over taxation, one of the most intense issues is what should be taxed. The decision about *what* to tax is really a decision about *whom* to tax and how heavily. Those with influence on decision makers try to get special tax treatment for themselves and other taxpayers in their group. What seems to motivate almost every group is the principle that the best tax is the one somebody else pays. The three most common political rationalizations for taxing various social groups differently are (1) to regulate their behavior, (2) to tax them according to the benefits they receive, and (3) to tax them according to their ability to pay.

Real property
Land and buildings.

Personal property
Tangible possessions other than real estate.

Tax rate
The amount per unit of taxable item or activity.

Tax base
The object or activity taxed.

Broad-based tax
A tax designed to be paid by a large number of taxpayers.

Regulatory Taxes Taxes do more than simply pay for the services of government; they often serve as a tool for social or economic control. Rewarding approved behavior with lower taxation or punishing socially undesirable action with a higher tax can have a definite effect on conduct.

Regulatory tax

A tax imposed with the intent of exerting social or economic control by reducing taxes on approved behaviors or imposing higher taxes on undesirable activities.

Most state **regulatory taxes** are designed to control isolated individual choices, especially those with moral overtones, and are sometimes called "sin taxes." The most prominent example of such state regulatory taxation is the "use" tax to discourage the consumption of items such as alcohol or tobacco. Texas has an excise tax (selective sales tax) on alcoholic beverages, and its cigarette tax of $1.41 per pack is among the greatest in the nation. Although it is being challenged in court, another of Texas's "sin" taxes is the one charged for admissions to sexually oriented businesses, sometimes called the "pole tax" in reference to a prominent stage prop in strip clubs.

Texans continue to drink, smoke, and frequent strip clubs, so such state use taxes do not entirely prevent "sin," but they place a substantial share of the tax burden on the "sinner." The regulatory intent of use taxes may be a rationalization to place the tax burden on others; the most vocal advocates of alcohol and tobacco taxes are those who abstain. Proponents argue that regulatory taxes have some effect on behavior without extensive enforcement. The small annual decline in cigarette sales in Texas may be partially attributed to cost and young people may be deterred from smoking by the high price of cigarettes.

Benefits Received On the surface, nothing would seem fairer than taxation according to benefits received—let those who benefit from a public service pay for it. Americans have become accustomed to believing that this principle operates in the private sector of the economy and should be applied in the public sector as well.

Benefits-received tax

A tax assessed according to the services received by the payers.

An example of a **benefits-received tax** in Texas is a 20-cent-per-gallon tax on gasoline Three-fourths of the income from gasoline and diesel fuel taxes is directed into the Texas highway trust fund, which also includes the state's share of license plate fees (much of which is retained by the counties). The amount of fuel used should represent the benefits from highway building and maintenance.

REGULATORY TAXES, TAX SUBSIDIES, AND "LOOPHOLES"

What critics call loopholes in the federal income tax structure are examples of regulatory taxation. "**Loopholes**" are tax subsidies designed to encourage favored behavior by excluding certain kinds of income from taxation. Exclusions exempt from taxation income derived from certain economic activities such as interest earned on municipal bonds. Deductions exempt taxes on certain expenditures such as mortgage interest payments or charitable contributions. Tax credits allow taxpayers to subtract portions of their income or expenditures from their actual tax bill such as credits to install energy-saving equipment. Such subsidies are designed to encourage such economic activities as donations to charity, home ownership, and the purchase of municipal bonds.

These goals may be highly desirable, but the general effect of most tax subsidies is to make the federal income tax less progressive and to benefit of high-income taxpayers. Although some tax subsidies are available to low- and middle-income taxpayers, these citizens are not as financially able to spend their money in ways favored by the federal tax structure. People who are unable to provide themselves with adequate shelter, clothing, and medical care can scarcely be expected to take deductions for drilling oil wells or making large charitable contributions, and few of the poor or middle class invest in tax-free municipal bonds. These tax loopholes or subsidies also contribute enormously to the length and complexity of the Internal Revenue Code, and they create most of the taxpayer's confusion during the tax filing season.

Loopholes

Federal income tax subsidies designed to encourage approved behavior by excluding certain income from taxation or allowing credits against taxes.

Although not strictly a tax, tuition paid by students in state colleges and universities is determined on the basis of the benefits-received principle. Although most of the cost of public college education in Texas is paid out of state and local tax revenues, an increasing share of the cost of higher education is paid by student tuitions on the presumption that a student should pay a larger share of the cost of the service from which he or she so greatly benefits. Likewise, revenues from hunting and fishing permits are used for wildlife management.

The benefits-received principle seems reasonable, but few government services are truly special services that are provided only for special groups. Although the student is a major beneficiary of state-supported higher education, society also benefits from the skills that are added to the bank of human resources. Even the elderly widow who has never owned or driven a car benefits from highways when she buys fresh tomatoes from the supermarket or goes to the hospital in the event of illness. Most services of government, like highways, schools, or law enforcement, take on the character of a public or collective good whose beneficiaries cannot be accurately determined.

The benefits-received principle cannot be applied too extensively. Although private businesses efficiently provide services on a benefits-received basis, a major reason for government to provide a *public* service is to make that service available to all. Many could not afford to pay the full cost of vital public services. For example, few people could afford to attend Texas's public colleges and universities if they had to pay the full cost of higher education.

Ability to Pay Most taxes are rationalized according to some measure of taxpayers' ability to pay them. The most common **ability-to-pay taxes** are levied on property, sales, and income. Property taxes are determined by the premise that the more valuable people's property is, the wealthier they are and hence the greater is their ability to pay taxes. Sales taxes are determined by the premise that the more a person buys, the greater is the individual's purchasing power. Income taxes are based on the assumption that the more a person earns, the greater is that person's ability to pay.

No base is completely adequate as a measure of a person's ability to pay. During Europe's feudal era, property reflected a person's wealth. With the coming of the commercial revolution, real wealth came to be measured in terms of money rather than land. Nevertheless, the taxes on real estate remained, while more modern forms of ownership, such as stocks, bonds, and other securities, are seldom taxed.

Taxes based on money (income or expenditure) also are an inadequate measure of true wealth. Income taxes reflect current taxable income and do not account for wealth accumulated in past years. Furthermore, exemptions allow the taxpayer to legally avoid taxes, even on current income. Taxes on consumption and spending (sales taxes) are an even less equitable measure of the ability to pay. Sales taxes measure wealth only as it is spent. Money saved or invested is not spent and not taxed. Because it is a general rule of economic behavior that the wealthier a person is, the more the person saves or invests, sales taxes weigh disproportionately on the "have-nots" and "have-littles," who must spend the largest portion of their income on the necessities of life.

Ability-to-pay taxes
Taxes apportioned according to taxpayers' financial capacity.

TAX RATES: PROGRESSIVE OR REGRESSIVE TAXES?

Most people would like to pay as little in taxes as possible, but it turns out that they pay quite a bit. The average working American works almost one-third of the year (from the first day of January until about mid-April) to pay taxes to all levels of government—federal, state, and local.

However, these averages obscure the real effect of taxes on the individual taxpayer. The so-called loopholes in the federal income tax structure have been well publicized, but every tax—federal, state, and local—treats various taxpayers differently. What in the political world is used to justify the unequal burden of taxation?

Figure 12.3

Federal Income Tax Rates for Single Individuals, 2010. Compare the five columns representing various levels of individual taxable income and the rates that apply. Notice that, regardless of total taxable income, the tax rate on the first $8,375 is 10 percent (blue), the 15 percent rate (green) applies only to the income between $8,375 and $34,000, and so on.

Source: Internal Revenue Service, Individual Federal Income Tax Rates for Single Individuals 2009.

What are the arguments for and against taxing individuals with higher income at higher rates?

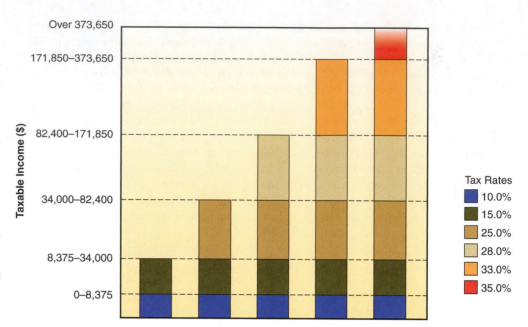

Progressive tax rates

Tax rates that increase as income increases; for example, the federal income tax is assessed using progressive rates.

Regressive tax rates

Tax rates that place more of a burden on low- and middle-income taxpayers than on wealthier ones; for example, sales taxes and most other consumption taxes are regressive.

Progressive Tax Rates Progressive tax rates, such as federal income tax rates, increase as income increases. Citizens at the very bottom of the financial totem pole have no taxable income and pay nothing, but as incomes increase, the rate increases stepwise from 10 percent to 35 percent. However, the greater rates apply only to *marginal* increments in income. For example, a single person with $400,000 in taxable income pays 10 percent on the first $8,375, just as lower-income taxpayers do; a rate of 15 percent applies only to taxable income above $8,375 and less than $34,000; and so forth as shown in Figure 12.3. The highest rate, 35 percent, applies *only* to the amount greater than $373,650 and not to an individual's entire income.

Liberal citizens and other supporters of progressive taxation argue that persons with greater incomes can better afford to pay greater tax rates and that lower-income persons should be left with enough of their incomes to maintain the necessities of life. Lower-income persons also spend a larger share of their incomes on consumption, which is the largest driving force in the economy.

Such arguments have not convinced Texans, who adopted a state constitutional amendment that forbids a state income tax unless voters approve. Even then, it can be used only for education and property tax relief.

Regressive Tax Rates By contrast, Texas has **regressive tax rates**, whereby the rate declines as income increases. For example, the state general sales tax (6.25%, among the highest in the nation) is proportional to the value of sales, but because of patterns of consumption, the effective rate actually declines as a person's income increases. Table 12.1 shows that if a family's income increases, so does its general sales tax payment. That fact seems reasonable—one would expect the purchases of taxable items to increase as income increases. But note that as income increases, an ever smaller *percentage* of that income is used for taxable purchases. Presumably, more money is saved, invested, or spent on tax-exempt items. Thus, despite exemptions for certain essential items, the effective rate of the Texas general sales tax

TABLE 12.1 TEXAS GENERAL SALES TAX PAID IN DOLLARS AND AS A PERCENTAGE OF TAXABLE INCOME, 2009*

Follow the income column down and notice that, as income increases, sales tax payments in dollars increase, but the rate declines as a percentage of income. What are the arguments for this kind of regressive taxation?

Taxable Income	Texas General Sales Tax	% of Taxable Income
$ 10,000	$ 259	2.59%
25,000	438	1.75
35,000	534	1.53
45,000	620	1.38
55,000	698	1.27
65,000	771	1.19
75,000	841	1.12
85,000	907	1.07
95,000	970	1.02
110,000	1,055	0.96
130,000	1,173	0.90
150,000	1,279	0.85
170,000	1,386	0.82
190,000	1,485	0.78
1,000,000	1,997	0.20

*For single individuals.

Source: Internal Revenue Service, Form 1040, 2009, p. A-13.

declines as income increases; a working-class individual with an income of $25,000 pays an effective sales tax *rate* more than twice as high as an individual with an income of $190,000 annually. Similarly, taxpayers pay a smaller percentage of their incomes in property and excise taxes as their incomes increase.

There is a simple explanation for the regressive quality of most consumer taxes—the **declining marginal propensity to consume**. As income increases, a person saves and invests more, thus spending a smaller percentage of that income on consumer items. Compare two smokers. One earns $20,000 per year and the other $200,000 per year. Does the typical smoker who earns $200,000 per year smoke 10 times as much as the one who earns $20,000? Of course not! Let's assume that each smoker consumes one pack of cigarettes a day; each therefore pays $514.65 a year in Texas tobacco taxes. For the low-income individual, tobacco taxes represent almost 7 days of earnings, but the other smoker earned the money to pay tobacco taxes in only 5 hours and 21 minutes.

Consumption of most items follows a similar pattern. The mansion represents a smaller share of the income for the millionaire than a shack does for a poor person. Proportionately, the Rolls-Royce is less of a burden to its owner than the old Chevrolet to its less-affluent owner. Obviously, there are exceptions, but appetites do not increase proportionately with income. Consequently, almost any tax on consumption will not reflect ability to pay. Yet Texas's state and local taxes are based on some form of consumption—property taxes, general sales taxes, gross-receipts taxes, or selective sales taxes.

Even business taxes may be regressive for individuals because of **tax shifting**. Businesses regard their tax burden as part of their operating cost, and much of that cost is shifted to customers in the form of higher prices. When property taxes increase, landlords raise rents. When business taxes are imposed, prices of consumer items usually increase as those taxes are passed on to customers as hidden taxes. Thus many business taxes become, in effect, "consumer" taxes and, like other consumer taxes, regressive relative to income.

Declining marginal propensity to consume

The tendency, as income increases, for persons to devote a smaller proportion of their income to consumer spending and a larger proportion to savings or investments.

Tax shifting

Businesses passing taxes to consumers in the form of higher prices.

TABLE 12.2 TEXAS MAJOR STATE AND LOCAL TAXES AS A PERCENTAGE OF HOUSHOLD INCOME, FISCAL 2011*

Look across each row in the table to see how major state and local taxes burden low- and middle-income taxpayers more. Why do such consumer taxes burden high-income families least? How can a business tax like the margins tax weigh most heavily on low-income families?

	Lower Income	Lower Middle	Middle Income	Upper Middle	Upper Income
General Sales Tax	5.4%	3.2%	2.7%	2,4%	1.7%
Franchise (Margins) Tax	0.8	0.5	0.4	0.4	0.3
Gasoline Tax	0.7	0.4	0.4	0.3	0.2
Motor Vehicle Sales Tax	0.5	0.3	0.3	0.3	0.2
School Property Tax	4.8	2.8	2.4	2.4	2.3

*Estimates based on an economic model that takes into account the effect of tax shifting. Household incomes are categorized by quintiles from the lowest one-fifth to the highest one-fifth, each representing 1,818,160 households.

Source: Texas Comptroller of Public Accounts, *Exemptions and Tax Incidence,* February 2009, pp. 47–66.

Taking into account all state and local taxes and tax shifting, Texas has one of the most regressive tax structures among the 50 states. Table 12.2 shows the final incidence of major state and local taxes on Texas families. Those with the lowest fifth of household incomes paid 5.4 percent of their income in general sales taxes—more than three times the percentage that upper-income households pay. Lower-income households paid an effective school property tax rate more than twice as high as upper-income households. And, for low-income households, the gasoline tax represents more than three times the burden that it does for the

HOW DOES TEXAS COMPARE?
TAXES—WHO PAYS? AND, HOW MUCH?

★ State taxes remain low in Texas compared with other states (see Figure 12.4). Only New Hampshire and South Dakota collect a smaller percentage of their residents, incomes than Texas, which collects approximately 4.6 percent; the average state collects 6.4 percent. Alaska has the highest tax rate in the United States, because of its huge severance tax revenue, but much of this tax burden is "exported" to other states that use Alaskan oil.

★ One way Texas has kept state taxes low is by using unfunded mandates that require local governments to provide services usually funded at the state level. Nevertheless, including local taxes and even the taxes that Texans pay in other states, the Tax Foundation calculated that Texans paid only 8.4 percent of personal income in all state and local taxes in 2009; residents of only seven states paid less.

★ Most states rely heavily on sales and gross-receipts taxes, but few states are as dependent on them as Texas. Only Nevada depends more on various sales taxes (especially its gambling taxes) than Texas. Because Texas relies so much on consumer taxes, it has one of the ten most regressive tax systems in the nation.

★ Texas is one of seven states without a progressive personal income tax and one of only four states without a corporate income tax. By contrast, progressive personal and corporate income taxes generate more revenues than regressive sales taxes in 21 states.

FOR DEBATE

★ *Do Texas's low tax rates attract business and promote economic growth? What is the effect of low state tax rates on the quality of state services?*

★ *Should Texas follow the lead of many other states by adopting more progressive tax policies that are less dependent on consumer taxes? Why? Why not?*

Sources: U.S. Department of Commerce, U.S. Census Bureau, Governments Division, *2007 Survey of State Government Finances,* March 2009: Council of State Governments, *Book of the States, 2009,* pp. 389–396; Legislative Budget Board, *Fiscal Size-Up, 2010–2011,* p. 48; Institute on Taxation and Economic Policy, *Who Pays? A Distributional Analysis of All 50 States* (3rd ed.), 2009, http://www.itepnet.org/whopays.htm; Tax Foundation, http://www.taxfoundation.org/research/topic/60.html

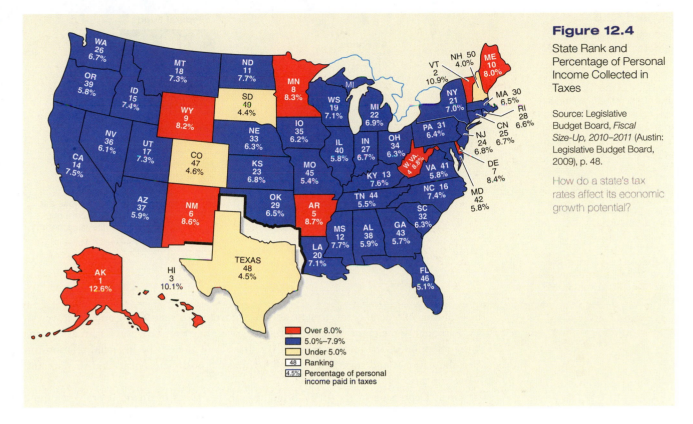

Figure 12.4

State Rank and Percentage of Personal Income Collected in Taxes

Source: Legislative Budget Board, *Fiscal Size-Up, 2010–2011* (Austin: Legislative Budget Board, 2009), p. 48.

How do a state's tax rates affect its economic growth potential?

Legend:
- Over 8.0%
- 5.0%–7.9%
- Under 5.0%
- 48 Ranking
- 4.5% Percentage of personal income paid in taxes

upper-income households. Lower-income families even bear a disproportionate share of the state's franchise tax on business.

Although they usually oppose business taxes, conservatives and high-income groups who support other regressive taxes argue that taxes on higher-income individuals should be kept low to allow them to save and invest to stimulate the economy—this is known as **supply-side economics**. They argue that applying higher rates to higher incomes is unfair and that sales and property taxes are easier to collect, harder to evade or avoid, and generally less burdensome than progressive income taxes. Some advocate a national sales tax, also known as the "fair tax," to replace the progressive federal income tax.

Supply-side economics

The theory that higher-income taxpayers should be taxed less because their savings and investments stimulate the economy.

Non-Tax Revenues

FEDERAL GRANTS-IN-AID

Much federal money is provided for Texas state and local government programs. For the 2010–2011 biennium, Texas will receive approximately $65.5 billion in federal funds, which represents 36 percent of state revenues (see Figure 12.5). A large majority of what Texas spends for health and human services and approximately 45 percent of what it spends for transportation originate as federal grants. Although there has been movement toward consolidating federal grant-in-aid programs, they are so numerous that it is only possible to generalize about them.

Figure 12.5

Federal Funds (in billions of dollars) as a Share of All Texas Funds, 2010–2011. The pie chart shows that about 36 percent of Texas revenues came from the federal government. Notice that most of these federal funds are for health and human services and stimulus funds for a variety of programs.

*Stimulus funds are mostly temporary funds made available by the American Recovery and Reinvestment Act of 2009.
**Primarily highways.

Source: Legislative Budget Board, *Fiscal Size-Up, 2010–2011* (Austin: Legislative Budget Board, 2009), pp. 31–32.

How can availability of these federal funds impact on policy decisions at the state level?

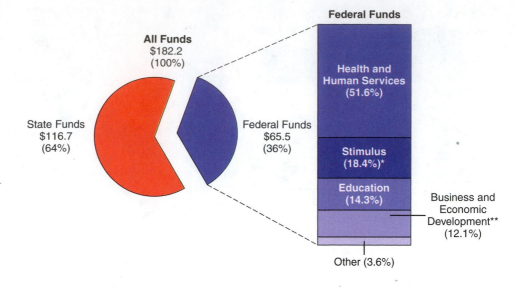

All Funds
$182.2
(100%)

State Funds $116.7 (64%)

Federal Funds $65.5 (36%)

Federal Funds

Health and Human Services (51.6%)

Stimulus (18.4%)*

Education (14.3%)

Business and Economic Development** (12.1%)

Other (3.6%)

Categorical grants

Federal aid to state or local governments for specific purposes, granted under restrictive conditions and often requiring matching funds from the receiving government.

Block grants

Federal grants to state or local governments for more general purposes and with fewer restrictions than categorical grants.

Devolution

The attempt to enhance the power of state or local governments, especially by substituting more flexible block grants instead of restrictive categorical grants in aid.

The evolution of federal grants to state and local governments has a long and controversial history. Although some grants from the national government to the states began as early as 1785, the adoption of the income tax in 1913 drastically altered the financial relationship between the national and state governments by making possible extensive aid to state and local governments.

The Great Depression of the 1930s brought with it a series of financial problems more severe than state and local governments had previously experienced. Increased demand for state and local services when revenues were rapidly declining stimulated a long series of New Deal grant-in-aid programs, ranging from welfare to public health and unemployment insurance.

Most of these early grant-in-aid programs were **categorical grants**. Under such aid programs, Congress appropriates funds for a specific purpose and sets up a formula for their distribution. Certain conditions are attached to these grant programs:

1. The receiving government agrees to match the federal money with its own, at a ratio fixed by law (between 10 and 90% of the cost of the program).
2. The receiving government administers the program. For example, federal funds are made available for Medicaid, but it is the state that actually pays client benefits.
3. The receiving government must meet minimum standards of federal law. For example, states are forbidden to spend federal money in any way that promotes racial segregation. Sometimes additional conditions are attached to categorical grants, such as regional planning and accounting requirements.

Most federal aid, however, now takes the form of newer **block grants** specifying general purposes such as job training or community development but allowing the state or local government to determine precisely how the money should be spent. Conditions may also be established for receipt of block grants, but state and local governments have greater administrative flexibility than with categorical grants. Federal transportation, welfare, and many other grants have been reformed to allow for significant **devolution** of power to the states through block grants.

The latest expansion of federal grants was a temporary response the economic collapse that began in 2007. In an attempt to stem the effects of the great recession, Congress passed a series of massive economic stimulus and bailout bills. Among them was the American

Recovery and Reinvestment Act of 2009 that pumped $12.1 billion of mostly temporary federal funds into Texas's treasury during the 2010–2011 budget period. More than one-half of these stimulus grants were spent on education, with much of the remainder going to state programs such as transportation, Medicaid, and unemployment benefits.

Although the infusion of these funds allowed the legislature to balance its budget despite plummeting state tax revenues, these temporary stimulus grants were extremely controversial. Governor Perry took a very high-profile stand against several grants that he believed placed too many restrictions on the state. For example, the state refused approximately $500 million in unemployment aid because the funds were conditioned on the state expanding eligibility for the program. Although resistance to stimulus funds was particularly intense, the tension between federal and state power will continue to be a feature of the American federal system, as it has been throughout the nation's history.

Texas Comptroller of Public Accounts Susan Combs is the state's chief tax collector and financial officer. Her financial estimates are binding on the legislature during the appropriation process.

How effective are Texas's balanced budget requirements? Should the national government also be required to balance its budget? Why? Why not?

BORROWING AND OTHER REVENUES

At the beginning of each legislative session, the comptroller of public accounts reports to the legislature the total amount of revenues expected from current taxes and other sources, and the legislature can in turn appropriate no more than this amount unless it enacts new tax laws. The few exceptions to this general limit are (1) the legislature, by a nearly impossible four-fifths vote, may borrow in emergency situations, and (2) the 1876 state constitution has been amended to provide for the issuance of bonds for specific programs.

State bonds are classified as (1) **general-obligation bonds** (to be repaid from general revenues), which have been used to finance prison construction, the veterans' real estate programs, water development, and higher education; and (2) **revenue bonds**, to be repaid with the revenues from the service they finance, such as higher education bonds financed by tuition revenue.

Other non-tax revenues account for a small share of its income from the lottery; various licenses, fines, and fees; dividends from investments; and the sale and leasing of public lands. For example, despite the continuing publicity it receives, Texas's net lottery proceeds account for less than one percent of total revenue.

General-obligation bonds

Bonds to be repaid from general taxes and other revenues; such bond issues usually must be approved by voters.

Revenue bonds

Bonds to be repaid with revenues from the projects that they finance, such as utilities or sports stadiums.

The Budgetary Process

Having discussed the various sources of state revenue, it is appropriate to turn to the other end of the money stream—budgeting and spending. There are two basic steps in setting spending priorities for the state: First, a budget plan must be formulated. Then the legislature must appropriate the funds necessary to implement the plan.

BUDGET PLANNING

Every state has developed some sort of central budgeting agency. Typically, such agencies are set up within the executive branch and are provided with a staff to analyze and evaluate budget requests before submitting a comprehensive budget to the legislature for its consideration. In some states, budget preparation is the joint responsibility of both the legislative and executive branches.

Texas has established a dual system of budget preparation in which the legislative and executive branches each have separate budgeting agencies: (1) the Legislative Budget Board (LBB), a legislative agency composed of the presiding officers of the Texas House and Senate plus four other members from each of the two houses; and (2) the governor's office.

These two budgeting agencies engage in some joint activities. A full year before the legislature meets, they jointly prepare forms on which the state's operating agencies submit their budgetary requests. After these requests are submitted, joint hearings are held, but the LBB's staff and the governor's staff make independent proposals. These two proposed budgets differ considerably because each of the two branches has its own distinct perspectives, goals, and political considerations. Finally, the two budgets are submitted to the appropriate legislative committees for consideration.

There is also a strong tendency toward **incremental budgeting** as agencies base their current budget requests on past appropriations plus some provision for increase. In the rush of the short 140-day session, the legislature cannot conscientiously evaluate billions of dollars in budget requests, so it reviews ongoing programs in light of past expenditures, whereas new spending programs are viewed more critically. Reformers frequently advocate **zero-based budgeting**, which would not assume that past appropriations reflect current needs but would instead evaluate existing programs as if they were new programs for which funding had to be justified.

THE APPROPRIATIONS PROCESS

It is through the **appropriations** process that the legislature legally authorizes the state to spend money to provide its various programs and services. Appropriations bills follow the same steps (described in Chapter 7) as other legislation, through standing committee consideration, floor action, conference committee compromise, final voting, and then approval by the governor. And during most of the legislative process, the recommendations of the LBB (because they tend to reflect the wishes of the legislature's powerful presiding officers) carry greater weight than those of the governor.

Perhaps the governor's most effective influence in the spending process results from the line-item veto. Texas's chief executive can veto particular items of expenditure without killing the whole bill. Although all vetoes may be overridden by a two-thirds vote of the legislature, in practice, item vetoes on appropriations bills are final. The legislature finishes its work on the appropriations bill so late in the session that it has usually gone home by the time the governor takes it up; obviously, such after session vetoes are immune to an override attempt.

THE POLITICS OF STATE SPENDING

A wide variety of factors affects the level of state spending and complicates efforts toward rational public spending. Nowhere is the dynamic nature of politics so evident as in public finance; nowhere is the conflict between competing economic interests more visible than in the budgetary process. Behind the large figures that represent the state's final budget are vigorous conflict, compromise, and coalition building. Most of society's programs are evaluated not only according to their merit but also in light of the competing demands of other programs and other economic interests. Government programs and problems compete for a share of the public treasury—highways, education, urban decay, poverty, crime, the environment—in short, all the problems and challenges of a modern society.

Powerful political constituencies, interest groups, and their lobbyists join forces with state agencies to defend the programs that benefit them. This alliance between administrative agencies and interest groups brings great pressure to bear on the legislative process, especially targeting the powerful House Appropriations Committee, the Senate Finance Committee,

Incremental budgeting

Basing an agency's budget requests on past appropriations plus increases to cover inflation and increased demand for their services, assuming that past appropriations justify current budgetary requests.

Zero-based budgeting

Evaluating budget requests for existing programs as if they were new programs rather than on the basis of past levels of funding.

Appropriations

The process by which a legislative body legally authorizes a government to spend specific sums of money to provide various programs and services.

and presiding officers. Individual legislators trade votes among themselves (a process called **logrolling**) to realize increased funding to benefit their districts or their supporters.

Dedicated funds also prevent the legislature from systematically reviewing the state's expenditures. For example, three-fourths of motor fuel tax revenues are dedicated to the State Highway Fund and one-fourth to the Available School Fund. Earnings from state lands are automatically directed to the Permanent University Fund and the Permanent School Fund. Contributions to the Teacher Retirement Fund may be used only for their specified purpose. The Texas Constitution and state statutes automatically channel 45 percent of state revenues to specified purposes with little or no legislative involvement.

Of course, federal grants, court orders, and other restrictions also limit the legislature as it adopts appropriations bills. One-fifth of the state's budget is discretionary spending (unaffected by federal, state, statutory, or court requirements).

Biennial legislative sessions themselves add irrationalities to the appropriations process. It is impossible to predict with precision how many students will enroll in a college for the upcoming semester, yet the legislature is expected to predict the state's financial needs two years in advance on the basis of how many students enroll in all public colleges in the state as well as elementary and secondary schools, how many applicants will be found eligible for unemployment and welfare benefits, how many potholes will develop along state highways, how many criminals will be sentenced to state prison, how many patients will be admitted to state hospitals, and so on. Inevitably, some agencies will be overfunded and others will have too little money to spend. Overfunded agencies always find ways to spend whatever money they have, while others literally run out of money during the biennium.

REFORMS

Because waste, fraud, and abuse plague public finance, Texas has made some attempts at reform. For example, voters amended the Texas Constitution to give the governor and Legislative Budget Board some budget execution authority. Acting jointly, they may make emergency transfers of existing appropriations from one program to another.

In another reform, the legislature directed the LBB to conduct a continuing systematic review of state spending and agency efficiency—the Texas Performance Review. Past reviews have resulted in the creation of the Health and Human Services Commission to coordinate related agencies. The Performance Review has also identified other examples of waste and inefficiency, but much still needs to be done.

Logrolling

Trading votes among legislators, especially to fund local projects to benefit their constituents.

Dedicated funds

Revenues dedicated for a specific purpose by the constitution or statute.

HOW DOES TEXAS COMPARE?
BUDGETING, BORROWING, AND SPENDING

★ Congress and most state legislatures work with a budget plan submitted by the chief executive as they begin the appropriations process. In Texas, however, the chief executive's budget proposals have less influence than the recommendations submitted by the Legislative Budget Board; Texas's governor is not truly the state's chief budget officer.

★ Unlike the national government, most states require that either their governor must submit a balanced budget or that the legislature pass one. Texas restrictions against borrowing are more effective than most—the average per capita state debt is more than three times higher than in Texas.

★ Unlike the U.S. president, 43 state governors (including Texas's) have a line-item veto. Reformers have advocated that the president should also be given this power to cut wasteful federal spending and to eliminate specially earmarked pet projects (pork barrel) inserted by members of Congress during the appropriations process. However, the experience in the states has not been promising—per capita state spending and state debt is not significantly lower in states where the governor has the item veto than in states where the governor lacks this power. In 2009, Governor Rick Perry item vetoed only 0.2 percent of the appropriations bill.

CHAPTER SUMMARY

* Although state budgets set records every two years, state spending as a percentage of personal income remains fairly constant, and state tax rates also remain low.

* Less than one-half of state revenues are raised through taxes. A substantial portion (more than one-third) comes from federal grants-in-aid, and miscellaneous sources account for the rest. State borrowing is limited.

* Although political self-interest determines which kinds of taxes are used, taxing decisions may be rationalized as serving some regulatory purpose or reflecting benefits received or ability to pay. Both narrow- and broad-based taxes are used in Texas.

* The largest single state tax is the general sales tax, which is regressive relative to income because it falls most heavily on middle- and lower-income people. Most state taxes, including selective sales taxes and gross-receipts taxes, are also consumer taxes and regressive relative to income. Even business taxes are shifted onto consumers.

* Local ad valorem and sales taxes also burden those least able to pay. Among taxes that Texans pay, only the federal income tax is somewhat progressive.

* Besides tax revenue, the other major sources of state revenue include traditional categorical and more flexible block grants from the federal government. Temporary stimulus grants also boosted the state's revenues in the 2010–2011 budget period.

* The LBB dominates the process of proposing Texas's state budget as the state legislature frequently follows its recommendations during the appropriations process. The governor's most effective tool in spending decisions is the item veto.

* Incremental budgeting, dedicated funding, biennial legislative sessions, logrolling, restrictions on state borrowing and the disproportionate influence of certain powerful interest groups limit rational budget planning and implementation.

* The spending process is political. Perhaps no other type of decision evokes more consistent and passionate political efforts from interest groups and administrative agencies. The outcome of this process is discussed in Chapter 13.

HOW TEXAS COMPARES

* Texans pay a smaller percentage of their incomes in state and local taxes than in most states.

* Only Nevada relies more heavily on sales taxes than Texas. Because Texas local governments also rely on regressive taxes, Texas state and local taxes weigh more heavily on poor and middle-income families than most states. As one of only four states with neither progressive personal nor corporate income taxes, Texas has no progressive tax resources.

* Although the governor has the line-item veto on appropriations, like 42 other governors, that power generally shows little effect in reducing wasteful state spending or earmarks for special legislative projects.

KEY TERMS

ability-to-pay taxes	declining marginal propensity	incremental budgeting	revenue bonds
ad valorem tax	to consume	logrolling	selective sales (excise) tax
appropriations	dedicated funds	loopholes	severance tax
benefits-received tax	devolution	personal property	supply-side economics
block grants	general-obligation bonds	progressive tax rates	tax base
broad-based tax	general sales tax	real property	tax rate
categorical grants	gross-receipts tax	regressive tax rates	tax shifting
	hidden taxes	regulatory tax	zero-based budgeting

REVIEW QUESTIONS

1. Discuss the major types of taxes imposed by state and local governments. How does Texas compare with other states?

2. What are the advantages and disadvantages of regulatory taxes? Of taxes based on the benefits-received principle? Of taxes based on the ability-to-pay principle?

3. Define *progressive* and *regressive* tax rates. What are the arguments for and against each type? Which social groups benefit from each type?

4. Outline the major steps in the budgetary and appropriations process.

5. How should Texas reform its tax structure? Why?

LOGGING ON

The key site for taxes and the budget is the Window on State Government of the Comptroller of Public Accounts at **http://www.window.state.tx.us**. Scroll down to "Find a Comptroller Publication." Some of the most valuable publications for research are as follows:

✴ *Texas in Focus: A Statewide View of Opportunities*

✴ *Biennial Revenue Estimate, 2010–2011*

✴ *Exemptions and Tax Incidence, 2009*

✴ *Texas Revenue by Source*

✴ *Annual Financial Reports*

✴ *American Recovery and Reinvestment: A Texas Eye on the Dollars*

Research tax and budget issues at the Texas Legislative Budget Board website **http://www.lbb.state.tx.us**. The most useful research tools include:

✴ General Appropriations Act for the 2010–2011 Biennium

✴ Budget 101: A Guide to the Budget Process in Texas

✴ Texas Fact Book

✴ Fiscal Size-Up 2010–2011 Biennium

Taxes, Social Services, and the Economic Impact of Illegal Immigrants

Brian K. Dille
Odessa College

INTRODUCTION

At least some undocumented immigrants benefit from virtually every service that the state of Texas offers. Although they drive up the cost taxpayers must pay to provide public services, illegal immigrants also contribute to the economy and pay taxes. In fact, Texas relies heavily on sales and use taxes that illegal immigrants cannot easily avoid. This article weighs the costs of state services provided to illegal immigrants against the taxes they pay. Its conclusions about what might be considered "net costs" have interesting implications for the debate over illegal immigration.

Much has been written and debated about the economic impact of illegal immigrants in the United States and Texas, ranging from the potential security threat since 9/11, the displacement of Americans and legal immigrants in the job market, and the financial burden they place on the social services of the state and nation. The controversy can be summed up by this question: Is the presence of illegal immigrants primarily a benefit to the nation, or is it a huge drain on its resources? This debate has intensified during the 2008 presidential campaign, particularly within the Republican Party. Anti-immigrant groups frequently argue that the costs of their presence in the state far outweigh the advantages, often ignoring or underemphasizing the benefits they provide. Proimmigrant groups typically argue that the benefits we receive from their presence exceed the resulting costs, downplaying the costs. The truth is not always easy to determine but lies somewhere between those two extreme positions. The challenge in weighing the benefits and costs is made more difficult by the fact that most illegal immigrants do not advertise their status, making exact and accurate data "guestimates." Further complicating this attempt is the fact that studies on this issue are often contradictory. The focus of this article is on the impact of illegal immigrants on the social services of Texas. An attempt will be made to determine whether the taxes they pay are greater or less than the cost of the services they use. The controversy over whether undocumented immigrants should or should not be recipients of these social services will not be the focus of this article.

BACKGROUND

The Pew Hispanic Center estimates that 30 percent of the foreign-born population is undocumented. (The undocumented include both those entering illegally and those overstaying their visit. The Immigration and Naturalization Service (INS) estimated that in 1996, about 41% of illegal immigrants living in the United States had entered the country legally but had overstayed their visit.[1]) The Center estimates that in 2005 the

---

[1] Carole Keeton Strayhorn, Texas Comptroller of Public Accounts, *Window on State Government*, April 2005, p. 8, http://www.window.state.tx.us/border/ch11.html

United States had approximately 11.1 million undocumented immigrants. The 2008 estimate, according to the Federation for American Immigration Reform (FAIR), is 13,175,000.[2] About 60 percent live in just six states: California, Texas, New York, Florida, Illinois, and New Jersey.[3] The Pew Center concludes that between 1.4 and 1.6 million (as of 2005) reside in Texas.[4] Texas is estimated to have about 14 percent of all undocumented immigrants in the United States.[5] The greatest number come from Latin America, with the majority coming from Mexico (56% of the total).[6] Adults comprise the largest number of undocumented immigrants—84 percent, and males account for 58 percent of all adults.[7] Most undocumented immigrants work in low-wage occupations not requiring a high level of education: 31 percent in service occupations, 19 percent in construction, 17 percent in cleaning, 15 percent in installation and repair, 12 percent in food preparation, and 4 percent in farming.[8] The foreign-born are found primarily in urban areas, and 88 percent are found in 7 council of government regions: Houston/Galveston, North Central Texas, Lower Rio Grande Valley, Upper Rio Grande Valley, Alamo Area, Capital Area, and South Texas.[9]

NATIONAL STUDIES

Many Americans are convinced that the cost of illegal immigrants comes not only from American citizens and legal residents who are displaced in the job market but from the social services the undocumented use. Although it is true that illegal immigrants do use social services, they are not eligible for a number of them: federal public assistance food stamps, Medicaid/Medicare, Supplemental Security Income (SSI), public housing assistance, federal student financial aid, unemployment insurance, cash welfare (TANF),[10] child care and development, and job opportunities for low-income individuals.[11] In the 1970s the states began reducing or eliminating illegal immigrants' eligibility for state and federal programs. That trend continued throughout the 1980s and 1990s, even affecting the eligibility for legal immigrants.[12]

It is also important to remember that illegal immigrants pay a variety of taxes: income, property, sales, and others (fees, etc.). The General Accounting Office released a report in 1995 summarizing national studies that weighed the costs and benefits resulting from illegal immigrants. Each study attempted to compare the tax revenue paid by the undocumented to federal, state, and local governments with the costs in social services, criminal justice, and so forth.[13] In a study by the Urban Institute, Jeffery Passel concluded that costs exceeded benefits by $2 billion. Passel calculated that immigrants pay more than $70 billion in taxes annually.[14] A second study by economist Donald Huddle, updating estimates from a 1993 report for the Carrying Capacity Network (an environmental group concerned over rapid population growth) concluded the costs were $19 billion. He estimated that only $20 billion was being paid in taxes by illegal immigrants.[15] A third study by Stephen Moore pointed out that the undocumented are paying into the Medicare and Social Security systems while their own parents are not collecting benefits. This results in a "one-generation windfall" to the Social Security system that will help cushion the increasing costs caused by the 40 million baby boomers retiring.[16] Another study concluded that undocumented immigrants pay into Social Security and Medicare, by the use of fake Social Security numbers, approximately $8.5 billion annually.[17] Each year, the U.S. Social Security Administration retains between $6 billion and $7 billion of Social Security contributions in an "earnings suspense file," an account for W-2 tax forms that cannot be matched to the correct Social Security Number. In just 2002, this revenue file accounted for $56 billion in earnings. It is assumed that the majority of these unmatched numbers belong to undocumented workers who do not claim their benefits.[18] Finally, in 2005 the National Research Council estimated that immigrants on average (not distinguishing between illegal and legal immigrants) pay $1,800 in taxes to federal, state, and local governments *above* their costs in services and benefits received.[19]

---

[2]*USA Today* Magazine, January 2008, Vol. 136, No. 2752, p. 7.

[3]Ibid.

[4]Pew Hispanic Center, *The Size and Characteristics of the Unauthorized Migrant Population in the U.S.* (Washington, DC, March 7, 2006), p. 4.

[5]Ibid., p. 11.

[6]Ibid., pp. 5–6.

[7]Senator Eliot Shapleigh, *Lifting the Lamp Beside Texas Door: Addressing the Challenges and Opportunities of Immigration in Texas for the 2007–2009 Biennium*, January 25, 2006, p. 27, http://shapleigh.org/system/reporting_document/file/167/ImmigrationChapter-Jan07.pdf

[8]Ibid., pp. 10–11.

[9]U.S. Census Bureau, Census 2000 Summary File 3, PCT19, Place of Birth for the Foreign-Born Population: Texas (County) and Census 1990 Summary Tape File (STF-3), PO42, Place of Birth.

[10]U.S. Department of Justice, Fact Sheet: Illegal Immigration Reform and Immigrant Responsibility Act of 1996, http://library.findlaw.com/1999/Jun/1/127033.html#15

[11]Carole Keeton Strayhorn, Texas Comptroller of Public Accounts, Special Report—Undocumented Immigrants in Texas: A Financial Analysis of the Impact to the State Budget and Economy, December 2006, p. 1.

[12]John Sharp, Texas Comptroller of Public Accounts, Immigration: Crossing the Line, July 1998, p. 167.

[13]General Accounting Office, *Illegal Aliens: National Net Cost Estimates Vary Widely* (Washington, DC: U.S. Government Printing Office, 1995).

[14]Jeffrey Passel, *Immigration and Taxes: A Reappraisal of Huddle's Cost of Immigration,* (Washington, DC: Urban Institute, 1994); Jeffrey Passel and Rebecca Clark, *How Much Do Immigrants Really Cost?* (Washington, DC: Urban Institute, 1994).

[15]Donald Huddle, *The Costs of Immigration* (Washington, DC: Carrying Capacity Network, 1993).

[16]Stephen Moore, *A Fiscal Portrait of the Newest Americans* (Washington, DC: National Immigration Forum and the Cato Institute, 1998).

[17]"Health Care Expenditures of Immigrants in the United States: A Nationally Representative Analysis," *American Journal of Public Health*, Vol. 95 (August 2005), p. 1431.

[18]Shapleigh, p. 46.

[19]Michael LeMay, *Illegal Immigration: A Reference Handbook* (Santa Barbara, CA: Contemporary World Issues, 2007), p. 58.

TEXAS STUDIES

There are two major studies on the economic impact of illegal immigrants on Texas: a 2005 FAIR study and a 2006 study done by Texas Comptroller Carole Keeton Strayhorn. The FAIR report concluded that undocumented immigrants are costing Texas taxpayers more than $4.7 billion annually for education, incarceration, and medical care. They argue that tax payments by illegal immigrants "can generously be estimated at slightly less than $1 billion a year."[20] This results in a net loss of $3.7 billion annually for Texas taxpayers. FAIR estimates the annual educational costs (K–12) at more than $4 billion, health care costs at $520 million, and incarceration costs at about $150 million.[21]

The second study that focuses on undocumented immigrants in Texas is a Special Report issued by Texas Comptroller Carole Keeton Strayhorn in December of 2006. According to Strayhorn, this study was "the first time any state ha[d] done a comprehensive financial analysis of the impact of undocumented immigrants on a state's budget and economy, looking at . . . revenues generated, taxes paid, and the cost of state services."[22] The facts cited below come from that report.

Strayhorn's report repeated what the national studies have concluded—up to a point. The costs of illegal immigrants as the result of their use of social services comes primarily from education, medical expenses, incarceration, and the effects of the low-paid undocumented workers on the salaries of legal residents. The "revenue gains" come primarily from taxes that cannot be avoided: sales taxes, various user taxes such as gasoline, and various fees such as motor vehicle inspection fees.[23] Because undocumented workers are more likely to work in the "underground economy," where wages paid are often in cash and no income tax is paid, states with income taxes are hurt. In contrast, Texas, with no state income tax, relies more on consumption taxes for state revenue. These taxes, in the opinion of the Strayhorn report, most likely "capture" a higher percentage of all the taxes that should be paid from the economic activities of illegal immigrants.[24]

Strayhorn's report emphasizes that calculating the impact of illegal immigrants on Texas's economy and budget "is at best an educated guess."[25] It is particularly difficult to count a group who does not want to be counted. Thus, the Strayhorn report uses the estimates of the Pew Hispanic Center to determine the number of undocumented immigrants in Texas.

The Strayhorn report arrived at the following costs (for fiscal 2005 unless otherwise noted) from illegal immigrants using the following social services:

1	Public Education	$957 million (for 2004–2005)
2	College Education	$11.2 million (Fall 2004)
3	State Medicaid	$38.75 million
4	Children with Special Health Care Needs	$7.2 million
5	Substance Abuse Services	$287,700
6	Mental Health Services	$3.8 million

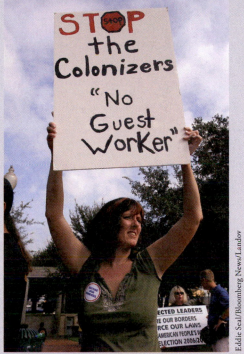

Eddie Seal/Bloomberg News/Landov

👆 *A major argument against illegal immigration is that many undocumented workers benefit from state services without paying taxes. Although it is true that many of them are part of an "underground economy" in which wages are often paid in cash and income taxes are not paid at all, the Texas Comptroller reports that they pay a considerable amount in consumption taxes such as state general sales taxes.*

How much do illegal immigrants cost Texas state and local governments? How much do they pay in taxes?

7	Women and Children's Health Services/ School Based Programs	$674,000
8	Public Health	$3.9 million
9	Emergency Medical Services	$3.4 million
10	Incarceration	$130.6 million
	Total State Expenditures on Undocumented Immigrants Local Government and Entities Expenditures:	**$1,156.4 billion**[26]
11	Local (Sheriff Dept.) Law Enforcement Costs	$49.1 million[27]
12	Texas Hospitals— Uncompensated Care (local entities)	$1.3 billion[28]

[20]Federation for American Immigration Reform, *Costs of Illegal Immigration to Texans: Executive Summary*, April 2005, http://www.fairus.org/site
[21]Ibid.
[22]Carole Keeton Strayhorn, Texas Comptroller of Public Accounts, *Special Report—Undocumented Immigrants in Texas: A Financial Analysis of the Impact to the State Budget and Economy*, December, 2006, p. 1.
[23]Ibid.

The estimated revenue from undocumented immigrants for fiscal 2005 indicates that state revenue from undocumented immigrants does exceed state expenditures for illegal immigrants, as the following figures show:

1	Major Consumption Taxes and Fees	$866.7 million
2	Lottery	$60.9 million
3	Utilities	$19.5 million
4	Court Costs and Fees	$20.6 million
5	All Other Revenue	$31.2 million
	State Revenue Subtotal	**$989.9 million**
	School Property Tax	$582.1 million
	Total Estimated Revenue	**$1,581.1 billion**[29]

CONCLUSIONS

The findings of Strayhorn's study are contrary to two recent reports on the costs versus benefits of undocumented immigrants: FAIR's "The Cost of Illegal Immigration to Texans" and the Bell Policy Center's "Costs of Federally Mandated Services to Undocumented Immigrants in Colorado." FAIR's report included the costs in education for legal children to undocumented parents, whereas the Comptroller's report focused only on the costs "directly attributed to undocumented persons" and did not include the costs of the "legally resident children of illegal immigrants." Also, the Strayhorn report estimates $581 million more in undocumented immigrant tax revenue than does the FAIR study. In conclusion, according to Comptroller Strayhorn's study, "illegal immigrants produced $1.58 billion in state revenues, which exceeded the almost $1.16 billion in state services they received." The report did acknowledge, however, that local governments "bore the burden of $1.44 billion in uncompensated health care costs and local law enforcement costs not paid for by the state."

The report emphasized that the largest costs from undocumented immigrants is to local governments and hospitals, primarily the costs of uncompensated incarceration and health care. These costs were estimated as $1.3 billion for hospitals and $141.9 million for local incarceration. These costs exceeded the estimated $513 million paid in local taxes by illegal immigrants. Thus, in 2005 undocumented immigrants cost local governments and hospitals $928.9 million above the $513 million in local tax revenue received from the illegal immigrants.[26] Clearly, although the state government receives more tax revenue than they spend on the social services for undocumented immigrants, the opposite is true for local governments and hospitals.

JOIN THE DEBATE

1. Do consumption taxes capture revenues from an "underground" economy better than income taxes? What contributions, other than tax payments, do illegal immigrants make to the Texas economy? Does the availability of low-wage immigrant workers make it possible for some businesses to operate?

2. Besides the costs of social services and law enforcement, what are the other economic costs of illegal immigration? Do low-wage illegal immigrants compete to drive down incomes of legal resident workers? Do employers of undocumented workers cut wages and workplace standards because their employees do not usually have legal recourse against them?

3. On balance, do the costs of illegal immigration outweigh its benefits? Should undocumented immigrants be denied the right to use state services? What problems do you see for Texas's future if undocumented immigrants were denied access to education and emergency health care? How should humanitarian concerns figure into the immigration debate?

[24]Ibid., p. 2
[25]Ibid.
[26]Ibid., pp. 4–20
[27]Ibid., p. 15.
[28]Ibid., p. 11.
[29]Ibid., p. 20.
[30]Ibid., pp. 1–2, 20.

Chapter 13

Spending and Services

CONTENTS

LEARNING OBJECTIVES

- ★ Explain competing views of government power and how state services create controversy.
- ★ Identify major state expenditures and how state spending reflects Texas's political culture.
- ★ Outline the major political issues surrounding each of Texas's most expensive state services.
- ★ Identify the decision makers who make important public choices for each major public policy focus in Texas.
- ★ Define the vocabulary of political controversy about Texas's public services.
- ★ Be able to take an informed position on public policy issues.

★ GET ✦ ACTIVE ★

Decide where you stand on education, the environment, health care, transportation, energy, privatization, crime, and corporate welfare.

Tap into Texas-based "think tanks" with public policy websites that offer contrasting conclusions about a wide range of issues. Although they are funded by special interest groups, they can still provide interesting perspectives and useful information. Visit think-tank websites and determine where your views fit into the conservative or liberal spectrum.

Conservative Groups

★ The Institute for Policy Innovation at **http://www.ipi.org/**. Probe the group's positions on health care and poverty.

★ Lone Star Foundation at **http://www .lonestarfoundation.org/**. Check out the conservative position on health care and welfare.

★ Private Enterprise Research Center at **http://www.tamu.edu/perc/**. Investigate the center's view of health care, welfare, and taxes.

★ Texas Conservative Coalition Research Institute at **http://www.txccri.org/**. Nose around this group's stand on health care, outsourcing, and privatization.

★ Texas Public Policy Foundation at **http://www.texaspolicy.com/**. Peer into the conservative philosophy about dealing with health care, education, and crime.

Liberal/Progressive Groups

★ The Center for Public Policy Priorities at **http://www.cppp.org/**. Probe the liberal view of poverty and health care.

★ Public Citizen—Texas State Office at **http://www.citizen.org/texas/**. Acquaint yourself with energy and environmental issues.

★ Texas Center for Policy Studies at **http:// www.texascenter.org/**. Check out liberal positions on the environment.

★ Texans for Public Justice at **http://www .tpj.org/**. Spot the influence of money and corporate power in Texas politics.

★ Find out which organizations and experts are front groups for corporate interests at **http://www.sourcewatch.org/**

Libertarian Groups

★ Sample the libertarian viewpoints at the national Cato Institute website **http:// www.cato.org/**. Search the site for "corporate welfare" to find such examples as those at **http://www.cato.org/pubs/ handbook/hb105-9.html**

Get the facts on health care in Texas and the rest of the nation at the Kaiser Family Foundation website at **http://www.state-healthfacts.org/**

Team up with those who agree with you on toll roads.

★ Plug into the Department of Transportation plans for privately funded highways in Texas at **http://www.txdot.gov/**

★ Fight privatization of Texas highways with Texans Uniting for Reform and Freedom at **http://www.texasturf.org/**

Get practical about your self-interest.

★ Get help paying for college at the Texas Higher Education Coordinating Board website at **http://www.collegefor texans .com/** and the Texas Comptroller's website at **http://www.everychanceeverytexan .org/**

★ Find lower electric and telephone rates, get help paying utility bills, and stop unwanted telephone solicitations at the Public Utilities Commission website at **http://www.puc.state.tx.us/**. Find competitive utility rates at **http://www .powertochoose.org/**

★ Compare your health insurance options at the Texas Department of Insurance sponsored site **http://www .texashealthoptions.com/**

★ Check out your doctor at the Texas Medical Board site at **http://www.tmb.state.tx.us/**

Two long-term and conflicting attitudes weave themselves through the American political culture. One emphasizes the potential of government to abuse its power by denying citizens their dignity and fundamental rights. The other regards government power as a positive instrument by which citizens can collectively provide for themselves those services that no other institution or individual can furnish.

Distrust of political power is amply justified. The history of government through the ages is blemished by the abuse and misuse of power and the rise and fall of successive dictatorships. Even in the United States, a bureaucracy has been constructed that too often seems uncontrollable and unresponsive. Texans, more than most Americans, have developed a political culture based on a conservative and cynical view of government power. They are not long removed from an era when a simpler rural life required little service from government. Even where the complexities of metropolitan living demand a growing role for government, Texans have remained suspicious.

However, Texans are also coming to expect more and more from the natural and social environments, demanding higher salaries and profits from economic institutions, more and better schools, more hospital beds, and more and better highways. The psychology of growth demands ever-increasing public services. These increasing expectations contribute to the growth of government spending.

Population growth and urbanization have also become expensive political and economic problems. Government is called on to supervise and regulate the economy in complex and costly ways, ranging from attempts to guarantee economic stability to efforts to prevent pollution. Just as the one-room schoolhouse can no longer meet our educational needs, neither can simple, inexpensive programs manage terrorism, poverty, crime, cultural tension, and other problems in the 21st century.

No single decision better typifies the political character of a state than its budget. The whole pattern of spending is, in a sense, a shorthand description of which problems the state has decided to face and which challenges it has chosen to meet. The budget shows how much of which services the state will offer and to whom. Figure 13.1

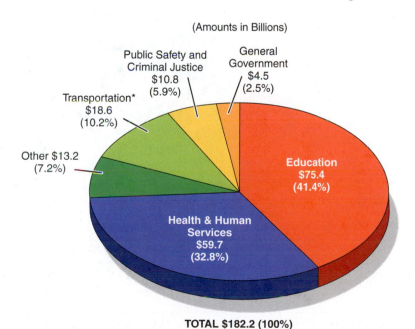

(Amounts in Billions)

Public Safety and Criminal Justice $10.8 (5.9%)

General Government $4.5 (2.5%)

Transportation* $18.6 (10.2%)

Other $13.2 (7.2%)

Education $75.4 (41.4%)

Health & Human Services $59.7 (32.8%)

TOTAL $182.2 (100%)

Figure 13.1

State Appropriations by Function, 2010–2011. The largest slice of Texas's budget pie goes to education, but the portion spent for health care is rapidly increasing.

*Primarily highways.

Source: Legislative Budget Board.

Explain why state spending decisions generate political controversy?

shows how Texas spent its state revenues in the 2010–2011 biennium. The most costly service in Texas is education. Public and higher education accounted for 41.4 percent of the state budget. Health and human services (including Medicaid and social services) were the second most expensive, accounting for 32.8 percent. Transportation, primarily highways, consumed 10.2 percent. These three services consume more than four-fifths of the state's budget, with a wide variety of miscellaneous services using up the remainder.

Both individuals and groups benefit from government services, and seeking these benefits, while denying them to others, is what motivates most political activity in the state. Political controversy develops because state services affect various groups differently and these groups evaluate state programs according to their competing self-interests and their conflicting views of the public interest. It is important to outline the state's most significant services and then explore some of the major political issues surrounding them.

Education in Texas

The educational system in Texas includes elementary and secondary schools (the public schools) and the college and university system (higher education).

HOW DOES TEXAS COMPARE?
SPENDING FOR PUBLIC SERVICES

Recently, Texas ranked last among 50 states in per capita spending (30% below the national average). Texas per capita expenditures for education ranked 44th among the 50 states and 48th for public welfare. The state ranked toward the middle in per capita spending for highways (28th) and hospitals (24th).[1]

FOR DEBATE

★ *Why would supporters argue that these budget items are "investments" in the state's future? If they are truly investments, how will the state realize economic gains from them?*

★ *Would higher rates of state spending in Texas drive up taxes and discourage economic growth in the state?*

[1]Legislative Budget Board, *Fiscal Size-Up, 2010–2011* (Austin: Legislative Budget Board, 2009), p. 54.

ELEMENTARY AND SECONDARY SCHOOLS

History Public schools were accepted institutions in the North by the early 19th century, but they did not take root in the South (including Texas) until after the Civil War. Not until the constitution of 1876 provided that alternate sections of public land grants be set aside to finance schools did the state begin to commit itself to locally administered, optional public schools.

Meaningful state support for public education started with a compulsory attendance law, enacted in 1915, and a constitutional amendment that provided for free textbooks in 1918. In 1949, the Gilmer-Aikin law increased state funding and established the Texas Education Agency (TEA), which carries out the state's educational program.

Recent Trends Sweeping changes in education resulted when House Bill 72 passed in 1984 to establish statewide **accountability** standards for student performance and teacher competence. Former President George W. Bush later took the use of "high stakes" testing nationwide with his "no child left behind" program.

Although the standards used to measure public school performance are sometimes controversial, there has been a recent trend toward their use to bring market forces to the public school system. Some teachers and administrators receive "merit pay," bonuses for improved student achievement. To introduce the element of competition among schools, the state legislature authorized the State Board of Education to establish schools with innovative special program charters, able to recruit students from across existing school district boundaries. Many state legislators now also favor adding even more school competition through *privatization* by providing vouchers to help students to buy their education from private businesses and organizations.

Today, public elementary and secondary education has grown from a fledgling underfinanced local function into a major state–local partnership. The TEA administers approximately 29 percent of all state expenditures, helping local school districts educate the approximately 90 percent of Texas students who attend public elementary and secondary schools. Public policy decisions affect the knowledge, attitudes, and earning potential of these 4.7 million students and the approximately 300,000 teachers who teach them.

Public School Administration As in other states, the Texas public school administration has three basic aspects:

1. Substantial local control in a joint state–local partnership.
2. Emphasis on "professional" administration supervised by laypersons.
3. Independence from the general structure of government.

State Administration The Texas Constitution, the legislature, and the State Board of Education (SBOE) have established the basic decision-making organizations and financial arrangements for public education in the state. The legislature approves the budget for the state's share of the cost of public education and sets statutory standards for public schools, but many policy decisions are left to the State Board of Education, the Texas Education Agency and local school districts.

Members of the State Board of Education are elected to 4-year overlapping terms in 15 single-member districts, and together they establish general rules and guidelines for the TEA. The SBOE approves organizational plans, recommends a budget to the governor and the Legislative Budget Board, and implements funding formulas established by the legislature. It sets curriculum standards, establishes guidelines for operating public schools, and requires management, cost-accounting, and financial reports from local districts. The SBOE leaves most routine managerial decisions to the Commissioner of Education.

Accountability

Responsibility for a program's results; for example, using measurable standards to hold public schools responsible for their students' performance.

The commissioner is appointed by the governor with consent of the senate to serve as the state's principal executive officer for education. With a number of assistant and associate commissioners and professional staff, the commissioner carries out the regulations and policies established by the legislature and the SBOE concerning public school programs.

Local Administration   Texas's 1,030 regular school districts (more than any other state) are the basic structure for local control. Voters in independent school districts elect seven or nine members (depending on the district's population) at large or from single-member electoral districts for either three- or four-year terms. These trustees set the district's tax rate and determine school policies within the guidelines established by the TEA. They approve the budget, contract for instructional supplies and construction, and hire and fire personnel. Their most important decision is the hiring of a professional superintendent, who is responsible for the executive or administrative functions of the school district.

Elected state and local school boards usually follow the recommendations of professional administrators (the commissioner and the superintendents). Most educational decisions are made independently of general government. Nevertheless, one should not conclude that independence from general government, localization, or "professionalism" keeps education free of politics. On the contrary, elected boards, especially the State Board of Education, have become quite politically assertive in recent years. Whenever important public decisions are made, political controversy and conflict arise.

THE POLITICS OF PUBLIC EDUCATION

One of the most important decisions concerning public education is what education should be. Should it promote traditional views of society, reinforce the dominant political culture, and teach "acceptable" attitudes? Or, should it teach students to be independent thinkers, capable of evaluating ideas for themselves? Because the Texas state educational system determines the curriculum, selects textbooks, and hires and fires teachers, it must answer these fundamental questions.

Curriculum   Most of the basic curriculum is determined by the SBOE. Some school districts supplement this basic curriculum with a variety of elective and specialized courses, but it is in the basic courses—history, civics, biology, and English—that students are most likely to be exposed to issues that may fundamentally affect their attitudes. How should a student be exposed to the theory of evolution? Should sex education courses offer discussion of artificial birth control or present abstinence as the only reliable method of birth control? In the social sciences, should the political system be pictured in terms of its ideals or as it actually operates, with all of its mistakes and weaknesses? How should the roles of women and minorities be presented? How should elective Bible courses be taught and by whom? Should students who do not speak standard English be gradually taught English through bilingual education, or should they immediately be immersed in the core curriculum taught in English?

Aside from social and political content, the substance of education in Texas has other important practical consequences as well. Although a large proportion of public school students will never enroll in an institution of higher learning, much educational effort and testing have been directed toward college preparatory courses that provide graduates with few, if any, usable job skills.

Historically, vocational, agricultural, and home economics programs were viewed as "burial grounds" for pupils who had failed in the traditional academic programs. Today, almost one-half of high school students are enrolled in "career and technology" programs, and one in five are in "family and consumer sciences." Although program titles have changed, much remains to be done to meet the need for highly skilled technical workers who possess other practical life skills.

TEXAS'S SOCIAL STUDIES CURRICULUM AND THE "CULTURE WARS"

After adopting controversial science and literature curriculum revisions in recent years, Texas's State Board of Education caused an even louder uproar in 2010 when it largely ignored the advice of professional educators and voted along party lines to establish the social studies curriculum standards for the upcoming decade.* Critics charged that the SBOE had hijacked the state's educational apparatus to impose a conservative, Christian fundamentalist political agenda on public school students.

Critics focused on standards that require teaching the political beliefs of conservative icons like Phyllis Schlafly, Newt Gingrich, the moral majority, and the National Rifle Association. Meanwhile, students will be taught that Senator Joseph McCarthy's anticommunist crusade may have been justified. Confederate President Jefferson Davis's inaugural address will be taught alongside Abraham Lincoln's speeches, and the role of slavery as a cause of the Civil War is downplayed.

Requirements that students learn the concept of "responsibility for the common good" (which one board member described as "communistic") has been removed from the curriculum. Students will learn that the United States is a "constitutional republic" rather than a "democratic society" and that the "separation of church and state" is not in the constitution. Students will evaluate how the United Nations undermines U.S. sovereignty and learn about the devaluation of the dollar including the abandonment of the gold standard. The curriculum standards emphasize the biblical and Judeo-Christian influences on the founding fathers and the benefits of free enterprise, which is mentioned more than 80 times in the curriculum requirements.

The state's new social studies standards attracted nationwide attention because of their implications for other states. Publishers develop textbooks and teaching materials to meet Texas standards and then attempt to market those publications in other smaller states. In the one state with enough market share to resist Texas textbook leadership, California legislative leaders considered legislation to require school authorities to screen for Texas-approved learning materials as a threat to the California education code requirement that public schools be nonpolitical.

FOR DEBATE

★ Is it possible to avoid political controversy in social science? Would a fact-based social science curriculum have political implications?

★ What is your position on the political issues raised by Texas's new social science curriculum standards?

*The Texas Essential Knowledge and Skills (TEKS) curriculum standards are available on the TEA website at http://www.tea.state.tx.us/

Textbooks The SBOE selects a list of approved textbooks that the state may buy for public school courses. The selection process generates intense political battles between conservative groups (such as the Texas Public Policy Foundation and Texas Freedom Works) and liberal groups such as the Texas Freedom Network. The conservatives have dominated the battle, and some publishers have withdrawn their text offerings or changed the content of their texts to satisfy the SBOE.

Legally, the SBOE can only determine the "accuracy" of textbooks, but it has used this power to pressure publishers to submit texts that reflect the political and religious values of its members. One publisher eliminated references to "fossil fuels formed millions of years ago" from a science text because it conflicts with some interpretations of the timeline in the Bible. Another eliminated sections that were too kind to Muslims by asserting that Osama bin Laden's actions were inconsistent with commonly accepted Islamic teachings (even though this is the official policy view of the U.S. government). An environmental science text was rejected because it favorably mentioned the Endangered Species Act and warned of the threat of global warming—one group argued that it was unpatriotic to refer to the fact that the United States represents 5 percent of the world's population but produces 25 percent of greenhouse gases. Under pressure from religious conservatives, publishers submitted health textbooks that presented an abstinence-only approach to sex education, excluding essential information about how to prevent unwanted pregnancies and sexually transmitted diseases. A Texas government text was rejected because it dared to include an article that asserted that the SBOE is influenced by religious conservatives!

Because Texas controls the second-largest textbook market in the nation, the state's textbook decisions have historically determined the content of texts used in public schools in much of the nation. In the future, however, school systems in other states may have more

ARE EDUCATORS PAID AS PROFESSIONALS?
The average annual earnings for Texas physicians is $164,020; lawyers,$124,600; pharmacists, $108,630; and elementary school teachers, $45,860.[2]

alternatives to Texas-preferred texts. Electronic books, specialty publishing, and custom options are replacing market-dominant, fixed-content texts, and the national textbook market is becoming much more competitive.

Faculties   Although the state board for educator certification establishes standards for qualification, conduct, and certification of public school teachers, actual hiring of teachers is a local matter. Most districts do not follow a publicly announced policy of hiring or dismissing teachers because of their political viewpoints, but in many districts, teachers are carefully screened for their attitudes. The absence of strong statewide policies requiring tenure for public school teachers makes them wary of controversy.

Salary and working conditions are perpetual issues of dissatisfaction among teachers because they affect morale and recruitment. Although student–teacher ratios remain typical in the 50 states, increasing public demands for accountability have added reporting and other paperwork to teachers' workloads beyond the standard expectations for lesson planning, grading, and communicating with parents.

Expected income is certainly a factor when people choose their careers, and education simply does not compare favorably among the professions. Texas teachers earn even less than public school teachers in other states. The National Education Association reported that Texas teachers' average salary of $46,179 in 2007–2008 was 11 percent less than the national average. The TEA reported that one-third of beginning teachers leave the profession by their fifth year.

Another issue for teachers has been the use of "high stakes" testing such as the Texas Assessment of Knowledge and Skills and the National Assessment of Education Progress ("The Nation's Report Card"). Teachers' groups have objected to the use of these test results in retention, promotion, and salary decisions on the grounds that they do not accurately measure the full range of teachers' contributions to student knowledge and that their use causes faculty to "teach the test" while ignoring other valuable skills and knowledge that are not included in standardized tests.

Students   Public schools have changed considerably in recent years. The number of students attending Texas public schools has been increasing at a rate of approximately two percent per year, and that increase is expected to continue for the next the decade. Figure 13.2 shows that students are also becoming more ethnically diverse and are increasingly from low-income backgrounds. This changing student population seems to present a challenge to public schools as a significant achievement gap remains between the performance of Anglo students and that of African Americans and Latinos.

Scores on the Texas Assessment of Knowledge and Skills (TAKS) test measure student achievement in lower grades and end-of-course exams in core classes are used to evaluate high school student performance. Student accountability programs have placed some limits on **social promotion** (promotion to the next grade on the basis of age rather than level of learning), and students failing TAKS are offered accelerated instruction in appropriate subjects. Perhaps as a result of these efforts, student performance on standardized tests has

Social promotion

Passing a student to the next grade on the basis of his or her age rather than level of learning.

[2]U.S. Department of Labor, Bureau of Labor Statistics, *May 2008 State Occupational and Wage Estimates*, Texas table.

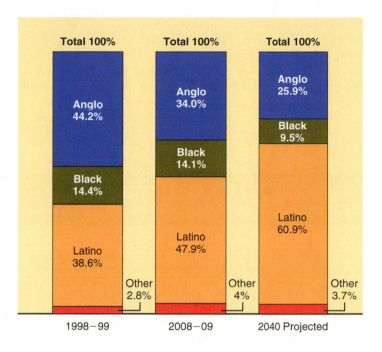

Figure 13.2

Ethnicity of Texas Public School Students. Compare the ethnicity of Texas public school students in 1998–99 (left column) with 2008–09 (center column) and projections of future enrollment (right column) to see the increasing diversity among students. The TEA also reports that about 57 percent of public school students are from low-income families.

Source: Texas Education Agency and Texas State Data Center.

What challenges do ethnic diversity and poverty present to public schools?

been improving somewhat during the past several years, and the gaps between performance between ethnic groups have narrowed. In 2009, 24.5 percent more Anglos passed TAKS than African Americans. whereas 17.7 percent more Anglos passed TAKS than Latinos.

Public School Finance In 2007–2008, expenditures for current public school operations in Texas were $7,987 per student (19% less than the national average). The actual distribution of these funds is governed according to extremely complex rules and mathematical formulas that occupy six chapters totaling more than 75,000 words in the Texas Education Code. Although public school accountants and financial officers must understand the nuances of these rules to maximize funding for their respective districts, students will need to understand only the system's most basic features to engage intelligently in the public debate that surrounds public school finance. The following discussion is organized around the three basic sources of public school funding—federal, state, and local.

Federal grants increased substantially in recent years. In addition to ongoing federal programs for child nutrition and special-needs, military, and low-income students, the American Recovery and Reinvestment Act of 2009 (known as the stimulus bill) pumped $6 billion into Texas public schools during the 2010–2011 budget period. These temporary federal funds were designed to offset the shortfall in state and local revenues caused by the recent economic recession. Such funds are not expected to be available in future years, and as a result, the state and local school districts will strain to fill the gap left in the absence of these one-time federal grants.

State funding comes from a variety of sources. The Permanent School Fund was established in 1854 and invests receipts of rentals, sales, and mineral royalties from Texas's public lands. Only the interest and dividends from this permanent endowment may be spent. Earnings from the Permanent School Fund and one-fourth of the motor fuels tax make up the Available School Fund, some of which is used for textbooks; the remainder is distributed to local school districts based on student average daily attendance. Basing distribution of state funds on attendance focuses a school district's attention on truancy.

The Foundation School Program (FSP) accounts for the largest portion of state and local funding by far. State funds from general revenues, a margins tax on business (the franchise tax), and a portion of tobacco taxes are distributed to districts according to formulas based on district and student characteristics. The FSP is structured as a state–local partnership to bring some financial equality to local districts despite vast differences in local tax resources.

Local funding comes primarily from ad valorem property taxes. The market value of property is determined by the county appraisal authority for all local governments within the county, and local district boards then set the property tax rate stated as an amount per $100.00 of property value. Local school district trustees may set the property tax rate for maintenance and operations up to $1.17 per $100.00 valuation.

HOW DOES TEXAS COMPARE?
RANKING TEXAS PUBLIC SCHOOLS AMONG THE 50 STATES

Several indicators are frequently used to measure states educational efforts and their outcomes, but students should be extremely careful in interpreting the meaning of state rankings among the 50 states. For example, Texas's ranking 45th among the 50 states in *per capita* spending for public education is a statistic derived by simply dividing total public school spending in a state by its population. Although this statistic may represent one measure of the state's educational effort, it does not take into account that Texas also has a larger proportion of young people to educate among its population than 48 other states.

A better measure of resources available to educate students is expenditure per student; Texas ranks 44th. However, even this statistic fails to take into account the growth rate in student enrollment. Because Texas has one of the fastest-growing school systems in the nation (three times the national average), it must devote a considerable amount of resources to new construction of physical facilities and assembling new school programs.

In addition, the rankings of average teacher salaries are not always fair indicators of educational inputs because they do not take into account that the cost of living varies a great deal from state to state, nor do state rankings by percentage of adults that have graduated from high school adequately measure public school performance because many Texas residents migrated to the state after their education was completed. Even comparison of high school graduation rates is suspect because states currently use different methods of reporting graduation and dropout rates. Likewise, comparison of SAT scores among the 50 states is problematic because not all students take the test. States in which a large portion of students are encouraged to take the test might be expected to have lower average scores than in those states where only a select few high-achieving students are tested.

Although no single statistic alone adequately describes the resources and performance of Texas public schools, their consistently low ranking on a variety of measures indicates that they do not compare favorably to public schools in much of the rest of the nation.

Measure	Texas's Rank
Population and Resources	
Per capita spending for elementary and secondary education*	45th
Percentage of population under 18**	2nd
Current expenditures per student**	44th
Average teacher salary*	34th
Results	
Percentage of population older than 25 with high school diploma**	50th
High school graduation rate**	41st
Scholastic Aptitude Test (SAT) scores**	46th

*Legislative Budget Board, *Fiscal Size-Up, 2010–2011* (Austin: Legislative Budget Board, 2009), pp. 219–223.

**Texas on the Brink, 2009: How Texas Ranks among the 50 States*. This publication can be accessed at El Paso Senator Eliott Shapleigh's website, http://www.shapleigh.org/reporting_to_you

FOR DEBATE

How can Texans evaluate the performance of its public school system? Is there any way to objectively determine how much spending on education is enough?

These property taxes are used to pay approximately 55 percent of the FSP basic operating expenses, with the state paying for the remainder. The state supplements local funds to ensure that each district has a basic allotment per student of $4,765 and guarantees that each additional cent in local tax above the minimum must yield at least $31.95 per student.

The system of basic allotments and guaranteed yields is designed to provide some financial equity among local school districts. However, local revenues from property taxes vary so much among school districts that the state has also been forced to establish certain "recapture" requirements. Richer districts such as those with taxable property of more than $319,000 per student may, under certain circumstances, be required to share their local revenue with poorer districts. They may choose one of several mechanisms to provide aid directly to poorer districts, but most send money to the state for redistribution to other districts.

Some local tax revenues are not subject to these "recapture" requirements. Without aiding poorer districts, wealthier districts may tax up to an additional 50¢ per $100 for construction, capital improvements, and debt service, and they may also collect a small amount for educational enrichment.

School Finance Reform The current finance system resulted from more than two decades of struggle, litigation, and failed reform efforts. Because the old state funding system failed to overcome significant inequalities resulting from heavy dependence on local property taxes, a lawsuit attacking the Texas system of educational finance was filed in federal court. Parents of several students in the Edgewood Independent School District in San Antonio charged that funding inequalities violated the Fourteenth Amendment to the U.S. Constitution, which guarantees that no state shall deny any person the equal protection of the laws. Ultimately, the U.S. Supreme Court declined to strike down Texas's system of school finance because it failed to find a fundamental U.S. constitutional right to equally funded public education.[3]

Later, the battle over inequality shifted to the state level. In 1987, a state district court decided a different challenge to the funding system, *Edgewood* v. *Kirby*, under a variety of provisions in the Texas Constitution guaranteeing a suitable and efficient school system. The wealthiest school district had property wealth per student 700 times greater than the poorest, and the court cited numerous other disparities resulting from heavy reliance on local property taxes.

In 1989, the Texas Supreme Court unanimously upheld the lower court decision in *Edgewood* v. *Kirby* (777 S.W.2d 391) that the funding system was unconstitutional. After a series of aborted attempts and adverse court rulings, the legislature enacted the current system as its best effort at **school finance reform**. Revenues per student now depend primarily on the tax rate (tax effort) because the state guarantees that a particular local property tax rate will produce a specific amount of revenue or the state will make up the difference. The recapture requirement that wealthier districts share their revenues with poorer districts outraged some parents and school officials, who described the system as "socialistic" or a **"Robin Hood" plan** that interfered with local control and the right to educate their children.

Despite the changes, there is still some disparity in revenues per student among school districts. For example, the Dallas Independent School District still has $29,600 more revenue for a class of 20 students than does the Huntsville Independent School District. Yet ironically, the poorer school district's students perform better on standard tests. And despite more equalized revenues, suburban school districts like Plano and Alamo Heights continue to have far more students passing TAKS than urban school districts like Dallas and Houston, who include the largest share of minority students and those from economically disadvantaged families. Table 13.1 shows that student TAKS test scores—and the factors sometimes thought to affect them—vary dramatically from district to district in Texas.

School finance reform

Changes in public school financial system resulting from a Texas Supreme Court ruling that significant inequality in school financial resources violated the state constitution; changes in any public policy are considered "reform" by their advocates.

"Robin Hood" plan

School finance reform program requiring the transfer of taxable property resources from wealthier to poorer school districts.

[3]*San Antonio Independent School District* v. *Rodriguez*, 411 U.S. 1 (1973).

TABLE 13.1 SELECTED TEXAS SCHOOL DISTRICT PROFILES

This sample of school district profiles is arranged by size of enrollment. The right column shows that some financial inequity remains among school districts. Follow the Percent Meeting 2009 TAKS Standard column (column 6) down and notice that there is very little relationship with district revenues per student. Now, look at ethnicity (Percent Minority, column 3) and Percent Economically Disadvantaged students (column 4) to see if these factors relate to the TAKS scores (column 6).

School District	Enrollment	Percent Minority*	Percent Economically Disadvantaged	Student/ Teacher Ratio	Percent Meeting 2009 TAKS Standard**	Revenue per Student***
Houston I.S.D.	199,524	92.2%	81.0%	16.6	69%	$ 9,969
Dallas I.S.D.	157,174	95.4	86.1	14.4	64	10,248
Plano I.S.D.	53,906	49.3	20.7	13.3	89	10,012
Edgewood I.S.D.	11,608	99.2	90.8	14.5	60	10,626
Huntsville I.S.D.	5,996	52.8	56.5	14.7	75	8,768
Alamo Heights I.S.D.	4,618	38.0	17.3	14.4	85	10,105
West Orange-Cove I.S.D.	2,591	73.4	80.7	13.5	51	9,939
Wink-Loving I.S.D.	322	36.0	36.3	7.4	73	23,161
Statewide	**4,728,204**	**66.0**	**56.7**	**14.4**	**74**	**9,739**

*African American, Latino, Native American, Asian, or Pacific Islander.
**The Standard Accountability Indicator among all grades tested.
***Actual revenues from all sources.

Source: Texas Education Agency, *2008–2009 Academic Excellence Indicator System*, District Reports.

Private-school vouchers

Taxpayer-funded payments to private schools to pay for the education of students transferring to them from public schools.

School Privitization Adjustments to the school funding system will continue indefinitely. Among recent proposals for school finance changes are various **voucher** plans to use public funds to enable students to attend private and parochial schools. Supporters, often including conservatives and particular religious groups, argue that voucher plans offer poorer parents the choice to transfer their children out of underperforming public schools, an alternative now available only to wealthier families. They believe that increasing competition between public and private schools should stimulate improvements in public education.

Opponents, including teachers' organizations, charge that vouchers would damage public schools by draining their financial resources and some of their best students, leaving public schools to educate students with special problems and learning disabilities. They argue that public funds should not subsidize special private privileges; therefore, any fair voucher plan must include requirements that private schools adopt open-admissions, open-meetings, and open-records policies.

State funding invites state controls and threatens the separation of church and state. Short of vouchers for students to attend private schools, a number of programs offer school choice and foster competitiveness within the public schools. Local school districts have established magnet schools; charter schools and

Texas public opinion surveys indicate that Texans are divided about programs to divert money from public schools to private and parochial schools. ☞

What are the arguments for and against school vouchers?

Bob Daemmrich/The Image Works

VOUCHERS AND RELIGIOUS LIBERTY

In 2002, the U.S. Supreme Court ruled that a Cleveland voucher program did not violate the establishment clause of the U.S. Constitution because the program provides funding to individuals rather than religious organizations. Because those individuals may choose to use the benefits at any private or parochial school, it does not favor religious over nonreligious education.*

However, state constitutions remain an issue. A Florida court ruled that the state's voucher program violated its state constitutional provision that prohibits funding for churches and other sectarian institutions. If Texas adopts such a program, it might violate Texas's constitution; Article 1, Section 7, prohibits appropriations for the benefit of any sect or religious society.

Zelman v. *Simmons-Harris*, 536 U.S. 639 (2002).

district home rule are also now available options. Opponents can point to research indicating that similar students perform as well in public schools as they do in similar private schools.

HIGHER EDUCATION

Like public schools, higher education is a major state service, accounting for 12 percent of state expenditure during the 2010–2011 budget period. Figure 13.3 shows that public institutions enroll 90 percent of all students in Texas higher education. Texas public institutions of higher education include 35 general academic institutions and universities (with three more scheduled to emerge), nine health-related institutions, and one technical college with four campuses. Fifty public community colleges operate on 80 campuses.

Administration of Colleges and Universities The Texas Higher Education Coordinating Board was established to coordinate the complex system of higher education. Its 18 members are appointed by the governor with the consent of the senate, and they serve for six-year terms. The Coordinating Board appoints the commissioner of higher education to supervise its staff. Together the board and staff outline the role of each public college and university and plan future needs for programs, curricula, and physical plants. Because Texas's colleges and universities were not established systematically, the Coordinating Board has difficulty imposing a rational, coherent system upon their operations. Politically powerful boards of regents complicate the Coordinating Board's efforts as they compete to impose their views on higher education, as do other groups.

Boards of regents or trustees set basic policies for their institutions, within the limits of state law and the rules and guidelines established by the Coordinating Board. Governing boards provide for the selection of public university administrators including system-wide administrators (chancellors), campus presidents, deans, and other officers. Certain boards govern institutions located on several campuses:

★ The University of Texas System includes The University of Texas at Austin (with the nation's largest student population on a single campus) and other campuses located at Arlington, Brownsville, Dallas, El Paso, Permian Basin, San Antonio, and Tyler, as well as University of Texas–Pan American and several medical and health units.
★ The Texas A&M System has its main campus at College Station, with additional campuses at Corpus Christi, Commerce, Texarkana, Galveston, Kingsville, Prairie View A&M, Tarleton State, West Texas A&M, Texas A&M International, and several smaller campuses.
★ The Texas State University System includes Sam Houston State, Texas State University at San Marcos, Sul Ross State, and Lamar University.
★ The University of Houston has its main campus in Houston, as well as a downtown campus and campuses at Clear Lake and Victoria.

Figure 13.3

Texas Higher Education Enrollments, Fall 2008. Higher education is over-whelmingly a responsibility of the state (left pie chart) and a majority of public college students enroll in community colleges (right pie chart).

Source: Texas Higher Education Coordinating Board and Legislative Budget Board, *Fiscal Size-Up 2010–2011*, p. 238.

What challenges do growing enrollments present to Texas's institutions of higher learning? How successful are these institutions at retaining and graduating students that have enrolled in them?

Community college approach

Higher education policy based on open admissions, maximizing accessibility, and incorporating technical, compensatory, and continuing education among the traditional academic course offerings.

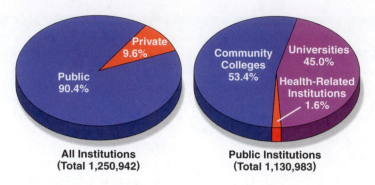

**All Institutions
(Total 1,250,942)**

**Public Institutions
(Total 1,130,983)**

★ The Texas Tech System includes the main campus at Lubbock, several other western Texas campuses, health science centers, and Angelo State University.

★ The remaining boards each govern mainly single-campus institutions.

Authorized and financed largely by the state, community colleges are also generally supervised by the Coordinating Board. However, unlike four-year institutions (which are usually designed to attract students from larger regions of the state and nation as well as international students), community colleges are established by voters in one or more school districts primarily to serve area residents. They are usually governed by independently elected boards.

The traditional role of the junior college has been to offer academic courses to freshmen and sophomores who would later transfer to senior colleges. Although most of their students are enrolled in transferable academic courses, two-year colleges have responded to the demands resulting from economic diversification by adopting a **community college approach**, adding adult, continuing, and special-education courses as well as technical specialties. The curriculum, low cost, and geographic and financial accessibility of community colleges have resulted in increasing enrollments, especially in academic programs. Figure 13.3 shows that a majority of Texas students enroll in two-year institutions.

THE POLITICS OF HIGHER EDUCATION

It is difficult to measure objectively many of the benefits of higher education, such as personal satisfaction and contribution to society. Individual financial benefits, however, are very clear. Texas high school graduates have an average annual income of $31,283; those with an associate's degree earn $39,506; and those with at least a bachelor's degree have an average income of $67,155.[4]

The economic benefits from investments in higher education seem quite impressive as well. According to a study funded by the Bill and Melinda Gates Foundation, every $1.00 invested in higher education yields $8.00 in enhanced productivity, greater ongoing capacity, reduced social costs, and stimulus to research and development.[5]

Despite its benefits, legislative bodies and boards of regents and trustees have often been critical in their evaluations of higher education and its results. Calls for faculty and student accountability have been frequent. Yet there are no generally agreed upon answers to the questions raised about higher education: What should its goals be? How should it measure success in achieving those goals? To whom should it be accountable? We examine some issues concerning higher education in the remainder of this section.

[4]U.S. Census Bureau, Current Population Survey, *2009 Annual Social and Economic Supplement,* Table PINC-04.
[5]The Perryman Group, *A Tale of Two States—And One Million Jobs,* March 2007, published by the Texas Higher Education Coordinating Board at http://www.thecb.state.tx.us/reports/PDF/1345.PDF?CFID=8408072&CFTOKEN=72550084

Faculty Issues Salaries are a perpetual issue when Texas institutions of higher education recruit new faculty. Average full-time public college and university faculty salaries, for example, are still significantly below the national average.

Rationalizing their attempts as an effort to promote faculty accountability, college and university administrators have long sought to dilute job-protection guarantees for professors. State law requires governing boards to adopt procedures for periodic reevaluation of all tenured faculty. Faculties generally fear that such policies can be a threat to academic freedom and a tool for political repression by administrators.

Financial Issues Financing higher education is a continuing issue. Like elementary and secondary schools, most colleges and universities in Texas must struggle with relatively small budgets. Meanwhile, increasing college enrollments and demands for specialized, high-cost programs are increasing at a time when unemployment compensation, social services, health care, and other services are also placing more demands on depressed state revenues. Revenues in turn are limited by the legislature's reluctance to increase taxes.

Student Accessibility Proposals to cope with financial pressures include closing institutions with smaller enrollments, reducing duplication, restricting student services, increasing tuitions, and delaying construction plans or implementing new degree programs. Most of these policies have the effect of limiting student access to higher education, but increasing costs represent the greatest obstacle to a college education for most students.

Because the Texas legislature deregulated tuitions, college and university boards have dealt with increasing costs by raising tuitions, mandatory student fees, and residence costs. Between 2003 and 2008, average tuition and fees for full-time students at Texas public universities increased 63 percent, to $6,089. At community colleges, tuition and fees increased to $1,639.[6] Financial accessibility of higher education is a growing concern, especially because the size of Pell grants and other forms of financial aid are not keeping pace with increasing costs, and students are financing more of the increased cost of higher education by borrowing. Figure 13.4 shows the recent trends in costs of higher education for Texas students.

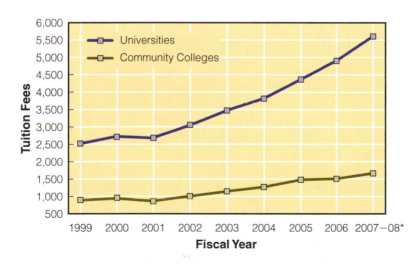

Figure 13.4

Texas Resident Tuition and Fees, 30 Credit Hours

*2007–2008 is for academic year.

Source: Texas Higher Education Coordinating Board. *College Costs, Fall 2003–Fall 2008,* http://www.thecb.state.tx.us/Reports/PDF/1759.PDF

Evaluate the alternatives to raising tuitions in Texas's institutions of higher learning.

---

[6]Texas Higher Education Coordinating Board, *College Costs, Fall 2003–Fall 2008,* http://www.thecb.state.tx.us/Reports/PDF/1759.PDF; Susan Combs, *Texas in Focus: A Statewide View of Opportunities* (Austin: Office of the Comptroller of Public Accounts, January 2008).

Student Diversity In addition to affordability other cultural, structural, and historical factors have limited access to certain populations that have traditionally been underserved by Texas institutions of higher learning. Economically disadvantaged people, those who live in rural areas, and ethnic minorities are notably underrepresented in colleges and universities.

Institutions of higher education have struggled with minority student recruitment in an effort to increase **ethnic diversity** and offer more access to underserved populations. Those efforts became especially difficult when the federal Fifth Circuit Court of Appeals ruled that race could not be considered in **affirmative action** admissions policies.[7]

Many states attempted to achieve diversity by considering low family income and other special nonracial obstacles that make it difficult to meet standard admission criteria. The Texas legislature responded by requiring that general academic institutions (except now for The University of Texas at Austin) must automatically admit students from the top 10 percent of their high school graduating class regardless of test scores. More female, African-American, Latino, low-income, and rural students have been admitted to state universities under the "10 percent" rule than under traditional admission criteria.

Meanwhile, more recent U.S. Supreme Court decisions have allowed race to be considered directly in college admissions policies as a last resort when other minority recruitment efforts have not produced a diverse student population and so long as specific point advantages are not assigned to minorities.[8] These decisions have, once again, sent some college administrators scrambling to find acceptable affirmative-action policies.

Student Retention Of course, admission to institutions of higher learning is hardly the only measure of success. Although students may benefit from even a short experience in college and employers credit applicants for it, graduation or completion of occupational curriculum programs is society's respected measure of success. Unfortunately, high costs, lack of course availability, inadequate academic preparation, and personal factors all contribute to the problem of student retention. Among full-time degree seeking students at public universities, 24 percent graduate within 4 years, and 57 percent receive degrees within 6 years. In addition, community colleges have a much more difficult challenge to retain and graduate students—within 3 years, only 11 percent graduate and 20 percent transfer to a senior institution.

Quality However, even graduation rates do not fully measure the success of institutions of higher learning. Measuring the success of Texas colleges and universities must take into account their two major functions: (1) teaching, that is imparting existing knowledge to students, and (2) research, that is creating new knowledge.

By one measure, Texas has two of the top 100 national public universities in the nation— The University of Texas at Austin ranks 15th and Texas A&M University ranks 22nd.[9] Other rankings show that these are the two most recognized public institutions of higher learning in the state.

Perhaps their rankings partly reflect the resources available to these institutions. General legislative appropriations have been relatively more generous for The University of Texas (UT) at Austin and Texas A&M University. Furthermore, the state constitution has earmarked more than 2 million acres of public land for the Permanent University Fund. Two-thirds of the earnings from the Permanent University Fund are used for construction and

---

Ethnic diversity

Inclusion of significant numbers of nonwhites such as Latinos, African Americans, Asian Americans, and Native Americans.

Affirmative action

Positive efforts to recruit ethnic minorities, women, and the economically disadvantaged. Sometimes these efforts are limited to publicity drives among target groups, but such programs sometimes include use of ethnicity or gender as part of the qualification criteria.

---

[7] *Hopwood* v. *Texas*, 85 F.3d 720 (5th Cir., 1996).

[8] *Grutter* v. *Bollinger*, 539 U.S. 306 (2003); *Gratz* v. *Bollinger*, 539 U.S. 234 (2003).

[9] Best Colleges: Top Public Schools: National Universities, *U.S. News and World Report*, http://colleges.usnews.rankingsandreviews.com/best-colleges/national-top-public. These imperfect rankings are based on reputation, exclusiveness in admissions, and financial resources.

The National Center on Public Policy and Higher Education published *Measuring Up 2008: The National Report Card on Higher Education.** Here is its summary of how Texas's higher education system stacks up against other states.

Affordability—Texas students spend 21 percent of their annual family income to pay for the cost of attending public community colleges after receiving financial aid; the net costs of attending a four-year public college represents 26 percent of family income. California offers significantly more affordable access to college through its community college system.

Preparation—85 percent earn a high school diploma or GED by age 24. Seven states do better.

Participation—30 percent of Texans ages 19–24 are in college. Forty-four states score higher.

Completion—One-half of four-year college students earn a bachelor's degree within six years. Forty-three states have better completion rates.

Benefits—Higher education provides greater economic benefits in 20 states.

*http://measuringup2008.highereducation.org/

other educational enhancements at The University of Texas System campuses, and one-third goes to Texas A&M University campuses. The UT and A&M systems have concentrated many of their resources on their flagship campuses in Austin and College Station rather than other institutions within their systems.

To help the other universities in Texas, voters amended the state constitution in 2009 to create the National Research University Fund out of the former Permanent Higher Education Fund to provide a source of funding to enable emerging research universities in Texas to achieve national prominence. Proposed Tier One research universities include the University of Houston, North Texas University, Texas Tech University, and University of Texas campuses at San Antonio, Dallas, Arlington, and El Paso. Of course, the results of these ambitious efforts cannot yet be fully foreseen or evaluated.

Health and Human Services

The second most costly category of state spending can be broadly classified as health and human services, which encompass public assistance, Medicaid for the poor, and a variety of other programs. In the 2010–2011 budget period, these programs cost $59.7 billion (32.8% of the state's total budget). However, approximately 60 percent of this funding originates as grants-in-aid from the federal government.

Figure 13.5 shows that the Texas Health and Human Services Commission provides a variety of social services, including Temporary Assistance to Needy Families, Medicaid, and the Children's Health Insurance Program. The commission also coordinates planning, rule making, and budgeting among its four subsidiary social service agencies, the Department of Aging and Disability Services, the Department of Assistive and Rehabilitative Services, the Department of Family and Protective Services, and the Department of State Health Services.

HEALTH PROGRAMS

Although opponents of government's assuming responsibility for public health describe it as "**socialized medicine**," health has been a concern of public authorities since Moses imposed strict hygienic codes on the Jews during their biblical exodus from Egypt. In the United States, the federal government began to provide hospital care to the merchant marines in 1798.

Socialized medicine

Strictly defined, socialized medicine is a health care system in which the government hires medical practitioners who work at government-owned facilities to directly provide health care as in Great Britain and in U.S. veterans and military hospitals. However, the term is often applied to health care systems in which the government provides health care insurance (such as Medicare), but benefit payments are made to private health care providers.

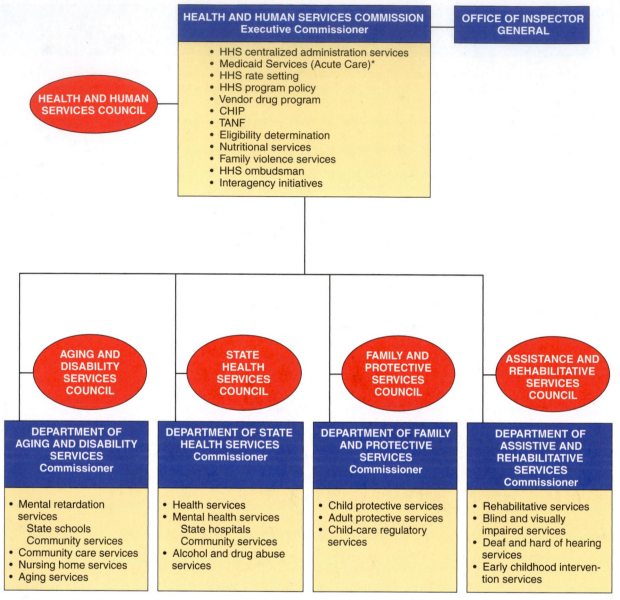

Figure 13.5

Texas Health and Human
Service Agencies

Source: Health and Human
Services Commission.

Why is it important for a single
commission to coordinate so
many of the state's human
services?

Today, health care has evolved into a growing public–private partnership and the second most expensive service that Texas provides.

The state has three levels of involvement in health care: (1) In some instances, the state is the provider of direct health services; for example it provides health care for certain special populations. (2) In other instances, the state is the payer but not the provider. When it acts as a public health insurer as it does with Medicaid, it pays for the medical services offered by private practitioners. (3) The state also acts as a regulator and buyer of private health insurance.

Direct Health Services Texas's Department of Health Services provides personal health services for special populations. For example, the health department operates a lung and tuberculosis hospital in San Antonio and a general services hospital in Harlingen. The

Department of Health Services operates general psychiatric hospitals and funds local mental health community centers and chemical dependency programs as well.

County hospitals and clinics are legally responsible for providing medical care for uninsured indigents, and therefore, they have become the health providers of last resort. County hospitals are usually operated by county hospital districts that have the authority to collect property taxes that partially fund their operations. Several government institutions also manage teaching hospitals that provide care to both indigent and nonindigent patients.

Instead of using county-funded hospitals and clinics, many uninsured and indigent patients access medical services through hospital emergency rooms because federal and state laws usually require them to accept patients regardless of their ability to pay. The cost of such treatment is often uncompensated and passed on to paying patients and insurance companies—a practice partially responsible for the recent dramatic increase in health insurance premiums.

State Health Insurance Programs Texas operates two major health insurance programs for those who qualify. **Medicaid** and the **Children's Health Insurance Program (CHIP)** are fairly comprehensive insurance programs designed to provide a minimal level of care for low-income individuals and families who have enrolled.

Texas spends one-fourth of its state budget on the Medicaid program, but more than 60 percent of Medicaid costs come from the federal government. Medicaid reimburses providers for most health services, including eyeglasses, prescription drugs, physicians' fees, laboratory and X-ray services, family planning, ambulance transportation, Medicare Part B premiums, and a wide variety of other medical expenses. Generally, these providers are in managed care (HMO-type) systems.

Medicaid should not be confused with **Medicare**, which is available to all persons older than 65 years of age regardless of income, and is administered by the U.S. Department of Health and Human Services. In contrast, the Medicaid program is administered by the state and is available only to certain medically indigent individuals: (1) categorically eligible persons eligible for Temporary Assistance for Needy Families (TANF) or Supplemental Security Income (SSI); (2) individuals seeking medical assistance only, low-income persons residing in institutions who qualify for SSI except for certain income requirements; (3) children up to 19 years of age whose family financial status would qualify for TANF but who reside in families with two able-bodied parents; (4) pregnant women who would qualify for TANF but have no other children; (5) children ages 6 through 18 who reside in family's with income below the federal poverty level; (6) children younger than 6 whose family's income is at or less than 133 percent of the federal poverty level; (7) pregnant women and infants younger than 1 year of age who reside in families with income less than 185 percent of the federal poverty level.[10] Of Texas's 3.2 million Medicaid recipients, 90 percent are elderly, disabled, or children.

CHIP helps insure children of parents with incomes less than 200 percent of the poverty level and who do not qualify for Medicaid. Even though 500,000 children are insured by CHIP and 2.2 million are enrolled in Medicaid, 1 in 5 Texas children remains uninsured.

Private Health Insurance Although approximately 17 percent of nonelderly Texans have some sort of public insurance coverage such as Medicaid or CHIP, most rely on private insurance companies to pay for their medical expenses. Employer-sponsored plans cover 51 percent of Texans and private individual policies cover five percent. The state itself pays private insurance companies for part of the premiums for its employees and teachers. As a result,

Medicaid

A program to provide medical care for qualified low-income persons; although funded largely by federal grants-in-aid, it is a state-administered program.

Children's Health Insurance Program (CHIP)

Program that provides health insurance for low-income children. It is administered by the state but funded largely by federal grants-in-aid.

Medicare

A federal program to provide medical insurance for most persons older than 65 years of age.

---

[10]Health and Human Services Commission, "Texas Medicaid Program," http://www.hhsc.state.tx.us/medicaid/index.html

HOW DOES TEXAS COMPARE?
HOW PEOPLE GET HEALTH INSURANCE

One of every six Americans and one in four Texans has no health insurance coverage. Texas has the nation's highest percentage of uninsured residents. In 2008, approximately 5.9 million Texans, or 27.7 percent of the state's nonelderly population, were uninsured, including more than one in five Texas children.

Nationally, about 60 percent of the nonelderly were covered by employment-based insurance, whereas only 51 percent had employment-based health insurance in Texas.* Texas ranked 47th among states, including the District of Columbia, in the percentage of people with employer-sponsored insurance.

Nationwide, 62.2 percent of businesses with fewer than 50 employees offered health care benefits, whereas only 49.8 percent of those companies in Texas offered such benefits. Nationally, 43.7 percent of employers with fewer than 10 employees offered health insurance, but only 31.3 percent of similar Texas businesses do so.

Increasing health insurance costs partly explain the large number of uninsured. Between 2001 and 2007, health insurance premiums across the nation rose by an average of 78 percent, whereas inflation rose only by 17 percent.** By 2008, the average premium cost for employer-sponsored family coverage in Texas was $11,967.*

The fact that many Texans are uninsured poses problems for individuals, businesses, and state and local governments, who bear extra costs to pay for uncompensated care. Medical providers of all types are forced to raise paying patients' fees to cover losses resulting from unpaid medical services to the uninsured. Costs that are not reimbursed are passed on to Texans in the form of higher taxes and insurance premiums. In 2005, Texas insured families spent an extra $1,551 in premiums to cover the unpaid health care bills of the uninsured. Meanwhile, rising premiums cause private employers to drop employee insurance coverage altogether, thus compounding the problem.**

FOR DEBATE

To what extent should health care insurance be a public policy concern? What measures could be adopted to cut health care costs?

*Kaiser Family Foundation, *State Health Facts* at http://www.statehealthfacts.org
**Susan Combs, *Texas in Focus: A Statewide View of Opportunities* (Austin: Comptroller of Public Accounts, 2008). This publication can be accessed online at http://www.window.state.tx.us/specialrpt/tif/index.html

---

businesses, government, and individuals have been seriously impacted by health insurance premiums that have skyrocketed more than 80 percent since 2001 and costing about $12,000 for the average family premium.[11] High premium costs have caused some businesses to drop coverage for their employees, and many individuals have chosen not to buy private coverage, leaving Texas as the state with the largest share of uninsured persons in the nation.

THE FUTURE OF TEXAS HEALTH INSURANCE

In an effort to cope with the increasing cost of private health insurance, the large number of uninsured Americans, and objectionable insurance company practices, Congress passed the controversial Patient Protection and Affordable Care Act of 2010 also known as **Health Care Reform** (HCR).

Because Texas has the largest percentage of uninsured persons of any state in the nation, HCR will have a more dramatic effect in Texas than in most states. It will expand Medicaid and CHIP eligibility by 2.1 million persons. Individual mandates, small business subsidies, affordability subsidies for middle-income families, and large business incentives will reduce the number of uninsured by as many as 4.3 million depending on how

Health Care Reform

A comprehensive federal program expanding health insurance coverage with broader Medicare coverage, "individual mandates," "guaranteed-issue" requirements, health insurance subsidies, and exchanges.

Texas "Tea Party" protesters attacked health care reform as being too much big government. ☞

How does HCR expand the role of the state and federal governments? Evaluate the need for the "individual mandate" and government regulation of the health care industry.

AP Images/Deborah Cannon/*Austin American-Statesman*

---

[11]The Kaiser Family Foundation. See how Texas compares at http://www.statehealthfacts.org

HEALTH CARE REFORM: HOW IT WORKS

Health care reform will come to impact Texans in stages as its provisions are implemented over time. The act will end some of the most unpopular insurance company practices as its first priority in 2010 and 2011. "Rescissions" will no longer be allowed as health insurance companies can no longer arbitrarily drop beneficiaries when they get sick or because they have reached lifetime limits. Insurance companies may not deny insurance to children because of preexisting conditions, and adults with preexisting conditions such as diabetes or high blood pressure will be allowed to buy subsidized insurance through a new high-risk pool. Insurance companies must also allow parents to keep their children covered under their family policies until age 26.

Small businesses will have tax credits to help them buy insurance for their employees during the first phase of health reform, but the most significant and controversial elements of the reform package will begin in 2014. Then insurance companies will be subject to a **guaranteed issue** requirement that they must insure all applicants even if they are sick—a requirement that insurance companies will be able meet only because they will be able to spread risk over a larger pool of customers. Everyone will be required to have health insurance or pay a fine to the federal government—the **individual mandate**.

To make health insurance affordable, states (with 90–100% aid from the federal government) will expand Medicaid eligibility to all persons with incomes less than 133 percent of the federal poverty level and maintain their CHIP program. Other uninsured individuals and small businesses will be allowed to buy health insurance through state insurance exchanges in which insurance companies compete by offering qualified plans with clear and comparable information on coverage options like, Travelocity or Expedia, for example. States may agree to allow their residents to buy health insurance in their exchanges across state lines. Individuals purchasing health insurance on these exchanges will be eligible for subsidies on a sliding scale based on their incomes up to four times the federal poverty level ($88,200 in 2010). Some low-income individuals will also qualify for subsidies for a portion of out-of-pocket expenses.

FOR DEBATE

Should government have the power to compel individuals to buy insurance or any product from a private company? How will health care reform affect the quality and availability of medical care for those who already have insurance?

Source: U.S. Department of Health and Human Services, http://www.healthreform.gov/reports/statehealthreform/texas.html; Center for Public Policy Priorities, http://cppp.org

---

many choose to ignore the individual mandate. The remaining uninsured will be mostly illegal immigrants who are ineligible and eligible persons who choose to pay a fine rather than buy health insurance.

The Texas Department of Insurance will be given substantial powers to enforce new federal health insurance regulations and to monitor hikes in insurance premiums. In addition, the state will assume the responsibility for operating an insurance exchange and for qualifying new Medicaid and CHIP clients. And, although the federal government will provide substantial grants to pay for new Medicaid benefits and administrative costs, Health and Human Services Executive Commissioner Tom Suehs estimates the expansion of Medicaid and the Children's Health Insurance Program will cost the state $27 billion between 2014 and 2023.

Guaranteed-issue requirements
Requirement that insurance companies will sell health insurance to applicants despite preexisting conditions.

Individual mandate
Requirement that individuals get health insurance or face a federal fine.

INCOME SUPPORT PROGRAMS

Temporary Assistance to Needy Families Among social service programs, Temporary Assistance to Needy Families (TANF) is designed for children whose parents are incapable of providing for children's basic needs. More than two-thirds of TANF recipients are children. Unless they are disabled or needed at home to care for very young children, adult TANF and food stamp recipients are referred for employment counseling, assessment, and job placement.

The TANF-Basic program serves those who are deprived of support because of the absence or disability of one or both parents and whose income is at least 87 percent less than the poverty level. TANF grants are available for two-parent families in which the principal wage earner is unemployed and the family income does not exceed the criteria established for the basic program.

IN MILLIONS

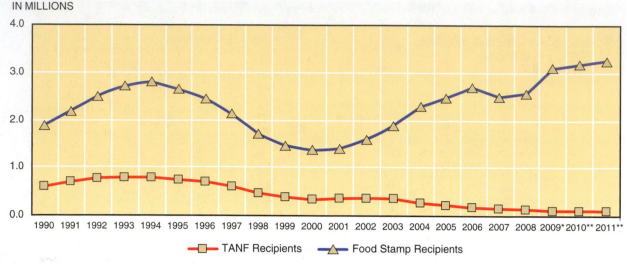

Figure 13.6

TANF and Food Stamp Caseloads, 1990–2011. Follow the TANF and food stamp lines across through the years. Notice that the state cash grant program (TANF) dramatically declined after federal welfare reform in 1996 when TANF ceased to be an entitlement program. Meanwhile, the federal food stamp program available to most citizens below the poverty level has fluctuated as economic conditions have changed.

*Estimated.
**Appropriated.

Source: Texas Department of Human Services.

What are the arguments for and against such income support programs?

Unemployment insurance

Benefit program for certain workers losing their employment; a joint federal–state program financed with a tax on employers.

Federal and state regulations now require recipients to cooperate in identifying an absent parent and, with few exceptions, limit TANF benefits to citizens; adult eligibility is usually limited to two years at a time, with a maximum five-year lifetime benefit. By making welfare less of an entitlement, these welfare reforms were intended to force able-bodied individuals out of dependency and into productive work. Some federal funds are now distributed as block grants to the states to allow them flexibility to develop support services, child care, job training and placement, and rehabilitation programs to help welfare recipients in finding work. Figure 13.6 shows that these reforms have substantially reduced the number of TANF recipients in Texas.

In 2010–2011, the maximum monthly TANF grant for a family of three was $260, considerably below the national average. The Texas median TANF grant is about one-half the national median. Adjusting for inflation, TANF benefits have declined considerably over the years. Today, Texas spends only 0.1 percent of its budget for this income-assistance program for the poor.

Unemployment Insurance Whereas TANF is designed as an income supplement for the poor and is administered by the Health and Human Service Commission, unemployment compensation is designed as partial income replacement for those who have lost their jobs. Unlike TANF, which is a welfare program determined by need, unemployment compensation is a social insurance program financed by employer-paid premiums and eligibility is based on previous earnings rather than on need or family size.

The U.S. Congress established the system of **unemployment insurance** under the Social Security Act of 1935 as a partnership between the states and the federal government. This act imposed a tax on covered employers to establish a nationwide system of unemployment insurance administered by the federal government. However, the act provided that most of this tax would be set aside in all of the states that adopted an acceptable state program. Thus every state was pressured to adopt state systems of unemployment insurance. Benefits are financed from state taxes on employers, but some administrative costs are paid with federal funds. These programs are actually administered by the states.

In Texas, unemployment insurance is administered by the Texas Workforce Commission (TWC), a three-member board appointed by the governor, with the consent of the senate, for six-year overlapping terms. Outside the authority of the Health and Human Services Commission, the TWC administers benefit payments. Usually, the maximum is 26 weekly benefit payments, but Congress usually extends the period of eligibility and pays for much of cost of the extension during periods of severe recessions when jobs are scarce.

Under Texas's rather restrictive laws, a worker must register for job placement with the TWC and is usually ineligible to receive benefits (at least for a time) if he or she voluntarily quits or was fired for cause. Because the rate at which employers are taxed is based on claims made by former employees, employers have an interest in contesting employee claims. For these reasons and others, only 35 percent of the unemployed Texans received benefits in 2009.

Until recently, handling unemployment insurance claims has not been a major priority among TWC's activities; its major functions have been providing a workforce for employers, gathering employment statistics, enforcing child-labor laws, and providing various special job-training and rehabilitation services. Able-bodied welfare recipients are referred to the TWC for training and child-care services. Regional workforce development boards plan one-stop career development centers in 28 areas across the state.

THE POLITICS OF "WELFARE": MYTHS AND REALITIES

Defining Welfare More myths and misunderstandings affect welfare than probably any other public service. The very concept of "welfare" has no uniformly recognized definition. The broadest view is that welfare is any unearned, government-provided benefit. The national government provides direct subsidies to businesses and corporations that far exceed TANF and food stamp costs. Such corporate welfare includes financial bailouts, most subsidies to agribusiness, and grants to weapons manufacturers to sell weapons to foreigners.

Programs that primarily benefit the middle class, such as federal income tax deductions for mortgage interest, are also more costly than poverty programs. Because Social Security recipients now receive more benefits in the first three years of retirement than they paid in Social Security taxes during their working lifetimes, even Social Security is largely an unearned benefit and may be seen as a form of middle-class "welfare." Because these programs are supported by powerful special interests or large numbers of middle-class voters, they are relatively secure from serious political threat.

More commonly, the term *welfare* refers to the often controversial programs explicitly designed to assist the poor. Accordingly, old-age, survivors, and disability insurance (commonly referred to as Social Security), as well as unemployment insurance, are **social insurance** programs, not public welfare programs. Eligibility for social insurance programs is based not on poverty alone (that is, eligibility is not based on a **means test**) but on the tax paid by beneficiaries and their employers. In this respect, they are like private insurance programs, differing primarily in that they are operated by the government, and are compulsory for most employers and employees. Such programs are not aimed directly at the poor. In fact, many persons now receive public assistance for the very reason that they were ineligible to participate in adequate social insurance programs.

Welfare Myths There is a mistaken impression that any poor person may be eligible for state public assistance benefits. Although more than 4 million Texans live in poverty, fewer than 5 percent receive TANF, and the only significant group of able-bodied adults now receiving income assistance is parents with sole custody of young dependent children.

There is no general program of cash assistance for able-bodied adults without children, even though they may be unemployed or in need. However, food stamps, the Supplemental Nutritional Assistance Program (see Figure 13.6), and Medicaid are available to most who fall below the federally defined poverty level, and federal SSI may be available to the aged, blind, and disabled.

Social insurance

Public insurance programs with benefits based on tax premiums paid by the beneficiary or his or her employer; for example, Social Security and unemployment compensation are social insurance programs that are not based on need alone.

Means test

A standard of benefit eligibility based on need.

Resentment can be expected when shoppers waiting in grocery checkout lines to part with hard-earned cash see the customer ahead paying with federally funded food stamps. Nevertheless, contrary to popular myth, there are few new Cadillac drivers who are legally on Texas welfare rolls, because benefits furnish less than the bare essentials of life.

Nor does it seem likely, as some critics suggest, that welfare mothers have more children just to increase their monthly TANF checks. The maximum monthly TANF grant is $260 per three-person family; even when these payments are combined with food stamps and Medicaid, the average TANF child lives in a home with resources approximately 23 percent below the poverty level for a family of three. Children intensify the problems of the poor. Large family size probably results from carelessness, promiscuity, or ignorance of birth control techniques rather than a deliberate effort to increase welfare payments.

There are several reasons for the myths that have grown around public welfare. Because welfare benefits people according to their needs rather than according to their efforts, it seems to violate the widespread American attitude that everyone ought to be paid according to the work one does. Consequently, even the lowest wage earner often feels superior to the welfare recipient. Most Texans prefer to identify themselves with the economically secure rather than with the poor. There is also prejudice against some of the groups that benefit from welfare because a disproportionate number of welfare recipients are mothers of children born out of wedlock or members of ethnic minority groups. Whatever the cause, these myths and prejudices remain major elements in the debate over public assistance.

Welfare Realities There are serious substantive questions concerning public welfare. Cheating and overpayment cost taxpayers money and dilute the limited resources that would otherwise be available for those in genuine need. It is difficult to estimate the amount of cheating, Although Texas's Lone Star Card was developed as a form of positive identification to reduce fraud, it is difficult to determine the amount of cheating that occurs during the application and qualification processes.

Probably the most serious problem for the welfare system today is that it alleviates rather than cures. Most public assistance programs are designed only to relieve the most severe pains of poverty, not to cure the disease. Welfare or other assistance programs may prevent starvation, but they offer little hope that recipients will someday escape poverty and dependence. The vast majority of Texas welfare recipients are children, too young to do much about their problems. But for the able-bodied, poverty is a symptom of a disease that affects both the individual and society at large. Typically, the poor have dropped out of school at an early age and lack the education and skills necessary to earn a living wage. They also exhibit varying degrees of despair, alienation, hopelessness, emotional insecurity, or lethargy. Many lack a feeling that they can do much about their problem; others lack a sense of responsibility.

Transportation

HIGHWAY PROGRAMS

In the early days of Texas history, road construction was primarily the responsibility of the county. Most Texas counties still maintain a property tax dedicated to the construction and maintenance of roads, and in rural areas, road building remains a major function of county government. But the efforts are too small and too poorly financed to provide the expensive, coordinated statewide network of roads needed by highly mobile Texans in the modern world.

In contrast to county roads, state highways in Texas are better financed. In 1916, the national government encouraged state governments to assume the major responsibility for highway construction and maintenance. The 1916 Federal Aid Road Act made available

TABLE 13.2 THE TEXAS HIGHWAY SYSTEM

Type of Committees

Type of Roadway	Total Miles	Percentage of Traffic Accommodated
Interstate highways	10,302	27
Farm-to-market roads	40,969	11
Federal and state highways	28,459	36

Note: Figures do not include more than 225,349 miles of city streets and county roads, which accommodate approximately one-fourth of traffic.

Source: Legislative Budget Board, *Fiscal Size-Up, 2010–2011,* p. 425.

federal funds to cover one-half of the construction costs for state highways. To become eligible for those funds, a state was required to establish an agency to develop a coordinated plan for the state highway system and to administer construction and maintenance programs. Texas responded by establishing the Texas Highway Department, now known as the Texas Department of Transportation (TxDOT). The department is supervised by a five-member commission appointed by the governor, with the consent of the senate, for six-year overlapping terms. The commission appoints an executive director who oversees the department and supervises the work of regional district offices.

Newer federal aid programs and increased funding for existing ones have expanded TxDOT's responsibilities. The earliest highway-building program was designed to provide only major highways along primary routes. Federal funding later became available for secondary roads, and Texas established the farm-to-market program to assume state maintenance of many county roads as the rural road network was paved, extended, and improved. Finally, beginning in 1956, Congress made funds available for 90 percent of the cost of construction of express, limited-access highways to connect major cities in the United States. Today, the 80,000-mile state highway system carries about three-fourths of Texas's motor vehicle traffic (see Table 13.2).

THE POLITICS OF TRANSPORTATION

The Good Roads and Transportation Association, a private organization supported by highway contractors and other groups, lobbied for the establishment of the state highway fund and for increases in motor fuel taxes and still attempts to guard the fund against those who would spend any part of it for other purposes. Despite the organization's efforts, per capita state highway funding is slightly below the national average.

Funding for the highway program is a joint federal–state responsibility. In 2010–2011, the federal government, mostly from the federal gasoline tax, provided more than 40 percent of the transportation department's revenues. This large federal contribution has allowed the national government to demand such restrictions as meeting clean air standards and setting a minimum drinking age of 18 as conditions for receiving federal aid.

State monies account for about 60 percent of TxDOT funding. The state highway fund is mostly supported by motor vehicle registration (license plate) fees and three-fourths of the 20-cent-per-gallon motor fuels tax which has not been raised since 1991. Although the motor fuels tax is about average for the 50 states, Texas has been maintaining the second most extensive highway network in the nation with limited revenue sources.

As a result, the state has been forced to look to alternative revenue sources to pay for new highway construction in one of the fastest-growing states in the nation. In a conservative state reluctant to raise motor fuels taxes or general revenue sources such as the state general sales taxes, Governor Perry and other state leaders turned to the idea of privatizing new highways.

Highway Privatization TxDOT planned to use Comprehensive Development Agreements with private entities to develop a highly ambitious and controversial 50-year program to supplement existing highways. The $200 billion, 4,000-mile **Trans-Texas Corridor** would have included superhighways (with separate freight and commuter lanes), railways (with high-speed, commuter and freight lines), and utility corridors (for water, electricity, natural gas, petroleum, fiber-optic telecommunications, and broadband lines). Funded by both state taxes and private investment, the project was to be operated largely by private enterprises such as toll companies.

Pro-business, free market, low-tax conservatives championed the Trans-Texas Corridor. They argued that the project was necessary to accommodate cross-border traffic generated by free trade agreements and to relieve congestion resulting from the state's huge population growth in metropolitan areas. Supporters contended that development of the new transport system would stimulate massive economic development with minimum public funding by harnessing private investment capital to keep state taxes low.

Other conservatives, such as property rights advocates, resisted the Trans-Texas Corridor as a state "land grab" of 584,000 privately owned acres. These opponents pointed out that not all of the seized land was to be used for public right-of-way, and land seized for "ancillaries" could legally be leased to investors for any commercial, industrial, or agricultural purpose that the government chose. Opponents argued that that the state intended to sacrifice property rights to profit influential campaign contributors and foreign investors. (See "The Eminent Domain Controversy in Texas" box in Chapter 11.)

Nativists feared the influence of foreign investors in the project, the influx of foreign goods along the vast new network of roads, and the economic integration that would result from expanding commercial interdependence. Others opposed the project on the grounds that the plan bypassed major metropolitan areas, and therefore, would have a minimum impact on urban traffic congestion. Consumer advocates simply opposed the very concept of toll roads.

In the face of stiff opposition, TxDOT abandoned the expansive Trans-Texas Corridor plan in favor of smaller more localized projects, but it has not yet given up on the concept of highway privatization or the use of tolls to fund new highway construction. The future of highway funding remains a tough political problem for the Texas legislature and the state's political leadership.

Mass Transit Texans, like most Americans, remain unreceptive to **mass transit** as an alternative to individual motor vehicles. Only four to six percent of Texas residents regularly commute by urban mass transit. By contrast, mass transportation is a popular, viable alternative to the personal vehicles in northeastern areas where one-third of all users of urban mass transit live in the New York City metropolitan area.

Automotive transportation is as close to the hearts of Texans, and no other mode of transportation seems as convenient because no other is as individualized. Buses and trains cannot take individuals exactly where they want to go exactly when they want to go there. Automobiles have become a way of life, and their manufacture, maintenance, and fueling have become dominant elements of the economy.

Trans-Texas Corridor

Mostly in planning stages, an extensive superhighway, railway, and communications system to be jointly financed by public funds and private toll road developers.

Critics of the Trans-Texas Corridor argue that it amounts to a state "land grab" to benefit private investors. ☞

What are the arguments for and against highway privatization?

Mass transit

Transport systems that carry multiple passengers such as train and bus systems; whether publicly or privately owned, mass transit systems are available to the general public and usually charge a fare.

Bob Daemmrich Photography

Mass transit proponents point to the enormous social and personal costs of automotive transportation. Texas's annual highway death toll is close to 4,000, and thousands more are injured. The motor vehicle is also the single most important contributor to atmospheric pollution, a major factor in climate change, a cause of thousands of highway deaths and injuries, and a significant source of refuse that finds its way into junkyards and landfills. As the least efficient mode of transportation presently available, dependence on the individual motor vehicle is in direct conflict with the need to conserve energy and reduce our "addiction to foreign oil" (a strategic factor in terrorism and foreign wars).

Urban mass transit was widely used before the end of World War II, and supporters of mass transit argue that adequate public funding could once again make railroads and buses rapid and comfortable alternatives to automotive transportation. When gasoline prices increase, more Texans seem to be receptive to the use of mass transit where it is available.

Critics argue that making mass transportation a viable alternative to motor vehicle transportation would require a massive investment of public funds. And, given Texans' love affair with the automobile and their strong cultural individualism, they are skeptical that the public will respond to a costly investment in mass transit with increased ridership unless there is a catastrophic energy or environmental crisis. In Texas's conservative political environment, it is doubtful that Texas will readily increase public funding for local mass transit authorities, but high energy prices might drive the market for other fuel-efficient alternatives.

CHAPTER SUMMARY

✶ Education, health and human services, and transportation are the major services that state government offers, together constituting four-fifths of the total cost of Texas's state government. These services have a significant effect on the way Texans live and even on the way they think. It is nearly impossible to evaluate them objectively because they affect different groups so differently.

✶ The educational system of Texas is generally decentralized. The chief administrative unit at the local level is the independent school district, and at the state level it is the Texas Education Agency. School boards, administrators, and curricula are conservative, as is much of Texas politics. Major political controversies in public education surround questions relating to the curriculum, textbook selection, student accountability, school finance reform, and private school vouchers.

✶ Public higher education includes public universities and several health-related institutions administered by boards of regents appointed by the governor. Community colleges are governed by locally elected boards of trustees. Major political issues surrounding public education are increasing costs, maintaining access, affirmative action, and accountability.

✶ Health and human services account for approximately one-third of the state's total spending. Among these services, health care presents the most serious challenges to policy makers because of the increasing costs of providing better

services to more people. Among publicly funded health insurance programs, the state-administered Medicaid program (already one-fourth of state expenditures) is becoming increasingly costly. National health care reform will dramatically expand private health insurance in Texas, but it is likely to benefit some Texans considerably more than others.

✶ In many ways, the Texas system of public welfare reflects the same conservative values as the state educational system. Income support (i.e., Temporary Aid to Needy Families) is poorly financed, and the public assistance programs that the state has adopted were established only with the financial support of the national government. Few of these programs are designed to eliminate the root causes of poverty.

✶ Financed largely by motor fuels taxes and federal funds, the cost of maintaining the extensive highway system is growing faster than revenues. Construction of new highways to relieve traffic congestion has become problematic as the state seeks alternative funding sources such as tolls. Facing budget limits, it is unlikely that TxDOT will substantially increase funding for local mass transportation authorities.

✶ Individuals and group's positions on these and virtually all public policies differ according to who benefits and who pays the cost for which public services. The process of allocating costs and benefits is the very essence of politics.

HOW TEXAS COMPARES

★ Fewer employers provide health insurance that in most other states, and as a result, a smaller proportion of Texans are insured to cover increasing health care costs than the residents of any other state. More Texans are likely to benefit from health care reform, but because of their individualistic culture, they are more likely to resent federal mandates than in most states.

★ Compared with other states, per capita expenditures for education are below average. Per student expenditures, like teacher salaries, are also considerably below average. College faculty salaries, income support for the poor, health care, investment in mass transit, and spending for virtually every public service lag behind much of the rest of the nation.

★ Although it would be tempting to attribute the Texas low-tax, limited public service environment to a basic distrust of government, some of its other public policies indicate a considerable willingness to use the power of government to control the population. More than most states, Texas limits same-sex relationships, implements the death penalty, restricts abortion, controls illegal drug use, and incarcerates a large percentage of its population. Texas's unwillingness to use the power of government is primarily a reluctance to tax, spend, and regulate business. Texas's political culture is supportive of government power to enforce traditional values but skeptical of government intervention in the economy. In short, Texas's public policies support economic individualism and social conservatism more than most states.

KEY TERMS

accountability
affirmative action
Children's Health Insurance Program (CHIP)
community college approach
ethnic diversity
guaranteed issue requirement
Health Care Reform
individual mandate
mass transit
means test
Medicaid
Medicare
private-school vouchers
"Robin Hood" plan
school finance reform
social insurance
social promotion
socialized medicine
Trans-Texas Corridor
unemployment insurance

REVIEW QUESTIONS

1. Describe the functions of state and local institutions in governing Texas public elementary and secondary schools. What are the major issues that these institutions face?

2. How are public schools financed? How has the state attempted to correct the problem of unequal funding among local districts?

3. Define *welfare*. Explain and justify your definition. Why are public assistance programs controversial?

4. Explain why health care is the state's second largest expenditure. How will national health care reform affect Texas?

5. Describe the state's role in providing transportation. What major political controversies have developed in planning for future transportation development?

LOGGING ON

You can also keep up with the 50 states policies and politics at **http://www.stateline.org/**. Use the "Issues" links or the drop-down menu for "Texas" where you can read and subscribe to the latest news on policy issues.

The Texas Education Agency is the key site for public education at **http:// www.tea.state.tx.us**. Go to **http://www.capitol.state .tx.us**. Click on "Statutes" and then on "Education Code." Scroll to Chapters 41, 42, and 43 to examine the complex funding of Texas public schools. The best national source of information about educational achievement is the National Center for Education Statistics at **http://nces.ed.gov/**

Special interest groups have very different views about public school textbooks and curricula. For the conservative view, click on "Publications" and then "Curriculum" at the Texas Public

Policy Foundation site, **http://www.texaspolicy.com/**. For the liberal view, browse the Texas Freedom Network site, **http:// www.tfn.org**. To learn about the official process for textbook adoption, go to the Texas Education Agency site at **http://www .tea.state.tx.us/textbooks/adoptprocess/index.html**. See how Texas public schools compare to other states at the Chamber of Commerce website at **http://www.uschamber.com/icw/report-card/default**. Note the standards used for comparison.

Use the Legislative Budget Board website at **http://www.lbb .state.tx.us** to learn about the financing of public education and all other state services. At the Legislative Budget Board site, read the full text of the state appropriations bill (H.B. 1) and *Fiscal Size-Up for 2010–2011 Biennium*. The Comptroller of Public Accounts also provides excellent resource material to begin the study of education, health care, economic development, and other major state services at **http://www.window.state.tx.us/specialrpt/tif/**

Find services and assistance at the Health and Human Services Commission website, **http://www.hhsc.state.tx.us/index .shtml**. Go to the Texas Workforce Commission site at **http:// www.twc.state.tx.us/** for information on unemployment benefits or to apply for a job.

Keep up with transportation issues at the Texas Department of Transportation (**http://www.dot.state.tx.us/**), and

read the latest research at the Texas Transportation Institute (**http://tti.tamu.edu/**). Sleuth out whether General Motors and its allies once conspired to snuff out mass transit in the U.S. Search "National City Lines" and "The Great Streetcar Conspiracy."

God, Man, and the Texas State Board of Education

Malcolm L. Cross
Tarleton State University

INTRODUCTION

Among the state's most important public policy decisions are what education should be and what public school students should be taught. These decisions have a major impact on the thinking of future generations of Texans and, as this article makes clear, have a significant influence in much of the rest of the nation as well. This article provides a perspective on the debate about the teaching evolution in the public schools.

What should we teach our children in Texas's public schools about God and man? Did humans evolve from lower life forms, or were they specially created by God himself?

Perhaps no issue in public education is more contentious. Political and religious activists, regardless of party, ideology, or faith, see the classroom as a battleground in the war to shape

children's minds. "I would rather have a thousand school board members," said Ralph Reed, former head of televangelist Pat Robertson's Christian Coalition, "than one president and no school board members."[1]

No school board in America has more power over curriculum issues than the Texas State Board of Education. Its 15 members, elected by party to 4-year terms, approve the curricula for Texas's public schools, and each year buy or distribute 48 million textbooks to its children.

And the influence of the SBOE extends well beyond Texas. Texas is the largest state with centralized adoption and purchase of textbooks. Therefore the nation's textbook publishers, eager to do business in Texas's vast market, produce books to conform to the SBOE's curriculum standards. Other state and local school boards, knowing the reluctance of publishers to produce alternative versions of their texts, accept Texas's guidelines and purchase books initially written for the Texas market. It is estimated that currently as many as 47 states use books written for Texas's schoolchildren.[2]

Of particular interest to SBOE observers are its guidelines for teaching biology, which it has had to develop within the context of the long history of legal and political conflict over how—or even whether—Charles Darwin's theory of evolution should be taught in America's public schools. Since Darwin first published *The Origin of Species* in 1859, Christian creationists and social conservatives have continuously challenged the validity of Darwin's ideas.

Creationism is the doctrine that life, humanity, and the universe itself were created by a supernatural being. Whether creationism and evolution are in conflict is debatable. Darwin wrote that all life forms today share a common ancestry—all, including humans, are descended from primordial microscopic organisms, from which they gradually evolved during the course of billions of years through natural selection. Many theologically liberal Christians who consider the Bible allegorical accept evolution, considering God the Creator and evolution the humanly

[1] Russell Shorto, "How Christian Were the Founders?" *New York Times Magazine*, February 14, 2010. The Ralph Reed quote is on p. 2 of the article as posted on http://www.nytimes.com/2010/02/14/magazine/14texbooks-t.html?em=&pagewanted=print. The article is a fascinating and invaluable analysis of the politics and processes by which the Texas State Board of Education develops curriculum standards, although its focus is on the development of social science standards.
[2] Ibid.

discernable means by which He creates. But more conservative Christian creationists interpret the Book of Genesis to say that God created each species of animal suddenly and independently of all others, and created man to exercise dominion over all other life. They further note that Darwin, an agnostic, made almost no mention of God in *The Origin of Species* other than a perfunctory reference, in the last sentence of the book, to "life, with its several powers, having been originally breathed by the Creator into a few forms or into one…." The apparent conflict between Darwin's views and Genesis, and Darwin's failure to attribute to God any meaningful role in evolution, lead Creationists to see evolution as an argument for atheism. Many atheists, in fact, do cite Darwin's work as contributing to their lack of religious faith.[3]

Some social conservatives charge Darwin with undermining values on which Western civilization is based. For example, the Seattle-based Discovery Institute, a leading social conservative think tank, says, "The proposition that human beings are created in the image of God is one of the bedrock principles on which Western civilization was built," and influenced the development of "representative democracy, human rights, free enterprise, and progress in the arts and sciences." But by "debunking the traditional conceptions of both God and man," Darwin helped call into question the idea that humans were "moral and spiritual beings," subject to inflexible laws governing human behavior. The Discovery Institute blames Darwin, along with Karl Marx and Sigmund Freud, for the rise of moral relativism and the decline in a sense of personal responsibility.[4] Other critics have charged Darwin with contributing to the rise of racism, Nazism, and communism.[5]

One of the earliest attempts to fight evolution was the passage of laws such as Tennessee's Butler Act, in 1925, which made it illegal, in the Tennessee public schools, "to teach any theory that denies the Story of the Divine Creation of man as taught in the Bible and to teach instead that man has descended from a lower order of animals."[6] In the only trial based on the Butler Act, the 1925 Scopes Monkey Trial, three-time Democratic presidential nominee William Jennings Bryan prosecuted teacher John T. Scopes for teaching evolution in a high school biology class. Scopes, defended by legendary defense attorney Clarence Darrow, was convicted, but his conviction was overturned on a technicality. The Bryan–Darrow clash, featuring Darrow's cross-examination of Bryan on the witness stand, was immortalized in

Inherit the Wind, a Broadway play which has been made into a theatrical film and three made-for-TV movies.[7]

The Butler Act itself was repealed in 1967. In 1968, the United States Supreme Court declared the teaching of creationism in public schools an unconstitutional violation of the First Amendment's Establishment Clause, which prohibits government promotion of religion. In 1987, the Supreme Court, again citing the Establishment Clause, likewise banned the teaching in the public schools of creation science, a branch of creationism which says the creation story and other events in Genesis are supported by science.[8]

These rulings stimulated the development of the newest prospective rival to evolution, Intelligent Design (ID). The Discovery Institute defines ID as the doctrine that "certain features of the universe and of living things are best explained by an intelligent cause, not an undirected process such as natural selection," on which evolution is based. In other words, some aspects of life are so complex they could not have merely evolved without guidance. Therefore, they must have been designed. Left open is the question of who the Designer really is, but the rational inference is that the Designer is God.[9]

But in a 2005 trial over whether ID could be presented as an alternative theory to evolution in biology classes taught in the public schools of Dover, Pennsylvania, federal Judge John E. Jones, III, ruled that ID was simply a restatement of creationism, and teaching it was therefore unconstitutional. Indeed, trial testimony established that the leading ID textbook that the Dover students were urged (but not required) to read was simply an updated edition of a text based on creation science.[10]

The response of evolution's opponents on the SBOE reflects the latest strategy to challenge evolution with creationism. Of the 15 members currently on the SBOE, 5 are Democrats and 10 Republicans. Seven Republicans have formed a Christian conservative voting bloc attempting to promote creationism by questioning the strength of the evidence for evolution. For example, evolution stresses the gradual modification of species over time as they develop from their ancient ancestors. But evolution's critics say that the fossil record shows gaps. While evolution's supporters argue that with each passing year paleontologists are discovering more fossils of intermediate species, the critics say

---

[3]Darwin's quote can be found in any edition of *The Origin of Species*. Of the numerous books discussing the relationship between religion and evolution, a representative sample would include Lee Strobel, *The Case for a Creator: A Journalist Investigates Scientific Evidence That Points toward God* (Grand Rapids, MI: Zondervan, 2004); Kenneth R. Miller, *Finding Darwin's God: A Scientist's Search for Common Ground between God and Evolution* (New York: HarperCollins Books, 2000). Strobel and Miller are both devout Christians. Strobel rejects evolution in favor of Intelligent Design, while Miller is one of America's leading defenders of evolution.

[4]The quotations and summary of the Discovery Institute's views can be found in "The Wedge," a statement published by the Discovery Institute's Center for the Renewal of Science and Culture and accessible at http://www.antievolution.org/features/wedge.pdf

[5]A fascinating summary of the political uses to which evolutionary theory has been put can be found in James Burke, *The Day the Universe Changed* (Boston and Toronto: Little, Brown and Company, 1985), pp. 260–273.

[6]The complete text of both the Butler Act (Section 49, 1922, *Tennessee Code Annotated*) and the 1967 law which repealed it can be found at http://www.law.umkc.edu/faculty/projects/ftrials/scopes/tennstat.htm

[7]The trial is formally known as *Scopes v. The State of Tennessee*. Also see Jerome Lawrence and Robert E. Lee, *Inherit the Wind* (New York: Ballantine Books, 2003). The play was first produced in 1955.

[8]The relevant cases are *Epperson v. Arkansas* (1968) 393 U.S. 97 (1968); *Edwards v. Aguillard,* 482 U.S. 578 (1987).

[9]See http://www.discovery.org/csc/topQuestions.php for the Discovery Institute's discussion of Intelligent Design. The Discovery Institute denies that ID is either based on the Bible or the same as creationism, and claims to be "agnostic regarding the source of design…"

[10]The relevant case is *Tammy Kitzmiller et al. v. Dover Area School District et al.* (400 F. Supp. 2d 707, Docket no. 4cv2688). The text in question was Percival Davis and Dean H. Kenyon, *Of Pandas and People: The Central Question of Biological Origins* (Richardson, TX: Foundation for Thought and Ethics 1989, 2nd ed. 1993). Copies of the text had been donated to Dover's schools.

gaps exist because evolution is wrong—the Designer created the species suddenly, as Genesis says.

So far, the Christian conservatives on the SBOE have had mixed results. In 2009, when the SBOE reviewed and revised its standards for science textbooks, it voted eight to seven to remove language requiring students to study the "strengths and weaknesses" of evolution and other scientific theories, and also rejected a requirement that students study the "sufficiency or insufficiency" of evolution. Supporters of evolution, believing that questioning it might permit the reintroduction of ID, hailed these votes as a triumph. But the SBOE did vote to require students to "analyze, evaluate and critique" evolution and other theories, and examine "all sides" of issues in science—decisions which the Discovery Institute hailed as victories for evolution's critics.[11]

So the battle over evolution continues, with the SBOE's decisions of 2009 giving support to both sides in the conflict. Moreover, the issues raised are increasingly reflected in other fights before the SBOE. In 2010 the SBOE has been reviewing and revising standards for social science textbooks, and a major question has been whether America is a Christian nation. In one sense, the answer is undeniably yes—after all, about 75% of Americans say they are Christians. But some religious conservatives argue that America was actually created by God to spread Christianity to the rest of the world, and that the Declaration

of Independence and the Constitution of the United States are divinely inspired and based on biblical principles. How this issue will be resolved in 2010, how long whatever decision is reached will actually stand, and how important to the rest of the country whatever the SBOE decides remains to be seen. SBOE membership is changing, and textbook publishers are developing new digital publishing technologies to facilitate publishing and distributing different versions of the same book for different states. But the overall issue of man's relationship to God will no doubt continue to be debated as long as God and man exist.

JOIN THE DEBATE

1. Do you believe in evolution, creation, intelligent design, or some other idea about human origin? How should public schools deal with culturally sensitive issues in a democracy?

2. Do you agree or disagree with court rulings that the teaching of creationism, creation science, and intelligent design are unconstitutional because they are based on religion?

3. Do you believe the issue is settled, or do you think the debate will continue? What new arguments can be made for or against the teaching of evolution?

---

[11] A sample of articles on the debate before the SBOE includes Stephanie Simon, "Texas Opens Classroom Door for Evolution Doubts," *The Wall Street Journal*, March 28, 2009, http://online.wsj.com/article/SB12381975141561761.html; Gordy Slack, "Texas on Evolution: Needs Further Study, *Salon.com*, March 28, 2009, http://www.salon.com/environment/feature/2009/03/28/texas-evolution-case/index.html; Terrence Stutz, "Conservatives Lose Another Battle over Evolution, *The Dallas Morning News*, March 29, 2009, http://www.dallasnews.com/sharedcontent/dws/texassouthwest/stories/DN-evolution; "Texas Board Comes Down on Two Sides of Creationism Debate," CNN.com, http://www.cnn.com/2009/US/03/27/texas.education.evolution/. The Discovery Institute hailed the outcome of the SBOE's deliberations at http://www.evolutionnews.org/2009/03/dallas_news_ofers_alt.html. Also, visit http://www.tea.state.tx.us/index3.aspx?id=1156 for the Texas State Board of Education official records.

Tuition Deregulation and the Future of Texas's Higher Education

Kevin T. Davis
North Central Texas College

Data Collection by *Jenna Morgan*
North Central Texas College

INTRODUCTION

Texas government had a big problem in 2003. The Texas Constitution mandated that the Texas budget be balanced, but the state was going to start with a $10 billion deficit! Where was the state going to find new money? There were only two answers: raise taxes or find ways to cut the budget. Speaker of the Texas House of Representatives, Tom Craddick, pushed to cut the budget by cutting $260 million from Texas's higher education budget and deregulating Texas's colleges and universities, which would allow them to set their own tuition. Colleges and universities offset these cuts by raising their tuition prices. The $18 billion budget deficit of 2011 will be especially challenging to address, and will necessitate more cuts in higher education, which will mean more tuition increases for students.

Back in 2003, the state of Texas faced a $10 billion shortfall. Texas leaders looked for ways to cut the budget without resorting to a tax increase. Because Texas subsidized all of the state's education programs, Speaker Craddick thought that deregulating the tuition at Texas colleges and universities would help save some money. Therefore, instead of the state paying more to colleges and universities, students pay more in tuition to cover the difference. Without the legislative controls in place, the tuition of many universities has risen substantially, and students and parents are complaining. With an even bigger budget deficit in the next legislative session, the state will be hard pressed to fully fund all our colleges and universities. Thus students should expect higher tuition costs.

The increasing tuition costs at Texas's colleges and universities were only a natural consequence of the state of Texas cutting back on its funding. Back in 2003, deregulation saved the state $260 million, which the schools had to recoup through higher tuition. In the words of state Senator Florence Shapiro of Plano, "We had a ten-billion-dollar shortfall. We didn't have the money to fund them appropriately."[1] Governor Perry agreed to this deregulation because he felt it would be better than a tax increase. Because a majority of Texas's budget goes to help fund our state's education, cutting back on our budget meant cuts in all our education programs.

After the Texas legislature cut back on their funding, colleges and universities have made several increases in their tuition. According to the records of several major Texas universities, and the Texas Board of Higher Education, tuition at Texas universities has increased dramatically during the last decade. Although some schools, like The University of Texas at El Paso, have managed to keep their increases to a minimum, other schools, like Texas Tech University, have increased their tuition substantially.[2] Texas Tech University increased their tuition almost 600% during the last 10 years![3] Texas A&M University recorded an increase of almost 300%, and other universities saw almost 200% increases.[4] Although community colleges have done better with their tuition increases, some of the more rural community colleges increased their tuition significantly. Obviously, these kinds of increases are making college degrees more expensive and thus tougher for poor and middle-class students to afford.

Texas will see the effects of the latest recession in the 2011 legislative session. Although Texas accepted more than $10 billion dollars of federal stimulus money to balance our budget back in 2009, there will be no help for 2011. Texas has approximately $9 billion in a Rainy Day Fund, but how much of that are we supposed to spend? Some legislators say we should spend all of it, since this is what we saved it for. Others will argue that we should hold some back, in case the economy does not come back over the next two years. Whatever the legislature decides, here will still be a major deficit to cover and we will still need to make cuts. Those cuts will affect the funding for our education programs, and Texas colleges and universities will have to make do with less.

Our colleges and universities will be facing several challenges. As with most economic downturns, colleges and universities are seeing an increase in student enrollment. At the same time, the state will be cutting back to save money, so Texas colleges and universities will have to find ways to accommodate the extra students without extra funding from the state. Although the state has spent more on education

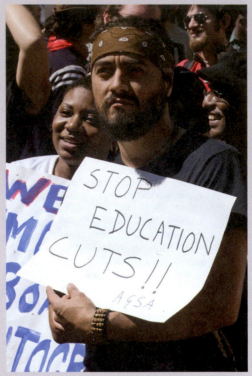

Students at The University of Texas-Austin protest proposed cuts in state funding for higher education.

through the years, the funding per student has slowly been decreasing because the number of students has grown faster than the funding. This slow decrease of support from the state has led many colleges and universities to rely more on part-time faculty and increase their class size. These changes have brought into question the quality of the education our students are getting and what the money is being used for.

Colleges and universities have been conscious of the fact that their tuition is getting very expensive for the average Texan. As such, they have been trying to save money as best they can. Many colleges and universities have put off building projects, delayed maintenance and hired fewer faculty and administrators. At the same time, they are trying to accommodate more students, while trying to keep their academic standards high. Most colleges and universities are succeeding, but they can't keep this up forever, and eventually they will be forced to raise their tuition again.

It is highly unlikely that Texas will ever reregulate tuition costs. Reregulation would be extremely expensive for the state, and would necessitate new, or higher, taxes. Because the citizens of Texas are very conservative, they especially dislike tax increases, which means that tuition costs will continue to increase. How fast the tuition costs rise will be up to the state of our economy, the Texas legislature, and the needs of our colleges and universities.

[1] Patricia Kilday Hart, "(Much) Higher Education: Does Tuition Deregulation Mean That UT and A&M Cost Too Much? It's All a Matter of Degrees," *Texas Monthly*, February 2005, http://www.texasmonthly.com/2005-02-01/hart.php

[2] Texas Higher Education Coordinating Board, Tuition and Fees Data: 2002–2008, http://www.thecb.state.tx.us/Reports/PDF/1759.PDF

[3] Texas Tech University Electronic Archive, http://www.depts.ttu.edu/officialpublications/archives/index.php

[4] Texas A&M University Electronic Catalog, http://www.tamu.edu/admissions/catalogs/

UNDERGRADUATE UNIVERSITY TUITION INCREASES 2000–2009[5]

College	Year	Tuition & Fees for 12 hours	% Increase
University of Texas–El Paso	2000/1	888	
	2002/3	1104	24.3%
	2004/5	1512	36.9%
	2006/7	1572	4%
	2008	1820	15.8%
	2009	1922	5.6%
		Increase since 2000	**116.4%**
		Average Annual Increase	**12.9%**
University of Texas–Austin	2000/1	1643	
	2002/3	1967	19.7%
	2004/6	2608	32.6%
	2007	3678	41%
	2008	4525	23%
	2009	4525	0%
		Increase since 2000	**175.4%**
		Average Annual Increase	**19.4%**
University of North Texas	2000	1239	
	2001	1302	5.1%
	2002	1446	11%
	2003	1803	24.7%
	2004	2261	25%
	2005	2361	4%
	2006	2484	5%
	2007	3046	22.6%
	2008	3233	6%
	2009	3501	8.3%
		Increase since 2000	**182.6%**
		Average Annual Increase	**20.3%**
Texas A & M University	2000	960	
	2001	1008	.5%
	2002	1056	.5%
	2003	1979	87%
	2004	2150	8.6%
	2005	2460	14.4%
	2006	3333	35.5%
	2007	3333	0%
	2008	3517	5.5%
	2009	3517	0%
		Increase since 2000	**266.4%**
		Average Annual Increase	**29.6%**

[5]From college and university archives on line or through the schools registrar offices.

College	Year	Tuition & Fees for 12 hours	% Increase
Texas Tech University		480	
		480	0%
		1056	120%
		1104	4.5%
		1488	34.8%
		1548	4%
		1780	15%
		1930	8.4%
		3034	57.2%
		3339	10%
		Increase since 2000	**595.6%**
		Average Annual Increase	**66.2%**

COMMUNITY COLLEGE TUITION INCREASES 2000–2009[5]

College	Year	Tuition & Fees for 12 hours (In-District)	Tuition & Fees for 12 hours (Out of District)	% Increase (In-District)	% Increase (Out of District)
Brookhaven College (Dallas CC District)	2000/1	300	516		
	2002/3	312	552	4%	7%
	2004/5	360	600	13.3%	8.7%
	2006/7	468	864	30%	44%
	2008/9	492	912	5.1%	5.5%
			Increase since 2000	**64%**	**76.7%**
			Average Annual Increase	**8.0%**	**9.6%**
Odessa Junior College		422			
	2001/2		542		
	2003	492	612	16.6%	12.9%
	2004/6	576	696	17.1%	13.7%
	2007/8	636	816	10.4%	17.2%
	2009/10	696	936	9.4%	14.7%
			Total since 2000	**64.9%**	**72.7%**
			Average Annual Increase	**8.1%**	**9.1%**
Houston Community College System	2000	420	708		
	2001	468	812	11.4%	14.7%
	2002	516	1044	11.1%	28.5%
	2003	564	1212	9.3%	16.1%
	2004	588	1236	4.25%	2%
	2005	612	1250	4.1%	1.9%
	2006	639	1287	4.4%	3%
	2007	669	1317	4.7%	2.3%
	2008	684	1332	2.2%	1.1%
	2009	690	1338	0.9%	0.5%
			Increase since 2000	**64.3%**	**89%**
			Average Annual Increase	**7.1%**	**9.9%**

College	Year	Tuition & Fees for 12 hours (In-District)	Tuition & Fees for 12 hours (Out of District)	% Increase (In-District)	% Increase (Out of District)
Tyler Junior College	2000	312	492		
	2001	384	636	23%	29%
	2002	432	684	12.5%	7.5%
	2003	492	804	13.9%	17.4%
	2004	528	876	7.3%	8.9%
	2005/6	552	936	4.5%	6.8%
	2007	576	960	4.3%	2.5%
	2008	648	1068	12.5%	11.25%
	2009	768	1248	18.5%	16.85%
			Increase since 2000	**146%**	**153.6%**
			Average Annual Increase	**16.2%**	**17.1%**

JOIN THE DEBATE

1. What arguments can be made for placing the burden of higher education on students, who benefit most directly from higher education? For some ideas, review the benefits-received concept of financing public services in Chapter 12.

2. To what extent is higher education a collective good from which all of society benefits? Give examples of costs to society if high tuitions reduce the number of college graduates.

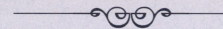

Chapter 14

Local Government

CONTENTS

LEARNING OBJECTIVES

* Explain how initiative, referendum, and recall powers allow voters to directly participate in local government.
* Compare different forms of government used by municipal governments.
* Compare different election systems used by municipal governments.
* Describe the different sources of revenue used by municipalities.
* Summarize current issues and trends facing municipalities.
* Describe how Texas county government is organized.
* Summarize contemporary issues and trends facing county governments.
* Explain the advantages and disadvantages of special-district governments.
* Describe how Councils of Governments facilitate regional development.

★ GET ACTIVE ★

Apply for membership on a city advisory board or commission. Go to your city's official website and check out the many boards and commissions that offer you the chance to advise the city council and city officials on matters of critical importance to your community such as health, education, transportation, housing, and ethics.

Participate in a local campaign. Candidates often need volunteers to help organize campaign rallies and get-out-the-vote drives, stuff envelopes with campaign literature for mail-outs, work phone banks, and pass out campaign literature. You will find the names of city council candidates listed on the election ballot at the official websites of Texas cities. For county elections, you will find the candidates listed on the ballot by going to the official websites of county governments.

Write a letter to the editor of a newspaper about a local issue that is important to you. Your letter could spark an exchange of ideas in your community. It could also lead local officials to take action.

Attend a city council meeting or a county commissioners court meeting. Sign up to speak during the time of the meeting set aside for public comments. Let city or county officials know what improvements you think could be made in your community.

S hould a city place red-light cameras at high-traffic intersections? Or annex a neighboring unincorporated area against the wishes of those who live there? Or pass antiloitering laws to curb the presence of the homeless? How should counties provide for mentally ill prisoners or fund the burial of indigents with no known next of kin? These are just a few issues that have been placed on the agendas of local governments throughout the nation, including Texas.

The aforementioned examples are of a local nature, but a visit to the websites of the U.S. Conference of Mayors and the National Association of Counties underscores the following point: Issues of national importance also are highly relevant to local governments. In 2008, the U.S. Conference of Mayors emphasized several objectives, including anticrime measures, climate protection, public housing assistance, infrastructure improvements, and youth employment opportunities in "Strong Cities . . . Strong Families . . . for a Strong American Mayor's 10-Point Plan." That same year, the National Association of Counties legislative priorities focused on a variety of goals, including food safety, renewable and alternative energy, reauthorization and expansion of the State Children's Health Insurance Program, improving health care for veterans, and selected the theme of "Protecting Our Children" for National County Week. Both organizations stressed Homeland Security concerns. The sheer number of local governments in Texas can challenge even the most interested members of a community who want to contact local officials occasionally or on a routine basis about pressing concerns ranging from potholes, the need for better street lighting and more police, and the increase in the number of homeless families. (See Table 14.1 for a comparison of local governments in Texas and in the United States as a whole.) Anyone who lives in a metropolitan area is likely to be governed by several **special districts** (such as a hospital district, a metropolitan transit authority, and a municipal utility district), in addition to the two **general-purpose governments**, municipal and county governments.

Although information about local governments is available in a variety of print and electronic media, adequately covering thousands of local governments is no small challenge.

Special district

A local government that provides one or more services to a jurisdiction that are not provided by general-purpose governments. Examples of special districts include municipal, utility districts, hospital authorities, and transit authorities.

General-purpose government

A municipal or county government, providing a wide range of services. Compare *special district*.

There are thousands of local governments in the U.S. and Texas. Different governments often work together to meet critical needs. For example, In 2008 the Texas Commission on Environmental Quality' Border Initiative was established to meet environmental needs on the U.S.–Mexico border. Cooperative efforts between cities and counties in both countries include air and water quality monitoring, and scrap tire management. ☞

What other policy needs can be effectively met by intergovernmental cooperation? What obstacles make cooperation difficult?

TABLE 14.1 LOCAL GOVERNMENTS AND PUBLIC SCHOOL SYSTEMS, UNITED STATES AND TEXAS, 2007

	Total	County	Municipal	Town or Special	Special Districts	School Districts
United States	89,476	3,033	19,492	16,519	37,381	13,051
Texas	4,835	254	1,209	0	2,291	1,081

Source: U.S. Census Bureau, 2007 Census of Governments, http://www.census.gov/govs/cog/GovOrgTab03ss.html

Political scientist Doris A. Graber has observed that when it comes to local media, "Reporting, of necessity, becomes highly selective and superficial."[1]

Nor can the public depend on local political parties to provide information and generate interest about all local governments. In Texas, political parties do not nominate candidates below the county level. Municipal and special-district elections are nonpartisan; that is, there is no mention of party affiliation on the ballot. It is not surprising that in the absence of party labels, voter turnout tends to be low in municipal and special-district elections.

In an effort to shed more light on the inner workings of local government, we examine in the following sections the various institutional features of cities, counties, and special districts. We also look at issues and trends facing local government. Finally, given the growing interest in finding regional solutions to local problems, we discuss the role of councils of government (COGs) at the local level.

The 2008 presidential election saw an increase in the number of young voters. ☞

What political issues today motivate students to engage in additional forms of political participation such as signing petitions, attending rallies, and contacting elected officials? What obstacles do students who want to engage in political activism face and what measures can be taken to overcome these obstacles?

Yellow Dog Productions/Getty Images

Municipalities

How are municipalities relevant to our lives? Cities hire police and firefighters to protect the community. Cities enforce building and safety codes, pass antilitter ordinances, issue garage sale permits, maintain recycling programs, launch antigraffiti programs, impound stray animals for the safety of the community, and enforce curfews. These are just a few examples of how cities routinely affect our day-to-day lives.

Cities also become involved in high-profile, controversial issues. For example, in May 2007 voters in Farmers Branch, a Dallas suburb, approved a ban on the rental of apartments to illegal immigrants (with some exceptions) by a more than a 2-to-1 margin. As of March 2010, two court rulings striking down the ban had not deterred the city council from appealing the rulings. In 2010, a controversial state law was passed in Arizona requiring police officers who stop individuals for lawful reasons to check their immigration status if they suspect they are in the country illegally; the law was amended to ban racial profiling in its enforcement. In reaction to the Arizona law, the Austin City Council passed a resolution banning (with some exceptions) city employee trips to Arizona and official business dealings with the state.

All local governments are bound by federal and state laws as well as the United States and Texas constitutions. The relationship between states and local governments follows

---

[1]Doris A. Graber, *Mass Media and American Politics*, 8th ed. (Washington, DC: CQ Press, 2010), p. 267.

TABLE 14.2 MUNICIPAL GOVERNMENTS IN TEXAS, 1952–2007						
1952	1962	1972	1982	1992	2002	2007
738	866	981	1,121	1,171	1,196	1,209

Sources: U.S. Census Bureau, *2002 Census of Governments, Volume 1, Number 1, Government Organization*, GC02(1)-1 (Washington, DC: U.S. Government Printing Office, 2002), http://www.census.gov/prod/2003pubs/gc021x1.pdf; U.S. Census Bureau, 2007 Census of Governments, http://www.census.gov/govs/cog/GovOrgTab03ss.html

from the fact that states, including Texas, have a **unitary system of government**. Municipalities—like counties, special districts, and school districts—are creatures of the state and have only as much power as the Texas Constitution and Texas legislature grant them. Texas has seen a marked increase in the number of municipalities in the state since the 1950s (see Table 14.2).

GENERAL-LAW AND HOME-RULE CITIES

Texas cities are classified as either general-law or home-rule cities. A **general-law city** is an incorporated community with a population of 5,000 or less and is limited in the subject matter upon which it may legislate. A city with a population of more than 5,000 may, by majority vote, become a **home-rule city**. This means that it can adopt its own **charter** and structure its local government as it sees fit as long as charter provisions and local laws (also called ordinances) do not violate national and state constitutions and laws. Municipal home rule was established in 1912 by a state constitutional amendment.

The Texas Constitution allows a home-rule city whose population has dropped to 5,000 or less to retain its home-rule designation. According to the Texas Municipal League, the vast majority of Texas cities—about 75 percent—are general-law cities, and more than 5,000 unincorporated communities have no municipal government.

Direct Democracy at the Municipal Level Home rule permits local voters to impose their will directly on government through initiative, referendum, and recall. According to the Texas Municipal League, most home-rule cities have all three provisions. With the initiative power, after the people obtain a designated percentage of signatures of registered voters, they can force a sometimes reluctant city council to place a proposed ordinance on the ballot. If the proposal passes by a majority vote, it becomes law. The following are examples of issues that have been resolved in Texas cities by popular vote as result of the initiative power:

★ Should a city allow stores within the city limits to sell beer and wine?
★ Should a city freeze the property tax exemption for seniors and people with disabilities?
★ Should a city increase the minimum wage?
★ Should a city impose a cap on the property tax rate?

Voters who wish to remove an existing ordinance also can petition the council to hold a referendum election to determine whether the law should remain in effect. For example, College Station voters approved by referendum the removal of red-light cameras. Smoking bans were put to a referendum vote in Lubbock and Baytown. In both cases, voters decided to retain the ban. A referendum election called by a city council can also permit voters to determine whether a law will go into effect. Finally, voters can, by petition, force the council to hold a **recall election** that would permit the people to remove the mayor or a member of the council. Texas Attorney General Greg Abbott ruled that recalled members of a city council must step down once the election results are certified—even if that leaves the council without a quorum.

As general purpose governments, municipal governments provide a variety of services that are critically important to the well-being of communities. As mayors and city councils attempt to prioritize the needs of their communities, what factors should they take into consideration?

Unitary system of government
A centralized governmental system in which local or subdivisional governments exercise only those powers given to them by the central government.

General-law city
A city with a population of 5,000 or fewer whose structure and organization are prescribed and limited by state law.

Home-rule city
A city with a population of greater than 5,000 whose structure and organization comply with state law.

Charter
The organizing document for a corporation or a municipality.

Recall election
An election that permits voters to remove an elected official.

HOW DOES TEXAS COMPARE?
CITIES AND RED-LIGHT CAMERAS

According to the Insurance Institute for Highway Safety, by July 2010, red-light cameras were used in approximately 475 U.S. cities in 26 states (including Texas) and the District of Columbia, and in 21 other countries.

In 2007, the Texas legislature imposed several restrictions on cities with red-light cameras. For example, signs must be placed at least 100 feet from the cameras to warn approaching drivers. Fines cannot exceed $75. Cities are entitled to only one-half of the money collected, and that amount is earmarked for local "traffic safety programs." After expenses, the other one-half of the revenue will be set aside for a Regional Trauma Account.

Sources: The Insurance Institute for Highway Safety (http://www.iihs.org); Ben Wear, "Rules for Cities Pursuing Red Light Cameras," *Austin American-Statesman*, June 22, 2007; SB 1119, Legislative Budget Board, Fiscal Note, 80th Legislative Regular Session, May 26, 2007.

Mayor-council form of government

A municipal government consisting of a mayor and a city council. In the *strong-mayor form of government*, substantial authority (over appointments and budget) is lodged in the mayor's office. The mayor is elected at large. In the *weak-mayor form of government*, an elected mayor and city council share administrative responsibilities, often with other elected officers.

Council-manager form of government

A form of government that features an elected city council and a city manager who is hired by the council. The council makes policy decisions, and the city manager is responsible for the day-to-day operations of the city government.

The Limits of Home Rule Although home-rule cities have wider latitude than general-law cities in their day-to-day operations, they must still contend with state limitations on their authority. For example, state law determines the specific dates on which municipal elections can be held. Voters are free to amend city charters, but the Texas Constitution permits cities to hold charter elections only every two years. An election establishing a metropolitan transit authority can be held only in cities that meet a population requirement determined by the Texas legislature. Local governments in Texas are subject to "sunshine" laws such as the Public Information Act and the Open Meetings Act. Because Texas is covered under the federal Voting Rights Act, all state and local election law changes must first be approved (the "preclearance" requirement) by the U.S. Justice Department or a federal district court in Washington, D.C.

FORMS OF GOVERNMENT

There are three common forms of municipal governments: council-manager, **mayor-council**, and commission.

Council-Manager System In a **council-manager form of government** (see Figure 14.1), an elected city council makes laws and hires a professional administrator who is responsible for both executing council policies and managing the day-to-day operations of city government and who serves at the pleasure of the council.

The powers of the city manager come from the city charter and from the delegation of authority by the council through direct assignment and passage of ordinances. For example, the city manager is responsible for selecting key personnel and for submitting a proposed budget to the council for its approval. The city council will likely seek the manager's opinion on a wide variety of matters, including what tax rate the city should adopt, whether or not the city should call a bond election, and the feasibility of recommendations made by interest groups. But these issues are ultimately up to the council, and the city manager is expected to implement whatever decisions the council makes.

The salaries of the mayor and council members are minimal compared with that of a full-time city manager. However, a 2008 survey of 20 Texas cities conducted by the City of Corpus Christi Legal Department revealed that some council-manager cities provide council members expense or travel allowances, cell phones, laptops, and BlackBerry devices—all for official use—and health insurance. In 2008, a district judge ordered the City of Corpus Christi to discontinue allowing members of the city council health insurance benefits because the provision was not in the city charter.

In a council-manager form of government, the mayor may be either selected by the council from among its members or independently elected by the voters. The mayor presides over

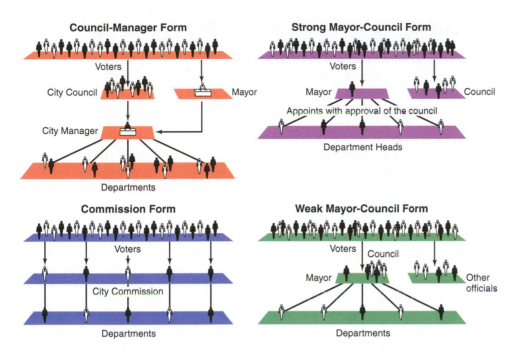

Council-Manager Form

Voters

City Council   Mayor

City Manager

Departments

Strong Mayor-Council Form

Voters

Mayor   Council

Appoints with approval of the council

Department Heads

Commission Form

Voters

City Commission

Departments

Weak Mayor-Council Form

Voters   Council

Mayor   Other officials

Departments

Figure 14.1

Common Forms of Municipal Government. Voters are the ultimate authority in each of the common forms of municipal government.

What measures can the public take to make their views known to city officials in a way that makes City Hall more accountable to the people?

council meetings, has limited or no veto power, and has for the most part only the same legislative authority as members of the council. The mayor also has important ceremonial powers, such as signing proclamations and issuing keys to the city to important dignitaries. Although the office is institutionally weak, a high-profile mayor can wield considerable influence. Henry Cisneros, who served as Secretary of Housing and Urban Development under President Bill Clinton, first achieved national attention as mayor of San Antonio in the 1980s. Ron Kirk, U.S. Trade Representative in the Obama administration, and former Texas Secretary of State, made history in 1995 as the first African American elected to the position of mayor in Dallas's history. San Antonio and Dallas are the two largest Texas cities using the council-city manager system.

Council-manager government was initiated as part of a reform movement during the Progressive Era (1900–1917). Reformers were attempting to substitute "efficient and businesslike management" for the then prevalent system of "boss rule," in which politics was the key consideration in city hall decisions. Although the council-manager system is seen as a means of separating politics from the administration of city government, critics charge that its principal shortcoming is that the voters do not directly elect the chief executive officer of the city.

Mayor-Council System There are two common approaches to the mayor-council form of government, and each comes with many variations. In the **strong-mayor form of government** (see Figure 14.1), the mayor (who is elected at large) is both chief executive and legislative (council) leader. The mayor makes appointments, prepares the budget, and is responsible for the management of city government. The mayor also sets the council agenda, proposes policy, and in many cities may veto council actions.

AP Photo/David J. Phillip

Strong-mayor form of government

In the *strong-mayor form of government*, substantial authority (over appointments and budget) is lodged in the mayor's office. The mayor is elected at large.

☞ *Houston has a strong mayor-council form of government, which gives the mayor substantial authority when it comes to setting the council agenda and proposing the budget.*

How do the priorities of big-city mayors differ from those set by mayors of smaller communities? What challenges do all mayors face regardless of the size of their cities? What are key leadership traits that every mayor should have?

Critics of the strong-mayor system fear that the office is too powerful and may become too politicized to distribute services fairly or efficiently. This system conjures up the image of 19th-century urban political party machines led by mayors who appointed political cronies as department heads, hired campaign workers as city employees, and awarded contracts to supporters.

Although the target of criticism of early 20-century reformers, the strong-mayor form of government did not die out but was often restructured to include an elected city comptroller (or controller) to separate the mayor from the city treasurer. (Houston, for example, elects a city controller who serves as the chief financial officer for the city.) Rules were also adopted to require that contracts be awarded to the lowest and best bidder. Other restrictions in place today that political bosses did not have to contend with include nonpartisan elections; ethics and campaign finance laws; Voting Rights Act coverage in many states, including Texas, that protects minority voting rights; and mayoral and city council **term limits** in cities throughout the nation.

Term limits

Restrictions on the number of times that a politician can be reelected to an office or the number of years that a person may hold a particular office.

The **weak-mayor form of government** (see Figure 14.1) lacks unified lines of authority because the mayor and council share administrative authority. Power is, in effect, decentralized. However, it is difficult for voters to know who to hold accountable when problems and mismanagement occur. This type of government is usually found in small cities and is not common in Texas.

Weak-mayor form of government

In the *weak-mayor form of government*, an elected mayor and city council share administrative responsibilities, often with other elected officers.

Houston and Pasadena are the two largest Texas cities with a mayor-council form of government. El Paso was the second largest city with a mayor-council system until 2004. That year, El Paso voters approved the establishment of a council-manager form of government and a city manager was hired. In 2005, Dallas voters rejected two attempts to replace the city's council-manager system with a strong-mayor form of government.

Commission form of government

A municipal government that permits members of the city council to also serve as heads of city departments.

Commission System The **commission form of government** (see Figure 14.1) is another approach to municipal government. Here voters elect one set of officials who act as both executives and legislators. The commissioners, sitting together, are the municipal legislature, but individually each administers a city department. A manager or administrative assistant may be employed to assist the commissioners, but ultimate administrative authority still remains with the elected commissioners.

Commissioners may possess technical knowledge about city government because they supervise city departments. However, because power in the city bureaucracy is fragmented among separately elected commissioners, coordination is difficult, and the check-and-balance system is impaired.

HOW DOES TEXAS COMPARE?
HOME RULE AND LOCAL GOVERNMENT FEATURES

Dye and MacManus observe that "Beginning with Missouri in 1875 more than half the states have included in their constitutions provisions for the issuance of home rule charters. About two-thirds of the nation's cities with populations over 200,000 have some form of home rule."* More than 90 percent of the Texas cities with a population greater than 5,000 have adopted home-rule charters.**

A survey of U.S. municipalities revealed that a majority of cities have (1) nonpartisan elections; (2) the council-manager form of government; (3) at-large election systems; and (4) powers of initiative, some form of referendum, and recall.*** These features are also found in a majority of Texas home-rule cities,

according to a survey of those cities.**** In cities throughout the nation, as is the case with Texas home-rule cities, a combination of features, such as election systems that include both at-large and single-member district seats, can be found.

Sources: *Thomas R. Dye and Susan A. MacManus, *Politics in States and Communities* (Upper Saddle River, NJ: Pearson Prentice Hall, 2007), p. 367; **Terrell Blodgett, *Texas Home Rule Charters* (Austin, TX: Texas Municipal League, 1994), Foreword; ***Susan A. MacManus and Charles S. Bullock III, "The Form, Structure, and Composition of America's Municipalities in the New Millennium," *The Municipal Year Book 2003* (Washington, DC: International City/County Management Association, 2003); ****Blodgett, *Texas Home Rule Charters*.

Home-rule cities are unlikely to use this form of government. The commission system has been largely replaced by the city manager option. The commission system also fell out of favor because of its association with other municipal early 20th-century reform features, including at-large elections, an election system minority groups have challenged in court as diminishing minority voting power.[2] In Texas, the commission system is found in general-law cities, but it does not resemble the plan described here. According to the Texas Municipal League, "In a general-law city, one commissioner, acting alone, has no individual power; only the commission acting collectively, exercises power."[3]

According to the National League of Cities: "Recent studies indicate that the distinctions between the mayor-council and the council-manager forms are becoming smaller and smaller. City officials continually change the structure of the municipal government. Those cities with a primarily mayor-council form often adopt features to improve management, while council-manager cities adopt features to increase their political responsiveness and leadership."[4]

If this trend holds, we can expect to see more cities engaged in public debates about what form municipal government should take and what impact government structure changes will have on city hall and the community as a whole.

MUNICIPAL ELECTION SYSTEMS

A considerable amount of legal and political controversy has revolved around the types of election systems used by Texas municipalities. The debate has primarily focused on two basic forms—at-large and single-member district elections.

At-Large Systems versus Single-Member District Systems **At-large elections**, which are city-wide elections, usually take two forms. In the **pure at-large system**, the voters elect all the members of the city council. The voters simply choose from all the candidates to fill the available council seats, with the winning candidates being those who receive the most votes. In the **at-large place system**, each candidate runs for a specific seat on the council (place 1, place 2, and so forth) and is elected by either a plurality or a majority of votes cast citywide for that particular seat. Variations of either system may require a specific candidate to live in a particular district of the city, but the candidates are still elected by all the voters in the city. In contrast, in a system with single-member districts, individual council members are elected from districts by the voters who live in each of those districts.

Supporters of at-large elections say that they promote the public interest because council members must take a citywide view of problems. They charge that council members elected from districts are focused on the needs of their district rather than the interests of the community as a whole. Opponents of **single-member districts** also claim that the election of individuals who have an outlook limited to their district makes it difficult for the council to build a consensus about the future of the city.

Critics of at-large elections maintain that the system allows a simple majority of voters to elect all council members (most of whom come from privileged backgrounds) and that consequently the interests of racial, ethnic, and ideological minorities in the community are not represented at city hall. Supporters of single-member districts charge that effective neighborhood representation serves the interest of the entire city and is more likely to occur when there are representatives on the council from all main areas of the city.

At-large elections
Citywide elections.

Pure at-large system
An electoral system in which candidates for city council run citywide and the top vote getters are elected to fill the number of open seats. Compare *at-large place system*.

At-large place system
An electoral system in which candidates run for a particular seat on the city council.

Single-member districts
Election districts in which one candidate is elected to a legislative body. In city council elections, single-member districts are contrasted to at-large citywide elections. Members from single-member districts tend to feel greater loyalty to the residents of their own neighborhoods because they are not elected citywide.

[2]*Handbook of Texas Online*, "Commission Form of City Government," http://www.tshaonline.org/handbook/online/; Amy Bridges, *Morning Glories: Municipal Reform in the Southwest* (Princeton, NJ: Princeton University Press).
[3]Texas Municipal League, *Handbook for Mayors and Councilmembers: General Law Cities* (Austin: Texas Municipal League, 2001), p. 9.
[4]National League of Cities, "About Cities: Cities 101," http://www.nlc.org/About_Cities/Cities_101

Although major Texas cities usually resisted single-member districts, successful legal action by minority groups in the federal courts by civil rights organizations such as the Mexican American Legal Defense and Educational Fund, the League of United Latin American Citizens, the American GI Forum, the National Association for the Advancement of Colored People, the Texas Rural Legal Aid, and the Southwest Voter Registration Education Project forced them to abandon at-large elections. Several cities have instituted a mixed system in which a majority of the council members live in and are elected from single-member districts, whereas the mayor and a number of additional council members are elected at large. One study found that Latino candidates in some Texas cities were more likely to win the district positions than the at-large seats in mixed systems.[5] Another investigation drew similar conclusions about African-American candidates in the state but found that for Latino candidates, "the pattern was less clear primarily because they were sharply underrepresented in both components."[6]

According to the National Association of Latino Elected and Appointed Officials (NALEO) Educational Fund, in 2007 there were 2,127 locally elected Latino officials in the state. Furthermore, Texas ranks number one among the states in the number of Latinos holding elective office, and the vast majority (98%) are local officials. In 2001, according to the Joint Center for Political and Economic Studies, of the 5,452 African-American county and municipal elected officials in the nation, 302 were elected in Texas.

Cumulative voting

An at-large election system that permits voters to cast one or more votes for a single candidate. For example, if a voter can cast up to five votes in a city council election, all five votes could be cast for one candidate or spread among several candidates.

Cumulative Voting Although the single-member district election system has served as the primary means of increasing minority representation on city councils, attention has also been drawn to other ways of achieving this goal. One alternative system is **cumulative voting**. Under this plan, members of city councils are elected in at-large elections, and the number of votes a voter can cast corresponds to the number of seats on the council. If, for example, there are five seats on the city council, a voter can cast all five votes for a single candidate. Or a voter can cast three votes for one candidate and the remaining two votes for another candidate. In other words, voters can distribute their votes among the candidates in whatever

HOW DOES TEXAS COMPARE?
PUBLIC FINANCING AND MUNICIPAL ELECTIONS

According to the Center for Governmental Studies, local jurisdictions that provide public financing for candidates running for public office are found in 10 states, including Texas. The jurisdictions are:

Albuquerque, NM	Los Angeles, CA	Oakland, CA
Long Beach, CA	New York, NY	Sacramento, CA
New Haven CT	Richmond, CA	Tucson, AZ
Portland, OR	Suffolk County, NY	Chapel Hill, NC
San Francisco, CA	Boulder, CO	
Austin, TX	Miami-Dade County, FL	

Although most of the jurisdictions use public financing for city council and mayoral elections, some also allow it for other city and county elective offices. Eligibility requirements vary. In Austin, funding is disbursed only in run off elections.

Source: "Local Public Financing Charts (2009)," Center for Governmental Studies.

[5]L. Polinard, Robert D. Wrinkle, Tomas Longoria, and Norman E. Binder, *Electoral Structure and Urban Policy: The Impact on Mexican-American Communities* (Armonk, NY: Sharpe, 1994), p. 55.

[6]Robert R. Brischetto, David R. Richards, Chandler Davidson, and Bernard Grofman, "Texas," in Chandler Davidson and Bernard Grofman (eds.), *Quiet Revolution in the South: The Impact of the Voting Rights Act, 1965–1990* (Princeton, NJ: Princeton University Press, 1994), p. 252.

way they choose. Theoretically, members of a voting minority in the city could cast all their votes for a single candidate and increase the chances of that candidate's winning in an at-large system. However, Brischetto and Engstrom conclude that such systems "guarantee no electoral outcomes. Minority voters must be mobilized and vote cohesively to take advantage of the opportunities [cumulative voting] provides."[7]

A ban on the rental of apartments to illegal immigrants (with some exceptions) was passed in Farmers Branch in 2007. The ban was struck down by the courts, but the city council appealed.

Should local governments take actions to crack down on illegal immigration? Or is immigration enforcement a responsibility of the federal government?

According to the organization FairVote, more than 50 local jurisdictions in Texas have adopted cumulative voting since the 1990s, most of them school districts. In approximately 20 percent of the communities in which cumulative voting is used, the method has been adopted by both the school board and the city council. Civil rights organizations such as the National Association for the Advancement of Colored People and the Mexican American Legal Defense and Educational Fund have backed cumulative voting in litigation, and the adoption of this election system is credited with leading to the election of minorities in two Texas independent school districts (ISDs)—Atlanta and Amarillo. The Amarillo ISD is the largest jurisdiction in the country to use this election system.

REVENUE SOURCES AND LIMITATIONS

Municipal Budgets According to Chapter 102 of the Local Government Code, all Texas cities must adopt annual budgets. The process of adopting a budget is a challenging one. Political scientists Thomas Dye and Susan MacManus have noted that "There are very few government activities or programs that do not require an expenditure of funds, and no public funds may be spent without budgetary authorization. The budget sets forth government programs, with price tags attached. The size and shape of the budget is a matter of serious contention in the political life of any state or community."[8]

The local political culture determines expectations about appropriate standards of services and tolerable levels of taxation. External forces—such as a downturn in the national economy, the closing of a military base, the downsizing of industries, federal and state mandates, and natural disasters—also influence the economic climate of a community.

The sources and amount of revenue used to meet a city's budgetary obligations vary greatly among Texas municipalities according to various factors, including the following:

★ The size of the city's population
★ The amount and type of taxes a city is allowed and willing to levy
★ The total assessed value of taxable property within the city limits
★ The needs of the residents

[7]Robert R. Brischetto and Richard L. Engstrom, "Cumulative Voting and Latino Representation: Exit Surveys in Fifteen Texas Communities," *Social Science Quarterly* 78 (December 1997), p. 973. For an examination of cumulative voting and representation issues, see Shaun Bowler and Todd Donovan, "Cumulative Voting and Minority Representation: Can It Work?" in *Diversity in Democracy: Minority Representation in the United States* (Charlottesville, VA: University of Virginia Press), pp. 232–250.

[8]Thomas R. Dye and Susan A. MacManus, *Politics in States and Communities* (Upper Saddle River, NJ: Pearson Prentice Hall, 2007), p. 295.

Sales tax

A broad-based tax collected on the retail price of most items.

Sales Tax Since the statewide one percent **sales tax** was introduced in 1968, Texas cities have become heavily dependent on it. Although all taxes are affected by economic conditions, sales tax revenue experiences more rapid ups and downs than property taxes during economic cycles of inflation and recession. Because the budgetary problems of state and national governments also make their assistance to cities unreliable, cities need to build into their budgets a reserve fund to compensate for these somewhat inconsistent sources of revenue.

Property Taxes Municipalities (as well as school districts and counties) are heavily dependent on (ad valorem) property taxes, in which the tax rate is a percentage of the assessed value of real estate (see Table 14.3). In a community with a low tax base, or total assessed value, the local government has a limited capacity to raise taxes from this source. Thus a "poor" city must have a high tax rate to provide adequate services. Furthermore, any loss in property values causes a decline in the city's tax base.

Texas has established a countywide appraisal authority for property taxes, and all local governments must accept its property appraisals. However, Texas state law does not require full disclosure when it comes to the price of home sales, which poses challenges when attempting to appraise property with accuracy. According to a 2003 survey by the Texas comptroller's office, chief appraisers concluded that a mandatory disclosure law would increase property values by more than $18 billion. Attempts to pass a mandatory disclosure law in the Texas state legislature in 2007 were unsuccessful.

The property tax rate of general-law cities depends on the size of the city, but the maximum property tax rate of a general-law city is $1.50 per $100 of the assessed value of a city's property. Home-rule municipalities can set property tax rates as high as $2.50 per $100 of assessed value.

Limits on Property Taxes Some Texas cities have taken measures to limit increases in property taxes. For example, a property tax cap of $0.68 per $100 valuation of property is written into the Corpus Christi city charter. (Tax hikes that are tied to voter-approved bonds are not applied toward the cap.) In 2003, Texas voters approved Proposition 13, which allows cities, towns, counties, and junior college districts to freeze property taxes for the disabled and the elderly. Once the freeze is in place, the governing body cannot repeal it. Texas cities (as well as counties and hospital districts) may also call an election to lower property taxes by raising sales and use taxes.

HOW TO PROTEST YOUR PROPERTY TAXES

Your local property taxes are based on the appraised value of your real estate. Local governments in your area use a central county appraisal district (CAD) that is usually accessible online. The CAD determines the value of your property. You can protest the appraised value of your property with this appraisal authority. You may find your efforts rewarded—in some jurisdictions, fewer than 10 percent of owners protest their property appraisals, but as many as 75 percent of those who do succeed in lowering their taxes.

According to the Texas Comptroller's Office, you can base your protest on the following:

Excessive Value. If you believe the CAD's value on your home is too high.
Unequal Appraisal. If you believe the CAD appraised your home at a higher proportion of its value than most properties.

Failure to Grant Exemptions. If the chief appraiser denied your exemption application.
Failure to Provide Notice. If the CAD failed to provide notice that the value of your home had changed.

When protesting the appraisal of your property, be prepared with photos, specific measurements of floor space and land area, and a list of any defects that might diminish the value of the property (for example, a cracked foundation slab). You can research the appraised values of other comparable properties in your neighborhood to help you determine what the appraised value of your property should be. The value of your property and comparable property values are a matter of public record and are available in the appraisal district of the county where you live. Go to **http://www.txcountydata.com** to locate your county appraisal district and to find out the appraised value of any property.

TABLE 14.3 PROPERTY TAXES LEVIED BY TEXAS LOCAL GOVERNMENTS IN 2008

Type of Local Government	Maximum Tax Rate per (in dollars) $100 Valuation	Amount Levied
Counties	0.80	6.3
General-law cities	1.50	} 6.4
Home-rule cities	2.50	
Special districts	Varies according to law	4.9
School districts	*	21.2
Total		38.9

*The maximum school district property tax for construction and debt service is 0.50. The maximum for maintenance and operations has been 1.50, but a 2006 special legislative session reduced the limit to 1.33 for 2007 and 1.00 for 2008 and future years.

Note: Totals may not add due to rounding.

Source: Texas Comptroller of Public Accounts, Property Tax Assistance Division , http://www.window.state.tx.us/taxinfo/proptax/

Rollback Election Rising costs, the increased need for local funding, and changing taxpayer attitudes have led to pressure on the state legislature to increase citizen control over local government. Voters in nonschool district jurisdictions (cities, counties, and special districts) may petition for a **rollback election** to limit an increase in the property tax rate to no more than eight percent (plus additional revenue to meet debt service requirements). For school districts, an election to decide whether a tax increase will stand is automatically held if the increase exceeds 6 cents (no petition is necessary). According to the Texas Comptroller's Office, close to 400 local governments have held rollback elections since 1982.

User Fees Sales and property taxes are important sources of revenue for Texas's cities because state aid represents a considerably lower percentage of municipal revenue than is the norm for many other U.S. cities. **User fees**—charging citizens for services received—are also increasingly popular for two reasons: citizen opposition to higher taxes and the notion that people should pay for what they actually use. These user charges may be fees for city-provided electricity, water, sewage, and garbage collection, as well as swimming pools, golf courses, and ambulance services. The Texas Municipal League has found that user fees bring in approximately 20 percent of municipal revenue. Permits, business licenses, and inspection fees round out the usual sources of city revenue.

Public Debt Local governments use **public debt** (normally bond issues that must be approved by the voters in a referendum) to fund infrastructure projects such as roads, buildings, and public facilities. The amount and use of the debt are determined by the same legal, political, economic, and cultural factors that determine the source and amount of tax revenues. The law in Texas explicitly limits the amount of long-term debt to a percentage of assessed valuation of property within the boundaries of the government. This restriction is intended to keep governments from going bankrupt as they did during the Great Depression of the 1930s.

ISSUES AND TRENDS

A series of trends and issues are important in understanding the current circumstances of Texas municipalities. These include population changes, economic development issues, federal and state mandates, annexation issues, and term limits for local officials.

Population Growth Table 14.4 shows the population of the 15 largest counties and cities in Texas on the basis of 2009 U.S. Census Bureau estimates. A community's size as well as its rate of growth can have a significant impact on the public policy decisions made by local

The property tax is the principle source of revenue for local governments in Texas. What are the advantages and disadvantages of the property tax as a major source of funding for local services? What other funding mechanisms can be used instead of the property tax?

Rollback election

An election that permits the voters to decide if a property tax increase (of more than 8 percent) approved by a local government will remain in effect or be reduced to 8 percent.

User fees

Charges paid by the individuals who receive a particular service, such as city-provided electricity or garbage collection.

Public debt

Money owed by government, ordinarily through the issuance of bonds. This source of funding is frequently used by local governments to finance major projects. Whether or not a local government will incur public debt is usually determined by the voters.

officials. Even a city with overall limited growth may see an internal shift in population, with one area of the city facing dramatic growth in a short span of time, while other areas contend with a loss of population and businesses.

Like other local governments, cities must be aware of demographic changes that produce new demands on city services. For example, a survey of more than 1,000 local governments revealed "challenges in meeting the needs of or planning for older adults," including the

Although large cities and counties can generate substantial revenue from property taxes, they sometimes find it necessary to seek additional funding from the federal and state governments. For example, In 2009 the Texas legislature granted $20 million to the eight largest cities in the state to assist these cities in aiding the homeless. The assistance goes to a variety of services, including housing, job placement, and shelter facilities. The expenditure is administered by the Texas Department of Housing and Community Affairs. Which local services are best funded by local tax dollars and which by the state?

TABLE 14.4 2009 POPULATION ESTIMATES AND 2000 CENSUS FOR THE 15 LARGEST COUNTIES AND INCORPORATED PLACES IN TEXAS

Geographic Area	Population		Percentage Increase
	2009	2000	
COUNTY			
Harris	4,070,989	3,400,578	19.7%
Dallas	2,451,730	2,218,899	6.8
Tarrant	1,789,900	1,446,219	23.7
Bexar	1,651,448	1,392,931	18.5
Travis	1,026,158	812,280	26.3
Collin	791,631	491,675	61.0
El Paso	751,296	679,622	10.5
Hidalgo	741,152	569,463	30.1
Denton	658,616	432,976	52.1
Fort Bend	556,870	354,452	57.1
Montgomery	447,718	293,768	52.4
Williamson	410,686	249,967	64.2
Cameron	396,371	335,227	18.2
Nueces	323,046	313,645	2.9
Brazoria	309,208	241,767	27.8
CITY			
Houston	2,257,926	1,953,631	15.5%
San Antonio	1,373,668	1,144,646	20.0
Dallas	1,299,542	1,188,580	9.3
Austin	786,386	656,562	19.7
Fort Worth	727,577	534,694	36.0
El Paso	620,456	563,662	10.0
Arlington	380,085	332,969	14.1
Corpus Christi	287,439	277,454	3.5
Plano	273,613	222,030	23.2
Laredo	226,124	176,576	28.0
Lubbock	225,859	199,564	13.1
Garland	222,013	215,768	2.8
Irving	205,541	191,615	7.2
Amarillo	189,392	173,627	9.0
Brownsville	176,859	139,722	26.5

Source: Table 1. Annual Estimates of the Resident Population for Incorporated Places Over 100,000, Ranked by July 1, 2009 Population: April 1, 2000 to July 1, 2009 (SUB-EST2009-01). U.S. Census Bureau, Population Division, September 2010, http://www.census.gov/popest/cities/SUB-EST2009.html

"accessibility, availability, affordability" when it comes to housing.[9] Cities can also feel the impact of countywide trends on such variables as income. According to the Census Bureau's 2006 American Community Survey, of the ten counties in the nation with the lowest median incomes, five are in Texas: Lubbock, Nueces, El Paso, Hidalgo, and Cameron.

Economic Development The **Development Corporation Act** allows many Texas cities to adopt a sales tax for economic development projects, subject to voter approval. The adopting cities have either a 4A or 4B designation, and the classifications determine how the money can be spent. According to the Texas Attorney General's *Economic Development Handbook for*

Development Corporation Act

A state law that allows certain Texas cities to raise the sales tax for economic development. The tax increase, which is subject to voter approval, has been approved in more than 500 cities.

ECONOMIC DEVELOPMENT AND TAX ABATEMENTS

Cities look for ways to generate revenue, create jobs, expand their tax base, and plan for the future. How well or poorly they achieve these objectives will affect the financial stability of their governments and the quality of life of those who call cities their home. Cities see economic development as instrumental toward meeting these goals. One means of achieving economic development is by attracting new industries. Cities create incentive packages in an effort to lure industries searching for more profitable locations. Incentive packages include a variety of features such as grants, loans, tax credits, job training, the creation of enterprise, tax increment and reinvestment zones, and revenue from sales tax elections.

One incentive feature that generates considerable controversy is the tax abatement. A tax abatement is a tax reduction or exemption that a local government grants to an industry or a business in exchange for some type of benefit to the community, such as jobs. Tax abatements are also granted to residences and to existing businesses (1) whose expansion would produce jobs and revenue for the city or (2) whose relocation to another city would negatively impact the local job market. In Texas, incorporated cities, counties, and special districts can grant tax abatements for a maximum of ten years. School districts can no longer enter into abatement agreements. According to the Texas comptroller, more than 1,900 tax abatement agreements were reported to that office between 1997 and 2005.

YES TO ABATEMENTS

Supporters of tax abatements maintain that the competition for new businesses and industries is so fierce that cities must have every incentive at their disposal. Abatements are so common, they argue, that businesses expect that they will be part of the incentive package, and communities fear being caught short. Cities can limit abatements to "targeted industries" that must produce a certain number of jobs and pay a particular wage. Cities can also target abatements for "distressed areas" in an effort to revitalize parts of cities that have suffered decline. Such targeting could spur additional development in neighboring areas. As a safeguard, cities can include

claw-back provisions in their abatement agreements that require the industry to compensate the city if it does not live up to its end of the bargain. For example, if a business, in exchange for a tax abatement, agrees to produce 100 new jobs and fails to do so, the city can seek to recoup the tax revenue that was lost as a result of the abatement.

NO TO ABATEMENTS

Critics of abatements believe that relocation decisions hinge so heavily on other factors, such as the available workforce, the quality of the schools, and other quality-of-life considerations, that abatements should not figure into the equation at all. They maintain that industries that are attracted to a community will likely relocate there even without the abatement. Opponents also charge that some cities have been too generous in granting abatements, and have created lopsided agreements that wind up costing cities more money than expected. The presence of a new industry may require additional spending for a city. Businesses that are not eligible for abatements, as well as private property owners, may wind up partially covering the cost. Finally, even if claw backs are in place, the bottom line question for most policies can still be raised: Are the claw back safeguards enforced?

To learn more about tax abatements and other economic development measures used by Texas cities, read the *Economic Development Handbook 2008* at the Texas Attorney General's website (**http://www.oag.state.tx.us/**; click on "Publications").

FOR DEBATE:

Should a city provide a more generous tax abatement for businesses and industries that want to relocate in "distressed areas" rather than in other areas of a community? Why or why not? Should the granting of a tax abatement be subject to voter approval? Why or why not?

Sources: Esteban G. Dalehite, John L. Mikesell, and C. Kurt Zorn, "Variation in Property Tax Abatement Programs among States" *Economic Development Quarterly*, 19(2) (May 2005), pp. 157–173; L. A. Lorek, "Tax Abatements Not Always Good as Gold," *San Antonio Express*, December 14, 2004; "Tax Abatement," City of Corpus Christi, http://www.cctexas.com/? fuseaction=mainview&page=2278

[9]Evelina R. Moulder, "The Maturing of America: How Local Governments Are Preparing for a Wave of Retirees," *The Municipal Year Book 2007* (Washington, DC: International City/County Management Association, 2007), p. 9.

Texas Cities (2008), 4A status is open only to cities that meet certain population standards, while all cities are eligible for the 4B designation. Sales tax revenue based on 4A is used for projects related to industry and manufacturing and can be tied to a decrease in the property tax rate. Cities can submit to the voters a joint resolution proposing a 4A sales tax hike and a separate sales tax increase for property tax relief. Voters must either approve or reject the entire joint resolution. The 4B designation is considered more expansive in scope, allowing cities to use revenue for a wide range of projects, including professional and amateur sports facilities, public park improvements, and affordable housing. Since 1989, more than 500 cities have approved a sales tax hike for economic development under one of the designations, and more than 100 have passed increases under both the 4A and 4B designations. The tax has generated more than $370 million for economic development at the local level.

Government Mandates Texas cities—like most cities in the nation—have seen both a decline in federal and state dollars and an increase in the number of mandates imposed by both governments. A mandate is a law passed by Congress or a state legislature requiring a lower-level government to meet an obligation. Some notable examples of federal mandates are the Americans with Disabilities Act, the National Voter Registration Act (Motor Voter Act), the Help America Vote Act, and the No Child Left Behind Act. Supporters of mandates argue that they permit the federal and state governments to meet important needs in a uniform fashion. Critics charge that mandates—particularly those that are unfunded—impose a heavy financial burden on the governments that are required to fulfill the obligations they impose.

In the late 1990s, the Texas legislature passed House Bill 66, which established the Unfunded Mandates Interagency Work Group. The state auditor, comptroller, director of the Legislative Budget Board, a senator (selected by the lieutenant governor), and a representative (selected by the speaker) make up the group. Its charge is to keep a record of unfunded mandates that are passed by the legislature so that lawmakers have a sense of the impact these mandates have on other governments. However, several types of unfunded mandates are exempt from the list, including those that are passed in compliance with the Texas Constitution, federal law, or a court order, as well as those that are established as a result of a popular election.

HOW DOES TEXAS COMPARE?
POPULATION CHANGES IN LARGE U.S. CITIES

2009 POPULATION ESTIMATES AND 2000 CENSUS FOR THE 10 LARGEST U.S. CITIES

Rank	Place	State	July 1, 2009	2000 Census
1.	New York	New York	8,391,881	8,008,278
2.	Los Angeles	California	3,831,868	3,694,820
3.	Chicago	Illinois	2,851,268	2,896,016
4.	Houston	Texas	2,257,926	1,953,631
5.	Phoenix	Arizona	1,593,659	1, 321,045
6.	Philadelphia	Pennsylvania	1,547,297	1,517,550
7.	San Antonio	Texas	1,373,668	1,144,646
8.	San Diego	California	1,306,300	1,223,400
9.	Dallas	Texas	1,299,542	1,188,580
10.	San Jose	California	964,699	894,943

Source: Table 1. Annual Estimates of the Resident Population for Incorporated Places Over 100,000, Ranked by July 1, 2009 Population: April 1, 2000 to July 1, 2009 (SUB-EST2009-01). U.S. Census Bureau, Population Division, September 2010, http://www.census.gov/popest/cities/SUB-EST2009.html

Annexation According to the Texas Municipal League, "The inherent power to unilaterally annex adjoining areas is one of the most important home rule prerogatives."[10] Big cities in Texas have suffered less than many other U.S. cities from "white flight," urban decay, the evacuation of industry, and declining tax bases; one reason they have escaped some of the worst of these problems is the state's liberal **annexation** laws. The Municipal Annexation Act establishes a buffer area known as **extraterritorial jurisdiction (ETJ)** that extends 1/2 mile to 5 miles beyond the city's limits, depending on the city's population. The city may enforce zoning and building codes in the ETJ, and new cities may not be incorporated within the ETJ. The law also gives home-rule cities the power to annex as much as ten percent of their existing area each year without the consent of the inhabitants of the area to be annexed.

With this protection and long-range planning, Texas cities can keep from being boxed in by suburban "bedroom" cities. The strategy involves annexing "fingers" of land outward from the existing city limits and placing the area between the fingers into the ETJ. The unincorporated areas within the ETJ may then be annexed as they become sufficiently populated to warrant such action. Cities that plan ahead are therefore free to extend their boundaries and recapture both the tax base and the population that earlier fled the city center.

In recent years, some outlying areas have raised strong objections to the state's municipal annexation laws. Critics resent the fact that their jurisdictions can be annexed without their permission. They fear higher taxes without comparable levels of services. The Kingwood subdivision, which was annexed by Houston in 1996, is a notable example of a jurisdiction that strongly opposed annexation.

A comprehensive annexation bill—the first in more than three decades—was passed by the legislature in 1999. Senate Bill 89 requires cities to give notice of annexation plans three years in advance, participate in arbitration with areas to be annexed, and deliver services within two-and-a-half years. (Exceptions to the last requirement can be triggered under certain circumstances.) Outlying areas face limits regarding what they can do if they want to avoid annexation, such as lowering the tax rate.

What happens when a colonia is annexed? A **colonia** is a severely impoverished unincorporated area that contends with a multitude of problems, including substandard housing, unsanitary drinking water, and lack of proper sewage disposal, for which it may receive state assistance. The Texas Attorney General's Office has identified more than 1,800 colonias in 29 Texas counties, most of them along the U.S.–Mexico border. In 1999, the Texas legislature passed House Bill 1982, which states that a colonia that is eligible for state aid can continue to receive such aid for five years after annexation by a city.

Term Limits Although there are no term limits for members of Congress, 15 states limit the terms of their state legislatures, according to the National Conference of State Legislatures. In a 2003 survey of cities, responses revealed that only nine percent have term limits for their chief elected official or the city council, but the measure is more likely to be adopted in larger cities.[11]

Proponents of term limits believe that city hall is best governed by new blood and fresh ideas and that limiting the number of terms for council members is the best way to achieve that goal. Opponents worry that cities stand to lose experienced, effective council members.

According to the Texas Municipal League, term-limit laws have been approved by the voters in more than 60 cities in the state, with the bulk of the adoption occurring in the

---

Annexation

A policy that permits a city to bring unincorporated areas into the city's jurisdiction.

Extraterritorial jurisdiction (ETJ)

A buffer area that may extend beyond a city's limits. Cities can enforce some laws such as zoning and building codes in ETJs.

Colonia

A severely impoverished unincorporated area that faces a variety of problems, including substandard housing, unsanitary drinking water, and lack of proper sewage disposal.

---

[10]Texas Municipal League, *2010 Handbook for Mayors and Councilmembers* (Austin: Texas Municipal League, 2009), p. 12.

[11]Susan A. MacManus and Charles S. Bullock III, "The Form, Structure, and Composition of America's Municipalities in the New Millennium," *The Municipal Year Book 2003* (Washington, DC: International City/ County Management Association, 2003), pp. 9, 15.

early 1990s. These laws are not uniform. Corpus Christi, for example, allows a person who has held a seat for four two-year terms to run again for the seat after sitting out one term. In Austin, a council member is limited to two consecutive three-year terms, but with a petition of five percent of registered voters (the number of signatures depends on whether that person is holding an at-large or single-member district seat), that limit can be waived. In Dallas, city council members are subject to term limits, but the mayor is not.

Attempts to weaken city term-limit laws by state law or by litigation have been unsuccessful. In 2000, voters in Austin rejected a proposition that would have repealed the city's term-limit law. Four years later, San Antonio voters said no to a ballot measure that would have permitted council members to serve beyond two terms. However, in 2008, a proposal for a limit of four two-year terms passed in San Antonio.

Counties

The responsibilities of county governments also have a direct impact on the public. For example, the March 2008 Democratic primary and precinct conventions (caucuses)—commonly referred to as the "Texas two-step"—saw a huge turnout as a result of the intense competition between Barack Obama and Hillary Clinton for the Democratic Party nomination. It was the county commissioners court that decided the precinct voting locations in each county. The County Clerk is responsible for early voting, issues marriage licenses, and records birth and death certificates. Property taxes are paid to the County Tax Office, which also issues license plates and stickers, and processes vehicle transfers. County Dispute Resolution Services help to resolve conflicts between landlords and tenants through mediation. Like the counties in most other states, Texas counties are established and structured by the state constitution and the legislature. The county serves as a general-purpose government *and* as an administrative arm of the state, carrying out the state's laws and collecting certain state taxes. Although the county is an arm of the state, state supervision is minimal.

HOW DOES TEXAS COMPARE?
COUNTY HOME RULE

Texas state law does not permit county home rule. However, according to the National Association of Counties, "37 states provide some 'home rule' authority to counties, while other states mandate county government structure."*

*Source: National Association of Counties, Glen Whitley's 2010-11 Presidential Initiative County Government Works: An Initiative to Raise Awareness and Understanding of Counties, http://www.naco.org/programs/countiesdo/Documents/Talking%20Points%20for%20Whitley%20Initiative.pdf

Courthouses are the nerve center of county government, where courts conduct trials, the commissioners meet, taxes are collected, and vital records are kept. In Texas county officials are elected in partisan elections. In the 2010 midterm election, Republicans made substantial gains nationwide and in Texas, yet Democrats retained control of countywide offices in Dallas County. ☞

What are the advantages and disadvantages of commissioners, judges, and other major officials such as the sheriff running for office on party labels?

Rodger Mallison /MCT/Newscom

With 254 counties, Texas has more counties than any other state. County government is far less flexible than municipal government in its organization and functions. Texas counties do not have home rule. At one time a constitutional provision that authorized county home rule was so poorly written and so difficult to implement that no county in the state was able to use it to reorganize, and it was subsequently removed. Because counties cannot pass ordinances unless specifically authorized by the state, new statutes or constitutional amendments are often necessary to allow the county to deal with contemporary problems. The needs of Harris County, for example, with an estimated population of 4,070,989 in 2009, (see Table 14.4) are significantly different from those of Loving County which had only an estimated 45 inhabitants in that year. Yet, Texas law allows only modest variations to accommodate these differences. (Many state laws, however, are unique to specific counties because of their population or their location—a law pertaining to a coastal county, for example.)

In the area of property taxes, the county is limited to a rate of 80 cents per $100 of assessed valuation, but it has the power to collect additional taxes beyond this limit (if voters approve) to cover long-term debt for infrastructure such as courthouses, criminal justice buildings, farm-to-market roads, flood control, and county road or bridge maintenance.

FUNCTIONS OF COUNTIES

County government is responsible for administering county, state, and national elections but not those for municipalities, school, and other special districts. County government acts for the state in securing rights-of-way for highways; law enforcement; registering births, deaths, and marriages; housing state district courts; registering motor vehicles; recording land titles and deeds; and collecting some state taxes and fees.

County government also has optional powers specifically authorized by state law, and they are found in various state codes. For example, according to the Local Government Code, a county government may establish and maintain libraries, operate and maintain parks, establish recreational or cultural facilities (such as an auditorium or a convention center), appoint a county historical commission, and regulate sexually oriented businesses. According to the Health and Safety Code, a county government has the authority to maintain a county hospital. A county government may also enter into an agreement with another local government to provide a service or program. One example—county–city authority to purchase and maintain a park, museum, and historical site—is listed in the Local Government Code. The Interlocal Cooperation Act, which is a part of the Government Code, authorizes various local governments, including counties, cities, and special districts, to contract with each other for the provision of various "administrative functions," such as tax assessment and collection and the management of records, and "governmental functions and services," including police and fire protection, streets and roads, public health and welfare, and waste disposal.

STRUCTURE AND ORGANIZATION OF COUNTIES

County government consists of a number of independently elected officials (see Figure 14.2). The county governing body, the **commissioners court**, consists of the county judge and four county commissioners. It is not a judicial body but a legislature of limited authority that approves the budget for all operations of the county, sets the tax rate, and passes ordinances. The commissioners court does not have direct control over the many elected department heads of county government, but it wields considerable influence through its budgetary power. The sheriff, for example, is responsible to county voters for enforcing the law and maintaining order and security in the county jail. However, the commissioners court must provide the funds to build the jail and approve its staff, authorize expenditures for each vehicle and its gas and repairs, and authorize deputies, clerks, and their salaries. The sheriff, then,

County government

A general-purpose local government that also serves as an administrative arm of the state. Texas has more counties (254) than any other state.

Commissioners court

The policy-making body of a county, consisting of a county judge (the presiding officer of the court), who is elected in a countywide election to a four-year term, and four commissioners, who are elected from individual precincts to four-year terms.

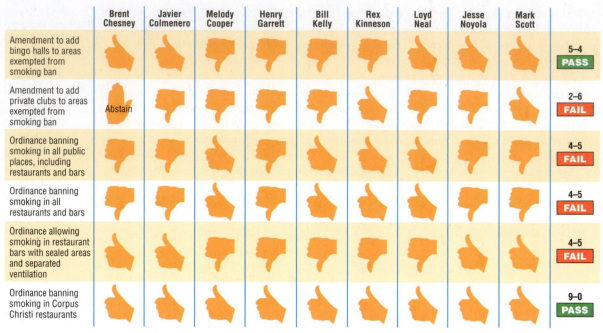

	Brent Chesney	Javier Colmenero	Melody Cooper	Henry Garrett	Bill Kelly	Rex Kinneson	Loyd Neal	Jesse Noyola	Mark Scott	
Amendment to add bingo halls to areas exempted from smoking ban	👍	👍	👎	👎	👍	👎	👍	👍	👍	5–4 PASS
Amendment to add private clubs to areas exempted from smoking ban	Abstain	👎	👎	👎	👎	👍	👎	👎	👍	2–6 FAIL
Ordinance banning smoking in all public places, including restaurants and bars	👎	👍	👍	👍	👍	👍	👎	👍	👎	4–5 FAIL
Ordinance banning smoking in all restaurants and bars	👎	👍	👍	👍	👍	👍	👎	👍	👎	4–5 FAIL
Ordinance allowing smoking in restaurant bars with sealed areas and separated ventilation	👍	👍	👎	👍	👎	👎	👍	👍	👍	4–5 FAIL
Ordinance banning smoking in Corpus Christi restaurants	👍	👍	👍	👍	👍	👍	👍	👍	👍	9–0 PASS

Figure 14.2

Developing a City Smoking Ban. An ordinance may undergo many changes from the time it is first voted on to the time it is finally approved.

Source: Leane Libby, "Smoke Ban Passes," *Corpus Christi Caller-Times*, January, 12, 2005, p. A5. Copyright 2004 Caller-Times Publishing Company. Reprinted with permission.

What factors make it difficult to pass local laws? What specific steps can local officials take to resolve differences of opinion on city councils and in the city as a whole?

County judge

An official elected countywide to preside over the county commissioners court and to try certain minor cases.

must be accountable to the voters and to other elected county officials who have their own constituents.

The **county judge** is elected for a four-year term from the county at large to preside over the commissioners court. According to the Texas Comptroller's Office, the powers of the county judge are delineated in more than 50 provisions of the Local Government Code, and additional authority is assigned to the office in numerous other state codes as well. The Texas Association of Counties lists numerous powers held by a Texas county judge. They include preparing the budget (a responsibility the county judge shares with the county clerk or auditor in counties with less than 225,000 population); supervising election-related activities (the calling of elections, posting of election notices, and the receiving and canvassing of election results); conducting hearings for beer and wine permits; performing marriage ceremonies; conducting hearings on state hospital admittance for the mentally ill and the mentally retarded; and serving as the head of civil defense and disaster relief for the county. In addition, a county judge may have judicial authority, but the obligations in this area depend on the county.

Four county commissioners comprise the remaining membership of the court and are elected for four-year terms. Commissioners are elected in single-member districts (or precincts, as they are called in Texas). In 1968, the U.S. Supreme Court ruled that commissioner districts must be drawn on the basis of the one-person, one-vote principle.[12] During the next

[12] *Avery* v. *Midland County*, 390 U.S. 474 (1968).

HOW DOES TEXAS COMPARE?
COUNTIES AND POPULATIONS

2009 POPULATION ESTIMATES AND 2000 CENSUS FOR THE 10 LARGEST U.S. COUNTIES

Rank	Geographic Area	July 1, 2009	2000 Census
1.	Los Angeles County, CA	9,848,011	9,519,338
2.	Cook County, IL	5,287,037	5,376,741
3.	Harris County, TX	4,070,989	3,400,578
4.	Maricopa County, AZ	4,023,132	3,072,149
5.	San Diego County, CA	3,053,793	2,813,833
6.	Orange County, CA	3,026,786	2,846,289
7.	Kings County, NY	2,567,098	2,465,326
8.	Miami-Dade County, FL	2,500,625	2,253,362
9.	Dallas County, TX	2,451,730	2,218,899
10.	Queens County, NY	2,306,712	2,229,379

Source: Table 7. Resident Population Estimates for the 100 Largest U.S. Counties Based on July 1, 2009 Population Estimates: April 1, 2000 to July 1, 2009 (CO-EST2009-07). U.S. Census Bureau, Population Division, March 2010, http://www.census.gov/popest/counties/CO-EST2009-07.html

two decades, county governments faced many legal challenges because of malapportioned precincts. For example, between 1974 and 1984, the Mexican American Legal Defense and Educational Fund and the Southwest Voter Registration Education Project filed voting rights lawsuits in more than 80 counties.[13]

Commissioners are frequently called "road commissioners" because they are responsible for the county roads and bridges within their precincts (unless a county engineer has been hired to do that job). Each is given a certain amount of money and has almost total authority to determine how it will be spent on roads and bridges. Residents who reside in rural areas often consider the building and maintenance of rural roads the primary responsibilities of the commissioners.

Law enforcement officers are the county sheriff and constables. **Sheriffs**, next to the county judge, are usually the most powerful county officers because they have a relatively large budget and staff of deputies to assist them in enforcing state law throughout the county. In the corporate limits of cities, they usually refrain from patrolling to better use scarce

Courtesy of Mark Randolph, City of Waco

City councils throughout the nation appoint high school students to youth commissions or councils in an effort to learn more about the challenges facing young people in their communities. Although youth commissioners serve only in an advisory capacity, their perspectives are of great value to mayors and council members, whose votes on safety, education, recreation, and health issues can have a direct bearing on a city's youth.

What qualifications should a student have in order to be appointed to a city's youth commission? How can youth commissioners make young people more aware of the role city government plays in their lives and engage them in the political process?

Sheriff

The chief county law-enforcement officer. Although the sheriff is an elected official in Texas, his or her budget must be approved by the commissioners court.

---

[13]David Montejano, *Anglos and Mexicans in the Making of Texas, 1836–1986* (Austin: University of Texas Press, 1987), p. 296.

Constable

A county law enforcement official who is elected to serve as the process officer of justice of the peace courts and also has general law enforcement powers.

Tax assessor-collector

A county financial officer whose responsibilities include collecting various county taxes and fees and registering voters.

County treasurer

In many counties, the official who is responsible for receiving, depositing, and disbursing funds.

County auditor

A financial officer whose duties may include reviewing county financial records and, in large counties, serving as chief budget officer.

County clerk

The chief record keeper and election officer of a county.

The sheriff is usually the most powerful county officer, next to the county judge, because he or she has a relatively large budget and a staff of deputies to assist in enforcing state law throughout the county. But the budget must be approved by the commissioners court. ☞

What should the commissioners court and the public look for to determine if a sheriff's office is effectively meeting the county's law enforcement needs?

resources and avoid jurisdictional disputes with the city police. The sheriff's department also operates the county jail and delivers and executes court papers (such as court orders).

Constables are elected from the same precincts as justices of the peace and serve as process officers of that court. They are also general law enforcement officers. In metropolitan counties such as Harris and Montgomery, constables have added many deputies and have become important law enforcement agencies.

In some counties, the constable office has remained unfilled for years, but because the office is provided for in the Texas Constitution, the only way to abolish it has been by constitutional amendment. In 2002, voters approved an amendment that allows a commissioners court to abolish a constable office that has been vacant for seven years or more. An abolished office can be restored by the commissioners court or by voter approval.

Financial officers of the county include the tax assessor-collector, the treasurer, and the auditor. The **tax assessor-collector** is probably the most important of these. The responsibilities of the office include collecting various county taxes and fees; collecting certain state taxes and fees, particularly motor vehicle registration fees (license plate fees) and the motor vehicle sales tax; and registering voters.

The **county treasurer** is responsible for receiving, depositing, and disbursing funds. The legislature is occasionally petitioned to abolish the treasurer's office in a specific county and to transfer the duties to other county officers. Because a general constitutional amendment to abolish the office throughout the state is unlikely, further abolitions will occur one county at a time, as the commissioners court must petition the legislature for a constitutional amendment to allow its county's voters to eliminate the county treasurer's office. The most likely recipient of the treasurer's duties would be the auditor.

The **county auditor** reviews all county financial records and ensures that expenditures are made in accordance with the law. Whereas other key county officials are elected, the county auditor is appointed for a two-year term by district judges.

Clerical officers in the county are the county and district clerks. The **county clerk** serves as the county's chief record keeper and election officer. In some ways, the office parallels that of the Texas secretary of state. The county clerk's duties include serving as clerk for the commissioners court; maintaining records for justices of the peace, county courts, and district courts in counties with a population of less than 8,000; recording deeds, mortgages, wills, and contracts; issuing marriage licenses and maintaining certain records of births and deaths; and serving on the county election board, certifying candidates running for county office, and carrying out other "housekeeping" functions in connection with elections, including preserving the results of state, county, and special-district elections.

Courtesy of Sheriff Greg Hamilton, Travis County Sheriff's Office

The **district clerk** in counties with a population of more than 8,000 assumes the county clerk's role as record keeper for the district courts. (The county clerk continues to maintain records for the constitutional county court and any county courts-at-law in existence.)

Legal officers, known as **county attorneys** or **district attorneys**, perform a variety of functions. In counties having only one county or district attorney, the official prosecutes all criminal cases, gives advisory opinions to county officials that explain their authority, and represents the county in civil proceedings.

If a county has both a district attorney and a county attorney, the district attorney specializes in prosecuting cases in district court, whereas the county attorney handles lesser cases. District attorneys are not subordinate to county government in Texas, nor are they considered county officials, but their office space and salaries are partly paid by the counties. County attorneys are wholly county officials.

Other executive officers may exist, depending on actions of the commissioners court and the electorate. There may be five or more members of the county board of school trustees, a county superintendent of schools, a county surveyor, a county weigher, and even a county inspector of hides and animals. Counties may authorize such appointive officers as the county election administrator, county health officer, county medical examiner, county agricultural agent, and home demonstration agent.

ISSUES AND TRENDS

The institutional features of Texas county government are largely a product of the 19th century, yet the demands of modern society are placing an increasingly heavy burden on this level of government. The following discussion focuses on some frequently cited criticisms of county government and the measures counties can take to deal with contemporary problems.

Constitutional Rigidity The great mass of detailed and restrictive material in the Texas Constitution creates problems of rigidity and inflexibility. Controls that are not embedded in the constitution are scattered throughout *Vernon's Civil Statutes*. The result is a collection of legal requirements that is applied equally to the four largest counties in the state—Harris, Dallas, Tarrant, and Bexar—as well as the more than 100 counties that have populations of less than 20,000. This standardized approach gives little consideration to the special needs of individual counties. The general observation made by Berman and Salant that the nation's "state legislatures have exercised virtually unlimited authority in prescribing the limits of county discretion"[14] clearly applies to Texas. At present, change has to come from the state legislature.

Long Ballot So many county officials are independently elected and the operations of county government are so decentralized that the voters may find it difficult to monitor the many positions involved. Reformers recommend a **short ballot** with fewer elected (and more appointed) county officials in conjunction with the establishment of the county manager system or the elected county executive. Defenders of the **long ballot** counter that the current system provides for the direct election of public officials to ensure that government remains responsive to the needs and demands of the voters.

Unit Road System The **unit road system** takes the day-to-day responsibility for roads away from individual county commissioners and concentrates it in the hands of a professional engineer. The engineer is responsible to the commissioners court for efficient and economical

District clerk
The record keeper for the district court in counties with a population exceeding 8,000.

County attorney
A county legal officer whose responsibilities may include giving legal advice to the commissioner's court, representing the county in litigation, and prosecuting felonies and misdemeanors. In a county that has both a county attorney and a district attorney, the latter prosecutes felonies.

District attorney
A county officer who prosecutes felony cases.

Short ballot
The listing of only a few independently elected offices on an election ballot.

Long ballot
The listing of several independently elected offices on an election ballot.

Unit road system
A system that concentrates the day-to-day responsibilities of roads in the hands of a professional engineer rather than individual county commissioners. The engineer is ultimately responsible to the commissioners court.

---

[14]David R. Berman and Tanis J. Salant, "The Changing Role of Counties in the Intergovernment System," in Donald C. Menzel (ed.), *The American County: Frontiers of Knowledge* (Tuscaloosa: University of Alabama Press, 1996), p. 24.

construction and maintenance of county roads. The voters may petition for an election to establish the unit road system, or commissioners may initiate the change themselves.

Supporters of this system maintain that it brings greater coordination and professionalism to the building of roads in rural areas. The current practice in most counties—dividing funds for roads and bridges among the four commissioners—is defended by those who believe these activities should remain the *direct* responsibility of elected officials.

Spoils System versus Merit System The **spoils system**, which is the primary method of hiring employees, is often criticized by students of government because it makes job security dependent on the continued election of and allegiance to one's employer. When a new official is elected, there may be a large turnover of county employees. Political loyalty rather than competence may be the main factor in the recruitment and retention of employees.

Opponents of these practices propose a **merit system** that bases employment and promotion on specific qualifications and performance. Because it would also prohibit termination of employment except for proven cause, the merit system offers job security, which should attract qualified personnel. Supporters of the merit system maintain that it encourages professionalism, increases efficiency, and allows uniform application of equal-opportunity requirements.

In contrast, supporters of the spoils system point out that the elected official is responsible for the employee's performance and therefore should have the authority to bring in more employees than just the personnel at the top echelon. They also argue that an elected official would be foolish to release competent employees simply because they had gained their experience under a predecessor. Finally, they argue that the merit system provides so much job security that complacency and indifference to the public may result.

Texas counties with a population of 200,000 or more may establish a **civil service** for county employees, and counties with populations of more than 500,000 may establish a civil service system for the sheriff's office. According to the Texas Association of Counties, a civil service exists in one-half of the 20 counties that meet the eligibility requirement. All seven counties that can establish this system in their sheriff's department have done so.

Consolidation Students of county government reform point to city–county consolidation as a means of reducing both the number of local governments and the duplication of government services, as well as providing greater government efficiency. With **consolidation**, a county and local governments within the county are merged into a single government. According to the National Association of Counties, 41 city–county consolidation proposals have been approved by voters since 1921.

There are several major challenges to the consolidation of governments. Consolidation requires action on the part of the state legislature, followed by local voter approval. Independently elected officials at the local level are likely to resist a move that would merge local responsibilities and reduce the number of political offices. Leland and Thurmaier conclude that "The most critical elements that can affect the passage or defeat of the consolidation attempt involve the county sheriff, the status of the new chief executive, taxation, minority representation on the new city–county council, public employees' job security, and the status of minor municipalities."[15]

In addition, "public choice" theorists maintain that government fragmentation is preferable to a monopoly, smaller governments are more responsive than larger ones, and the current system forces governments to be competitive.[16] Although many cities and counties enter into agreements to provide services, city–county consolidation bills have failed to win passage in the Texas legislature.

Spoils system
A system that gives elected officials considerable discretion in employment and promotion decisions.

Merit system
An employment and promotion system based on specific qualifications and performance rather than party affiliation or political support.

Civil service
An employment system used by governments that takes merit into account in hiring and promotion.

Consolidation
The merging or joining of responsibilities by counties and other local governments.

[15]Suzanne M. Leland and Kurt Thurmaier, "Lessons from 35 Years of City–County Consolidation Attempts," *The Municipal Year Book, 2006* (Washington, DC: International City/County Management Association, 2006), p. 8.
[16]A thorough discussion of metropolitan fragmentation can be found in Virginia Gray and Peter Eisinger, *American States and Cities*, 2nd ed. (New York: Longman, 1997), Chap. 11.

TABLE 14.5 SPECIAL DISTRICTS IN TEXAS, 1952–2007						
1952	1962	1972	1982	1992	2002	2007
491	733	1,215	1,681	2,266	2,245	2,291

Sources: U.S. Census Bureau, *2002 Census of Governments, Volume 1, Number 1, Government Organization*, GC02(1)-1 (Washington, DC: U.S. Government Printing Office, 2002), http://www.census.gov/prod/2003pubs/gc021x1.pdf.; U.S. Census Bureau, 2007 Census of Governments, http://www.census.gov/govs/cog/GovOrgTab03ss.html

Special-District Governments

Special districts are local governments that provide single or closely related services that are not provided by general-purpose county or municipal governments. (Although the more than a thousand independent school districts in Texas constitute a type of special-purpose government, other districts are the focus of this chapter. School districts are discussed in Chapter 13.) Special districts do not always receive attention comparable with cities and councils, but they are no less important when it comes to serving the needs of the public. In a suburban area outside the city limits, for example, a special district may be established to provide water and sewer facilities for a housing development. This government unit will have the authority to borrow to build the system and may assess taxes and user fees on property owners and residents.

The number of special districts has grown considerably since the 1950s, as shown in Table 14.5. In fact, special districts are the most numerous of all local governments in Texas (see Table 14.1). Some examples are airport authorities, drainage districts, hospital authorities, municipal utility districts, library districts, navigation districts, metropolitan transit authorities (see Figure 14.4), river authorities, rural fire prevention districts, and noxious weed control districts. According to the U.S. Census Bureau, two-thirds of the special districts in Texas provide a single service. The rest are classified as "multiple-function districts," and most of those provide sewerage and water supply.

Some individuals who serve on the governing boards of special districts are elected, whereas city councils and county commissioners appoint others. In some cases, council members and commissioners serve on these boards themselves.

DEPENDENT AGENCIES

Special districts should not be confused with dependent agencies. The Census Bureau recognizes some government entities as "dependent agencies" rather than special districts because they are more closely tied to general-purpose governments and do not have as much independence as special districts in budgeting and administration. An example of a **dependent**

➤ *Special districts have been on the rise since the mid-20th century. Some special districts have their own elected governing boards that have the authority to impose a property tax.*

What are the benefits of having a specialized approach to providing government services? What are the drawbacks? What issues might encourage special districts to collaborate with cities and counties, and what challenges might make collaboration difficult?

Dependent agency

A classification created by the U.S. Census Bureau for governmental entities that are closely tied to general-purpose governments but do not have as much independence as special-district governments.

Figure 14.3

Texas County Officials Elected by Voters. Each of the 254 Texas counties has several officials who are each independently elected in partisan elections.

Should counties have fewer elected offices and nonpartisan elections, as is the case with Texas municipalities? Or are the voters better served in terms of government accountability by the current county organizational structure?

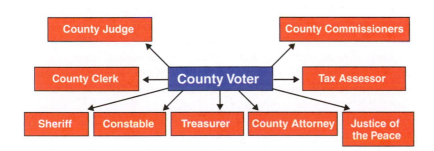

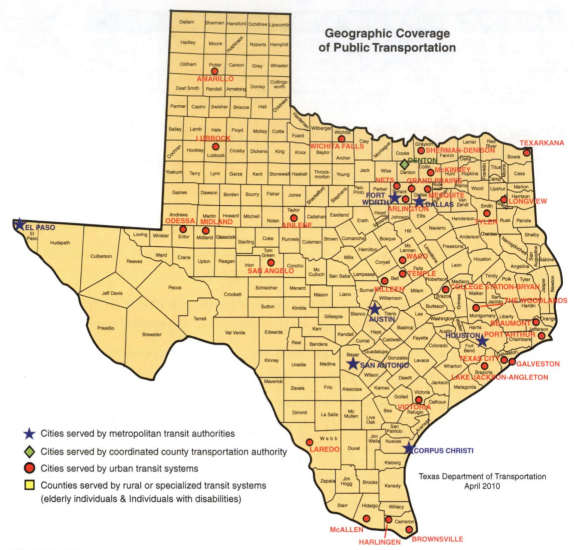

**Geographic Coverage
of Public Transportation**

Texas Department of Transportation
April 2010

★ Cities served by metropolitan transit authorities

◆ Cities served by coordinated county transportation authority

● Cities served by urban transit systems

□ Counties served by rural or specialized transit systems
(elderly individuals & Individuals with disabilities)

Figure 14.4

Cities and Counties Served by Public Transportation Systems

Source: Texas Department of Transportation (October 2010).

Should Texas cities invest more in public transportation? What factors are likely to encourage the public to use mass transit?

agency is a crime control and prevention district, which is subject to voter approval and remains in existence for only a designated number of years unless the voters approve an extension. A crime control district (as it is sometimes called) also collects a voter-approved sales tax. This type of dependent agency has become increasingly popular since the 1990s, particularly in cities located in Tarrant County. Fort Worth was the first city in Texas to approve the district in 1995. In 2009, the Texas Comptroller's Office reported more than 60 crime control districts with most collecting either a one-half cent or one-fourth cent sales tax. In some communities, an increase in the number of police officers is due to money generated by a voter-approved Crime Control and Prevention District.

Having a service provided by a special district rather than a general-purpose government is appealing to many people for a variety of reasons. A city or county may have limited revenue because of a downturn in the economy, the loss of a major industry, new unfunded **mandates**, or fewer federal dollars. The general-purpose government may have hit its sales tax ceiling (2%) as mandated by the state. Popular or political sentiment may be that city and county **property taxes** are already too high, and there may be a strong antitax organization in the community eager to make that point. Little or no support may exist for increasing taxes or cutting other services to accommodate another service responsibility. Furthermore, the service need in question may be unique to only a small area within a city or county. Why tax the entire jurisdiction? A district may be created for the benefit of "underserved areas," as is the case with the 15 library districts in Texas, according to the Texas Comptroller, that serve rural and suburban areas. Finally, the demand for a service may extend beyond a single jurisdiction, calling for a special district that is multicity or multicounty in scope. For a host of reasons, a special district as an alternative revenue source can become an attractive option.

ISSUES AND TRENDS

Multiple Governments Special districts can be dissolved. If a special district is annexed, according to the Local Government Code, the municipality takes ownership of the district's property and assets and assumes responsibility for the district's debts, liabilities, and services. The national trend, though, has clearly been toward an increase in the number of special districts, and this trend is also evident in Texas (see Table 14.5).

The rise of special-district governments is of concern for two reasons. Special districts are sometimes called "hidden" governments. For one thing, the actions of district officials and employees are less visible than if a county or city provided the services. In addition, when special-district elections are held at times or places other than those for general elections, voter turnout is quite low.

Cost Because special districts are often small, they may purchase in limited quantities at higher prices than larger governments. In addition, if special districts have little or no authority to tax, they are forced to borrow money by issuing revenue bonds, which are paid from fees collected for the service provided, rather than **general-obligation bonds**, which are paid from tax revenue. Because revenue bonds are less secure than general-obligation bonds, special-district residents are forced to pay higher interest rates just to service the bonded indebtedness. Special districts may also have a lower bond rating than larger, general-function governments, which also increases their cost of borrowing.

A study of special-purpose governments in more than 300 U.S. metropolitan areas concluded that the special-district approach to governing is more costly than the general-purpose approach. Moreover, "social welfare functions" (such as hospitals, housing, and welfare) tend to receive more revenue in metropolitan areas with fewer special districts. "Housekeeping functions" (including fire protection, natural resources, and police protection) and "development functions" (including airports, water, and highways) tend to receive more revenue in areas in which districts are more prevalent.[17]

Mandate
A requirement or standard imposed on one level of government by a higher level of government.

Property tax
A tax levied as a percentage of the assessed value of real property.

General-obligation bonds
Bonds to be repaid from general taxes and other revenues; such bond issues usually must be approved by voters.

[17]Kathryn A. Foster, *The Political Economy of Special-Purpose Government* (Washington, DC: Georgetown University Press, 1997), pp. 221–224.

As stated previously, local governments sometimes enter into interlocal governments to meet the needs of their respective jurisdictions. Many governments also recognize that problems and fiscal challenges often transcend city, county, and special-district jurisdictions and that solutions of a regional nature must be sought.

A 2004 survey of city officials conducted by the National League of Cities revealed that "three-fourths of city officials (75%) rate their municipality's relations with other cities in their region and metropolitan area as either excellent (28 percent) or good (47 percent),"[18] which is encouraging to those who seek intergovernmental cooperation. However, the survey also shows that the degree of cooperation among municipalities varies depending on the policy. For example, cities are more optimistic about working together on traffic congestion problems and business development issues than on concentrated poverty and the physical conditions of neighborhoods. Further, by looking at the three classifications of cities—central, suburban, and rural—the authors of the survey conclude that "different types of cities within a region perceive the benefits of interlocal and regional cooperation in different ways."[19]

Councils of Government

Councils of government (COGs)

Advisory bodies consisting of representatives of various local governments brought together for the purposes of planning and cooperation.

Councils of government (COGs) represent an attempt by the state to encourage coordination of local government activities on a regional basis. The first COG in Texas was formed in 1966, and today there are 24, encompassing all regions of Texas. According to the Texas Association of Regional Councils (TARC), more than 2,000 general-purpose and special-district governments in Texas belong to COGs. Most of the members are municipal and county governments. A COG is not a government and has no jurisdiction over the various local governments within its borders. Rather, it is a voluntary grouping of governments that have not relinquished any of their self-government rights. COGs provide several significant services to their membership, including regional planning, technical services, and help in applying for grants. When requested by member governments, COGs conduct research into problem areas and organize and operate training facilities such as police academies. One of the major issues on the agenda of Texas COGs is homeland security. TARC is working with the Texas Engineering Extension Service and the governor's Texas homeland security coordinator to facilitate the implementation of the state's Homeland Security Project. The TARC website (**http://www.txregionalcouncil .org**) lists the many homeland security training workshops that were held at the various COGs throughout the state on topics, including counterterrorism training, multihazard programs for schools, weapons of mass destruction, and radiation safety training.

According to the TARC, the South East Texas Regional Planning Commission, Deep East Texas Council of Governments, and the Houston/Galveston Area Council have distributed $40 million of Hurricane Rita relief money to Southeast Texas. In 2008, the Bexar County Commissioners Court commissioned the Alamo Area Council of Governments to establish an inventory of all greenhouse gases in the county.

By bringing local officials together, COGs provide a base for the exchange of ideas and knowledge. Although COGs do not solve the problems that local governments face, they do encourage local officials to recognize the magnitude of these problems and cooperate to manage some of them.

---

[18]The State of America's Cities 2004: The Annual Opinion Survey of Municipal Elected Officials (Washington, DC: National League of Cities, 2004), p. 10.
[19]Ibid.

CHAPTER SUMMARY

★ Although local governments are responsible for providing services that are unique to the communities they serve—that is, reducing traffic violations, fixing potholes, maintaining parks—they also must contend with issues of national importance, such as immigration, homelessness, and homeland security. Municipalities, counties, and special districts provide numerous services that have a direct impact on our daily lives.

★ The examination of local governments is challenging because they number in the thousands, and they do not receive the media attention of the national and state governments. Municipal and school district elections in Texas are nonpartisan and are commonly met with a low voter turnout.

★ Municipalities with a population greater than 5,000 may adopt home rule, which allows them considerable latitude when it comes to governing. These cities can write their own charters (which are comparable with a constitution) and ordinances, as long as they do not conflict with state or federal laws or constitutions. Cities that do not meet that population requirement must operate within the structure of a general-law charter established by the state.

★ The municipal reform movement of the 20th century had a major effect on Texas cities. Key features of the reform era—nonpartisan elections, the council-manager form of government, and at-large elections—are characteristics of many Texas cities. Some cities with Latino and African-American populations have (often by court order) replaced at-large elections with single-member districts, modified election systems, or cumulative voting. In addition to participating in city council, county, (and some) special-district elections, local voters may also influence their communities through initiative, referendum, and recall elections; rollback elections; term-limit elections; and economic development sales tax elections.

★ Local governments are frequently on the receiving end of mandates imposed by Congress or the state legislature.

★ Although unfunded mandates are of particular concern to local governments, supporters of mandates contend that they allow governments to address pressing needs in a uniform fashion.

★ Texas maintains liberal annexation laws that facilitate the jurisdictional expansion of home-rule cities. But the policy is subject to criticism by unincorporated areas that are annexed against their will. In the late 1990s, the Texas legislature passed a sweeping annexation bill designed to facilitate greater planning and quicker service delivery when it comes to annexation.

★ Texas county government does not have home rule. Its structure and organization is determined by the Texas Constitution and the Texas legislature. Texas counties range considerably in terms of population, yet they are quite similar when it comes to structural features, sources of funding, and functions. County law enforcement, financial officers, and clerical officers are independently elected. The spoils system remains a feature of county government; however, counties that meet certain population requirements may establish civil service systems.

★ Although city–county consolidation of governments is nonexistent in Texas, local governments can establish interlocal agreements that promote regional cooperation.

★ Local governments rely on a variety of revenue sources—property and sales taxes, user fees, public debt, and state and federal dollars—to provide services.

★ Government is largely fragmented at the local level. Although there can be friction between governments (for example, in the area of annexation), there can also be cooperation (such as interlocal agreements). Nevertheless, any significant changes in the structural relationship between cities, counties, and special districts will likely continue to be more incremental than sweeping.

HOW TEXAS COMPARES

★ Like state governments, local governments are often subject to comparison on the basis of their structural features. Municipal home rule is a common feature in most states—including Texas, which allows its adoption in cities with a population of more than 5,000, contingent on voter approval.

★ The city manager form of government, nonpartisan elections, and at-large elections have been widely adopted by municipalities throughout the nation, including Texas home-rule cities.

★ Combinations of distinct features, such as election systems that include at-large and single-member district seats, may also be found. Term limits have not been widely adopted by municipalities nationwide or in Texas.

★ Texas has more counties than any other state. Whereas most states permit some variation of home rule, Texas counties are not authorized by the state to adopt home rule.

KEY TERMS

annexation
at-large elections
at-large place system
charter
civil service
colonia
commission form of
    government
commissioners court
consolidation
constable
council-manager form of
    government
councils of government
    (COGs)

county attorney
county auditor
county clerk
county government
county judge
county treasurer
cumulative voting
dependent agencies
Development Corporation
    Act
district attorney
district clerk
extraterritorial jurisdiction
    (ETJ)
general-law city

general-obligation bonds
general-purpose
    government
home-rule city
long ballot
mandate
mayor-council form of
    government
merit system
property tax
public debt
pure at-large system
recall election
rollback election
sales tax

sheriff
short ballot
single-member district
special district
spoils system
strong-mayor form of
    government
tax assessor-collector
term limits
unit road system
unitary system of
    government
user fees
weak-mayor form of
    government

REVIEW QUESTIONS

1. Why do cities adopt home rule? What are examples of limitations that are imposed on home-rule cities?

2. Compare and contrast at-large and single-member district election systems. Describe the cumulative-voting election system alternative.

3. Explain the mayor's role and authority in the council-manager, weak-mayor, and strong-mayor forms of government.

4. Discuss the various revenue sources used by local governments, including property taxes, sales taxes, and user fees.

5. Explain how initiative, referendum, recall, and rollback elections allow voters to influence local governments.

6. Why do proponents of economic development support tax abatements? What reasons are given to oppose them?

7. Explain how county government is organized. What are the responsibilities of the county commissioners court?

8. What are the advantages and disadvantages associated with special-district governments? Is the trend toward special districts a positive feature of local government? Why or why not?

9. What services do councils of government provide local governments?

LOGGING ON

Visit the websites of the following organizations to stay informed about local government issues:

★ National Association of Counties: **http://www.naco.org**

★ Texas Association of Counties: **http://www.county.org**

★ U.S. Conference of Mayors: **http://www.usmayors.org**

★ National League of Cities: **http://www.nlc.org**

★ Texas Municipal League: **http://www.tml.org**

A useful source is the U.S. Census Bureau's "State and County QuickFacts," which provides an abundance of data on Texas counties and Texas cities and towns with a population of more than 25,000. Go to **http://www.census.gov**, click on "QuickFacts," and then select "Texas" on the U.S. map.

Go to the website of the Texas Association of Regional Councils (**http://www.txregionalcouncil.org**) to see how councils of government assist local governments.

Go to the FairVote website (**http://www.fairvote.org**) to learn more about various local election methods, including cumulative voting.

Growing Cities Reach Out to Sports Teams

Allan Saxe
The University of Texas at Arlington

INTRODUCTION

Issues that drive almost every city's political debate are economic development, budget priorities, traffic congestion, revitalization, and eminent domain. This article shows how several growth-oriented North Texas cities dealt with these issues and how their decisions had dramatic consequences for residents' quality of life. Spot how these cities competed to outbid each other in offering special subsidies and benefits to a privately owned business when it threatened to relocate.

The famous Dallas Cowboys football team for many years did not play in their namesake city Dallas, but in nearby Irving, Texas. Ironically, Dallas chose not to build the Cowboys a new stadium, believing that the old Cotton Bowl located in Dallas's Fair Park area was sufficient. Therefore, the Cowboys organization decided to relocate to Irving because of the city's motivation to construct a new stadium.

The new stadium would be named "Texas Stadium" and featured a large opening at the top which fans liked to quip "so God could watch the Cowboys play football." The new Texas Stadium opened on November 24, 1971, with a capacity of 65,675 at a cost of $35 million. Impressive for its day, the structure consisted of imposing concrete and steel. It was located at the intersection of several major highways. Initially, this was a good and accessible location, but as the Dallas–Fort Worth area grew larger the traffic increased dramatically at the site. Furthermore, the Dallas–Fort Worth Airport was located nearby and added to the congestion. Soon, it would take much time for vehicles to enter and leave the stadium.

Texas Stadium was a very hospitable home for the Cowboys, and many legendary games and players left imprints on the turf. After many years Texas Stadium aged as new and more impressive venues opened for a variety of NFL teams throughout the country. The City of Irving, Texas, owned the stadium and understood the need for renovation as the Cowboy ownership under Jerry Jones pressed for an up-to-date stadium.

A number of ideas were discussed. The cost of constructing an entirely new stadium was too large an undertaking for the City of Irving. They had nearly exhausted their sales tax base, and other financial avenues seemed closed. The discussion moved to the construction of a new and retractable roof on Texas Stadium. This would require new roof support structures and still

would not make the stadium competitive with the more modern and larger NFL stadiums being built.

The owners of the Cowboys began to discuss the possibility of moving the Cowboys to another city capable of helping finance a state-of-the-art sports stadium. All eyes initially turned to the namesake city of Dallas. The prospect of moving the team from Irving to nearby Dallas would again run into barriers, political and financial.

Some Dallas leaders proposed constructing the stadium in the Fair Park area, near the old Cotton Bowl where the Cowboys had played in their formative years. The Fair Park area had become an aging and economically depressed part of Dallas. It was home to the Texas State Fair, which had located there in the 1930s Depression. Some Dallas leaders envisioned a new and modern professional football stadium that would invigorate the Fair Park area. Others wished to locate a new professional football stadium in the immediate downtown area, apart from Fair Park. However, the obstacles to building a new stadium in Dallas would also meet with resistance.

Dallas had reached the ceiling on its sales tax use by an earlier vote in the late 1990s for the building of a new sports arena for the Dallas Mavericks of the National Basketball Association and the Dallas Stars of the National Hockey League. Partial financing for the center would come in the form of a tax on hotel room occupancy and car rentals. American Airlines would eventually purchase the naming rights, and the American Airlines Center would open in 2001. The vote on the new sports center barely passed voter scrutiny. During the heated campaign to raise the sales tax in Dallas, there was discussion that if the tax election failed perhaps the new center could locate to a new place: Arlington, Texas. Indeed, Arlington civic leaders were already mapping out plans to attract the Dallas Mavericks and Stars if the election failed in Dallas, which it nearly did.

Arlington was already home to a sports stadium constructed for a professional baseball team, the Texas Rangers. The stadium was a state-of-the-art structure located alongside Interstate 30, midway between Dallas and Fort Worth. Arlington had a history of being growth-oriented and part of that vision had been implemented by attracting the Washington Senators baseball team to relocate and become the Texas Rangers. The new baseball stadium was designed by a world-renowned architect. This would be an attractive magnet for Arlington if it would make a bid to woo the Dallas Cowboys away from Irving or other potential venues competing for them.

Many fans of the Cowboys in Dallas still had hope that their namesake team would eventually wind their way back home to Big D! The stumbling blocks were mounting. Having reached the limit on the use of sales taxes, the mayor at the time was not very enthusiastic on the use of public money for sports facilities. If Dallas was serious about luring the Cowboys to a new stadium there would be a bruising political battle like the preceding close election to build a center for the Mavericks and Stars.

With Dallas stumbling over whether and how to build a new football stadium and Irving lacking the financial heft to keep the team there, other cities joined the discussion. Some leaders in nearby Grapevine, a city also attuned to growth, floated an idea about joining with Irving to construct a new Cowboys Stadium. Each city alone would not have the financial muscle, but together it might work. Yet, the idea never gained much traction.

Arlington meanwhile had gathered together a team to make a serious bid for the new football stadium. Arlington had the population size of nearly 400,000 for a sales tax base, and more importantly, it had at least one-half cent of sales tax available for the enterprise. The revenue bonds on the Texas Rangers baseball stadium had been paid off almost ten years early and that released new sales tax money. A very attractive location would put the football stadium near the new baseball stadium. Arlington had it all in place for a serious bid—a great location at the center of the North Texas region, available sales tax, and a unified mayor and city council all in favor of attracting the Dallas Cowboys to its town.

Arlington Mayor Robert Cluck had spoken to the Cowboys owner Jerry Jones and this opened up communication between the city and the team owner. Both were enthusiastic and serious. An election had to be called to allow for sales tax use for a sports enterprise. The initial estimated total cost was $650 million dollars. Arlington said it could not contribute more than $325 million of the total. As the proposal gained momentum, opposition groups rose up in the city. Their main arguments against the stadium centered on the sales tax use and the issue of public assistance for a private sports team. Opponents also rose up to oppose the use of eminent domain, which would be limited but necessary, and some concerns were raised over traffic congestion.

An election enabling sales tax usage was called by the city council for November 2004 to coincide with a national election that might draw more voters to the polls. Bumper stickers and yard signs appeared over the city designating for or against the proposal to use one-half cent sales tax to construct a new sports stadium. Bumper stickers appeared critical of Cowboys owner Jerry Jones. Jones himself would spend over $5 million dollars backing the measure. Former Cowboy players made radio and television appearances in favor and the famous Cowboys Cheerleaders were even enlisted to lead cheers for the ballot proposal.

The sales tax passed by a margin of 55–45 percent. A crucial argument made by those in favor was that the city had reached an important crossroad. Its total tax base at the time was eroding. Affluent families were moving to the growing and prosperous suburbs of Colleyville, Southlake, and Grapevine. With tax revenues in decline, city services were increasing as a result of the large amount of rental and low-cost housing. The new stadium would bring a revitalization of the city both economically and psychologically.

The new Cowboys Stadium eventually would cost $1.2 billion dollars, with Arlington's share limited to $325 million. The stadium would attract national attention for its modern architecture, retractable roof, crowd capacity of over 100,000, and the largest video screens in the world.

Near the end of construction of the stadium, the nation slipped into an economic recession. As the 2009 football season approached, national media attention began to focus on the new facility. In addition to record-breaking attendance at Cowboy games, other sports events and concerts brought fans and

AP Photo/Matt Slocum

👆 *Fireworks are launched during a ribbon cutting ceremony outside of Cowboys Stadium, the new home of the Dallas Cowboys football team, Wednesday, May 27, 2009, in Arlington, Texas.*

What are the costs and benefits of establishing a sports stadium for a community? What should the public and elected officials take into consideration to determine if the benefits outweigh the costs?

curiosity seekers to Arlington, helping to cushion the effects of the recession. The new Cowboys Stadium produced rave reviews from sports fans, event attendees, commentators, and writers. New highway improvements paved the way for better stadium access. Arlington's longtime goal of growth and entertainment was coming to fruition.

JOIN THE DEBATE

1. Should local governments be allowed spend taxpayer money and take private property by eminent domain to provide facilities for highly profitable businesses like the Dallas Cowboys? Should public officials bend to the demands of team owners that threaten to move their operations to competing cities? Should cities provide taxpayer subsidies and special treatment to retain or attract other businesses?

2. Do such economic development subsidies pay for themselves by stimulating new business activity and by generating higher tax revenues? Do these stimulus policies enhance a city's profile and reputation and improve local residents' quality of life?

From the Mayor's Desk: Lessons in Governing a City

Paul W. Wilson
San Antonio College

INTRODUCTION

The author of this article was a mayor of a small town in South Texas. His very personal insight into a mayor's day-to-day activities shows the difficulties of satisfying competing political demands generated in a close-knit community. And most of the lessons in decision making that this article teaches apply to larger cities, states, and the national government as well.

When you are the mayor of a small town, your phone rings a lot. Usually, the call is about the condition of the streets, an interruption in water service, or another stray dog. This call was about neither of those things—it had to do with something happening at our new city park.

"I want to make a complaint," the unidentified caller said, "I've got small kids that go down to play at the park and the older kids that are always there pick on them. Why aren't the police down there more often to keep this from happening? The police are never there."

Alone this conversation was not unusual, what made it a lasting impression is the next call that came 20 minutes later.

"Are you the mayor?" caller number two demanded.

After assuring her I was, I asked the nature of her concern.

"I have some teenage boys that like to go over to the park with their friends after school, but they don't want to go anymore because they say the police are always down there giving them a hard time."

Every time I hear someone say that an elected official's job is to do just what the voters want—I think of those two calls. Each caller was seeking relief within the same context, but with two totally different perspectives and two divergent requests for the action they wanted to see taken. Of course I recognized that I had no way of knowing how many others were unhappy about the police presence in the city park, and of those that possessed a concern I had no way of knowing which caller's perspective they shared. All I could do is raise the topic with the city manager and the police chief and have the department be both present and judicious at the site.

People who hope to study politics would be well advised to live in a small town for just a short time. In the national media, they talk about "retail politics" taking place when Iowa

holds their presidential caucus and New Hampshire hosts the same candidates in the very personal campaigning leading to their primaries. That is a quadrennial event. If you want retail politics every day, move to a rural community. In rural Texas, most mayors and city council members serve without pay. They are, in fact, generally driven by a sense of civic purpose. They serve with no pay and have no staff to assist them. They are as responsible for the governance of a municipal corporation as their big city counterparts, but with fewer resources to execute them. Of course, they do have specific motivations like holding down the tax rate or promoting singular projects, like the city park I mentioned. People know each other in small towns and their personalities and motivations are known by the voters on a personal level.

If the two contradictory phone calls demonstrated the elected official's role of providing constituent services to me, the following vignette clarified another political phenomenon to me.

In the 1980s, the United States economy took a dive amidst the failure of financial institutions known as Savings and Loans (S&L) Associations. At the macro level, the whole affair, like most economic downturns, is best left to the economists to explain. I live in a small town and my experiences allow me to offer a micro-level explanation of how the S&L failure impacted government. The S&L located in our town failed and was closed by federal regulators on a Friday. At the city council meeting the next week, we were approached by a leader in the local business community. He appeared before us as the president of the local Little League. It seems the boys and girls had been playing ball on fields that sat on property owned by the S&L. They had no contract to use the fields; it was allowed on "a handshake-kind of arrangement." The federal program closing down the S&Ls planned to sell the land the fields had been built on at auction if the Little League could not buy them at a price set by the regulators. The Little League did not have the money, and the citizen was before the Council asking if the city could save this recreational venue for the town's children. He conceded that it was deep within our budget year and he was requesting a sizeable expenditure that we had not planned for or foreseen. His plea was a logical and well-reasoned presentation. However, it was not over.

"One more thing," he said, "As vice-president of the Chamber of Commerce (in a small town the civic minded wear many hats) I would like to formally ask the city to provide a vehicle and trailer when we represent the city at out-of-town events like parades and other activities."

However, he was not done yet.

"And the street in front of my business needs repaved."

He still was not done.

"Finally, I just want to say that I don't understand why the Council keeps raising taxes. You're killing us. It's time to cut back a bit."

Now let me say, I have the utmost respect for this citizen. He was concerned, he was articulate, and he was involved. He saw problems and he saw answers. What he never saw were the inherent contradictions in his requests. He wanted three ball fields purchased, use of city-owned equipment, and street improvements. Along with the wish list came a demand for lower taxes.

Plato said to understand the actions of men you had to understand society, because society was just human nature writ large. I will never be accused of belonging in Plato's intellectual company, but I think to understand big government in America you can watch small-town politics in Texas. The big picture comes with financing wars, maintaining Social Security and Medicaid, containing the damage when financial institutions collapse, and altering the tax code through the complexity of congressional operations. The small picture is Little League parks and city taxes. Either way, we see citizens making additional demands on a government while resisting the taxes it takes to meet those demands. This thinking leads candidates to pledge, "I will tax you less and give you more—Vote for me." Do I even have to ask if that sounds familiar?

Rural government stories can be examined as allegories to urban, state, and national policy making. That is what I hope my first two stories tell. The last tale I wish to tell is about how rural governance is different.

I was presiding over a council meeting in which bids were being opened for a municipal project. One of the losing bidders unleashed his rather vocal displeasure at the outcome in an unexpected breach of decorum. I let the citizen have his say as he vented his disappointment. After the meeting, our financial consultant (a resident of one of Texas's larger cities) confided that he was surprised that I had allowed such an outburst and that it was not my typical way of handling a meeting. I had to remind the consultant that I lived in a small town. Our wives

could easily meet in the grocery store, and, I would certainly see his son in my classroom the next day. I knew this citizen and was well aware of the many contributions he had made to the community. Tomorrow I may well go to the citizen's business and buy something.

In rural governance, you cannot avoid the personal impact of every decision you make. That is the real nature of rural city governance, the reminder that every policy is personal. All sizes of government at all levels would be well served to remember that.

JOIN THE DEBATE

1. Is it ever possible to reconcile citizen demands to provide improved city services while trimming the budget? How does cynicism about government develop when citizens present self-contradictory demands?

2. How do personal relationships affect government decision making? Should public officials be sensitive to the effects of their decisions on individuals, or should they try to be "professional" by making policies that benefit the community at large without regard to their effects on particular individuals.

Glossary

Ability-to-pay taxes Taxes apportioned according to taxpayers' financial capacity.

Access The ability to contact an official either in person or by phone. Campaign contributions are often used to gain access.

Accountability Responsibility for a program's results; for example, using measurable standards to hold public schools responsible for their students' performance.

Acquitted Found not guilty in a court of law.

Ad valorem tax A tax assessed according to value, such as the tax on *real property* and *personal property*.

Ad-hoc committee A temporary committee.

Administrative law The rules and regulations written by administrators to administer a law. The effectiveness of a law is often determined by how administrative law is written.

Administrative review Administrators' study and interpretation of a law and writing the rules and regulations to implement the law's enforcement. All laws undergo administrative review, whereas relatively few undergo *judicial review*, which is the courts' interpretation of the law.

Adversary system The legal system used in English-speaking countries in which two contesting parties present opposing views and evidence in a court of law.

Advocacy Promotion of a particular public policy position.

Affirmative action Positive efforts to recruit ethnic minorities, women, and the economically disadvantaged. Sometimes these efforts are limited to publicity drives among target groups, but such programs sometimes include use of ethnicity or gender as part of the qualification criteria.

Annexation The incorporation of a territory into a larger political unit, such as a country, state, county, or city.

Antitrust legislation Legislation directed against economic monopolies.

Appellate jurisdiction The power vested in an appellate court to review and revise the judicial action of an inferior court.

Appropriations The process by which a legislative body legally authorizes a government to spend specific sums of money to provide various programs and services.

Arraignment A prisoner's initial appearance before a magistrate in which the charges and basic rights (to an attorney and bail) are explained.

Astroturf lobbying The fabrication of public support for issues supported by industry and special interest groups, but which give the impression of widespread public support.

At-large elections Citywide elections.

At-large place system An electoral system in which candidates run for a particular seat on the city council.

Attorney general's opinion Interpretation of the constitution, statutory laws, or administrative laws by Texas's attorney general. Government officials may request opinions, and although they are not legally binding, government officials usually follow them.

Australian ballot A ballot printed by the government (as opposed to the political parties) that allows people to vote in secret.

Bail The security required for release of a suspect awaiting trial.

Benefits-received tax A tax assessed according to the services received by the payers.

Beyond a reasonable doubt The standard used to determine the guilt or innocence of a person criminally charged. To prove a defendant guilty, the state must provide sufficient evidence of guilt such that jurors will have no doubt that might cause a reasonable person to question whether the accused was guilty.

Bicameral Consisting of two houses or chambers; applied to a legislative body with two parts, such as a senate and a house of representatives (or state assembly). Congress and 49 state legislatures are bicameral. Only Nebraska has a one-house (unicameral) legislature.

Bicultural Encompassing two cultures.

Biennial regular session Regular legislative sessions are scheduled by the constitution. In Texas, they are held once every two years, hence they are biennial.

Bills marked up Bills that have been amended or otherwise changed while in a legislative committee.

Binational Belonging to two nations.

Block grants Federal grants to state or local governments for more general purposes and with fewer restrictions than categorical grants.

Blocking bill A bill placed early on the senate calendar that will never be considered by the full senate. Its purpose is to require two-thirds of the senators to vote to suspend the senate rule that requires bills to be taken off the calendar in chronological order. The effect is that any bill appearing later on the calendar must have the support of two-thirds of the senate if it is to be allowed to come up for debate and passage.

Blue-ribbon commission A group assembled by the governor (or legislature) that may have both fact-finding and recommending authority. It often contains public personages or authorities on the subject that is being considered. Such commissions can help measure public reaction to proposals and may also let the governor delay consideration of issues that may be politically uncomfortable.

Brief A written argument prepared by the counsel arguing a case in court that summarizes the facts of the case, the pertinent laws, and the application of those laws to the facts supporting the counsel's position.

Broad-based tax A tax designed to be paid by a large number of taxpayers.

Budgetary power The power to propose a spending plan to the legislative body; a power limited for Texas's governor because of the competing influences of the Legislative Budget Board.

Burden of proof The duty of a party in a court case to prove its position.

Bureaucracy The system of nonelected officials administering government policies and programs.

Bureaucratic oversight The legislative function of monitoring administrators to make sure they are administering the laws according to legislative intent.

Cabinet system A system that allows the chief executive to appoint and remove top-level administrators, thereby giving the chief executive more control over the administration.

Calendar The list of bills reported out of committee and ready for consideration by the house or the senate.

Categorical grants Federal aid to state or local governments for specific purposes, granted under restrictive conditions and often requiring matching funds from the receiving government.

Chad The small pieces of paper produced in punching data cards, such as punch-card ballots.

Challenge for cause A request to a judge that a certain prospective juror not be allowed to serve on the jury for a specific reason, such as bias or knowledge of the case.

Change of venue A change in the location of a trial.

Charter The organizing document for a corporation or a municipality.

Checks and balances The concept that each branch of government is assigned power to limit abuses in the others, for example, the executive veto could be used to prevent legislative excesses.

Chief of state The governor, who serves as the symbol of Texas and who performs ceremonial duties and represents the state at meetings with foreign officials and other governors.

Children's Health Insurance Program (CHIP) Program that provides health insurance for low-income children. It is administered by the state but funded largely by federal grants-in-aid.

Civil law Nonpenal law dealing with private rights and responsibilities.

Civil service (merit) system An employment system used by governments that takes merit into account in hiring and promotions.

Clemency powers Executive authority to grant relief from criminal punishment; Texas's governor's clemency powers are very limited.

Clientele interest groups The groups most concerned with the laws and policies being administered by a government agency.

Closed primary A type of primary where a voter only can participate in the primary for the party of which they are a member.

Closed shop A workplace in which management hires only labor union employees (illegal in Texas).

Cloture A parliamentary move to stop legislative debate and force a floor vote; also known as *closure*

Colonia A severely impoverished unincorporated area that faces a variety of problems, including substandard housing, unsanitary drinking water, and lack of proper sewage disposal.

Commission A body that systematically evaluates most government agencies and departments and may recommend restructuring, abolishing, or altering the jurisdiction of an agency.

Commission form of government A municipal government that permits members of the city council to also serve as heads of city departments.

Commissioners court The policy-making body of a county, consisting of a county judge (the presiding officer of the court), who is elected in a countywide election to a four-year term, and four commissioners, who are elected from individual precincts to four-year terms.

Committee of the whole The entire senate acting as a committee. Its purpose is to allow the senate to relax its rules and thereby expedite legislation.

Common law Customs upheld by courts and deriving from British tradition.

Common-law marriage A marriage without an official ceremony made legally binding by mutual agreement and legally established conditions.

Community college approach Higher education policy based on open admissions, maximizing accessibility, and incorporating technical, compensatory, and continuing education among the traditional academic course offerings.

Community property Property acquired during marriage and owned equally by both spouses.

Compulsory process A procedure to subpoena witnesses in court.

Concurrent powers Powers shared by the national government and the states.

Conference committee An ad-hoc committee that meets to resolve differences between senate and house versions of the same legislation.

Conference committee report A compromise between the house and senate versions of a bill reached by a conference committee. It may not be amended by either house but must either be rejected, accepted, or sent back to the committee for more work.

Conflict of interest The situation that exists when a legislator, bureaucrat, executive, official, or judge is in a position to make a decision that might result in personal economic benefit or advantage.

Conservative A political ideology marked by the belief in a limited role for the national government in economic regulation and helping individuals, support for traditional values and lifestyles, and a cautious response to change.

Consolidation The merging or joining of responsibilities by counties and other local governments.

Constable A county law enforcement official who is elected to serve as the process officer of justice of the peace courts and also has general law enforcement powers.

Continuance Delay of a trial.

Co-optation The "capturing" of an institution by members of an interest group. In effect, in such a situation, state power comes to be exercised by the members of the private interest.

Council-manager form of government A form of government that features an elected city council and a city manager who is hired by the council. The council makes policy decisions, and the city manager is responsible for the day-to-day operations of the city government.

Councils of government (COGs) Advisory bodies consisting of representatives of various local governments brought together for the purposes of planning and cooperation.

County attorney A county legal officer whose responsibilities may include giving legal advice to the commissioner's court, representing the county in litigation, and prosecuting felonies and misdemeanors. In a county that has both a county attorney and a district attorney, the latter prosecutes felonies.

County auditor A financial officer whose duties may include reviewing county financial records and, in large counties, serving as chief budget officer.

County clerk The chief record keeper and election officer of a county.

County government A general-purpose local government that also serves as an administrative arm of the state. Texas has more counties (254) than any other state.

County judge An official elected countywide to preside over the county commissioners court and to try certain minor cases.

County treasurer In many counties, the official who is responsible for receiving, depositing, and disbursing funds.

Creole A descendant of European Spanish (or in some regions, French) immigrants to the Americas.

Criminal law Law prosecuted by the state, seeking punishment for violations of public concepts of morality.

Crossover voting When members of one political party vote in the other party's primary to influence the nominee that is selected.

Cumulative voting An at-large election system that permits voters to cast one or more votes for a single candidate. For example, if a voter can cast up to five votes in a city council election, all five votes could be cast for one candidate or spread among several candidates.

De novo Latin for "anew"; a *de novo* trial is a new trial conducted in a higher court (as opposed to an appeal). In *de novo* cases, higher courts completely retry cases. On appeal, higher courts simply review the law as decided by the lower courts.

Deadwood State constitutional provisions voided by a conflicting U.S. constitutional or statutory law; also provisions made irrelevant by changing circumstances.

Dealignment The situation that arises when large numbers of voters refuse to identify with either of the two parties and become increasingly independent of party affiliation.

Decentralization Exercise of power in political parties by state and local party organizations rather than by national party institutions.

Declining marginal propensity to consume The tendency, as income increases, for persons to devote a smaller proportion of their income to consumer spending and a larger proportion to savings or investments.

Dedicated funds Revenues dedicated for a specific purpose by the constitution or statute.

Delegated powers Powers granted to t he national government by the U.S. Constitution.

Delegation The legal transfer of authority from an official or institution to another official or institution.

Dependent agency A classification created by the U.S. Census Bureau for governmental entities that are closely tied to general-purpose governments but do not have as much independence as special-district governments.

Deterrence Discouragement of an action, especially of criminal acts, by threat of punishment.

Development Corporation Act A state law that allows certain Texas cities to raise the sales tax for economic development. The tax increase, which is subject to voter approval, has been approved in more than 500 cities.

Devolution The attempt to enhance the power of state or local governments, especially by substituting more flexible block grants instead of restrictive categorical grants in aid.

Direct primary A method of selecting the nominees from a political party where party members elect the candidates that represent them in the general election

Directive authority The power to issue binding orders to state agencies; the directive authority of Texas's governor is severely limited.

Discharge petition A legislative process for rescuing a pigeonholed bill from a committee. It is seldom used.

Discretion The power to make decisions on the basis of personal judgment rather than specific legal requirements.

District attorney A county officer who prosecutes felony cases.

District clerk The record keeper for the district court in counties with a population exceeding 8,000.

Division of powers In a federal system, the granting of certain powers to the national government and others to the regional or state governments.

Docket The schedule of court activity.

Double jeopardy A second prosecution for the same offense after acquittal in the first trial.

Down-ticket Describes a candidate for political office relative to others located higher on the ballot.

Due process The following of proper legal procedures. Due process is essential to guaranteeing fairness before the government may deprive a person of life, liberty, or property.

Early voting The practice of voting before election day at more traditional voting locations, such as schools, and other locations, such as grocery and convenience stores.

Elective accountability The obligation of officials to be directly answerable to the voters for their actions. This allows elected administrators to ignore the wishes of the chief executive.

Electronic voting Voting using video screens similar to e-ticket check-ins at most airports.

Eminent domain Government taking private property for public purposes with compensation.

Ethnic diversity Inclusion of significant numbers of nonwhites such as Latinos, African Americans, Asian Americans, and Native Americans.

Evangelical (fundamentalist) Christians A number of Christians, often conservative supporters of the Republican Party, who are concerned with such issues as family, religion, abortion, gay rights, and community morals.

Ex officio Holding a position automatically because one also holds some other office.

Examining trial An initial court hearing to determine if there is sufficient evidence to send a case to a grand jury.

Exclusionary rule The requirement that illegally obtained evidence not be used against the accused.

Exclusive powers Powers delegated to the national government but not to the states.

Expressed powers Powers explicitly granted by the U.S. Constitution to the national government; also known as *enumerated powers*.

Extraterritorial jurisdiction (ETJ) A buffer area that may extend beyond a city's limits. Cities can enforce some laws such as zoning and building codes in ETJs.

FBI index crimes Crimes used as a national barometer of the crime rate (murder and nonnegligent manslaughter, forcible rape, robbery, aggravated assault, burglary, grand theft, and motor vehicle theft).

Felony In Texas, a serious crime punishable by state institutions.

Filibuster An attempt by a senator to delay a bill by unlimited debate. The speaker hopes to focus attention on the bill, elicit a compromise on some point, or force the withdrawal of the bill from consideration. Unlike a U.S. senator, a Texas senator may not surrender the floor to another sympathetic senator in order to continue the filibuster.

Floor The part of the capitol building where the senate or the house meets. The term can also be applied to the senate or house acting as a whole to debate, amend, vote on, enact, pass, or defeat proposed legislation.

Floor leaders The legislators who are responsible for getting legislation passed or defeated. Their job is to negotiate, bargain, and compromise because they are in the center of political communication.

Formal (legal) powers Powers stated in rules, a law, or a constitution.

Fourteenth Amendment The amendment to the U.S. Constitution that places restrictions on the states and sets certain national standards for state action. Its "due process" clause and "equal protection" clauses have been used to void many state actions.

Fragmentation Division of power among separately elected executive officers. A plural executive is a fragmented executive.

General sales tax A broad-based tax collected on the retail price of most items.

General-law charter A document authorizing the establishment of a city with a population of 5,000 or fewer whose structure and organization are prescribed and limited by state law.

General-law city A city with a population of 5,000 or fewer whose structure and organization are prescribed and limited by state law.

General-obligation bonds Bonds to be repaid from general taxes and other revenues; such bond issues usually must be approved by voters.

General-purpose government A municipal or county government, providing a wide range of services. Compare *special district*.

Gerrymander A district or precinct that is drawn specifically to favor some political party, candidate, or ethnic group.

Grand jury In Texas, 12 persons who sit in pretrial proceedings to determine whether sufficient evidence exists to try an individual and therefore return an indictment.

Grassroots The lowest level of party organization. In Texas, the grassroots level is the precinct level of organization.

Gross-receipts tax A tax on the gross revenues of certain enterprises.

Guaranteed-issue requirements Requirement that insurance companies will sell health insurance to applicants despite preexisting conditions.

Health Care Reform A comprehensive federal program expanding health insurance coverage with broader Medicare coverage, "individual mandates," "guaranteed-issue" requirements, health insurance subsidies, and exchanges.

Hidden taxes Taxes included in the retail prices of the goods and services.

Hierarchy A pyramid-shaped administrative organization in which several employees report to a single higher administrator until there remains only one person with ultimate authority at the top.

Home-rule charter A document organizing a municipality with a population greater than 5,000 and allowing it to use any organizational structure or institute any program that complies with state law.

Home-rule city A city with a population greater than 5,000 whose structure and organization comply with state law.

Homestead An owner-occupied property protected from forced sale under most circumstances.

Hung jury A jury that is unable to agree on a verdict after a suitable period of deliberation; the result is a mistrial.

Impeachment Officially charging an office holder with improper conduct in office.

Implementation The carrying out by members of the executive branch of policy made by the legislature and judiciary.

Implied powers Powers delegated to the national government as a result of interpretation of the "necessary and proper" clause in the U.S. Constitution.

Incremental budgeting Basing an agency's budget requests on past appropriations plus increases to cover inflation and increased demand for their services, assuming that past appropriations justify current budgetary requests.

Incumbent The current holder of an office.

Independent expenditures Money that individuals and organizations spend to promote a candidate without working or communicating directly with the candidate's campaign organization.

Indictment A formal written accusation issued by a grand jury against a party charged with a crime when it has determined that there is sufficient evidence to bring the accused to trial.

Indirect appointive powers Texas governor's authority to appoint supervisory boards but not operational directors for most state agencies.

Individual culture A political subculture that views government as a practical institution that should further private enterprise but intervene minimally in people's lives.

Individual mandate Requirement that individuals get health insurance or face a federal fine.

Informal (extralegal) powers Powers that are not stated in rules, a law, or a constitution but are usually derived from these legal powers.

Information A written accusation filed by the prosecutor against a party charged with a minor crime; it is an alternative to an indictment and does not involve a grand jury.

Initiative An election method that allows citizens to place a proposal on the ballot for voter approval. If the measure passes, it becomes law (permitted in some Texas cities but not in state government).

Interest group An organization that expresses the policy desires of its members to officers and institutions of government; also known as a *pressure group*.

Interim committees Committees that meet between legislative sessions.

Internationality Having family and/or business interests in two or more nations.

Intestate Without leaving a will at the time of death.

Iron Texas Star A model depicting policy making in Texas by a coalition of interests that includes interest groups, the lieutenant governor, the speaker, standing committees, the governor, administrators, and boards and commissions.

Iron triangle A working coalition among administrative agencies, clientele interest groups, and legislative committees that share a common interest in seeing either the implementation or the defeat of certain policies and proposals.

Issue network Collections of individuals in organizations who are interested in a policy area and get involved in policy making as topics affect their interests. They are not consistently in alliance or opposition with other groups or networks. Internet "blogs" are an example.

Item veto Executive authority to veto sections of a bill and allow the remainder to become law

Judicial review The power of the courts to rule on the constitutionality of government actions.

Ku Klux Klan (KKK) A white supremacist organization. The first Klan was founded during the Reconstruction era following the Civil War.

La Réunion A failed French socialist colony of the 1800s located within the city limits of modern Dallas. Its skilled and educated inhabitants benefited early Dallas.

Late train contributions Campaign funds given to the winning candidate after the election up to 30 days before the legislature comes into session. Such contributions are designed to curry favor with individuals whom the donors may not have supported originally.

Legislative Audit Committee The body that performs audits of state agencies and departments for the legislature.

Legislative Budget Board The body responsible for proposing the legislature's version of the proposed biennial budget. The governor also proposes a budget to the legislature.

Legislative Council The body that provides research support, information, and bill drafting assistance to legislators.

Legitimacy General public acceptance of government's right to govern; also, the legality of a government's existence conferred by a constitution.

Liability insurance Insurance against negligence claims such as those arising from auto accidents.

Libel Published falsehood defaming a person's character.

Liberal A political ideology marked by the advocacy of positive government action to improve the welfare of individuals, government regulation of the economy, support for civil rights, and tolerance for political and social change.

Little legislatures Another name for standing committees because most of the work of legislation occurs in committees.

Lobbying Direct contact between an interest group representative and an officer of government.

Lobbyist In state law, a person who directly contacts public officials to influence their decisions. Registered lobbyists are paid to represent the interests of their employers.

Logrolling Trading votes among legislators, especially to fund local projects to benefit their constituents.

Long ballot The listing of several independently elected offices on an election ballot.

Loopholes Federal income tax subsidies designed to encourage approved behavior by excluding certain income from taxation or allowing credits against taxes.

Mandate A requirement or standard imposed on one level of government by a higher level of government.

Maquiladora A factory in the Mexican border region that assembles goods imported duty-free into Mexico for export. In Spanish, it literally means "twin plant."

Mass transit Transport systems that carry multiple passengers such as train and bus systems; whether publicly or privately owned, mass transit systems are available to the general public and usually charge a fare.

Mayor-council form of government A municipal government consisting of a mayor and a city council. In the *strong-mayor form of government*, substantial authority (over appointments and budget) is lodged in the mayor's office. The mayor is elected at large. In the *weak-mayor form of government*, an elected mayor and city council share administrative responsibilities, often with other elected officers.

McCarthyism A false or unproven attack on the character, integrity, or patriotism of a political opponent.

Means test A standard of benefit eligibility based on need.

Medicaid A program to provide medical care for qualified low-income persons; although funded largely by federal grants-in-aid, it is a state-administered program.

Medicare A federal program to provide medical insurance for most persons older than 65 years of age.

Merit Plan A method of selecting judges based on the candidate's qualifications rather than politics. Under this system, the governor fills court vacancies from a list of nominees submitted by a judicial commission, and these appointees later face retention elections. Also known as the Missouri Plan.

Merit system An employment and promotion system based on specific qualifications and performance rather than party affiliation or political support.

Message power The influence a person gains merely by being in the public eye. For example, message power allows the governor to focus the attention of the press, legislators, and citizens on legislative proposals that he or she considers important. The visibility of high office draws instant public attention for the officeholder's proposals, a power that led Teddy Roosevelt to refer to the presidency as the "bully pulpit."

Mestizo A person of both Spanish and Native American lineage.

Metroplex The greater Dallas–Fort Worth metropolitan area.

Misdemeanor A minor crime punishable by a county jail sentence or fine.

Missouri plan See *merit plan.*

Mistrial A trial not completed for legal reasons, such as a hung jury; a new trial may be possible.

Moralistic culture A political subculture that views government as a positive force, one that values the individual but functions to benefit the general public.

Mores Society's strong beliefs about right and wrong.

Negative campaigning A strategy used in political campaigns in which candidates attack opponents' issue positions or character.

Negligence Failure to act with the prudence or care that an ordinary person would exercise.

No bill A grand jury's refusal to return an indictment filed by the prosecutor.

No-fault insurance An insurance plan allowing the insured person to collect from the individual's own insurance company regardless of who is at fault in a vehicular accident.

North American Free Trade Agreement (NAFTA) A treaty between Canada, Mexico, and the United States, that calls for the gradual removal of tariffs and other trade restrictions. NAFTA came into effect in 1994.

Office-block ballot A type of ballot used in a general election where the offices are listed across the top, in separate columns.

Ogallala Aquifer A major underground reservoir and a source of water for irrigation and human consumption in northern West Texas and the Texas Panhandle, as well as other states.

Ombudsman An official who hears complaints of employees and citizens concerning government administrators or policy administration. Ombudsmen usually lack authority to force administrative

compliance, but they can bring the complaints to the proper authorities and represent the interests of the complaining individual within the administration.

Open primary A type of party primary where a voter can choose on election day in which primary they will participate.

Open-meetings laws With some exceptions, laws that require meetings of government bodies that make decisions concerning the public interest to be open to public scrutiny.

Open-records laws Laws that require most records kept by government to be open for the examination of the parties involved.

Original jurisdiction The authority of a court to consider a case in the first instance; the power to try a case as contrasted with appellate jurisdiction.

Pairing Placing two incumbent officeholders in the same elective district through redistricting. This is usually done to eliminate political enemies.

Parole Early release from prison under official supervision.

Participation paradox The fact that citizens vote even though their votes rarely influence the result of an election.

Partisan elections General elections in which candidates are nominated by political parties and their party labels appear on the ballot.

Partisan identification A person's attachment to one political party or the other.

Party platform The formal issue positions of a political party; specifics are often referred to as planks in the party's platform.

Party realignment The transition from one dominant-party system to another. In Texas politics, it refers to the rise and possible dominance of the Republican party in recent years.

Party–column ballot A type of ballot used in a general election where all of the candidates from each party are listed in parallel columns.

Peremptory challenge A challenge made to a prospective juror without being required to give a reason for removal; the number of such challenges allotted to the prosecution and defense are limited. Also called a *peremptory strike*.

Permanent School Fund A small source of funding for the Texas public school system. Leases, rents, and royalties from designated public school land are deposited into the fund. The school system uses the interest and dividend income from this fund for public education.

Personal property Tangible possessions other than real estate.

Personal recognizance A defendant's personal promise to appear; sometimes allowed instead of cash bail or bond.

Petit jury The jury for a civil or criminal trial.

Pigeonholed Eliminated from consideration by committee vote. If the committee considering a bill votes to table the bill, it has been pigeonholed and is effectively killed.

Plaintiff The private person bringing a civil suit.

Plea bargaining Negotiations between the prosecution and the defense to obtain a lighter sentence or other benefits in exchange for a guilty plea by the accused.

Plural executive An executive branch with power divided among several independent officers and a weak chief executive.

Plurality vote An election rule in which the candidate with the most votes wins regardless of whether it is a majority.

Pocket veto Chief executive's power to kill legislation by simply ignoring it at the end of the legislative session; this power is not available to Texas's governor.

Point of order A formal question concerning the legitimacy of a legislative process. A successful point of order can result in the postponement or defeat of legislation.

Political action committees (PACs) Organizations that raise and then contribute money to political candidates.

Political culture The political values and beliefs that are dominant in a nation or state.

Popular recall A special election to remove an official before the end of his or her term, initiated by citizen petition (permitted in some Texas cities but not in state government).

Pragmatism The philosophy that ideas should be judged on the basis of their practical results rather than on an ideological basis. American political parties are pragmatic because they are more concerned with winning elections than with taking clear uncompromising stands on issues.

Precedent A previously decided legal case used as a guiding principle for a current or future case.

Precinct convention A gathering of party members who voted in the party's primary for the purpose of electing delegates to the county or district convention.

Preponderance of the evidence The amount of evidence necessary for a party to win in a civil case; proof that outweighs the evidence offered in opposition to it.

Presession bargaining Negotiations that let the governor and the legislative leaders reach the necessary compromises prior to the start of the legislative session. This usually ensures passage of the legislation.

Presidential preference primary A primary election that allows voters in the party to vote directly for candidates seeking their party's presidential nomination.

Pressure group See *interest group*.

Prima facie **case** Sufficient evidence to convict if unchallenged at trial; the amount of evidence necessary to indict a defendant.

Primary An election held by a political party to nominate its candidates. Texas party primary elections are usually held in the spring.

Private-school vouchers Taxpayer-funded payments to private schools to pay for the education of students transferring to them from public schools.

Privatization The hiring of private contractors to perform government services and functions.

Probable cause Sufficient information to convince a reasonably cautious person that a search or arrest is justified

Probate The procedure for proving the validity of a will.

Probation A judge's sentence of an offender to serve outside a correctional institution but under specific restrictions and official supervision.

Progressive movement A political movement within both major parties in the early 20th century. Progressives believed that the power of the government should be used to restrain the growing power of large corporations, as well as to provide services for its citizens.

Progressive tax rates Tax rates that increase as income increases; for example, the federal income tax is assessed using progressive rates.

Prohibition Outlawing of the production, sale, and consumption of alcoholic beverages.

Property tax A tax levied as a percentage of the assessed value of real property.

Proposal of constitutional amendments In Texas, the proposal of a constitutional amendment must be approved by two thirds of the total membership of each house of the Texas legislature.

Public debt Money owed by government, ordinarily through the issuance of bonds. This source of funding is frequently used by local governments to finance major projects. Whether or not a local government will incur public debt is usually determined by the voters.

Public interest The good of the whole society, without bias for or against any particular segment of the society.

Punitive damages Judgments in excess of actual damages intended to punish a defendant in a civil suit.

Pure at-large system An electoral system in which candidates for city council run citywide and the top vote getters are elected to fill the number of open seats. Compare *at-large place system*.

Ranchero culture A quasi-feudal system whereby a property's owner, or patron, gives workers protection and employment in return for their loyalty and service. The rancher and workers all live on the *ranchero*, or ranch.

Ratification Approval of a constitutional amendment by a majority of voters.

Real property Land and buildings.

Reapportionment The redrawing of district and precinct lines following the national census to reflect population changes.

Recall election An election that permits voters to remove an elected official.

Recidivist A criminal who commits another crime after having been incarcerated.

Recorded vote Votes in which the names of those who cast the vote are recorded in the house journal.

Reduction veto The power of some governors to reduce amounts in an appropriations bill without striking them out. Texas's governor does not have this power.

Referendum An election that permits voters to determine if an ordinance or statute will go into effect.

Regressive tax rates Tax rates that place more of a burden on low- and middle-income taxpayers than on wealthier ones; for example, sales taxes and most other consumption taxes are regressive.

Regulatory tax A tax imposed with the intent of exerting social or economic control by reducing taxes on approved behaviors or imposing higher taxes on undesirable activities.

Rehabilitation The effort to correct criminals' antisocial attitudes and behavior.

Remedy The means to redress an injury, including relief from ongoing injury or compensation for past damages.

Removal powers The authority to fire appointed officials. The Texas governor has limited removal powers; they extend only to officials he

or she has appointed and are subject to the consent of two thirds of the state senators.

Reserved powers Powers belonging only to the states and not shared with the federal government.

Retainership system A special interest group or organization's placing lawyers who are also legislators on retainer with the intent of legally purchasing their support as legislators.

Revenue bonds Bonds to be repaid with revenues from the projects that they finance, such as utilities or sports stadiums.

"Revolving door" The interchange of employees between government agencies and the private businesses with which they have dealings.

Right-to-work laws Laws that prohibit union shop agreements requiring new employees to join a union.

"Robin Hood" plan School finance reform program requiring the transfer of taxable property resources from wealthier to poorer school districts.

Rollback election An election that permits the voters to decide if a property tax increase (of more than 8 percent) approved by a local government will remain in effect or be reduced to 8 percent.

Runoff primary A second primary election that pits the two top vote-getters from the first primary, where the winner in that primary did not receive a majority. The runoff primary is used in states such as Texas that have a majority election rule in party primaries.

Sales tax A broad-based tax collected on the retail price of most items.

School finance reform Changes in public school financial system resulting from a Texas Supreme Court ruling that significant inequality in school financial resources violated the state constitution; changes in any public policy are considered "reform" by their advocates.

Secession The separation of a territory from a larger political unit. Specifically, the secession of southern states from the Union in 1860 and 1861.

Selective sales (excise) taxes Taxes levied on specific items only; also known as *excise taxes*.

Senatorial courtesy The tradition of allowing a senator to reject the governor's appointment of a political enemy from the senator's district. The senator declares the appointee "personally obnoxious," and the other senators vote to reject the appointee.

Separation of powers The principle behind the concept of a government with three branches—the legislative, executive, and judicial.

Severance tax A tax on raw materials (such as oil and natural gas) when they are extracted from their natural state.

Sheriff The chief county law-enforcement officer. Although the sheriff is an elected official in Texas, his or her budget must be approved by the commissioners court.

Shivercrat A follower of Governor Allan Shivers of Texas (1949–1957). Shivercrats split their votes between conservative Democrats for state office and Republicans for the U.S. presidency.

Short ballot The listing of only a few independently elected offices on an election ballot.

Single-member district system A system in which one candidate is elected to a legislative body in each election district.

Single-member districts Election districts in which one candidate is elected to a legislative body. In city council elections, single-member

districts are contrasted to at-large citywide elections. Members from single-member districts tend to feel greater loyalty to the residents of their own neighborhoods because they are not elected citywide.

Slander Spoken falsehood defaming a person's character.

Social insurance Public insurance programs with benefits based on tax premiums paid by the beneficiary or his or her employer; for example, Social Security and unemployment compensation are social insurance programs that are not based on need alone.

Social promotion Passing a student to the next grade on the basis of his or her age rather than level of learning.

Socialized medicine Strictly defined, socialized medicine is a health care system in which the government hires medical practitioners who work at government-owned facilities to directly provide health care as in Great Britain and in U.S. veterans and military hospitals. However, the term is often applied to health care systems in which the government provides health care insurance (such as Medicare), but benefit payments are made to private health care providers.

Soft money Money spent by political parties on behalf of political candidates, especially for the purposes of increasing voter registration and turnout.

Special district A limited-purpose local government that provides a narrow range of services not provided by general-purpose local governments such as cities or counties. Examples of special districts include municipal utility districts, hospital authorities, and transit authorities.

Special district A local government that provides one or more services to a jurisdiction that are not provided by general-purpose governments. Examples of special districts include municipal, utility districts, hospital authorities, and transit authorities.

Special session A legislative session called by the Texas governor, who also sets its agenda.

Spindletop Spindletop was a major oil discovery in 1901 near Beaumont that began the industrialization of Texas.

Spoils system A system that gives elected officials considerable discretion in employment and promotion decisions.

Standing committees Permanent committees that function throughout the legislative session.

Stare decisis The principle of following precedents in deciding legal cases.

Statute-like detail Detailed state constitutional policies of narrow scope, usually handled by statutes passed by legislative bodies.

Statutory law Law passed by legislatures and written into code books.

Strong-mayor form of government In the *strong-mayor form of government*, substantial authority (over appointments and budget) is lodged in the mayor's office. The mayor is elected at large.

Subcommittees Divisions of a committee that consider specific subtopics of a committee's primary jurisdiction.

Suffrage The legal right to vote.

Sunset Advisory Commission A body that systematically evaluates most government agencies and departments and may recommend restructuring, abolishing, or altering the jurisdiction of an agency.

Supply-side economics The theory that higher-income taxpayers should be taxed less because their savings and investments stimulate the economy.

Supremacy clause Article VI of the U.S. Constitution, which makes the national constitution and laws supreme when they conflict with state rules and actions.

Suspension of the rule The setting aside of the rules of the legislative body so that another set of rules can be used.

Swing voters People who cast their ballots on the basis of personality and other factors rather than strictly on the basis of party affiliation.

Tagging A senate rule that allows a senator to stop consideration of a bill by the standing committee for 48 hours.

Tax abatement A reduction of or exemption from taxes (usually real estate taxes); typically granted by a local government to businesses in exchange for bringing jobs and investments to a community.

Tax assessor-collector A county financial officer whose responsibilities include collecting various county taxes and fees and registering voters.

Tax base The object or activity taxed.

Tax rate The amount per unit of taxable item or activity.

Tax shifting Businesses passing taxes to consumers in the form of higher prices.

Tenant farmer A farmer who does not own the land that he or she farms but rents it from a landowner.

Tenth Amendment U.S. Constitution provision that all powers not delegated to the national government are reserved for the states and the people—the basis for states' rights arguments.

Term limits Restrictions on the number of times that a politician can be reelected to an office or the number of years that a person may hold a particular office.

Texas Ethics Commission A constitutionally authorized agency charged with accepting reports of candidates and lobbyists and making them public. It also establishes standards of conduct for officeholders, candidates, and lobbyists.

Texas Register The official publication of the state that gives the public notice of proposed actions and adopted policies of executive branch agencies.

The Lobby The collective characterization of the most politically and economically powerful special interest groups in the state.

Threat of veto An informal power of the Texas governor. Threatening in advance to veto legislation enhances the governor's bargaining power with legislators, enabling the governor to shape the content of legislation while it is still in the legislature.

Ticket splitters People who vote for candidates of more than one party in a given election.

Tidelands A submerged area that extends three leagues (about 10 miles) off the Texas coast. The tidelands controversy developed when offshore oil was discovered and the federal government contended that Texas's jurisdiction extended only three miles into the Gulf of Mexico.

Tipping A phenomenon that occurs when a group that is becoming more numerous over time grows large enough to change the political balance in a district, state, or county.

Tort A private or civil injury or wrong other than a breach of contract.

Tort reform Efforts to limit liability in civil cases.

Traditional culture A political subculture that views government as an institution to maintain the dominant social and religious values.

Trans-Texas Corridor Mostly in planning stages, an extensive super-highway, railway, and communications system to be jointly financed by public funds and private toll road developers.

True bill An indictment returned by a grand jury.

Two-party system A political system characterized by two dominant parties competing for political offices. In such systems, minor or third parties have little chance of winning.

Umbrella organization An organization created by interest groups to promote common goals. A number of interest groups may choose to coordinate their efforts to influence government when they share the same policy goal. The organization may be temporary or permanent.

Unemployment insurance Benefit program for certain workers losing their employment; a joint federal–state program financed with a tax on employers.

Union shop A workplace in which management requires all new employees to join a union or pay dues as a condition for employment (illegal in Texas).

Unit road system A system that concentrates the day-to-day responsibilities of roads in the hands of a professional engineer rather than individual county commissioners. The engineer is ultimately responsible to the commissioners court.

Unitary government A system of government that places primary authority in a central government. Subordinate governments have only as much authority as is permitted by the central government.

Unitary system of government A centralized governmental system in which local or subdivisional governments exercise only those powers given to them by the central government.

User fees Charges paid by the individuals who receive a particular service, such as city-provided electricity or garbage collection.

Valley (of the Rio Grande) An area along the Texas side of the Rio Grande River known for its production of citrus fruits.

Veto The executive power to reject a proposed law unless an unusual majority of the legislature (usually two-thirds) votes to override the governor's opposition. This is almost an absolute power in Texas because the legislature is seldom in session when the governor issues the veto.

Victimless crime A crime such as prostitution, gambling, or drug possession that primarily victimizes oneself rather than society at large.

Voice vote Vote cast by lawmaker but that is not recorded in the official record as that lawmaker's vote.

***Voir dire* questioning** The initial questioning of jurors to determine possible biases.

Voter turnout The percentage of people who are eligible to vote who actually vote.

Voting-age population The total number of persons in the United States who are 18 years of age or older regardless of citizenship, military status, felony conviction, or mental state.

Weak-mayor form of government In the *weak-mayor form of government*, an elected mayor and city council share administrative responsibilities, often with other elected officers.

Whistle-blowers Government employees who expose corruption, incompetence, and criminal acts by other government employees.

White primary The practice of excluding African Americans from Democratic Party primary elections in Texas. First enforced by law and later by party rules, this practice was found unconstitutional in *Smith v. Allwright*, 321 U.S. 649 (1944).

White-collar crime Bribery, tax fraud, business fraud, embezzlement, and other nonviolent crimes usually committed by more prosperous individuals than those who commit street crime

Winter Garden The Winter Garden is an area of South Texas known for its vegetable production.

Writ of habeas corpus A court order requiring that a prisoner be presented in person and that legal cause be shown for imprisonment; also used in some civil cases.

Writ of injunction A court order to compel or restrain a particular action.

Zero-based budgeting Evaluating budget requests for existing programs as if they were new programs rather than on the basis of past levels of funding.

Note: Bold page numbers are illustrations

Concurrent powers of federal and state governments, 44

Conference committees, 199–200, 202–203; Conference committee report, 200; description of, **180**; function and membership of, 178–179, 180

Conflict of interest: among judges, 283; among legislators, 193–194; among lobbyists, 153; defined, 137, 147; Department of Agriculture and agribusiness, 235; and legislative salaries, 183–184; public administration and politics, 242, 243

Congress of Racial Equality (CORE), 15, 16

Connally, John B.: 1962 election of, 15; conservative Democratic support, 111; and farm labor movements, 16, 38

Connally, Wayne, 187

Conservatives. *See also* Republican Party: among Republicans, 115; defined, 109–110; faction in Democratic Party, 110–112; fundamentalist Christians, 115; ideology of, 109–110; State Board of Education, 161; Texas crime rate, 307; traditional constituency of, 111

Consolidation, 392

Constables, 296, 390

Constitution, current Texas. *See* Constitution of 1876

Constitution of 1869, 63–64, 228

Constitution of 1876, 40–60; adoption of, 5; amendments to, 57, 58; attempts to revise, 58–59; Bill of Rights, 50–51; compared nationwide, 61; Constitutional convention of 1875, 48–49, 64; delegates to convention, **49**; early republic and state constitutions, 47–49; establishment of public schools, 339; executive branch of government, 53–55; gubernatorial authority granted, 226, 228; judicial branch of government, 55; legislative branch of government, 51, 53; local government authority, 55, 57; modern implications, 49–50; opposition from railroad interests, 49; procedural requirements for legislature, 53; purpose and influence of, 49, 50; rights guaranteed, 133; rigidity of, 391; separation of powers, 51; suffrage, 57; and U.S. Constitution, 42–46; voting rights, 57

Constitution, U.S. *See also individual amendments to U.S. Constitution:* powers assigned to federal government, 42–43; rights guaranteed, 133; state constitutions, 42–46; supremacy clause of, 44; Texas Bill of Rights, 50

Constitutional amendments: procedures nationwide, **58**; ratification of, 57, 58; voter participation in, 57

Constitutional convention of 1974, 17, 58–59

Constitutions: compared nationwide, **60**; purpose and influence of, 41–42; structure and purpose of, 59

Consumption, 323

Continuance, 302

Conventions, 76; county district, 117; Senatorial district, 117; state, 117–119; Superdelegates to, 127

Conventions *vs.* primaries, 76–77

Cook, John, 313

Cooper, Cynthia, 251

Co-optation, 137

CORE. *See* Congress of Racial Equality

Cornyn, John: 2002 election, 112; election to U.S. Senate, 214; tenure as Attorney General, 233

Corporate charters, 288

Corporate sponsorship, 224

Corporation courts. *See* Municipal courts

Council-manager government, 374–375

Councils of Government (COG), 396

Counsel, right to, 300–301, 304

County Board of Elections, 84

County courthouse, **386**

County courts, 266–268; cases disposed in, **267**; county jails, 310; courts-at-law, 266–267; established by Texas constitution, 55; place in Texas judicial structure, **263**; size of juries, 274

County district conventions, 117

County governments, 386–393; civil service for employees, 392; consolidation with city, 392; elected officers in, 390–391, **393**; functions of, 387; issues and trends in, 391–393; malapportioned precincts in, 389; Republican-held offices, 113; role in administering elections, 84–85, 85; structure and organization of, 387–391

County-level party organization, 119

Court of Criminal Appeals: appeals controversy, 271, 272; appeals process, 305; dual courts of last resort, 269; election of Morris Overstreet, 93, 280; established by Texas constitution, 55; photo of judges, **272**; place in Texas judicial structure, **263**

Courts, 300–305. *See also* Court of Criminal Appeals; Juries; Supreme Court, Texas; Texas Judiciary; Trials: of appeals, 261–262, 268–269, 305; appeals court districts, **270**; attorney addressing jury, **259**; county courts, 266–268; court-appointed counsel, 300–301; courts-at-law, 266–267; district courts, 268; juvenile courts, 305–306; lobbying before, 153–154; municipal courts, 262, 264; national courts and federalist system, 42; as organized in Texas, 262–273; of record, 262; types of cases heard, 259–260

Cowboys Stadium, **400**

Craddick, Tom, 20; actions as Speaker of the House, 178; appointment of Bill Ceverha, 179; election to Speaker of the House, 177, 181; establishment of House Research Organization, 182; governor's influence on

2003–2004 state budget, 223; lobbyists on transition team, 216; ties to special interest groups, 147; tuition deregulation, 365, 366

Creationism, teaching of, 363–365

Creole culture in South Texas, 24

Crime: clearance rates for major crimes, **297**; detection of, 296–297; deterrence of, 306; elements of, 290–294; federal crimes, 290; felony crimes, 290, 297; frequency of, 294; prevention of, 296; ranking among 50 states, 33; rates, 306, 307

Crime victims, characteristics of, 293–294

Crime Victims Compensation Fund, 294

Criminal Justice, Board of, 242

Criminal Justice, Department of, 242–243; diagram of organizational structure, **244**; public support for, 247; role of, 306, 308, 309

Criminal *vs.* civil cases, 261

Criminal *vs.* civil law, 286–287

Criminals, characteristics of, 292–293

Cross, Malcolm L., 363–365

Crossover voting, 81

Crystal City, 24, 38

Cultural diversity in Texas: 2000 Census figures, 29; table illustrating, **30**

Cultural regions across Texas, 22–28, **23**

Culture wars and social issues, 160–162, 341

Cumulative voting, 378–379

Cunningham, Minnie Fisher, **7**

Customs and Border Protection agency, U.S., 313

D

Dallas: Democratic Party strength in, 122; and Fort Worth Metroplex, 28; judicial elections in Dallas County, 277; *La Réunion* colony, 28; political culture in 1963, 125

Dallas Cowboys, 399–400

Danburg, Debra, 199

Daniel, Price, 14, 15

Davis, E. J., **5**; beginning of Democratic Party dominance, 108; Constitution of 1869, 48; corruption of administration, 112; effect on present state constitution, 213; reaction to tenure, 228; *Reconstituting Texas: E. J. Davis and His Legacies* (essay), 62–64; Reconstruction and, 5–6

Davis, Edwin S., 139

Davis, Kevin T., 365–369

Davis, Wendy, 164–165

De La Cruz, Laura K., 100–102

De Salvo, Albert, legislative honors for, 52, 185

Deadwood, constitutional, 53

Dealignment, 122

DeAnda, James, 14–15

Debates in Legislature, 197–199

Decentralization: among political parties, 106–107; graph depicting, **107**; of legislative power, 177

Dedicated funds, 329

Defense industry, 28